MANY MINDS
ONE HEART

MANY MINDS
ONE HEART

SNCC's Dream for a New America

WESLEY C. HOGAN

The University of North Carolina Press | Chapel Hill

© 2007 The University of North Carolina Press
All rights reserved
Manufactured in the United States of America

Designed by April Leidig-Higgins
Set in Minion by Copperline Book Services, Inc.

The paper in this book meets the guidelines for permanence and durability of the Committee on Production Guidelines for Book Longevity of the Council on Library Resources.

This book was published with the assistance of the Z. Smith Reynolds Fund of the University of North Carolina Press.

Chapter 5 was originally printed in *Pennsylvania Magazine of History and Biography* (July 2002); reprinted with permission.

Library of Congress Cataloging-in-Publication Data
Hogan, Wesley C.
Many minds, one heart: SNCC's dream for a new America / Wesley C. Hogan.
p. cm.   Includes bibliographical references and index.
ISBN 978-0-8078-3074-1 (cloth: alk. paper)
ISBN 978-0-8078-5959-9 (pbk: alk paper)
1. Student Nonviolent Coordinating Committee (U.S.) — History.   2. Student Nonviolent Coordinating Committee (U.S.) — Biography.   3. African American political activists — Biography.   4. African American civil rights workers — Biography.   5. Oral history.   6. African Americans — Civil rights — History — 20th century.   7. Civil rights movements — United States — History — 20th century.   8. United States — Race relations — History — 20th century.   9. Southern States — Race relations — History — 20th century.   10. Social movements — United States — History — 20th century.   I. Title.
E185.61.H693 2007
323.1196'073 — dc22   2006029922

cloth   11 10 09 08 07   5 4 3 2 1
paper   12 11 10 09 08   5 4 3 2 1

To Corbett

Contents

Illustrations

Abbreviations

ASCS	Agricultural Stabilization and Conservation Service, U.S. Department of Agriculture
CIG	Civic Interest Group of Baltimore
CNAC	Cambridge Nonviolent Action Committee
COFO	Council of Federated Organizations
CORE	Congress of Racial Equality
CR groups	Consciousness-raising groups
DNC	Democratic National Committee
ERAPS	Economic Research and Action Projects of SDS
FBI	Federal Bureau of Investigation
FELD	Fund for Educational and Legal Defense
FOR	Fellowship of Reconciliation
FOS	Friends of SNCC
ICC	Interstate Commerce Commission
MFDP	Mississippi Freedom Democratic Party
NAACP	National Association for the Advancement of Colored People
NAG	Nonviolent Action Group, Howard University
NCLC	Nashville Christian Leadership Council
NSA	National Student Association
NSM	Northern Student Movement
SCLC	Southern Christian Leadership Conference
SCOPE	Summer Community Organizing and Political Education of SCLC

SDS   Students for a Democratic Society

SNCC   Student Nonviolent Coordinating Committee

SPAC   Swarthmore Political Action Club

VEP   Voter Education Project of the Southern Regional Council

YDCA   Young Democratic Clubs of America

MANY MINDS
ONE HEART

Introduction

Sweat beaded on twenty-one-year-old Charles McLaurin's forehead as he opened the car door and got out. His stomach felt weak, his knees unsure. What he called "the fear" was upon him. A handsome, broad-shouldered man from Jackson, he stood up as three elderly women emerged from the back seat and started toward the courthouse on a hot August day in 1962. He stopped behind them, watching the pride with which they moved, the strong convictions that they held, "as if this was the long walk that led to the Golden Gate of Heaven, their heads held high." Earlier in the car, the women had told stories of the years gone by while McLaurin drove "with knees shaking, mouth closed tightly so as to not let them hear the fear in my voice." When they passed through Sunflower, Mississippi, one of the women said, "Won't be long now." McLaurin's heart jumped, "realizing what danger could lie ahead for us, especially me." The women, whose ages ranged from sixty-five to eighty-five, "knew the white man and his ways, they knew him because they had lived with him, and worked for him." At the courthouse in Indianola, McLaurin stayed by the car as each woman walked up to the white registrar and said, "I want to vote."

Charles McLaurin spent the next four years "registrating." That is to say, in the majority-black Mississippi Delta, he encouraged African Americans to exercise their right to vote. Eventually, those who registered and those who were stopped from registering combined forces to invent something entirely new in American politics — a party structure made up of "legal" and "illegal" voters. At the Democratic National Convention in Atlantic City in 1964, they captured the nation's attention with their creation: the Mississippi Freedom Democratic Party (MFDP).

Yet nothing in 1964 marked the high point for McLaurin. Nor did any event later in the decade. His peak moment occurred when three elderly ladies had acted in a way that gave him "the spirit to continue." He recognized the existence of a "slavery mentality" that kept people from registering, and he had learned in the movement that it was not just a black problem, but a human problem. It was a problem of submission — people are helpless when young and

Charles McLaurin, who spent the years 1962–65 encouraging African Americans to exercise their right to vote. (From *Student Voice*, courtesy of Dr. Clayborne Carson)

learn subservience to survive. The women McLaurin drove to the courthouse found a way to rise above this submission and attempted to reside in the world as free persons. So this is why McLaurin remembered that day in 1962. He fixed in his mind how to live.[1]

As a member of what came to be a central group in the civil rights movement, the Student Nonviolent Coordinating Committee (SNCC or, as its members called it, "Snick"), Charles McLaurin symbolized where the organization stood at a critical juncture between 1960 and 1966. Inside the group, people learned to identify the specific nature of their grievances and to act on them in a way that brought new meaning to their lives.

The practice of segregation in America was a fundamentally crazed undertaking. Civil rights activists found that the way out of craziness was not always to take small, carefully programmed steps of rationality. The young people of SNCC invented particularly ingenious experiments in freedom. In so doing, they caught a glimpse of an America not-yet-lived.

SNCC activists felt like pioneers — "in a strange place and an unknown land," as McLaurin put it. They tried to provide "light," or follow a light, or perhaps even be a light that illuminated a New World of political activity. Drawing upon American traditions and Gandhian sources, they imagined and put into practice fresh models of resistance — the sit-ins of 1960 and the Freedom Rides of 1961. They dug out footholds in the rural Deep South, in Albany, Georgia, and Greenwood, Mississippi, in 1962, and they set up the innovative, unauthorized Freedom Vote in 1963. In these very different experimental departures from what everyone understood as "normal politics," SNCC people created workable ways to democratize America. Sometimes (actually, most of the time), mainstream black and white Americans saw these strange "Freedom Riders" as actors almost from another planet. It was not that they were unbelievable; what they were trying to achieve was very much needed. Most everyone understood that. Nevertheless, their conduct electrified onlookers. Official resistance appeared overwhelming — police power, judicial power, state power. All of it unrelenting. The striking fact was that the young people of SNCC kept on. And most difficult of all, despite everything, they managed to achieve a series of victories.

SNCC's declaration of independence from America's racial caste system and the high drama of its efforts at self-definition recruited others out of the generation coming of age in the early sixties. Their boldness triggered a cascade response. By 1964, youth throughout the nation followed SNCC's path to challenge racial segregation, South and North. Soon the targets expanded to include foreign policy (particularly the war in Vietnam), sexual mores, and even styles of music. The resulting counterculture appeared to spring up all over the country, all at once, with startling speed. Young Americans everywhere had adapted and experimented with the SNCC folkway of "acting as if you were free to act."

Their own cultural transformations, all the ways they had attempted to live "as if" segregation did not exist, generated inside SNCC an unstable combination of rising expectations and accelerating tensions. SNCC people recognized the need for change, as well as the need to develop a democratic method of achieving it. The two together demanded an experimental approach. Early on, the members' ability to act this way became SNCC's great strength. Within the group, this technique required a genuine tolerance for error. Indeed, it was the faith in the lessons coming out of trial-and-error experience — its seemingly effortless capacity for improvisation — that most dramatically stamped the organization's style and also its appeal. If SNCC had anything to say about it, the new desegregated America would be a more open, generous society.

People with little connection to SNCC or the movements that followed from it often felt this push for a more democratic society as a threat to the way they as Americans were used to doing things. Mounting resistance from the political establishment combined with police repression forced wider the gap between the political perceptions of people in SNCC and those of the larger society. President Lyndon B. Johnson's landslide victory in November 1964 did not resonate within either of the contending parties in the Mississippi Delta: the hardline segregationists anchored in the White Citizens Councils or the movement activists who had built the MFDP. Despite some concessions by the president, the Mississippi movement felt rejected by regular Democrats. To wit: by the time Johnson settled into his new term of office at the beginning of 1965, SNCC knew they were no longer riding a promising tide of popular understanding and support. Their rebuff at Atlantic City proved that. So, frustrated as they were, and feeling betrayed, they turned inward and began to argue with each other. In a remarkably brief time, they lost much of their hard-won momentum.

By the late summer of 1965, McLaurin found the Greenwood project staff "divided and about to kill one another and the project not doing a thing." He worked hard and soon felt he had got things back on track, determined to keep on "until more than 10,000 Negroes are registered to vote in LeFlore County."[2] But he found the hazards too imposing. One of many who tried to deflect quarrels in the name of preserving SNCC's focus on the grass roots in the towns and hamlets of the South, McLaurin found his driving energy seeping away. After 1965, in every locale except SNCC's cutting-edge outpost in Lowndes County, Alabama, all of the McLaurins working at the base of southern society had found their actions effectively blunted. What was once excruciatingly hard had now become all but impossible. By the end of 1966 SNCC ceased, in any programmatic sense, to exist.

Precisely how this happened has remained, for almost four decades, something of a puzzle. What later became apparent was a subtle but unclear connection: the American civil rights movement began to wane at about the same time as SNCC faltered. Yet the two were not the same. The goals we associate today with the civil rights movement — desegregation, equal rights for African Americans, the "dream" of peaceful coexistence and harmony between the races — all can be seen as a kind of sacred ground. Today, few people question these accomplishments. Somehow the "civil rights movement" began to occupy terrain beyond reach, beyond interpretation, beyond analysis. In the minds of many citizens, a kind of sanctified mist hovers over this landscape, rendering the subject awesome and regal, but difficult to see. Subjecting the movement to critical examination appears akin to the idea of correcting the grammar of the Gettysburg Address.[3]

As the late historian Herbert Gutman astutely observed, however, it is not possible to honor people by romanticizing them.[4] Today, forty years after the fact, many young people are quietly doubtful of the idealized narrative of the civil rights movement they are often handed on Martin Luther King Jr. Day, or by Hollywood filmmakers. Discussion of the movement is seen as just "old folks talking." They are mostly bewildered as to how the movement might relate to their own lives. Even those who do not know much about the inaugural dramas of the sit-ins and the apocalyptic Freedom Rides, or the magisterial achievement of the MFDP, cannot grope their way to any sort of genuine historical understanding because they are, like everyone else, trapped within the aura of sainthood surrounding the movement.

This is not to say that this book constitutes a dramatic break with tradition, because, simply enough, it begins and lives on this sanctified terrain. It must — and for a very elemental reason: In the 1950s, the rituals of a racial caste system rooted in three hundred years of lived experience persisted in the cities, towns, and countryside of the American South. A scant ten years later those rituals lay shattered. The achievement was profound, the cost for many people was severe, and the long-term meaning is still to be acted out on the stages of the nation's history. It was not perfect. But it happened.

There is a stark reason why romanticizing the civil rights movement fails young people. It is not supported by the facts. In the first decade of the twenty-first century, the door to opportunity wedged open by the freedom movement of the 1960s swings shut on more African Americans than it did in the 1970s. Nothing is settled. Although legal segregation has been dismantled, segregation in neighborhoods and schools across the country is once again reaching the levels of the 1950s: four out of every five whites live outside cities and 86 percent of whites live in neighborhoods where minorities make up less than 1 percent of the population. In contrast, 70 percent of blacks and Latinos live in cities or inner-ring suburbs. Disparity in wealth accumulation is stunning. As sociologist Dalton Conley reminds us, "Unlike income or education levels, wealth has the particular attribute of tending to reproduce itself" from one generation to the next, with dramatic effects on where people live and where their children go to school, the investments they can or cannot afford to make, and the security and support they can offer their children. Conley's numbers are stark: African Americans owned 0.5 percent of the total wealth of the United States at the end of the Civil War; by 1990, they owned 1 percent of the nation's total wealth.[5] Though Jim Crow is dead, the evidence is overwhelming that the culture of white supremacy prevails in a more protected form than was ever possessed by the necessarily embattled idea of Jim Crow.

A new racial contradiction has gradually come to haunt the landscape of contemporary America. A change of historic proportions has been achieved and a debilitating caste system finally laid to rest. Yet at the same time, a tenacious residue of white nationalism has remained a central feature of daily life. Today it rubs against African Americans in benign and abrasive ways, a continuous rhythm too dispiriting to be easily ignored, yet too tiresome to be energetically engaged.[6]

Despite this convoluted present, the cultural rising of the nation's black citizenry in the 1960s stands clear as one of the defining moments of the American experience. When the day is fairly won, and at last the whole nation learns how to confront the racial agony it has had to weather, perhaps we will acquire the poise to put away the sacred drums and trumpets on the parade grounds and quietly acknowledge the imagination and steadfastness of those who took great risks to warm our racial glacier. Even at this premature date, however, one historical result can be referred to in the past tense: the freedom movement that burst upon America in the 1960s is too rich in tragedy and rebirth to be sanded off, polished, and then domesticated under a chorus of "We Shall Overcome."[7]

What follows, then, proceeds from a premise that is both ordinary and undeniable: fallible human beings gave the sixties its inimitable shape. They did so with resolve, with imagination, and while in thrall to grand dreams. They also, on occasion, proceeded in error. At their best moments, they were quite a bit ahead of where we are today. Fifty years after the momentous *Brown v. Board of Education of Topeka, Kansas* decision, and forty years after the civil rights legislation of 1964 and 1965, it may be time to acknowledge that we cannot go much further up the road until we find a way — with the benefit of hindsight — to be precise about what happened inside the movement. How could it alter so many rhythms in the United States and yet suddenly collapse when its most crucial work remained before it? Just as important, what do the movement's events mean to those living in its wake?

A surprise or two lurks within this puzzle. The civil rights movement's teaching power increases exponentially when its failures are arrayed alongside its successes. Our affinity for the historical comfort and clarity of sacred ground has left us without the patience to see the most critical moments. Often these have appeared as "details" in prior histories. At times, then, the story demands a small amount of poise in reading. This becomes particularly necessary at the movement's climax when SNCC's internal tensions flash to visibility during the crisis at Waveland, Mississippi, at the end of 1964.

The aura of the civil rights movement as sacred ground is now part of American culture. To transcend it, we have to find ways to sustain self-criticism as well as affirmation, to be demanding as well as generous, and to acknowledge sober realities as well as intoxicating dreams. There is immense hope and achievement in what lies ahead. And deep tragedy.

ormer SNCC communications director Julian Bond has effectively satirized the way popular understandings of the civil rights movement have fundamentally distorted what actually happened: "Rosa [Parks] sat down, Martin [Luther King] stood up, and the white kids came down and saved the day."[8] This gross caricature contains just enough truth to make its underlying falsity hard to erase, for who can dispute the facts of the Montgomery bus boycott in the mid-1950s; Birmingham on an Easter Sunday in 1963; white kids in the Mississippi Delta and the Civil Rights Act in 1964. Closure on segregation and, therefore, at long last, on slavery. Closure, finally, on the troubling issue of race.

Many who teach the history of the 1960s in the nation's secondary schools and universities propagate the popular version that Bond so effortlessly satirized. And most teachers who do so are unaware that it fosters the white supremacist assumptions they oppose. In contemporary classrooms young students learn that SNCC's democratic ideas came from SDS, or that blacks could not have claimed their rights without the help of sympathetic whites. Granted, the death of Jim Crow was long overdue, and as conservative representatives such as William F. Buckley Jr. have belatedly conceded, a number of Americans like himself wrongly opposed the movement for civil rights. Nevertheless, in the fullness of time it all happened. In this easy manner, students are invited to believe that white supremacy is a cultural barnacle that has now been scraped off the ship of state.[9]

So many civil rights histories start with a quiet, dignified woman named Rosa Parks who refused to give up her seat on a bus in 1955, or with a pack of national guardsmen escorting nine black children to Little Rock High School in 1957. The story can also begin as student sit-ins flashed across the South in 1960. Yet for many, the first truly apocalyptic moment came in the late spring of 1961, when mobs firebombed the lead bus and blocked the exits on the first Freedom Ride — outside Anniston, Alabama. By the barest of margins, no one died that day, but the idea of the "Freedom Ride" seemed to be as shattered as the bus itself. The incident led to one of the Freedom Riders, a young man named John Lewis, immediately turning to fellow student Diane Nash. He discovered that she felt even more strongly than he that "the future of the movement would be cut short if the Freedom Rides are stopped by violence."

Lewis and Nash agreed that the integrated journey by bus therefore had to continue, even if it meant a longer trek into chaos. They recruited nineteen young people to join them. And so began the second Freedom Ride of 1961, whose participants — twenty-one students, every one of whom was from Nashville, Tennessee — were warned by the fearless minister Fred L. Shuttlesworth:

"You might be killed." Nash replied, "If they stop us with violence, the movement is dead. The students have decided. We're coming. We just want to know if you can meet us." We start, then, with these students.

But we cannot intelligently make sense of them in 1961 when they step into the international spotlight. We go back to 1959, when it really all began, in a very small room in an annex of the redbrick First Baptist Church in Nashville. Here, just blocks away from the state capitol, a group gathered every Tuesday night throughout the fall of 1959. Most of the chairs were folding metal, so during the workshop people often stood up to move around. Later, it would seem remarkable that such a modest, cramped space helped bring into existence events that transformed the political horizon of the nation. There, ten to twenty students from Fisk University, Vanderbilt University, Meharry Medical College, and American Baptist College discussed William Penn, Jesus of Nazareth, Gandhi, and the Europeans who resisted Nazi aggression. To an outside observer, it appeared not much different from thousands of college classrooms or Bible studies across the country. Only one thing made this group unusual: the participants were trying to figure out how to act on their ideas.

This history begins in the annex of the First Baptist Church because the young people taking part in such workshops became the lifeblood of the early years of SNCC. SNCC was never, by itself, the civil rights movement. Many organizations contributed. The National Association for the Advancement of Colored People (NAACP) specialized in litigation. The Congress of Racial Equality (CORE) focused on direct action in the North. Martin Luther King Jr.'s organization, the Southern Christian Leadership Conference (SCLC), had its base in southern black churches. King called SNCC's young people the "storm troopers" of the region who could push the movement forward because "they do not have to think of their families, their positions and who's going to preach next Sunday like we do." Of course, there were exceptions: NAACP youth councils often engaged in direct action, and CORE worked in the South, particularly Louisiana and Mississippi; when they did, SNCC and CORE workers walked many of the same roads, experienced many of the same transformations. But for a time between 1960 and 1965, SNCC served as the movement's most powerful energy machine, experimenting with new ways to act that catapulted the freedom struggle to new levels.[10]

To get a clear understanding of how SNCC unfolded, we must go back to the Nashville workshops. Here, students created experiences for themselves in order to learn some basic tenets of nonviolent practice. These workshops overlapped with SCLC meetings held throughout the region. Yet none of these prior SCLC efforts carried the power to move people from ideas to action as consistently and successfully as did the workshops run by a young Methodist minister at Nashville's First Baptist.

His name was James M. Lawson Jr. Martin Luther King Jr. made it a habit to be present each time Lawson ran a workshop at SCLC meetings. In this manner, King emphasized to his staff how vital he thought the workshops were. King possessed unmatched rhetorical skill, and he used it to interpret the meaning of the movement struggle to the American people in a language they could understand. He built on the mainstream history of the country in which he himself believed. Still, he understood that his strengths, though widely celebrated, were not in organizing. In Lawson, King saw a superior mastery of the crucial democratic skill of training people to move from idea to action.[11] It was this capacity that those who received the training later adopted to such remarkable ends in the sit-ins, Freedom Rides, and perilous voter registration campaigns that are explored in Part I of this book. Lawson, in conjunction with legendary organizers Ella J. Baker and Myles Horton of Tennessee's Highlander Folk School, passed on America's democratic organizing tradition to SNCC youth as they attempted to reinvigorate the nation's political culture.[12]

As its members invented a new path forward in the South, SNCC became a magnet for northern students trying to "do something," yet unsure how to proceed. Part II of this book tracks how and what the movement taught the nation's youth. People from Yale University, the University of Michigan, Oberlin College, and the University of California at Berkeley closely followed the activities of southern black youth during the sit-ins and Freedom Rides. Frequently when northern students met SNCC activists, they were awed by what SNCC people had learned — and they were thunderstruck when they discovered what SNCC people had lived through. But they were almost never able to connect the two — to grasp public experimentation as the necessary forerunner to a new politics. As the subsequent actions of most northern students proved, they did not readily view SNCC people as political "organizers" but rather as vivid new kinds of radicals. This shortfall was a central one, and it had unanticipated effects down the road. For the time being, most northern students who visited the South functioned in a way analogous to town criers, passing on the ideas and experiences of the southern movement to the North and West. Deep South organizing experiences got transferred to northern students through SNCC's project in Cambridge, Maryland. These same students and others influenced by them subsequently generated a cross-current involving Cambridge, Swarthmore College in Pennsylvania, and working-class black neighborhoods in Cleveland, Ohio, and Newark, New Jersey. In this way they affixed their newly acquired SNCC practices to their own SDS project in the urban North.

SNCC people also achieved an unparalleled success in moving beyond their own group to bring local people into civic life across the South — climaxing with the MFDP's arrival in American politics. Part III is therefore suffused with initiatives that are imaginative, dramatic, and sometimes even breathtaking, yet also misunderstood (sometimes willfully, sometimes not) by the rest of the nation, with outcomes that were generally disappointing, frequently violent, and now and then agonizing.

The concluding section, Part IV, explores how and why this civic movement began to split up — spinning its members into Black Power, the women's movement, draft resistance, or other struggles.

The entire saga of the freedom movement in the United States is perhaps most usefully viewed as part of a worldwide uprising of people after World War II against the globalized culture of white supremacy. Plainly, the task of coming to grips with white supremacy is daunting.[13] Indeed, how strange the behavior of SNCC people may seem to young people today: youth changing the nation through their self-activity. How odd. How bewildering. Above all, how seemingly impossible. But we have a truly powerful blueprint lingering in front of our eyes. As Charles McLaurin began to internalize in 1962, it carried the potential to be not only a rich experience, but a transforming one as well. The need, of course, is to understand this experience. It is too useful to be walled off as sanctified terrain. For our own sake, the remarkable lessons provided by SNCC need to be excavated from the sacred ground.

PART ONE
A MOVEMENT EDUCATION

CHAPTER ONE

The Nonviolent Anvil

The encounter was both simple and crude: the white man spit on James Lawson. As divinity student Bernard Lafayette looked on, Lawson, a black minister in his early thirties, asked his assailant for a handkerchief. Momentarily baffled, the young spitter handed him one. Lawson wiped off the spit, handed the handkerchief back, and asked the white man if he had a motorcycle or a hot rod. A motorcycle, the man said. Lawson, tall, gentle, distinguished-looking with black-rimmed glasses, maintained this casual manner, asking technical questions about how the bike had been customized, until the two men appeared simply involved in conversation. Watching in amazement, Lafayette realized that not only had Lawson refused to engage the man on the level of retaliation, but also he had forced his enemy to see him as a human being.

For Lafayette, the performance by Lawson was a revelation: The black minister no longer felt the need to explain to people why he believed in nonviolent action. This was hardly the nonviolence of "begging white folks to accept us." Lafayette, whose trim frame and open expression belied an iron will, had been raised by devout parents who gave him two pieces of advice seemingly impossible to follow when yoked together: he should always stand up for his rights, and he should avoid trouble with whites. The problem with nonviolence was that not only did it appear weak or unmanly, it also provoked whites. Yet what Lawson demonstrated was as simple as it was transformative: there was no reason to "shout out" that he was doing something as an "act of courage, not an act of fear."[1] Lawson's gift to Lafayette provided a subtle illustration of how to overcome the contradiction. It was an offering that Lawson would supply to many other potential young activists from the South between 1959 and 1965.

Lawson first learned of nonviolence through the teachings of his mother in the 1930s. When he was ten years old, a small white child called him "nigger" from a car window. Lawson did not hesitate. Possessing little fear of whites, he ran over and slapped the child as hard as he could. Returning home, he recounted the story to his mother. Philane Lawson stood cooking, her back turned to him. When he had finished, she asked, "What good did that do, Jimmy?" He felt "absolute surprise" at her response. "We all love you, Jimmy," she continued. "And God loves you, and we all believe in you and how good and intelligent you are. We have a good life and you are going to have a good life. I know this Jimmy. With all that love, what harm does that stupid insult do? Jimmy, it's empty. Just ignorant words from an ignorant child who is gone from your life the moment it was said." Years later, Lawson recognized the incident as a "sanctification experience," a moment when his life seemed to stop — and then permanently change. In subsequent decades, whenever he got angry or found himself in a confrontation, he remembered those words: *Jimmy, what harm did that stupid insult do? Jimmy, you are loved.*[2]

If his parents got young Lawson off to a promising start, veteran pacifist A. J. Muste and the Fellowship of Reconciliation (FOR) proved a vital link to the possibilities of justice on a global scale. Originally an organization formed to support conscientious objectors (COS) during World War I, the FOR had in later years become a major channel for the transmission of Gandhian practices and philosophy to U.S. activists. In his first year at Ohio's Baldwin-Wallace College in 1950, Lawson heard Muste, FOR's executive secretary, speak on campus. Lawson joined FOR, and Muste soon became an important mentor.[3]

FOR's influence would be evident to Lawson later in 1950, when the Korean War draft board sent him a U.S. Army classification form. Lawson refused to fill out the draft card (a violation of federal law), and soon the army issued a warrant for his arrest. He turned himself in. Undoubtedly he could have qualified for a student, ministerial, or CO's deferment, but to act on conscience, Lawson felt, one had no moral right to take a deferment.[4]

Once in prison, Lawson confronted the primary barrier facing all who consider using nonviolent tactics: the almost overwhelming human need to protect one's own body. He felt most personally challenged by the threat of prison rape. Would he use violence to defend himself? After an agonizing self-examination, he determined that if someone hurt him, he could not control that person's behavior; his responsibility was to his own conscience. Anything that happened would not ride on personal choice. Rather, it was just "one more thing you have to endure in order to be true to [God]. It is part of the test He set out for you."[5] It would be hard to overestimate the impact of this trial on Lawson — coming as it did years before he began the fateful dialogue with the Nashville students who sustained the sit-ins and the Freedom Rides. That impact was both simple and profound: Lawson's prison experiences allowed him to relate to the deepest fears of the Nashville students. It was — absolutely — the central challenge each nonviolent practitioner had to face: "How do I respond if someone attacks me or my family?"

After his release from prison in 1953, Lawson left for India to work as a youth minister at a Presbyterian college in Nagpur. While still in college, he had grown wary of work with traditional civil rights groups in the United States. He believed that the NAACP possessed no programs or organizational forms capable of harnessing the growing collective self-respect of black southerners, especially World War II veterans, who were trying to find ways to end segregation in America. Having initially learned about Gandhi through the black press, he had taken a special interest in nonviolence after reading about Gandhi's 1936 meeting with Howard Thurman, at the time one of the most distinguished ministers in the United States. Thurman asked Gandhi if he had a message for Americans: Gandhi replied that since events in America captured the attention of the rest of the globe, perhaps an African American would succeed where he had failed, by making the practicality of nonviolence visible worldwide. To Lawson, Gandhi's teachings and actions represented what the Christian God would do if he found himself an Indian subject to British authority or an Afro-American subject to Jim Crow.[6]

When Lawson heard about the astonishing events unfolding during the Montgomery bus boycott in 1955–56, he quickly made plans to return home. On meeting the Montgomery movement's young spokesman, Martin Luther King Jr., in the fall of 1956, Lawson mentioned his experiences in India. He told King that he wanted to work in the South after receiving his doctorate — in about five years. "Don't wait! Come now!" King said. "We don't have anyone like you down there. We need you right now. Please don't delay. Come as quickly as you can." Lawson understood King's sense of urgency. Events in the boycott appeared to be happening so fast, no one had time to sit down, converse, and plan where to go next. Few in the movement found it easy to reflect carefully on previous actions. "At best we were all inspired amateurs," Nashville minister Kelly Miller Smith wrote of this early period. "Much of what had been done had been based on the trial and error method." Or, as Lawson later explained, "We are becoming teachers when we are still so young that we ought to be nothing but students." Lawson responded to King's call at the beginning of 1957, becoming FOR's field secretary for the South, and set out to canvass the region.[7]

Lawson began traveling as part of a two-man "reconciliation team" with Glenn E. Smiley, a white minister from Texas and a conscientious objector during World War II. Smiley had brought nonviolent methods to the leaders of the Montgomery bus boycott. Now Smiley and Lawson ran nonviolent workshops throughout the region to show people — experientially — how to act to end

James Lawson in Nashville, 1960. Martin Luther King Jr. made it a habit to sit in the first row each time Lawson ran a workshop at SCLC meetings. (Nashville Public Library, The Nashville Room)

segregation. Most workshops, which were sponsored by a church, civil rights organization, or student group on a college campus, lasted two or three days. They started with devotions, songs, and an overview of nonviolence, followed by question-and-answer sessions, break-out groups, and more singing. Then participants engaged in small group discussions and sometimes role-plays.[8]

Nashville: A Laboratory for Many Montgomerys

Hoping to create a base for nonviolent activism, Lawson moved to Nashville in 1958 and entered Vanderbilt University Divinity School. By this time, veteran civil rights activists had pulled together a new group called the Southern Christian Leadership Conference, led by Martin Luther King Jr. and other African American ministers. SCLC member Kelly Miller Smith, a professor at Nashville's American Baptist College and pastor of the First Baptist Church in Nashville, encouraged Lawson, making him the social action leader of the local SCLC affiliate, the Nashville Christian Leadership Council. When SCLC began, Smith recalled, the group recognized the need for "a small disciplined group of non-violent volunteers. These persons should receive intense training in spirit technique." Smith had "no idea how this could be done," but he believed that SCLC would have to provide the training. Thus, when Lawson arrived in Nashville, Smith immediately asked him to hold workshops in the First Baptist Church on nonviolent philosophy and its applications. Smith was a slightly older minister who had been purposefully laying the groundwork for a civil rights movement. Lawson later described him as dedicated to "social action, social change, and justice." Smith served as one of the key black players in the city's cautious efforts at integration over the 1950s. Many regarded the members of his congregation as the black elite of Nashville, and the slow pace of change forced Smith to face "the most seductive pulls which went with his job — public rage and private depression." In Lawson, he recognized a new spirit that gave him a lift.[9]

L awson "intended to make Nashville a laboratory for demonstrating nonviolence." He wanted "many Montgomerys," and he thought he knew how to create them. For his idea to flower, he needed people willing to face the same hurdles he had. When Lawson settled in Nashville, he organized a series of workshops that began on 26 March 1958. With Kelly Miller Smith's support, Lawson worked with ten or so local ministers each week.[10]

A standout in this group was a student of Smith's at American Baptist named John Lewis. Lewis, an earnest and devout young man from rural Alabama, drew closer to Lawson because Lawson served as a field secretary for the FOR. Lewis had been impressed by the pamphlet FOR had published a year earlier on King and the Montgomery bus boycott. It explained how nonviolent action could desegregate public facilities in the South. FOR executive secretary Alfred Hassler directed the pamphlet "primarily to Negroes" and aimed to "avoid any indication of hostility toward whites." He tried to illustrate "the whole struggle in nonviolent, Christian, potentially reconciling terms rather than with violence and bitterness." The pamphlet — presented in comic book form with vivid graphics and clear examples of the dignity of noncompliance — "wound up being devoured by black college students across the South," Lewis later explained.[11] So when Lawson first offered a workshop under FOR's sponsorship, Lewis decided that "this is something I should really attend."[12]

In the spring of 1959, NCLC took the first step of what Lawson termed a "nonviolent scientific method" — namely, "investigation, research, and focus." Lay people, including women, joined the group, and together they surveyed the needs of Nashville's black community. Not only did they target the "white"

First Baptist Church, Nashville, where Lawson ran nonviolent direct action workshops every Tuesday night throughout 1959. (Nashville Public Library, The Nashville Room)

and "colored" signs, Lawson explained, but they also aimed to "break open job opportunities for people. There were no black cashiers in downtown Nashville. There were no black bank tellers. There were no black secretaries working in corporate offices, there were no black reporters in the two newspapers. There were no black folk in communications." Except for a few blacks on the council persons, city government was wholly segregated. Though Nashville had a large pool of African American professionals, there were no blacks in the police department hierarchy, in other city services, or on the bench. "Black lawyers had a tough time in the courts because of the abject racism, the segregated restrooms in the courthouse, the lack of reading facilities for black lawyers," Lawson remembered. Black teachers had only recently won a hard-fought court battle for equal salaries.[13]

Life in the workshops signaled the future of the civil rights movement in the South: discussions routinely grew heated and ranged over many subjects — education and segregation of the schools, police brutality and harassment of black people, the segregated job market, and meager job opportunities. In May

1959 NCLC decided to launch a campaign to desegregate downtown Nashville, envisioning a ten- to fifteen-year struggle — "however long it would take." This created a much larger task than what had been achieved in Montgomery. "Based upon that tenet," recalled Lawson, "I began to draw up the plan for workshops in September."[14]

It was not difficult to recruit students. The word spread through social and church networks that Lawson was developing practical tactics to fight segregation. People flowed in from Fisk University, Tennessee State, Meharry Medical School, Vanderbilt, and American Baptist. "A year earlier we rarely had ten people in that room," Lewis noted. By the fall of 1959, however, "there were often more than twenty, black and white alike, women as well as men." Lawson now looked to create a movement "that will involve thousands of people. A public relations man is not our answer. We need [a] program at [the] local level. . . . A wide movement of nonviolence."[15]

One of the new recruits was Diane Nash, who quickly emerged as a leader. Intense and poised, Nash, a former beauty queen, had been raised by Mississippi parents who moved to Chicago before her birth. A devout Catholic, she had excelled in the city's parochial schools before entering Howard University in Washington, D.C.; she then transferred to Fisk. Lewis noticed that she arrived "with a lot of doubt at first." Nash "came to college to grow and expand, and here I am shut in," she explained of her reaction to Nashville's segregation. During her first few days at Fisk, she "learned there was only one movie theater to which Negroes could go. I couldn't believe it, it took about ten people to convince me." When she realized that students at Fisk spent most of their time on campus because they could not eat at restaurants or go to most theaters, "I felt chained." Nash's status as a beauty queen — light skin, long hair, and light eyes — reflected an attitude widespread among middle-class blacks in the pre – Black Is Beautiful era. Her willingness to walk away from the access her appearance provided to the upper crust of black society indicates her early determination and commitment. She asked around campus, "Who's trying to change these things?" A friend told her about the workshops. She went.[16]

Kelly Miller Smith brought some of his most ambitious and intelligent students to Lawson's workshops, not only Lewis, but also divinity students Bernard Lafayette and James "Jim" Bevel, a veteran raised in rural Mississippi. Lithe, short of stature, and bald, Bevel had what one colleague later described as "the burning eyes and visionary intensity of a Russian mystic. He was always arguing, passionately, some highly original, far-out position." His hitch in the U.S. Navy proved Bevel to be a rising star: brave, fiercely intelligent, determined to excel. A few years into military service, a chance friendship with an African American cook introduced him to Tolstoy's *The Kingdom of God Is Within*

You. Bevel left the navy within weeks, persuaded by the novelist's argument that Christians could not be true to their faith and kill others. A sermon taken from Isaiah convinced him of his calling, and by January 1957 he had saved enough money to enter American Baptist. Lewis, Lafayette, and Bevel would go on to lead major campaigns within the civil rights movement. At this early stage, the three southerners stood out for their determination to live in light of the Christian gospel's teachings.[17]

Five months before the Greensboro, North Carolina, sit-ins would electrify the nation, the Nashville group set out to teach themselves how to act nonviolently. Initially, the members traced the idea of nonviolence from the early Christians, pausing at length on New Testament concepts of love. They discussed John Woolman's efforts against slavery, William Penn's experiment to peacefully coexist with Native Americans in colonial Pennsylvania, and the Freedom Rides of the 1840s in Pennsylvania and New England. Lawson shared his understanding of Gandhi and the goals of the nonviolent struggle in India, stressing "the Gandhian idea of our being engaged in an experiment where you have to keep figuring out what happened and why, and what didn't happen."[18] Through historical example, in other words, he taught them something that became centrally useful as the civil rights struggle in Nashville intensified: how to reflect on and analyze their past activity before acting again.

The point is not that Lawson was introducing into the culture of black Nashville the intellectual tradition of nonviolence that stretched through so many Eastern and Western religions. He accomplished something much more profound — he brought these settled positions to people who were trying to find a way to act. Thus, Lawson began to serve as a central pivot by which ideas about equality moved to action in the American South.[19] Finally, the students examined the Montgomery bus boycott. "We started mostly with talk," said Lewis, "but later we turned to what we called sociodrama." In essence, they relived the boycott, from early planning, through the first carpool, to final action.[20] In this manner the workshops began to fundamentally reshape the students' sense of political possibility.

The first important discovery of the workshops now emerged: the students were not alone. Lawson's broad historical context allowed them to draw from a rich lode of previous experience. "This was eye-opening stuff for me," remembered Lewis. "Learning that the feelings I'd had as a boy, the exclusion and unfairness that I had witnessed growing up in Alabama, the awful segregation that surrounded all of us there in Nashville — throughout this entire nation — was nothing new." For Lewis, the workshops were "mind-blowing." "To learn that the tension between what was right and what was wrong that had torn at me since I was old enough to think had a historic context, that people of all cultures and all ages had struggled with the same issues, the same questions, the same brutal realities . . . that was mind-blowing."[21]

Warned for so many years by parents and other authorities not to discuss the way segregation made them feel, the words, once let loose, would not stop. All of them had suffered the indignities of Jim Crow: had sat in the ragged balconies of movie theaters, had lived on unpaved streets, had been denied seats on buses. All had attended elementary and secondary schools transparently inferior to nearby white schools. Many had seen siblings, parents, or grandparents humiliated by whites — or worse — without consequence. Talking about these profoundly personal incidents as a group, they saw in a new way how a lifetime of such experiences could diminish a person's sense of self. A menacing, existential fear controlled them. Yet as they began to share these private stories in workshops, they realized that it was possible to hold higher expectations of themselves and the broader society. And they brought this new understanding to their recruits, noting that segregation "made thousands of Negroes feel that they are 'nobodies' and that they have no right to aspire to nobler things." They identified *segregation* — not individual weakness — as the "wicked thing," because it "penalizes a person for being what God has made him." Such a hard-earned vision promoted intense bonds.[22]

The students also began to see how to apply Gandhian philosophy to their own lives. As Lewis later wrote, the beauty of these ideas lay in their practicality: they "applied to real life, to the specifics of the world we walked in. They applied to Byrd's drugstore and to the Troy [Alabama] theater. They applied to the buses I rode to high school and to the all-black classes in which I sat. They applied to the men and women who refused to serve black people at the lunch counters of downtown Nashville."[23]

Unexpectedly, Lawson did not seize upon such energy by advocating immediate action. Rather, he explained, before acting on these wounds, they first must control their fear and scrutinize their feelings of worthlessness. Once they accepted that they did not deserve segregation, they could see clearly why they *could* challenge this system: it unfairly relegated an entire group of people to second-class status and engendered feelings of powerlessness and worthlessness for no reason other than an unchangeable and arbitrary physical characteristic. They must develop compassion to try to relate to the insecurities that drove their oppressors. Here surfaced a startling political component of nonviolent direct action: Compassion might be practical.[24] If they treated others with civility and dignity, they increased the chances that they would be treated the same way. Even if a man had just spit in one's face, he was capable of handing over a handkerchief.

The problem of verbal or physical assault raised profound yet practical questions. As Lawson put it, "If segregationists were truly powerful or confident or well loved," they would not feel the need to assault others. To face such individuals, workshop participants would need a "bedrock of inner strength and confidence" to "rise above" the instinctual emotional response of retaliatory violence. He pushed them "to be their better selves." Only at that point would their behavior compel respect from those actively denying them their rights as well as those watching from the sidelines.[25]

Lewis's friend from American Baptist, Jim Bevel, started off as a reluctant, infrequent participant in the workshops. Yet he soon grew fascinated by Lawson's argument: If a man had enemies, it was easy to hate back. Still, what good did it do? Who benefited? Bevel's visceral animosity toward selfishness and his experience in reading Tolstoy now combined to make him open to Lawson's teaching: this simple act of insisting on the respect due any human by another was the only thing that could end the cycle of hate and violence.[26]

Lawson pushed the students, and they pushed each other, to talk through the reasons why they should not honor the impulse to fight back. Lawson recalled it as "a mutual learning process. The notion of self-defense is an essential notion, . . . but it doesn't necessarily mean only violence." People might be reluctant to admit it, he noted, but most resist insults, and subsequent hostile situations, by turning the other cheek. "Folk who believe so much in violence fail to recognize that in violence somebody always loses. It's a strategy that's only fifty percent effective." On the other hand, where nonviolent approaches work, "it's a win-win for everybody. When you don't retaliate with a personal insult, but instead offer a friendly, generous gesture, that's what Jesus meant when he said 'turn the other cheek.' You cause the other person to do searching." Lawson admitted that if the perpetrator of violence possessed a real criminal mind, "he may insult you again, and push you some more, or hit the other cheek without qualms. That can happen. But a good part of the time, the hostile person experiences surprise at the response, and feels inward chagrin, and or shame, and/or inward disturbance that they acted so chauvinistically, and the other person [acted] graciously." Again, the experience of thinking through and debating the various responses took time and energy — in some cases, it took an enormous amount of time. Lawson's presence as the guiding force, and his willingness to meet with the students once a week, proved pivotal. He taught patience and persistence, and, at the center of the workshop, an ethic of compassion began to develop.[27]

In Lawson's words, they worked to create "the beloved community." The first time Lawson used this phrase, Lewis immediately felt that it defined his own vision. In the workshops, participants began to understand this as "nothing less than the Christian concept of the kingdom of God on earth." Throughout human existence, people "from ancient Eastern and Western societies up through the present day, have strived toward community, toward coming together," observed Lewis. Though this community might be delayed or interrupted by evil, hatred, greed, revenge, or the lust for power, "believers in the Beloved Community insist that it is the moral responsibility of men and women with soul force, people of goodwill, to respond and to struggle nonviolently against the forces that stand between a society and the harmony it naturally seeks." The struggle, Diane Nash wrote in 1961, freed each individual "to grow and produce to his fullest capacity." The phrase summarized, not just for Lewis and Nash, but for the hundreds and later thousands of people who would join in its pursuit, a vision of the world they wanted to create, "where the barriers between people gradually came down and where the citizenry made a constant effort to address even the most difficult problems of ordinary people." In other words, the "community" represented the group's ability to live in the solution.[28]

At this point, the Nashville students could consider Lawson's example of asking the street tough who spit on him for a handkerchief in a new light: how could *they* reproduce this kind of dramatic initiative in different situations? They began to ask: What would I do if someone spit on me? How would I respond if someone called me a "black bitch"? How can I claim my dignity when a white calls me "boy"?[29] In essence, the students tried to take ownership of public life — not only their own conduct, but also the overall environment in which they interacted with whites. It understates their achievement to see this as an effort to alter customs of white supremacy — even if the object was such a sweeping set of rules as the southern caste system. They succeeded where thousands of others tried but failed: they innovated *concrete* ways to throw over an entire array of deferential behavior and ideas. They reviewed what had happened in the street between Lawson and the white tough, then continued to practice the technical skills needed to assert themselves (nonviolently) as equal citizens. As Lewis explained, "We actually acted out roles, trying to foresee the varieties of possible alternatives, and how we could apply nonviolence to different situations." Parents warned them that challenging segregation meant certain harm and possible death. Yet Lawson's example demonstrated a new way to claim the respect and dignity that segregation systematically denied them. Furthermore, it offered the prospect of doing so without engaging in physical violence. It thus brought people nearer to the day when they could act on their own — not just during a sit-in, but in numerous situations, under varying conditions.[30] In political terms, the Lawson workshops allowed individuals to move from private talk to public action — again and again. The choices they shared together — whether or not to risk injury or death by engaging in the sit-ins — would be difficult to understand for those who did not participate in these workshops. To make sense of SNCC, the workshop experience needs to be grasped as one of the core moments of the entire SNCC story.

The participants in the Nashville workshops experimented with carving out space for the creation of egalitarian public relationships. How they created this democratic political space and then maintained it (or failed to maintain it) arose as a compelling dynamic that pulsed through SNCC and the civil rights movement through all the volatile years of the 1960s. This point merits emphasis. Sustaining a campaign of nonviolent direct action — such as the sit-ins — involved an internal strategic change of massive proportions. Engaging in a sit-in — in the face of mass arrests, white violence, and expulsion from school — required the participants to adopt specific steps, steps that people had to learn how to take. Lawson's immersion in the idea of nonviolent action prompted him to approach the subject with considerable care. How could they make nonviolent methodology a reality in their lives? Here the group gave itself permission to act out this mode of self-assertion with poise, confidence, and determination. "In training for nonviolence," Lawson asserted in 1959, "study, discussion, and fellowship" all became essential components.[31]

A key element of Lawson's teaching was that he did not talk continually. Rather, he demonstrated the importance of listening. In so doing, he established his respect for others' knowledge, experience, and opinions. He later explained it as part of the nonviolent method, which "doesn't pretend to have the answers in given situations." When entering a new locale, he felt it imperative to "spend a lot of time listening. And observing. And looking." Such an approach opened space for learning about others' experiences in the context of searching for self-understanding. John Lewis, one of the first workshop participants from American Baptist College, later noted Lawson's patience, attentiveness, and calm. "There was something of a mystic about him," Lewis wrote, "something holy, so gathered [in] his manner, the way he had of leaning back in his chair and listening — really *listening* — nodding his head, saying 'Yes, go ahead,' taking everything in before he would respond." Over time, workshop participants grew to trust Lawson and each other, enough to be increasingly forthright — approaching what might be described as routine candor. When they risked telling him some truth about themselves, their family, or their hometown, he did not ridicule them. When they expressed vulnerability, raising concerns about wanting to defend themselves or their families, Lawson took them seriously. He gave people the means to prevail.[32]

In cultural terms, Lawson understood the "emotional conflicts" that nonviolent action could produce, for instance, when young men imagined *not* hitting an attacker. The resulting candor and respect fostered a new sensitivity within each participant and became a tangible component of the group itself. Instead of telling others what he thought he knew, Lawson wanted them to find the discovery he had already made: if they acted justly in a country where the laws were unjust, they would no longer be people living in a caste system; they would escape it.

Participants reached none of these transcendent plateaus quickly — the workshops went on and on, as did individuals' analysis of their condition. Eventually the day came when all creative reflection had to be stored in the bank and replaced by practical testing. Graduates of the workshops had to assess their ability to act. Lawson used two kinds of role-plays. He directed the first, a "socio-drama," toward an individual. All of the participants confronted a violent scene, one-on-one. They had to "work out in their minds" how to respond, then act it out "to help them deal with the violence that they would feel inside. The hurt they would feel in the insults. Push them around, try to figure out why a nonviolent approach on that personal matter was the best way of handling it." Lawson gave illustrations of how others had responded in similar situations before the students acted it out again. After the individual sessions, Lawson initiated a second kind of role-play, setting off part of the room as a lunch counter, or a restaurant. He asked some people to pretend to sit-in, while others yelled insults, acting as harassers. "We'd try to stage it realistically. I'd say, 'You have to cuss them out, call them bad names. Put yourself in that mood, and act it.' So we'd try to get people to *act out* potential scenes. And they did good work of it. People learned. People were confronted by it." Afterward, Lawson walked around the role-play "to teach them to dissect it, both from the inward perspective, and then [gave the] fellow strategies used to resist."[33]

The role-plays drained people, angered them, exhilarated them. Some participants began to eat together beforehand and ride home together afterward. In their free time, they talked about their lives, and many became friends. They often attended one another's church services; when Lawson married a few years later, many participants attended the wedding. The idea of a beloved community was coming to life among the Nashville students.

After eight or nine sessions with the enlarged group that gathered in the fall of 1959, Lawson challenged the students to translate their commitment from the theory of nonviolence into a blueprint for change. In the previous spring, he had listened to the older women's descriptions of their humiliating ordeal when shopping downtown: "'You husbands don't do the shopping. You men don't know about these matters. You can stay away, especially you black preachers who pastor black churches in good facilities. You don't have to face this stuff. But we have to shop. We sometimes have to drag our children with us. There's no place we can stop to rest our feet. There's no place we can stop for a cup of coffee or a sandwich.'" Lawson recalled one "particularly grating story," at Harvey's department store. On the fourth floor, the owner had erected a beautiful children's carousel. Yet black children were forbidden to play on it. Nor were their mothers allowed to sit in the adjacent tea room. White mothers could stop and rest their feet while their children played on the carousel. "'Shopping is hard work, especially with one child, two children, sometimes three children with you,'" the women told Lawson. "'They're tired. You have to keep them from getting into trouble, like from drinking in a white fountain. You have to help them follow the customs, use the segregated restrooms.'"[34]

For Lawson, the women "carried the day." He asked the students to consider these downtown Nashville stores as their initial target. First, he suggested, they could study the possible outcomes of any actions they proposed and then, if they found the target suitable, reach a consensus on action. Fisk University economist Vivian Henderson provided what Kelly Miller Smith called "enlightening figures on the amount of business Negroes did in the Nashville area." Smith continued: "We figured that the merchants would want to keep the nearly $8 million that Negroes spent annually on Church Street [downtown] alone, and the 100 million dollars Negroes in the trade area of ninety miles brought to Nashville each year."[35]

In November 1959, groups of four to eight students sat-in at Harvey's department store and Cain-Sloan's various downtown lunch counters. They intended these initial demonstrations not to provoke arrests, but simply to be "a continuation of the experiment, giving people a feel" for nonviolent action, Lawson reported. "Every group was assigned to bring back basic information about each restaurant or counter," he later related. "They were to see the layout, and what the waiters and supervisors were like. They would try to talk to people. When refused, they would try to get hold of a supervisor, or a manager, or boss who was prepared to talk." The students hoped "to find out who [the manager] was, what his posture was." Was he hostile or friendly? Did they know why the facility did not serve black people? Upon their return, the students presented a report to the rest of the group. "It was not just a laboratory to show what could be done," Lawson emphasized, "but again it was a part of the focusing in — that these places are going to be our targets down the road." They ran the experiments right up until the week before Christmas and agreed to reconnect early in the new year.[36]

Greensboro: Sit-ins Sweep the South

In an orderly and logical world, the great wave of student sit-ins that washed across the South early in 1960 should have flowed outward from Nashville.

They did not, of course. The source of the momentous sit-ins was Greensboro, North Carolina, and the students were from North Carolina A&T State University—not Fisk, or American Baptist, or Meharry. Though the Nashville students had planned to start their sit-in in January 1960, Lawson recalled that they "lolly-lagged" and had trouble getting back together after the Christmas break. Lawson himself had been preoccupied with final exams and traveling for the Fellowship of Reconciliation. "February 1 [1960] happened, and woke us up," he said. On that date, four students at North Carolina A&T—Franklin McCain, Ezell Blair Jr., David Richmond, and Joseph McNeil—sat down at the Woolworth's lunch counter in Greensboro. They purchased school supplies in the store, then approached the lunch counter, ordering coffee and doughnuts. When the waitresses refused to serve them, McCain and McNeil spoke up: "We wonder why you'd invite us in to serve us at one counter and deny us service at another." Police officers arrived and while in the store began heckling them. McCain described his reaction as he watched a white policeman fuming nearby: "If it's possible to know what it means to have your soul cleansed . . . I probably felt better on that day than I've ever felt in my life." His guilt and shame appeared to vacate the premises. "I felt as though I had gained my manhood, not only gained it, but had developed quite a lot of respect for it. Not only as an individual, but I felt as though the manhood of a number of other black persons had gotten some respect from just that one day." The next day, 40 other A&T students joined them, then sympathetic whites from UNC-Greensboro. Spurred by their success, other students conducted sit-ins elsewhere throughout the South—two thousand by the end of the spring semester alone. In the end, these demonstrations signaled a new phase of the civil rights movement in which student activists moved to center stage.[37]

The night after the Greensboro sit-in, Douglas Moore, the minister advising the Greensboro A&T students, called his friend Jim Lawson. Would Lawson's students sit-in at the Nashville Woolworth's as well? The Nashville students mounted a "ready response." After all, they had been planning just such an event throughout the previous fall. "We called a mass meeting at Fisk," Lewis later reported, and "more than five hundred students showed up."[38]

On 13 February 1960 the Nashville students staged their sit-in. The core group of workshop participants now moved in as instructors, training other students. The plan was to enter as many stores as possible, using a "human wave technique—as one group was arrested, another group would take its place." The intended effect was to give local authorities pause: How many people had the will to take part? The central glue holding the action together would be rigid adherence to nonviolent resistance—"under no conditions were they to strike back, either physically or verbally." The core group invited those students who

had expressed doubt about their ability to remain nonviolent "not to participate in the specific demonstration but to go do something else, get involved in
the other support works, transportation, making the sandwiches, painting the
posters," Lawson recalled. The group drew up specific rules, and Lawson passed
them out, stating that they must "follow these instructions to the letter": "Do
not strike back nor curse if abused. Do not laugh out. Do not hold conversations with floor walker. Do not leave your seat until your leader has given you
permission to do so. Do not block entrances to stores outside nor the aisles
inside. Do show yourself friendly and courteous at all times. Do sit straight;
always face the counter. Do report all serious incidents to your leader. Do refer
information seekers to your leader in a polite manner." Those who broke the
rules "would undermine the sacrifice of everyone else." The list of rules ended
with a caution to "Remember the teachings of Jesus, Gandhi, Martin Luther
King. Love and nonviolence is the way." As he handed out the rules, Lawson
added a verbal exclamation mark: "Remember this: violence of spirit is even
worse than striking back."[39]

The students stopped by the church office as they departed for the demonstration, leaving behind nail files, pocket knives, and anything else that could
be construed as weapons. They walked to Eighth Avenue, then south to Church
Street, and sat-in at the five-and-dime store. The first action involved 124 students from American Baptist, Fisk, and Tennessee A&I State University. On 18
February, 200 students participated; on 20 February, 300 students sat-in. Their
numbers swelled to 400 when, on the twenty-seventh, white youths began to
stand in the aisles at Woolworth's, "insulting us, blowing smoke in our faces,
grinding out cigarette butts on our backs, and finally pulling us off our stools
and beating us," reported a blond, mustached Fisk student named Paul LaPrad.
LaPrad was the first attacked: "Hey, what's this white guy doing sitting with all
the rest of them?" "That's right — Nigger lover; Let's get him! Let's get him!"
LaPrad stated that "none of us attempted to fight back in any way. Failing to
disrupt the sit-ins, the white teenagers filed out. Two or three minutes later,
the police entered and told us we were under arrest." Once jailed, the students
became aware that a large segment of Nashville's black community was pulling behind them — first by raising bail money, then by conducting a boycott of
downtown stores. NCLC served as the pivot through which African Americans
and liberal whites could financially support the student movement.[40]

Throughout this hectic period known as the "sit-ins," the core group saw
to it that the time-consuming workshops continued. They were essential. As
Fisk student Peggi Alexander noted, "Throughout the movement the process
of learning took place." With the help of Lawson and another impassioned and
astute NCLC member, Reverend C. T. Vivian, "students saw, through practice,

Paul LaPrad (center) in Nashville sit-in. Whites shouted, "Hey, what's this white guy doing sitting with all the rest of them? . . . Let's get him!" (Nashville Public Library, The Nashville Room)

Young men in jail for sitting-in, Nashville, March 1960. (Nashville Public Library, The Nashville Room)

Flyer from the Nashville nonviolent movement, 1961. H. G. Hill hired African Americans only for warehouse work and as truck drivers and paid them below-union wages. Stores in black neighborhoods refused to hire black cashiers or personnel. Nashville students concluded that "the refusal of businesses to hire perfectly qualified Negro individuals" was "one of the worst weapons of discrimination in this nation. . . . As the educational level rises, so aspirations rise. And how tragic it is for the Southland when a majority of Negro college graduates seek employment in the North because so many doors are closed below the Mason-Dixon line." (Kelly Miller Smith Papers, Vanderbilt University Special Collections)

H . G . HILL

If you Hire - We will Buy

Do you know that...

1. More Negroes shop at **Hill Stores** than at any other chain store?

2. More **Hill Stores** are located in Negro neighborhoods than any other section of the city?

3. When approached about Negro Employment Hill's Management answered:
   "WE DON'T HIRE NEGRO CLERKS AND HAVE NO INTENTION OF HIRING THEM!"

4. **H. G. Hill Stores** are home-owned chain stores and reputedly had its origin in a Negro neighborhood.

IMPORTANT NOTE

OUR DUTY AS CITIZENS OF AMERICA AND AS CHRISTIANS IS TO BREAK DOWN ALL FORMS OF SEGREGATION BY PEACEFULLY RESISTING

DO NOT SUPPORT SEGREGATION

DO NOT BUY WHERE STORES WILL NOT HIRE YOU ON A FAIR BASIS.

Nashville Christian Leadership Council

the truth and beauty of the profound words 'Love thy neighbor as thyself.'" But NCLC members grew concerned: if a young man saw his girlfriend or sister abused, would he be able to maintain nonviolence? Lawson was confident that the workshop ties were strong enough.[41]

To sustain nonviolent direct action—*actively* challenging the segregated system as opposed to choosing not to ride a bus—required a different array of internal resources. The workshops provided space to develop these resources. Here, participants refined their capacities to live with the uncertainty of the immediate future: they felt sustained by a slowly solidifying belief in each other and in each others' values. When the students found out that there might not be bail money for them, for instance, Bevel believed that "something will happen in the situation that will provide the solution." As Kelly Miller Smith later wrote, Bevel "thus exhibited a faith far superior to that shown by our seasoned minds." Diane Nash and Angeline Butler agreed, but the older members of the NCLC were not so sure. The students "were certain that to wait another day would be worse than facing the situation right then without worrying about consequences to themselves," recounted Smith. These were "young people armed with a dream."[42]

The students decided that they needed a different structure from that provided by the parent organization of Nashville ministers. Once their meetings grew from twenty to several hundred, and those hundreds were demonstrating in the streets, the core group put in place a "central committee." Observing that Diane Nash responded well under pressure, the group asked her to chair the new policy-making body. This committee "met night and day, late at night, early in the morning, and planned the strategy from week to week." The central committee became the laboratory, Lawson recalled. "We used it as an opportunity to analyze nonviolence, to analyze what we were doing, and to learn more about nonviolence. I went to many of those meetings, and tried to persistently help people keep their focus on the nonviolent anvil, so that practical problems were discussed around a nonviolent ethos."[43] It was this quality of reflection, conversation, and commitment to intellectual and moral examination in the ongoing workshops that differentiated the Nashville movement from the thousands of other protest sites across the nation.

After all, people had challenged Jim Crow from its very implementation. The Nashville students were certainly nowhere near the first serious challenge to segregation. What made the Nashville group so powerful not just in comparison to prior activists but to others sitting-in in 1960 was this ability to work as a group, grounded in shared experiences over a long period. Workshops provided internal strength and cohesion, as well as a fierce determination to act despite dangers, which drew others in the first year after the 1960 sit-ins began.

At work in Nashville was something rarely seen in modern society: the workshops became the means through which people could develop intense civic relationships. By discussing the options and their own reasons for wanting to act, and using the belief of nonviolence as a new way to think about both, the students began to map out the implications of possible actions. The deeper these relationships became, the more candid they became with one another. Once they experienced this no-bullshit environment, the students worked to protect its integrity by demanding of themselves and of each other that it be maintained.

Meanwhile, each individual grappled with his or her own fears. Nash, for example, felt that if she could not act, she should not order others to do so either. Because she doubted her ability to follow through on the sit-ins, she asked herself how she could in good conscience send others to sit-in if she could not face down her own fears? Would she have to absent herself from all aspects of the sit-in, including the community she took a central part in creating? "I made a deal with myself," she said later. "I'd take five minutes during which I'd make a decision that I was going to either put the fear out of my mind and do what I had to do, or I was going to call off the sit-in and resign." Despite her uncertainty, she forced herself to act. Although she risked expulsion from Fisk as a result of her involvement, she wanted "a good America, and I want it just a little bit more than I want a degree."[44]

When Nash did participate, the reaction of the police was profoundly reassuring. "They were confounded," she reported. "No matter where they looked, there was another line of students waiting." Demanding treatment as a dignified human being, Nash "felt of value to herself." She "found courage in myself that wasn't there [before], and I found beautiful things in people who would care enough about other people to put their bodies between another person and danger. A lot of things started making sense to me through the learning of nonviolence as well as the practice of it. And I developed it as a way of life." Another southern student declared: "I myself desegregated a lunch counter, not somebody else, not some big man, some powerful man, but little me. I walked the picket line and I sat in and the walls of segregation toppled. Now all people can eat there." Thousands of other students throughout the South reported a similar feeling. For a brief moment, in Lewis's memorable phrase, they lived "democracy as a reality."[45]

Her participation in the sit-ins placed Nash in a fundamentally new relationship to those who routinely imposed segregation upon her. In the later 1960s, some people in the movement explained their turn to other forms of protest in part because they did not grasp the nature of transformations such as Nash experienced. Some dismissed nonviolence as a weak "appeal to the conscience of whites," as if Nash and her colleagues were acting as victims waiting for someone to recognize the moral righteousness of their cause. That was not Nash's understanding, however. She — and others in the nonviolent struggle like Bayard Rustin and Martin Luther King — believed that people and institutions tended toward corruption, and that evil was pervasive. Yet nonviolent activity could compel others to make a moral decision. Nash felt that she moved decisively away from victimhood: secure in a morally unassailable position, she grabbed the initiative and invited others to be their best selves as well. Her experience gave her a new sense of who she was and what her life might be.[46]

Local judges found Nash and the others who sat-in guilty of disorderly conduct. Lewis refused to pay the $50 fine and spent thirty-three days in the county jail. In the old days of routine segregation, jail brought shame on a family. Yet in this new context created by the movement, "it was like a holy crusade. It became a badge of honor," said Lewis, echoing Nash. "I had never had that much dignity before. It was exhilarating, it was something I had earned — the sense of independence that comes to a free person."[47]

In the spring of 1960, the students found increasing support from the larger black community: social clubs contributed funds, sororities and fraternities donated money earmarked for their annual functions, as did beneficent organizations such as the Nashville Council on Human Relations and the United Church Women. In April, ever greater numbers boycotted downtown stores. As white southern author and civil rights activist Anne Braden commented, "The sit-ins brought back the life-blood of citizen participation that had been scared out of our parents by the witch hunts and McCarthyism."

Amid the growing economic pressure on merchants in Nashville, on 19 April unknown assailants firebombed the house of Z. Alexander Looby. Dark-skinned, handsome, and stately, Looby served as city councilman and NAACP leader, and though born in the Caribbean, had long been considered Nashville's foremost champion of civil rights law. Quickly, four thousand mostly black citizens gathered to march to City Hall. Some of the demonstrators sang church songs, but, C. T. Vivian noted, "as we came closer to town, it was merely the silence of the feet." White workers lining the avenue on their lunch break "didn't know what to do. All you could hear was our feet as we silently moved." Nash recalled that "one of the things we had learned from Gandhi's movement was to turn the energy of the violence that was perpetrated against us into advantage." The attack on Looby backfired — he was highly respected in many parts of the community. "It was no longer the students and a few civil rights activists and SCLC people," Lewis stated. "Blacks and whites from all over came and participated. It was the total community, white people and black people."[48]

The marchers stopped on the steps of City Hall, and Mayor Benjamin West came out to meet them. Face to face on the steps, Reverend Vivian condemned the mayor, and an angry shouting match followed. Then Diane Nash, shy and vulnerable in private life, stepped forward to speak. She felt great respect for Lawson, and she knew her peers to be good and intelligent people, but during the fall workshops she had doubted they could implement their dream. "We are children and we are weak," she had thought. "We have no police force, no judges, no cops, no money." Now, as she actually participated in the nonviolent demonstration, Nash felt differently. She could look authority in the eye, even the mayor.[49] She started to speak in a calm, distinctly nonconfrontational manner that immediately changed the tenor of the interaction. West later described what happened as a kind of "soul-searching." "Mayor West," she asked directly, "do you feel that it's wrong to discriminate against a person solely on the basis of his race or color?" In response to her question, West attempted "as best I

Nashville mayor Benjamin West, Reverend C. T. Vivian, and Diane Nash. West stated: "They asked me some pretty soul-searching questions. Nash's question was addressed to me as a man; I tried as best I could to answer it frankly and honestly, that I could not agree that it was morally right for someone to sell them merchandise and refuse them service." (Nashville Public Library, The Nashville Room)

could to answer it frankly and honestly." He said that it was morally wrong to sell someone merchandise and refuse them service. He later received criticism for his statement but stood by it. "It was a *moral* question," he asserted, "and one that a man and not a politician has to answer." "It was a turning point," recalled Nash. Three weeks later, blacks were served at Nashville's lunch counters.[50]

SNCC: Debating Nonviolence

All of their preparation would now pay off and in a way that exceeded the Nashville students' expectations, if not precisely in the manner they had anticipated. After the first wave of sit-ins swept across dozens of southern cities, veteran civil rights organizer Ella J. Baker, then serving as acting executive director of SCLC based in Atlanta, recognized the sit-ins' potential to energize the movement she had spent a lifetime advancing.[51] She prevailed upon Martin Luther King and SCLC to provide some gas money for the students to gather at her alma mater, Shaw University in Raleigh, North Carolina. She did not want to see a stall in momentum now. The students had broken through; if they could compare experiences and coordinate their future activities, more progress might be made. It proved to be a fateful meeting.

Most colleges sent two or three students to the Shaw conference in April 1960. Baker asked Nashville to dispatch five students—the largest number invited from any city. Nashville sent three cars carrying sixteen people. Their experience in the Lawson workshops and extended sit-ins gave them an aura of audacity and resoluteness that attracted other students. They also provided a model of interaction: they trusted one another. Atlanta delegate Julian Bond was "very taken by their group personality. Not just the panache and confidence they had in each other," he remembered, "but how far they had already gone." Unlike the sit-ins in Atlanta in which Martin Luther King and SCLC dominated, the older leadership in Nashville—ministers like Kelly Miller Smith—allowed the Nashville students to make the critical decisions themselves.[52]

To keep open strong lines of communication after they dispersed, the participants in the Shaw meeting formed a temporary body and named it the "Student Nonviolent Coordinating Committee." At the conference, where young and not always sophisticated egos banged up against each other, Ella Baker's poise and experience helped bridge everyone over the shoals. It is also where the Nashville group moved to the forefront. In May, participants at a second SNCC meeting worked on a statement of purpose. The task became the first challenge for the Nashville students faced with exporting their experience to the emerging movement. To get their ideas across to others who had not shared the workshops and conversations that *predated* the demonstrations and jailings, the Nashville group took on virtually the whole second meeting in May. Lewis stated that there was "a great deal of debate and a great deal of discussion and even verbal fights on the whole question of nonviolence." "Some people," he explained, "opposed the whole idea of basing the movement on the Judeo-Christian heritage—a belief in love and nonviolence." The Nashville students, particularly Lewis, Nash, Bevel, Lafayette, and, of course, Lawson, had "thought through" and "acted through" the key components of the nonviolent message. Perhaps most important, that message had enabled them to desegregate Nashville's lunch counters. As Nash said, "Success is very persuasive."[53]

The development of a statement of purpose marked the beginning of the "Nashville Era" of SNCC, a period between 1960 and 1962 when the Nashville students exerted a formative influence on the organization as a whole. The Nashville group won other pivotal converts, including Charles "Chuck" McDew, a self-possessed student from South Carolina State College who would soon be named chairman of SNCC. McDew recalled that at the Shaw conference, the "very eloquent people from Nashville" talked about "a redemptive community." The debonair McDew had grown up in northern Ohio and converted to Judaism when he went south for college — the local rabbi was the only religious leader in town who did not discriminate. McDew and his associates in Orangeburg had been using nonviolent direct action "strictly as a tactic." Yet once they encountered the Nashville advocates, "we learned so much." Lawson "spent hours talking with us. But we still didn't have the grasp of the concept as well as people from Nashville did." Some activists, like Ella Baker and Howard University's Stokely Carmichael, grasped the concept but could not apply the "spiritual evangelism" of the final step: establishing a moral human contact with the aggressor. If moral suasion worked, fine. But if it took legal proscription or even force of arms, that worked too. As Carmichael said: "I never saw my responsibility to be the moral and spiritual reclamation of some racist thug. I would settle for changing his behavior, period."[54]

But "changing behavior" undergirded the campaign to erase Jim Crow from American life. The point was critical: the idea of nonviolence was embattled within SNCC from the start, because few found it easy to understand and most felt it harder still to put into action. McDew said that the debate over nonviolence as a tactic versus nonviolence as a way of life marked the site of "continuing struggle within the organization." The fact that the "struggle" persisted verified a tenacious truth about the emerging movement. Almost everyone who attended the Shaw conference in April 1960, as well as a critical meeting the following October, could be regarded as an activist. Almost all of the conferees had been to jail. They had gotten their feet wet. Yet most of the them had not lived through an extended evaluative, reflective training workshop even remotely akin to the experience the Nashville students put themselves through in 1959 – 60.[55] Many consequently lacked a commitment to what Lawson called "revolutionary" nonviolence grounded in values recently honed individually and hammered out collectively amid lengthy, candid, and confrontational discussions.

People needed to "grow into a commitment" to nonviolence, Nash said. "As we widened the movement on a national basis, many of the participants had never been in a single nonviolent workshop, and some of those in SNCC had been in one or two or three, so that was very different from our experience." In other words, most people did not see nonviolence as a powerful alternative to the status quo. Nonviolence certainly did not characterize many — or even most — approaches used within the three-hundred-year-long black freedom struggle. It did not easily mesh with the political tradition of most African Americans living in the rural South who followed Ida B. Wells's 1892 counsel that "a Winchester rifle should have a place of honor in every black home, and it should be used for that protection which the law refuses to give." Indeed, SNCC activists would soon find the house of veteran Mississippi civil rights activist Amzie Moore a veritable armed fortress. Lawrence Guyot, a large, jovial man who joined SNCC early and drew on his Mississippi heritage to energize his nonstop canvassing work, remembered that "whenever anyone was threatened, Moore was an individual protection agency. He had successfully fought against the [Ku Klux] Klan, both politically and physically."[56]

As Stokely Carmichael stated, in "American cultural terms, particularly the cowboy, mountain-man, outlaw, carbine-and-six-gun culture of the American frontier, popularized over the media, nonviolence is clearly aberrant." Carmichael added that in Harlem, the group he called "the 125th Street nationalists" attacked nonviolence in street corner stump speeches and mocked its practitioners for "begging white folks to accept us." But this, of course, was a bit of street theater — dramatic but devoid of the enduring day-to-day dignity that nonviolent direct action sought to spread across America. Passively watching or listening to a sidewalk debate did not change behavior; it could even reinforce passivity. Throughout the twentieth century, the vast majority of black southerners never viewed themselves as pacifists even though thousands were willing to march in nonviolent demonstrations at various points. Instead, many saw nonviolence through the lense of their own experiences and that of the dominant culture, where nonviolence often seemed impractical, weak, or unmanly. Certainly it was always counterintuitive. The Nashville students addressed this issue in 1961 when they wrote: "Some people say we are cowards; some believe that we seek publicity; others feel we are only looking for excitement and that we cause violence. Still others hold that nonviolence asks too much of the individual." Robert F. Williams, head of the Monroe, North Carolina, NAACP chapter, invoked an even more powerful idea in 1962, when he asserted that "massive civil disobedience is a powerful weapon under civilized conditions," but "where there is a breakdown of the law, the individual citizen has a right to protect his person, his family, his home and his property." None of the sit-in activists in Monroe was "even spat upon," he believed, because "we'd shown the willingness and readiness to fight and defend ourselves." Many people in the movement felt like Assata Shakur, who eventually resolved to challenge the state's monopoly on violent methods: "I still couldn't get used to the idea of letting somebody spit on me."[57]

In the spring of 1960, those debates still had not run their course. Indeed, among nonviolent practitioners, wide-ranging discussions raged over various interpretations of nonviolence as well as the degree to which one could and should practice it. One catches a glimpse of this complexity in historian Stewart Burns's apt description of Martin Luther King's philosophical evolution during 1955–56. King's "faith-based nonviolence," Burns argued, differed from that of

FOR workers Bayard Rustin and Glenn Smiley "in that [King] faced sin squarely, without illusion, like the Hebrew prophets. He grasped that love could not endure without power to defeat the evil that revolts against love — and that this power of justice and righteousness required coercion as well as suasion." Throughout the Montgomery bus boycott, King's "nonviolent philosophy changed inflection depending on his audience." Black mass meetings heard him preach about "the ubiquity of evil" where the devil lurked in white supremacy; white audiences in the North listened to his eloquent, scholarly call to white redemption. Eventually, King renounced any use of violence, even in self-defense.[58]

So at this early juncture in SNCC's formation, the well-tested ideas of the Nashville group prevailed — a testament to their experience and discipline, as well as to their individual and collective verbal skills. SNCC's founding statement pledged to "affirm the philosophical or religious ideal of nonviolence as the foundation of our purpose, the presupposition of our faith, and the manner of our action."[59]

The Sit-ins' Recruiting Power

The sit-in example jump-started others. As Lawson later noted, "The kinds of relationships in Nashville that formed, that became genuine relationships of community and understanding and of commitment to the common good, [were] repeated in other places." The FOR, in fact, hired Charles Jones from Charlotte, North Carolina, as its student secretary, to "interpret the sit-in movement in various campuses across the whole nation" during the fall of 1960. Jones, the son of a Presbyterian minister and an English teacher, early on learned that "between Jesus of Nazareth, Hegel, Homer, I believed that this country was based on sound, solid Christian principles." He could not square man being basically good with what was happening to black folk in the South. So nonviolence, as interpreted by King and Lawson "with all of the European finesse," was a fresh ray of light. He quickly carried this idea of nonviolent relationship into other areas of the South through FOR workshops.[60]

Charles Sherrod, a divinity student at Virginia Union University in Richmond, heard of the sit-ins through newspapers. He had grown up poor in Petersburg, raised by his mother and grandmother to strive for a better day. Tall, slim, and resolute, Sherrod possessed an infectious enthusiasm and a passion for life. Later, he would be known throughout the movement as "the wild man of nonviolence — dramatic, devout, daring." But in early 1960, he sat on the sidelines. Reading about the sit-ins, a friend asked him, "Why don't we do it?" Sherrod habitually read the *Afro-American, Journal and Guide,* and *Pittsburgh Courier,* all of which printed articles about a minister in Nashville named James

Lawson. On 22 February 1960 Sherrod and others staged a sit-in at Thalheimer's department store in Richmond, integrating the lunch counter.[61]

Even though he lived in the North, New Yorker Robert P. "Bob" Moses felt a strong connection with the southern black college students involved in the first sit-ins. Raised by politically astute and educated working-class parents in Harlem, young Moses earned a bachelor of arts degree from the overwhelmingly white Hamilton College and a master's degree in philosophy from Harvard University. Back home to help support his family after his mother's death in 1959, he was teaching math at the prestigious Horace Mann School when the sit-ins began. "I could feel myself in the faces of the people," he said later. Immersed in white society at Hamilton, Harvard, and Horace Mann, Moses taught himself to "repress my feelings, or at least expression of my feelings whenever I felt humiliated — to hide them." The sit-ins offered a new way forward. Over the spring break, Moses went to Virginia to visit an uncle who taught at Hampton Institute. In Newport News, he sat-in for the first time at a Woolworth's, "finally finding a way to personally take on prejudice and racism — to engage." It created in him "a feeling of great release." The sit-ins "hit me powerfully, in the soul as well as the brain." Soon Sherrod and Moses — two of the most determined and brilliant of SNCC's later visionaries — were invited to participate in SNCC gatherings as a result of their involvement in the Virginia sit-ins.[62]

The sit-ins also spurred the creation of new cultural forms, especially songs. The first time Albany State College student Bernice Johnson marched around City Hall in Albany, Georgia, to protest segregation, she realized that she had walked on Pine Street only once before. As a teenager, tall and radiant with poise beyond her years, she was well regarded for her ability as a song leader in church. Yet the Pine Street protest was scary. "Once you do something that is new, you can't walk too far," she noted. Thus the group soon retreated to the black institution closest to City Hall — Union Baptist Church. When someone asked Johnson to begin a song, the first one that came to mind was an "old song. I'm doing this new thing, ain't never been done before." She began to sing "Over My Head." The first line traditionally began, "Over my head I see trouble in the air." Yet inspired by their action, she sang, "Over my head I see freedom." She "didn't feel any trouble and I knew I could not sing 'trouble.' Also I was given permission to mess with a sacred song. The permission came because I had walked around City Hall. And if you're bad enough to walk around City Hall in Albany, Georgia, you can change the words to this old song."[63]

The music, then, fought the fear that each participant felt. Lining a song — where one person sang a line and others repeated it together, gave people what SNCC worker Zohorah Simmons called a "spirit force that was like taking on armor."[64] It made tangible the courage they needed to challenge the received culture and reassured them that they were not alone. Before and during the protest, then in jail, singing rooted many of the participants in the church hymns and spirituals their parents sang when they were young. Singing reminded people of the strength they already possessed by virtue of growing up in their own church-based communities. The lyrics and structural forms embodied modes of survival and resistance to oppression that had sustained African Americans for generations.[65]

Across the South, the sit-in tactic — almost always accompanied by song — worked to compel *adults* to address segregation. At Voorhees Junior College in South Carolina, Cleveland "Cleve" Sellers and other students sitting-in forced the college president's hand: that is, whether to let the students protest downtown or expel them. The Board of Trustees advised expulsion. "We were on the right side of a gigantic moral chasm," Sellers wrote, one that had been created out of "greed, prejudice, and ignorance. The Board of Trustees was attempting to act as if a middle ground existed. We knew that there was no middle ground."[66]

Though it drew many new people into the struggle, the sit-in movement faltered in the fall of 1960. Publicity declined as the novelty of protests wore off and as local white governments refined the practice of co-opting black college administrators dependent on the local power structure. These stumbling blocks led to the decision at a SNCC conference in October 1960 to coordinate protests under a more formal organizational structure, rather than simply under a clearinghouse committee.[67]

Miss Baker

Ella Baker nurtured the young organization. It was not too much to call her, in the words of one SNCC activist, "one of the most effective political organizers this country has ever produced." She had worked at the top of the NAACP as well as SCLC, and knew the leaders of CORE and the Urban League. Though she had long been "close to the centers of power within the black community," she always worked as "a critical and conditional insider." As her biographer Barbara Ransby wrote, Baker chose this marginality throughout the 1940s and 1950s by "criticiz[ing] unchecked egos, object[ing] to undemocratic structures," and protesting unilateral decision-making. In the early 1960s she made time to attend SNCC meetings by moving from the Atlanta-based SCLC to a job at the national YWCA, also in Atlanta. When trying to reach consensus, the young people often veered off on tangents and lost the central issue under discussion. Baker used a technique she had developed through long years of organizing: she asked questions. "I was not too sure that I had the answer," she later admitted. While this may have been true, her precise questions and nondirective style helped SNCC members to focus on the most important issues, as well as to respond authentically. Diane Nash was puzzled, at times even devastated, by civil rights leaders who seemed more concerned with their own organization, public relations, or fund-raising than with being honest. She once commented that Baker was her "only trustworthy guide. She made things make sense for me."[68]

Baker's approach provided an important model — "crucial to the dynamic and tone of these early [SNCC] meetings" — that students like Nash and Charles Sherrod subsequently adopted. As activist and historian Joanne Grant put it, Baker showed people "that everyone had something to give, thus helping them learn to respect each other." She "would pick out a kernel that was a good idea," said Chuck McDew. "Somebody may have spoken for eight hours. Seven hours and fifty-three minutes was utter bullshit, but seven minutes was good. She taught us to glean out the seven minutes." Stokely Carmichael added: "She was so patient with us, very patient." She avoided dogma at all costs "because she clearly understood the danger of becoming that against which you are fighting." Everyone in SNCC took their tough questions to Baker because "she knew way more than we did and we all knew that." Distrusting dogma of any kind, she almost never gave an advice-seeker a direct answer. "Usually she preferred to answer with another question and then another, forcing us to refine our thinking and to struggle toward an answer for ourselves." She did not agree with every conclusion reached, "but she truly believed *we* had to make our own decisions so long as the process was open, inclusive, and rigorous."[69]

Baker took a decisive step when she publicly opposed the proposal of SCLC leaders Martin Luther King, Ralph Abernathy, and Wyatt T. Walker to make SNCC a youth wing of SCLC. Baker, "outraged by the ministers' plans," walked out of a meeting where they discussed how to convince the students to join their organization. Baker viewed the sit-ins as a fresh approach. Her departure from SCLC, according to Grant, "signaled the beginning of a new phase for the civil rights movement. It was no longer to be controlled by a stodgy ministerial or bureaucratic presence." Instead, student energy and daring would control the direction of the movement.[70]

Bob Moses returned to New York after the sit-ins, but kept his eye out for a way to return to the South. Bayard Rustin soon sent him to Atlanta. There Moses met Ella Baker and Jane Stembridge, a white poet from Georgia and at that time the only full-time SNCC staff member. As Stembridge began to organize the October 1960 SNCC conference, she saw that she had no names of people living in rural Georgia, Alabama, Mississippi, or Louisiana — which together constituted the heartland of the caste system. Stembridge asked Moses to travel through the region seeking recruits for SNCC. He agreed, and he, Stembridge, and Baker compiled a list of Baker's grassroots contacts in those states that might be useful.[71]

Through long conversations in the summer of 1960, Ella Baker took it upon herself to get to know Bob Moses as a person. As Bernice Johnson Reagon later explained, "in the middle of the most intense movement crisis, Miss Baker would always ask you about your person, your home, your children, your food, your thinking." This is how she taught everyone "that no movement could exist without individuals," and that any movement's organization had to take care of the people who made up the movement. In all this, she was "extremely mat-ter-of-fact," focused always on "[how] did this action here that you were doing really affect the long range or overall goal of the movement, or of people?"[72] Yet, in its ultimate application, Baker's persistent interest in the personal aspects of people's lives served as more than an organizing method. It was the social cornerstone of political life: for a movement to be democratic, one had to work with its people in a democratic manner.

Baker's approach to politics was more than merely pragmatic. It was so broad as to be ideologically undefinable. She "seemed to know that however much we think and talk, and however important that is, it is action that makes social change happen. She was always directed toward action, thoughtful ac-tion." Baker's "notion of the need to raise up new leaders, to rotate leaders, far from being intellectual, was totally practical, based on years of experience in seeing folks join the leaders' club when they became leaders, leaving their constituents behind."[73] Her long-standing emphasis on building a leadership capability among local people would have a marked influence on the direction of SNCC — and on Moses in particular — and through both, on the civil rights movement as a whole.[74]

Baker's practical and strategic concern to make mutual respect a social pivot would reappear as a central issue within SNCC in the fall of 1964, when some members accused Moses and others who shared this broad vision of being "short-sighted." But in 1960, with the crisis still to come, it seemed that Law-son's workshops, Baker's mentoring, and their dual ability to counsel while encouraging the black-led southern movement to develop the voices of local people, provided cohesion for the energy radiating outward across the South.

No Longer a Small Group

Scholars and journalists paid a good deal of attention to the sit-ins, but almost none of their accounts penetrated deeply into the movement or were able to explain the source of its power. From Lawson's workshops, one can see how the sit-ins harnessed enough muscle to kill Jim Crow — at least at urban lunch counters in southern cities. The Nashville sit-ins took on a distinctive quality because Lawson pulled together a group of people with whom he met regularly, people who considered how to apply "historical" examples to Nashville in the present day. "We had the feeling that we were going somewhere," recalled Lewis. "We were going to do something. But it's strange. We were very patient."[75]

That job — pulling people together on a regular basis to reason about how they might change their immediate circumstances — sounds simple. Yet, throughout human history, it has proved to be one of the more difficult activities to *maintain*. Some people simply decide that they do not have an extra hour or two in their week to meet for such discussions. Others choose a pseudo-conclusion in place of civic conversation: "What is all this mere talk going to do, anyhow? It's pointless." People who have the time and understand the need may be discouraged by the potential risks to themselves or their families. Still others may not continue because they dislike the facilitator, or their only friend in the group stops going so they feel uncomfortable attending alone. Or they get sick. Or they get married. Or, as frequently happens, they use minor disagreements as justification for their withdrawal. Any of these things may halt the group's momentum, but the biggest roadblock of all is a sense of the remoteness, perhaps even of the hopelessness, of the desired goal.

To counter these potential barriers, Lawson emphasized the power of their vision. "Your idea is not small," he kept saying, "and because your idea is not small, your numbers will not be small either." Although they lived ordinary lives without visible power, if they acted on their conscience, on their vision, they would have to take terrible risks. Their actions in the face of this danger would transform them — they would no longer be ordinary. The power of this idea mesmerized them. "The greater the injustice, then the greater the force of the idea which opposed it." Action encouraged others to do the same, serving as a potent recruiting mechanism for those who shared their desire to end the caste system.[76]

This last idea inspired the students at a time when it seemed almost impossible to imagine that any small group could have an impact on the behemoth of segregation in the American South. Lawson knew that people could not be persuaded to act on their beliefs if they felt that action would have no effect. Their unstated fear — "no one will pay attention to a bunch of black college students" — immobilized them. Lawson countered with a prudent but provocative insight: others out there think like you do — but you have to stand up and become visible so they can see and join you. In this manner, Lawson confronted the final hurdle — moving people to act.

This formulation worked to recruit and develop leaders into a movement. First they were discovering — experiencing — a community of like-minded individuals who increasingly felt responsible for themselves individually and for one another. Second, they learned how to bring forth their own finest instincts — their capacities to imagine a just world and act on that vision. Third, as Bernard Lafayette later explained, Lawson's seminars integrated the religious and political components of life, offering participants a new kind of wholeness. For many students, all three reasons were interwoven, making the workshops, as Lewis observed, "the most important thing we were doing." Along with an extraordinary group of protégés, Lawson re-created, in essence, the community he had experienced as a child as part of a large black Methodist church. There it felt "safe for black people to release their most private and powerful emotions," a space that "was not merely religious but political as well."[77] By allowing others' experiences and ideas to become central to the workshops, they no longer existed as "Lawson's workshops." They belonged to all of the participants who contributed. The day following Diane Nash's confrontation with Mayor West, Martin Luther King visited Nashville. He came to the city, he said, "not to bring inspiration, but to gain inspiration from the great movement that has taken place in this community."[78]

CHAPTER TWO

Come Get My Mattress and I'll Keep My Soul

Freedom Riding

Two-inch newspaper headlines shrieked across the continent when Freedom Riders arrived in Anniston, Alabama, on Mother's Day in May 1961. Images of bloody Riders, club-wielding white thugs, and a burned-out bus flashed around the globe. Fearful of the consequences if they continued, CORE leaders canceled the Freedom Rides they had started ten days earlier in Washington, D.C. As Bob Moses recalled, at this point it was "only the Nashville student movement [that] had the fire to match that of the burning bus."[1] What happened was this: the Nashville students reignited the stalled Freedom Rides by traveling to Alabama and then Mississippi. The difference between what had been accomplished in the Nashville sit-ins and the more impromptu sit-ins that occurred across the South now became vividly evident in the students' response to the white violence in Alabama.

Riding through Mississippi, members of the group from Nashville were subsequently arrested in Jackson for breaching the peace. Soon joined by other black and white Freedom Riders, the students wound up in the maximum security unit of the infamous Mississippi State Penitentiary at Parchman. There, prison staff forced Riders to parade around the cell block naked and tortured them with electric cattle prods, fire hoses, and wrist-breaker cuffs. The new inmates answered these terrorist tactics with hunger strikes and a joyfully defiant outpouring of freedom songs. John Lewis and Bernard Lafayette wrote to their peers in Nashville that, despite the extreme molestation in Parchman, the group's "spirit is high, and shall remain high until this sleeping nation awakens to its most degrading problem — segregation." If need be, they resolved to remain in Mississippi jails "until the moral weight of the universe is brought to a focus on Mississippi and the South in general."[2]

The idea for the Freedom Rides came from a widely ignored Supreme Court ban on segregated bus and train terminals in the 1960 case *Boynton v. Virginia*. Despite the Court's ruling, blacks still had to ride in the back. In response, CORE resurrected a strategy first tried in 1947. Interracial groups would travel on buses; blacks would sit in the front and whites in the back, or they might sit together in the front. At every rest stop, blacks would enter the white waiting room and whites the black waiting room. If they were asked to move, they would refuse. "We felt we could then count upon the racists of the South to create a crisis, so that the federal government would be compelled to enforce federal law," explained James Farmer, the head of CORE. Much more than domestic policy hung in the balance. As the Cold War divided the world into two halves, TV broadcasts of violence against peaceful civil rights activists would intensify the pressure on President John F. Kennedy to intervene on the side of racial justice. In 1961 international pressure on the young president was intense, particularly after the Bay of Pigs debacle exposed him to charges of weakness in the face of the communist threat. CORE knew that Kennedy was keeping a wary eye on his upcoming summit in Vienna with Soviet premier Nikita Khrushchev, scheduled for 3 June. Kennedy wanted to look tough, in charge, and holding the upper hand. To maximize the chances of Kennedy's intervention on its behalf, CORE scheduled the Freedom Ride to begin on 4 May.[3]

The first group of CORE volunteers met in Washington in April 1961. John Lewis joined twelve others, all of whom had experience in nonviolent activity. Lewis was among the youngest; he, Charles Person, from Morehouse College in Atlanta, and Hank Thomas, an undergraduate at Howard University, were the only students. After a week of intensive training, six black and seven white Freedom Riders departed for New Orleans.[4]

There were few confrontations in the Upper South. Through Georgia, all was quiet. Then on 14 May, outside of Anniston, a white mob firebombed the lead bus and blocked the vehicle's exit. SCLC leader Fred Shuttlesworth had to send a convoy from Birmingham to rescue the Riders and escort the injured to the hospital when the police refused and the bus itself was destroyed. The second bus was boarded by the Ku Klux Klan; one Rider, a retired Detroit school administrator named Walter Bergman, suffered permanent brain damage from a beating, and another, Jim Peck, required over fifty stitches. The Klan also attacked the Freedom Riders in Birmingham. These incidents marked the momentous clash of integrationists and white supremacists that Farmer had anticipated. After the Klan attacks, no one from Greyhound Bus Lines was willing to drive the buses on to Montgomery. Shaken by the ferocity of the assault in Alabama, Farmer called off the action and put the Freedom Riders on a plane to New Orleans.[5] Apparently, white supremacist violence could defeat the Freedom Rides.

But the veterans of the Nashville workshops refused to surrender. Lewis flew to Nashville and met with Diane Nash, Jim Bevel, and Bernard Lafayette. Lewis sensed that, if anything, Nash was more determined than he. As she later said, "I strongly felt that the future of the movement was going to be cut short if the Freedom Rides had been stopped as a result of violence." It would have given the impression "that whenever a movement starts, all that has to be done is that you attack it with massive violence, and the blacks will stop." Lewis also felt that one of the most basic tenets of nonviolent action was "there can be no surrender in the face of brute force or any form of violent opposition," because "backing down in a situation like that means that other values matter more than the issues or principles that are at stake."[6]

If the Nashville students could restart the Freedom Rides, not only could they keep their movement alive, they might also be able to force the president to choose between what he knew was morally right and the *realpolitik* of a Democratic Party still dependent on the all-white party machinery in the South. To make the moral choice, however, Kennedy would have to make a stand against the commanding director of the Federal Bureau of Investigation (FBI), J. Edgar Hoover, a longtime enemy of the civil rights movement.[7]

The week after the CORE Freedom Rides disbanded, twenty-one students — the mainstays of the 1960 Nashville workshops — prepared to leave for Alabama. Funded by NCLC, the Nashville students determined to mount the challenge despite the pleas from parents and the threats from their universities. They selected ten volunteers to continue the ride: six black men, two black women, one white man, and one white woman. The rest would serve as backup. All of the participants were "mentally, physically, and psychologically prepared," thanks to Lawson's workshops and their own self-generated experiences in Nashville. "You might get killed," Shuttlesworth warned when Nash told him they were coming. "If they stop us with violence," she replied, "the movement is dead. The students have decided. We just want to know if you can meet us."[8]

Upon their arrival in Birmingham, the police immediately jailed two Nashville Riders for refusing to move to the back of the bus and held the remaining eight in protective custody until they promised to leave the city. On 19 May all ten students went on a hunger strike, which they intended to maintain until released "as free men with the rights of regular citizens." The Birmingham police drove the eight black members of the Nashville delegation to the Alabama-Tennessee state line at 4:30 A.M. and dropped them off by the side of the road. Despite fear of a Klan ambush, they returned to Birmingham in a car arranged by Nash; there they were met by eleven more Nashville students arriving by train and car.[9]

As the Nashville students had suspected, it was only when they put Robert Kennedy on notice, telling him they were willing to sacrifice their lives to desegregate interstate travel—by going back to Alabama—that the attorney general became "really involved."[10] Only then did the physical protection of the students become as important to him as the political protection of his brother, President Kennedy; or to put it more bluntly, only then did protecting the president mean protecting the Riders. At that point the attorney general demanded that Greyhound find a bus driver and called Alabama Governor John Patterson to insist on state protection.[11]

While the federal government tried to resolve the transportation issues with the state of Alabama and Greyhound, the Nashville students continued to gain information from new allies in the media. Some reporters with colleagues who covered the U.S. Justice Department, the White House, and the Alabama state capitol "kept passing on what they were hearing [from these colleagues] to the Freedom Riders, trading information as reporters traditionally do," writes David Halberstam, then a reporter in Nashville. "The bigger the story got, the less darkness the Freedom Riders operated in, the more information they were given."[12] Information was power—though different from the power of putting one's body on the line—and the Freedom Riders, through their own pluck and determination, had plugged in to a very valuable resource.

On 20 May the Freedom Riders rode from Birmingham to Montgomery under police escort. On the outskirts of the city, the state troopers disappeared, and Montgomery police did not appear at the bus station. "There was no one, so quiet, peaceful; nothing," Lewis said. Then, "all of a sudden, just like magic—white people, sticks and bricks. 'Nigger—kill the niggers!'" recounted Frederick Leonard, another Freedom Rider from the Nashville workshops and a student at Tennessee State. The Riders realized that if they exited from the back of the bus, "maybe they wouldn't be so bad on us," Leonard continued. "They wanted us to go off the back of the bus. We decided no, we're going off the front of the bus, and take what's coming to us." Jim Zwerg, a white student from Wisconsin who had been spending a semester at Fisk, took the brunt of the beatings. "I think that's what saved me, Bernard Lafayette, Allen Cason—because

Jim Zwerg walked off the bus in front of us," said Leonard. "He had a lot of nerve." Leonard's voice cracked with emotion, remembering Zwerg's stunning courage. William Barbee and John Lewis were also beaten, and Barbee suffered permanent paralysis.[13]

Robert Kennedy's rage now burst forth — both at the lack of control of the Alabama state government and at the behavior of two FBI agents who stood by doing nothing as his top aide, John Seigenthaler, was beaten by the mob. The attorney general immediately sent U.S. marshals to Maxwell Air Force Base outside Montgomery.[14]

Martin Luther King also flew in to lead a rally at Montgomery's First Baptist Church to support the Riders. Before long, a white mob surrounded the church, followed soon afterward by Kennedy's unarmed and reluctant U.S. marshals. When the white crowd threatened to burn the church and shoot everyone who ran outside, the marshals admitted that they could not control the situation. King called Kennedy from inside the church, demanding federal protection. Kennedy, in turn, called Governor Patterson, who refused to protect King.[15] During an eight-hour, overnight standoff, two cars were overturned and set on fire, and bricks were thrown through the church windows, shattering glass over the heads of those inside. Finally, in the wee hours of the morning, just as Robert Kennedy ordered in federal troops, the governor declared martial law and dispersed the mob with state troopers.[16]

The Freedom Riders' actions had forced both the federal and the state government to protect the constitutional rights of movement activists — and, thus by extension, the rights of all Americans. Two days later, on 24 May, Greyhound buses left with Freedom Riders for Jackson, Mississippi. Unbeknownst to the Riders, Robert Kennedy had made a secret deal with the state of Mississippi — he would not enforce federal law in the state in return for a pledge that there would be no visible, public violence inflicted upon the Riders. Kennedy's compromise had the effect of undercutting the Riders' intent to compel federal enforcement of U.S. law in the Deep South. Worse, Kennedy negotiated without consulting a single Rider. The compromise thus put the Freedom Riders at the mercy of Mississippi's police, judges, and jailers: in Jackson, each Rider was sentenced, for "breach of peace," to sixty days in the state's infamous penitentiary at Parchman.[17]

In response to Kennedy's betrayal as well as his request for a "cooling off period," SNCC, CORE, SCLC, and the Nashville nonviolent movement formed a coordinating committee to take prompt action in Mississippi. The members of the coordinating committee then issued a nationwide call for volunteers to travel in integrated teams to Jackson to keep the pressure on the federal government to enforce its laws in the state. Ordinary people came from many places: Lula

Mae White, an African American elementary school teacher born in Alabama, joined the Freedom Ride because "I feel each individual has a responsibility to participate directly in projects which aim to destroy segregation. I feel a moral obligation as a citizen who believes in direct action to achieve a more democratic society." Jeanne Herrick, a white housewife from Chicago, participated because "by the use of nonviolent resistance we show that we can help all to a 'better' more merciful solution to the problem." She wanted her daughter "to be able to eat ice cream cones anywhere with any of her friends. I do not want her to have to learn to take in discrimination — that is only something of the past."[18]

All summer long, Freedom Riders continued to pour into Jackson, and over three hundred had been arrested by the end of August. Throughout, Soviet news services continued to ridicule U.S. claims to leadership of the free world in light of the jailing of hundreds of people for simply riding a bus. When Attorney General Kennedy called a meeting of SNCC and CORE to complain that the Freedom Rides were no longer productive and to ask for another cooling off period, he suggested that civil rights workers should register voters instead. At this point Charles Sherrod jumped out of his seat: "You are a public officer, Sir. It is not your responsibility, before God or under the law, to tell us how to honor our constitutional rights. It's your job to protect us when we do." Later that year Nash wrote: "If one acknowledges the God within men, would anyone ask for a 'cooling off period,' or plead for gradualism, or would they realize that white and Negro Americans are committing sin every day that they hate each other and every day that they allow an evil system to exist without doing all they can to rectify it as soon as they can?" The answer, she felt, was "to stop sinning and stop now!" Burke Marshall, assistant attorney general for civil rights enforcement, later admitted that the Freedom Rides were an education for himself, the attorney general, and the president. So important to the Cold War battle did the Freedom Rides appear to Secretary of Defense Robert McNamara and Secretary of State Dean Rusk that they publicly encouraged the Interstate Commerce Commission (ICC) to expand the Justice Department's capacity to enforce desegregated facilities. Finally, in September 1961, the ICC issued stronger regulations. In the space of one summer, the Freedom Rides had eliminated Jim Crow from the nation's interstate highways.[19]

The Rides' second major accomplishment was to bring "student energy into the state," reported organizer Bob Moses. When he arrived in Mississippi in 1960, "no one could know or tag me with anything." But when Moses returned in July 1961 — after the first Freedom Riders stepped off the buses in Jackson on 24 May — and "walked the dusty roads of Beartown, in McComb, little children would point us out and whisper, 'There goes some Freedom Riders.'" In fact, from that point forward, local blacks throughout the South called all civil rights workers

"Freedom Riders" — a testament to the courage it took to challenge the caste system. This shift in consciousness, recalled Moses, became intertwined with how SNCC got off the ground in Mississippi.[20]

Parchman Farm

The narrative of the Freedom Rides seems to end with this victory. Yet the Riders themselves remained in Parchman prison for sixty-day terms. Surpisingly, prison soon proved a central experience to the freedom struggle. "In Parchman [State Penitentiary], we were only allowed one book, the Bible. So we did a lot of singing," remembered Frederick Leonard. To keep their morale high, they sang freedom songs. The guards tried to silence them, but when the men heard the women singing on the other side of the facility, it only strengthened their resolve. "They'd sing to us and we'd sing to them," Leonard said. The guards threatened to take their mattresses if they continued to sing. "Everything else was cold and hard." It was very threatening to have nothing left to sleep on, noted James Farmer. Jim Bevel, who had also joined the Rides and was now in Parchman, held: "What they're trying to do is take your soul away. It's not the mattress, it's your soul." At this moment a Rider began yelling for the guards. When they appeared, Bevel said: "Come get my mattress, I'll keep my soul." The activists began singing: "Ain't gonna let nobody turn me round, turn me round, turn me round / Gonna keep on a-walking, gonna keep on a-talkin / Keep on walkin to the Promised Land." The guards took the mattresses, "and people sang as they had never sung before." Though the guards brought in fire hoses and hosed the whole row, everyone kept singing. "We thought we were winning the battle," Farmer stated, and "they were on the run."[21]

For many, the jail experience produced this kind of solidarity and mutuality. Yet it was often purchased at the price of great individual suffering. For example, when SNCC leaders shifted to a "jail-no-bail" strategy in Rock Hill, South Carolina, in February 1961 — three months before the Freedom Rides — they found that thirty days in jail provided a new type of experiential learning, one as important as that of the sit-ins.[22]

Ruby Doris Smith (later Robinson) was one of the fastest learners. A newcomer to Spelman College in Atlanta, the seventeen-year-old joined SNCC veterans Diane Nash, Charles Sherrod, and Charles Jones on the trip to Rock Hill. Smith, whose grit, intelligence, and fierce dedication to the sit-in movement soon became legendary, was raised in Atlanta by self-sufficient, devout Methodist parents. She "kneeled-in" during the summer of 1960 at local white Methodist churches, stunned by white ushers and congregants who blocked her entry and stared at her with looks of "pure hatred." She soon moved on to lunch counter sit-ins and to the center of the Atlanta student movement along-side her older sister Mary Ann. Though the more-experienced Mary Ann had been chosen to go to Rock Hill, she began to get "more weak in the knees." As she said, "I started thinking about all the little things I had in the making for the next year. Fellowships and what have you. What's going to happen if I [get] up there and spend all this time in jail?" Ruby Doris, disappointed that she had not been selected originally, kept talking it up and Mary Ann let her sister go in her place.[23]

After their arrest at Rock Hill, Sherrod and Jones were assigned to the chain gang, digging drainage ditches and laying pipe along highways. Armed guards with shotguns on horseback surrounded them. At any moment, they knew, they could be whipped or even shot for looking these deputies in the eye. Jones recalled that their intense punishment "galvanized" others in SNCC: "All we had done was sit down and ask for Coke and a hot dog. . . . That began the regional, national movement of students through SNCC . . . educating a lot of people in the country." It also was a turning point in Sherrod's life. Having lived through the possibility of imminent death, he came out of the jail "transformed," his philosophy firmly rooted in his survival of that experience. "If I accept death, then there's nothing that anybody can do to me." If he could learn to handle the "ever-present threat of death, then jail is just another house." Sherrod wrote later to others in SNCC: "If we represent something the people consider impor-tant, they will identify with us. Our best selling point is that we are students with nothing but our bodies and minds, fearlessly standing before the monster who killed our mothers and castrated our fathers — yet we stand with Love." It was grand, perhaps overly so. Yet it seemed very real.[24] Sherrod shared this understanding "with all the people that I came in touch with" subsequently,[25] and it proved decisive for the SNCC project he led in southwest Georgia the fol-lowing year.

The young women lived through a very different kind of incarceration. Nash remembered the thirty days in Rock Hill as one of the best and most peaceful periods of her life. Put in jail for a political crime, absolutely sure she was right and the jailers were wrong, she felt the pain was marginal. She discovered "a surprising spiritual side to her time there." She could find solitude when she chose to, and she had time to reflect on her recent actions. She read a good deal, finishing Gandhi's autobiography and the Acts of the Apostles.[26]

Southern authorities intended jail as a humiliation, a punishment for violat-ing the region's social norms. Yet after the concentrated emotional and social pressures Nash had faced since she began to work and act with Lawson's work-shop group in the fall of 1959, jail came almost as a reprieve. Here, she did not have to make life-and-death decisions. She faced no struggle within herself, nor with others, to figure out the right thing to do. The pace of life suddenly flowed with a slow and predictable regularity. Nash could finally begin to meditate in a sustained, detailed way about the events that had tumbled by in rapid-fire fashion ever since the sit-ins began. She had been a key member of one of the few communities committed to this kind of reflection — the Lawson workshops. By the spring of 1961, however, these sessions had been discontinued. Events had overtaken the Nashville group, as its members traveled and worked in various locales. Thus, at the same time that the student group grew large, it lost many of its internal mechanisms to process in all the new people. The small, intimate gatherings — in which the students had methodically explored attempts at human freedom ranging from the works of Jesus of Nazareth through Gandhi and the Montgomery bus boycott — now appeared far-flung and dispersed. Jail in Rock Hill gave Nash some time to reflect on this powerful set of experiences. Had her recent actions meshed with her beliefs? What mistakes had she made? What mistakes had the sit-in movement made? Should she return to college and get her degree, or should she work for the movement full time? Nash imagined the Fisk dean's goals for "nice young girls": to get their degree "and marry some black doctor, and live a black life parallel to the life of the wife of a white doctor." Nash grew acutely alert to "the difference between the real world as she saw it as an activist, and the tidier, more antiseptic world which seemed to be taught at Fisk," with what seemed to her "its unconscious acceptance of a segregated, evil order." Once released from jail, she felt spiritually renewed and certain of her commitment. She quit school.[27] Ironically, the punishment — intended to end the student movement — unintentionally provided some activists the quiet space and forced inactivity to think about their futures in a new way.[28]

The individuals incarcerated in Parchman in the summer of 1961 had faced the same test as the Rock Hill four in February and James Lawson in the 1950s: Were they willing to go to jail for their beliefs? Seriously compromise their relationships with parents and other significant people in their lives? Experience torture? Risk death? Those who survived would be forever altered.[29] One of Jim Bevel's teenage recruits to the Jackson movement, Willie Rogers, described solitary confinement at Parchman. "It's a cell about six foot square, which they call the hot box. Long as they don't turn the heat on, with three in there, you can make it." Sometimes nine, and then thirteen, were in the hot box at one time, reported another teenager, Jesse James Glover. Glover spent a total of thirteen days in the box. "We were making it okay about thirty minutes with the fan off, breathing in this oxygen, letting out this carbon dioxide — and the air was evaporating on top of the building and it got so hot the water was falling off the top of the building all around the sides like it was raining." A guard let them out but then hung Rogers and SNCC activist MacArthur Cotton on the bars for singing freedom songs. Seventeen-year-old Fred Harris spent 160 hours in the Parchman hole. SCLC minister C. T. Vivian refused to accept the guards calling him "boy" — "My denomination normally ordains *men*, not boys" — so guards beat his head bloody.[30]

"We remained a close brotherhood and sisterhood of shared experience," Stokely Carmichael wrote of those jailed in Parchman during the Freedom Rides. "For us, that prison experience would be life altering, a rite of passage, a turning point." It is pertinent to note a gradation of experience in these comments. The Freedom Riders' prison experience often forged bonds exponentially stronger than Lawson's workshop training, which had in turn created relationships exponentially stronger than those established in people's ordinary lives.[31]

The women activists were not exempt from horrendous abuse in prison. Elizabeth Hirshfeld, a twenty-four-year-old white graduate of Cornell University then working in a lab in Ithaca, New York, decided to go on a Freedom Ride as soon as she heard the call from SNCC. Flying to Washington en route to Nashville, "we went right over all the national monuments. I looked out of the window, at all the key places, and I thought, 'this is really what being an American is all about,' going on the Freedom Rides. Making America the way Lincoln and Washington meant it to be. That may have been kind of naïve, but it was really a fundamental part of what made me go down there. To do what I did was to be an American."[32]

Sixty days in Parchman, for a "naïve" young white woman who had grown up in a suburban, Midwestern, "rock-ribbed" Republican family, "forever marked my life."[33] Hirshfeld witnessed firsthand the intense commitment to nonviolence shared by many Freedom Riders, none more so than SNCC's Ruby Doris Smith. As the wardens prepared the women for showers, Smith refused to take her clothes off. "She was really into nonviolence, and she just wasn't going to do anything that she thought was contributing to an unjust society. So they took her clothes off and they scrubbed her with a wire brush." The women listened to Smith's screams for twenty minutes.[34]

What would compel someone to endure pain like that? "I lost my fear," another Rider reported. "It happened to all of us in that jail!" When people did not cooperate, despite the brutality and threats of death, "we all realized that we were much more powerful than them. That's when we all became noncooperative." Smith's biographer, historian Cynthia Griggs Fleming, reported that life in Parchman made the choice between freedom and its opposite unusually clear: Smith saw "fifty, sixty Negro men in striped uniforms, guarded by a white man on a white horse. It reminded you of slavery."[35]

Forced into solitary cells with nothing to do all day, the Riders had the opportunity to explore with new depth and "quiet time" life in the United States.

For Hirshfeld, it was a six-week course in political education—a very intensive seminar. In Parchman, for the first time, she became conscious of the all-white nature of her previous environments in Detroit and at Cornell. Someone asked her, "'Why do you think you didn't know anybody [black]?' I just had never thought about it (it was one of those 'a-ha' experiences), and I got it—pretty immediately."[36] What was the point of going South, she realized, "when this is going on in the North. I'm from the North, and I sound like a northerner, a particularly Midwestern northerner. I ought to go home and figure out what to do there, and maybe SNCC will tell me. SNCC said 'Raise money! Raise money!'" After her release, Hirshfeld met SNCC's Detroit contacts and over the next year began to raise money for SNCC in the North. She was just one of the hundreds of northerners who came out of Parchman "completely committed to the struggle," explained CORE field secretary Debbie Louis. "Exposure to the southern judiciary, and personal suffering stemming from the limitations of federal as opposed to state power . . . served to teach lifelong lessons to those young people in American democratic reality," Louis observed. "Most left jail to become full-time movement personnel, or to return to their home communities in the North to awaken people to the realities they themselves had just discovered."[37]

Until the spring of 1961, northerners had been restricted to supporting the southern freedom struggle through sympathy boycotts of northern chain stores like Woolworth's. But the Freedom Rides catapulted the southern struggle onto the national stage, for the first time giving northerners the opportunity to take direct action, wrote Anne Braden of the Southern Conference Educational Fund. Northerners like Hirshfeld went home with new insights.[38]

T he Freedom Rides changed the geography of the movement. Most sit-ins had occurred in the urban centers of the South where college youth gathered —none took place in rural Alabama or Mississippi. No one even thought it possible until something like the Freedom Rides "penetrated daringly . . . into these two citadels of caste," wrote Leslie Dunbar, head of the Southern Regional Council in Atlanta.[39] The Rides had shown SNCC that they *could* go anywhere to challenge the southern caste system. It amply demonstrated that there were places the sit-ins had not touched. SNCC members, seared by their time in Parchman and increasing their close connections as the dangers intensified, now decided to "go home"—to help others to break through in precisely the places where the caste system had by 1961 changed the least: the rural areas of southwest Georgia and Mississippi.

The Inner Life of Recruiting

Fear—that was what stood in the way of any purposeful action. The student movement had to find a way to deal with it. As Charles Sherrod put it, "There's got to be some settling done there, some coming to terms with your insides." New recruit John O'Neal remembered that the first time Sherrod drove him back to Albany, Georgia, from Atlanta, he pulled the car off the highway as they left the city and said "'Let's pray.'" Sherrod bowed his head for what "seemed like three hours. And then after a while he took his handkerchief and wiped the tears from his eyes and said, 'Amen.'" O'Neal, who was from Illinois and had been scared ever since entering the South, felt that Sherrod was unnecessarily "trying to make me afeared." But the SNCC organizer "went on to explain that he always prayed before he got on the highway because he didn't know whether he was going to get to where he was going. And he gave us the number and the address of the project office in Albany and the number of the office in Atlanta and the name of the person in Albany" in case they got stopped or arrested and something happened to him. This was one way Sherrod had discovered to continue despite his fear.[1]

By the end of 1962, SNCC had established two "hubs" of voter registration in regions considered among the most hostile in the South. One hub centered on Albany and the three counties in southwest Georgia that surrounded this small city of 60,000 people. The second hub would eventually cover most of Mississippi. The projects' most intense years of registering black voters were between 1962 and 1965. In order to work in these areas, SNCC activists had to find ways to operate under the constant threat of terror.[2]

Voter registration in southwest Georgia and Mississippi *was* direct action. This was a surprising discovery. Voter registration was just as threatening to the racial caste system as a sit-in or a Freedom Ride, so there was no meaningful difference between these kinds of actions. Before they entered the rural South, SNCC people had developed two effective tactics: one was the workshop pioneered by Ella Baker, James Lawson, and the Highlander Folk School, which built the fortitude and interpersonal trust to sustain an ongoing challenge to segregation. The second experientially grounded tactic was the sort of direct action epitomized by the sit-ins and the Freedom Rides, which had become the vehicles to mount that challenge. Yet SNCC organizers had not yet worked in significant numbers with anyone but themselves. After the Freedom Rides in Jackson, "we got the idea of mobilizing the whole community from the way people responded in Jackson," Sherrod recalled. "Local folk stood up against the system as they never had before — many went to jail with the Freedom Riders."[3] How could they find and work with local people in other communities? They also had to cope with the fact that their tactics could be altered, changed, and ultimately driven by white violence. While finding ways to proceed on these different fronts, they created democratic practices that would subsequently be exported to other struggles for citizenship across America in the 1960s. In this way, the country discovered that it housed a "movement."

Mississippi, 1960–1961

In Mississippi in 1960, out of 500,000 eligible blacks, a mere 23,000, or 4.6 percent, were registered to vote. Just to make sure things stayed that way, reported historian John Dittmer, whites in the state banned books, censored speakers, and cut off network TV programs in mid-sentence. As one white resident claimed, "I don't think that just to be 21, alive, and a citizen gives people the right to vote. I don't think these people have yet demonstrated the intelligence and responsibility required of a voter." To be certain that subversive voter registration campaigns did not operate underground, "the legislature created the State Sovereignty Commission, a secret police force that owed its primary allegiance to the [White] Citizens' Council." In the southwestern corner of the state, comprising Pike, Amite, and Walthall Counties, 200 out of a possible 16,000 black voters were registered. Bob Moses set up SNCC's first voter registration schools in these three counties.[4] Moses arrived in McComb, Pike County — reputed as the most antiblack area of the most hard-core antiblack state in the South — in the summer of 1961. C. C. Bryant, a longtime activist in McComb, made this possible. Moses set up classes to teach people how to register to vote, then accompanied them to the county courthouse, in Liberty, to register. After the registrar refused their applications and Moses was beaten, a dozen other SNCC workers went to McComb to support the project. Local high school students, eager to act now that "Freedom Riders" were in town, staged a sit-in at a local restaurant.

In the wake of the violence against Moses and other SNCC voter registration workers in the fall of 1961, a long-limbed, blue-eyed attorney in the U.S. Justice Department, John Doar, arrived in McComb to investigate. After all, in the midst of the Freedom Rides, Attorney General Robert Kennedy had promised to protect SNCC workers who stopped "direct action" and instead began to register voters. On 24 September Doar and Moses asked a local black farmer and leader in the voter registration campaign, E. W. Steptoe, if there was any danger in the area. "Steptoe told us that EH Hurst, who lived across from him, had been threatening people and that specifically Steptoe, Herbert Lee and George Reese were in danger of losing their lives," Moses recalled. Lee, a farmer and the father of nine, had been working constantly with Moses, arranging contacts, finding facilities for meetings, and extending himself as a community leader to encourage others to register. The next day, after Doar departed, E. H. Hurst picked a fight with Lee on the pretext that Lee owed him money. Although Hurst was a state representative and a childhood friend of Lee's, neither circumstance prevented him from shooting the unarmed Lee (Hurst later claimed self-defense). Moses, who identified the body, described what happened next: "Lee's body lay on the ground that morning for two hours, uncovered, until they finally got a funeral home in McComb to take it in. . . . No one in Liberty would touch it. They had a coroner's jury that very same afternoon. Hurst was acquitted." He did not spend a single hour in jail. "I remember reading very bitterly in the papers the next morning," continued Moses, "a little item on the front page of the *McComb Enterprise Journal* said that a Negro had been shot as he was trying to attack EH Hurst." No facts surrounding the shooting were given. "Might have thought he'd been a bum. There was no mention that Lee was a farmer, that he had a family, nine kids, beautiful kids, and that he had farmed all his life in Amite County. It was as if he had been drunk or something and had gotten into a fight and gotten shot."[5]

The Moses-Lee relationship was strategically important for the simple reason that if the federal government did not protect the right to vote in Mississippi, people like Herbert Lee were not going to become full citizens: they would be dead. As Lawrence Guyot, a SNCC field secretary, remarked: "It took a long time for SNCC internally to realize this, that when you're attempting to secure power in the South, it doesn't matter whether you're sitting at a lunch counter or you're attempting to register to vote. The most threatening of the two was attempting to register."[6] Therefore, it was historically incorrect to see voter registration as a "retreat" from direct action. To white authorities in Mississippi, no action by blacks was "moderate"; only total passivity and total acquiescence to all the customs and expectations of a white supremacist society were considered acceptable conduct.

Despite this climate of unpredictable racial terror, SNCC members worked to recruit others. It was a challenge faced by all insurgent movements: how to expand the base of people who were able to act? In July 1961, when Moses first arrived in McComb, Webb Owens, a retired railroad employee and treasurer of the local NAACP, picked up Moses and "began making the rounds" to "every single black person of any kind of substance in the community." For two weeks, during each visit, Moses conversed with these leaders about his proposal to undertake a month-long voter registration project. Other SNCC staff members would come to help, he promised, if the community raised money to support them. At that point, Owens moved in as a "closer." A smart, slim, cigar-smoking, cane-carrying, sharp-dressing gregarious man known in the community as "Super Cool Daddy," liked and trusted by all, Owens solicited contributions of five to ten dollars per person. Before the rest of the SNCC staff arrived, the black community not only supported the project, it financed it as well.[7]

Surfacing here is one of the central causal dynamics of the civil rights revolution in the South of the 1960s. While SNCC people may not have broken down the recruiting process into its component parts, these components are now (and were at the time) quite visible: Moses would approach a local leader — in this case, Webb Owens. He then listened to Owens's ideas and, in so doing, built a relationship. Impressed, Owens led Moses to all of the potential leaders in the community, in the process exposing himself to great risks as a local NAACP leader. When he extended himself on behalf of Moses and asked citizens to financially support a voter registration drive, things began to happen. "The quality of the local person that you go to work with is everything in terms of whether the project can get off the ground," Moses later explained. The McComb voter registration drive would not have taken off without someone like Owens.[8]

Moses' work in Mississippi has often, in retrospect, been termed "community organizing." But Ernesto Cortes, an organizer for the Industrial Areas Foundation, described this as just "a fancy word for relationship building. No organizer ever organizes a community. What an organizer does is identify, test out, and develop leadership. And the leadership builds the relationships and the networks and the following that does the organizing."[9] Moses' work can be seen as the initial formation of these key relationships. Ella Baker had developed this modus operandi to the level of high craft, and other effective field secretaries in SNCC gravitated toward it. Rather than mobilize people based on what SNCC wanted them to do, Moses tried to give local people an expanded sense of possibility. "If I want to organize you," Cortes said, "I don't sell you an idea. What I do, if I'm smart, is try to find out what's your interest. What are your dreams? I try to kindle your imagination, stir the possibilities, and then propose some ways in which you can act on those dreams and act on those values and act on your own visions. You've got to be the owner. Otherwise, it's my cause, my organization. You've got nothing!" Mississippian Charles McLaurin, a virtuoso organizer, later described this approach: "Talk with the people, laugh with them, joke with them; do most anything that gets some kind of conversation. It is very important to learn what bugs them. It may happen that they are thinking about trying to get the vote. You'll know when they talk." Moses built relationships through individual meetings. He tried to find out: What did people value? What did they want to do? In each meeting, he identified leaders and encouraged them to give themselves permission to act on their beliefs.[10]

In this way, with the initial network provided by Amzie Moore, C. C. Bryant, and Webb Owens, voter registration caught on in McComb. It had all begun with Moore — for years a giant in the Mississippi movement. In the 1950s, while singing in a gospel quartet, Moore had traveled the rural countryside signing people up for the NAACP. And he had mounted countless voter registration efforts. Moses considered Moore his "movement father." On Moses' first visit to Mississippi in 1960, Moore had told him that the vote could be a strategy for breaking down the caste system. ""No use sitting-in at lunch counters in the Delta,'" Moore said. "'Not enough food on the table.'"[11]

It would be difficult to overstate the role of Moore and other movement elders in creating community networks and safe meeting spaces, as well as serving as mentors of the SNCC workers. Moore, like Owens, introduced Moses to the black leaders in McComb, described the larger strategy, and sent young people in the state to work with Moses. In short, Moses found open minds in McComb because he learned from Moore that many blacks perceived the vote to be a logical, long-term goal pivotal to changing life in Mississippi. Moses then worked through already-existing networks of activists in the area — networks created by World War II veterans, fraternal organizations, church auxiliaries, and local NAACP groups that offered their spaces and resources for his project.[12] Finally, parting with their hard-earned money gave people a sense of responsibility to *and* ownership of the emerging program.

Moses quickly became well known to law enforcement circles in Mississippi. A week after the voter registration school opened in McComb, a county marshal stopped him for no apparent reason, then arrested him for "impeding an officer in the discharge of his duties." He asked Moses: "'Are you that Negro who's been trying to register our niggers?'" Moses was fined fifty dollars and spent two days fasting in jail. Suddenly life moved very fast in McComb. Young people in the town helped Moses and other SNCC staff to canvass, but they also wanted to organize a sit-in. Charles Sherrod and Marion Barry, just coming off of the Freedom Rides in Jackson, joined Moses in August to train youths in nonviolent direct action. On 26 August two nineteen-year-old friends from rural Pike County, slim and clear-eyed Hollis Watkins and tall, powerfully built Curtis Hayes, went to the Woolworth's in McComb to sit-in. They were arrested and spent thirty-six days in jail. It was the first student action in rural Mississippi. A few days later, black people in McComb began to protest the jailing of Watkins, Hayes, and Moses. The SNCC staff held a mass meeting for local people to decide how to act on their feelings.[13]

Two hundred McComb citizens attended the mass meeting — a huge turnout for rural Mississippi. They made two decisions. First, a group of three high school students would conduct a sit-in at the Greyhound bus terminal; they were arrested the next day for breach of peace and failure to obey a police officer. Second, SNCC would escort adults to the courthouse to register to vote. Upon arrival, the registrar denied the blacks' applications and threatened them. Inspired by the example of Moses and his local recruits, other SNCC workers traveled to McComb over the course of the fall, including Reginald "Reggie" Robinson from Baltimore, John Hardy from the Nashville student movement, Ruby Doris Smith from Atlanta, Travis Britt from Howard University's Nonviolent Action Group, Charles Jones, and Chuck McDew. All of these outsiders watched Moses carefully. After the development of relationships with community leaders, his most successful recruiting tactic was going door-to-door with registration forms. He asked residents: "Have you ever tried to fill out this form? Would you like to sit down now and try to fill it out?" People could then try to visualize themselves as voting citizens. But more violence followed. The repetition of such incidents made Moses "very, very depressed," he admitted later. Moses' state of mind was in fact a prime example of the toll movement work took on people, noted Constance "Connie" Curry, a white adviser to SNCC from its earliest days in Atlanta who frequently traveled to SNCC projects in the South. "I don't think that anybody ever envisioned the long years of struggle and violence — anguish," she acknowledged. "I don't think they were really aware of it." She remembered "watching the changes in Bob Moses" over time. "It was just a terrible, terrible, toll . . . it broke his heart. . . . He used to get hurt every time anybody would look mean at him, literally. He would feel it, and you could imagine that kind of sensitivity in Mississippi where people wanted to kill him."[14]

After the murder of Herbert Lee, SNCC could no longer find adults willing to register. Yet the area's young black workers refused to slow down. On 3 October 1961 SNCC held a mass meeting to raise money for Lee's family. Brenda Travis, a teenager arrested at a Woolworth's sit-in, voiced a desire to return to school, although she had been expelled for taking part in the sit-in. The day after she was denied readmittance, over one hundred students walked out of school and asked SNCC workers to help them plan a mass protest downtown. SNCC's first campus traveler, a white Alabamian named Bob Zellner, showed up in Mc-Comb to meet people and to get a feel for the field. The brown-haired, gentle "preacher's kid" realized during the mass meeting that he had to decide quickly whether his participation in the upcoming protest would endanger his "quiet sort of work" with white southern students, or whether he wanted to assert to these black high schoolers — and to himself — his place in the movement.[15]

It was a significant moment of choice. Many whites were afraid to enter the fray. What if their picture appeared in the paper and people back home saw it? Joining a sit-in or a picket line or a protest march "was such a public step," one southern white worker recalled. "It put you against everybody else"; it made you an outlaw in your homeland.[16] Nonetheless, Zellner joined the march along with two other SNCC workers the following day as the students marched downtown through the watchful Negro community. When they reached the steps of City Hall, Curtis Hayes and Hollis Watkins began a "pray-in." All 114 demonstrators were arrested for breach of the peace. White onlookers assaulted all of the SNCC staff members.

Zellner, as the only white marcher, stuck out. As he approached City Hall, the mob began to scream "Bring him to us, bring him to us." Hemming him in on all sides, white men grabbed at Zellner while Moses and McDew tried to shield him with their bodies. Then, as the chief of police held Zellner down, "men began to beat him and to pull him into the crowd. He clutched at the railing, and tried to crawl up the steps. While policemen watched, Zellner was punched and kicked, his face scratched, his eyes gouged, and while on the ground he was kicked repeatedly in the head until he passed out." At one point, Zellner held his gouged eyeball in his hand. Denied medical treatment, he and the other SNCC staff members were jailed for contributing to the delinquency of minors.[17]

Despite the high schoolers' attempts to keep the voter registration movement alive in McComb following Lee's murder, SNCC workers knew few adults who were willing to continue. The project sputtered. "It's okay to put our own lives in jeopardy," McDew recalled. "But when you can cause somebody else to get killed, then that's a different question." "We knew in our hearts and minds that Hurst was attacking Lee because of the voter registration drive," said Moses. "I suppose that we all felt guilty and responsible, because it's one thing to get beat up and it's another to be responsible, or to participate in some way in a killing." After wrestling with their consciences, the staff decided to leave McComb for a time and test other areas of Mississippi, but resolved that they would not be turned back from their goal. When SNCC workers temporarily closed their office, a local resident put up a sign on the door: "SNCC done Snuck." It made the group all the more determined to find another way to challenge white supremacy in the state. "Nothing would happen in Mississippi, and in the South, unless somebody was willing to die," Moses believed. "They will have to kill us to get us out."[18]

The startling events in McComb in 1961 produced long-term consequences. First, to recruit in rural areas, SNCC had to rely on young people, especially teens who did not yet have families dependent on them for support. Youths knew the community, could take risks, and showed up for long hours to do the arduous and repetitive tasks of canvassing for new recruits and financial support. Having long since heard of the sit-ins and Freedom Rides, they were ready to move when SNCC came to town. Second, both SNCC staff and local black high school students learned from their attempts to register voters. As in the Freedom Rides, participants' experiences permanently altered their understanding of themselves and their environment. Because SNCC workers tried to cover his body when he was attacked, for instance, Bob Zellner subsequently felt "welded" to the movement "by a feeling so deep that it was akin to a religious experience." Thirty years later, as a result of this and other experiences, Zellner would say that he had lived his life "disguised as a white man" who saw America through black eyes. Zellner's move to solidarity not only changed his life, it also jolted the students' general distrust of whites, providing what historian and SNCC adviser Howard Zinn termed "an opening wedge for a new understanding about the tyranny of race."[19]

Meanwhile, the police paroled the McComb minors to their parents on the condition that they sign an affidavit admitting that activism was "detrimental to the harmony of the school." Eighty refused to sign and were expelled. To continue their education, SNCC staff opened a "Nonviolent High School" for these expelled students at Campbell Junior College in Jackson. Within this ad hoc idea for the "Nonviolent High School" lay the kernel of a design for the subsequent "Freedom Schools" that became an integral part of the Mississippi Summer Project of 1964.[20]

T he nonviolent direct action in Mississippi revealed parts of the democratic process that had been previously invisible. By trying to implement one of the basic rights of American citizenship — voting — the SNCC staff drew people to them who were willing to work. The violent reaction of local whites to the registration effort provided stark evidence that, in fact, blacks could not gain even this basic right. Moreover, white Mississippians denied blacks numerous other constitutionally guaranteed rights, including access to decent schools. By pushing the boundaries, movement participants could see more clearly what was at stake. The events in McComb made vivid the process through which the civil rights movement grew: people saw a small number of individuals taking action and were inspired to join them; through the experiences they then shared, the activists and their recruits developed an understanding of what was possible — one that differed considerably from that of most blacks and whites in Mississippi. Acting on this new understanding became the means of recruiting even more people to their movement. Loyalty to the other SNCC activists grew quickly despite divergent philosophies and ideologies, due to the harsh, repressive atmosphere in which they worked. This was the experiential reality of life in the American civil rights movement of the early 1960s.

This reality in McComb forced SNCC to change, and change dramatically, in the fall of 1961: the coordinating committee, which was essentially a group of leaders from decentralized movements, named a permanent staff and developed a new strategic approach to accomplish its mission. This change came in large part after a three-week seminar held in Nashville during 30 July – 26 August 1961. Tim Jenkins, vice chairman of the National Student Association (NSA) and SNCC activist, put it together, and the New World Foundation financed it. Jenkins's express intent was to transform SNCC from "an amorphous movement to an organization" and give its most active members "a solid academic approach to understanding the movement." Led by sociologists, the seminar "concentrated on the social structure of the South and the possibility of a political confrontation of human problems which would create a personally fulfilling social system." Following this workshop, Chuck McDew replaced Marion Barry as chairman of SNCC, Diane Nash was put in charge of direct action, and Charles Jones was selected to head up voter registration activities. Everyone who joined the permanent staff by the spring of 1962 had attended the three-week seminar, except Moses, who was in McComb; Zellner, who was at the NSA Southern Human Relations Seminar in Madison, Wisconsin; and James Forman, a Chicago schoolteacher and CORE activist, who spent much of the summer in Monroe, North Carolina, working with Robert F. Williams of the state's NAACP chapter. Nash soon recruited Forman as SNCC's executive secretary. Born in Indianola, Mississippi, Forman had maintained his roots in the region and, since the Fayette County sharecropper strike in 1960, had returned South repeatedly looking for a way to work in the movement full-time. In what marked a pivotal change for the organization, Forman would have full responsibility for fund-raising and managing the now permanent SNCC staff in the fall of 1961. Also established were an executive committee — composed of Moses, Jim Bevel, McDew, Jones, and Nash — and an advisory board. The Nashville seminar and the activity in McComb thus served as mutually reinforcing developments turning SNCC into a bona fide organization.[21]

With this formalization, SNCC ceased to be just a "coordinating committee" of activists. Now some members performed the work of "field staff," and others were primarily responsible for operations in SNCC's home office in Atlanta, though they often visited the field. This creation of two divergent sets of day-to-day work experiences made the "all staff" meetings and workshops — held three to four times a year — increasingly important as a means of interstaff communication.[22]

nside McComb's jail in the fall of 1961, SNCC workers began to reconsider their relationship to the federal government. Following the Freedom Rides, the Kennedy Justice Department had encouraged the students to redirect their energies from direct action to voter registration by telling SNCC that Justice officials would accept collect calls at any hour from civil rights workers involved in voter registration. Despite the fact that Robert Kennedy had betrayed the Freedom Riders in May 1961, he and his senior staff — John Doar and Assistant Attorney General Burke Marshall — at first took the calls from Moses and other voter registration workers directly. Unbeknownst to SNCC leaders, however, Kennedy, Doar, and Marshall soon decided that they could not offer much protection. Though the Justice Department *could* devise a legal argument for sending in federal marshals and the marshals might have some value as a deterrent or as a symbol of federal concern, administration officials believed that only something tantamount to a military occupation could protect the workers, and this they were unwilling to undertake. So Kennedy, Marshall, and Doar promised SNCC that they would answer the desperate phone calls from civil rights workers imprisoned in southern jails, surrounded by white officers "about to eat [them] up with billy clubs and dogs," in the words of Tim Jenkins. But when the SNCC workers made their one call — collect — to the Justice Department in Washington, it was often "refused on the technical grounds that the federal government can't receive a collect call," said Jenkins. "You tell me that's not a recanting of [their] original commitment." The SNCC people felt grossly deceived.[23]

In late 1961 Moses and the rest of the SNCC staff regrouped in Jackson to assess their efforts in McComb over the past six months. Of nearly forty attempts by residents to register, only six had succeeded. The sit-ins had not integrated the town. People had lost jobs and businesses. Herbert Lee was dead, leaving a widow and nine children.[24] It was time for a reevaluation. SNCC faced the hard fact that black churches and businesses, or anyone dependent on white economic support, could not be counted on when needed. Therefore, the organization must rely on young people, those economically independent of any sector of the white community and able to act as free agents. Moses and other SNCC members recruited two of the most active students in McComb, Hollis Watkins and Curtis Hayes, to become the first two project directors in Mississippi.[25]

Meanwhile, the new, small SNCC staff in Atlanta held nonstop meetings on the ongoing crises in McComb, especially after Lee's murder.[26] Diane Nash and Jim Bevel, now married, continued a nonviolent direct action campaign in Jackson that had come out of the Freedom Rides. James Forman arrived in Atlanta to assume his full-time responsibilities for fund-raising and personnel. He subsequently established SNCC communications and research departments to facilitate intramovement exchange of ideas and information, as well as to generate publicity and funds for the fledgling organization. Gradually over 1962–63, he pulled together a national fund-raising network. A tireless worker willing to do anything, from sweep the office floor, to call liberal fund-raisers, to sit up all night in Greenwood, Mississippi, and watch for night riders, Forman became a pillar of SNCC during this period. As Stokely Carmichael later observed, Forman "turned a loose association of contentious, widely scattered, diffuse student groups into an effective organizational force" by creating the administrative base to make SNCC "the most spiritually unified, focused, creative force in the movement."[27] Yet as SNCC activist Muriel Tillinghast noted, this required tactics that some considered decidedly undemocratic. Forman knew the local banker, he knew the fund-raisers nationwide, he knew the donors — in other words, he knew where the money was. Furthermore, "Forman used to manipulate SNCC [members]" to outmaneuver those who disagreed with him, Tillinghast said. "If he wanted to get a vote through, he knew exactly who to pigeonhole, how long to hold them in the meeting and when to bring the vote up and usually votes were around 2 A.M. and everyone would be stoned asleep."[28] He used that power not to dictate, but to steer SNCC toward the making of what he thought was a black revolution for dignity and equality. For the time being, however, the imperfect and undemocratic fund-distribution system worked because most people agreed on the means to achieve SNCC's goals.

Albany, 1961–1962

Over the course of the next two years, the SNCC group based in Atlanta would focus on supporting the work of Bob Moses and his band in Mississippi, as well as the southwest Georgia project Charles Sherrod would soon assemble in

Albany. Sherrod's Albany project foreshadowed the question SNCC raised but had not yet answered: What would the new integrated society look like?

Sherrod, now wiser for his experiences in Mississippi, decided to apply the organizing tactics learned in McComb to another part of the Deep South, southwest Georgia. Born in rural Surry County in southeast Virginia and raised in Petersburg, Sherrod arrived in Albany at the age of twenty-three to register black voters. Years later, when asked what led him to his uniquely bold innovations in nonviolent practice, he related a story from Surry. At the turn of the century, his grandfather verbally protested the lynching of another black man, who was "burned, hanging from a tree, while his genitals were burning in another tree." His grandfather was forced to flee the county for nothing other than having spoken up against this horrific public lynching. "Stories like that were part of my consciousness. That was what was passed down." Yet young Sherrod had also learned from his grandmother that as a Christian, if he acted humbly and in step with the teachings of Jesus, he need not fear any man.[29] Together with Charles Jones and Cordell Reagon of the Nashville workshops, Sherrod initiated a chain of events in Albany that would have important consequences for both SNCC and the broader civil rights movement as a whole.

Sherrod, Jones, and Reagon went to Albany because they had been invited. Their first hurdle was to find meeting space. Some ministers were afraid that if they let SNCC use their churches for meetings, whites would bomb the churches. "If we were to progress," Sherrod stated, "we knew we must cut through that fear. We thought and we thought," and the results in McComb led them to target the same group in Albany: students. Sherrod and Reagon visited Albany State College, the city's one institution of higher education for blacks. They initially brought the students together to rectify an incident earlier in the year when a group of whites in cars had driven through campus, throwing eggs, firing guns, and trying to run people down.[30]

Soon Sherrod read in the paper that the ICC — under pressure from the Kennedys following the Freedom Rides — had issued an edict for all states to comply with the desegregation of interstate travel facilities by 1 November 1961. Sherrod and Reagon decided to test the 1 November date. When students from Albany State and the Youth Council of the local NAACP wanted to join, SNCC set up workshops to explain the concepts and have the participants practice the skills of nonviolence. One crucial recruit was Albany State's Bernice Johnson, whose student activism on the city's Pine Street foreshadowed the fiercely determined and loving presence she would come to hold in SNCC. Johnson told Sherrod and Reagon that she understood the *student* and *committee* in SNCC's name, but what did they mean by *coordinating* and *nonviolent*? Reagon said, "'Nonviolence is love, love for your fellow man,' and it just clicked a blank in my head," she recalled. The students showed up at workshop after workshop, held at different churches each night, where Sherrod reported "some shocking responses in role-playing" that "marked a significant point in our recruitment and education of the people." The workshops, he noticed, met "the need to unify emotion and direct common anxieties." On 22 November the students sat-in at the white waiting room of the bus terminal, which was "full of men in blue," and tried to get served at the lunch counter. Sheriff Laurie Pritchett, not wanting to appear in violation of the federal edict, detained the students for "failing to obey the orders of an officer." Sherrod encouraged them to remain in jail, explaining that the longer they stayed, the easier it was to get other students to join them. Only fifteen or twenty tested the injunction, and they were expelled from Albany State. "So then they became our staff," Sherrod stated. "They had nothing else to do. So we used them to spread even wider."[31]

SNCC workers' bold actions — proceeding as if they were free to act in the white supremacist culture — caught the attention of many blacks in Albany. Local ministers were initially distant, yet before long Sherrod and other workers won over Dr. William G. Anderson, a prominent community leader. The young SNCC people, Anderson said, "sort of infiltrated all the social, civic and religious organization[s] in the community and became a part of us." Sherrod, Reagon, and Jones sounded out deacons and other church elders, who began to urge ministers to come on board. "Soon," said Jones, "there was so much interest from the grass roots that the leadership — the traditional leadership — had to either get into the process or try to fight us." A larger, economically independent black middle class enabled Albany's elders to be more supportive than their peers had been in McComb. These participants soon elected Anderson president of the Albany movement.[32]

This critical sequence of events repeated itself across the South wherever Freedom Riders came to town. "This was history's moving edge," Sherrod asserted. "One little step led to two larger steps. There were no models for us to follow" other than the one they themselves had made through the sit-ins, Freedom Rides, and actions in McComb. As Sherrod said, "We looked behind at failures and successes." In Albany, SNCC pulled together tools from the Lawson workshops, with insights gained from Ella Baker's mentoring, and the knowledge absorbed during retreats run by the Highlander Folk School.[33]

"We just pushed: pressure, pressure, pressure," said Sherrod. "Sometimes we don't know who controls this [political organization], who controls the other. So we stomp and stomp, and see whose feet we get. And then somebody's going to holler, 'Oh, you got me.' So then, when he hollers, that's the direction we go in. And that was the general strategy." In short, the SNCC workers initially played it by ear — but as this became an increasingly bold and sensitized organ of hearing, their planning was more purposeful and reflective.[34]

Reflection is one more important innovation that SNCC people emphasized in the civil rights movement. SNCC workers not only acted to provoke a reaction from others, they also studiously reflected upon the interaction afterward and incorporated their findings into their next action. For all its simplicity, this process took advantage of a remarkable quality of SNCC: the ability to innovate and remain open to new approaches despite careful planning. Sherrod arrived in town initially to test the federal injunction against a racist registrar in Terrell County, then picked up on the ICC ruling effective 1 November, and eventually created an interracial strategy for the city of Albany. In a movement in which events happened in rapid succession, and where each event demanded an immediate response, SNCC's very deliberate habit of reflection gave leaders a measure of poise when their next step remained uncertain.

The mission of Sherrod and colleagues quickly moved from voter registration to complete desegregation of this small, semirural city. If Pritchett arrested them for "trespass" or "failing to obey an officer," they would fill the jails so that the city would have to submit to their goals. "We were going to break the system down from within," Sherrod stated. "Our ability to suffer was somehow going to overcome their ability to hurt us." Martin Luther King spoke in similar terms when he said that the oppressed were often the only ones willing to bear the burden of the quest for justice, but the struggle itself was redemptive.[35] Remarkably, within a week of the first arrests, the SNCC workers had seven hundred people in jail. "Doctors and lawyers and teachers and domestics walked together to jail, and got to know each other in the cells, as they sat next to each other, and felt, breathed, and slept the passion that they had about their own desires to be free," recalled Sherrod. "But more than that, they came to know each other as people, and not as classes." Local activist Janie Culbreath remembered that in jail, people were deeply engaged with one another. After their release, the community was "not the same anymore. You find people walking together, people talking together. People who would never think they would speak to this person, or that person" were now standing in solidarity.[36]

Trying to implement Gandhi's tactic of filling the jails until the police no longer had the capacity to make arrests, SNCC people had not anticipated the effective mass incarceration Sheriff Pritchett was able to carry out. "We had made no provisions for these people going to jail because we did not anticipate the mass arrests," Anderson said. He and other local leaders felt enormous frustration. In his own earthy description, Sherrod noted that with hundreds of people in jail, all kinds of things happened. "Kids are being hurt, females had physical needs, somebody's getting smacked." After Sherrod and Reagon were arrested, Anderson and other movement leaders met to evaluate the situation. We "recognized that we had never been involved in mass demonstrations, mass arrests." They had no provisions for posting bond and "no provisions for taking care of families of people who were in jail," Anderson recalled. Feeling isolated, unsure of SNCC's capabilities, and overwhelmed, they called Dr. King of SCLC.[37]

Why did the "fill the jails" strategy not work as it had during the sit-ins? Pritchett later admitted that FBI agents had alerted him that the civil rights movement was coming to Albany.[38] Researching Martin Luther King's methods, Pritchett discovered that King advocated Gandhi's strategy in India: fill the jails and publicize police brutality through the media. The sheriff then began an "orientation of the police department into nonviolent movement — no violence, no dogs, no show of force. I even took up some of the training the SNCCs originated there — like [having my men sit] at the counter and being slapped, spit upon. I said, 'We're going to out-nonviolent them.'" Pritchett won agreement from all police chiefs and sheriffs within a sixty-mile radius to use their jails as holding cells. In this way, the Albany protesters could not force the city to give in because of the lack of jail space. Laurie Pritchett, it turned out, was the smartest and most tactically adroit policeman the civil rights movement encountered in the 1960s. He was able — initially, at least — to prevent one of the most common and successful methods of nonviolent *realpolitik*: using the violence of the oppressor against him politically.[39]

Three weeks after the first Albany State students were jailed, Martin Luther King arrived, gave a speech, marched with protesters, and was arrested. When King returned six months later to serve his time, Pritchett asked local whites to pay the bond rather than incur the glare of the national media that would follow King into the Albany jail. Most important, during this time the city attorney was able to obtain a *federal* court order preventing King and other leaders from demonstrating. "When the federal court started ruling against us," Coretta Scott King reflected, "that created a whole different thing in terms of strategy." Up to that point, her husband "had been willing to break state laws that were unjust laws, and our ally was the federal judiciary." Yet now, "if we would take our case to the federal court, and the federal court ruled against us, what recourse did we have?"[40]

The Albany movement stalled in the face of Pritchett's tenacious response. During the lull, long-simmering conflicts between SCLC and SNCC began to surface. The sheriff's determination to deny the participants a high profile for their activities appeared to be working. Yet he could not train every jailer in the county in "non-brutal" techniques. His most horrific failure occurred when

Marion King, the wife of respected local black leader Slater King (no relation to Martin Luther King), took food to demonstrators in the Camilla jail. Seven months pregnant, she carried a one-year-old in her arms and held her three-year-old by the hand. As she approached the officer on duty, he viciously kicked and punched her to the ground. She lost the baby a month later. Fifteen-year-old Joanne Christian was dragged to the same jail by her hair and kicked into a cell, whereupon an officer brought a police dog in and threatened to unleash it.[41]

Albany's black citizens were outraged when they learned about the beatings. Yet movement people struggled, and failed, to find a way to focus the community's rage on a nonviolent action that would invite the national attention and moral authority of the Montgomery bus boycott or the student sit-ins. At most, some blacks in Albany hurled bottles and bricks at the police. The movement lost momentum, and Dr. King left the city in August 1962, depressed.[42]

Broken Promises

It is striking that, although they worked through different models, both SCLC and SNCC began to develop a deep sense of betrayal over the continued refusal of the U.S. Justice Department to take action against the forces of segregation in the South. Assistant Attorney General Burke Marshall, who was responsible for civil rights enforcement, maintained that the department had failed to act because it lacked proof: the Justice Department could not prosecute if the FBI would not collect the evidence it required. "If somebody beat somebody up on the streets of Albany, that violates justice," said Marshall. "It violates a city ordinance in Albany, it may violate the law of the state of Georgia," he continued. "But it doesn't violate, normally, any federal law, so the FBI will say that it's none of their business. And it will say that it's none of their business not only to investigate it afterwards, but that it's doubly none of its business to interfere with what's going on at the time, since Bureau agents are not policemen, they're investigators." FBI agents had a different job: "to produce evidence to go into court later and not to interfere."[43]

This logic was inconsistent: Marshall later noted that FBI agents *did* interfere with a bank robbery in progress. He later suggested that because of the "anti-civil rights movement" outlook and "highly bureaucratic mind" of FBI director J. Edgar Hoover, his agents avoided interceding in crimes that violated blacks' civil rights. Whenever a Justice official requested an investigation of alleged infringement of black citizens' civil rights in Albany, Hoover would balk, arguing that it would violate federal law.[44] This intra-agency divergence between Justice and the FBI seemed irrelevant to movement leaders, who condemned both agencies. Indeed, the reality was indisputable: federal help would not be forthcoming. Bureaucratic disagreements in Washington could not be justified in light of the Herbert Lee homicide. This was movement wisdom by 1962.

And it was wisdom that had to be acted upon to maintain the momentum of the movement. SNCC workers explored how federal law might be interpreted to aid the campaign to allow blacks in the Deep South to vote. The constitutional right to speak freely, distribute literature, assemble peacefully, and petition the government for redress had been consistently denied by southern officials.[45] By the end of 1962, SNCC had filed hundreds of affidavits at the Justice Department, with no result. In moments of physical peril, the students had also made desperate phone calls for immediate protection. The department's disregard of those calls had left SNCC workers open to intense harassment, point-blank shootings, bombings, and death.[46]

Even without federal protection, SNCC resolved to soldier on. After SCLC left Albany in 1962, Sherrod and other SNCC staff continued to organize voter registration drives in the three surrounding counties. Mass meetings and protests against the city's segregated facilities continued. None ever succeeded until the Civil Rights Bill became law on 2 July 1964. The next day, on 3 July, all facilities were opened to African Americans. "We're not going to give Martin Luther King any reason to come back," one local official spat.[47]

In the face of Albany's intransigence and the federal injunction, Sherrod, in 1962, centered his fighting strategy at the root: "the idea that white is superior. That idea has eaten into the minds of the people, black and white." Regardless of the federal injunction, he could continue this fight in Albany with campaigns for voter registration. Segregation could be destroyed only "if they see white and black working together, side by side, the white man no more and no less than his black brother, but human beings together." In subsequent voter registration campaigns, Sherrod defied the fundamental, devastating, and surprisingly tenacious stereotype promoted by segregation: black meant inferior, white meant superior.[48]

The commitment to create space for equality in counties notorious for their racial terrorism took an uncommon individual. There can be little doubt that Charles Sherrod was then, and remained, a remarkable person. As Anne Braden, a longtime white civil rights activist visiting from Louisville, Kentucky, commented in 1962, "Anyone who would go into an area like this with interracial teams of registration workers has to be a little bit wacky; either that, or he has to be gripped by a vision of a whole new world." Sherrod's courage and vision pulled in local people of similar strength of character, such as Carolyn Daniels. "Carolyn Daniels was an extraordinary woman," SNCC staff member Prathia Hall asserted years later. Hall and other workers lived with Daniels, a beautician. One night someone shot into her house, wounding SNCC field secretary Jack Chatfield. The shooting "did not unnerve" Daniels, a single mother struggling to make ends meet. She was "steel, she was strength for all of us, and she took all of us, with our technicolor selves and our strange ways, and some northern and some southern. She wasn't that many years older than many of us, but she mothered us."[49]

The larger point here is that Sherrod found Daniels and others — as they discovered him — equal to the challenge. Prathia Hall, whose parents had deep southern roots, was another such person. The daughter of a Philadelphia minister, she became one of the movement's most powerful young preachers. Tall, gentle, and fearless, Hall effortlessly reconciled a northern élan with southern roots and folkways. Merely transcribing her sermons on a typewriter drew tears from SNCC staff in Atlanta. Yet she also drew on Carolyn Daniels's courage. Years later, Hall said that it was in southwest Georgia — not Philadelphia — where she found "freedom faith, this sense that I'm not a nigger, I'm not a gal, not a boy. I'm God's child. It may cost me my job, it may cost me my life, but I want to be free. So I'm going down to the courthouse, I'm going to sign my name. I'm going to trust God to take me there . . . and bring me back." Sherrod used such examples as proof of the quality of ordinary people. The organizing process that Sherrod brought to southwest Georgia and that Bob Moses developed in Mississippi encouraged scores of Carolyn Daniels to emerge in the South. They were the soul of the movement at the local level, and it was there that the new vision for black America and for all of America tried to anchor itself.[50]

The Albany voter registration drive was built on details so straightforward that it is easy to pass over them: SNCC staff sought out residents to attend meetings on voter registration and then arranged their transportation to the courthouse to register. Yet embedded in these two seemingly simple activities was individual and group conduct within the community that fundamentally challenged American segregation. These activities lay at the heart of the American civil rights movement.

The people recruited by Sherrod, Jones, and Reagon did not banish their fears. Rather, they learned how to keep acting despite these fears. Sherrod's highway prayer was but one invention to meet this day-in, day-out challenge. Another was the example set by people like Albany's Reverend Samuel Wells, who kept by his side an old leather-bound ledger of past registration efforts dating back to the 1940s, inspiring in the young SNCC workers "the greatest reverence for the patience and persistence with which the long effort was made and the laborious entries were set down." The staff meeting became another way of working through this problem in public — out in the open, so to speak. As Sherrod explained, "We'll talk about it together and then we'll go to meet the man with a smile, look him in the eye and say, 'I'm afraid, but I'm not a coward.'" The activists lived "by a strict personal discipline" in the early days, with no drinking or behavior "that could even give the appearance of anything but strict morality." When Anne Braden visited the site, she sensed "an atmosphere of exuberance about them." They seemed to have "a deep personal joy" in carrying forward this important work.[51]

As repression continued, Sherrod developed an uncanny talent (some combination of wit, patience, and wry cunning) for taking routine situations generated by the caste system and standing them on their head. In July 1962 he persuaded some reporters, including Claude Sitton of the *New York Times* and Bill Shipp of the *Atlanta Constitution*, to attend a voter registration meeting at Mount Olive Church in "Terrible" Terrell County. "Twenty white citizens stood on the steps of the small wooden church, and said a few things to us as we were going in, uncomplimentary," field secretary Ralph Allen remembered. The head of the local movement, Lucius Holloway, finished his report of the week's activities, and then Sherrod read scripture. He invoked the earliest Judeo-Christian ideas of equality and brotherhood: "Do you really believe in God?" he asked. "If you believe in God, do you also believe that God said 'Thou shalt have no other God before me?' Are you not making of the white man a god, if you afraid of this white man?" Years later Sherrod noted that fear was reasonable, but he "messed with them. I asked, 'Why can't you vote? You are scared of the white folk. What do you believe? Do you really believe you are going to heaven? Do you really believe that nothing can separate you from the love of God?'"[52]

According to Allen, as Sherrod spoke the words "'If God be for us, who can be against us?'" Sheriff Z. T. Matthews and a dozen other white men came charging through the door, boots pounding on the unfinished pine. Matthews had earlier told the reporters that whites were "a little fed up with this voter registration business. . . . We want our colored people to live like they've been living for the last hundred years—peaceful and happy." Matthews took over the meeting as the reporters continued to write. "'Hey there, boy, put that pencil and paper away. Who you anyway?' One of them said, 'I'm Claude Sitton from the *New York Times* and I'm a native Georgian, just like yourself.'" "Sheriff Matthews could not have hung himself any higher if we had asked him to perform in a play or something. That was Sherrod."[53]

The incident illustrated how daily life in the movement educated the press. Six weeks later, the Mount Olive Church, "with Jesus and the American presidents on the walls," burned to the ground. Subsequent meetings on voter registration were held in a tent. More SNCC workers were arrested and beaten, and drive-by shootings riddled the homes where they were staying. Sheriff Matthews ordered SNCC people not to sing in jail: "When you come in here you lose all your rights." Sherrod told him: "We would like to have two devotional periods a day, as we are religious people." But Matthews stood firm: "There'll be no singing and praying." When Sherrod responded, "We may be in jail, but we're still human beings and still Christians," Matthews hit him in the face, then took him into an office where another policeman hit him again in the face. With his mouth full of blood, he was led to a cell by himself.[54] Sherrod, simply by the strength of his actions, not only taught the reporters Sitton and Shipp what the movement was trying to do: he made it clear to the sheriff that a person's dignity could not be taken away by a mere punch in the mouth.

In short, Sherrod, like James Lawson, insisted that, by acting democratically, he could change the way people saw themselves, their community, their institutions, and, eventually, their nation. He demonstrated that blacks did not have to remain within the powerful but hopelessly outmoded behavioral code called "segregation." The price of this education was, for an extended time, the survival of continued terror.

After people had experienced overwhelming repression, Sherrod's mass meetings renewed their resolve. The gatherings embodied SNCC's main strategy: teaching people to become their own leaders and to think for themselves. This was the real meaning of the phrase "political consciousness." Sherrod taught others to value their own experiences as vital knowledge, the most central information of their lives. Whether they were farmers, janitors, undertakers, teachers, grocers, or students, all risked their livelihoods and lives to attend the meetings. He emphasized that it was *they*, not him, who knew best how to solve their problems. Sherrod's role was to encourage them, to urge them to give themselves permission to tackle those problems.

Anne Braden reported on one such gathering in Terrell County. First, they sang. Then, asking field secretary Jack Chatfield, a northern white volunteer, to stand, Sherrod told the group that Chatfield remained despite having been shot the second night he arrived in Terrell. The two men shook hands. " 'Remember this handclasp,' " said Sherrod. " 'As we work together, all of us, don't you forget it. Not Negro and white shaking hands, but Charles Sherrod and Jack Chatfield — human beings together. That's the way it is.' " Black people were tired, he declared. " 'All our lives we've had to bow and scrape, laugh when there was nothing funny and scratch our heads and say "yes sir." We want to change that. We want to be men; that's what the power of the vote can do.' " Sherrod, of course, was already a man. In fact, his actions up to this point showed him to be a "man" — a person who was self-defining and self-determined — in ways that most people never were. But Sherrod used the handshake, the stories of terror and how to act despite it, to teach incipiently free people a way to act so that they could become literally free. He closed by affirming that it was people like themselves who would change America. " 'And we'll do it together.' "[55]

This issue was the "commanding sentiment" with Sherrod, Chatfield observed: "To craft a social movement that symbolized a new approach to race" that would "bridge the gap that centuries had constructed. It was a very difficult thing to do, but every fiber of our being was devoted to doing this." Chatfield recalled his long conversations with Les Holly, a blind African American, "who spoke movingly about our work in Terrell County, as though he was describing the dawning of a whole new world that could not have been imagined." At dusk one day, as Chatfield and James Crawford returned from driving people to register in Lee County, their car broke down. The two volunteers came upon the home of a black man with a telephone and called Sherrod in Albany. Suddenly four white men in a black Ford drove up, an Oldsmobile behind them. The homeowner loaded his shotgun and asked the SNCC people to leave, tears visible in his eyes. Chatfield, Crawford, and the registrants took off across a field and remained secluded until they saw Sherrod's car pull up. They raced back and hopped into the car. As Sherrod sped off, the Oldsmobile followed in pursuit. It slammed into his bumper once, then a few more times, and finally left. Chatfield had arrived at Trinity College in Hartford, Connecticut, with the idea that "there is nothing but the self." Howard Zinn reported that after his experiences in southwest Georgia, Chatfield believed that "there is nothing but other people."[56]

To those Americans unfamiliar with the grim truths of racial terrorism, remarks like Chatfield's can be easily dismissed as movement pieties or even propaganda. Such comments fail to address the central question raised by terror: how do people survive it? Nothing in Chatfield's comment was a romanticization: on his second day in the South, he got shot. He stayed because he felt sustained by other activists he met who had borne even greater risks.

The individuals drawn to the Albany movement formed a diverse group. They tended to see the normal political loyalties of the time very differently from those in power. In the face of continued terror, they welcomed anyone who was willing to put a body on the line to end this oppression. This extended to all people, black or white, and believers in all known ideologies. "I don't care who the heck it is — if he's willing to come down on the front lines and bring his body along with me to die — then he's welcome!" Sherrod stated. SNCC's southwest Georgia project soon became an oasis *and* served as an incubator for many organizers and activists who later traveled to other projects or joined other freedom movements.[57]

In contrast to some members of the Mississippi Summer Project of 1964, Sherrod did not try to maintain a black base among the organizers in Albany. Early on he decided to bring in white northerners to raise money. His experience growing up in Petersburg, Virginia, where he had sung with the Police Boys'

Club, and his participation in the Virginia Human Relations Commission in 1956–58 had long since convinced him that white people were the same as black people. Sherrod used the racism in Albany creatively, to the movement's advantage. For instance, when segregationists burned a church, a reporter would go "straight to the white person" on his project for information. Yet, based on extended conversations with Sherrod previously, the white SNCC member would send the reporter right back to Sherrod. In this way, the movement taught the American press the merits of desegregated news sources. When racial tension arose within his staff, Sherrod tried to show the SNCC workers that racial tension among *them* was not the real problem. He kept people focused on the task at hand, asking, "What are we here for?" The dramatic community he created as a result of bringing in white as well as black northerners put the Albany movement in the papers for the whole year preceding the Mississippi project of 1964.[58]

Most important, in Albany SNCC achieved its initial goal: building local leadership. Before the students arrived, Albany was a "society where there were very clear lines," recalled Bernice Johnson Reagon. The movement destroyed the lines based on immutable characteristics like color. This experience taught people "that if something puts you down, you have to fight against it," Reagon said. "That's what the Albany movement did for Albany, Georgia." The people who got involved "made a determination within their own minds that they would never accept that segregated society as it was, anymore," said movement president William Anderson. Attaining this new self-recognition marked the biggest achievement of the Albany movement. Some activists like Reagon took this lesson further. The movement, she said, gave her the "power to challenge *any* line that limits me."[59] It was a feeling that had the potential to transform American culture.

The Mississippi Movement, 1962–1963

When Bob Moses left McComb in the fall of 1961 and returned to Jackson for a lean winter during which SNCC just tried to "hang on," he worked as the "submerged campaign director" for black minister, R. L. T. Smith, who had decided to run for Congress. Through this campaign, SNCC, CORE, and the NAACP joined together to run the state's voter registration program under the banner of a coalition they named the Council of Federated Organizations (COFO). Moses was field director and David "Dave" Dennis, CORE's most active field secretary in Jackson, was assistant field director. COFO, which Moses later said was a "direct response to the extraordinary repression" in Mississippi, was unique: in no other state were civil rights groups able to work in this coordinated fashion. On the Smith campaign, Moses had made an important discovery: participation in an election might allow him to organize around direct involvement in politics, "even though there wasn't a chance of winning." People unwilling to support SNCC as a civil rights organization still might support Reverend Smith's run for Congress.[60]

At that time, the Stern Family Fund and Taconic and Field Foundations gave $870,000 to the Southern Regional Council in Atlanta to disburse to the NAACP, the Urban League, SCLC, CORE, and SNCC for voter registration activities. The organization subsequently created to disseminate the funds was called the Voter Education Project (VEP). The Southern Regional Council quickly realized what Martin Luther King had noted earlier: initially, only students could and would do voter registration work. In 1961–62, CORE, which had engineered the Freedom Rides, was more concerned with immediate desegregation of public accommodations, recalled Leslie Dunbar, then head of the Southern Regional Council. SCLC, rooted in urban churches with a membership tied to families and jobs, was "unable to reach the rural population because of the necessity to live and share with these people the poverty and tension of their lives." However, a SNCC volunteer could work in these situations. Having "rejected middle-class values" and lacking responsibilities that put limits on their involvement, SNCC workers were restricted only by their "own personal courage." SNCC got enough money to continue its voter registration activities in Mississippi during the spring of 1962. As Dunbar said in 1965, "The most important idea which developed within SNCC from late 1961 on was the idea that we must work with the majority of the Negro people of the South and not the [black] middle-class."[61]

Moses later regarded the period up to the fall of 1963 as a time when he and others were "consciously trying to build a group of young people in Mississippi who would work and view themselves as having the right to work" on voter registration. Before SNCC, young blacks headed for higher education did not view community organizing as a legitimate career option. But a "certain tone, rationale, [and] spirit" began to develop among the twenty-five young people who were mostly from Mississippi and worked on voter registration. It was on the basis of their work that "all the other work [in Mississippi] rose," Moses explained.[62] "We saw that students were the only ones economically free enough to do anything," recalled Lester McKinnie, a veteran of the Nashville workshops. "So we were obligated to launch this movement." Through this core group of young Mississippi blacks, Moses set up seven voter registration projects in the summer of 1962. In that part of the Delta, Moses said, "it was only Amzie [Moore] who would open up his house to Freedom Riders." Standing at 614 Chrisman Street in Cleveland, Mississippi, Moore's house became "the beachhead from which student leaders would penetrate the Delta" and a safe house. The young people participated in a week of orientation workshops at the Highlander Folk School. Here "Myles Horton opened up his school for us," Moses stated, "and gave the benefit of his experience" to the young Mississippians who mostly viewed themselves at this point as summer volunteers. McKinnie went to Laurel; Curtis Hayes and Hollis Watkins, the two young men from McComb, went to Hattiesburg. Frank Smith, a Morehouse student from Georgia, went to Holly Springs. Mississippians Willie (Wazir) Peacock, Charles McLaurin, Colia Lafayette, and Dorie Ladner worked in Ruleville, and Sam Block settled into Greenwood, where Lawrence Guyot and Luvaughn Brown soon joined him. James Jones was assigned to Clarksdale and Emma Bell to Greenville.[63]

What Sherrod did for Georgia, Moses did for Mississippi. Moses set an example of living in the communities he was trying to organize, and the SNCC workers followed his lead. Local people tended to be much more responsive to activists who tried to become part of the community. Frank Smith, for instance, spent his first days in Holly Springs "just loafing around," trying to find "the most trusted and respected leaders" in town. The son of a homemaker and a farmer, Smith had spent his high school years as a member of the New Farmers of America, debate team, choir, and drama club. Before finishing Morehouse College, he joined the civil rights movement. In Holly Springs, he began by sending a "very vague" letter, which "mentioned voter registration only slightly," to seventeen black leaders in the town, announcing a meeting. Sixteen people showed up, one of whom gave Smith permission to use his Catholic school to hold meetings on voter registration. A week after the first meeting, these leaders organized a "door-to-door committee." Of the 1,000 residents contacted by the committee, 150 took the voter registration test. The committee also provided transportation to the registrar. Once white authorities became aware of Smith's presence, the sheriff began riding by his meeting place, writing down license plate numbers. Black citizens who attended the meetings soon discovered their cotton acreage allotments reduced and their taxes suddenly raised. In Holly Springs, no one shot at or assaulted black people attempting to vote. Instead, Howard Zinn reported, "the Chancery Court sells the land for taxes and the farmer is forced to move, and in the meantime the banks refuse to give him a loan." Such economic reprisals made SNCC intensely aware that the movement needed an independent economic base. Smith, however, continued to do the "slow, respectful work" of developing community leadership that characterized SNCC's efforts in Mississippi.[64]

Recruitment: The Role of Nonviolence

When civil rights workers arrived in Ruleville in the summer of 1962, a middle-aged resident named Fannie Lou Hamer participated in the first church meeting, encouraged by a longtime family friend, Mary Tucker. Once there, Jim Bevel's speech moved her to get involved. "Our being able to use the church as a meeting place, and to have a minister speak the social gospel about why we should register to vote — what impact that would have on our lives — influenced Mrs. Hamer and 21 other people," remembered Lawrence Guyot. "She decided to go with us the next day to Indianola to register to vote."[65]

Yet this evidence does not reveal what motivated people to register to vote. Adults with full-time jobs, children to support, and bank loans risked all they had worked for — indeed, their very lives. So why did Hamer go to Indianola after attending the meeting? What did SNCC — and Bevel — do that day that "worked" to recruit her? "By the time I was ten or twelve I just wished to God I was white," Hamer later said. "Because [whites] didn't work, they had food to eat; they didn't work, they had money, they had nice homes. And we would nearly freeze, we didn't have food, we worked all the time and didn't have nothing."[66] Hamer's anger at the lifetime inequities she had experienced made her a prime candidate to become involved. Yet anger alone was not enough: SNCC needed to convince her and the others present that they could change things, or at least that they should try.

At that first meeting, Bevel spoke from a spiritual stance. How could the residents think of themselves as Christian if they did not vote? He quoted the twelfth chapter of Luke, where Jesus talked to the Jews. Here, Jesus explained why it was easy to look at the sky to divine the weather, but hard to discern equally clear moral and ethical signs. Bevel then translated this into the present day for blacks in Mississippi. If they were good Christians, they would come forward and fight for the right to vote — it was a right given to them by their God and could not be taken away by anyone, not even Senator James Eastland and his friends in Sunflower County.[67]

Using language and metaphor that resonated with those at home in the southern black church, Bevel called people to vote as a self-affirmation. They *deserved* to vote, they did not have to ask for it. Hamer's faith was strong — and her parents taught her not to hate. She discovered early that "there were many things 'dead wrong' with the lives of Blacks and whites in Mississippi. 'I used to think . . . let me have a chance, and whatever this is . . . I'm gonna do somethin' about it.'" Bevel, James Forman, and the other SNCC workers provided her and others "the chance to act as people with power."[68]

Most people, however, did not see how getting beaten up while trying to register would make them "people with power." Nonviolence might be easy to understand at a lunch counter sit-in, but how did it facilitate voter registration in rural Mississippi? In Hamer's own Sunflower County, the heart of the Delta, people could not imagine a purely nonviolent movement succeeding. Hamer's mother had carried a 9 mm Luger in a covered bucket to the fields each day to protect her children from abuse by the bossman. How would suffering give them anything but a heavier burden to bear? Why did SNCC people talk so much about suffering, anyway?[69]

Nonviolent direct action would become almost wholly discredited in the late 1960s. This development makes it extremely difficult in the present day to recognize the impact of nonviolent ideas on recruiting blacks in the Deep South — people like Fannie Lou Hamer — to register to vote in the early years of the decade. Yet there is a surprising amount of evidence describing the tools that the practitioners of nonviolence contributed to voter registration campaigns. In the summer of 1965, movement veterans trained northern volunteers to work on SCLC's Summer Community Organizing and Political Education (SCOPE) projects. The volunteers — few of whom had any familiarity with nonviolence — both listened to these advocates of nonviolence speak and asked questions before heading off to work. The resulting transcripts provide a dramatic picture of the practices that materialized in the movement through the first half of the 1960s.[70]

At a SCOPE orientation in June 1965, Bevel spoke on self-defense. If someone attacked the volunteers, would they be acting within the bounds of nonviolence if they defended themselves? This, of course, was the dilemma James Lawson had faced in prison as a draft resister. Self-defense was not immoral, Bevel stated. It caused problems only when someone "got all bogged down" in the complexities of self-defense, rather than addressing the issues most crucial to the people with whom he or she worked. Bevel gave an example: he had worked in a northern city with a "very able Negro leader" who organized his people by telling them to buy guns. "I was sitting on the platform with him and I was against buying guns, but I thought, 'Well, this is fine.' I told him that I thought this was great." But, he cautioned the leader, "'This is the problem: you don't have adequate houses and you don't have classroom space and you don't have adequate education and nobody is jumping on you anyway: now what are you defending?'" In nonviolence, he now said to the students, "you have to think of what's important. What is it that you want?" If somebody *did* want to ambush you, there was not much you could do about it, he continued. You could certainly defend yourself. "A fellow was telling me the other night that 'if a policeman is beating me, I'm going to beat him back.' Fine. Okay. But are you going to have the public reading about one-eyed policemen, or about the voting problem and police brutality? You have to weigh this out."[71]

A student volunteer challenged Bevel's thesis. "You're not doing the community any good if they can't defend themselves against, say, a beating," the student rebutted. "If you're lying out on the street, you're not doing anybody any good." He asked Bevel to elaborate on personal defense, rather than on organizing tactics. Bevel answered, making sure to address the young volunteer's point. "People ask me, 'What do you do when you are hit?' Well, I always fall," Bevel laughed. "If you get shot, sometimes you die." In such situations, rather than defend his body, Bevel said he kept his mind focused on the question: "In this situation, can I communicate? How can I let my mind keep this situation from deteriorating, so that communication can continue?" In Selma, Alabama, a sheriff's deputy once said to him on the street, " 'I wish I could get you alone somewhere. I'd beat your brains out.' " Bevel replied, " 'Oh, no you wouldn't. You'd sit and talk with me.' " The two men had another confrontation in jail. Bevel had caught pneumonia and passed out in a cell. When he awoke, "this posseman was standing over my bed watching me, and the truth of the matter was that he did just stand and talk."

Bevel stressed the importance of "communicating, rather than getting bogged down in just trying to protect your body, which I doubt very seriously you can do anything about." Love can be defined as "undiscouragable good will," he suggested. Bevel, in his own inimitable way, extended this goodwill to any opponent. "I'll go into the Sheriff's office, I'll go into the Klan's meetings, I'll go into the mob, thinking not in terms of how I'm going to protect my being, but how am I going to communicate my humanity and force them to deal with me as a human being?"[72]

Taking his turn at the podium, Reverend Andrew Young illustrated this in a slightly different manner. Young said that he had learned a great deal about nonviolent practice from SCLC organizer Annell Ponder. In Winona, Mississippi, the police forbade Ponder and others from sitting in the white section of the bus terminal. Ponder took out a pad and pencil and jotted down the license number of the patrol car parked out front. At that point, the demonstrators were arrested and beaten severely in jail. The next day, Young accompanied Bevel and Dorothy Cotton to the jail, "not without some nervousness and fear." Ponder emerged bruised almost beyond recognition. "And when Annell walked by, she told the sheriff and the deputy sheriff, 'Well, so long. Hope I'll see you again some time.' And walked out of there very cheerfully." Young was stunned. "When I got outside of the jailhouse, I said, 'Annell, who was it that beat you all like that?' And she said, 'Those men in there.' "[73]

This story showed "a strange kind of phenomenon — of men who are capable of being very decent human beings and also capable of being beasts when their interests are being threatened," observed Young. A second lesson was that the essence of nonviolent practice was the attempt to bring out the decent side of people. Young used the word "appeal": "You seek to appeal to the very best in the man." Despite the way the media often portrayed nonviolent activists — as innocent lambs attacked by white thugs — Young did not mean "appealing to the conscience of the oppressor," addressing some kind of allegedly preexisting consciousness. The purpose, rather, was to offer to closed people the opportunity to discover a more open way to live.

Ponder understood the realities of moral confrontation in the same context as Lawson: Evil acts served as "examples of man's separation from God and from his own truest self." The level of hatred and violence that Ponder faced was intense, which makes her response all the more remarkable. Fannie Lou Hamer, incarcerated in Winona with Ponder, described the jail beating: "I started hearing screaming like I had never heard. And I could hear the sounds of the licks, but I couldn't see nobody. And I hear somebody when they say, 'Cain't you say yessir, nigger? Cain't you say yessir, bitch?' Hamer heard Ponder answer, "'Yes, I can say yessir.'" The officer said, "'Well, say it.'" And Ponder answered, "'I don't know you well enough.'" Ponder "never would say yessir, and I could hear when she would hit the flo', and then I could hear them licks just soundin'." Softly, almost at a whisper, Hamer continued: "That was somethin'. . . . She kept screaming, and they kept beatin' on her, and finally she started prayin' for 'em, and she asked God to have mercy on 'em, because they didn't know what they was doin'." The people who beat her were not evil themselves, Ponder felt; they needed "training and rehabilitation." Her actions echoed those of Charles Sherrod, who believed that the movement's capacity for suffering would overcome their opponents' ability to inflict harm.[74]

The movement needed such actions as Ponder's encounter with the sheriff and his men, Young maintained. Suffering, he emphasized, was essential to their tactics. Still, it was not enough. Civil rights activists also wanted calls made to the Winona jail — from the media, from the Atlanta SCLC office, from the FBI. The calls would alert the Winona sheriff to the fact that he and his men existed "in a community situation. It's not the isolated violence that they're going to be able to get away with and nothing will ever come up about it." The movement needed both the personal encounter — Ponder's willingness to suffer and her determination to address her torturers as human beings — and the demonstration of community to transform the situation in Winona at the individual and structural levels.[75]

Lawson ended the orientation session with a rousing explanation of the practical aspects of nonviolence. "Nonviolence is not docility," he maintained. "Nonviolence is the courage to be—in very personal terms. It is the tenacity in insisting upon one's own life." Violence discriminates, he continued. "It chooses between which individuals are worth living and which individuals are not worthy of life. And what single person knows that much about any other man to declare that that person is no longer worthy of being allowed to live?"[76]

A student who was confused by these concepts asked Lawson to address the fact that people had been killed for attempting to register. Lawson answered: "Violence doesn't guarantee you any safety at all. We can protect ourselves and we do protect ourselves in more ways than violence."[77]

As in his earliest Nashville workshops in 1959, Lawson still represented nonviolence as a basic approach to daily life, a way to maintain one's poise and dignity in the midst of a degrading caste system. Yet many young people on the Mississippi staff—particularly those who had never taken part in Lawson's workshops—did not view nonviolence as a way to live, but as *one* of several powerful tools for breaking open the "closed society." They made clear that they would not oppose local blacks who armed themselves in self-defense against KKK night riders and even local law enforcement.

Still, those who believed in nonviolence as a way of life strengthened the rural voter registration projects by giving sustained attention to two principles. First, everyone was valuable and potentially a leader, and thus a humane relationship had to be established with every single person, adversary or friend. This relationship created the opportunity to break through stereotypes to see the multifaceted person at the core. While Bevel and others spoke about seeing adversaries as complex and reachable human beings, Ella Baker perceived the impact on relationships within the movement as well: people "were so keen about the concept of nonviolence that they were trying to exercise a degree of consciousness and care about not being violent in their judgment of others." SNCC scholar Charles Payne called this one of the "moral anchors" that helped regulate relationships within the movement, enabling people to keep working together.[78]

The second principle was that by withdrawing support from a system—not a person—that oppressed them, people no longer saw themselves as victims. When a person was able to identify his or her responsibility in the maintenance of systems of oppression, "it puts you in a position of power," Diane Nash explained, "because then you are able to withdraw your participation and therefore end the system."[79] This reinforced an ironclad rule of organizing: never do for other people what they can do for themselves. In fact, it recast that rule: not only should organizers not do for others, they *could not* do for others. Thus the nonviolent workshops had provided another avenue for ideas already brought forward through people who came out of the tradition of armed self-defense such as Amzie Moore, Amite County activist E. W. Steptoe, and, to some extent, Ella Baker.[80] Whether they got to be fully self-owning human beings by practicing nonviolent direct action or armed self-defense, it was only when many people overcame their deference that the system of oppression itself collapsed.

Both nonviolence and armed self-defense fed the trail to freedom.

Greenwood as a Model

No matter how they challenged the state's white supremacist system, SNCC workers provided rural black Mississippians with new ways to understand their struggle that justified the suffering they were likely to endure. Fannie Lou Hamer's readiness was typical rather than extraordinary: people got ready to move when the student activists came to town. Over the years Hamer had watched the NAACP organize only those who owned homes, but she saw that SNCC was open to *everyone*. Working with SNCC provided her first opportunity to be "treated like a human being, whether the kids were white or black."[81]

As Hamer joined SNCC in the summer of 1962, the voter registration campaign in Greenwood, the seat of LeFlore County, gathered a momentum unlike any yet seen in Mississippi. The pattern of action in Greenwood became a new model for SNCC and other civil rights workers throughout the rural Black Belt. As student organizers moved into Greenwood, whites responded with violence. Regardless, the SNCC workers stayed and became part of the community. Sam Block — young, thin, intense — arrived first and moved with care among the black citizenry. Mostly, he listened. If he saw an opening, he talked about voter registration. Older people were the most responsive, especially World War II veteran Cleveland Jordan, who had first tried to vote in 1951. The contact proved critical: Jordan provided space for local leaders to meet at the Elks Hall. Block asked for their involvement "but never pressur[ed] them to make a total commitment."[82] Greenwood, situated in the center of the Delta, was also the state headquarters of the White Citizens Council — white businessmen and bankers who saw themselves as "respectable" enforcers of the system of racial caste. They put a stranglehold of economic pressure on any resident — black or white — who was not overtly hostile to civil rights workers.[83]

Initially, Block felt stymied. Then in late July 1962 the police arrested a fourteen-year-old boy for breaking into a white woman's house. Though he insisted he had been in the fields all day, the officers forced the boy to strip and "beat him with a bull whip as he lay naked on the concrete floor," wrote Howard Zinn. "When someone came near, a buzzer was sounded, and a television set was turned on to drown out the boy's screams."[84]

The stunning cruelty toward this youngster drew from Block a passion for justice so strong that it overcame the normal human response to flee from an overpowering enemy. Block obtained an affidavit from the boy, took photographs of his wounds, and gave the evidence to the U.S. Justice Department. "From then on it was Sam versus the police," remembered Bob Moses. Block organized the voter registration drive around this case. His courage inspired other SNCC staff as well as local people. More black citizens showed up to talk with him and more tried to register.[85]

As a matter of course, a crisis occurred. Moses took an emergency call from Block in the middle of the night: Greenwood police had surrounded the SNCC office while whites drove up and down the street. Then the police disappeared. Moses immediately called the Justice Department, where an official told him to keep in touch with Block and call the local FBI. Meanwhile, Block was "crouched in the office, looking out the window, talking on the phone in a very hushed voice, describing people downstairs with guns and chains milling around outside his office." He subsequently escaped out of a second-floor window. Soon afterward, the Greenwood sheriff told Block that he better not see him in town again if he wanted to live. Block retorted, if that was the case, the sheriff better pack and leave. Block announced he would be there tomorrow and the next day — and the day after that.[86]

While it is unclear whether Block saw himself operating as a practitioner of nonviolence, James Lawson later cited the young activist's determination as an example of the way nonviolence could protect people. "Now Sam is still around working, and moving, and acting, because [he had] the courage to be. That excited the sheriff in the kind of way that in fact protected [Block]," Lawson said. "Fear has been a major weapon in keeping things under control in the Southland. Beating and death. And here is Sam walking into the lion's den and saying to the sheriff, 'You don't have anything in the world, sheriff, that you can do about me because I'm going to be here as long as I can and I'm going to keep on working.'"[87]

Over the summer of 1962, SNCC organizers in Mississippi exchanged information about ways to refine the mass meeting as a tool for recruitment. They taught citizens how to register, they chopped wood and hauled water for them, they sang freedom songs. During long hot days walking dusty back roads, they learned what issues animated local people. The objective was a simple one: how to get black residents to act — to register to vote. Each successful registrant gave substance to the idea that the movement meant freedom. As in Albany,

Georgia, the meetings in Greenwood created a shared experience that further encouraged each person's growing sense of possibility.

The meetings at churches represented the culmination of weeks of one-on-one conversations and served as what Moses called an "energy machine." John Dittmer portrayed such gatherings as a "combination of spontaneous testimony, old-fashioned preaching, wickedly hilarious observations about the character of the white opposition, and inspiring oratory from the young organizers." In these "community meetings" that were not yet "community organizations," people "began to acquire a new sense of themselves as a people in the community and in that county who were willing to take a stand and take some risk around this voting."[88] People, in other words, developed a collective self-respect.

"It was out of those meetings that you began to get the hook-up between people in one county who would go visit another county meeting," observed Moses. The cross-fertilization of people and ideas then became more deliberate; joint meetings were planned. "These were run as COFO meetings, so that people, in, say, a Holmes County meeting got a sense of themselves as a unit in COFO and they would go to COFO meetings which were meetings where people from other units" gathered to explain what they were doing and plan programs. Organized around voter registration, these community meetings became the basis of the later MFDP, the structure that would challenge the legitimacy of the state's regular Democratic Party. The blueprint of this challenge began to take shape in the summer of 1962 and continued, although at a very slow pace, through the following summer.[89]

The plan became most visible in Greenwood after brutality and terror failed to drive Sam Block and the other SNCC workers away. County officials next tried economic strangulation: they discontinued the federal surplus food program in October 1962, "leaving 22,000 people to face a lean Delta winter." Yet, as Charles Payne noted, this "awkward reprisal" put many blacks in a position where they no longer had anything to lose by joining the movement. By punishing those "innocent" as well as those "guilty" of civil rights activities, it illuminated the connection between the right to vote and the power to control basic needs like access to food, and "gave COFO a chance to show that they were more than the bunch of rag-tail kids they might appear to be."[90]

Informed of the decision to stop the surplus food program, Friends of SNCC (FOS) groups throughout the North and West initiated a food and clothing drive. This marked something of a turning point in SNCC as an organization. For the first time, SNCC was able to demonstrate an ability to provide direct aid to the black community, as northern college students arrived with truckloads of food, clothing, and medical supplies. The distribution attracted new recruits on the local level, gave those in the North something to organize around, and provided SNCC workers considerable experience with large-scale organization.[91]

In February 1963, amid the food collection and distribution, Sam Block was arrested for the seventh time in Greenwood. A few days later, SNCC worker Jimmy Travis was shot in the neck while driving from Greenwood to Greenville with Bob Moses and Randolph Blackwell, the field director of the Voter Education Project. The attack served as a clarion call: at least fifty civil rights organizers went to LeFlore County during the next month. Further violence ensued: the homes of two sympathetic white citizens were fired upon, and whites shot into a carload of civil rights activists, all of whom were injured by flying glass. As a result, people joined the mass meetings in ever greater numbers. High school senior Euvester Simpson, for example, became a full-time SNCC worker in voter registration: "First I would introduce myself. I would tell them that I was from Itta Bena to let them know that I was not from out of state." She admitted that "I'm scared too, but I think that this is something that's important enough to risk even going to jail." As in Albany, local people's courage inspired the civil rights workers to continue despite the terror.[92]

SCLC and SNCC

At times throughout this period, SNCC work brushed against the mobilizing efforts of SCLC ministers in the Deep South. At other times, the two organizations worked in concert. The sophisticated resistance orchestrated by police chief Laurie Pritchett in Albany had put great strain on local black resources, so when the SCLC ministers and others had appealed to Martin Luther King for help, he responded. But the alacrity with which the national press followed King's every move exasperated the young circle of activists rallied by Sherrod. To them, King was not the story—instead, it was the initiative of "ordinary people" like Carolyn Daniels and Samuel Wells that lay at the heart of movement work. Journalists therefore were surprised, if not stunned, to hear some SNCC workers derisively refer to the dignified King as "De Lawd." In ways that most of the news media did not remotely grasp, Sherrod and company had acquired (and knew they had acquired) extensive and hard-won knowledge about organizing people against the caste system. King's rhetoric inspired, but it did not get people to the courthouse. SNCC's anger extended to the white press, which, in the minds of some activists, had undermined the movement by exalting the brand of leadership that King represented.

The differences between SNCC and SCLC were, in fact, routinely misread in most of white America. Since these distinctions all surfaced between 1962 and

1964, affecting what happened as well as affecting perceptions of what happened, it is useful to compare the strengths and weaknesses of the two organizations.

The visible activism that had materialized during the sit-ins and Freedom Rides of 1960 – 61 had been the work of young cadres of activists who had taken it upon themselves to assert systemic demands in the name of all of the nation's black citizens. But when Charles Sherrod moved into southwest Georgia and Bob Moses took up station in the Mississippi Delta, they were not only "shifting their base" (in the manner of military commanders launching a new campaign), they were also engaging in something much more profound — the recruitment of a new, active citizenry drawn from the rank and file of black America. These "ordinary people" did not sit passively on the sidelines watching Freedom Riders perform kamikaze acts of daring-do; rather, the "grassroots folks" spoke for themselves.

This involvement of people at the base of society cannot be credited to the young field secretaries of SNCC. The concept of a broad-based assault on a key institution of Jim Crow had been pioneered in 1955 with the citywide bus boycott organized in Alabama by the Montgomery Improvement Association led by Jo Ann Gibson Robinson, E. D. Nixon, and Martin Luther King. In one way or another, virtually the entire black population of Montgomery had been drawn into the elaborate car-pooling and telephone networks that became the organizational backbone of the successful year-long bus boycott.[93]

In the Montgomery boycott, local black ministers tapped into the readiness of average citizens to take a measured stand against segregation. It is not enough to say that thousands of blacks stopped riding Jim Crow buses in the city. Everyone participated. But it is important to note that the acts they performed stopped short of being "active" assertions against authority. They were, rather, assertions passively carried out. People did not have to confront authority directly; they merely had to *not* ride a bus. The emotional achievement — the social achievement — was nevertheless transforming. One small event, appropriately historicized as the title of a book on the boycott, illustrates the point fully. As the car-pooling got under way in Montgomery, the participants quickly gained confidence that they would, indeed, be able to transport the entire black working population to their jobs. Spotting an elderly woman trudging down a sidewalk, men in one packed car pulled over and offered to make room for her. She smilingly assured them she could make it on her own: "My feets are tired, but my soul is rested," she said.[94] She was removing Jim Crow from her life.

Yet Sherrod in Georgia and Moses in Mississippi were asking people to explore an even more demanding path: to face The Man at the courthouse, to face police in the streets — all to register to vote, all to challenge other facets of a Jim

Crow system of commerce, justice, and politics. These "ordinary people" were threatened, intimidated, intermittently beaten, and often jailed. From SNCC's standpoint, this struggle was of a different order—whether Martin Luther King understood it or not, whether the press knew it or not.

Nevertheless, for a number of young workers, much of the grousing about King or about other alleged "Uncle Tom" leaders in various southern towns was simply rhetorical hype—self-serving, self-promoting, and not, by any standard, beneficial to the cause. Among those who so believed was Jim Bevel, a veteran of Nashville's workshops and the Freedom Rides. Bevel joined forces with the SCLC leader in an effort to capitalize on King's oratorical flair and demonstrable status to aid in organizing at the grass roots.

It would be in this shifting maelstrom of experimentation and tension that America experienced the coming of the Freedom Vote in Mississippi and the unveiling of King's "Letter from a Birmingham Jail" in 1963. While Moses and others brooded over different strategies for shaping movement activities that year, one of America's great ministerial figures of the 1960s, Fred Shuttlesworth, moved to place his congregation at the forefront of the struggle in Birmingham, Alabama. Shuttlesworth pushed SCLC's program of nonviolent direct action into the streets in response to some unconvincing posturing by self-styled white moderates engaged in a political struggle against T. Eugene "Bull" Connor, the commissioner of public safety. Connor's brutal style of law enforcement vastly complicated Shuttlesworth's efforts to recruit from the city's respectable black families. He asked for Martin Luther King's help and got it. And so it was in the Easter Boycott campaign of April 1963 that King made an impassioned call for recruits, marched down the aisle of St. Paul Methodist Church and out into the street, and was followed not by the congregation he had addressed but, from the surrounding neighborhood, hundreds of largely teenage youngsters who had been recruited, organized, and briefed by Bevel. The nation watched in shocked amazement as Bull Connor's police dogs and fire hoses routed the marchers in the next few days, washing people against walls and down streets. King's subsequent arrest, incarceration, and, above all, "Letter from a Birmingham Jail," supplemented the graphic TV images that flooded the nation's living rooms. In the aggregate, these developments were the immediate catalysts for the passage of the first effective legislative victory over the Jim Crow system, the Civil Rights Bill of 1964.[95]

Bevel did not regard these events as any sort of personal vindication. He was defeated in his attempt to persuade SCLC to join the Moses-led COFO project in Mississippi and refused to participate in King's alternative effort in St. Augustine, which occupied SCLC throughout much of the summer of 1964. The Mississippi campaigns would prove to have considerably longer legs; in fact, they led to the political high point of the southern civil rights movement — namely, the construction and deployment of the MFDP in 1964.

Putting Beliefs to the Test

The only thing in the twentieth century that encouraged blacks in the South to test out their "courage and determination" had been SNCC, Amzie Moore concluded.[96] It was precisely this quality of SNCC organizing and mobilizing that led a fiery Charles McLaurin to call SNCC's voter registration activity "revolutionary." "People going to the courthouse, for the first time. Then telling their friends to go down." What is not captured in this shorthand is the colossal battles black Mississippians experienced in their own minds about whether or not to go to the courthouse. Despite thunder and lightning, over one hundred people had stood with McLaurin in front of Bryant's Chapel in Indianola during July 1964. "They felt the meaning of ONE MAN ONE VOTE," reported Eddie Johnson. "To vote out police brutality; to vote out officials that keep the Negro down. To vote in people that care about people — black and white. They saw a policeman ask to talk to McLaurin. And they saw McLaurin say, 'Wait till I'm finished talking.' And McLaurin went on and talked. And they sang 'Ain't gonna let no policeman turn us around.' Brave people ready to join you in the fight for freedom." Such activity was not only ground-breaking, it helped win the revolution against the caste system of segregation. SNCC organizers in both Albany, Georgia, and rural Mississippi, after two years, refused to run, "despite the trumped-up prosecutions, the inordinately long jail sentences, the brutal beatings, and the constant threat of death." They built new offices when segregationists set fire to the old ones. They drove only at night, without headlights, so that racists bent on running them out could not find them. Yet to borrow from James Baldwin, they did not foresee the price of the ticket. At every moment, SNCC people lived in a world of high anxiety.[97]

The events in Mississippi and Albany, Georgia, make it possible to see more clearly what happened on a larger scale in 1962 – 64. The initial creativity of SNCC became visible as discrete events: the sit-ins, the Freedom Rides, the Mississippi movement, the Albany movement. Through their own innovations, and by building on older organizing networks led by prominent figures such as Amzie Moore, C. C. Bryant, E. W. Steptoe, Herbert Lee, and William Anderson, SNCC activists began to work with people outside their own group. Their first recruits were young black southerners like Charles McLaurin, Bernice Johnson Reagon, Rutha and McCree Harris, Hollis Watkins, Curtis Hayes, and Sam Block. Soon drawn into this decisive effort were northern black students, including Ivanhoe Donaldson, Stokely Carmichael, and Martha Prescod, among many others.

Joining this visionary group were a very small number of whites, such as Bob Zellner from Alabama and Jane Stembridge from Georgia.

Each nonviolent direct action taught participants new lessons and gave them concrete ideas about what might work in the future. Whether or not subsequent innovations "worked" or not, they could not be repressed by the received culture supporting the caste system. Movement activists continued to engage in new tactics because they had escaped from the immobilizing consequences of their own fear. They did not resign or otherwise give up, which is precisely what made them "activists." Many others who could not find ways to cope with doubt and fear did not, in consequence, "act." They were not, therefore, "activists."

PART TWO
HOW DEMOCRACY
TRAVELS

Bridges to the North

No one at the University of Michigan in 1962 had ever heard anybody like Curtis Hayes before.* The young man from Mississippi simply knocked people flat, and he did it without even trying. Previously isolated in small hamlets, the field secretaries of the southern movement realized that northern college campuses were particularly responsive, to put it mildly, to blow-by-blow accounts of the freedom struggle. Hayes, who led the first sit-in at the bus terminal in McComb and subsequently signed up as one of Bob Moses' original staffers on the voter registration projects, soon spoke at the University of California at Berkeley, the University of Wisconsin, and the University of Michigan. Dickie Magidoff, a Michigan sophomore, remembered Hayes's visit to campus: "Hayes was a very young man, very shy. He was only about twenty. He came up, and spoke at a couple of churches, and a few house meetings." Magidoff grew up in New York familiar with the Old Left and its perceptions of what constituted radical politics. He felt comfortable with what he considered sophisticated political debate. Yet he was thunderstruck by Hayes's capacity to act, "how willing Hayes was to risk his life. And it was clear he *was* risking his life." For Magidoff, Hayes had "unimaginable courage."[1]

Six months after his beating in McComb, Bob Zellner went to Ann Arbor as well. Zellner tried to explain how the southern movement had changed his understanding of political effectiveness. "We had a big argument about nonviolence," Magidoff said. Zellner was "sitting here, in our kitchen, saying that if they sicced a dog on him, and the dog was chewing on his balls, he would prob-

---

*The next three chapters explain how SNCC electrified those outside the South. Readers who want to follow the narrative of SNCC in the South may prefer to skip to Chapter 7 and return to Chapters 4–6 later.

ably not fight the dog!" It was too much for the Michigan activists. " 'You're just saying that!' " they retorted. "We were getting exasperated, although we all got along very well," said Magidoff. "It was early groping with very difficult ideas. Zellner was such an absolutist about it."[2] It was hard to believe and harder still to ignore.

These stories, however dramatic and even dazzling to students like Magidoff, did not show people how to find ways to act in their own communities. As one interested Harvard theologian observed, such a connection was very difficult to make: "Chuck McDew has been here for several days and has done a lot to provide some identity with your work 'down there' and what the group in Boston is doing. This gap is sometimes hard to bridge."[3]

Places like Michigan and Harvard mattered to SNCC. True, people there were not engaged in the central civic work to destroy Jim Crow. No one stunned and electrified the sedentary residents the way Moses and Sherrod were doing in the Deep South. Yet even Moses and Sherrod were largely invisible outside of their project areas. Vulnerable to local sheriffs and hostile white communities, they needed outside support. Northern students from prominent families had one major benefit: many were idealistic and could bring money, human resources, and the national media South.

In peculiar ways, this northern front of the civil rights movement would also challenge the national culture of white supremacy. Though many northern whites were committed to racial equality, they had almost no experience with making it happen. The racial divide was in everyone, they would discover. They would have to change themselves. Some did. Some could not. The young whites who got involved early were part of something else aborning — kindred spirits who would spin off in frustrated splinters, some of which tipped into violence. But in 1962 that was all in the future, and the spirit in Ann Arbor was bravely optimistic. If we join forces, they believed, we can change the country.

It was still unclear *how* SNCC could explain to these northern students what it was doing in Mississippi and Georgia. Yet it had to if it was going to survive.

Into this breach stepped a bridge builder of pivotal importance — Sandra "Casey" Cason, who entered the student movement through the sit-ins. Between 1960 and 1963, Casey moved to the center of SNCC in the South. She also strengthened an early, central connection to the major student group in the North, Students for a Democratic Society (SDS). From these two vantage points, she worked as SNCC's "Northern Coordinator" to translate the immediacy and desperation of the southern situation for interested northern students. To communicate effectively, Casey needed to craft specific, fresh explanations that could cut through conventional political language. For example, how could she find a visceral way to explain that southern field secretaries of SNCC were not interested in Democratic or Republican Party politics, but instead worked to survive everyday terror in order to register voters in Albany, Georgia? Her first effort was widely successful — a pamphlet called "You Can Help" that circulated across campuses in the North and West. Then she started a newsletter so northern supporters reading it in a suburb of St. Louis, Oakland, or Philadelphia could better grasp what black people experienced in the South. Casey created links among people who had vastly different experiences. Her work therefore represented an innovative form of political leadership emerging in the student movement of the 1960s.

There were not many Caseys in the southern movement. A tall, blonde, white woman with an intense, philosophical bent, she had been raised by a single mother in Victoria, Texas. Both her mother and her grandmother taught her that "people should be honest and kind to each other." She entered the University of Texas at Austin in 1957 and soon moved to the Christian Faith and Life Community, the only integrated housing on campus. There she joined wide-ranging seminars under Reverend Joseph Matthews. Matthews asked the students to read and discuss the philosophers appearing in the wake of World War II devastation. The voices of European philosophers in particular resonated with this young group of interracial students in the segregated South of the late 1950s. People's experiences with Nazi Germany led them to the idea that while political systems could not prevent the occurrence of evil, one could still insist on one's values. Casey felt that these "small, intensely confrontational seminars" proved "far more challenging than any of my classes at the university."[4]

The participants, white and black, regarded the Bible as a book of history and found value in the symbolic meaning of the stories. As the existentialists suggested, there were no meaningful ways to make sense of the world — no history, no truths — except the actions one took every day. When an individual worldview that a student had fashioned prior to coming into contact with the Faith and Life Community began to break down, the group called it a "Christ event" — a sanctioned crisis. As Casey put it, "there was talk about pushing people to their limit. They did not use the phrase ego-death, but that's what it was, where there was a collapse of systems. And what happens at that point is that you're still here standing on the basic ground." That ground "is what they called God." Those willing to release their attachment to belief systems came together, creating a symbolic and ritual life around the idea that "you live in community and you *only* live in community." In fact, Casey concluded, the idea of an independent self existing apart from anything else was a lie.[5]

This intense, philosophical experience was in some ways comparable to the Lawson workshops taking place at exactly the same time in Nashville. In the late 1950s, Casey shared leadership in national YWCA groups with black chairpersons and taught in urban, primarily black, vacation Bible schools. She lived in integrated housing and was active in integrated groups. "I had heard black people *talk* about white people and their hatred and their fear and their anger and their forgiveness and I'd been part of that and cried. I'd done a lot of emotional work before I ever came to SNCC." Needless to say, few young Americans had sustained such an intense experience — daily, for two or three years — of human relations work. Even fewer had engaged with members of another racial group. Casey's efforts in this community and her participation in the YWCA on the Austin campus gave her an unusually sophisticated understanding of the new interracial and intraracial terrain that was just becoming visible on the horizon. This understanding turned out to be extremely practical. Casey emerged from the Austin community well prepared to work within both the "act now" environment of SNCC and the highly intellectualized, debate-dominated SDS.

When the sit-ins began in the spring of 1960, Casey joined the fight for free, unfettered access to her black friends: "I loved the black community. The music and the culture and the hip guys and the hip girls, and it was a drag to not have access to that," she recalled. Her participation in the discussions of the Christian Faith and Life Community, where she had debated the utility of the Christian existentialist philosophers, prompted her to view the civil rights movement in ways different from most southern white students. "As it was developing — even before the self-sacrificial living and loving your enemy," she stated, "it just seemed to me that the black community was morally superior." To not have access to such a world was a restriction on her. Segregation, she realized, "was about me." She and her black friends "were comrades in a common thing."[6]

Casey centered her emotional and social life in the fragile interracial community in Austin. Still, she considered herself a guest in the black community — that is, working under black leadership and within a black framework. Once the sit-ins started, Casey believed that nonviolent direct action was a transforming experience — "a new self was created." She was "released from older and lesser self-definitions" — not completely free, but closer. "We assumed a new identity," Casey explained. The process was similar to the one John Lewis, Diane Nash, and others lived through in Nashville: their experiences in the student movement gave them a new sense of who they were and what they thought their lives might become. They no longer had to wait for others but could choose to act on their own beliefs.[7]

In the spring of 1960, as Casey participated in Austin's sit-ins, Atlanta activist Connie Curry visited the Austin campus to enlist students for the NSA's Southern Student Leadership Seminar. Curry recruited Casey by telling her the story of the Nashville sit-ins. "When we sat together in a little restaurant on the

Drag and heard that story, a new life began for me," Casey remembered. At the NSA seminar that summer, Casey met SNCC activist Chuck McDew, who told her that before he could participate in movement actions, he had to be willing to die. He also said that "in the movement we are many minds, but one heart." Casey described McDew as unlike anyone else she had met but "just the first of the many new friends who would guide my life in the years to come." During the seminar, she began to understand the civil rights movement as regional, affecting blacks and whites both. It was a "serious response to our region's failings."[8]

SNCC invited Casey to Atlanta University in the fall of 1960 to present a workshop on school integration based on her work in Austin. Also speaking at the workshop was James Lawson. Casey understood Lawson's explanation of nonviolence as a way of life that "took one out of [being a] victim and put her in total command of her life." She explained: "This was freedom as an inside job, not as external to myself, but as created, on the spot and in the moment, by our actions." In effect, Lawson gave her words to describe her experiences in the Austin sit-ins. "By acting in this way, in which the act itself was of equal value to its outcome, and by risking all for it, we were released from old and lesser definitions of ourselves in terms of race, sex, class," she wrote. The SNCC conference that fall was "powerful far beyond any expectations I had."[9]

The workshop Casey led on school integration was one of many she ran during this period on southern campuses — first in SNCC and later in SDS. Collectively they possessed rich theoretical implications for democratic practice. "Workshops," she believed, "carved out public space for people to be"; workshops had parameters that helped to "line out" the discussion. "Lining out" described the way rural southerners sang in church. In the absence of songbooks or widespread literacy, the leader would sing the line and the congregation would repeat it. In these workshops, she led by introducing a topic, then by promoting discussion of it. In some cases she might start conversation by giving information to the group; in other cases she asked for information. "Then there would be response from the group. Then on to the next topic. Then response. In this way the parameters of a topic [were] established, a framework within which it can be understood as a topic, and information [was] exchanged." As Lawson had done so effectively in Nashville between 1958 and 1961, Casey established an environment that provided room for everyone to contribute. The seminar leader did not try to overpower others. The customary word to describe this kind of exchange is "egalitarian." But the objective was actually a new level of engaged conversation that went beyond egalitarianism. Facilitators like Casey were looking for ways to fashion "joint ownership of the learning situation between participant and leader." The skills one needed to establish such a workshop "were simply clarifying, questioning, recruiting, watching people emerge," Casey recalled. This method echoed Ella Baker's longtime organizing approach. Still, it contained a view of leadership as yet quite indistinct and only prefigurative of larger changes in leadership styles over the next quarter century. For the moment — 1960 – 62 — "it was the way to go, as opposed to lectures or intellectual debate," Casey wrote.[10]

Casey represented the forward edge of a larger trend. Young people began to create personal links between South and North, as SNCC activists traveled around the country between 1961 and 1965. Though the links between North and South seem natural now, in the first years of SNCC's existence few individuals took the steps necessary to become deeply connected to people in both regions. The dapper and savvy Tim Jenkins, a black graduate of Howard and subsequently a law student at Yale, pioneered connections between the early SNCC organization and the Northern Student Movement (NSM) while simultaneously serving as vice president of the NSA. Though he never held a formal position in SNCC, Jenkins was a major architect of its early policies. Maria Varela, dark-haired with clear, piercing eyes, was a Latino writer and photographer who attended Emmanuel College in Boston. She participated in early SNCC meetings as well as SDS's historic conference in Port Huron, Michigan, in 1962 and by 1963 had moved into SNCC full time as an organizer and literacy educator. Peter Countryman, a white undergraduate at Yale drawn to the spiritually purifying aspects of southern direct action, started NSM in the fall of 1961 "to man the supply lines — that means money, man," in the words of James Forman. NSM became a major vehicle to mobilize financial support and publicity for the activities of SNCC and CORE in the South.[11]

Students for a Democratic Society

Many northerners went South to see what SNCC was doing. Inspired by SNCC's work, students at the University of Michigan breathed new life into campus activism by creating SDS. Later generations would recognize that these two organizations, SNCC and SDS, were critical components of what, by the end of the decade, became popularly known as the New Left.

At the time, it was less clear that this was happening. For example, a perceptive student leader at Michigan, Alan Haber, headed an obscure national student group, the Student League for Industrial Democracy. As an active socialist, Haber was a radical scholar who believed that intellectuals were central to social change. He scheduled a conference on "Human Rights in the North" to be held in Michigan in April 1960. It would have been "just another conference," recalled Helen Garvy, a later SDS activist, except that on 1 February Ezell Blair

Jr., Franklin McCain, Joseph McNeil, and David Richmond of North Carolina A&T State University sat down at Woolworth's lunch counter in Greensboro. The sit-ins spread like wildfire across the South that spring. Haber immediately invited the young men from Greensboro to the April conference, where they electrified the other participants.[12]

"I once thought politics was what you were for and against—not what you did," said Bob Ross, also a freshman at Michigan that spring. "But here [at the sit-ins] were people who were doing something." And they needed help. Over the next year, northern students organized themselves as Friends of SNCC groups and picketed Woolworth's and the Kress store in northern campus towns to publicize the freedom struggle in the South. In April 1960 Haber also attended the founding SNCC conference at Raleigh's Shaw University and met Ella Baker and other SNCC activists. He then traveled from campus to campus, looking for recruits. "This became the kernel of SDS," said Garvy.[13]

Sharon Jeffrey, an early Michigan activist, had organized sympathy pickets in Ann Arbor to protest southern segregation at Woolworth's and Kress and helped Haber to arrange the human rights conference in the spring. The picket was extended to include a local women's apparel store that refused to allow black women to try on clothing. Among those who joined the picket line was Dickie Magidoff, the student "blown away" by Curtis Hayes.[14]

Just as SNCC organizers discovered in the rural voter registration campaigns, house meetings, mass meetings, and even parties following an action served as essential gathering spaces. Participants compared notes, exchanged information, and deepened their relationships. This combated the sense of fear and impotence threatening individuals' impulse to act. It therefore helped sustain people's energy. The social ties developed and strengthened at these events were incipient *political* ties as well.

After working to organize the picketing against the dime stores in Ann Arbor, Jeffrey traveled to Miami during the summer of 1960 to attend a CORE workshop on nonviolence and met Martin Luther King. Returning to Ann Arbor in the fall, she felt even more impelled to participate in Haber's group. "It had vision, it had purpose, it had meaning. [Haber] was also smart enough to know that you have to organize around specifics. That's everything that I really responded to." Magidoff also was attracted to Haber's intellectual capacities. Listening to Haber talk "was like hearing the inside of my head. He was able to conceptualize views, values, perspectives, judgments, reactions—it was amazing." Both Jeffrey and Magidoff later became key organizers for the young SDS.[15]

Looking back on that period, Magidoff recalled with some incredulity "how optimistic I was. And also how incredibly potent I felt." Hearing about the North Carolina A&T students who took this step "pushed the whole thing forward." As Jeffrey said, "I don't know if SDS would have taken off without the Southern students. . . . They gave incredible energy to us, because who could say they were wrong?" Throughout the North, it suddenly became easy to organize students to picket under the slogan "We Walk So They May Sit."[16] The southern sit-ins encouraged northern students to feel that action based on one's values was possible.

Recruiting Tom Hayden

Another pivotal figure in this early group, Tom Hayden, wrote for the *Michigan Daily*. Initially, he was simply a curious student journalist who covered the sympathy pickets Jeffrey and others assembled against Woolworth's in March 1960. Talking with the picketers led Hayden to learn more about the civil rights movement. He also read Jack Kerouac's *On The Road*, then resolved to hitchhike to California. When school ended in May 1960, Hayden thumbed his way to Berkeley to meet the students who had led a fight earlier in the year against the House Un-American Activities Committee. Covering the Democratic National Convention in Los Angeles that summer for his college newspaper, he interviewed Martin Luther King. King told him that "each of us had to be more than neutral and objective. We had to make a difference."[17]

From the convention, Hayden traveled to a NSA conference, where he first encountered SNCC in the persons of chairman Charles McDew and Sandra Cason, then representing the University of Texas. In her speech calling for the national student group to support the southern student sit-ins, Cason gracefully agitated for action on the part of NSA:

> I do not see the law as immutable, but rather as an agreed-upon pattern for relations between people. If the pattern is unjust or a person does not agree with the relations, a person must at times choose to do the right rather than the legal. I do not consider this anarchy, but responsibility. . . . I cannot say to a person who suffers injustice, "Wait." Perhaps you can. I can't. And having decided that I cannot urge caution, I must stand with him. . . . I am more concerned that all of us, Negro and white, realize the possibility of becoming less inhuman humans through commitment and action, with all their frightening complexities.[18]

Many northern students in the audience were deeply affected by Casey's appeal — a fact that verified a new American political reality: northern youths were being recruited to activism by the southern black movement and by its representatives, black and white.

Casey's speech recruited Hayden, who after some initial hesitation, became one of the best-known and durable activists of the decade. To Hayden, Casey "held a position of great authority within the group because of her ability to think morally, express herself poetically, and have practical effects." He wanted to know even more about the civil rights movement and why Casey identified the sit-ins as part of her self-interest.[19]

Hayden met Casey again at the October 1960 SNCC conference, where she led another workshop on school integration. Hayden, as the new editor of the *Michigan Daily*, felt pressure to take political positions on the paper. Following the conference, Hayden corresponded with Casey and, through her, learned of SNCC's work in Atlanta and Fayette County, Tennessee. Soon, Casey and Hayden traveled together to Fayette and observed the demonstrations for better wages and living conditions. There, they witnessed evicted sharecroppers living in tents in the snow and then found a group of white toughs waiting for them with belts and clubs. When Hayden called the police, "they just joined the toughs. We got in our car and raced out of town. The [police] followed us for fifty miles before we lost them." After that experience, Hayden no longer wanted to stay on the sidelines. The crucial ingredient that Casey brought to Hayden was not the words she was speaking but the sites she was taking him to — the schoolrooms that SNCC was in the process of creating in Mississippi, Georgia, and Tennessee.[20]

In the fall of 1960 Casey was a graduate student in English and philosophy at Texas, focusing much of her energy on SNCC. She continued to exchange long philosophical and passionate letters with Hayden following their encounter at the NSA over the summer. Years later, when asked to pinpoint the beginning of his long involvement in the movement, Tom Hayden first cited the "direct action quality of the sit-ins where you were able to live what you believed and take the consequences." Reconsidering, however, he said "it wasn't even that," so much as "getting personally involved with some of the people who were in the civil rights movement."[21] The "truth of the matter is that I fell in love with [Casey]," he said. That personal connection made him feel "more compelled than I might otherwise have been by watching people or listening to speeches." Hayden "won me over with his correspondence," Casey later wrote, "sending mammoth letters and whole boxes of books he'd read and loved . . . madly underlined." Meeting SNCC people, Hayden recalled, "was a key turning point, the moment my political identity began to take shape." Changed by the experience, he began to see "proof there [in the South] that ordinary people can change conditions."[22]

A SNCC Identity

To be closer to Hayden, Casey took a job in the spring of 1961 as program director at the University of Illinois YWCA. They married in Austin in the fall, and after the ceremony drove through the night and next day to Atlanta.[23] Ella Baker had recruited Casey as a campus traveler for a YWCA human relations project. Both Baker and Casey chose to work on the project because it allowed them, as Casey said, "to be near the black students who were setting us all on fire." Baker served as a role model of a "great soul and a true organizer" for Casey. Tom Hayden, meanwhile, agreed to become SDS's regional traveler in the South. "Our marriage vows and SNCC's vow to be there on the edge even at the risk of death now merged in my life," Casey remembered.[24]

During the fall of 1961, Casey traveled to black and white campuses throughout the South, running integrated "human relations" workshops for college students "trapped in the cage of race," who saw these programs as "a way out." She discovered that SNCC's work overlapped with the workshops, as many black campus leaders who attended were also local movement leaders. Her work in human relations "undermine[d] and defeat[ed] segregation on the personal level," just as the wider civil rights movement crushed legal barriers that could defeat segregation politically.[25] Again, rich theoretical implications emerged from her experiences: it was not enough to change the laws against segregation: one had to *also* defeat segregation in one's own personal relations.

In between these trips, Casey often acted as recorder for the SNCC meetings at B. B. Beamon's restaurant on Auburn Avenue in Atlanta. The discussions, as Charles McDew noted, could ramble — "Somebody may have spoken for eight hours, and seven hours and fifty three minutes was utter bullshit, but seven minutes was good." Casey's dexterity in human relations was evident in these meetings as she became skilled in the development of consensus — an absolutely critical component of SNCC's functioning at that time. Majority rule would not suffice: "Consensus was important in nonviolence, because the final arbiter of one's behavior was one's conscience." Whoever lost in a vote, therefore, following their conscience, "might have to leave the group."[26] So in SNCC, unity came first. Yet it was hard to achieve. Black Mississippian Joyce Ladner said that the staff meetings in which she participated sometimes lasted days. "You'd think you're going to arrive at a decision after all this dialectical stuff goes on, and then someone jumps up and says, 'Well, who gave you the right to decide?' and then you start all over again." Casey recalled that "it took real effort to find the line of thinking, and make it clear without distorting anything. If I could do that, I could assist in the development of consensus."[27]

For Atlanta activist Julian Bond, SNCC's program at this point was "to encourage college students to take a year or two out of school to come down in the South and try to convince Negroes just to register to vote." As Charles Sherrod later said, "When we got together and we decided to commit ourselves to the movement, we were talking about jumping down in the South, and in three or four years, knocking it out. And then going back to school, about our business," he laughed. "But when we jumped down in here to fight, we got a bigger fight than we thought we'd get." The task of registering voters and developing grass-roots organizations to mobilize those voters was a slow and sometimes tedious process.[28] Above all, it was an uncharted route to political self-determination. SNCC people lived through experiences that immediately distanced them from their peers who remained in college. They felt an enormous obligation to the individuals they were trying to register: field secretaries could not simply leave after a summer or a semester and go back to school when those with whom they had worked had so little and remained so greatly threatened. And SNCC workers needed to come to terms with two facts: as a result of their experiences, they differed from other college students, and despite their strenuous efforts, their work was far from complete.

Slowly, through 1961–62, SNCC activists began to develop a distinct and powerful group identity: "They worked, ate, socialized and slept together," Cleve Sellers reported. They "read the same books and wore the same kind of clothing. They had a definable lifestyle. They were *SNCC people* and they considered themselves different from those who had not shared their unique experience. SNCC had become a way of life" — in both its personal and political manifestations. "Although they frequently had sharp arguments," especially over tactics, "they were bound together in a community of common commitment." As Stokely Carmichael explained, joining SNCC often produced a feeling of "relief bordering on euphoria." Coming from a large West Indian family in New York, as he did, "it was a lot like finding a long-lost family that you hadn't previously known about, but with whom you instantly recognized your kinship." In 1962 Casey Hayden was one of the few whites involved at the center of this developing community. Not only was she part of a group actively resisting segregation, but by living with its members, she was also literally "living in the solution." She learned "to reject the absolute constructs and abstractions of civilization, following the lead of the existentialists in response to the horrors of World War II. I learned to believe my own experience."[29]

As Casey moved to the center of SNCC work, Tom Hayden learned — through Casey's participation in the Atlanta meetings — about SNCC's first voter registration project in McComb, Mississippi. It routinely produced drama beyond anything offered by formal educational institutions. One day Bob Moses called the Atlanta office from Ernest Noble's Cleaners in McComb, reporting that he and others from SNCC were hiding among the clothes while police and other white men surrounded the building, threatening to kill them. Hayden wanted "to go to Mississippi and do a quick report and take it to the Justice Department and try to write something for the national press to get protection." When he flew to McComb in October 1961, Moses sneaked him into town from the airport, arranging "by clandestine means" to meet a car in an unlit section of a black neighborhood. Hayden wrote back to his comrades in SDS: "We had to be let out of a rented car, and lie on the back floor of a parked car in a parking lot." The shutters drawn and windows reinforced, Hayden met secretly in the basement with Moses and others. "We were having to use, at that point, clandestine means to discuss the most conventional kind of tactic, namely the registration of voters, because what we were up against was a whole organized system that was out to kill us." Hayden concluded: "That was a very devastating thing to discover."[30]

Such activity became increasingly common as SNCC activists drew the attention of northern students, who began to visit SNCC projects in larger numbers in the winter of 1961–62. Hayden struggled with his own position. In Michigan, he felt he had lived in a stifling, alienating world. Now, suddenly, others' life-and-death commitment confronted him. "The whole emotion of defining not only yourself, but also your life by risking your life, and testing whether you're willing to die for your beliefs, was *the* powerful motive," Hayden told journalist James Miller in 1985. SNCC staff, he wrote to SDSers in the North, "have decided that it is time right now — not in a minute, not after this one more committee meets, not after we have the legal defense and court costs promised — to give blood and body if necessary for social justice." As it turned out, Hayden's visit, while just one in a series of unexpected developments in McComb during October 1961, boosted the movement in the North. Published by SDS as a pamphlet in the late fall, Hayden's reports from Mississippi and Atlanta recruited numerous people for SDS.[31]

At this juncture, Tom Hayden's personal development appeared uneven. He had not yet experienced the difficulties — and thus not yet learned the lessons — of how to organize a campaign in the same way as had Sherrod, Moses, or Hollis Watkins. Yet as a reporter with good strategic instincts, Hayden understood that something of great importance was occurring in the SNCC projects, even if he did not yet understand its fundamental dynamics. The changes the SNCC experience caused in his beliefs truly seemed to surprise him: "I began to unlearn everything I had been taught at college. Mechanics, maids, unemployed people taking things into their own hands. I kept wondering, where did these people come from? Really, where have I been?" It marked the beginning of

Hayden's belief in the possibilities of participatory democracy. This echoes the experience of Prathia Hall, who worked in the southwest Georgia SNCC project: "I learned there some of the most important lessons I will ever learn in my life. I had been to college before I went South, and I've been to school a lot of years since. But the most important lessons that I ever learned, I learned in those rural counties from people who could not read or write their names."[32]

Precisely in this way the movement politics of the early 1960s began to challenge received traditions about the components necessary for truly democratic politics in America—traditions that turned on basic assumptions about how people learned the realities of public life in America, about how things actually worked, and what people could do, or attempt to do, to transform the culture itself. Virtually every significant "ex-student" organizer in the movement—South or North—repeated some version of this story that Prathia Hall told: the most important educational institution they attended was the southern movement itself. It is interesting to note after the fact how quickly people who had not lived the movement routinely labeled such thinking "romanticization of the poor." Such terminology distorted what may be one of the most important factors in middle-class students' adoption of values quite different from those they had absorbed at home. When black and white students left the university and began to organize, they often reported their surprise at watching "ordinary" citizens finding ways to break free from a system that not only deprived them of a voice in the political order, but also denied their essential humanity. Raised in an environment where people accepted competition and hierarchy as the norm, college students, black and white, began to revalue all they had come to assess as "worthy" or "worthless." Confronted with the complexity and strength of character in the ordinary people they encountered, students like Tom Hayden and thousands of others rather effortlessly moved on to a new vision of a democratic America, one that, on a most basic level, flowed from the discovery that each person had value.

At different speeds, and with varying degrees of personal intensity, young people in the North began to respond to the initiatives welling up out of the South. SNCC staff went North to raise money to keep people in the field. They publicized the activities and the reprisals increasingly common across the South, in the hope that the federal government could be prodded to overcome its reluctance to intervene. They also went North to "find a quiet place" away from the constant strain and tension of their work in the South.[33] SDS's primary role during the first two years of its existence was to be one of several groups trying to link eager northern students to what was rapidly becoming one of the most dramatic democratic initiatives in the nation's history.

The Basement versus the Kitchen:
The Search for Serious Politics

Though SDS was new, small, and not yet engaged in direct action, the fledgling student organization stood out in the context of the U.S. political culture of the early 1960s. First, like SNCC, SDS did not exclude anyone willing to take on its vision, regardless of political affiliation and personal background. Second, its leadership quickly determined to be a multi-issue organization, rather than focus on only one part of a larger problem. The Student Peace Union, for example, addressed only peace issues. SDSers, on the other hand, were concerned with peace, civil rights, democratic politics, and social reform. Furthermore, they believed that these concerns were interrelated. In discussions they created games like "Connect the Issues," where someone would say, "OK, rainforests in British Columbia, and apartheid in South Africa, how do they connect?" Another would reply, "Rainforests in BC, you've got loggers, the loggers are selling their product to the Japanese. The Japanese are trading with the South Africans." Later students like Colorado native Robert Pardun would be attracted to SDS for precisely this reason: "Things actually did interconnect, and those things were affecting people's lives."[34]

Though SDS's policy of nonexclusion and its attempt to address multiple issues made it unusual, the group still had not produced a public statement that summed up these beliefs for the general public. Alan Haber, Sharon Jeffrey, and Bob Ross first energized SDS at Michigan through their determination to connect with and support the sit-ins in the South. In December 1961, after whites harassed and assaulted Tom Hayden during his McComb visit in October and white police in Albany arrested him for violating segregation laws in November, SDS's national executive committee felt a pressing need to define "what we are personally and collectively prepared to give and produce."[35]

SDS sought to build a political and educational framework embracing the civil rights struggle in the South, activists and researchers in the peace movement, and others who shared a commitment to "democratic and humane values as a basis for political action." Above all, the group needed to define what it meant by *democracy*. How did the term apply to industry, education, the arts, colonial revolutions, economic development, and the USSR? At bottom, SDS hoped to provide a "much needed statement of conviction and program for the young left in America."[36]

In late 1961 Haber, Jeffrey, and Ross turned to Tom Hayden, then in Atlanta with Casey, to write an initial draft of what would become SDS's most successful recruiting document, the "Port Huron Statement." Together with Martin Luther King's "Letter from a Birmingham Jail," it proved to be one of the seminal

American political manifestos of the twentieth century. Hayden's central role in its construction, conceptually and literally, verifies the range of his creative political imagination. Hayden wrote the first draft based in part on the ideas of those he had studied as an undergraduate: C. Wright Mills, John Dewey, Paul Goodman, and Albert Camus in particular.[37] It called others to follow the lead of SNCC: to reinvigorate the democratic political tradition in the North. On a personal level, the "Port Huron" period also marked a turning point for Casey Hayden. She and Tom moved North, removed from the daily support of the SNCC community, and she began to develop a feminist perspective.

It would be difficult to overestimate Casey's influence on Tom during this period. Her experiences in challenging arbitrary power in Austin, Atlanta, and elsewhere in the South during the previous three years had been substantial. Her ability to reflect clearly and critically on those experiences and then articulate their meaning in the vernacular of philosophy made her a vital partner for Tom in the weeks in which he wrote and rewrote drafts of the "Port Huron Statement." Both Tom *and* Casey were philosophers, and though Tom has been credited as the author of the document, Casey's substantial, if largely unrecognized, influence on the thinking of the time grew from the fact that for several prior years, she had tried to live her democratic values in the southern crucible.

As the statement evolved, Casey began to discover some of the ways the culture immobilized young women. In her words, "the guys were more independent. The girls all felt bad because they couldn't be." In this respect, Casey became a more representative figure of where the culture was headed than her much more famous spouse. Indeed, she came to act on a vision of equality that traveled well beyond Tom's, certainly one more precient on gender equity, women's liberation, and the idea that the personal is political. But all of this would only come later. In 1962 in Michigan, Casey's vision did not yet grab the hundreds of thousands it later would. In Casey's most prominent memory of the 1962 Port Huron conference, held during 11–15 June, where the statement was debated and approved, she disagreed with the phrase, "We regard *men* as infinitely precious and possessed of unfulfilled capacities for reason, freedom, and love." This wording conflicted with her belief in existentialism, which led her to think of everything in terms of process rather than end result. Instead of viewing people through the lens of liberal politics, where people forever progressed toward greater freedom and expanded their capacities for reason and love, she saw "Sisyphus pushing the rock up the hill, and it rolls back down. Another way to say that [is] there's no millennium. We're all in this together and we're never going to get out."[38]

The only way to proceed under such circumstances, she felt, was to act now as they wanted the world to be. In practical, strategic terms, she later observed, SNCC helped her realize that movements grew by creating a small community that lived its values and thus attracted others. "Creating the new world in the shell of the old [was] a strategy for change as well as a philosophical position." This connected the philosophies of nonviolence and existentialism. Despite Casey's objections to the "unfulfilled capacities" phrase, the wording was left in place because Tom argued for perfectibility as a goal, one that could never be reached. The repetition of the word "independence" in the document probably reflected, at least in part, the youth of its authors. "If you're independent, you don't have to talk about it." This cannot be said to have seriously diminished the statement, Casey observed, given "what adults were like then, what the world was like." Later, she viewed the emphasis on individual freedom as "a flaw of the guys, and I see this sense of interdependence or interbeing that the women brought to the situation as more valuable, more needed then. But at the time, the heroic individual was the ideal." Thus, the "Port Huron Statement" called upon Americans to rethink politics as an "art of collectively creating an acceptable pattern of social relations," but SDSers did not agree on what "an acceptable pattern" might be. Even though the document highlighted the need for "human brotherhood" and "interdependence," many in the group still clung to the received culture's emphasis on individual independence as the culmination of human freedom.[39]

After the Port Huron conference, the Haydens moved from Atlanta to Ann Arbor so Tom could enter graduate school. Through Tom, Casey grew close to the emerging national leadership of SDS then centered in Ann Arbor. In addition to Al Haber and Sharon Jeffrey, this group consisted of intellectuals Richard "Dick" and Mickey Flacks, who were a bit older than the others. Oberlin graduates Paul Potter and Rennie Davis also went to Michigan for graduate school. Over the next year the Haydens' basement became SDS headquarters and a "social action center." "You could show up anytime — three o'clock in the morning," Bob Ross remembered. "Tom would be in the basement, his shoes off, sitting in front of a typewriter, the phone next to him. He was constantly getting calls from the South about guys getting shot or arrested. You'd walk in and he'd say something like 'Make these ten phone calls for me, get some food down to Mississippi, raise $100 to get this guy out of jail.'" Casey got a job to support them while Tom was in school.[40]

Casey continued to "interpret SNCC" to those in the North, supporting civil rights work in the South through food, clothes, and money drives. She worked with Martha Prescod (later Norman) from the University of Michigan and Ivanhoe Donaldson from Michigan State, both of whom would soon become important SNCC staff members. Prescod, whose parents had been active in the

Progressive Party in 1948, went to Michigan to connect with blacks who were active in politics. Among her first contacts were black sorority sisters who were embarrassed to bring up civil rights issues. When she heard Curtis Hayes speak at Michigan, Prescod immediately formed a FOS group on campus with three other students. For two years, she raised money, sold records, arranged for speakers, and planned cocktail parties. She also got stories out to the newspapers and organized support demonstrations for SNCC.[41]

In April 1962 Casey, with Tom Hayden, Peter Countryman of NSM, Alan Haber, Tim Jenkins, and Paul Potter from Oberlin ran an intercollegiate conference on civil rights at Sarah Lawrence College in Bronxville, New York. The conference brought together several hundred students to talk about the southern movement and the possibilities of adapting similar strategies in the North. With her friend from the Christian Faith and Life Community, Dorothy Dawson, and Dawson's partner, another Texan named Robb Burlage—all three of whom were now in the North—Casey also strategized how to create an SDS in the South.[42]

The core SDS group in Ann Arbor discussed strategy and tactics at weekly meetings held in the Haydens' basement. Mickey Flacks noted that a complex if unarticulated dynamic was "a constant theme through the year." The men—desperately trying to act on their beliefs, but unsure as yet how to do so outside of the South—did not feel sufficiently confident in their own political rectitude. In the absence of such confidence, they tried to be "serious" all the time. Serious meant meeting, debating, and writing position papers. According to Flacks, Bob Ross insisted that they meet on Saturday nights, "which was his way of stating that he was different than the undergraduates, than the fraternity boys. They were going to carouse on Saturday nights, and we were going to do serious study." Yet the women "hated it; they didn't feel that to do social things on Saturday night was being like the fraternity boys. . . . But nobody would say that because it would sound frivolous." Instead, when the meetings started at 7:00 P.M., one by one the women would "drift up to where Casey lived. We would be socializing among ourselves, without the men," said Flacks. "One or two guys would often drift up with us, those who weren't afraid of being seen as selling out."[43]

The personal relations reflected different political priorities. This cannot be overstated. What happened within this small group in Ann Arbor in 1962 could be seen hundreds of thousands of times throughout the next two decades, in small groups and national conventions, in fringe political organizations, and in the very halls of Congress. Personal beliefs about political values and priorities played out in ways that either dramatically strengthened or dissolved civic bonds.

Casey, secure in her political acumen, felt the activity in the basement to be important. But crucially, she could compare it to that of SNCC, where the basis of political activity *was* building relationships—both among blacks and between blacks and whites. This political self-assurance precipitated one of the first insurgencies within SDS which—while low-key—later emerged as a significant moment of growing political consciousness. It happened at a New Year's Eve meeting of the SDS National Council, held in the Michigan Student Union. As midnight approached, Mickey Flacks related, the men were still meeting, though all the women had long since drifted out to talk to Casey. "Nobody threw [the women] out" of the meeting, Flacks asserted. "Nobody said, 'as women, we want to leave.'" Yet the women had felt that the meeting was crazy, thinking: "'Why are we sitting here,'" what were they trying to prove to themselves by sitting there talking serious politics? Flacks was sure that the men felt the same way but "suppressed that desire in themselves." So, at quarter to twelve, "led by Casey," the women went back into the meeting and broke it up, "insist[ing] that we were going to have a New Year's Eve party." Tom Hayden, Flacks remembered, was extremely angry at this interruption.[44]

Guided by Casey, the women contested the Ann Arbor men's understanding of what constituted "serious" political engagement. These women understood the central—if unexpressed—importance of social relations in building political strength. Such knowledge was in part a product of their gendered acculturation. Nonetheless, these conversations took place nearly seven years before the women's movement gave people a common language to express such an understanding. The women were certainly not frivolous. In what Flacks recognized as the experiences that "provided the earliest ideology of the women's movement," the women in this group "were concerned with interpersonal relations within the organization. Some of the men felt they had to suppress those needs in themselves, in order to be effective organizers."[45]

The movement was developing two distinct models for a "good organizer": the heroic individual and the relationship builder. This individual situation is important because it came to represent a pattern visible throughout the politics of the 1970s, the idea that the heroic individual could not create a strong civic culture. Indeed, the reaction *against* this new vision came to political life in the ascendancy of Reagonomics, the Christian Right, and the cowboy-style vision of the George W. Bush administration: "you're either with us or with the terrorists." Casey remembered that "when the [basement] study group's analysis of the objective world was not meaningful to me, I'd invite the women upstairs to talk about our lives."[46] It was, in effect, an early version of a consciousness-raising group. Thus, despite the determination of the "Port Huron Statement" to improve the quality of one-on-one social relations as the very building blocks of participatory democracy, many SDSers were unable to perform serious work on these relations. In particular, most of the men did not yet know how to act on their announced intentions.

This tension over what constituted "serious politics" was only one of the challenges the Haydens faced. Their romance represented the challenges faced by many in the movement who tried to live out their political beliefs in their private lives. It foreshadowed the difficulties faced by other movement couples. Casey felt that they had "held together as a couple well in the South" during 1961–62. Yet in Ann Arbor the following year, despite her work linking northern students to SNCC, she grew "homesick for the South, and for my strong sense of myself there." Casey's vital work of carrying SNCC experience and models to the North did not appear then — to her or to others — as crucial as it would in hindsight. Except for her relationship with Tom, nothing in the North engaged her as had the SNCC group centered in Atlanta. "I couldn't get into the style of intellectualism in Ann Arbor. I missed the spiritual and action elements of the southern experience," she later told Tom. Tom, for his part, admitted that he could have gone to graduate school in Atlanta rather than Ann Arbor. In 1987 he concluded sadly that he had been "too self-centered, my SDS involvement too intense, to have imagined such an alternative." While Casey longed for the South, Tom did not know how to help her. Years afterward, he recognized that he came from a family "where it was common, when faced with confusion, to shut down emotionally." Finding SDS "a chauvinist's paradise" where "the positions of power were dominated primarily by men, and the opportunities for unequal sexual liaisons were legion," he took a lover on the East Coast rather than maintain the integrity of his relationship with Casey. Casey stated that the only thing engaging her passion in Ann Arbor at this time was her marriage, which had replaced the Christian Faith and Life Community and SNCC as "the central covenant community of my life." When Tom started spending weekends with his lover, Casey returned to SNCC in Atlanta. "I was very sad," she wrote. "Even though I thought I had entered my marriage without illusions, I was brokenhearted when it ended."[47]

Hard as it may be to understand, this was in fact understatement: in the North, Casey and Tom Hayden shared no common intellectual framework for seeing their relationship as a political issue, which underlay Casey's "broken heart." Tom placed Casey's needs in the category of nonpolitical, or personal — their marriage was separate from their political life. Though Casey lacked the conceptual framework to articulate this at the time, she saw the clarification of the politics of the marriage as the foundation of her political activity.[48]

The Haydens' breakup at the end of 1962 was the first blow to the infectious optimism SDS espoused in the "Port Huron Statement." "It was very upsetting to all of us," said Sharon Jeffrey, "because we were really committed to the integrity of relationships." Tom later reflected that the break caused early SDS-ers to lose "some measure of confidence in ourselves. Mickey Flacks thought I was, plain and simple, an asshole. Others walked around in silent pain." Bob Ross told Tom that Tom's "political involvement [and] organizational intensity produced an intolerable situation" for Ross, as he "was still very young and the child of divorced parents. You [Tom] were the first sibling in my new 'family' to get divorced. It meant that our seamless, loving, and romantic community was breaking up." The split foreshadowed the enormous challenges inherent in a politics committed to the integrity of personal relationships.[49]

Northern Coordinator

Casey's return to Atlanta in the spring of 1963 was fortuitous. At the time, SNCC executive secretary James Forman was fervently working to expand his organization's northern connections to provide a financial base for the struggling voter registration projects. This effort signaled a structural change in the trajectory of SNCC's field operations. Between 1960 and 1961, during the sit-ins and Freedom Rides, SNCC had not needed much money to function. By 1963, however, the workers felt increasingly committed to sustaining registration efforts in the field. Even though SNCC maintained the largest staff of full-time voter registration workers of any civil rights organization during this period, it received less than $24,000 of the $500,000 distributed by the Voter Education Project.[50] Forman subsequently recruited people to run a national fund-raising network with hubs in New York, Chicago, the San Francisco Bay area, and Detroit, among other places. After Casey returned to the South, Forman appointed her to the new position of northern coordinator, one that maximized her already large contact base. Drawing on the skills she had developed working for Ella Baker two years earlier, Casey organized many more FOS groups on college campuses and in cities in the North, starting with the contacts she had made at Michigan.[51]

By establishing the FOS groups, Casey now felt centered, doing the work that enabled SNCC staff to stay in the field. "This position was a good fit for me," she wrote. "I was trained to organize and administer programs, had been on a Northern campus and knew what was needed to sustain support there, and had an enormous number of contacts by now through the Y, NSA, SDS, the Northern Student Movement, and all the traveling I'd done." From the beginning of 1963 until she left SNCC in 1965, Casey remained a support person behind the lines. "I preferred not to work where I would endanger my comrades, and being a white woman meant that wherever I was, the movement was visible, and where there was visibility there was danger." During this period, she put together a pamphlet called "You Can Help," which told northern students how to organize a civil rights committee. Many students she contacted became strong supporters of SNCC. They raised money, pushed newspaper editors to include information on the conditions SNCC faced in the South, sent people down to survey the situation and return to tell others, delivered SNCC speakers to campuses, and organized clothing and food drives. She provided guidance, assistance, and emergency trips to the field, and she trained others in Atlanta to help run the program and expand the network. By linking together FOS groups, SNCC created sustaining financial support. Equally important was the political support and pressure brought by FOS groups. These networks "were our only protection," she emphasized, the "source of calls to northern liberal politicians, and a lifeline to local press who could then ask the Associated Press for stories."[52]

This work built and expanded upon the organizing already being done by FOS groups in New York, Detroit, Los Angeles, and the San Francisco Bay area. Casey's former position at the inner core of SDS — which rapidly became the fastest-growing student group on campuses throughout the North — uniquely positioned her to mobilize and coordinate students nationwide to support SNCC. Anchored in Atlanta, she continued to travel across the country for her new job, carrying ideas, names, and contacts from one place to the next. Casey mixed and matched people and projects. "There were always people coming out here who just got out of jail in Mississippi and Louisiana," said Raymond Hewitt, a black activist in Los Angeles. "They would come to a demonstration and say, 'I got to be back in Mississippi in court in two weeks, but I'm going to stay here with you guys for a week enjoying your demonstration.' So it was one hell of a grapevine." Seeing it on television gave Hewitt an idea of the scope of the freedom struggle taking place, "but it was not really humanized and personalized until you began to deal with these people." This group of travelers, yo-yoing back and forth, "moved so fast the dross burned off," Casey recalled. "We burned down to our essential selves, and the relationships were intense."[53]

Northern people often traveled South to see the work of SNCC and CORE firsthand. Radcliff student Helen Garvy remarked that "you could read about cattle prods being used." Yet when one of her acquaintances from a Spanish class came back with scars on his back from a cattle prod, the experience became "real. This was a sweet white kid. Harvard. Click! Boy, if it could happen to him — *that* made it real."[54] Person by person, the movement traveled North, facilitated by SNCC's northern coordinator office, NSM, and FOS groups.

As a primary architect of the northern student networks of support for SNCC, Casey circulated information unavailable elsewhere to students at places such as Harvard, Illinois State University, and the University of Arizona. She typed SNCC field reports onto stencils, mimeographed them, and mailed them out.

Eventually an informal network for a whole range of northern initiatives duplicated SNCC's methods of organizing in the South. These included tutorial projects, public school democratization, welfare rights protests, and draft board protests. Collectively, the foundation stones of student activism for the 1960s were now in place, growing out of the southern civil rights movement.[55]

The leadership that developed this network remained largely unrecognized at the time. Indeed, SNCC workers' lack of a sense of ownership over it was striking. Casey — as well as Tim Jenkins, Peter Countryman, Maria Varela, and others — simply shared information about how to organize and about events in the South not covered in the media.[56] The democratic forms SNCC initiated in this period depended on the organization of many such groups — hundreds, then thousands — independent of established power bases. These were the building blocks of the "counter" culture based on democratic self-activity, mutuality, and a relative lack of hierarchy. Today, the term "counterculture" has come to refer to people who had a lot of sex and easy access to drugs, who lived life to a soundtrack of rock 'n' roll. But this is self-serving misrepresentation. SNCC workers' adherence to nonhierarchical ways of relating formed the initial "counterculture." It was not about self-gratification and the pursuit of sensual pleasure over civic duty. The SNCC counterculture created institutions that supported civic development of people toward a common good, the very fabric of the nation envisioned by Jefferson and Washington, and applauded by Tocqueville and Francis Lieber. To many outside the student movement, the counterculture that emerged in the mid-sixties seemed spontaneous and ubiquitous. But it was not spontaneous; it was the product of conscious organization.

More immediately, the organization of this informal network had two structural consequences. First, SNCC now had the financial base and press contacts to continue its voter registration projects. Second, the ties between SNCC workers and northern students created a pipeline, a way for SNCC's skill-based tactics and ideas to move to Ann Arbor, Philadelphia, and Berkeley — indeed, to many places throughout the North and West.

Testing the Southern Blueprint

In January 1962 black and white students launched a series of sit-ins on the Eastern Shore of Maryland. They targeted restaurants that refused to serve African Americans, precipitating volatile confrontations. When a petite, amiable, and spirited eighteen-year-old named Judy Richardson approached the Choptank Inn, a bar and grill near Cambridge, a "big burly white guy told me I couldn't come in." As Penny Patch, a white classmate of Richardson's at Swarthmore College in southeastern Pennsylvania, recalled: "A mob of white people gathered, shouting at us, waving sticks. It was very threatening." For Richardson, it was the first time white supremacy seemed so clear. "It was almost cathartic to me, to have a physical thing that could embody these subtle acts of racism that I had experienced growing up in Tarrytown [New York]. This man actually said, 'No, you are black and therefore you cannot come into this place.' But it also enraged me. How dare he?"[1]

That confrontation at the Choptank Inn was typical of movement strategies in the early 1960s. It is singled out here, however, because this episode was a first tentative step northward with the SNCC model. But the Eastern Shore sit-ins also became the building blocks of popular politics.[2] The growth of the movement in one key locale nearly astride the Mason-Dixon line demonstrates the way democratic conduct can develop in one place and subsequently spread to other parts of society. Swarthmore College, founded by Quakers southwest of Philadelphia, became an important point of contact between SNCC and the emerging student movement in the North. The intense experiences of Swarthmore students in the SNCC project in Cambridge, Maryland, prompted them to try to adapt SNCC's community organizing strategy in a northern urban context. In nearby Chester, Pennsylvania, SDS adopted SNCC methods as a blueprint for its Economic Research and Action Projects (ERAPs). The ERAPs electrified all other organizing efforts of SDS, and, after 1964, they blossomed as major outposts of democratic movement culture. The people supplying the initial experience, energy, and vision that molded these projects were students from Swarthmore who worked with SNCC beginning in 1960; many of them served in Cambridge between the sit-ins of early 1962 and the momentous summer of 1963.[3] They took SNCC's blueprint and refashioned it. The movement moved North, but not in a way either SDS or SNCC intended.

In 1960, shortly after the first SNCC sit-ins, a small group of Swarthmore students, who had initially been participants in a progressive study group, formed the Swarthmore Political Action Club (SPAC). SPAC's first action was to set up picket lines on Saturdays outside Woolworth's in Chester. Although Chester's lunch counters were not segregated, the students wanted to demonstrate support for the SNCC sit-ins in the South. Until then, activism on the Swarthmore campus had been characterized by support for the anti-apartheid movement in South Africa, rather than addressing issues closer to home. SPAC sent Jerry Gelles to the founding meeting of SNCC in April 1960, and he returned with enthusiastic reports. This led SPAC to send a delegation including Charlotte Phillips, Miriam "Mimi" Feingold, Blake Smith, Ann McCaghey, and Oliver Fein to SNCC's October meeting, which featured the Martin Luther King/Ella Baker debate over whether SNCC should form its own organization or be a youth wing of SCLC, Dr. King's organization.

Back in Pennsylvania, Charlotte Phillips began discussions with Richard James, a young black man from Chester who worked with her in the Swarthmore cafeteria. When she learned that James was active in the NAACP Youth Group in Chester, SPAC members began to meet with members of the Youth Group. Chester was a depressed industrial city of 63,000 on the Delaware River, south of Philadelphia and just two miles from Swarthmore. James suggested that SPAC and the NAACP Youth Group test a local roller rink reputed to have "white nights" and "black nights." On a "white night," two Chester black youths tried to buy tickets and were told the rink was full. Then, two white Swarthmore students went up to the window and bought tickets. This became the basis for an NAACP lawsuit against the roller rink. After the rink was integrated, black and white students from Chester and Swarthmore returned to skate together in the spring of 1961 and fall of 1962. Penny Patch, a freshman from New York, recalled these outings as "frightening." Hostile whites yelled at the activists, threatened them, and tripped them up. Yet the Chester and Swarthmore groups continued to test local accommodations. Often these

Oli Fein and Richard James, Swarthmore, Pennsylvania, 1964. James worked in the Swarthmore cafeteria and headed the local youth chapter of the NAACP. He and Fein helped to establish SNCC in the North. (Courtesy of Oliver Fein)

political actions were followed by parties, turning political alliances into social friendships.[4]

SPAC activities had profound effects on the participants. New Yorker Mimi Feingold joined the Freedom Rides during the summer of 1961, and in the fall Charlotte Phillips decided to spend part of her junior year at historically black Tougaloo College outside Jackson, Mississippi. Subsequently, SPAC became the SDS chapter on the Swarthmore campus. And so Swarthmore students flowed into the South-North network that sprung up around SNCC, SDS, and NSM.

During the 1961–62 school year, black SNCC activists from Morgan State University in Baltimore, Temple University in Philadelphia, and Howard University

Mimi Feingold and Charlotte Phillips, Swarthmore, Pennsylvania, 1964. Feingold and Phillips were two of the first northern white women to work in the South, Phillips as an exchange student at Tougaloo, Mississippi, in 1961, and Feingold as a Freedom Rider. They later participated in ERAP projects in Hoboken, New Jersey, and Cleveland. (Courtesy of Oliver Fein)

in Washington, D.C., put out a call for white students to join them in sit-ins along the Eastern Shore of Maryland.[5] Some of these black students — including Stokely Carmichael, Reggie Robinson, Dion Diamond, and Muriel Tillinghast — were active members of SNCC's national coordinating committee. Swarthmore was only two hours from the Eastern Shore, and a small group of its students responded enthusiastically. Most Swarthmore students were white, and many of them came from liberal or leftist backgrounds. Penny Patch had one of the more unusual upbringings in the group. With her father assigned to a U.S. diplomatic post in West Germany after World War II, Patch spent her early adolescence trying to reconcile the friends she had made in her German school with an early visit to Dachau. "When the movement came in front of my nose," she said, "it was not an option to *not* do anything." Any contact with SNCC people, or simply hearing about their work in the Deep South, was "totally inspiring." Given the opportunity to work with SNCC in the sit-ins along the Eastern Shore, she and other Swarthmore students eagerly jumped in.[6]

Despite its proximity to Washington, the Eastern Shore in 1961 resembled a pocket of the Deep South. Cambridge, Maryland, a small city of 12,000, became a key civil rights battleground in 1962 and 1963. All of its public facilities were segregated, including schools, housing, and health care facilities. Though the city had officially desegregated schools from the fourth grade on, the three black students who enrolled in Cambridge High School in 1962 withdrew after a few days as a result of intense harassment. The population was 30 percent black, yet the city refused to hire African Americans for white-collar positions in city government. Watching the 1960 sit-ins from Cambridge, local leader Gloria Richardson realized that it was "the first time I saw a vehicle I could work with. With SNCC, there's not all this red tape—you just get it done." Richardson, a charismatic Howard University graduate a bit older than most other SNCC members, ultimately led the Cambridge Nonviolent Action Committee (CNAC), an organization that formed in March 1962 to challenge local conditions.[7]

Although SNCC sent field secretaries to Cambridge to assist CNAC, the Cambridge committee remained autonomous. Richardson stood out: John Lewis described her as "fiercely independent, very militant, and very articulate." Her family had been part of the town's black elite for generations. Students in the nearby SNCC affiliate at historically black Howard University, the Nonviolent Action Group (NAG), learned an enormous amount in Cambridge. Led by Ed Brown, Bill Mahoney, and Muriel Tillinghast, among others, NAG members came up from Washington—sometimes on weekends, sometimes for a longer time—to take part in the Cambridge movement. NAG functioned as a "close-knit community of distinctively individual young people," united by "a conviction that youth could change the world." Stokely Carmichael, a witty and winsome Trinidadian raised in New York who later became one of the standout organizers in SNCC, joined them upon his arrival at Howard: "They struck me as smart, serious, political, sassy," he wrote. In Cambridge, he noticed a different pattern from other southern campaigns. Though launched as part of the nonviolent struggle, the members of NAG and CNAC—unlike the students and NCLC ministers in Nashville—"adopted nonviolence strictly as a tactic. It was a way to fight effectively and above all else NAG saw itself fighting for the race."[8]

White students like Mimi Feingold, Penny Patch, and Carl Wittman from Swarthmore participated wholeheartedly, if intermittently, in the Eastern Shore sit-ins of 1962. These events also attracted some of the few black students at Swarthmore. As opposed to the visits back and forth between South and North described in the previous chapter, the SPAC students' involvement in Cambridge provided the first sustained contact between full-time SNCC workers, university students affiliated with SNCC from NAG, and university students associated with SDS at Swarthmore.[9]

When Gloria Richardson went to jail, SNCC field secretary Reggie Robinson served in her stead. Robinson grew up in Baltimore. As an undergraduate at Morgan State in 1960–61, he worked with the Civic Interest Group of Baltimore

(CIG) to desegregate the city's public accommodations, joined the Freedom Rides, and worked with Bob Moses in McComb, Mississippi.[10] In 1962 a black Swarthmore undergraduate named Judy Richardson (no relation to Gloria Richardson) heard Robinson speak at a mass meeting in Cambridge. Richardson had been raised in Westchester County, New York, the daughter of a politically active mother and a father who was a union organizer. "I grew up listening to *Meet the Press* on Sundays," she recalled. Her father died on the assembly line at the local factory when she was seven, prompting her mother to go back to work as a civil servant. She encouraged Richardson to find her own way as a standout student and violinist. When a high school guidance counselor tried to place Richardson in the "business" rather than the college preparatory track, her mother refused to allow it. As a result, Richardson entered all-white college preparatory classes and headed for Swarthmore in 1962. "This was the year that they had decided they were going to really do something, good Quaker school that it was," Richardson said. "So for the first time, they got a large incoming class of black students, meaning eight. There was one black woman who was a senior, and one black woman who was a sophomore, and eight of us coming in as freshmen, four boys and four girls, presumably so we would not have to date outside the group," she laughed. "All of [us] were roomed with Quaker children, because it was assumed that [the Quaker children] would be more liberal about this."[11]

When Richardson heard Robinson speak for the first time at a mass meeting, she was amazed "to see that kind of energy, no holds barred, speaking truth to power." (As one supporter noted, "nothing builds support for SNCC like SNCC people who have been in the field.") Robinson "was just moving mountains," whereas "most of the [black] men that I knew did not have that kind of *political* strength." Richardson explained: "My mother's brothers were very strong men to me" and very protective. Yet Robinson possessed a willingness to confront injustice that was new. "Even the middle-class black guys that I saw when I first came up against the Urban League kids were *nice* guys. They were raised to go into middle-class America and be assimilated, and not stand out, except in terms of academic excellence and how well they spoke. But when they said 'how well they spoke,' they meant it in a certain way, which was the way white people said, 'and you're so articulate, you're a credit to your race.'"[12]

It was no coincidence that students at Swarthmore, located in the lower North, comprised the first large cohort from a predominantly white college to have protracted contact with the northernmost of SNCC's southern projects. Students from Brown, Yale, and the University of Rhode Island, among others, all participated in the Eastern Shore sit-ins. Yet despite the heavy involvement of Peter Countryman, who repeatedly traveled to the area to hook up north-eastern students with those he knew in SNCC, the practical limitations of travel allowed students from Philadelphia, Baltimore, and Washington colleges to engage in more sustained efforts on the Eastern Shore.[13] Swarthmore's commitment to Quaker values and the liberal arts provided a fertile ground on which activism could flower. The student body had maintained connections with larger peace and social justice movements since the Progressive era. Even in the 1950s, at the height of the Cold War red scare, Swarthmore students had mobilized to protest nuclear proliferation and advocate disarmament.[14]

The Cambridge sit-ins had the same effect on the participants from Swarthmore as similar actions had had on the students involved in Nashville, Greensboro, and Austin: the direct action forced them to think in new ways. As early as February 1962, Countryman noted that the "situation looks good here for organizing this as training ground for northern students." It took only one bad experience, such as one poorly organized sit-in, for participants to see what not to do the next time. In what became a critical development for the Swarthmore group's cohesion, Mimi Feingold's circle of friends in SPAC wrote and distributed reports on the Cambridge sit-ins to build collective knowledge about how to conduct such actions more effectively. This equipped the student group with the confidence and understanding to organize direct action protests over the next two years, well before most other whites in the North began to gain similar experience protesting conditions on campus or the Vietnam War.[15]

To prepare for a sit-in, students worked with CNAC to notify police, press, and local blacks through the churches, ran a call-in to gather support, and put one individual in charge of coordination. They lined up picket groups in churches beforehand and briefed them on each restaurant, the town as a whole, and the concept and practices of nonviolence. They chose group leaders among the students and met during the action to maintain unity. Once on the picket line, leaders needed to stay put, the group had to remain together, and someone had to keep counting to ensure that all the participants were accounted for. Afterward, each group reported on the sit-in. Precise evaluations led to observations that increased their confidence and likelihood of success in the next action. They learned to choose leaders carefully, emphasizing experience rather than seniority. Unseasoned leaders "neglected to talk to their groups about conduct or to take the names of persons within the group." Feingold and others decided that they should assemble the students before an action to set general plans and orient new participants on what to expect. They recognized that picketers needed more information, both logistical — where the home church was in relation to the establishments being tested — and political — what was the present status of negotiations between civil rights organizations and the city. To inform the picketers of what had happened during the day at other sites, they adopted the SNCC-CNAC approach of holding a mass meeting after the action to relay reports from group leaders.[16]

The experiences of Swarthmore students on the Eastern Shore fundamentally challenged their perspectives on what constituted popular politics, the same dynamics that created new vistas for African American students at sit-ins in Nashville, Atlanta, and elsewhere in the South. When, for example, on 30 March 1963 police jailed nearly thirty Swarthmore students for sitting-in at the Dorset Theater, Carl Wittman reported on a transfiguring encounter to his friend Mimi Feingold. Wittman, a white in his junior year, from an Old Left family in New Jersey, had been drawn to SPAC for its broad progressive politics, not just its civil rights programs. Now, he wrote from jail that he and other white Swarthmore men, while bunking with black men from Cambridge, were engaging in long conversations "about everything from morals to religion to the movement." As he and the others listened to one man describe a lynching in the 1940s, Wittman discovered that the candor lacing these discussions generated strong emotions. Just as in Mississippi and Georgia, extended jail sentences allowed relationships of mutuality and solidarity to develop among activists unlikely to have met and gotten to know one another in their lives outside the movement. It broadened the sense of the possible for everyone involved.[17]

As the students became acquainted in the Cambridge jail, SNCC's traveling "Freedom Singers" — most of whom were from the Albany, Georgia, movement — arrived to raise money for SNCC. The songs coming out of SNCC's second major voter registration hub "carried greater emotional force and were more often rooted in the Afro-American cultural heritage than was earlier the case," observed SNCC historian Clayborne Carson. The Freedom Singers subsequently carried these songs of triumph and struggle across the country.[18]

The singers received an overwhelmingly favorable response in Cambridge. Their performance provided yet another occasion where, amid rising emotion sparked by the jailings, people developed an increasing sense of solidarity across racial and class lines. "St. Luke's [African Methodist Episcopal Church] was filled to overflowing," Charlotte Phillips, a Swarthmore senior, wrote Feingold. "There was much foot-stomping, cheering, audience participation." It was all very southern. Indeed, Phillips, who had attended early SNCC conferences and spent time at Mississippi's Tougaloo College, wrote that the Cambridge actions made her feel "deeply at home again, so to speak." Home in this sense referred to a place where people joined together in pursuit of what they felt to be real political life.[19]

Carl Wittman, Swarthmore, Pennsylvania, 1963. Wittman wrote "An Interracial Movement of the Poor" and was a major architect of the ERAPs. Later in the 1960s he became a pioneer in the gay liberation movement. (Courtesy of Oliver Fein)

For many students, returning to campus after events like the sit-ins seemed pointless. After she had passed a weekend in jail, Swarthmore no longer was that important to Judy Richardson: "It's not exciting, it's not real. The *real* thing is Cambridge." By the fall of 1963, she had put college on hold and joined the SNCC staff in Atlanta. Mimi Feingold reevaluated her future plans as well. "The final question really is what I want to do with my life. If I really want to make a commitment to the movement, I shouldn't worry about academics, but I should work full-time in SNCC. . . . Where can I be most effective?" The process of working through the decision forged a bond of intimacy and trust among this generation of Swarthmore activists — a group that included Phillips, Feingold, Carl Wittman, Vernon Grizzard, David Levin, Connie Brown, Oliver Fein, and Nick

Egleson. Each of them wrestled with the issue of remaining in school to prepare for a professional career or continuing their "revolutionary involvement."[20]

This pattern echoed that of SNCC activists during 1961–62, as college-educated organizers like Diane Nash, Ruby Doris Smith, Prathia Hall, and Charles Sherrod began to consider their involvement in civil rights as the central work of their lives, not just a summer job. Some Swarthmore students — Carl Wittman and a younger cohort consisting of Connie Brown and Larry Gordon — decided to join the SDS's ERAP effort immediately after their graduation in 1964. Others such as Jerry Gelles, Oliver Fein, and Charlotte Phillips entered medical school to build skills useful to the movement. They supported one another's decisions not to follow traditional career paths, as well as the idea of committing fully to the movement. Like the students in Nashville and the early SNCC activists, these individuals sustained their insurgency against received cultural traditions by operating within a small, strong community of like-minded people.[21]

The vivid experiences in Cambridge, Maryland, also fueled sharp (if often unwanted) insights into how power worked. Feingold's direct encounter with the city's inflexibility prompted her to reconsider the possibilities for social change. Problems there seemed so intractable that she was given to moments of despair and apocalyptic speculation: "Only a revolution will do any good," she wrote Wittman upon her return from jail. "But — how do you develop the co-operative mentality" that such a revolution required? she wondered. Wittman believed that jail encouraged such thinking. "That might be a good way to gain adherents to the movement," he wrote, since the people he met in jail seemed eager to learn what they could safely do next. Aside from SNCC, the Swarthmore students saw no models for how this revolution might take place or what it might achieve. Despite the "sophistication" of SNCC project leader Gloria Richardson — and she met "at least ten other people like her" in Cambridge — Feingold still found the challenges of organizing for permanent change daunting. In the spring of 1963, after meeting with Malcolm X at a Philadelphia speaking engagement, she and other SPAC members explored the solutions offered by the Nation of Islam and other black nationalists. The Swarthmore students nursed doubts about the best ways to bring about change or how to act on that knowledge, but they were determined to do something. In the meantime, they continued to work with SNCC.[22]

Following a large nonviolent demonstration in Cambridge on 13 June 1963 against segregated schools and public facilities, a mob of 350 white men followed an equally large number of African Americans back to the black section of the city. Jeering whites surrounded blacks, heaving eggs and rocks at the praying and singing demonstrators. Maryland Governor J. Millard Tawes ordered in 400 state troopers to black neighborhoods only, outraging not just the city's activists but the black population generally.[23] The next day, the governor declared martial law in Cambridge. The resulting escalation carried ominous overtones. Lehigh University sophomore Mark Suckle wrote Feingold: "I am sitting here with a rifle to the left of me. Last night, it was my turn to do phone duty at Gloria's [Richardson]. I sat all alone in an arm chair with a shot gun across my lap. The community is an armed camp."[24] It was a hint of the breakdown of the nonviolent ethic in the face of a fast-developing repression and a lack of training workshops for what James Lawson termed "revolutionary nonviolence."

Angered by the presence of the state troopers and then National Guardsmen, Cambridge's black citizens joined the student movement in large numbers. This development considerably complicated SNCC's organizing task. "All elements of the community are now involved, most notably the guys I call the 'toughs,'" Vernon Grizzard informed Feingold. The larger number of people gave the movement more leverage with the city but caused internal conflicts. Adopting the descriptive terminology of the European Left, Grizzard offered the thought that the new recruits were "not committed to the bourgeois means of the civil rights movement. Negro leaders are fast put in a position of holding back, of pleading for nonviolence, of calling off demonstrations for fear of the outcome." In essence, how could SNCC take this flood of new volunteers rapidly through the time-consuming process of nonviolent workshops that shaped the thinking of the SNCC activists from Nashville? It took patience and persistence to convince any group of people of the political effectiveness and spiritual transformation possible through nonviolence. The appearance of the National Guard created a heightened danger for blacks in every part of Cambridge. To persuade members of the town's gangs of the adequacy of nonviolence as a response to the Guard's presence was not only unlikely but also impractical.[25] The white students failed to let local issues emerge from the locals themselves, either out of ignorance or out of latent white supremacy. This hinted at the future of blacks and whites working together in the movement, South and North, with very different understandings of what needed to be done. These issues materialized in Mississippi in full force by the summer of 1964, with devastating results for SNCC.

But in 1963, the SNCC-CNAC group decided that its best path would be to negotiate a settlement before activists less committed to nonviolence reacted to the National Guard in untimely and self-destructive ways. Any violence against the Guard or the white mobs, CNAC leaders knew, would only justify a crackdown on the black community. The tension increased on 14 July, when cars full of whites drove through the main street of the black neighborhood firing into houses; blacks returned fire in an exchange that lasted more than an hour. As Richardson said at the time, "unless something is achieved soon in Cambridge, then no one is going to be able to control these people who have been provoked by generations of segregation, by countless indignities — and now by uncontrollable white mobs in the streets."[26]

To end the immediate threat to the movement, Richardson and others signed the "Cambridge Accord," which called off the demonstrations in exchange for further desegregation of the public schools, the construction of low-income public housing for blacks, and the appointment of a biracial commission.[27] In such an environment, Wittman and Grizzard, having risked their lives to participate in the demonstrations, began to generalize mistakenly — and perhaps unfairly — about the country as a whole. The civil rights movement, "with its stated means and ends, is incapable of effecting any meaningful solution of the Negro's problems," they felt. As they saw it, economic inequalities lay at the heart of an oppression the Cambridge Accord had not addressed. The South was "on its way to becoming a tokenly desegregated society with poor housing, poor schools, and unemployment as the model, as the North now is." Forty-six percent of the Cambridge residents they interviewed over the summer noted unemployment as their most serious problem. "It is increasingly clear," Wittman and Grizzard wrote in their report on the summer project, "that the main problem of Cambridge is not the race-problem — for that is only exacerbated by the real problem: poverty and increasingly serious unemployment." Thus focused on economic inequality, they planned to devote their energies in the future to the urban North. Without a body of experience of the variety, intensity, and intractability of white terrorism, Grizzard speculated, "one problem with the South is that they can be satisfied so easily. Even militant CNAC is now demanding public accommodations and similar things which can be met without the whites having to give much at all." In a few years, the South might be completely desegregated, "enough to satisfy civil rights organizations, but not enough to solve the problems of poor schools and unemployment."[28]

Not having worked in direct action projects for an extended period, Wittman and Grizzard had not experienced the racial terror that SNCC and other civil rights organizations faced. They did not know enough to understand the dynamics of the National Guard's arrival in Cambridge. While they worked in that city, they were not privy to most of the strategy sessions held by Gloria Richardson and SNCC leaders.[29] Nonetheless, they fashioned future plans for activism out of their summer experiences in Cambridge, producing ideas instrumental in the formation of ERAPs in late 1963.[30]

Despite their flawed conclusions, the accumulated experiences of the Swarthmore students gave them a sense of urgency and a workable model that other northern white campus groups lacked in 1962 and 1963. After the intense spring and summer of 1963, the first Swarthmore contingent of activists began to disperse throughout the country. In so doing, they formed some of the most important and solid building blocks of the South-to-North activist network. Judy Richardson, Penny Patch, and Mark Suckle joined SNCC; Charlotte Philips and Oliver Fein moved to Cleveland to attend medical school at Case Western Reserve, later inviting an ERAP to start in Cleveland. Mimi Feingold went to rural Clinton, Louisiana, where she and seven members of CORE — six blacks and two whites — discovered that the list of registered voters had been purged, "reducing the number of [black] voters from 1500 to 82 in the whole parish."[31]

Carl Wittman, now a senior, returned to Swarthmore dispirited by events in Cambridge over the summer and looked for another place to get involved. He carefully examined the depressed industrial city of Chester near campus. Building on SPAC's earlier connection with Richard James from the Chester NAACP Youth Group, Wittman and some other students began to work with Stanley Branche, the Chester NAACP's executive secretary. They decided to mobilize Chester residents through a campaign to improve the Franklin Elementary School, which residents believed to be unsanitary and dangerous. Calling themselves the Committee for Freedom Now (CFFN), they demanded a new facility from the Board of Education and began to picket and boycott the school.[32]

The following week about 100 people, including many Swarthmore students, blocked the doors to the Franklin school and caused it to close for the day. The demonstrators then marched downtown. The boycott kept 60 percent of the students from attending class for the week. Police arrested 250 demonstrators for sitting-in at City Hall, and the School Board agreed to all of CFFN's demands.

Fatefully, CFFN failed to secure this pledge in writing. The School Board soon reneged on most of its promises. In analyzing the action a year later, SPAC students felt that multiple factors contributed to the measured success of their first activity in Chester. First, residents widely regarded Franklin as the worst school in Chester, making it an appropriate initial target. Second, the surrounding neighborhood included a housing project, which formed a fairly tight-knit community. Third, the proximity of the protesters' housing to the school facilitated high attendance at demonstrations. Fourth, the militancy of the demonstrations, their specific demands, and confident attitude apparently convinced people that things were finally going to change. And fifth, SPAC had caught the School Board and the city off guard. If the police had arrived early on the first day of protests and arrested people, they surmised, fewer residents would have joined the demonstrations. Momentum, and the subsequent building up of mass meetings each night, would have been impossible. Yet the group did not answer a central question: Why, initially, did so many Swarthmore students get involved in Chester?[33]

The answer appears fairly simple. First, the movement in the South, and

Cambridge in particular, primed Swarthmore students for greater involvement. Mimi Feingold's letters from rural Louisiana may well have played an important role in galvanizing Wittman and others at Swarthmore (see Appendix C). In Louisiana, state court rulings had enjoined her CORE project from engaging in direct action protests against segregated facilities. Local high school students were "raising hell," she wrote Wittman, demanding total integration of all schools, the rehiring of staff fired for demonstrating, and the firing of a superintendent who had slapped a black girl during a demonstration. "For four days straight, demonstrations were broken up with tear gas and billy clubs, and the church that was mutilated before was broken into again with the gas." Her accounts of the tenacity and courage of these *high school* students prompted great excitement at Swarthmore during the winter of 1963–64. SPAC students had an intense sense that they were "not in the real world" and were eager to get involved with the burgeoning developments in the nearby black area of Chester as a result.[34]

Second, Swarthmore students' exposure to the Cambridge project — and their sense that CNAC was not a place where all of their efforts would be appreciated — gave them additional incentive to start local projects.[35] Once engaged in Chester, many went to jail. The intensity of jail itself brought forward local leaders, just as it had in the wake of the sit-ins in Nashville, Atlanta, and Rock Hill, South Carolina, as well as in the aftermath of the Freedom Rides.

Moreover, many contacts established in jail between students and residents later proved essential. The jail experience gave people time to build stronger relationships. Wittman took the lead, searching out local leaders in three neighborhoods that surrounded the Franklin Elementary School. When the activists were released, these relationships became key to Swarthmore students' ability to build what they called "block organizations."[36]

Why did the group decide on block organizing? Quite simply, unlike SNCC in the South, the Swarthmore students could not use Jim Crow laws as a target. Indeed, their political work had few precedents. Civil rights activity could be organized largely on the basis of racial identity. Union organizing had a clear constituency in those who worked in the same factory or held the same kind of job. Block organizing emerged as a way to build collective identity in geographic communities of people, some of whom might have multiple interests. It could only be a temporary solution. Legal segregation might end, but economic apartheid remained entrenched. How to bring communities together to fight for economic justice would continue to vex urban organizers over the next four decades.[37]

Wittman and other SPAC members assigned specific streets to each organizer. The students went house-to-house, using previous contacts from the Franklin school boycott to find and develop community leadership. The crucial thing was to spend as much time talking, and listening, to each person as possible. They learned the issues that plagued the community and then pulled people together to talk. Each resident should be reminded, they noted, the afternoon before each meeting, "so there is little time to forget."[38]

Clearly the Swarthmore students, in little more than a year after their contact with SNCC's Cambridge project, had learned a crucial truism of popular politics: the importance of building relationships through one-on-one conversations. Although they did not know how to institutionalize this skill as a cornerstone of democratic politics, they recognized that personal engagement brought people out to meetings. On the other hand, they made some major mistakes that SNCC did not make. Swarthmore students told people what to ask for, rather than allow issues to be raised by the residents themselves. And they had trouble activating the existing leadership in a neighborhood, which would have increased the attendance at meetings. In contrast to the SNCC workers, the Swarthmore students lacked mentors of the caliber of James Lawson or Ella Baker. Besides providing a steadying, long-range perspective, Baker had introduced SNCC organizer Bob Moses to Amzie Moore. Moore, of course, proved to be Moses' most productive initial contact in the Mississippi voter registration project. Wittman never found someone who could provide him the same entrée in Chester. It was extremely difficult for the Swarthmore students to hook into older networks of Chester activists.[39]

Not long into the Chester project, a series of small incidents revealed that the executive committee of CFFN did not function "with complete regularity." The Swarthmore students gradually realized that CFFN was a top-down organization led by Stanley Branche, rather than a democratic body.[40] Despite Branche's tight grip on the committee, the students kept working with the community. The block organizations turned into much more than a means to keep the movement going. They became "the basis of any continuing organization in the city, for it became apparent that there was a tremendous difference between mobilizing people for a demonstration, and deeply involving them in decision-making and strategic planning."[41]

The students working in Chester felt on-task when picketing landlords and boycotting bad schools, yet they recognized that sometimes setting up a playground or a baby-sitting pool was "more easily accomplished initially and allowed people to have the experience of working together." Such small triumphs also encouraged people to feel that their community organization could succeed. Branche, then, did not struggle alone with leadership emanating from the grass roots.[42] The Swarthmore organizers felt a constant tension between organizing Chester residents to fight battles the students felt should be waged and trying to get them to take on the issues most important to the residents themselves.

Through their work in Cambridge and later in Chester, Swarthmore students learned a great deal about community organizing between 1962 and the spring of 1964. While they reflected on what worked and what failed, they did not create an institutionalized format for evaluation of their projects. Thus much of the knowledge gained through experience was retained by individuals rather than shared widely in discussions and meetings. These students did not self-consciously and methodically spread their model to other organizers, nor did they adapt or fine-tune it for use in Chester or other places. Two remarkable facets of their work stand out, however. First, despite the absence of a structure to support this, and despite heavy demands on their time both from their activism and their schoolwork, they were able to engage in sustained reflection on their experiences. Second, their commitment to the civil rights activities in the eastern Pennsylvania – Delaware – Maryland corridor surpassed other efforts from predominantly white campuses also located on the cusp of the Mason-Dixon line, such as the University of Pennsylvania, Bryn Mawr, Haverford, or Johns Hopkins.

Thus when national SDS organizers worked to carve out a plan of action in 1963 – 64, the Chester-Swarthmore example drew them like a magnet. SDS produced a voluminous literature list, and people throughout the Left respected the high caliber of SDS's young intellectuals. Yet as president-elect Todd Gitlin later sighed, SDS "was not known for *doing* anything on its own, either as a national group or (with few exceptions) in its chapters." Many of its central figures attended graduate school at Michigan and Harvard, but the degrees they sought seemed unrelated to the work they wanted to do. They yearned to find "some way to live that would not violate the way they believed." The university, Gitlin said, "begins to feel like a cage." The experiences Tom Hayden internalized between 1961 and 1962 with SNCC in Mississippi and Georgia weighed heavily on him throughout the spring of 1963 as his tenure as president of SDS came to a close. Hayden did not want to turn the organization into a think tank or unite it with other liberal voices. He did not want to see SDS "inevitably assigned to a vague educational role in a society that increasingly is built deaf to the sounds of protest."[43] He and newly elected SDS national secretary Lee Webb, who spent many weekends with the Swarthmore students in Chester's low-income neighborhoods, turned to these students to teach SDS how to bring SNCC North.

SNCC Teaches SDS How to Act

In 1963 it seemed like SDS was a debating club; SNCC lived the revolution. Daily life in 1963 for many SDSers consisted of going to class, gathering with friends at political meetings, debating how to change society, and traveling to conferences where more such talk occurred. It often boiled down to a lot of students in slacks and button-down shirts looking serious, drinking coffee, writing position papers, searching the library stacks, and mimeographing flyers. SNCC workers, on the other hand, walked people to courthouses to register to vote and sat-in at restaurants, all the while passing on their skills to people coming to life at the grass roots. SDS leaders like Tom Hayden visited SNCC projects and watched Amzie Moore drive SNCC workers from one local leader to the next, explain the voting campaign, and raise money for the operation. He observed Moore's wife Ruth fixing breakfast for the SNCC people and sending them out for another day of canvassing with a paper bag lunch and a warning to be back before dark. The southern SNCC workers took care of each other: northern white Jack Chatfield remembered the peace of southern SNCC friends on a shaded porch, placing damp tea bags over the sunburn of one of their peers after a hard day spent canvassing. Hayden, Chatfield, and other northerners believed that it was the local citizens working with SNCC — people like Amzie and Ruth Moore, Fannie Lou Hamer, and Carolyn Daniels — who lived the country's democratic ideals. Though the vision of participatory democracy reflected in SDS's "Port Huron Statement" grabbed the imagination of thousands of college students during the decade, those at the top of SDS lacked the knowledge SNCC possessed of how to breathe life into the dream. SDS people needed to act. "Otherwise, our criticisms of the labor unions and other groups for not organizing the poor were merely academic," Hayden asserted.[1]

Stokely Carmichael, in his denims, approached SDS members at the Bloomington, Indiana, NSA meeting in the summer of 1963. A Freedom Rider and SNCC activist, Carmichael had grown up in New York and knew some SDSers from civil rights activities there, as well as through NSA. Just back from the voter registration project in Mississippi, he suggested that SDS go out into the community and organize poor people, especially poor whites. SDS president Todd Gitlin remembered Carmichael's challenge as the "direct impetus" for setting up an SDS pilot project to organize whites in Chicago. In August 1963 the United Automobile Workers (UAW) union donated $5,000 to SDS for an education and action program focusing on economic issues. Having created the structure, SDS now needed to figure out how to find people.[2]

Swarthmore students in Chester were solving that problem in the fall of 1963. This attracted the attention of newly elected SDS national secretary Lee Webb, who spent many subsequent weekends in Chester. He canvassed, was arrested and jailed, witnessed firsthand what a community-organizing project might look like, and fed his insights back to others in SDS. Webb took Carl Wittman to Ann Arbor, where Wittman's stories about Chester's block organizations persuaded Tom Hayden. Finally, someone was bringing the work of SNCC to the North. The three men emerged from their intense discussions determined to promote expansion of SDS's nascent Economic and Research Action Project (ERAP) based on the Chester model.[3]

At the next SDS national council meeting in December Al Haber, the driving visionary behind the early SDS, believed that the Cambridge-Chester model might help students design "a labor-liberal-Negro coalition that is needed in the area as the vehicle of a comprehensive civil rights program." Rather than focus on discrete, small projects like a food and clothing drive or a tutorial program that other people could do, SDS students should direct their energies toward developing "a specific program of economic, political and social demands to meet fully the problems/needs of the particular Negro community in the vicinity of the school" they attended.[4]

At the December 1963 meeting, however, it quickly became clear how distant Haber's vision was from the ideas of Wittman and Hayden. Haber thought that ERAP should continue with an academic tilt: designing programs other people could then implement. As students, the SDSers' strength was in research and writing; he warned them against becoming proponents of a "cult of the ghetto." The latter direction could lead to an "anti-intellectualism, a disparagement of research and study, an urging of students to leave the university, a moral superiority for those who 'give their bodies.'" He feared that working "'in the world' ha[d] come to mean 'in the slum.'"[5]

However prescient Haber's fear would prove for certain elements of the student movement, it was not so for Hayden. The difference between what Hayden (or Penny Patch, or Martha Prescod) had learned on the Albany, Georgia, SNCC project and what Haber learned in the halls of academe was significant. And Hayden knew it. For at least two years, several like-minded people had expressed ideas in sync with those presented by Wittman and Hayden as to what SDS should do next. At the December 1962 SDS national council meeting in Boston, Peter Countryman of NSM had talked about an internal conflict, the feeling of being "torn constantly between infrequent exposure to SDS and consistent exposure to the SNCC people, to the people in Roxbury [and] New Haven, people with immediate problems." Countryman and his close friend Tim Jenkins from SNCC had decided that NSM should not just raise money for SNCC, but should also set up tutorial programs in the North.[6]

Countryman recruited others by passing on the dramatic and evocative stories Jenkins, Chuck McDew, and later Tom Hayden sent from Mississippi's voter registration projects. Relating a short history of SNCC, Countryman endeavored to explain the experimental process that brought SNCC into being: *how* students came together, why they decided on a certain internal structure, and their new strategy. He made it personal: How would you feel as a middle-aged black parent, he asked NSM members, if you thought "first of [your] son marching down to protests against a systematic injustice, and then of Herbert Lee"? How would you react to McDew's experience, "beaten in a public courtroom and taunted with threats of castration and lynching? What did it feel like to be in a black congregation, "weighted with fear, singing for the first time 'We Shall Overcome' instead of 'There is a Balm in Gilead'"?[7]

The civil rights movement was the seminal political struggle of the time, Countryman declared. "Is it not possible that there could be a student protest movement in the North, tied to that of the South, which could bring home to this society the basic falsity in its inter-relationship and create in turn an actualization of the democratic ideas which it professes"?[8]

One of the key organizers who responded to the call of both NSM and SDS was Sharon Jeffrey. During the summers while a student at Michigan, she had worked in Guinea, then on an NSA project to register voters in North Carolina;[9] following her graduation, NSM hired her as its research director, working out of Philadelphia. Jeffrey grew excited by the NSM activists: "They have captured the imagination of hundreds of college students and hundreds within the ghetto," she observed, through tutorials, campaigns for better housing, and school boycotts. NSM activities raised "many questions about [the] way SDS can, should, is thinking about forming an adult group to effectuate change." In other words, what actions should northern students be engaged in?[10]

By the end of 1962 NSM had drawn members in, but the NSM tutorials, Countryman felt, served as an agent for "student social work rather than student social change." Conversations with Tim Jenkins from SNCC led Countryman to envision "another answer, another technique. There is the possibility of students working in the North with technical problems and with basic democratic problems at the same time." If Jenkins could find a group of people to work with him, Countryman said, who would "for two months live in one room apartments and eat hamburgers and develop the very necessary close personal relationships that sustain SNCC, and sustain the necessary sacrifice, and go into that community, and talk the language of the people and be sensitive to their problems, and not be compromised by outside people," this was where the "Northern civil rights movement is going to have to go."[11]

Throughout 1963, SDS was acutely aware of the hardships endured by activists in the South. In fact, it was now possible for any suburban TV viewer to learn what southern blacks, sheriffs, registrars, ward politicians, country lawyers, and plantation owners had always known about daily life in the South. Television portrayed Bull Connor's police dogs mauling children in Birmingham, as well as "mass arrests in a dozen southern cities, and long jail sentences," Todd Gitlin noted. In February 1962 SNCC chairman Chuck McDew, Dion Diamond, and Bob Zellner had been arrested in Louisiana for "criminal anarchy," a charge carrying a sentence of ten years of hard labor, with little chance of parole. Black high school students involved in direct action continued to suffer under conditions of torture in the Mississippi State Penitentiary at Parchman for their participation in the 1962 nonviolent direct action campaign in Jackson. In Greenwood, Mississippi, SNCC had been so effective in organizing black citizens to claim their voting rights that the local power structure's clumsy retaliation was to cut off black welfare recipients en masse in the winter of 1962–63. This caused starvation and prompted a large-scale northern food and clothes drive that served to strengthen the freedom movement. At a November 1963 conference in Washington, D.C., at which whites predominated, John Lewis urged: "We as students must not sell out. We must stand up and stand up for what is right. . . . Negro and white students from the North must go into the black areas of the North, go into the ghettoes of Harlem, into the ghettoes of Chicago and Detroit, and organize a mass movement similar to what we have seen in the South." In addition to feeling like they should "be out there with the real people," Gitlin said, SDSers possessed "a very strong feeling of wanting to be active in comradeship with civil rights organizers. They wanted us to be doing stuff and they were organizing the poor, so we should." A more accurate description of what SNCC was doing at the time might have been registering people to vote, getting people to claim their full citizenship. Nonetheless, the solidarity SDSers felt with SNCC workers extended at some point to an "imitativeness which went so far as SDS people imitating the gestures and the speech patterns of SNCC people."[12]

Following the December 1963 national council meeting, Carl Wittman took a six-week road trip, something that would become increasingly common as SDS began to adopt SNCC's mobile, nonstop work style. Among his stops, Wittman spent two days in Cambridge, Massachusetts, three days in Washington, D.C., four days at historically black West Virginia State College, and ten days in Chicago. In each location he assessed what was happening and how people were organizing, trying to determine the quality of the local leadership. His presence energized people he met. On the way to Cambridge, he rode with a warm and energetic SDSer, Helen Garvy from Radcliff. Garvy later said that she kept "poking at him. I really wanted to know more of what they were doing [in Chester], because this was *the* model, this was the only model. The kind of organizing SNCC was doing was different." It was rural and southern. But Wittman had begun to figure out how to bring SNCC North. His work had immediate relevance for Garvy, reinforcing her intention to move out of NSM and into an organization that addressed broader concerns than tutoring alone.[13]

As Wittman traveled, he was, as Casey Hayden aptly commented, "carrying ideas and contacts, connecting folks to each other, welding, one by one, those crucial linkages." He stayed in intermittent contact with the twenty to thirty Swarthmore students who spent that January of 1964 — Swarthmore's intercession — working full-time in Chester to start a voter registration campaign and increase publicity for a citywide school boycott in February.[14]

This first sign of something concrete to do in the North galvanized several groups within SDS. In early 1964 Wittman, Tom Hayden, and Lee Webb recruited people to write proposals for each of ten incipient ERAPs.[15] Hayden and Wittman decided to work together in Newark, the only major city with a black majority. "Like Carl," Hayden later wrote, "I wanted to prove in action that an integrationist perspective stressing common economic interests could still work. So when Carl suggested that I join the budding Newark ERAP, I was interested."[16]

Both Wittman and Hayden were buoyed by the response of people in Ann Arbor to the ERAP idea. Nonetheless, most SDSers needed to be convinced before the organization made a commitment to community organizing projects like Chester. To galvanize this process, Hayden and Wittman decided to write an intellectual justification for the change. They crafted "An Interracial Movement of the Poor?" as an exploratory, "incomplete and unpolished" set of working notes. Living in communities with local people, they stated, was a new "organizational form" for SDS which would "permit the natural beginnings of a people-centered, instead of a student-centered, movement." The document served as the guiding rationale for the early ERAPs.[17]

In Chester, Wittman and other Swarthmore students brought to SDS a new capacity for reflection grounded in shared experiences. After the small victories in November 1963, the students noticed that city officials began to "harden their attitude" toward local activists in Chester, as well as toward Swarthmore students, "apparently finally convinced that it was not a one-shot affair." Long-dormant ordinances against leafleting without a permit were enforced, and the police refused to let demonstrators march in the street, either herding them onto the sidewalk or taking them into custody. Five Swarthmore students, including Wittman, were arrested and fined thirty-four dollars each for pamphleting in February. Chester activists responded by holding more demonstrations in late March. When the protesters blocked intersections, police arrived with riot sticks, resulting in six hospitalizations. After this, Cambridge leader Gloria Richardson and Philip Savage, tristate secretary of the NAACP, participated in another sit-in at the Chester Board of Education. In April 1964, police jailed Wittman and 106 Swarthmore students for demonstrations demanding an end to inadequate and segregated schools.[18] The city remained unresponsive, and the long jailings were "financially highly burdensome and discouraging." The activists looked for "a safer but equally effective tactic . . . to evolve a deeper commitment" to the struggle. Their success at raising issues but failure to bring home victories foreshadowed problems faced by all ERAPs in subsequent years. Still, Wittman and others in SPAC felt that they had begun to develop — partly from exposure to SNCC, partly from their own instinct, and partly from their interaction with SDS — a fairly effective model for organizing a community.[19]

Later ERAP workers who tried to apply the SNCC model of grassroots politics to urban situations described it as "mind-breaking." ERAP effectively encouraged a number of local people to develop their capacities as leaders.[20] Yet ERAPs never discovered things for local people to do to dramatize the economic inequalities of the region. Gloria Richardson and CNAC in Cambridge had the same problem. As they reported, "The people in Cambridge are demonstrating against unemployment, poor housing and segregated and substandard schools. Yet it is in these areas that they least know *what to do* or where to turn." In both the South and the North, as organizing efforts around economic issues failed, the activists tried to find new paths forward. After much frustration, they merely noted that their individual projects had disbanded.[21] SDSers thought they were using SNCC's model in their urban organizing efforts, but they were mistaken. They did not understand the differences in their approach because, despite their sincerity, many were still in the patronizing teacher mode, telling poor folks how to do politics. The only SDS organizers who escaped this trap were the women who were working with other women on welfare and the men who moved into antidraft organizing.

Five years later, when the last ERAPs collapsed in 1968, many organizers began to scale down their hopes for a democratically functioning society. Some retreated to lesser objectives — "by and large now we can only raise questions about who decides." In 1964 they had gone into poor areas in anticipation of a growing unemployment crisis and the possibility of making unemployed people the agents of change. That depression never came, and the activists who remained were unable to articulate precisely why they were there.[22] Lacking an organizing plan, the original intent remained: ERAPs were institutional sites where people who wanted a say in their local government could find support and training. While this certainly proved useful, it was a far cry from the grand aspirations of 1964.[23]

Subsequent observers therefore have been content to view ERAP as a failure. Kirkpatrick Sale, the first to study SDS in its entirety, stated that ERAP fell short because it "was never able to escape the fact that the poor are not 'the agents of change' in American society, whether there be massive unemployment or not. The poor," Sale opined, "want leaders, they do not want to lead; the poor are myth-ridden, enervated, cynical, and historically the least likely to rebel; the poor are powerless."[24] This statement did not lack sweep, but it was wrong. It represented white journalists' difficulty in informing the rest of the nation. Most moved on without understanding why they had failed to tell the central story, or how much they had misconstrued what black southerners had tried to teach them. Myths, cynicism, and the perception of powerlessness are not the sole domain of the poor. Furthermore, SNCC provided a working example of poor people taking control of their lives to become leaders of innovative democratic institutions. In the case of the Mississippi Freedom Democratic Party, this resulted in a realignment of the nation's major political parties. Most importantly, however, Sale's conclusion failed to consider the central experiences of the civil rights movement: analysis and insight alone did not translate into effective action. As all successful SNCC organizing efforts demonstrated, a movement could be sustained only through finding something people could do. Without specific, clear, and feasible goals around which to organize and act, there would be no movement. This was the immutable truth that SNCC learned from the totality of its efforts in the South.[25]

It is true that ERAPs ultimately failed to unify poor blacks and poor whites. Partly, this was a consequence of the climate of the counterculture, where patience was never a virtue. When SNCC, SDS, or ERAP encountered problems, their posture of militance and action could discourage or even deny cultural sanction to cautious reflection. Moreover, their collective commitment to participatory democracy on every level led some ERAP and SDS activists, in the opinion of sociologist Wini Breines, to "utilize participatory democracy inappropriately, unintentionally producing elitism and making it almost impossible to make decisions."[26] These shortcomings, however, enriched the nation's democratic heritage, providing a map of roads not to take for future organizers.

On the one hand, ERAP people did not perfect forms for making participatory democracy a reality in a large-scale organization. Yet this does not indicate, as James Miller concludes in a curiously resigned manner, that participatory democracy was unsuitable "even for a relatively small national group." As scholars like Jane Mansbridge and Carmen Sirianni have shown, other movements, most notably the women's movement, would go on "to confront issues of democratic representativeness, informal tyranny, imposed sisterly virtue, distorted communication, forced consensus, democratic accountability, and strategic efficacy" — all problems that SNCC, ERAP, and SDS faced — with significantly improved results. People within such voluntary social formations needed to hold those in their own structures accountable, so democratic morale could not only be maintained but also grow. Despite their ultimate lack of success, ERAP organizations created space wherein people could work out such issues in real-life situations. This was ERAP's most significant legacy.[27]

Democracy traveled North when those who had been South brought back to their homes in Michigan, California, or Pennsylvania an understanding of how to act collectively. People learned how to explain to those who had never gone to jail that it was okay to do so. Often, participation itself passed along a democratic understanding of how to be a citizen.[28] Going North was a difficult experiment. To many, it appeared a failure, despite good intentions. Yet some in ERAP ultimately internalized SNCC's teaching. They helped to seed the later community empowerment, peace, and black liberation movements in the North and the West. However, the thread of misaligned white-black purposes that emerged in ERAP continued, a growing source of stress and missed opportunity.

PART THREE

DELTA CIVICS: FASHIONING A NEW AMERICA

The Core Struggle

There was the war in Vietnam. There was numbing poverty in every region of the country. And there was the founding stain of the land — the blight of American racism — which, for blacks, remained the core struggle. But whatever else happened in the 1960s, hopes for a democratic transformation of American race relations remained centered in the Deep South.

In Mississippi, the civil rights movement encountered heightened terror. A typical incident occurred in 1963, when SNCC workers Ivanhoe Donaldson and Charles "Charlie" Cobb were canvassing the tiny Delta town of Rolling Forks, hometown of blues genius Muddy Waters (McKinley Morganfield). Donaldson, a black football player raised in Queens, New York, and a student at Michigan State, approached a woman sitting on her porch. "Good afternoon, Ma'am," he said. "Have you voted in the election yet?" No, she had not. As he began to describe the gubernatorial campaign of African American Aaron Henry, a white man in a pickup truck drove onto the property and exclaimed: " 'Nigger, we aren't going to have any more of this agitation around here. Niggers 'round here don't need to vote, so you and your damned buddy get out of here.' " The white threatened to kill both men and gave them a minute to leave. Later, a policeman put Donaldson in the back of his cruiser; then he pulled out a gun, cocked it, and held it to the student's temple. " 'You and the other goddamn Moses' niggers around here ain't gonna get nothin' but a bullet in the head!' " he announced. A second officer intervened, and the activist was released.[1]

Despite the hysteria that SNCC activism had produced among Mississippi officialdom, the organization was actually in crisis in the Deep South. The lack of funds barely allowed SNCC to support its existing staff and field workers. The lack of public visibility or federal protection continued to put people at great risk — not only organizers like Donaldson, Cobb, Charles McLaurin, and Hollis Watkins, but also the black citizens they tried to recruit and register. The blunt fact was that terror immobilized people across the Delta. And the lack of success in getting people to register sapped the morale of the movement. As Bob Moses wrote to SNCC's executive committee: "The Mississippi monolith has successfully survived the Freedom Rides, James Meredith at Ole Miss, and the assassination of Medgar Evers. The full resources of the state will continue to be at the disposal of local authorities to fight civil rights gains. The entire white population will continue to be the Klan."[2] Something had to change.

Down from Yale Law School during summer break in 1963, Tim Jenkins, a defining member of the early SNCC, picked up on the Mississippi staff's angry desperation. In particular, he zeroed in on Moses' analysis that "the only attack worth making is an attack aimed at the overthrow of the existing political structures of the state. The focus of such an attack must be on the vote and the Delta of Mississippi." Jenkins had brought some of his peers at Yale with him, and now they poured over Mississippi case law looking for something to break the deadlock. Eventually, they discovered a statute that allowed residents to cast protest votes in party primaries. Moses and others in the Jackson office agreed that the statute might have some potential.[3]

In SNCC, apartments where movement people slept were called "freedom houses." Pamphlets explaining how to register were "Freedom Primers." The cars donated to SNCC by the labor movement became the "Sojourner Truth Motor Fleet." Movement supporters who fed SNCC staff at their storefront eateries refused SNCC money, saying they had "put it on the freedom tab." In Greenwood, a stray cat inhabiting the local freedom house was simply called "Now." Interstaff memos as well as fund-raising letters often closed with "For freedom" or "Freedom!" True to form, the Mississippi staff took Jenkins's idea of casting protest votes in primary elections and began to think about a "Freedom Ballot." On the day of the gubernatorial primary in the fall of 1963, SNCC encouraged local blacks to submit their own ballots because 96 percent of blacks did not have access to the regular Democratic Party primary. So people went down to their local black church or SNCC freedom house and voted for a slate of freedom movement candidates. "Freedom balloting" had the added advantage of safety: instead of exposing citizens to the risks entailed in a trip to the county courthouse with its imposing two-story Doric columns and armed pot-bellied guards from the sheriff's office, SNCC worked with COFO to establish voting booths in convenient and safe locations. After the ballots were counted, some of these self-enfranchised voters went to the Greenwood courthouse anyway so that, in Martha Prescod's words, "we had some record of how many people had tried to vote." Moses knew he needed visible victories to sustain the morale of his organizers. The Freedom Ballot created a new public context for dramatizing the true situation: rural southern blacks were in no way satisfied with their condition.[4]

The Freedom Ballot did much more than produce evidence that whites excluded black Mississippians from political participation; it provided ways for people to act and interact in politically meaningful ways. For example, while casting their ballots, black citizens might engage in the following exchange. Someone says, "I want to be able to take my child to the doctor." Her neighbor responds, "Well, I think we just get the streets paved first, hire a Negro policeman." More people gather, and the conversation moves on to the highest priority if they had a black sheriff. "Well now, we get some of these church burnings investigated," according to one person. "Uh-huh," says another. "And take care of those white cops." Someone else adds: "We need a black tax assessor. Black people on the Board of Supervisors or Board of Education." Another concurs: "No more split season for the children." An older man notes, "They won't be able to weed us out with the literacy test then." "No," a landowner counters. "We ought to focus on land. How we could change the distribution of federal farm money if black farmers got elected to the Agricultural Stabilization Board. No more blacks cheated out of their cotton."[5] Bob Moses noted that in such small, informal meetings, black Mississippians challenged themselves, made demands on themselves, and in so doing, took the first step toward real citizenship.[6] The flowering of this growing collective political self-respect, in turn, restored the bruised morale of the young SNCC activists. The movement once more had a tangible goal — one that did not immediately put people into harm's way, and one that many African Americans responded to by going to meetings and organizing around next steps. Freedom Ballots, in short, not only revitalized the movement, they also expanded its site and scope.

This shift had been coming since 1962, but now throughout SNCC one could observe the beginning of the "Mississippi" era. It lasted through SNCC's critical Waveland conference in November 1964 (described in Chapter 10). SNCC's focus veered from nonviolent direct action to voter registration — an attempt to enter and democratize the Democratic Party. It did not take the movement staff long to realize that Freedom Balloting could easily become a more comprehensive tactic — namely, the "Freedom Vote." The idea possessed a galvanizing simplicity: to dramatize their exclusion from the democratic process, black Mississippians who could not vote in the general elections in November 1963 would cast their ballots at COFO-sponsored election stations. (The Council of Federated Organizations had been revived in 1962 as a good-faith effort on the part of different civil rights groups to prevent conflicts in fund-raising).[7] SNCC and COFO could then present these ballots to federal authorities and the Democratic National Committee (DNC) as legal evidence of their participation in the election.[8] Despite the mass arrests of those who had tried to register—and in the undiminished presence of terror—Moses and the other organizers felt the Freedom Vote provided a means to keep the Mississippi movement alive. The idea carried the movement—at long last—into the very center of southern black society.[9]

Organizing African Americans to exercise their franchise provided SNCC and CORE staffers an opportunity to explain the relevance of the electoral process to people's daily lives. Additionally, the strategy also led to a liberating discovery: unregistered voters actually "voting" was a low-risk innovation for participants. And should classic southern violence happen to erupt anywhere in the state, it could not be seen as "random" but would call additional attention to the Freedom Vote.[10]

As the idea of the Freedom Vote spread, so did white terror. Medgar Evers of the state NAACP had been murdered in June 1963. Court injunctions prevented political protest in Greenwood and elsewhere. Massive violence and heavy fines were slowing down COFO activity. In the midst of these traumatic events, an energetic Democratic Party organizer and white New Yorker named Allard Lowenstein first visited the COFO projects determined to find ways to increase the movement's visibility. During the summer Bob Moses and Charles Evers of the state NAACP agreed that if Lowenstein raised money and recruited northern white students to help get out the vote in November, they might be able to induce national media to cover the Mississippi movement for the first time. This, in turn, offered the possibility that federal protection, both legal and physical, might finally arrive on the ground.[11] Importing white students to assist the black activists addressed the continuing reality that the time-honored customs of segregation allowed southern police to beat and murder *black* people with impunity. Lowenstein began to recruit students through contacts developed as an instructor at Yale Law School and as dean of freshmen at Stanford. At rallies and in one-on-one conversations, he asked young college students to work in Mississippi for two weeks during the fall of 1963 to help publicize the Freedom Vote. Hundreds signed up.[12]

Although he certainly provided a willing labor pool, Lowenstein's style jarred many SNCC people, especially Ella Baker. At the initial meeting between SNCC and Lowenstein, Baker was "turned off," Bob Moses later reported, by the New Yorker's work habits: he was "on the phone calling big name people all the time." In attempting to mobilize publicity for the Freedom Vote, Lowenstein tended to emphasize how to project the campaign to outsiders, such as the media and national political figures. While publicity was a critical tactical goal, his approach contradicted the strategic practice SNCC had used since initiating the Mississippi project—a relentless focus on developing local, long-term leadership.[13]

In any case, in the short term, the Freedom Vote of November 1963 was a resounding success. Though only 20,000 blacks were registered to vote in Mississippi, 83,000 Freedom Ballots were cast across the state, dramatizing the white lockout of massive numbers of blacks from the electoral process. As Baker later observed, not only did Mississippi symbolize "that which has been the damnable curse of America: racism." The Freedom Vote also brought "to our attention the possibility of what can be done when those who are trampled upon by the powers-that-be can rise up and say, 'Thus far shalt thou go, and no farther.'"[14] The Freedom Ballot had been useful at the local level, as volunteers canvassed house-to-house persuading people to envision themselves as voters. At that point, Afro-Mississipians became citizens in their own minds and gave substance to that transformation by attending small community meetings at local churches or halls. There, people learned how to act as if they were free to act as full citizens.

Each small meeting then hooked up with larger meetings in other towns in the county. At many more meetings around the state, committees were organized to promote the campaign of Aaron Henry, who was running for governor on the Freedom Vote slate. Henry, a Clarksdale pharmacist, had a unique ability to attract black people regardless of age, social class, and ideology. A fearless, energetic, and unpretentious campaigner, Henry drew many new participants to the voter registration project. Following the election, Moses and others in Jackson called statewide COFO meetings once a month from December 1963 through June 1964. Across Mississippi, citizens met informally to discuss the issues and once a month got together a carful of neighbors and drove to the state meeting. There, the two hundred to four hundred people assembled exchanged stories of what was going on in Belzoni and Hattiesburg and Holly Springs, spoke with COFO staff, and worked out what to try next. Observing their growing numbers, they began to acquire a sense of themselves as a collective political presence. In this concrete way, black citizenship spread through the state.[15]

White Mississippi responded to the Freedom Vote "in traditional fashion," reported Debbie Louis of CORE:

In Biloxi, a church building where the NAACP was holding an integrated banquet was stoned by a white mob while police watched; in Columbus, a black woman was shot and killed near an Air Force base; there were five cross-burnings in Copiah County; in Goodman, the body of a black man was found in the Big Black River in a sack weighted with rocks; in Hattiesburg, volunteers were arrested and held incommunicado while their lives were threatened. In Natchez, Bruce Payne was attacked and beaten by four white youths, shot at, and later run off the road five times and shot at three times while driving with George Greene.

Yale and Stanford volunteers wrote their hometown newspapers demanding that editors cover the mock election and the terror inflicted on civil rights workers in Mississippi. L. K. Miller, editor of the *Berkshire Eagle* in Pittsfield, Massachusetts, received a communication from Yale student and British citizen Jonathan Middlebrook that began:

> This is a letter written in anger and shock at what I could not have believed could happen in a country I have admired from the perspective point of Europe. By being silent, the rest of this country pretends that it is not responsible for what happens in Greenwood, Meridian, or Yazoo City. . . . Like every democratic struggle, this one depends not only on freedom of the press, but on the decision of a responsible press such as *The Eagle* represents, to demand and get coverage for its readers. Help us![16]

In Jackson, SNCC set up a statewide communications structure to coordinate a response to the violence, as well as to synchronize activities for the Freedom Vote. The staff drew up a list of contacts from the state's five congressional district offices, which "became organizational bases for penetration into neighboring cities and towns." The Jackson office had one critical luxury: a WATS telephone line to facilitate long-distance calling. The WATS line immediately became the heart of SNCC's communications network, since information unmasking terror could now be passed on easily and rescue efforts coordinated throughout Mississippi.[17]

Thirty SNCC staff members met in Greenville in November 1963 for a five-day Highlander-run workshop to evaluate the Freedom Vote and decide how to capitalize on its momentum. The agenda was packed with ideas. Should SNCC press on, extending the campaign during the next summer? Should it challenge the Democratic Party system from within or create a new party altogether? How could it induce U.S. enforcement of the right to vote in Mississippi, as Diane Nash, John Lewis, and others had done to compel integrated interstate bus travel during the Freedom Rides? Would importing large numbers of white northerners force action in Washington? The debate centered on one key component of extending the Freedom Vote campaign: *Should* they draw on large numbers of white northern volunteers during the following summer to do some of the legwork in light of the staff's experience with those students during the Freedom Vote?[18]

After 1963, SNCC's original, straightforward mission became complicated by other pressing dynamics. In particular, how could it sustain movement? As more and more students—from both South and North—joined SNCC, who would decide what those students should do? This latter question took on a particularly thorny cast as white students traveled South in increasingly larger numbers. What should be their role? Though these issues were discrete, for SNCC staff they were increasingly difficult to address separately.

A grotesque repercussion of white supremacy now surfaced: SNCC's two years of organizing forced everyone to recognize that white injuries or deaths prompted a more immediate reaction from the federal government than did black injuries or deaths. Charles Sherrod had repeatedly used this fact for his own ends in southwest Georgia. He introduced northern whites in part to gain exposure and resources for the project. Still, such a profound inequity produced a necessary, inescapable, and unanswerable anger. "I can get my head bloodied down there in Dalton, Georgia, terrible Terrell County," he explained later. "I can get shot up in unbearable Baker; and in unmitigated Mitchell I can get my ass kicked black and blue, and nobody don't care a damn what happens to me. But come on sister!" he looked at a white woman in the room. "You were down there with me. But bring her down there, and let her big ass get hit! A white face, and a white tail, let her tail get whipped on, and it's all over AP and UPI and FBI! We're in the news! And when we're in the news we get a little chance to eat hearty now and then."[19] Sherrod's tactic had indeed attracted press attention and funds to areas where neither had been forthcoming—despite grave peril and momentous sacrifice on the part of black Americans.

Black SNCC staff in Mississippi had observed the same dynamic during the November 1963 Freedom Vote. When white students from Stanford and Yale showed up, the Justice Department for the first time had "people on hand in the *eventuality* of trouble." "I saw how the FBI followed around white volunteers," Mississippi native Lawrence Guyot recalled. "We could not move unless we bumped into an FBI agent as long as there were white people involved." He supported importing larger numbers of whites during the following summer, because it would bring "the wives, daughters, sons, nephews of the Binghams who were in Congress, the Rockefellers, into the Freedom Houses of Mississippi."[20]

Furthermore, Moses observed that the core staff in Mississippi—people like Hollis Watkins, Willie Peacock, Sam Block, Charles McLaurin, Emma Bell, and Curtis Hayes—were not only exhausted, but also "butting up against a stone wall." Story after story, such as Ivanhoe Donaldson getting a gun stuck to the side of his head in Rolling Forks, prompted Moses to wonder: "How long could you expect [the SNCC staff] to survive working in that kind of isolation?" At this point, Moses knew that the federal government would not make common cause with the voter registration workers. "Where was the help to come from?"

he said. "The civil rights organizations were not prepared to make Mississippi a focus."[21]

Despite the potential benefits, a majority of COFO workers expressed concern that northern whites would usurp leadership positions, draw publicity, and then leave; they could never contribute to SNCC's primary goal of developing local leaders. In fact, Greenwood project director Wazir Peacock and Hollis Watkins argued that the presence of educated white northerners in November 1963 had inhibited this development and increased local blacks' sense of inferiority. While the SNCC staffers at Greenville in late November anticipated that bringing down northern college students for what came to be called the "Mississippi Summer Project" would attract media attention to the state, they also had reason to fear that, as Watkins put it, "ultimately it would destroy the grassroots organizations that we had built and were in the process of building."[22]

Yet he could not deny that, for the first time, "local people . . . had begun to take the initiative themselves and do things." They were deciding "what moves to make next" and "where the organization should be going," both politically and economically. These people "had not even heard the word 'political power,' because it wasn't taught in the black schools," noted black Mississippian Unita Blackwell. They had just begun to learn that "there was such a thing as a Board of Supervisors, and what they did." The SNCC staff encouraged residents to find out who sat on the board and how they had voted in the recent past. Mississippi blacks then began to challenge the all-white control of local institutions with their own incipient democratic organizations.[23]

It was an agonizing irony that at the very moment local blacks began to take the initiative, some members of SNCC argued that only national publicity and federal intervention could sustain the movement in the face of the white terrorist response to that initiative. Watkins and others on staff feared that the summer volunteers — white and black — would surely overshadow their efforts. "The local indigenous people would feel," Watkins continued, that since "'[the northerners] are more educated than I am, maybe I should listen to them, do it their way, do what they say.'" In his own experience, Curtis Hayes understood this to be true. Perhaps not fully crediting the explosive impact he had had on northerners like Dickie Magidoff in Ann Arbor, Hayes recalled that he "always felt inferior to the northern students, personally. I thought they were smarter than we were. I knew that we knew more about Mississippi than they did, but they had the ability to carry out these long analyses, intellectual discussions about our environment that seemed like foreign language to us." Local blacks might "feel inferior and fall back into the same rut that they were in before we started the grassroots organizations." They feared that when the summer volunteers returned North, "people from Mississippi would have to start all over again."[24]

In organizing for the November Freedom Vote, SNCC staff had carefully navigated hundreds of discussions with white volunteers in an attempt to break them in on the process of how to develop local leaders. It was critical that the whites understand why a canvasser's initiation of a give-and-take conversation with local black Mississippians was more important than their actual registration. A Yale volunteer provided a vivid example of this problem. Shocked that Mississippi police greeted him with weapons drawn, the student retreated to canvassing plantations. At the end of the first day, he noticed that sharecroppers were averting their eyes and appearing to agree with anything he said. The volunteer subsequently stopped telling sharecroppers *why* they should register and simply told them *to* register. It would save time, he thought. A black SNCC worker then "admonished him to treat the sharecroppers with full respect." The SNCC man said that the explanation was as important, if not more so, than the actual vote. "Through the ensuing discussion," historian Taylor Branch recorded, "the Yale volunteer recalled that he and the SNCC worker 'spent a decade together in thirty-six hours.'"[25] At the Greenville meeting, SNCC workers wrestled with this issue: why devote so much energy to educating white volunteers?

The debate haunted SNCC people over the next year and a half. On the Mississippi staff were Martha Prescod from the University of Michigan and Jean Wheeler from NAG at Howard, both of whom had initially worked on SNCC's integrated southwest Georgia project. Both black women had moved on to Mississippi because they felt too many whites were working in Georgia. For Bob Moses, their departure signaled what later became a "huge problem in the organization." They "mirrored a kind of concern which existed within the Mississippi staff," most of whom were native to the state. They had had "very little working contact with white people" and were not eager to increase those contacts. After all, the staff had created the voter registration projects "out of nothing, and at great risk to themselves." "We had been trying to build a strong Black movement in Mississippi," Moses recalled, "unlike the SNCC project in southwest Georgia where Charles Sherrod consciously introduced whites to help define what integration was to be." Furthermore, "SNCC itself had never really resolved what it meant by integration and in Mississippi we more or less left the idea alone, the question open. We talked local leadership instead." Mississippi staffers had already voted down a suggestion to bring whites over from the Atlanta SNCC at the beginning of 1963. They had only "reluctantly" agreed to use whites from Yale and Stanford to help in the Freedom Vote with the understanding that the whites would leave immediately after the election.[26]

Willie Peacock, a black from Tallahatchie County, testified eloquently to these concerns. Quick-witted, passionate, with a talent for healing, Peacock had planned to enter medical school in the fall of 1962. Just before the end of that summer, Amzie Moore and Bob Moses went to his home and convinced him to begin working on SNCC's Greenwood campaign.[27] Peacock scrutinized the impact of those who came down for the Freedom Vote. For most of the whites, he observed, it seemed impossible to see black separatism as anything but reverse racism. Soon, in fact, some volunteers accused the Mississippi staff of precisely this. Peacock recognized, though, that when white Mississippians told black Mississippians what to do, the latter ignored the former at their peril. When northern whites appeared on the scene and told people to register to vote, it was "just another person who looks like the oppressor telling them to do something. It's not commitment. It's done out of that same slavery mentality." Sherrod saw this many times as well: "Two people, a black and a white, go to a door and knock, and a black comes to the door. Who are they going to look at? They're going to look at the white."[28]

Blacks who had "worked and sacrificed, labored and exerted influence" over a period of years, stated Sherrod, could not easily accept that a white who had been there just one week could "say something to the black people, and they'll do it, and it's taken you two years to get them to come to a meeting." On the other hand, if a local person was recruited by Peacock — himself a black Mississippian — that recruit could break through some of the deferential thought and behavioral patterns he or she had learned from childhood. "If I can get my brother committed," Peacock explained, "that's a true commitment." That recruit, he felt, would no longer be limited by the conviction that whites were superior. Once a person truly believed he or she was the equal of every other human being, it was impossible to go back to "the slavery mentality." Peacock and other staffers held that long-term political benefits would accrue to local blacks from building this kind of self-respect. The majority of SNCC's Mississippi staff, then, believed that white northern students could build only short-term organizations with no more than a superficial impact on black Mississippians.[29]

An additional fear stemmed from the previous year's experience in Greenwood, where some newly arrived white male volunteers "had not presented a very good image to the adult community — in reference to their daughters," Peacock reported. White men had long exploited young black girls and women, and they had often compounded the injury by demeaning the morality of black girls and women who had been victims — calling them sluts, whores, or worse. So when white male volunteers showed an interest in local young women, many of these black daughters were barred from the SNCC office by parents who wanted to keep their daughters safe from such an experience. If the whites were to come in, Peacock warned, they should "come in to work and keep hands off of black women." Then "they may be able to work [more] successfully."[30]

Another component of the debate on whites' role in the Mississippi movement, Mendy Samstein observed, stemmed from tensions over how decisions were made during the Freedom Vote campaign.[31] Samstein, one of the whites who arrived from Atlanta in the fall of 1963 at Moses' invitation, was a New Yorker teaching history at Atlanta's Spelman College. The office's WATS line and statewide communications network was a tremendous organizing tool, yet access to so much information gave the Jackson staff a good deal of power. SNCC's lack of a clearly defined decision-making process and the pace of the Freedom Vote campaign made it necessary, Samstein recalled, for some decisions, "if they were to be made at all, be made in Jackson and on the spot." White workers were clustered in the central office because they had been discouraged from working in the field. Furthermore, the office needed extra hands, as well as specialized people, and white volunteers could do this work. Finally, according to Samstein, "there was simply no one willing to come out of the field in order to work in the Jackson office." No solution emerged, and whites continued to wield undue influence.[32]

By the time of the Greenville meeting in November 1963, Bob Moses was keenly aware that black staff had a difficult time working so closely with whites after a lifetime of being subjected to white prejudice. At a previous meeting, he had seen a black Mississippian explode in frustration, emitting "a whole series of really racial statements of hatred." The rest of the staff, mostly black with a few whites present, sat stunned. "The white students were, in this case, now made the victims," Moses stated. How could the staff act together while they lived amid such extreme racial animosity? On the one hand, the influx of whites into SNCC offered the possibility for blacks and whites to live in the solution — "black and white together." On the other hand, given the weight of racial history everyone bore, the entry of large numbers of whites threatened the very integrity of the fragile democratic organizations that black Mississippians had labored to create.[33]

For his part, Moses saw merit on both sides of this argument. For very practical reasons, he felt that "the people who did the work should make the decision,"[34] and a majority of the staff did not want the Summer Project.[35] Yet Moses was forced to weigh this reality against the white terror that paralyzed all organizing, which risked the collapse of the whole movement through despair and resignation. Moreover, many staffers were "already burnt out," and SNCC had no rejuvenatory measures to offer them. While the flexibility and ad hoc nature of the organization had initially been an asset, it was not foolproof. Volunteer psychiatrists, weekends in California or New York, and visits from celebrities all helped the SNCC workers continue. But long-term recuperation was not an option. As Moses said, "We didn't have any resources; we didn't have any money."[36]

Also influential for Moses was the fact that local adult activists, as distinct from SNCC workers from Mississippi, had looked upon the Yale and Stanford students as helpful in the Freedom Vote. They felt that more white students would bring increased assistance. As Mississippi movement stalwart Victoria Gray stated, "I understood clearly that unless we found ways to focus national attention on what was happening in Mississippi," the whites in the state were "going to wear us down, or [do] whatever was necessary to stop us."[37]

The murder of Louis Allen in January 1964 pushed Moses decisively toward supporting the Summer Project. In 1961 an FBI agent had interviewed Allen, a middle-aged black farmer, as a witness in the murder of Herbert Lee. Allen told the agent that local deputies had forced him to lie to the coroner's jury about what he had seen. Six months later, a sheriff's deputy accosted Allen and repeated word-for-word the farmer's statement to the federal agent. From then on, Allen felt he was a marked man. He put his house up for sale and prepared to move to Milwaukee.[38]

The day before he planned to close the sale on his house and leave Mississippi for good, Allen was killed by three shotgun blasts in his front yard. If the Lee murder welded tight SNCC's commitment to remain in the state in 1961, Allen's death in January 1964 aroused Moses to do all in his power to force a change in Mississippi: "We had to do something." Determined to push for local empowerment, he nonetheless believed that he had to focus the national spotlight on the state. Moses spoke out for the Summer Project, "which I knew would tip the scales."[39] SNCC made its choice: the Summer Project went forward.[40]

CHAPTER
EIGHT

The High Summer of Transformation

In the summer of 1964 white Mississippi declared war on SNCC and COFO. A White Citizens Council leader exhorted his fellow citizens: "Don't you ever give up that gun! That's all you've got left to protect that little baby in that crib. Because these dirty devils will be in your home! That's what they want. They do not want equality. You know they don't want equality. They don't want something *like* you got, they want *what* you got—your women!"[1] Mississippi governor Paul Johnson talked bluntly about the Summer Project: "If we allow these invaders to succeed in their dastardly scheme, we will be guilty of a very costly error." The state prepared for battle with the nonviolent voter registration workers by buying tanks and armored cars, as well as hiring two hundred more state police officers. War, in traditional terms, carries the weight of finality only because victory or defeat is registered in the body count. For white supremacists in Mississippi, targets were easy to find: all blacks who attempted to register to vote were listed in local newspapers for two weeks at a stretch, and police took pictures of individuals who showed up at local courthouses to register.[2]

While white Mississippians prepared back home, SNCC people gathered in Ohio to train volunteers for the Summer Project. Each volunteer cohort spent one week in SNCC seminars, role-plays, and planning sessions. When a volunteer asked Hollis Watkins, "'What should we expect when we get to Mississippi?'" he replied, "If you're going to Mississippi, you should be prepared for at least three things. You should be prepared to go to jail. You should be prepared to be beaten. And, ultimately, you should be prepared to be killed."[3]

The Summer Project required new levels of organizing by SNCC. In the spring of 1964, a five-person "Mississippi Summer Project Committee" was created. The group included Moses, Ella Baker, Casey Hayden, Mendy Samstein, and Dona Richards (Marimba Ani). Richards, Moses' first wife, was a whip-smart, slightly bohemian black philosophy student from the University of Chicago. All five had spent extensive time on northern campuses, had wide-ranging networks of contacts there, and thus were key links in preparing for the entry of large numbers of white students from the North into the southern black, church-based movement. White volunteers from the North were needed not only as extra workers to canvass African Americans across Mississippi, but also to draw the national media to Mississippi for the Summer Project.[4]

Mississippi Freedom Democratic Party

In early 1964, having dramatized the plight of black disfranchisement in the 1963 elections and having been shut out of the state's regular Democratic Party, COFO workers moved to create their own political party. Beginning in the spring of 1964, they started to lay the legal groundwork for challenging the all-white Mississippi Democratic Party. The civil rights workers figured that the state's weakest point — technically, at least — was its lack of adherence to the national party's by-laws. In April, they announced the formation of the Mississippi Freedom Democratic Party, emphasizing that it was open to all state residents. Since it was an election year, COFO had a chance to bring the Mississippi situation to the attention of the nation at the Democratic National Convention, scheduled for August 1964 in Atlantic City. At the national convention, delegates traditionally drafted the party platform and elected a presidential candidate. The COFO workers planned to use the MFDP as the vehicle to contest the right of the (white-only) Mississippi Democrats to be seated in Atlantic City.[5] But they had to get the word out.

By March 1964 the Summer Project was gathering momentum. The students were coming. There was much to do and little time. As plans for the project proceeded, some members of SNCC had cause for hope in the strategy of importing white students from the North. Justice Department attorneys argued before federal judge Harold Cox that Cox should direct Foote Campbell, the circuit clerk in Madison County, Mississippi, to process black voter applicants more rapidly. This departure from Justice's pattern of inactivity occurred one week after Campbell had allowed only 5 of the 350 black Mississippians present at the courthouse to take registration tests. Throughout the hearing, Judge Cox referred to them as "a bunch of niggers." "Who is telling these people they can get in line and push people around, acting like a bunch of chimpanzees?" he asked. Nevertheless, the federal pressure moved the judge onto new ground: Almost 150 years after the passage of the Fifteenth Amendment, Cox directed the clerk to process at least 50 applicants a day.[6]

For many SNCC people, terrorist activity by white supremacists had prompted a reconsideration of the strategy of nonviolence. At an Atlanta staff meeting in June 1964, Charlie Cobb brought grim news: "Amzie Moore was told by a white that he, Mrs. Hamer, Moses and Aaron Henry were slated to be killed. . . . The feeling is that violence this summer will be directed at black staff members and leaders and not at white summer volunteers." Since staffers in Greenwood "felt they would be killed," they had acquired guns "for the house and the office with the idea of self-defense, to protect against the organized violence which is developing." Throughout the Second Congressional District, "people are arming themselves," Charles McLaurin reported. And Willie Peacock commented: "County people say they are going to defend themselves because they know the whites are not playing. They have set up a self defense structure so that if there is violence in an area anyone there must make an account of his presence." Since the FBI "was unwilling to track down the guilty parties" in the shooting of Louis Allen, whites knew they could kill blacks and "get away with it," Peacock continued. The challenge to the "formerly workable ways" of nonviolence, Lawrence Guyot acknowledged, had been given weight by the views of Max Stanford, a protégé of Malcolm X, who advocated armed self-defense. Stanford "exerted a great deal of influence" in the state, noted Ruby Doris Smith Robinson. Hollis Watkins summed up the changes he had observed since 1961. Early on, people had guns in their houses — "they were protecting their homes." But "there was a nonviolent attitude then." Now, in 1964, "things had changed." When a young boy was shot by a police officer in Albany, Georgia, in May, 1,200 people showed up at a mass meeting, Don Harris reported. "They were mad. Young people and people on the fringes of the movement were expressing themselves. That night they could have had as big a demonstration as ever," but when SNCC people began to talk about nonviolence, it had a chilling effect. In a scene reminiscent of the blowup in Cambridge, Maryland, Harris said, what right did SNCC have to stop people from doing what they wanted to do?[7]

Sam Block explained the escalating tension in Greenwood: "Mrs. McGhee has guns and has been able to stop some violence. What are we to say to her?" Longtime Quaker activist and Spelman historian Staughton Lynd had traveled to Mississippi to serve as the Summer Project's Freedom School coordinator. He had seen an equally troubling situation in Carthage, Mississippi. When SNCC volunteers tried to open a Freedom School, local whites claimed that the deed to the land was invalid. "They were talking about getting their guns and setting fire to the schoolhouse." A volunteer reported Lynd's dilemma: "In a situation like this, what do we do? It's necessary to ask other people to protect you, and this is something we are trying to avoid." Lynd said that he had "an uneasy feeling about getting someone else to do my dirty work for me. It seems to me that some time we are going to have to go one way or the other — either asking all the people in the movement to drop their guns, or picking them up ourselves." Courtland Cox provided a different perspective, one that echoed that of the Nashville workshops: namely, that armed self-defense was a step back, a retreat, not a step forward. "To the extent that we think of our own lives, we are politically immobilized," he suggested. "We volunteer for this situation knowing what's happening and we must accept the implications. Self-defense can only maintain the status quo, it can't change the existing situation." During the summer, staff and volunteers would be living with rural folks — nearly all of whom were armed, Charlie Cobb noted. What would happen if someone attacked a local person's home — someone who was housing SNCC people? Would SNCC stand by their workers who were there, "even though SNCC advocates nonviolence?" "Defending your home is dignity," continued white New Yorker Mike Sayer. "We can't assume what reaction will take place to self-defense. We can't be sure it won't lead to a holocaust."[8]

There was, of course, no way to reach consensus on the issue.[9] "When are we going into the white community with the idea of nonviolence?" McLaurin asked. Samstein reported that Ed Hamlett was beginning to develop a "White Folks Project" for the summer, but he was encountering many difficulties. In McComb, for instance, whites like Bob Zellner and Tom Hayden had been beaten almost upon arrival. McLaurin said that "when whites come down [from the North] they rush into the Negro community. That's why they're beaten." Instead, he proposed, white volunteers should try to organize southern whites to support integration. As a political argument, McLaurin's view made sense. But in terms of the political reality, it made no sense at all. The minute white workers broke the rules of the racial caste system, they were assaulted, regardless of whether they were on the white side or the black side of town. As comedian Dick Gregory quipped that summer, the only white moderates one could find in Mississippi were "cats who'll lynch you from a low tree."[10]

For many early SNCC activists, nonviolence had become part of their lives. But having guns in the home for self-protection was commonplace for black Mississippians — a by-product of living under Jim Crow. Therefore the question that loomed in 1964 was stark and unavoidable: Did nonviolence apply to all situations, no matter how great the threat to people's lives? Should local leaders, or families who housed activists, be encouraged to follow nonviolence, no matter how grave the consequences? In the end, was nonviolence merely a tactic, or was it a way of life? And what were the risks of its abandonment? A reign of violence by white supremacists could not only destroy the civil rights movement, but potentially cost hundreds or even thousands of lives. Who knew whether nonviolence or self-defense offered greater protection against terror? Perhaps it was simply an individual decision: every staff member could decide

Staughton Lynd and
John Lewis, 1964.
Lynd headed the Free-
dom Schools during
the summer of 1964.
(Courtesy of Staugh-
ton Lynd)

for himself or herself. Yet if everything was personal, how could SNCC formulate
a coordinated program? How could it provide any level of organization or co-
herence? By the summer of 1964, there were no easy answers in Mississippi.[11]

The June meeting in Atlanta ended with SNCC staffers coming together to
face the summer. They stood in a circle, arms around each other, and sang "We
Shall Overcome." "After we had sung all the verses we could think of," Lynd
recalled, "we hummed. John Lewis spoke over the humming. He told of how
the Nashville group decided to plunge ahead on the Freedom Ride after CORE
had called it off. They took buses to Birmingham where police chief Bull Connor arrested them." Plucking them from jail in the dark of the night, Connor
drove them to the Alabama-Tennessee border and dropped them off in Ku Klux
Klan country. They had no transportation and no money. Their strategic plan
lay in ruins. But, wrote Lynd, "John said as we hummed, 'We knew one thing.
We had to start back to Birmingham.'"[12]

Activists had to assess how much bottled-up emotion to unleash at staff meetings and how much to stifle. While everyone knew there was a problem with the society, it was not always understood as a caste system and thus a structural crisis of enduring proportions. As a practical matter, people did not always possess the intellectual and emotional room to think beyond short-term planning. The tendency to focus on the short run was often a substitute for clarity on specific strategic goals. Meanwhile, the time for the MFDP's precinct meetings had arrived, and the volunteers needed to be trained. For that to happen, SNCC workers had to prepare local people to take these volunteers in, as well as to prime new areas in which COFO had not yet worked. There was not enough time. Would the COFO staff hold together in the face of these challenges? Everyone was, as COFO lawyer Len Holt wrote, "tired — continuously, malnourished — continuously, tense — continuously, and frustrated — continuously."[13] It remained to be seen whether SNCC's emphasis on consensus would survive the influx of youthful college students, many of them white. Then, despite the grave reservations of most SNCC workers in the state, the Summer Project was upon them, bringing with it what Moses described as "a searchlight from the rest of the country on Mississippi."[14]

Oxford: Volunteer Training Ground

In the spring of 1964 SNCC had sent a call to historically black colleges and predominantly white colleges: "We need our best people in Mississippi," a field secretary told an audience at Stanford. "But don't come down with any high-minded notions. SNCC has no place for white liberals. When you come, come to help yourself, not the Negro." Many came to live out the values of freedom and democracy they perceived to be at the core of the country's mission, to better understand their own lives as Americans.[15] This is what SNCC people had learned from 1961 to 1963 and made into movement wisdom. Others had to learn it too before they could be helpful.

The training programs organized for the summer volunteers were necessary but insufficient. As Bob Moses said in June, the SNCC staff "must try to set a tone so that the summer volunteers can understand problems the staff has and understand what they're getting into, who they're working with."[16] Unfortunately, there was no way a one-week training session could convey the learning gained from the tumultuous experiences of the preceding two years. The new volunteers had not been shot at on country roads. The young women among them had not been leered at in rural counties by deputy sheriffs threatening rape. They had not been thrown out of courthouses by registrars, a shotgun pointed at the back of their necks. They had not awakened to the dull *thud* of a house

Staughton Lynd running a workshop for summer volunteers, Oxford, Ohio, 1964. (Courtesy of Staughton Lynd)

or church bombing. They had not encountered children who had only beans to eat for weeks. They had not seen Willie Peacock and Curtis Hayes spending hours or days educating white Yale and Stanford students as to why they could not just get local blacks to sign the Freedom Ballot and move on. They had not yet heard (or themselves offered) cutting remarks that daily life made inevitable when people experienced tense situations in close quarters. In short, they were not yet SNCC workers.

As a result, there were sharp limits on what could be conveyed in a quick training program in Oxford, Ohio, in June 1964. Indeed, SNCC staffers were themselves unsure of the shape of the immediate future. As Hollis Watkins put it: "We don't know what will happen with whites coming into the state. Neither do we know our own feelings and hatred of whites." He urged SNCC members to "deal with our own hates" before the summer. Fannie Lou Hamer argued that hatred of black for white solved nothing. "The white man is the scaredest person on earth." In the daytime, things were quiet, "but at night he'll toss a bomb or pay someone to kill. The white man's afraid he'll be treated like he's been treating the Negroes. I couldn't carry that much hate."[17]

The sessions in Oxford had been planned to expose the volunteers to SNCC experiences in all their variety. James Lawson presented a moving discourse on the nonviolent method. Symptomatic of the tension that would grow steadily larger, he was immediately and eloquently rebutted by Stokely Carmichael, who drew on recent events now visible within the wider movement. Nonviolence used to work, Carmichael announced. It was a novel approach. Attracted to the drama generated by early SNCC initiatives, newspaper reporters covered the actions week after week. Sometimes this media attention had contributed to the early success of nonviolent protests. Regardless, the nonviolent protesters had made only "minor" demands, such as access to a lunch counter or integrated buses. Carmichael argued that resistance to these changes was not "hard-core." "Stokely does not advocate violence," a summer volunteer wrote home after the session. "What he *is* saying is that love and moral confrontation have no place in front of a brute who beats you 'til you cry *nigger*." The volunteer, having heard both Lawson and Carmichael speak, made an assessment that, he felt, was shared by others in the group: "Nonviolence is a perverted way of life, but a necessary tactic and technique." The movement had come a long way from Nashville.[18]

Nonviolence fueled SNCC's original attack on the caste system. It was a centerpiece, not a sidebar, of the struggle. Certainly, it could not be defined, as this volunteer offered, as a "perversion." Lawson and Carmichael possessed a different understanding of life, a different understanding of politics, and a different understanding of democracy and how to attain it. Practically speaking, both self-defense and nonviolence provided a way for the politically powerless to carve out democratic space in a nation saturated with authoritarian institutions. Both offered the vision of a society where people could struggle to overcome internalized habits of authority and submission as well as external repression. What was more, nonviolent direct action and voter registration were practical ways to act on this vision. Yet the summer volunteer's reaction to the differing perspectives of Lawson and Carmichael showed precisely how difficult it was to convey — and absorb — a nonviolent approach within a short period. Characterizing nonviolence as "perverted" indicated a failure to understand how years of nonviolent direct action campaigns from 1960 to 1963 had wrenched open the segregated caste system.[19]

On 21 June 1964, a day after sending the first busload of volunteers to Mississippi, Moses began working with the second group of three hundred volunteers. He received a telephone call from Casey Hayden in Jackson. Andrew Goodman, a white SNCC volunteer who had arrived in the state only hours before, was missing along with CORE staff members James Chaney, a black Mississippian from Meridian, and Michael "Mickey" Schwerner, a white New Yorker. SNCC staff in Jackson assumed the three to be dead.[20]

Moses quickly assembled the volunteers in a large auditorium. The "problem was how to convey that to the volunteers so they could understand, so they could have a choice," he later reflected. Before they got to rural Mississippi, he wanted them to realize in a visceral way that "the die was cast . . . these were the stakes." To people so young, filled with a sense of their own immortality, how could he make the risk real? He stood, dressed in blue overalls and a T-shirt, looking at his feet. "This was one of my most profound experiences of leadership," said volunteer Pam Parker. "The director of the whole Summer Project, and he looked at his *feet*, shuffled them a bit, and talked about how he *felt*." Moses started by explaining that he had no doubt the three missing workers were dead. Now, seared by the knowledge he could be sending more to die, he borrowed an analogy from J. R. R. Tolkien's ring trilogy. Frodo the hobbit, he told them, was given the task of taking the Ring of Power to the Cracks of Doom so the ring would never afflict the world again. By the time Frodo reached the end of his journey, however, the ring had exerted its power over him — ultimately he was corrupted by it and could not destroy it. Moses said: "This is like leadership. Leadership affects you. It's like the Ring of Power. I know that to be true. I know that to be true about myself, but nevertheless, I for better or worse am in this position and think we should continue the summer project." Marshall Ganz, a California volunteer, recalled that Moses was saying "I don't want to put you at risk, but I have to put you at risk." Moses closed: "All I can say is I'll be there with you." Parker said: "I would have gone anywhere with him. . . . I trusted him that much."[21]

After Moses finished speaking, there was an extended silence. Finally, staff member Jean Wheeler stood. Her gentle oval face was marked by handsome features and attentive eyes that reflected experience in both Albany, Georgia, and the Mississippi Delta. She sang in an exquisite, strong voice from the back of the room: "They say that freedom is a constant struggle / They say that freedom is a constant struggle / Oh lord, we've struggled so long; we must be free." Robert Coles, a psychiatrist brought in to ascertain the mental fortitude of the volunteers, later wrote: "The emotional power and support of [that moment] can hardly be conveyed. One has to be there, feel the strength and reassurance of the words, the melodies, the young people united in saying and singing." At that point, "all of us stood and marched out behind Jean," said Ganz, years later still visibly moved by the memory.[22]

As the frantic federal search for Goodman, Chaney, and Schwerner continued, parents of the summer volunteers exhausted their contacts and resources in the subsequent days and weeks to insist that President Lyndon B. Johnson and the U.S. government protect the Summer Project workers. Marcia Rabinowitz read a formal list of demands over the radio in New York. Pam Parker's parents spent the week after the three young men went missing sending "letters, telegrams and telephone calls to everyone we knew with any influence, for help for the three boys and protection for all these beautiful young people." Friends of SNCC groups staged protest demonstrations in New York, Chicago, Philadelphia, Boston, and Cincinnati. In each locale, they demanded that the local federal attorney provide protection for civil rights workers in Mississippi. It was exactly this new kind of pressure bearing down upon Washington that SNCC people, in desperation after the Louis Allen killing in early 1964, had hoped would change national policy.[23]

Twenty-nine hours after the Jackson office's first call to Washington for help, four of the nation's six thousand FBI agents arrived in Philadelphia, Mississippi. It would take six weeks — and hundreds of additional law enforcement personnel — before the bodies of Goodman, Chaney, and Schwerner were found buried in an earthen dam near Philadelphia. Yet the missing workers represented only a tiny fragment of the repression — state-endorsed and otherwise — that grew until it verged on the surreal. First it had been Herbert Lee, then Medgar Evers, four little girls in church in Birmingham, and Louis Allen. Over the summer, the Jackson office prepared a running summary that graphically portrayed — through the bodies of those shot at, maimed, beaten, and killed — the miniscule range of democracy in the Deep South. By October 1964, fifteen people had been murdered, four wounded, and over one thousand arrested; thirty-seven churches had been bombed or burned. As a young staffer named Jane Stembridge put it, "America, we have paid a high price for your attention."[24]

SNCC's list of actual bombings in Mississippi does not include incidents too common to record — though they litter the oral histories of civil rights workers. In one instance, the Marshall County sheriff pulled over a SNCC car, ordered everyone out, then stepped in the face of Kathy Kunstler, a white woman from New York. " 'Which one of them coons is you fuckin?' " he growled, as a white crowd gathered to threaten the movement workers. Though the sheriff allowed the workers to leave, he warned them that they would be killed if they ever returned. Then he stood by and watched as a posse of twenty-one vehicles chased their car out of town at speeds exceeding one hundred miles per hour. Zohorah Simmons noted that such encounters wore down people's commitment to nonviolence. She learned to drive as a SNCC worker in Mississippi: "And on at least two or three occasions, I drove at speeds of over a hundred miles an hour, trying to outrun the Klan. But when you are a brand new driver, driving at those kinds of speeds, and not knowing if you are going to make it to town so that they turn off and leave you alone — this began to shake me. These things caused anger, resentment, in addition to the fear. So the nonviolent commitment has been a struggle for me over the years." "Almost nobody could get out in an automobile and drive anywhere without fear of being arrested for some trumped-up traffic violation," reported Wiley Branton, director of the Voter Education Project. One civil rights worker's car was confiscated by Hattiesburg police for "speeding," and when the owner later claimed it, he found syrup in the tank. Although such incidents never showed up in the official records of the violence that summer, their sheer repetition created an atmosphere of threat that civil rights workers understood could at any time move into physical torture and murder.[25]

Under such conditions, humor became necessary to sanity. When a northern lawyer working for SNCC picked up the phone and heard surveillance on the other end, including a male voice saying, "Gimme a pencil," another SNCC worker quipped: "That's okay. In some towns the cops can't even write. In Itta Bena the other day a SNCC man had to fill out his own ticket." While Curtis Hayes was driving a northern black Episcopal minister named Harry Bowie around the countryside, he "kidded me for my northern accent" and "not knowing the 'survival kit' and my inability to say 'yassuh.'" Bowie recalled: "And so I'd say, 'Oh, is this the way you say 'yes, sir?' And he'd say, 'No, no.'" The two were laughing and joking when suddenly three cars surrounded them. Hayes stomped on the accelerator and blew by the whites. He turned to Bowie: "'Harry, I'm worried.' At that point, we broke into laughter because I said, 'Yas-suh.' [Laughs] And as we were laughing, I'll never forget, he or myself—I don't know who said it—said, 'I'll bet Schwerner and Chaney and Goodman were laughing when they were being chased, too.' And the laughter was hysterical . . . we couldn't do anything but laugh, okay?"[26]

Each project required clear rules and stringent security measures to protect workers and residents. People had to be on the job by 8:30 every morning. Two-way radios ensured regular communication. COFO staff had to sign in and sign out. No one could travel after dark except on official business. All shades were drawn at night. Workers were advised that no interracial groups should travel downtown at any time, and local whites and police should be avoided at all costs. There could be no interracial affairs between staff members, nor between white women and local black men.[27]

Despite attempts to protect themselves, the best the staff and volunteers could do was to ensure that they knew where their cohorts were at any given time. The armed defense came from local residents. Jane Adams, a volunteer from Illinois, remembered the first night she arrived in Harmony, Mississippi. A group of people were "playing music, dancing, and having a good time." They heard a car coming down the road, and two brothers in her host family "picked up their guns, turned the lights out, opened the door, and looked at the car as it went by." After the vehicle passed without incident, "we turned the lights on and continued dancing." It was similar to Amite County, she noted, where "blacks didn't go anywhere without a gun."[28]

After a three-year absence, SNCC had, in fact, decided to return to the southwest region of the state. Beginning in July 1964, Bob Moses announced at a news conference, summer workers would go to McComb — home of Herbert Lee and Louis Allen. Five black men had been murdered there since December 1963, and no one had been indicted. The decision resolved the ongoing dilemma of whether COFO should ignore the black Mississippians there, "allowing all the violence to be taken out on local people," Moses recalled, or "share their terror with them."[29]

The volunteers in McComb shared the terror. Dennis Sweeney, a Stanford undergraduate, worked with classmate David Harris and Mario Savio from Berkeley. The first week, Sweeney heard a thud on the porch of the local freedom house, then the squeal of tires. Before he could move, a blast of dynamite collapsed the front of the building and blew a large hole in the driveway. No one was killed — the most serious injury was a concussion in Sweeney's eardrum, but the attack served as the opening volley of weekly firebombings of houses, cars, and churches in McComb. This incident coincided with the bludgeoning of a COFO rabbi in Clarksdale and the wounding of a nineteen-year-old female volunteer when a car full of whites fired into a black church in Moss Point. The situation in McComb, however, remained particularly dangerous throughout the summer. Later, three Klansmen would be brought before Mississippi judge William Watkins, to whom they revealed the local practice of drawing black activists' names from a hat each week in order to decide whom to bomb. Indicative of the widespread official endorsement of these tactics, Watkins sentenced the three — and eight others who had also pleaded guilty to bombing charges — to probation. Then he suspended the sentence. From the bench, he told the defendants that he made their punishment light because they had been "unduly provoked" by outsiders of "low morality and unhygene [sic]." Even FBI director J. Edgar Hoover, with his lengthy record of hostility toward civil rights activity, denounced Watkins for "blindness and indifference to outrageous acts." Still, the FBI did not move into McComb in force. By summer's end, blacks in McComb posted guards at their homes, businesses, and churches. Residents in isolated areas lit up their neighborhoods at night with makeshift streetlights draped on posts and trees in their yards.[30]

"Hate and viciousness seemed to be everywhere," wrote Cleve Sellers, a black South Carolina native who joined SNCC as a volunteer that summer. "We realized," he later admitted, that the only thing keeping us from death was "dumb luck. Death could come at any time in any form: a bullet between the shoulder blades, a fire bomb in the night, a pistol whipping, a lynching."[31] Robert Coles treated one volunteer who had stopped functioning in the midst of such terror. He feared losing his "gritty, tough, daring ways" and could not understand why — unexpectedly — he fell victim to tears, panic, and confusion. The young man was ravaged with dread of "assault — sexual, personal, moral, mental, and spiritual" and of losing "the complicated organization of mind and emotions which we spend so long building, and which is not meant to be tested by hells like this."[32] The volunteers now faced the problem Lawson, Nash, Lewis, Sherrod, Moses, and others had long confronted: How could one act despite this fear of death? Sellers, for his part, saw the SNCC staff in a new light. Now he too knew the severe and painful cost of trying to work under "constant tension and near-paralyzing fear."[33]

Living the Freedom Party

In ways that were hard for outside observers to grasp, the stress of living in an environment of terror was exacerbated by the commonplace tasks that staff and volunteers assumed in the painstaking day-to-day work of that summer. Forty-one of the forty-four summer projects had Freedom Schools, institutions that expanded the children's image of themselves.[34] Offering courses in African American history, French, and modern Africa, as well as basic reading and math, the schools taught children to value their own community's history and expanded their horizons to political and social realities outside of Mississippi. The teachers, who provided instruction through workshops rather than lectures, asked their students to question the white supremacist assumptions suffusing their official textbooks. The Freedom Schools not only impacted a generation of Mississippians but also reshaped the educational practices of thousands of teachers across the country.[35]

Twenty-three projects created community centers. After the ministers with movement connections started the Delta Ministry and opened offices in Hattiesburg and McComb, people supported by these community centers turned their attention to other areas of Mississippi life. Some worked to elect movement farmers to the county committees of the U.S. Department of Agriculture's Agricultural Stabilization and Conservation Service (ASCS). If black farmers could sit on these committees, they would have a direct say in the loans and subsidies they received — in other words, for the first time they would have at least some input on the way the county parceled out government farm programs. Other movement activists focused on health care and still others, on formal education.[36]

These community institutions laid down roots that offered the prospect of altering all manner of political and social relations in the state. Black people across America could thus see some of the most impoverished and disenfranchised people in the nation taking steps to shape their own political destiny. Members of the MFDP appeared to be living out the biblical injunction of "the last shall be first." By itself, the development of institutions independent of the state's white supremacist structure was a democratic achievement of considerable magnitude.[37] A final ingredient in this process of building political self-respect could be seen in hundreds of black voluntary associations. For a century following the Civil War, the single institution controlled by blacks in the segregated South had been the church. Now, independent black organizations of all kinds began as a result of the emerging political activity. Aside from the MFDP, local people created Freedom Schools, farm cooperatives, the *Mississippi Free Press*, and the Mississippi Child Development Group, among others. The Delta Ministry provided community organizers, financial aid, and logistical support to the MFDP and the Child Development Group. The Freedom Schools supported and expanded black Mississippians' quest for knowledge and self-improvement. African American farmers contested ASCS elections throughout the decade and into the 1970s, even though they had little success. Yet sustained efforts to break the white monopoly of every aspect of public life were traceable to the variety of local energies unshackled by the Mississippi freedom movement.[38]

Local people recognized this institution-building as a victory and welcomed the volunteers who expanded it. Sometimes the residents' warm greeting was returned by volunteers, other times not. Fannie Lou Hamer explained that she was called one night by someone who said "they was going to put me in the river, in the Mississippi River." Two white volunteers, Bill and Len, were staying with her. "And those two young men just begged me until I went over to Miss Carter's and I stayed over there and they stayed over here. Now what that meant, that they were willing to give their life for their brother. And I say brother; my husband *is* a black man . . . but if you concerned about human beings, you're brothers, under the skin." When she went home early the next morning, Hamer "saw a note, and they don't know today that I read that note, but there was a note in the chair, that they had wrote there in the dark, just in case something happened to them." The note avowed their determination to do *something* to protect Hamer and the movement her courage and spirit so deeply personified. In the summer of 1964, such experiences were not uncommon in the Mississippi Delta.[39]

Consensus on movement strategy and racial reconciliation was, of course, impossible. People bumped up against one another in endless varieties of understanding and misunderstanding, so that attempting to carve out racial generalizations of any kind became perilous and unrewarding. Nevertheless, almost everyone tried. For L.C. Dorsey, an MFDP leader from the town of Shelby, the most striking thing about the summer volunteers was their "demeanor, how they treated us, how they approached you." They were courteous and polite, and they "didn't talk down to you, talking to them. There was no consciousness of your 'place' when talking to them." Jeannette King, a black activist from Jackson, said that her "most outstanding memory" of the Summer Project was the "marvelous attempt on the part of people to tear down their own internal barriers in terms of getting in touch with other people." It was an "assault made on the political and social barriers that people had grown up with all of their lives." Black southerners, white southerners, and northern volunteers all made "an attempt to bridge the gap of class, of race, of religion that I've never been involved with before or since." The "intensity of involvement" among different people all coming from various experiences was the greatest legacy of that whole period of time, she said. Aaron Henry agreed, noting that the "deeply imbedded bitterness and hatred of whites in the minds of many" black Mississippians "began to subside" as white volunteers "continued to work with us and live in our houses, even when they were bombed and shot into." The summer volunteers, he concluded, "gave civil rights leaders an argument for our continued profession of love as the solution to our problems."[40]

But the many moments of racial transformation could not overcome the building tensions between the Mississippi-based COFO staff and the northern volunteers. It was these tensions — not the interracial cooperation between local families and volunteers — that had the greatest impact on the subsequent evolution of SNCC. COFO staffers — mostly native to the state — had to adjust to the fact that the tone, pace, and intimacy of the movement was no longer in their hands. The brilliance and talent of a Charles McLaurin or a Emma Bell refined in the fire of movement actions often remained unrecognized and thus disrespected by the students, who came from some of the most elite universities in the country. As James Forman remembered, black project director Dickie Flowers said that, as more northern volunteers arrived, he claimed that he attended Morehouse College " 'when I *know* I didn't go to Morehouse.' " The highly credentialed student volunteers doubted the COFO staffers, many of whom were not college graduates, had much to offer. Worse still, it was difficult for the staff to establish new criteria for assessing "intelligence" and "skill" — criteria that would give recognition to their own hard-won knowledge.[41]

McLaurin, Flowers, Hollis Watkins, Curtis Hayes, and others on staff grew increasingly alienated from the movement they had built. Prior to the summer of 1964, they had directed the movement's painstaking, costly nurturing of democratic self-respect, and institutions reflecting that self-respect, among black Mississippians. Northern whites, though courageous in their own right, had not experienced their sacrifices or ensuing learning processes. The black staff's internal equanimity was now at risk as they watched the local people's self-respect and institutions ebb in the face of the well-intentioned northerners. It maddened some SNCC veterans to see the confidence of native Mississippians recede in the presence of formally well-educated but culturally innocent volunteers. Furthermore, virtually none of this reality was transmitted to the larger public at the time. It was a reality that violated the sacred myths that comforted white America. It was a reality that required a respect for the democratic idea that most people simply did not yet possess. When the summer was over, COFO staffers knew, they would have to pick up the pieces. In certain ways, the entire scene constituted a mountain of contradiction with every nuance heightened by the constant violence that assaulted daily life. Though some veteran staffers maintained serious reservations about the decision to import northern whites, Moses had supported the project. Hayes saw Moses as a "little Jesus," repeatedly risking his life to bring civil rights to Mississippi. How could Hayes, Watkins, or Sam Block—who took the same risks—leave SNCC now? They stayed, despite the outrageous reality that the killing of white mothers' sons was more important to the nation than the killing of black mothers' sons. The resulting realpolitik was awash in irony: it seemed necessary to bring in whites to protect the voter registration workers.[42]

As northern volunteers began to occupy social spaces inside the movement, they often grew confused and agitated. It felt bizarre to live in one world but not completely belong to it, to be able to get on a plane at any time and return to the suburbs of Minneapolis, Buffalo, or Seattle. While these volunteers often rejoiced in the community growing around the voter registration project, they often experienced a long period of adjustment in which they felt alone and intimidated.[43]

And sometimes gender made a significant difference. During the Summer Project, COFO staffers made obvious distinctions between the jobs that male and female volunteers could undertake. They also drew divisions between what black volunteers should do and what whites should do. This gender- and race-based allotment of tasks developed as a direct response to staffers' understanding that the presence of whites, especially white women, provoked verbal abuse and violence from white southerners. Since staff members considered voter registration more dangerous than other work, males "sometimes imbued it with an air of macho derring-do," historian Sara Evans observed. Women, she found, were in some ways protected. They did not work in the most dangerous counties and often did not perform the more risky tasks, such as driving. People from different ethnic and regional subcultures perceived such gendered job-tasking differently. Joyce Ladner remembered the men driving and "pushing [women] to the floor when danger approached. I didn't want to sit in the front. For black people, black southern people, especially, we understood that as a kind of protectiveness, like a brother would protect." Someone else, she said, might see it differently. "If you were coming from the North, if you were white, if you had a different set of experiences, you might have perceived that to have been discrimination. Maybe you would have wanted to drive." Prathia Hall, a black Philadelphian, believed that while some like Sherrod tried to engage in that "loving kind of protection, it didn't work." If everybody was wounded, "then whoever could get up first was the one who had to get up first and move; that was just a reality."[44]

While this method of allotting jobs was based on what the staff considered the realities of working in Mississippi, some volunteers perceived a distinct but informal hierarchy as the unintended result. Since black men took the greatest risks, they held the preponderance of power in the organization. Black women and white men followed, with white women sitting at the bottom. The latter taught in Freedom Schools, performed office work, or staffed community centers. These assignments reflected gendered work stereotypes prevailing at the time, but they also minimized the provocation caused by visible white female activists.[45]

German playwright Bertolt Brecht famously noted, with respect to the World War II resistance to the Nazis in Europe, that even those who "wished to lay the foundations of kindness, could not ourselves be kind." The issue recurred in social movements through many eras and, indeed, around the world. The typical range of human behavior and emotions did not easily harmonize with a consistently respectful and candid manner toward others, even among people who wished to be allies. The pressure placed on a movement from external terror only increased the likelihood that emotional lives were lived at an intensified pitch.[46]

So it was in Mississippi during the Summer Project. Added to this consistent dynamic, white northerners often came South with great personal courage, but also with what Mimi Feingold, herself a white northerner, characterized as a "perfect obnoxiousness." Northern liberals "never shut up about race but were constantly telling racially oriented jokes, pointing out every stare, and mentioning their various exploits in the 500 causes they were associated with." Feingold's description might seem extreme—she was in the first cohort of northern whites of her generation to confront the disjuncture between northern liberal conceptions of the South and the South itself. Still, the archival record lends considerable support to Feingold's assertion. On returning from the Freedom Vote, Oregonian Dennis Sweeney spoke to his Stanford peers in an effort to publicize the grave injustices of the Magnolia State. "Any white Northerner who's had the good fortune to achieve even an average education in the North is going to be, just by virtue of this fact, so much more talented than the Negro leadership in the movement in the South, that in one day, he can make a significant contribution," Sweeney blithely offered. Though he was one of the few summer volunteers who had had previous contact with SNCC, his statement nevertheless contradicted the entire thrust of SNCC's effort in Mississippi, geared as it was to develop local leaders into strong public advocates of their own self-interest. Given the degree of condescension Sweeney displayed, it would be a challenge for him to understand how out-of-step and counterproductive he was.[47] Again, the northern media transmitted such pomposities — without criticism — to the wider American populace.

Sweeney's characterization of the activity in Mississippi not only contraverted SNCC's intent, it also grossly mischaracterized the reality in Mississippi. As Charles Payne aptly described the deeper meaning of the situation, local leaders created the "parameters to which others had to adjust." Those others included COFO organizers, traditional black leaders, and white vigilantes bent on terrorizing the movement. Yet Sweeney's difficulties in assessing the role of white volunteers was fairly common. According to one black summer volunteer, his white peers were "generally a good bunch," but a "few came in and wanted to take over. Their attitude was 'Okay, we are here, your troubles are over. We are going to put your house in order.'" In an extensive study of Summer Project volunteers, conducted in the 1980s, sociologist Doug McAdam discovered that despite their "supreme desire" to appear color-blind, northern whites often appeared to "believe the view put forth by the national media that it was *they* who had come to save the Mississippi Negro."[48]

In fact, only a handful of white individuals were able to come to terms with their own racial identity and successfully interact with blacks in SNCC. Notable among them were Casey Hayden, Penny Patch, Constance Curry, Bob and Dottie Zellner, Mendy Samstein, and Arkansas project director Bill Hansen. Reflecting later, Hayden said that she related well to blacks because she was loyal to the group. "I didn't want a place in the larger culture, I wanted a place in the beloved community. And you got that by being loyal to the community." She joined the movement in 1959 because segregation restricted her interactions with blacks: "It was a limit on me." She was effective not because she felt that white should help black, but because she had a stake in it for herself, a mind-set not shared by all — or perhaps most — white participants at the time. Casey was able to respond so wholly to the sit-in movement's ethos, she explained, because previously she had participated in efforts she later characterized as premovement groundwork — through the YWCA and the Christian Faith and

Life Community.[49] Few whites in the civil rights movement were able to match the political clarity or understanding of purpose that grew out of these experiences in the 1950s.

Thrust into an unprecedented situation with sparse training, white volunteers nudged face-to-face interracial relationships much higher up on the list of things SNCC had to address. First, these volunteers had little or no experience negotiating interracial etiquette prior to the summer of 1964. Second, enough brought a college-educated arrogance to taint the group as a whole. These two factors prompted some COFO staffers to conclude that white volunteers did not or could not show adequate respect for local Mississippians.[50]

It would be hard to imagine two American subcultures more alien to each other than those of rural blacks and northern, suburban whites. Fish fries and shaped-note singing and conjurers were foreign to those who had grown up in suburban cul-de-sacs. In his study of the Freedom Summer volunteers, Mc-Adam noted the attraction of some northerners to the "immediacy and strong communal base" of the black neighborhoods in which they worked. For many, this contrasted sharply with their own atomized suburban upbringing. The volunteers' exposure to the stark conditions in Mississippi—the terror, the living conditions, the poverty—could provoke intense emotions. "I was just seeing too much, feeling too much. Things weren't supposed to be like this," reflected one northerner. "I just remember feeling sad, guilty, and angry all at the same time." Heather Booth, a volunteer from New York, "grew up believing that the police were your friends. They were the crossing guards, the place to call if you ran into trouble." When she shared this sentiment with local movement leader Victoria Gray, Gray responded, "Well dear, I never ever thought of the police as my friends. Any time the police showed up in my neighborhood, it meant trouble."[51]

Understanding the arbitrariness of power was often a struggle for white volunteers. Marshall Ganz recalled his shock at "the feeling of being able to depend on *only* yourself and those most immediately close to you—that the courts, the law, the whole system was not there to defend you but was there to oppress you, to do you in. There's no appeal to rule of reason or rule of law." Whoever had the power made the rules. "That's a real powerful emotional experience. If you grow up in a safe middle class community, you don't experience that." The resulting "powerlessness and rage," Ganz said, "takes away your dignity."[52]

Sex brought yet another layer of complexity. In fact, the various strains that sex provoked frequently shaped the interactions between local Mississippians, COFO staffers, and volunteers. "We were all young, bereft of parental supervision, and strong-willed human beings, excited by the romance that we were involved with," explained John O'Neal. "So there was a lot of sex."[53] In Mississippi, northerners encountered what McAdam characterized as a "more sensual way of life" that encompassed new spiritual and visceral experiences. As one female volunteer stated: "I was young and impressionable and not very experienced sexually." She recalled the summer romance as "transporting . . . having sex in a field in the countryside where all you see are stars and I don't know, it just blew my mind. I don't know how to describe it. . . . I was frightened and awed by it."[54]

Though people tried to keep personal relationships private, their liaisons continually spilled over into the public realm. "Sometimes it got to be disturbing when there were meetings that were determined by who was fucking who," O'Neal remembered. Charles Sherrod learned that the volunteers' private lives required supervision if the SNCC staff was to stay intact. "You can't tell kids what to do in the daytime, and then expect them to go home and stay at the place where they're supposed to stay all night. Young people are not like that," Sherrod observed. "When you bring them down here you've got to supervise them 24 hours a day." With thirty or forty people on staff, and not enough accommodations, he put the women in one room, the men in the other, and slept at the door. Such arrangements "took a certain consistency, a certain amount of time and dedication to keep on top of them." Sherrod found that if he was able to contain inevitable personal eruptions, young people would "work all day and all night. They had a lot of energy."[55]

Many — but by no means all — of the interracial sexual encounters made a positive difference, broke through another barrier. In retrospect, interracial sex seems to have been a predictable consequence of SNCC's penchant for improvisation in pursuit of its broadly democratic objectives. Sex between black men and white women had had such severe repercussions in the South for so many earlier generations that when it occurred without those repercussions, it "helped to alleviate that fear," recalled Sherrod. Consensual sex between black women and white men — unions formed in the context of truly free choice — also could provide a new democratic vista.[56]

Nonetheless, the complicated emotions that sex provoked could be interpreted negatively as well. Some staff members and volunteers — mostly women — reported negative experiences with sexual interactions. As historian Cynthia Griggs Fleming noted, black women in leadership positions "often felt the need to cultivate a tough, assertive image. Some were convinced that dating a SNCC man could compromise that image and ultimately diminish their effectiveness." Willie Peacock remembered that often this view was persuasive: "We had some tough women with us. They were really tough, like Dorie Ladner. We'd be at Amzie Moore's home, and she'd come and crawl in bed with me, and I knew not to touch her — not in any kind of way. I was her sleeping partner. Nobody else. I knew better. It was just an understanding. It was quite clear. We were partners in the struggle, working together." Yet when Mary Rothschild interviewed 1964 summer volunteers in 1982, she found that "the most difficult task [was] to convey the throbbing pain in many of the interviews." Black women felt betrayed and invalidated when black men chose white sexual partners. Alice Walker's fictional civil rights worker Meridian Hill saw the situation as "strange and unfair" when black men left their black girlfriends to date white women. Meridian's boyfriend "made *her* ashamed, as if she were less." Some SNCC people recalled that when African American men were criticized by other blacks for "talking black and sleeping white," they claimed that "black female deficiencies had driven them to choose white partners." For their part, white women new to a project sometimes faced the "sex test": How would they handle sexual advances from black men in the movement? Vincent Harding raised this issue in the Oxford, Ohio, orientation: One response to three centuries of slavery and segregation on the part of some black men could be that "the only way that whites can prove they're really in the movement is by going to bed with a Negro." Peacock remembered how this dynamic differed from the early days of SNCC. Rather than everyone being equal, some white volunteers "were giving up guilt action to black men."[57]

For many women, black and white, sex did not always contain (or could not always provide) a new egalitarian context for intimacy. Indeed, as later social historians recognized on a broader cultural level, the availability of birth control in the 1960s "shifted the sexual balance of power so that [women] had neither the grounds to say no to men's pressing invitations nor to persuade men to commit themselves to the old terms of the sexual bargain, the exchange of sex for intimacy, fidelity, and economic support." In any case, some movement women adapted to the new terrain with enthusiasm, but at least one aspect of the old bargain prevailed — in SNCC as in the wider counterculture: "To take the sexual pleasure men offered still brought down the punitive force of the double standard."[58]

In ways that differed from the circumstances of their premovement lives, significant numbers of women became, as Doug McAdam found, "targets of a great deal of anger and hostility masquerading as normal sexual attention." This is not to say that movement men were any more likely than other men to commit sexual assault. The overwhelming number of assaults that summer were by southern white males attacking the movement. The vast majority of movement men did not engage in assaults of any kind. Yet when assaults did happen *within* the movement, black and white women were in the same position that black women had always occupied — they could get no outside help that did not endanger their own community.[59]

There was never much clarity on intraracial or interracial sex during this tumultuous period. On this issue, everyone remained befuddled. In retrospect, one can argue that sexual interactions, with the negative consequences that could ensue, contributed to the degradation of democratic social relations within the movement. Paradoxically, some of the most profound experiences between individuals took place in a sexual context. In fact, because sex was so personal, it could leave high levels of bitterness for some and an expanded sense of possibility for others.

One last dimension of the problem of internal relations seemed straightforward enough: prior to June 1964, those involved had been overwhelmingly southern and black. People like black northerners Diane Nash, Bob Moses, and Jean Wheeler, white southerner Casey Hayden, or white northerner Penny Patch were able to fit into the southern black community because they shared a bedrock of confidence in the capacities of local people and an ability to relate to a southern, black, church-based movement. Perhaps as important, they were relatively few in number and did not threaten the southern, black orientation of the organization. Moreover, they had been there long enough to develop close relationships with other members of the core staff.

All this changed with the Summer Project. The new volunteers rarely possessed the extraordinary perception of a Diane Nash or a Casey Hayden. Moreover, in the crush of time and the pressing obligations of the work, people did not have an opportunity to exchange experiences and develop a capacity for candor, as the original Nashville group and the Mississippi COFO staff had done over the course of many months. The civil rights movement had learned a great deal since four college students sat-in at Woolworth's in Greensboro, North Carolina; since James Lawson began his nonviolent workshops in Nashville, Tennessee; since Charles Sherrod appeared in Albany, Georgia. In fact, veteran workers were fairly certain they had learned enough to change America. Yet cultures are hard to change. And historically, they have proved almost impossible to change quickly.

The Freedom Party Encounters Conventional Hierarchy: The Movement versus the American Political Tradition

Within SNCC, confusion and disagreement over the MFDP challenge remained at the beginning of the summer and was clearly visible at the pre-summer staff meeting in Atlanta on 9–11 June 1964. The SNCC people could not agree on a strategy. Some staffers wondered why they were trying to enter the Democratic Party. Prathia Hall asked: "What do we intend to do concerning the existing structure [of the national Democratic Party]? Are we working within it in hopes of changing it?" Courtland Cox noted that they were "working within the Democratic Party because that's where the Negro is. It's practical." SNCC had to "move step by step." Doug Harris, a black staff member working in Mississippi, argued that running candidates would also educate local people. Charlie Cobb disagreed: There would be "negligible value in merely being part of the Democratic Party structure." Black officials could be manipulated by the national parties. At this point Bob Moses laid out his understanding of the challenge. "Our work with the convention challenge should at least give us an idea of what we do or don't understand" about current economic and political structures, he said. There was no danger that SNCC would be "sucked into the Democratic Party." The process of initiating the challenge would reveal dynamics they had not been able to see before. One example, he noted, was provided by sharecropper-turned-movement-activist Fannie Lou Hamer. Her campaign for Congress through the MFDP had embarrassed some blacks in Jackson, revealing class conflict among Afro-Mississippians. "She is too much of a representative of the masses [for elite blacks]," Moses observed. The whole endeavor, he suspected, might allow the emergence of a more concrete "definition of politics and economics," one that not just the usual black elite in Jackson participated in, but one that "everyone can understand."[60] The fact that SNCC staff did not see eye-to-eye on the purpose of the challenge from the beginning of the summer would have significant repercussions for the organization.

Nevertheless, voter registration was *the* primary work: forty-two of the forty-four Summer Projects engaged in this activity to strengthen the MFDP challenge. Canvassing thus formed the center of many volunteers' work. Decidedly unsensational, canvassing could be boring and repetitive to a maddening degree, and it rarely produced instant or tangible results. "There is nothing dramatic in the work" is the way volunteer Carol Rogoff described her daily routine. "It is canvassing from sunup to twilight, and then often a meeting in a church." Here, fear ruled. Stokely Carmichael captured the irony of the situation in a joke he repeated to the Greenwood office staff: "I was talking to a woman yesterday, trying to get her to go register, and she said, 'Our people are dirty, they don't go to school, they're lazy, they smell,' and that we weren't ready for the vote. We had to be more like white folks to be ready for the vote. 'That's right!' I said to her. 'We got to bomb their churches, shoot them at night, wear hoods, lynch them, beat on their heads, be just like they are, *then* we'll be ready for the vote!'" The depressing reality was that most people who were "canvassed" declined the opportunity to register. "When you ask a man to join you," asserted one worker, "you are asking for a confession that his life up until now has been lived upside down."[61]

Mechanics of the MFDP Challenge

In Jackson, preparations for the challenge, led by Dona Richards, Bob Moses, Casey Hayden, and Mendy Samstein, proceeded all summer. Mississippi had 1,884 voting precincts, and each precinct was supposed to elect a delegate to attend one of the eighty-two county conventions. Regular Democratic Party delegates were chosen in a series of elections that began at the county level. The county conventions then sent delegates to the five congressional district caucuses, which then selected smaller delegations to attend the state Democratic Party convention.[62]

To challenge the seating of the Mississippi delegates to the Democratic National Convention in Atlantic City, COFO would have to demonstrate that blacks in the state were denied entry to the Democratic Party precinct meetings scheduled to take place in June. Recruiting from their base, Moses and other staff explained at small house and church meetings that local blacks would need to find the precinct meeting place on 16 June 1964 at 10:00 A.M. — as specified by Democratic Party regulations — and then try to vote in them. Those who made these attempts discovered that three-quarters of the state's precincts did not actually hold meetings. In those that did meet, black citizens were allowed to attend ten of these meetings but were prohibited from voting, nominating delegates from the floor, or choosing people to tally the votes. Whites excluded blacks altogether at six precinct meetings.[63]

As SNCC and COFO expected, based on their three years' experience in trying to register blacks in Mississippi, white retaliation was swift. "I took those calls when they came in from the precincts," recalled Casey Hayden. "Many people suffered at those meetings physically." Going to the meetings "was a very, very dangerous thing to have done, and everybody who went knew that it was." Defenders of the all-white Democratic Party knew where the black activists lived, worked, and conducted their business. In ways hard for outsiders to grasp at the time, black Mississippians gambled their lives and those of their families for the right to be seated at the Democratic National Convention.[64]

Building the Mississippi Freedom Democratic Party

Local blacks had tried to participate directly in the regular Democratic Party, but the way was blocked at the local level. Statewide, black Mississippians affiliated with COFO now moved to phase two. According to state law and the by-laws of the national Democratic Party, they now had the right to establish their own party—the MFDP. Their first precinct meetings took place in late July, with 3,500 people participating.[65] Workers carefully followed regular Democratic Party regulations to protect the MFDP from accusations of electoral irregularities. In the precinct meetings, people learned firsthand the uncertainty and possibility of politics. For example, someone asks: "Well, if we are not going to support the regular party, what are we for? What should we recommend that our party stands for?" Someone else suggests, "Freedom." A third responds: "Well, I agree. But concretely, what do we stand for?" Talk continues, as people begin to formulate their ideas of what might be possible. "We want to elect some good people—our own people." A farmer suggests that black farmers must be on the federal ASCS board. Another counters that such an addition will be pointless unless farmers can escape the high interest rates charged by seed distributors and storage facilities. An old man gets carried away and stands to state clearly that the only solution is to take over the ASCS boards in every Mississippi county. Discussion continues: "How best can each child in the county be adequately fed?" "Getting the vote is the only way," they decide, and this declaration closes the first meeting. The repetition of such scenes throughout rural Mississippi in July 1964 formed a giant public experiment in popular politics.

Daily life in the MFDP built on thousands of such richly textured discussions, a politics unmatched anywhere else in the United States at the time. Each local group met to elect representatives to the county caucus and then to the state convention. COFO workers carefully documented every activity and filed affidavits with the Jackson office to send on to Atlantic City. The presence of terror required that each stage of the process be the focus of an immense, sustained organizing effort. When local whites learned that black people had gathered at local meetings, often the first question asked was: "Where did they meet?" As soon as someone said, "That little holiness church down Blue Lake Road," someone else said, "Well, let's go burn that thing down." Thirty-seven churches were burned that summer. Even though insurance companies often canceled the policies of other churches after such incidents, and movement workers had to find new places to meet, the violence only made people more determined.

In one case, after Dewey Greene Jr. of Greenwood applied to the University of Mississippi, night riders shot into his home. "But when they shot in my home they didn't dampen nothing," Dewey Sr. explained at the MFDP county convention. "Dewey Jr. was the only one then active in civil rights work. I have seven children. When you shot in there you got six more. The white people of this state shot me into politics. And to get me out, they'll have to shoot me out."

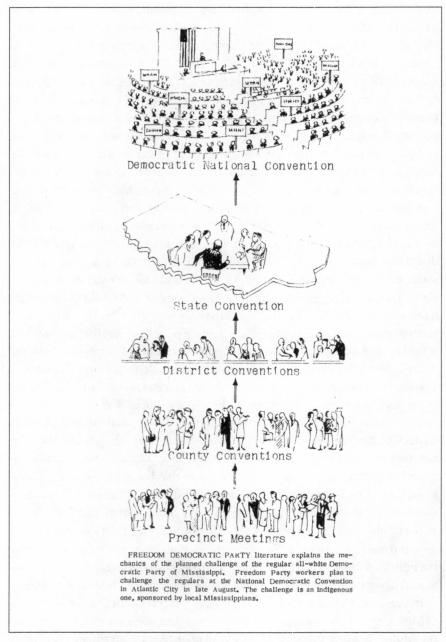

Democratic National Convention

State Convention

District Conventions

County Conventions

Precinct Meetings

FREEDOM DEMOCRATIC PARTY literature explains the mechanics of the planned challenge of the regular all-white Democratic Party of Mississippi. Freedom Party workers plan to challenge the regulars at the National Democratic Convention in Atlantic City in late August. The challenge is an indigenous one, sponsored by local Mississippians.

This diagram of how the MFDP would set up a parallel political organization in Mississippi was widely distributed in the spring and summer of 1964 among the disenfranchised in the state. (From *Student Voice*, courtesy of Dr. Clayborne Carson)

When it came time for the precinct members to elect delegates to represent them at the county convention, Greene received the most votes of anyone in the county — eighty-eight. "It was people taking on the system at the highest level," explained L. C. Dorsey. The national Democrats were the "folks who allowed people to be beaten to death, and shot, and lynched" and who had said nothing. By challenging the seating of the regular Mississippi Democrats, the MFDP might force the national party to finally address these outrages.[66]

As a mechanism for reaching into the whole population and catapulting ordinary people onto the "stage of history" for a sustained period of civic activity, there was nothing in the 1960s comparable to the MFDP. In November 1963's Freedom Vote, 83,000 blacks had registered; over 50,000 more registered with the party by the end of July 1964. These were people "who had not the slightest notion, including myself, of what the political arena was like," stated Victoria Gray, an MFDP leader from Hattiesburg. But they were "really out there, taking hold. They were setting up the precinct meetings, setting up the county meetings, setting up the district meetings. They, like us, knew that every step was taking us another step." To her, "it was heart-warming to see these MFDP people." Endesha Ida Mae Holland, a young COFO worker from Greenwood, remembered telling people, "If we can stick together, then we can take the seats up at the convention." She kept repeating to her neighbor: "They're gonna seat you all, Ms. Haynes." Summer volunteers supplied additional labor, working in areas as yet untouched by COFO and helping the MFDP to become a statewide organization by the fall.[67]

Over eight hundred delegates from forty Mississippi counties attended the MFDP state convention in Jackson on 6 August. Each delegate embodied the triumph of self-determination — or citizenship — over the cultural forces of white supremacy and the political forces of terror. In the words of historian John Dittmer, "The sight of delegates arriving from such embattled outposts as Ruleville and Liberty inspired all who attended." Victoria Gray recalled that "walking into the hall that Sunday morning, and seeing all these people here — and how pleased they were, and how proud they were with themselves and each other was just one fantastic reward for all the risk that had been taken up until that time." The MFDP convention elected forty-four delegates and twenty-four alternates — sixty-four blacks and four whites — to the Democratic National Convention in Atlantic City. "The sharecroppers, the maids, the *people*. Those who always looked elsewhere for their leadership, always looked to other people for their leadership."[68]

Now they were looking at themselves. The convention had nominated sixty-eight people to represent them. Soon the nation would hear from the officially unregistered voters who called themselves the Mississippi Freedom Democratic Party.[69] This rare and rich experiment in democracy — a political party assembled by the people themselves — went off to the national convention of the nation's oldest political party. There the MFDP delegates would encounter the limits of that institution's tolerance for democratic change.

PART FOUR
MOVEMENT
ECOLOGY

Contact with Power
Atlantic City

August 1964. In the sweep of four hundred years of American history, that single month was bizarre, excessive, and altogether unprecedented. August 1964 produced high achievement and shocking murders; enhanced expectations and abrupt, dismaying tragedy; and finally, an explosion of anger that poured up out of a funeral service in Neshoba County, Mississippi, and flowed into the towns and cities of America.

On 4 August 1964 three young civil rights workers—James Chaney, Mickey Schwerner, and Andrew Goodman—were found buried in an earthen dam five miles outside of Philadelphia, Mississippi. The night after the emotional high point of the summer—the MFDP's state convention in Jackson—Chaney was laid to rest in his hometown of Meridian, Mississippi. The service remained sedate and mournful until Dave Dennis, the medium-tall, light-eyed assistant director of the Summer Project, stood to give the eulogy. Dennis's persistence and attention to detail made him indispensable that summer. Having grown up near Shreveport, Louisiana, in an extended family that relished down-home cooking and wry humor, Dennis possessed a quiet, earthy manner and low-key wit that had served him well through countless crises on rural voter registration projects in Louisiana and Mississippi over the past four years. So he seemed well placed to follow the composed tone that started off Chaney's memorial. In fact, representatives of CORE's national office approached him before the service "to make sure that the speech given [would be] calm." There was a basic concern "about cooling things down because the country was angry," recalled Dennis. But as he waited for his turn to speak in the small Baptist church, he caught the eye of Chaney's eleven-year-old brother, Ben. An anger welled up inside, Dennis said, and his usually gentle manner and kind expression grew hard. "I was in a fantasy world, to be sitting up here talking about things gonna get better, and we should do it in an easy manner, with nonviolence." The America that he had known "operated then, and still operates, on violence. It's an eye for an eye, a tooth for a tooth. That's what we respect. So I just stopped and said what I felt. There was no need to stand in front of that kid Ben Chaney and lie to him." Nonviolence was never easy for its practitioners: Dennis was not saying it was. He did, however, want to make whites suffer the way James Chaney had suffered. Nonviolence, he asserted, was too easy for the whites toward whom it was directed.[1]

Through death, Chaney had gotten his freedom, Dennis began. "But we are still fighting for it." Dennis lambasted "the living dead" — the governor of Mississippi, the president, and other officials in Washington, D.C. These people, he charged, were just as responsible for Chaney's death as the men who pulled the trigger. "I'm sick and tired of going to the funerals of black men who have been murdered by white men," he thundered. "I've got vengeance in my heart tonight, and I ask you to feel angry with me!" He turned to the local people in the audience. "Don't just look at me and go back and tell folks you've been to a nice service." No longer could they "take what these white men in Mississippi are doing to us. . . . If you take it and don't do something about it . . . then God Damn your souls!"

COFO staffers, who had traveled from across the state to attend the service, responded keenly to this call of anguish. For years Dennis had been canvassing house by house, encouraging people to walk through the violence that kept Mississippi's county courthouses all white. He, Bob Moses, and others had imported northern white volunteers just so the killing of black citizens might stop. How could he continue to encourage black Mississippians to vote if the federal government would not enforce its laws, even when two white northerners were killed alongside Chaney? A central tenet of nonviolence — that the movement's capacity to suffer would eventually overcome the ability of the oppressors to hurt people — did not suffice under such circumstances, he argued.[2]

Public disclosure of various details of the Chaney case drove home Dennis's point. Unlike Schwerner and Goodman, who died from bullet wounds, it appeared to them that whites had literally beaten Chaney to death. The autopsy report noted that his "jaw was shattered, the left shoulder and upper arm were reduced to a pulp; the right forearm was broken completely across at several points, and the skull bones were broken and pushed in towards the brain," reported Dr. David Spain of the University of Mississippi Medical School Hospital. Spain concluded that "these injuries could only be the result of an extremely severe beating with either a blunt instrument or chain. The other fractures of the skull and ribs were the result of bullet wounds. It is impossible to determine whether the deceased died from the beating before the bullet wounds were inflicted." He added that in his "extensive experience of 25 years as a Pathologist and as a Medical Examiner, I have never witnessed bones so severely shattered, except in tremendously high speed accidents such as aeroplane crashes." Etching this evidence of depravity more clearly in the minds of movement activists, an FBI informer revealed that Chaney, Schwerner, and Goodman had met their deaths still trying to make what James Lawson called the vital human connection. As the three sat trapped in a police cruiser, Klansman Alton Wayne Roberts cursed his more hesitant comrades, bursting by them to pull Mickey Schwerner from the car. Roberts shoved a pistol into Schwerner's ribs, shouting, "'Are you that nigger lover?'" In the last moment remaining to him, Schwerner replied, "'Sir, I know just how you feel.'"[3]

Such reports prompted expressions of outrage and disgust as well as desperation so intense that it surfaced as brooding silence. In the weeks prior to the recovery of the bodies, anxiety-ridden stories on television, radio, and magazines across the nation had covered the long search for the three men. A national searchlight had fixed on the Magnolia State. Now that no one in the nation could deny the high price Freedom Democrats paid for their efforts, federal inaction was exceptionally galling. This, of course, was not true for seasoned activists, who had years of experience with the callous disregard of U.S. officialdom. White supremacist media coverage, "at its most blatant," recalled summer volunteer Sally Belfrage, "produced such references as on a northern network news program recapitulating 'the murders of Andrew Goodman' — cut to picture of Andrew, long pause; 'Michael Schwerner' — picture of Mickey, pause; 'and a Mississippi Negro youth.' For James, no picture, no name."[4]

The Johnson administration was not moved by the high-profile challenge of the Mississippi Freedom Democratic Party to the regular Democratic Party process. Cautious ambiguity marked the statements of officials within important sectors of the national party, including the labor movement and traditional black leadership. Indeed, nothing illustrated the fragility of the MFDP's position better than signs of equivocation in other quarters, namely the camp of Lyndon Johnson's likely running mate, Hubert H. Humphrey, who no longer appeared to be the same man who had stood resolutely against the Dixiecrat challenge in 1948.[5]

At the end of the summer, with emotional and political momentum building nationwide, Mississippi locals, summer volunteers, and COFO staffers focused on the Democratic National Convention in Atlantic City, New Jersey. If they could compel the party to open itself to Mississippi blacks, perhaps Chaney, Goodman, and Schwerner, as well as Herbert Lee and Louis Allen, would not have died in vain. While tensions within the Mississippi movement remained taut and sometimes fierce, people hung together in the hope that success in Atlantic City would ease the strains on all of them and justify the cost that participation exacted. In the final weeks leading up to the convention, few if any civil rights workers had a chance to assess the summer's developments or to explore the increasing complexity of their social relations. The timetable of the convention prevented a serious look at those dynamics. Thus saddled, the MFDP delegation — and the Mississippi movement and SNCC staff with it — headed for Atlantic City.

Bob Moses initially kept everyone on the SNCC staff focused. At the time, Casey Hayden — who had worked with him all summer — called Moses "a genius in the way he could simply just cut to the chase. He would just blow everything off, except what was really happening." Uppermost in Moses' mind was, of course, the outcome of the convention. Would the MFDP delegates be seated? Could they do anything at this point to ensure success? The groundwork for this challenge had been laid by those who paid the physical cost of a beating, a lost job, or a canceled mortgage. These sacrifices towered in the minds of many MFDP delegates traveling to the convention. With thirty-seven black churches destroyed, thirty black-owned homes and buildings bombed or burned, five civil rights workers dead, over one thousand arrested, and eighty brutally beaten, how could a rational, moral citizenry *not* seat the MFDP? As Moses said to the delegates assembled before the convention, "I don't think that if this issue gets to the floor of that convention that they can possibly turn [you] down. I don't see how they possibly can do it if they really understand what's at stake."[6]

Atlantic City

How participants (and subsequent historians) approached the volatile events in Atlantic City was a function of their point of view. Seen from the standpoint of power — the Johnson administration — the terror that constantly confronted black attempts to overthrow the southern caste system was destroying the white Democratic Party that had ruled the region since the end of Reconstruction. It was an unworkable politics, a litany of the past — ineffective in the short term and doomed in the long term. Yet, inasmuch as the one-party South routinely cast its votes for the Democratic presidential ticket, anything that altered the status quo was a threat to Johnson's reelection. In contrast, movement people saw Atlantic City as a beckoning future that heightened both their confidence and their anxiety.

In the end, for those in the Mississippi movement, two significant aspects of the Atlantic City events stood out: the outcome and the process that led to it. The outcome was simple enough: the Democratic Party offered the MFDP a Two-Seat Compromise.[7] This consisted of two "at large" votes, rather than seats in Mississippi's state delegation. And these two votes were to go to delegates Aaron Henry, the black gubernatorial candidate, and Ed King, a white chaplain from Tougaloo College in Jackson.[8] The MFDP delegates, not surprisingly to those inside the movement, turned down the offer, choosing to forgo participation in the convention rather than accede to what they perceived as an illegal and unjust procedure.[9]

Democratic Party regulars — as well as most political commentators nationwide — could not comprehend the reasons for the MFDP's rejection of the Two-Seat Compromise. Later, some observers suggested that MFDP delegates did not appreciate what they were offered. Reasonable people could differ, and, in the conventional wisdom, the way to resolve such differences was compromise — the core political activity in a democracy. To spurn such negotiations was irresponsible.[10]

To understand why the MFDP rejected the Two-Seat Compromise, then, one must consider the process by which it came about. Both the party regulars who supported the proposal and the MFDP insurgents who rejected it made points that each side felt were valid. Moses, the chief negotiator for the Freedom Democrats, wanted all sixty-eight MFDP delegates to be involved in any meetings between the MFDP and representatives of the national Democratic Party. Otherwise, how could the MFDP delegates reach consensus on whether to accept any compromise? Each MFDP delegate needed to be included in the sharing of information that took place between Freedom Democrats and party regulars.

Moses also believed that such information sharing was essential to the Mississippians' political education: by talking with and listening to national party representatives, they would learn how to sit at the table and negotiate with people who had power. In essence, they would learn — at yet another level — how to share power and govern themselves. If self-respecting people are not allowed to sit at the table and to share power, the only alternative left to them is, as James Forman would say later, to knock the legs off of that table.[11]

Moses' understanding of democratic dialogue was far more inclusive than the view held by party regulars. He also had a vivid picture of the psychological needs of the MFDP delegates. As he later wrote, the small meetings and workshops in rural Mississippi had opened space "within the Black community where people could stand up and speak, or in groups outline their concerns. In them, folks were feeling themselves out, learning how to use words to articulate what they wanted and needed." At Atlantic City, "they were asking the national Democratic Party whether it would be willing to empower people in their meetings in a similar way."[12] But the representatives of the national party only wanted to meet with the delegation's so-called male leaders — Moses, Aaron Henry, and Joseph L. "Joe" Rauh, the Washington lawyer and longtime Democratic Party activist whom Moses invited to represent the MFDP at the convention. "We felt there was no reason why the [MFDP] delegation couldn't sit in session," said Moses. "They were there, they had nothing else to do, and they could all sit, while we all talked and hashed out all the matters." After all, he and the other organizers saw the creation of the entire MFDP as "a process of education for the delegates, and so what better education than for them to sit through those meetings and find out, and try to hash through themselves? And the more people who were educated by that, the wider the fallout when you got back to Mississippi." Negotiating behind closed doors also contradicted the primary goal the MFDP (and SNCC) was fighting for: opening up the political process and the institutions of the country to all interested U.S. citizens.[13] Thus, the first significant development of the convention was that those negotiating for the national Democratic Party refused to include all of the MFDP delegates in the negotiations.

The second development was the reaction of the national Democrats to the evidence that the Freedom Democrats had marshaled on their own behalf. People in the Jackson SNCC office like Moses, Dona Richards, Casey Hayden, and Mendy Samstein had carefully followed the letter of the law in every phase of the MFDP challenge. They had brought to Atlantic City documentation gathered from people in the field and placed it in numerous file cabinets on the floor of the convention. Inside the drawers were thousands of affidavits attesting to people's attempts to register to vote and to attend Democratic Party precinct meetings. These sworn statements bore witness to the violence that had met black citizens in their quest for political inclusion.[14] The ruthless brutality attacking these civic assertions was clearly shown not only in affidavits but also by the more immediately compelling testimony of delegates Fannie Lou Hamer and Annie Devine, who described in person the terror they had undergone.[15] The MFDP delegates had traveled to the national convention to appear united behind Hamer and Devine as they stood to share the experiences of 93 percent of the adult blacks in Mississippi who met voting requirements but were denied the right to register and vote in the state. "Our position was valid and our cause was just," said Charles Sherrod. "No human being confronted with the truth of our testimony could remain indifferent to it."[16]

In hindsight, it is possible to see that it was the MFDP's careful adherence to Democratic Party rules that prompted such a strong Democratic counter-reaction and the party's decision to marginalize Mississippi's black representatives. In Jackson, Rauh had told the MFDP delegates that they needed only 11 votes of the 110-member Credentials Committee to take the issue to the convention floor, and only 8 states had to wave their placards to force a roll-call vote. When Hamer started shouting "Eleven and eight!" at the Jackson convention, others followed. President Johnson, Rauh later claimed, boiled over: He determined to stonewall the MFDP so that its challenge would never leave the Credentials Committee. Johnson swore to Rauh's boss, Walter Reuther: "'You tell that bastard god damn lawyer friend of yours that there ain't gonna be all that eleven and eight shit at the [Atlantic City] convention.'" Johnson would let nothing interfere with his coronation as presidential nominee in his own right. This, according to Walter Jenkins, Johnson's administrative assistant, made the MFDP challenge "the most important single issue" of the convention for the president.[17]

Johnson knew that if the MFDP had a chance to lay out its meticulously gathered evidence on the floor, the convention would vote to seat it. Johnson ordered his aides to stall for time. The president's team became a whirring hive of workers, calling in favors, large and small. The goal was to prevent the MFDP's story from getting out of the Credentials Committee — where the black delegates first had to present their case — and onto the convention floor, where delegates from all fifty states would hear it.[18]

At the same time, the FBI sent a special squad to the convention, wiretapping not only Martin Luther King's hotel room, but also the SNCC headquarters. Neither wiretap was specifically authorized by the attorney general. A Senate committee later investigating similar illegalities discovered that at the 1964 Atlantic City convention, Jenkins received extensive intelligence reports from the FBI surveillance operation, amounting to a steady stream of reports on SNCC's strategy in the struggle to seat the MFDP delegation. Jenkins passed this information directly to Johnson, who was then privy to "the most intimate details of the plans of individuals supporting the MFDP's challenge."[19]

As Joe Rauh later observed, "politics is a tough game. The president has more strength than everybody else put together at his re-nomination convention." Rauh was a leading Democrat in his own right — he had clerked for Supreme Court justices, served as general counsel for the United Automobile Workers, formed a close association with Hubert Humphrey, and recently finished a stint as head of the Americans for Democratic Action. For a time prior to the convention, he felt the MFDP had a chance to be seated. "We've got such a wonderful case against the other side, I told them we were going to win." On the boardwalk outside the convention hall, the MFDP parked the burned-out Ford station wagon that Chaney, Schwerner, and Goodman had been driving the day they were killed, alongside the bell from the church set afire in Philadelphia, Mississippi. In front of these graphic reminders of the cost of their quest for full citizenship, MFDP delegates stood every day, greeting other state delegations on their way into the hall. Aaron Henry recalled Rauh as a bit more pessimistic: Rauh, Henry said, told the MFDP delegates at the beginning of August that it would be very hard to get President Johnson to go along with the MFDP challenge. Still, Rauh contended in a speech inside the convention: "The Democratic Party has won over the years when it stood fast for principle. It cannot win this time by hauling down the flag [of principle]. . . . Your choice comes down to whether you vote for the power structure of Mississippi that is responsible for the death of those three boys, or whether you vote for the people for whom those three boys gave their lives." "We had anticipated appealing to the conscience of America, and America would stand up and say, 'No more, Mississippi,'" recalled summer volunteer Cleveland Sellers. Before the MFDP ever addressed the Credentials Committee, nine Democratic delegations and twenty-five members of Congress supported its seating as the official Mississippi delegation.[20]

Nonetheless, Johnson and his aides eventually prevailed — at least in part. The MFDP's challenge never got out of the Credentials Committee. The convention, however, did fulfill the goals Ella Baker had laid out in her keynote speech to the state MFDP convention in Jackson: she had urged MFDP delegates to treat the national convention as a classroom and to learn as much as possible. Significantly, she advocated the election of delegates who would remain loyal to the interests of the majority of the state's black people — the rural poor — rather than the interests of the black elite. And indeed, Atlantic City was an enormous national classroom for civil rights people — in both the MFDP and SNCC. As Aaron Henry remembered, "We did all we could and learned a great deal about the way things work up in the world of high-level politics — heartbreak and all." The Sunday evening before the convention opened, all of the black Democrats from other states' delegations met, Sherrod reported, "somewhat secret[ly]," at the Deauville Hotel. The black MFDP delegates had not been invited, but they were not turned away. "In a small, crowded, dark room with a long table and a blackboard, some of the most prominent Negro politicians in the country gave the 'word,' one by one," Sherrod recalled. Charles Dawson, the "black dean of politics," made the final statement. "We must nominate Lyndon B. Johnson," he said, as well as register more blacks to vote, and "we must follow leadership."[21]

At that point, Annie Devine of the MFDP asked to speak. "We have been treated like beasts in Mississippi," she told the room. "They shot us down like animals. We risk our lives coming up here. . . . Politics must be corrupt if it don't care none about people down there. . . . These politicians sit in positions and forget the people [who] put them there." As she continued to talk, tears of agony and frustration coursed down her face. Instead of rallying behind Devine's call to remain loyal to the nation's ideals, or to the people the delegates represented, the meeting was adjourned. There was no further action on the part of regular black Democrats to support the MFDP.[22]

The experience shattered many assumptions held by the MFDP. Sherrod recognized that black groups in other parts of the nation "had no power; they could show no power. One would suspect that it is part of the system to give [people these] positions [as] meaningless labels and withhold the real power. This is the story of the bond between our country and its black children."[23]

Finding themselves thus alone, the MFDP began to struggle in a "life-death grip, wrestling with the best political strategists in the country." Of these strategists, none was more talented or ferocious than the president himself. Arriving before the convention started, the MFDP secured verbal agreements from four times the number of people it needed on the Credentials Committee to guarantee a minority report, which would have brought the issue to the convention floor. In large part, this was a result of Ella Baker's hard work over the summer. As denim-clad COFO workers canvassed the back roads of Mississippi, she had put on her respectable gray suit and visited members of Congress, civil rights leaders, and stalwarts of the labor movement in her extensive political network to make sure the MFDP would receive a fair hearing in Atlantic City. Yet Johnson's men engineered a postponement of the initial vote.[24]

The president's aides then went to work on the people who had committed themselves to vote for the MFDP. As Fannie Lou Hamer said later, even Joe Rauh changed sides. Rauh approached her with "tears in his eyes and said: 'If this fight goes to the floor, [Humphrey] won't be nominated tonight for Vice President.'" Hamer asked Rauh if that meant Humphrey's position was "more important than 400,000 lives."[25] The answer appeared to be yes. "All of a sudden, we started getting all these reports back that people were having to change," recalled Marshall Ganz. A summer volunteer from California, Ganz had lobbied the delegates from his home state particularly hard. One of them, a black woman, "broke down crying after she'd been visited by one of the Democratic powers that be," said Ganz. She was "told that her husband was up for a judgeship, and she could just forget it if she voted for the FDP. Welcome to the real world of Democratic politics," Ganz bitterly summarized. A black congressman approached Courtland Cox, Bob Moses, Dona Richards Moses, and Fannie Lou Hamer and asked for the list of delegates on the Credentials Committee whom they believed were solidly behind the MFDP challenge. "Do you think this man is going to steal this list?" Cox asked Moses, who was reluctant to part with the names. But the congressman said he wanted to give the list to the Credentials Committee chair, David Lawrence, to demonstrate the MFDP's strength. Cox, who later felt he had been "ignorant," encouraged Moses to hand over the list. "What happened next was something unbelievable," Cox remembered. "Every person on that list, every member of that credentials committee who was going to vote for the minority, got a call." Loans, appointments, and other benefits the Democrats could deliver were threatened unless the committeeperson withdrew support for the MFDP. With such pressure, Johnson's aides cut the original number of supporters in half by Sunday. By Tuesday, only ten delegates remained committed to provide a minority report—one short of the eleven needed to bring the MFDP's case to the floor. "We can sit at home in Mississippi and watch things from the [segregated] balcony," Aaron Henry thundered. "But we will not accept that here!"[26]

In offering the MFDP the consolation of two seats "at large," the Johnson administration gave its sixty-eight delegates "seven hours to examine the compromise," Sherrod reported. Within that limited time, they had to "think about it, accept or reject it, propose the appropriate action, and do what was necessary to implement it." Many national leaders gave input, including Martin Luther King, Bayard Rustin, Senator Wayne Morse, Congresswoman Edith Green, and James Farmer. Speaking for SNCC were James Forman, Ella Baker, and Bob Moses. "Time had made the decision," Sherrod felt. "The day was fast spent" by the time discussion was opened to the delegation. Still, the Freedom Democrats rejected the Two-Seat Compromise.[27]

Despite this setback, the MFDP challenge had significant long-term results. First, the Atlantic City convention changed the guidelines by which all future state delegations could be admitted. By 1968, all delegations to the Democratic National Convention had to have a ratio of minority delegates to white delegates proportional to the state's overall racial composition. Each delegation had to pledge to support the national Democratic platform.[28] Even though the 1964 challenge did not succeed, black Mississippians still had their own institution—the MFDP—through which they could attempt to reorganize political life in the state. Most important, the MFDP challenge had given Mississippi blacks yet another democratic experience on which to build. "Going to the convention was an attempt to put the nation on the spot," recalled Holly Springs teenager Roy DeBerry. "At the very least, we could ask Lyndon Johnson to do what we thought was right, which was to unseat the regular Mississippi delegation and to seat the MFDP. I don't think we felt that was actually going to happen, but just going through the process itself was good." It gave African Americans like himself "an opportunity to participate in the political process at a level that we had not participated in before." Hamer, for example, asked Ella Baker, Jim Forman, and Bob Moses how they felt about the Two-Seat Compromise. Whatever they would have said, she remembered in 1966, she respected them enough to follow their advice. "They told me, I'll never forget this, everyone would say almost the same thing. 'Now look Mrs. Hamer, you're the people living in Mississippi. We don't have to tell you nothing, you make your own decision.'" Hamer paused, emphasizing the tremendous impact that reaction from the SNCC people had made on her. "See, we'd never been allowed to do that before."[29]

Hamer had testified before the Credentials Committee that if the MFDP delegation was not seated, she questioned the very foundation of the nation.[30] After all, according to the U.S. Constitution, sovereignty rested with the people. If the government colluded in the denial of voting rights to citizens, this violated the basic rules of the nation's political system. The MFDP challenge presented a philosophical question as well as a structural one: When should democracies compromise, and at what point should they refuse to engage with an authoritarian system operating from within?

Hamer and other MFDP delegates were not naïve; they understood the Democratic Party process all too well. But they had too much self-respect to accept a compromise that betrayed the sacrifice represented by the loaded file cabinets on the convention floor.[31]

At the time, print and TV commentators portrayed the MFDP's refusal of the Two-Seat Compromise as a sign of the delegates' naïveté, "as people who didn't understand the political process," Moses summarized, "and therefore brought tactics from the sit-in movement into a place where they didn't apply." Milton Viorst, for example, wrote: "What Moses chose not to take into account were the processes of democratic politics. His was a position of moral absolutism, which the MFDP believed it had earned during the Summer Project. This view may have had a place in abstract philosophy, but not in the political system. Moses' answer was to drop out of the system." Such responses were not only facile and condescending; they were, in their own right, deeply naïve. Moses was not trying to get the regular Democrats to recognize the moral nature of the MFDP's cause; rather, he was asking them to follow their own rules. The fact that this point was still widely misinterpreted years later speaks to the enormous burden of communication placed on the MFDP and SNCC — at the time and subsequently. And the claim that the MFDP was unwilling or too naïve to compromise is belied by the fact that its delegates were willing to go along with another alternative, the Green Compromise. Representative Edith Green of Oregon had suggested that half of the seats go to the regular Mississippi Democrats and half to the MFDP.[32] This was not pie-in-the-sky, hand-wringing romantic liberalism but a workable proposal that Johnson elected to brush aside.

Johnson's rejection of the Green Compromise opened up the progressive wing of the Democratic Party to accusations of betrayal from within the movement. Bayard Rustin, Martin Luther King, James Farmer, and Joe Rauh, all of whom had urged the MFDP to accept the Two-Seat Compromise, had to endure this charge repeatedly in the years that followed.[33] But the lesson for the MFDP was that there was room in the nation's Democratic Party for some people and not others. Roy Wilkins, chair of the NAACP, made this painfully clear to Fannie Lou Hamer in Atlantic City. "'Mrs. Hamer, you people have put your point across,'" he told her. "'You're ignorant, you don't know anything about politics. I have been in the business over twenty years. You have put your point across, now why don't you pack up and go home?'" Compared to the reaction of Ella Baker, James Forman, and other SNCC people, the attitudes of President Johnson and Wilkins sobered everyone. As Moses recalled of Aaron Henry and Ed King, "the professional people within our group were asked to become part and actually did become part of the Democratic Party." Significantly, however, the Democrats did not allow participation of "the sharecroppers, the laborers, the day workers." There was room for the latter "as recipients of largesse — poverty programs and the like," but not to share in real decision-making.[34]

SNCC and MFDP people understood that the real issues of the 1964 convention — how to integrate the citizens in Mississippi who had been disenfranchised for a hundred years — were simply not on the table. The larger public, including nearly all members of the media and Congress, did not understand this. The contrast between SNCC and MFDP's private knowledge and the larger society's ignorance frames a recurring paradox in U.S. history. Small "d" democrats reach for greater implementation of the nation's credo and are rejected, even as their efforts alter the structure of the dominant politics. After all, the MFDP did set the stage for the Democratic Party to eject segregationists at the 1968 convention. The MFDP constructed a concrete political institution that *was* able to confront the national Democratic Party — and the latter could no longer live with the stain of racist disfranchisement. It was an extraordinary accomplishment. But in the short term, MFDP workers had little to show for their sacrifice. SNCC worker Maria Varela remembered coming "back from Atlantic City, crowned in powerlessness," to face "evictions of striking cotton pickers and old people freezing to death under damp flour-sack sheets, the Klan still riding in celebration of Goodman, Chaney and Schwerner," while SNCC tried "to start all over again on lonely plantation roads."[35]

Johnson's landslide victory over Barry Goldwater in November 1964 could not be taken as the crowning defeat of Jim Crow. That work clearly remained to be done. In the short run, the doors to meaningful national political participation for southern blacks remained shut.[36] Thus, when SNCC activists gathered in the Mississippi Gulf Coast town of Waveland after the election, everyone understood it was time for the movement to take stock of itself. Few could imagine how agonizingly difficult that task would prove to be. For better or for worse, the effective grassroots phase of the Afro-American freedom movement now encountered a defining crossroads.

CHAPTER TEN

Desperate Initiatives
Waveland

As waves gently lapped at the dock, a dozen SNCC workers lounged on the weathered pier, staring at the stars and drinking red wine. Stokely Carmichael began one of his stand-up routines, poking gentle fun at his comrades and himself. The activists allowed the peaceful night to seep into them, soothing the scars from verbal confrontations during the day. They were all participants in the major SNCC staff meeting at Waveland, Mississippi, which provided a snapshot of their collective mind in the second week of November 1964. For many, the scene on the dock marked the last time SNCC staff found a way to come back together in song and mutual harmony after a day of fierce disagreements. This cohesion had been an innovative and essential feature of SNCC's democratic culture. The disintegration of this culture, one black woman staffer later wrote, left the circle broken.[1]

What happened inside SNCC? The morale of SNCC's key organizers had deteriorated and their anxieties had increased in the political aftermath of the Democratic National Convention. Voter registration efforts no longer seemed to offer a clear path to SNCC's strategic goals. Veteran organizers sent frantic memos between projects and began to engage in debates, some of which became increasingly acrimonious. A longtime SNCC supporter, entertainer Harry Belafonte read the signs and worried about burnout. He arranged for a number of SNCC's most engaged people to accompany him to Africa, where Bob Moses, James Forman, John Lewis, Fannie Lou Hamer, and other activists visited Guinea as the personal guests of President Sékou Touré.[2]

Meanwhile, SNCC's central office in Atlanta decided to hold several day-long staff meetings during September and October. These initiatives failed to revive the group. After the October meeting ended in gridlock, the Atlanta staff scheduled a week-long "reassessment" conference at the seaside campground facility at Waveland, Mississippi, in November.

At Waveland, people faced the realization that SNCC had reached an impasse. Some perceived "structural problems" traceable to confusion over program — a matter of deciding what to do next. For others, it was the sober reality that funds for field staff had almost dried up. For some, SNCC's tradition of improvisation threatened to become a license for aimlessness. Finally, quite a few people believed, uneasily, that SNCC had a race problem.

In preparation for Waveland, the Atlanta office called for position papers; over forty offerings were submitted on topics ranging from how SNCC's executive board should be chosen, to the proper place of women in the organization, to the role of education in organizing. While the number of participants fluctuated over the course of the retreat, between 80 to 140 people attended. Unlike the excitement and expectation characterizing the founding conference at Raleigh's Shaw University, or the bustle and energy of the gatherings leading up to the Summer Project, the interactions at Waveland included accusations of stealing one another's personal property and snubs aimed at old friends. At bottom, though, the conference was permeated with the tension over what to do next.

By no means were all the vibrations negative. The 1964 Civil Rights Act was the first real breakthrough since Reconstruction and the repression of voter registration made the entire country see for the first time the need to protect access to the ballot box in states of the former Confederacy. Movement activists were fairly confident that 1965 would see a comprehensive Voting Rights Act. Indeed, several people closely associated with the Mississippi Freedom Democratic Party regarded Atlantic City as a mere bump in the road — at worst a setback and certainly not a crisis. MFDP chairman Lawrence Guyot even considered it a success: "Despite the Convention's decision, Atlantic City was for us a great victory, because for the first time it told our story to the country and demonstrated our growing strength."[3]

It turned out that the voter registration projects that had matured between 1962 and 1964 created two distinct drives among organizers. The first focused on rank-and file residents: to live among the people and, by example and daily association, encourage them to see themselves as full citizens and to act on that understanding. This was the one sure way black Americans, by themselves, could destroy Jim Crow. The second objective was to compel the federal government to enforce its own laws in Mississippi. This entailed setting up a comprehensive system to keep the Justice Department constantly informed about voter registration abuses, alerting the ICC about Jim Crow transportation, and urging the Federal Communications Commission (FCC) to investigate violations of its equal-time policy on the airwaves. Charles McLaurin had posed a question about these two drives at the beginning of the summer: "What are we trying to do, develop Freedom Schools and work on voter registration, or get the federal government involved and open the eyes of the nation?" While the two objectives seemed distinct, in practice they were interwoven because the continued failure of the federal government to protect the right to vote threatened the entire cultural and political campaign against segregation. As movement experience demonstrated, when law enforcement did not protect voter registration campaigns, people like Herbert Lee and Louis Allen were murdered. Beyond this awesome truth, which the nation did not yet grasp, virtually the entire black population was exposed to physical beatings and to threats against their homes, their education, and their livelihood. McLaurin contended that if the goal was federal involvement, SNCC needed to go into places where there was certain to be violence against the student workers. White staffers should try to organize in white communities: "We should send whites into new communities where [white retaliatory] violence will occur." The failure of the Democratic Party to seat the MFDP in Atlantic City appeared to endorse — and, in fact, reinforce — the inaction of federal law enforcement. For SNCC chairman John Lewis as well as for the newest recruits on the field staff, what Atlantic City proved, once again, was that the caste system was still embedded in American society.[4]

If Washington was not going to protect voter registration or allow meaningful black participation in the Democratic Party, how could a registration campaign remain the major focus of SNCC work? SNCC could not have foreseen the massive opening for southern black political participation that would follow the 1965 Voting Rights Act. President Johnson had given no indication that this would be a priority. (Still, as SNCC historian Hasan Jeffries noted, after August 1965, Attorney General Nicholas Katzenbach dispatched federal registrars to less than 1 percent of the Mississippi counties that ought to have received them according to the 1965 Voting Rights Act.)[5]

For SNCC's Atlanta-based executive director, James Forman, the answer began with putting aside the organization's experimental tradition. Forman made this objective unmistakable by taking over the podium and delivering a formal speech at the opening of the Waveland retreat. SNCC conferences had rarely started this way, but Forman offered an arresting point of departure. Handsome, tall, and burly in his denim overalls, Forman had a penetrating voice and his authoritative certainty rang through the hall. SNCC revered Forman: he had served as mentor to many and encouraged every SNCC participant to find and develop personal strengths. He had always made sure people felt included. Bob Zellner remembered first meeting Forman in Atlanta: "'It's your turn on the broom,'" Forman greeted him, laying the broom handle in Zellner's palm. An advocate for many SNCC staffers, Forman by 1964 had become a constant, solid presence in Atlanta. When he rose to speak at Waveland, no one questioned his right or his purpose.[6]

But many SNCC people looked at each other curiously, "What is Jim doing?" "Where is this coming from?" "Where's our dialogue?" Forman believed that the aimlessness and confusion that beset the organization was caused by its decentralized structure. SNCC needed to "alter the over-all decision-making body within the organization, for the organization has been in limbo, because of the unresolved nature of this question." SNCC lacked leadership because its people continued to shy away from power, he said. SNCC was a vanguard institution, and Forman, for one, believed in vanguards. The only way it could maintain internal cohesion and unity was to establish a strong centralized executive structure.[7]

It proved too much to ask. Forman's proposed alteration of the movement's trajectory did more than contrast with SNCC's traditions, it contradicted them in a fundamental way.[8] Thus, from the outset, the organizers who founded and nurtured SNCC's flagship projects backed away from Forman's approach. Prominent among them were Bob Moses in the Mississippi Delta, Charles Sherrod in southwest Georgia, and Charles McDew, who preceded John Lewis as chairman of SNCC. Many other well-known local organizers, like Charles McLaurin and Hollis Watkins, also failed to rally to Forman's call. Nonetheless, SNCC's executive secretary was tenacious. Participants soon discovered that Forman was doing more than floating a trial balloon with his opening speech; when support failed to materialize, he tried again the next day and the day after. And he kept trying — throughout the Waveland conference and, as events unfolded, throughout 1965 and into 1966.

No one wanted to be seen participating in a public rebuke of this committed son of the movement. Yet Forman's unwillingness to acknowledge the absence of support for his position created a logjam. In response to his persistent call for a centralized structure, what surfaced instead was the staff's resolve to continue experiments at the grass roots. Sherrod's driving imperative was to determine whether SNCC people could agree on short- and long-range goals: What do we want? By what principles should we live? What is worth dying for?[9]

Sherrod's prerequisite for decision-making did not start at the top: "Who we are and who we will be should determine what we want, and what direction we go in." It could not be a centralized structure. "The problems we are facing are not problems of organization, but ideology." Insisting that rank-and-file southerners be included in any community decision-making associated with

SNCC, Sherrod consciously employed down-home idioms to illustrate the intelligence of black Georgians as part of the coming new America: "We must," he explained, "demand that the new society of democracy for which we strive be based on the wisdom of the pinched toe and the empty belly." A man may not know how to make a pair of shoes, but he was "not so ignorant that he doesn't know when a pair of shoes pinches him, or that the roof leaks or that white folks have power over the fact that his belly is empty." The founder of the Albany movement felt that no amount of intellectual theorizing could substitute for such experiential knowledge. If the organizers at Waveland formulated a program that helped SNCC stay loyal to its people, it could do what was necessary.

With the same focus on the hard-won knowledge of the field staff, Moses tried to be both strategic and tactical, for he believed that SNCC needed to recover its equilibrium and heal in the wake of the bruising developments of 1964. These injuries precipitated a kind of ad-libbed lashing-out at whites that now punctuated daily life on most local projects. Moses fully understood the emotions at work, but he did not think this new tendency was helpful. Black staffers needed to recuperate before they could be generous. African Americans needed to find a way to say to SNCC's white staffers, "We need to meet by ourselves for a while, behind closed doors." Because Moses felt that "it was worth whatever amount of time it took" for SNCC to "resolve the basic problems that had surfaced as a result of 1964," he waited patiently for the issues to emerge. This was Moses' style. It seemed Gandhian, which, of course, it was in part. But it grew straight out of the Mississippi realities that had been his primary schoolroom since he entered the Delta four long years earlier. Moses was persuaded that an internal struggle for power would wreck the culture of SNCC: he himself would not try to assume a formal leadership role in the group. SNCC was a "leaking boat afloat in the middle of the ocean," he told his brothers and sisters at Waveland. Everyone knew about the leaks and wanted to help rebuild the boat. The challenge was the simple fact that the boat had "to stay afloat in order to be rebuilt."[10]

SNCC therefore had to focus on itself. Taking models from other times or other places did not seem workable. Neither did a centralized structure or a provocative-sounding Black Belt Project. First, SNCC had internal work to do.

In this manner, Waveland came to have a whispered urgency about it. When speakers seemed to go off on tangents, people mumbled urgent and cosmic things to one another, such as "We need to change the structures and institutions that dehumanize black people"; "we need to get our own heads organized." Through it all, Forman pressed his proposal for centralization and maneuvered to put it to a vote. He did not get far because Moses and Sherrod — SNCC's two most prominent regional organizers — reminded everyone of the desperate strategic imperatives: solutions had to correspond to the survival needs of field staff. In addition, veteran staffers generated a number of well-argued responses grounded in their own experience. People were accustomed to acting as if they were free to act in local communities of the Jim Crow South. Forman, intent on turning SNCC into a centralized vanguard, could not build momentum behind his proposal. He had made an error that warred against SNCC's democratic culture: he did not enter into a conversation with SNCC, he launched a monologue. It was a decision that crippled the discussion at Waveland.

Nevertheless, irresolution carried its own momentum. The seven days at Waveland saw workshops, general sessions, the airing of position papers, and earnest sidebar discussions that began over meals and extended late into the evening. But during that time a major concern tended to get lost: the conference needed to come up with something concrete for people to do — something they could believe in and something they could work hard at. Perhaps then, they could organize a structure to support that work. But before they could concur on such a program, they had to work through the organization's problems. And the most immediate problem was money.[11]

Forman pointed out the advantages of employing a "lead dog" in the New York SNCC office as a symbol around which to raise funds. SCLC had Martin Luther King as its public representative, CORE could send off James Farmer. Yet Forman's key associate, Bob Moses, did not believe in front men — real or projected. Moses quietly told Forman that he "was not available for such a projection."[12]

Still, nobody had been paid in the weeks since Atlantic City. Often, there had been no gas for the cars. The everyday reality for SNCC people was that no one had money. As executive director of the organization, Forman controlled the disbursement of funds. After consulting the executive committee, he had obligated SNCC to buy a building in Atlanta to give the group a place to gather and institutionally root itself. This purchase put an immense strain on the funds he could get to the field. The budget had grown from roughly $75,000 annually between 1961 and early 1963, to $162,000 in 1963, to over $200,000 in 1964. The SNCC staff had soared from 20 members before 1963, to about 100 at the end of 1963, to over 170 by the fall of 1964.[13]

The "bonding agent" — the trust and accountability that had enabled SNCC to continue working — had begun to collapse as people expressed profound doubts about the procedures, or lack of them, that governed the decision-making process between the central office and field staff. Since Forman was in charge of fund-raising, he made the decisions, almost by default, on disbursing funds to workers. This had worked in the 1962–63 period, because, Forman explained, "certain non-democratic powers are often necessary in a period of rapid transition to build a structure which can eventually achieve democratic ends — like the war powers of Congress."[14] In 1964 this approach no longer worked. Who had the power to provide necessities? As one worker pointed out: "If you were new to the organization, and you didn't know people individually, or didn't know Jim [Forman], what then? Now, only Jim can decide or get you what you may need." Aside from Forman and a few of his staff, no one saw the budget breakdown and knew how much money was coming in or where it was going. Because Forman had such a strong work ethic, no one could doubt his dedication to the cause. He repeatedly asked for help in raising money, but no one else was willing to do what he did.[15]

Thus, money no longer went from Atlanta to Jackson. People in both offices were guilty of making decisions without consulting field staff. This happened not because functionaries in either Atlanta or Jackson wanted to be dictators but because, as one harassed worker put it, "decisions had to be made and there was no decision-making body." It was the same problem, writ large, that had emerged during the previous November's Freedom Vote. For Forman, there was only one remedy: a centralized executive. The monetary crisis could not be resolved until a decision was reached on structure.[16]

At this point, Sherrod suggested that the debate on structure be given a temporary rest so that participants might tackle something at least as threatening — namely, internal racial tensions. Everyone in SNCC was "prejudiced and insecure in our own identity and aspirations, black and white," he wrote in his position paper. "In fact, we are more prejudiced and bitter, frustrated and impatient and hateful than our parents because we have had more, and seen more, and *think we can get more* than they did and *we think we can get it now* because we have done miracles; we have most of the time surprised ourselves." Sherrod asked black staffers to consider the fact that whites had the same needs as "our own as regards recognition, fulfillment, status in our group." Racial animosity had no place among SNCC staff; hatred would make "slaves of us all." The primary question, as he saw it, was "whether SNCC is born to die, or to live in the new society, or to be the new society."[17]

Race had always been at the center of SNCC because race was the unacknowledged heart of the unfulfilled democratic promise of America. To many young people who had labored and suffered in the building of the MFDP, the seating of the white supremacist "regular" Mississippi delegation at Atlantic City was an act of public humiliation of all of black America. It suggested that the issue of race was an obstruction that SNCC could no longer surmount. Willie Peacock later contended that the summer volunteers had been more of a nuisance than an asset. They got "in the way of community organization and grass roots organization among black people." Martha Prescod Norman agreed. "I think most people came out of the summer feeling that it was a mistake to have brought in so many northern, white people," she said. "It tended to push the local people out of things, as well as the northern, middle-class blacks who were active. They got sort of overwhelmed."[18] Such views were by no means universal at Waveland, but they were deeply held by many and suggested the intensity of SNCC's internal agony.

Years later, people could find ways to talk about SNCC's internal race issue with some vividness. But in the immediate aftermath of the 1964 presidential campaign, it was not easily discussed. People in the Jackson office were determined to break through this evasion. To troubleshoot the situation, they had brought in a civil rights worker from CORE, who reported that "discipline has broken down so far that the state headquarters has had several race riots." Such hyperbole was a conscious effort to make people confront the issue. The CORE worker identified sexual tensions between local black youth and white female staff as one cause of the problem. Others were not so sure.[19]

Few in SNCC had sustained a committed organizing relationship across racial lines for as long as Charles Sherrod of the Albany movement. Early in 1962, Sherrod and white volunteers such as Jack Chatfield and Penny Patch had fashioned an intimate bond in the course of their daily civil rights work. Chatfield had been shot at on his second night in Terrell County but remained in the movement. Sherrod subsequently took Chatfield to a mass meeting, where the two men shook hands in front of the group. Sherrod had also noticed changes in SNCC between 1962 and 1964. No longer were the "people who started with deep commitment and feeling toward nonviolence" remaining in SNCC. In contrast to the Nashville students, workers in the voter registration projects had serious questions about nonviolence. "This has changed SNCC's whole outlook." In other words, the echoes from its Nashville era were very hard to hear.[20]

Sherrod would look back on Waveland from the perspective of 1979 and reflect that "some of us can't admit that we have hatred and hostility and where it comes from." Whites alone could not change society's system of decision-making. Blacks could not do it alone, either. "It's going to take all of us." Only if people were able to admit their hatred of other races, "and understand where that hostility comes from and why it's among us," did people have a chance at working together. At this point, a good fifteen years past Waveland, Sherrod needed to stop and call out a song: "Oh Freedom." Wazir Peacock, Sam Block, and Matthew Jones joined in and then began "This Little Light of Mine." So fortified in 1979, Sherrod was ready to continue his analysis of the racial confusion that had engulfed SNCC so many years before. Blacks and whites had to work together, he said. But to do so effectively, they had to admit "we got hatred in us." Sherrod himself acknowledged that even a dozen years after the movement's peak, he hated whites. "Can you take that? Can you work with me if I say I hate white folks?" He asked a white in the audience, "Can you work with me young lady? See, that's the problem, and that's why the system's going to whip your ass, and whip mine too." Developing a mechanism for overcoming their own internal race hatred, for being able to transcend "our feeling for self," Sherrod felt, was the only way to proceed interracially. This was his settled view in 1979. The fact that it was not expressed at Waveland in the fall of 1964 shows that even among SNCC people, honest interracial conversation proved immensely difficult to sustain.[21]

At Waveland, some participants struggled to say that interracial work was not necessarily what SNCC should be doing. Given the black-white tensions the group had experienced internally, an idea that had first surfaced during the summer of 1963 — namely, that whites should work with whites and blacks with blacks — found increased acceptance. Nonetheless, no one was ready to tell the whites to go (this would not happen until the end of 1966).* To their credit, some whites tried to raise this issue. "The problem is not that whites want to take over," wrote Elaine DeLott Baker, a white staffer in the Jackson office, "but simply that whites want to do a job. The question then is, do the blacks of SNCC want to do the same job?" If not, "then tell the whites and let them go."[22]

Black project director Silas Norman wrote a paper examining "the importance of racial considerations among the staff." Raised in Augusta, Georgia, Norman had served a stint as a second lieutenant in the U.S. Army and was completing graduate work in microbiology at the University of Wisconsin when he met Maria Varela at a civil rights initiative in 1963. He accepted her invitation to work during the summer of 1964 in Selma, Alabama, where Sheriff Jim Clark provided him with a firsthand introduction to cattle prod brutality. Soon afterward, Norman took over the project in Selma. "Whites and blacks should be used according to the functions which they best serve," he said at Waveland. Whites brought "wider publicity and thus wider support." On the other hand, whites in some areas regarded white women in the company of black men as a "declaration of war." Furthermore, a sort of "ethnic relationship" existed among black staff and local people that whites could not enter. Aside from these observations, Norman would not generalize. If integrated groups could "live and move together to do their job" productively, fine. Yet he

---

*In December 1966 the few whites remaining in SNCC would be asked to leave. The marrow of SNCC's democratic culture had long since been drained. For more specifics, see Carson, *In Struggle*; Curry et al., *Deep in Our Hearts*; and Richardson et al., "Hands on the Freedom Plow." The dismissal of whites gets far too much attention as a symbolic event. It was a by-product, not a symbol, of SNCC's loss of its own culture.

did not know if he was willing to work in an integrated project "simply to prove a point."[23]

Some white staffers found such declarations depressing. Others found them true, but no less depressing. The influx of northern whites for the 1964 Summer Project had offered SNCC people, most of whom were black southerners, the opportunity to participate in a seemingly interracial democracy — however edgy daily life might be. For a time, Moses and Sherrod had been able to keep workers focused not on internal racial tension but on the task at hand: breaking down the caste system. Yet when the black members of SNCC asserted their views and otherwise struggled for their own dignity, the entry of large numbers of whites threatened the integrity of these efforts. During the Summer Project, experiencing freedom often proved to be exhausting.

None of this was easily explained to outsiders, even to those who had come South specifically because they wanted to cease being "outsiders" to the freedom struggle. During the fall of 1964, blacks were not asking whites to leave permanently, but rather to understand that they needed to talk alone among themselves. The movement had created a great many questions for African Americans: How to unlearn a lifetime of "black step back, white is right"? How to find ways to cope with the unintended but often-present racism of progressive whites? What precisely were the advantages and the costs of the strenuous work necessary to all of this forgiveness? Most maddening of all, why did a disproportionate "obligation to make things work" fall on black people? What about the emotional costs? Wouldn't simple separatism provide a better alternative?

In this seldom-explored territory, the most elemental questions seemed to lurk: What does it mean to me to be American? What is black? It became increasingly urgent that black people in SNCC have a place to discuss these basic questions of identity without constantly feeling the need to justify their speculations to white cohorts. The atmosphere at Waveland fairly pulsed with the pent-up tensions, the disappointments, and the successes and near-successes of the movement.[24]

In the early to middle 1960s — the most intense years of movement innovation and tension — Bob Moses had made many attempts to find a way to get the black-white issue "into the open" and find space for black people to meet by themselves.[25] In the interests of the group's long-term health, it had to be done. That terrain proved to be exceedingly difficult to negotiate, however. Dona Richards later noted that even though these discussions had begun in Greenville in November 1963, the "talk was cut off. We didn't really grapple with the problems because people were ashamed of admitting their feelings. When the talk becomes moralistic, it gets shut off." Yet Moses felt black people needed to develop a stronger group identity in the process of claiming their full rights as individual citizens. It was the actions of people in the collective that helped to drive individuals toward a better understanding of their own potential.[26]

Black SNCC workers shared a growing sense that the segregated past and the slave past had left a residue that was more burdensome than people had previously understood. Black people needed to express their anger at the legacy of American history. Yet the expression of anger was not enough. It served a psychological need, not a political one. At the same time that it brought a measure of solace to blacks, it failed to be politically smart, because it alienated large numbers of nonblack people who would be useful to any ongoing politics of change.

Visible at Waveland, then, was a problem that would haunt American politics through the next two generations. A politics of anger produced political stasis with no policy payoff. Unpacking this dilemma was a massive project that had to be undertaken nationwide. It would prove to be a very long process, much longer than most people foresaw at the time.

As these tensions worked themselves out in black communities, almost no early help was forthcoming from white communities. While individual whites might undertake intensive self-examinations of their own inherited white supremacist modes of thought, and even begin to talk and write about it with poise and candor, such introspection of mainstream culture did not broadly materialize in twentieth-century America. On the contrary, the cultural habits of the vast majority of white Americans prevented them from perceiving black expressions of anger as more than antiwhite rancor. Ella Baker, who had spent a lifetime in steady combat with the American caste system, told SNCC workers that if they could find a way to successfully address the issue of white involvement, they would "have cracked the problem open."[27] At Waveland, SNCC began to look but could not find tools powerful enough to "crack it open."

Where all of this left SNCC at the end of 1964 was certainly not easy to see. On the one hand, the beguiling, Lawsonesque dreams developed in the Nashville workshops seemed to be increasingly ephemeral and politically impractical in the face of mushrooming white resistance. Those African American activists who reluctantly agreed to the 1964 Summer Project did so because they believed that the mere presence of white volunteers would provide some protection for black activists, preventing the murder of another Herbert Lee or Louis Allen. Now *whites* — Mickey Schwerner and Andrew Goodman — had been killed, and the federal government still refused to actively protect civil rights workers.

Evidence from McComb during September and October 1964 had fostered the climate of irresolution at Waveland. SNCC activists knew in their bones that a number of unwanted truths needed to be faced because the quality and scale of violent retribution against the Mississippi movement had worsened over the summer and fall. Each week saw another bombing, and SNCC staffers observed that anything they said to FBI officials was immediately conveyed to local police. The state police moved 147 officers to McComb, one-third of its total force. Over 200 local people were arrested and harassed, and some were beaten. Many on staff believed that McComb was the place where Mississippi authorities had begun a statewide rollback action now that so many volunteers (and the national spotlight) had returned to the North.[28] In light of the newly verified fact that the federal government would not protect civil rights workers, how should this latest level of terror be addressed? How should SNCC workers interact with activists who carried guns? Where did nonviolence fit in? Should SNCC workers themselves be armed? At Waveland, SNCC was forced to face all of these issues head-on — race, money, structure, and nonviolence.

What Do You Mean, Revolution?

Before the Waveland meeting, James Forman had undertaken to fill the vacuum of power he perceived within SNCC by proposing that it recruit black students to register voters from Virginia to Texas over the following summer. This so-called Black Belt Project could "serve to capitalize on the momentum of the Mississippi Project, but with our errors in Mississippi corrected, and [serve] to consolidate bases in regional structure with national potential."[29]

But, as it turned out, Forman's proposal was distressingly thin on specifics. Despite his intention to move forward "with our errors in Mississippi corrected," his concrete plans were derivative of COFO innovations developed in Mississippi in 1963 – 64. Thus Forman said that the project would have six staff positions: administrator, labor program coordinator, federal program coordinator, Freedom Democratic Party coordinator, community center coordinator, and Freedom School coordinator. In short, it offered no new departures from those pioneered in the Delta the year before.

In any event, there was no questioning Forman's personal courage or dedication. Over the preceding five years, he had faced down lynch mobs from Monroe, North Carolina, to McComb, Mississippi, and many places in between. To provide administrative support to those in the field, he had made countless drives on lonely country roads, always wondering if nearing headlights signaled a mere passing car or imminent death. He had stayed — and not bailed out of — jails in Albany, Greenwood, and Atlanta. Once, in Danville, Virginia, in 1963, he verbally challenged E. G. McCain, that city's malevolent police chief, to give demonstrators time to get away from McCain's fire hoses. Furthermore,

Forman had tirelessly maintained the material base of SNCC since 1961, setting up an administrative structure to raise funds and communicate with northern supporters — all despite serious health problems that led to multiple hospitalizations. Plain and simple, no one had consistently demonstrated more personal bravery, no one had worked more tirelessly than James Forman.[30]

Moreover, through all the violent chaos engendered by the Ku Klux Klan and condoned by southern police forces, Forman had kept the Atlanta office functioning. He had traveled extensively in the field, spending considerable time in local projects to better understand and assess local needs — and convey those needs to northern supporters. In the aggregate, he had volunteered for a greater variety of undertakings than the vast majority of Americans, the vast majority of activists, and, indeed, a goodly number of those present at Waveland. Yet, as he acknowledged in his opening speech at Waveland, each SNCC person could only know so much.[31]

Allowing for all of Forman's achievements, one significant area of organizing set him (and his experiences) apart from grassroots activists such as Charles McLaurin, Jesse Harris, and many other SNCC field staff. Forman's principal duties were in the Atlanta office. Though he routinely visited projects in the field, he had few opportunities to establish the face-to-face relationships with local people that made up the lifeblood of SNCC's fieldwork. Bob Moses described SNCC activities in obscure places like McComb as the "necessarily slow and patient work" that had to take place between organizers and local people for things to happen. Forman, on the other hand, sought details from local projects that he could convert into stories through which to raise funds from movement sympathizers in the North. This was desperately needed work, and there is evidence that Forman was good at it. But in conveying to Forman experientially grounded insight into the organizing process itself, such field visits carried serious limitations that were not easy for Forman himself to see. However fully it seemed reality was glimpsed, a substitute was in fact being sampled. In-and-out trips to the front lines could not illuminate the specific process through which ordinary people acquired that most sought-after attribute: political "consciousness," the ingredient that heralded the arrival of a person's capacity to act. It was not something that one learned by making a commitment, by deciding to become militant, or by reading an approved text that offered instruction on how to think. Rather, it was something the great majority of SNCC's most accomplished veterans learned through their own experiences. And because this social knowledge was experiential, it was reproducible. That is, it offered the prospect of an immense payoff because it brought ordinary citizens to commit public acts, and these acts permanently changed their consciousness.[32]

Forman's regular work schedule did not expose him to the daily realities of the process through which ordinary citizens moved from passive victims to active participants. It was a process that did not originate with high character or what is generally called "courage." Nor did it begin with high theory, what is commonly referred to as "ideology." But it did start with an encounter between citizen and organizer — a public relationship that was sustained over time. It began when a young Charles McLaurin, for example, met with some elderly women in the Delta and got to know them by talking about the nuts and bolts of registering to vote. SNCC's very patient time clock left room for people to think about such daunting activities and even to put the idea of "registrating" in their own words. All such things McLaurin and the elderly women had time for as they took a deep breath and talked about the possibilities of action and the consequences of inaction. It was a subject that could be explored over days and sometimes weeks, one that could be discussed in a car moving down a rural highway toward an awaiting crisis at a courthouse in Indianola. In such a drive in 1962, one elderly women said to McLaurin, "It won't be long now." Indeed so: they were going to "face the man" and they hoped and believed they were going to live to tell about it.[33]

Here we can see the human capacity to act — that elusive product of what social observers so easily call "consciousness." People like McLaurin possessed a different understanding from Forman's of how to give tangible meaning to a political descriptor such as "revolutionary." This was why, in 1964, Forman did not honor (in the experientially precise way McLaurin and Curtis Hayes honored) voter registration as an activity that could alter people's sense of themselves and thus transform their lives. "People going to the courthouse, for the first time. Then telling their friends to go down." When McLaurin spoke these words at Waveland, he condensed into one sentence those colossal battles black Mississippians had experienced in their own minds that determined which people went and which people did not go to the courthouses of the American South. The process carried much more meaning for McLaurin and other voter registration staff than it did for those who spent most of their time in urban offices.

At Waveland, Charles Sherrod gracefully but repeatedly challenged Forman's plan. Sherrod attempted to make the discussion of structure as concrete as possible.[34] The conversations at Waveland revealed that the gulf between them was not so much ideological as experiential. At one of the staff meetings leading up to Waveland, Frank Smith, a Morehouse student from Newman, Georgia, had noted the vastness of that gulf and prophesied that SNCC people would have to move to one side or the other. "[The Democratic National Convention at] Atlantic City," he said, "left many people with the feeling for the necessity to work in the political arena. Are we interested in building a political empire for SNCC, or in building local leadership?" he asked. "These two types of organizations are not compatible. We must discuss what SNCC is."[35]

However it was characterized, Forman's concept of revolution through top-down decision-making did not resonate with Bob Moses. Volunteers *had* to be trained by people as skilled and experienced as McLaurin had become. Yet this training took time and energy, and Moses felt "it was useless to try and go into another student project" to register voters when SNCC first needed to focus on its internal tasks.[36]

Twenty years after the fact, Forman would describe Moses' position at Waveland as a refusal to lead. In November 1964, he did not directly challenge Moses' sustained withholding of agreement. This was understandable, inasmuch as Moses' prestige within the movement was unsurpassed. Moses believed that he could not tell people what to do because he never in his own mind thought that was the underlying purpose of SNCC. "A basic principal in decision-making in SNCC is that people who do the work make the decisions," he said. "Decision-making should be geared to programs, not to hierarchy." Moreover, people did not learn to grow by being told what to do.[37]

Forman had a different understanding of politics. In his 1985 retrospective, *The Making of Black Revolutionaries*, he wrote that SNCC's mission had been to "outmaneuver the racists . . . hammer against the federal government . . . consolidate our power and extend our influence." He defined his supporters in the student movement as "Field Staff" and his opponents as the "Freedom High" group.[38] The latter had been influenced, according to Forman, by countercultural ideas from SDS. They possessed a "middle-class bias" and were "elitists."[39] It is instructive to note that none of these terms surfaced at Waveland because it would have been far-fetched to raise them. The suggestion that Moses, Sherrod, and their solid ranks of supporters at the core of SNCC were "elitists" and crippled by a "middle-class bias" would have been immediately hooted down in 1964.[40]

In fact, the philosophies and methodologies of Moses and Sherrod, on the one hand, and Forman, on the other, were so far apart that in hindsight it is difficult to see how the men worked in concert for so long. A plausible explanation may be that the singular determination to register black voters had been the shared agenda holding them together prior to the Summer Project.

In *Black Revolutionaries*, Forman asserted that in 1964 SNCC "had reached the point where it was necessary to become a revolutionary organization in every sense. . . . And an organization that is seeking revolution, and willing to use violence, cannot afford the fear of power. It cannot afford weak or vacillating leadership; it cannot afford liberalistic forms of self-assertion."[41] The objective was to establish what Forman called, without further elaboration, a "revolutionary organization in every sense"; this was by no means the way Forman cast his proposal at Waveland. There, he called for a greatly strengthened central authority that could make prompt decisions and increase efficiency. In contrast, Sherrod and Moses argued that the only way to increase popular power was by strengthening people at the grass roots, so they could strive to achieve their own goals. At root, the point of contention at Waveland was over the very meaning of democracy and how to work politically to realize it. The disagreement could not have been more fundamental.[42]

Forman's literary postmortem, written more than twenty years after Waveland, proved to be far more influential with outside observers than was his 1964 proposal.[43] This ex post facto achievement was grounded in Forman's recasting of the debate on structure first set in place at Waveland and repeated over the next eighteen months. In juxtaposing the descriptive labels, "Freedom High" and "Field Staff," he effectively achieved an orderly trajectory that otherwise did not exist throughout the week-long discussion in November 1964. This encouraged later observers, similarly seeking a logical explanation, to employ the same descriptive terminology.[44] Yet the two terms did not accurately describe the divisions at Waveland: it was not a matter of organizers on one side and dreamers on the other. Everyone present, including Forman, knew the challenge they faced turned on revitalizing SNCC's organizing agenda: they differed fundamentally on how to do that.

The dismissive term "Freedom High," which surfaced after Waveland, did not describe anyone at the staff meeting. Frayed nerve endings, especially racial ones, suffused the meeting, as did different ways of seeing things. Finally, an overarching financial crisis heightened anxieties across the board. As a result, uncertainty and confusion abounded. But there were no organized groups at Waveland. In his 1985 book, Forman crafted a rationale for his centralizing project. The Waveland meeting, he maintained, "revealed very clearly to me that we had a factional fight on our hands, and that it was necessary to organize in a way appropriate to such a fight."[45]

Forman encountered a wall of opposition from local organizers whose morale was grounded in their own experiences. One such person was Morehouse student Frank Smith, who had worked to create voter registration organizations in Mississippi since 1962. Smith saw the movement's amazing ability to transform life at the base of Delta society as a product of SNCC's own history — that is, of the lessons learned in the struggle itself. During the early sit-ins, he wrote, campus groups had sent representatives to SNCC's coordinating committee. Though the committee no longer existed in the fall of 1964, "there was a time when they did exist and they fought for their right to be the decision making body." After 1962 SNCC moved off campus and into black communities: "Today [1964], the staff is demanding its right to make decisions the same as the Coordinating Committee did when it was the base of SNCC. Today, the staff is the base and it should have the right to make decisions since it is the people . . . affected by those decisions and will have the job of carrying the decisions out."[46] In December 1963, when members of the Selma and southwest Georgia projects had met to discuss SNCC's role in the community, Phil Davis of Albany described the consensus that had developed in the field: "We should decide on the projects in the field, what we need, rather than being directed from Atlanta. Who decides where field workers are sent, which projects get money and cars? We should establish priorities, what we want to achieve in the predictable future so as to add objective, rational factors to these decisions."[47]

If decisions were to be made by staff, however, there were three prerequisites. First, everyone in the group must agree to the idea. Second, they needed to trust each other to follow through. Third, they had to be straightforward — to exchange information honestly on what they knew to be true. It was clear that these prerequisites did not exist inside SNCC during the fall of 1964 and into 1965. At some point, a small, rump group led by Forman began to believe that acting on his analysis was more important than holding the group together. Throughout 1965, this group attempted to take control of SNCC and implement its agenda, even as the near-absence of funds forced people to abandon local projects in state after state across the South. Simply enough, people who wanted power took it. But their victory was pyrrhic, as much of the organizing experience generated within SNCC was no longer present. Those who possessed the experience were gone.

Until the internal fragmentation, SNCC activists had significantly pushed the limit of democratic possibility.[48] Based on a voluntary staff whose only driving motivation was its dedication to bring those "on the bottom rail" into civic life, the lived experience of SNCC activism verified that hierarchical structure had very limited value in such a project. Steeped in the practice of democracy in everyday life, SNCC people resisted hierarchical decision-making. Their experiences bore out the merits of candor in personal relationships, the need to rely on each other, and the central importance of community-based leadership.[49]

Ella Baker vividly characterized what was lost: people "ate on each other," reproaching their comrades to justify their own vision. Forman was the most visible — but certainly not the only — such critic. He maintained that those who opposed his vision were weak, perhaps too close to whites, maybe smoking marijuana, or wedded too tightly to individualist or "liberalist" thought and prone to being misled by appeals to "participatory democracy." Interestingly, Forman

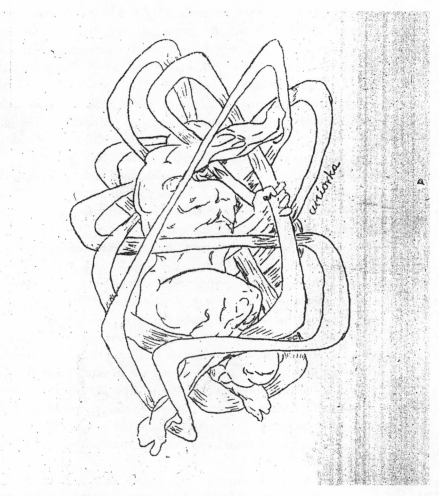

Drawing of SNCC "structure." (Frame 982, reel 11, SNCC Papers)

also referred to the opposition as a "small elitist core of self-perpetuating or-ganizers" who could not recruit masses of people into the organization.[50] The awkward fact, of course, was that the founding organizers of SNCC's two largest and most visible projects — its bellwethers — were Bob Moses of the Mississippi project and Charles Sherrod of the southwest Georgia project. Among SNCC's many local organizers across the country, none had more prestige than Moses and Sherrod, both of whom did not support Forman's centralizing objective.

As if this were not enough, the impasse over what values SNCC represented had an immediate and detrimental impact on the specific training SNCC would give the eighty-plus summer volunteers who wished to stay in Mississippi, as well as prospective organizers. Because veterans on staff now had diverging views on what the organization needed to do next, the question of what to teach new recruits was an issue. As Jean Wheeler described it, the work in Mississippi centered on "creating a trusting and loving atmosphere, a supportive atmosphere. . . . We let the person we were trying to organize, lead. We let him express what was important to him and then we followed. And having let him lead, we then did two things: we'd point out the contradictions" by asking the recruit, "You want this and this, they don't go together; could you look at this another way?" Then "we would offer an alternative solution to the solution [the recruit] had historically operated on. That is the way that I understood what I was doing when I was there."[51] Each man was his own leader, a female SNCC veteran said later. "Each man held, by himself, all together, and the idea was always teamwork. Bob Moses emerged very early as a leader, but as a leader among peers, not a [traditional] leader. And the only reason a hierarchy developed was because [we needed to train] the absolute novice." Another woman recalled that "who was the leader was not important until we were converged upon by thousands of people in the summer of '64."[52]

Diane Nash, a veteran of James Lawson's original workshops, retrospectively blamed the teachers, not the students. "I think education was the key." While "some people think it was the influx of northerners, of whites, that made the redemptive community idea dissipate, I don't agree," she stated in 1988. "I think it's possible for even a large-scale movement to operate as a band of brothers and sisters, a circle of trust. The reason wasn't that new people came in; I think we did not devote enough time and energy into the education of the people coming in."[53]

Nash's comments reveal two things. First, the size of the task implicit in developing widespread Lawson-style workshops to train people who joined SNCC was immense. Second, amid the drama of the civil rights movement and the terror of repression, this kind of experientially grounded workshop training was dropped. SNCC thus failed to educate its recruits the way activists like Nash, John Lewis, Chuck McDew, and Casey Hayden had been trained in 1959–61.

The rapid increase in staff without this "internal" education was a key factor in the abandonment of SNCC's democratic ethic and the drift away from the close, mutually supportive relationships between SNCC staff and local people. Most important, perhaps, was SNCC's failure to hold wide-scale workshops on "lessons learned" to permit reflective thinking about prior activities. Lawson's Nashville "laboratory" had harmonized the ardent wills of numerous strong-headed people toward unified action. Yet all of the hard-won lessons of that work seemed futile at Waveland, where some participants held that SNCC's innovative democratic processes lacked sophistication.

In 1964, it is likely that the participants themselves lacked what had been a hallmark of the early movement: patience. In preparing for the sit-ins over the winter of 1959–60, Lewis had noted that the Nashville students knew they were "going to do something. But it's strange. We were very patient."[54] It was a remark that meant much more to the sit-in participants of 1960 than to those who heard it later. What did Lewis mean by "patience"? It was not the patience called for by southern white authorities, needless to say. Nor was it "radical" patience. It surely did not call people to be patient relative to the external pace of change. Instead, it was an understanding possessed by each workshop participant while sifting through his or her own experiences and feelings. It was patience with each other, patience with one's own errors, patience with one's predecessors in the older generation, patience with larger African American constituencies across America. The persistent but calm behavior exhibited in Nashville allowed people to combine the ingredients necessary to act, and to do so with sustained poise. From the perspective of the Nashville workshops, Lewis's comment defines a type of democratic act. His form of patience allowed people raised in a hierarchical and segregated society to undergo a sequential process that prepared them for civic action.

This idea of democratic patience would be hard to summon in the crisis period following Atlantic City. For most people at Waveland, their sole experience outside of the civil rights movement had come from within hierarchical institutions — those of family, church, school, or business. In fact, few Americans had extensive experience with voluntary social forms. When the SNCC staff gathered at Waveland and put all of these matters on the table, it was difficult for most people to even envision, much less create, an efficient *and* nonhierarchical structure for their organization.

The nearly four days' deliberation of the staff's overriding concern — agreement on a future program — was interrupted when Forman passed around his paper proposing a new organizational structure. Amid a muddled discussion about why some were stealing others' belongings at the retreat, Forman and Ivanhoe Donaldson returned the focus of the conference to the agenda introduced by the Atlanta office. "We have to deal with the issues," Forman said, "so round up people who are outside and move on to proposals for structure."[55] This reflected the clear division between what people in the field thought was important and what staff in the Atlanta office needed. Whereas Forman believed that structure was the issue, project staff felt that programs desperately needed discussion. Janet Jemmott voiced the perspective from the field: "Let's talk about needs of projects, where has authority broken down, what have been our hang-ups? In workshops then [we can] discuss how we're going to get people responsible for fulfilling the needs." Yet "concern for [the] pressing time element [that] people felt brought about [a] halt of program discussions," the retreat minutes recorded.[56]

Forman's position paper laid out a structure to knit local groups together through a tightly controlled hierarchy. In it, the coordinating committee would meet three times a year to decide on policy, voting "very tightly and efficiently." An administrative body, the executive committee, would then form a finance committee to raise monies to disburse the budget created by the coordinating committee. An executive secretary "should be asked by [that] body to be the overall administrative officer of the organization." A single person — the program secretary — would be assigned to support people's work in the field. Even this was presented as more of an enforcer role than a supportive one: the role of the program secretary, Forman wrote, "will be to travel in the field to examine how programs are carried out and to report to the Executive Secretary his findings and to the Executive Committee."[57]

Two groups at Waveland — one led by Casey Hayden and Maria Varela, the other by Francis Mitchell — presented alternatives to the structure proposed by Forman. Hayden and Varela's group suggested that local groups could decide themselves when to draw together to show collective strength. Mitchell's group proposed what amounted to a compromise between the decentralized and hierarchical models, a "representative democracy" with an elected "interim committee" that met monthly and made decisions between full staff meetings.[58]

Moses had run the Mississippi projects in a decentralized manner except for the fact that the Atlanta office controlled the disbursement of funds. Both the Mitchell and Varela-Hayden groups built on Moses' Waveland paper, where he suggested they put decisions to be made in one of three categories: (1) crucial decisions "at the center of our work," (2) every-day decisions, and (3) working problems, which "fell between the 'crucials' and the 'every-days.'" "Crucial decisions," Moses said, should be talked out at length and then made by all of those affected. "Working problems" could be "cited and circulated. A group of staff who are interested [could] band together to work on the problems. They chunk out their work and carry it through. When it's over they disband." Finally, "every-day problems on the edge can be decided immediately by the person responsible in forum with himself or whoever."[59]

On the next-to-last day of the Waveland retreat, each group presented its proposal for SNCC's structure to the full staff. The ensuing discussion made one thing clear: Forman's proposal did not have the votes. The official notes of the

Waveland conference simply record that the discussion had to be cut short by time constraints, and the matter was left unresolved. The Waveland meeting, far from reenergizing SNCC's core organizers, had left people with a feeling of loss.[60] Most critically, the key component of their democratic culture was broken: the ability to disagree and still come together at the end of the day, a band of brothers and sisters, a circle of trust.

Vertigo

The series of SNCC meetings in 1964–65 centering on the Waveland conference can be understood as the culminating events of the decade. The immediate effect was felt only by those inside SNCC. But the clash of ideas and personalities observed at these staff gatherings followed patterns that would be repeated in other groups seeking social justice over the next ten years. Often these groups traced their origins to the innovative democratic forms that SNCC people created.[1] The Waveland conference, in other words, constituted one of the determining junctures of the 1960s in America.

In terms of drama and emotional impact, this is where the story ends. Certainly Hollywood would draw the curtain. Yet this is not how social movements come to a close. And this is not where SNCC organizers' work ended. It may be counterintuitive in hindsight, but at the time SNCC workers did not see this as the end of the group's innovation. As individuals, SNCC workers took what they had learned and kept on organizing, which they understood to be a series of trials and errors. The fact is, many creative initiatives resulted.

Without a group plan for what to do next, people did whatever they could define as movement work. Encouraging the development of indigenous democratic organizations among disenfranchised blacks in the South, workers enabled local people to defend their own self-interests. Many SNCC staffers thus remained loyal to their base in southern black communities—building agricultural cooperatives, challenging racist implementation of federal welfare programs like Aid to Dependent Children or FHA loans, or working with the Mississippi Student Union. Those who wanted to be allies of SNCC would have to support its respectful, slow organizing at the grass roots. In SNCC's Atlanta office, some staffers made valiant attempts to increase communications and improve relations between Atlanta and the field; others began to make decisions based on their own ideological preferences.[2]

The MFDP mounted a second (also unsuccessful) challenge to the right of the newly elected all-white Mississippi congressmen. At times relations between SNCC and the MFDP were strained, as SNCC people looked toward fundamental societal change, whereas some MFDP members did not. "How do we deal with people after they become organized?" one staffer asked. It was a thorny question: What should SNCC do when people used the vote that its workers had bled and died for in ways with which it disagreed? Work nonetheless continued in the other institutions generated in the wake of the Mississippi Summer Project. James Forman pursued the "Black Belt Project," while others participated in the Selma campaign in the spring of 1965. In Selma, the strategy that had worked reasonably well for SCLC in 1963 and produced the Civil Rights Bill of 1964 was employed again. That is, go to a town with a traditional southern style of law enforcement, augmented at the top by an especially authoritarian police chief. Attract the media, demonstrate, suffer through the resulting violence, agitate for a new, broader Civil Rights Bill. In Selma, the police chief was Jim Clark, the movement marched over the Pettis Bridge, and the on-camera charge of the mounted Alabama state police prompted enough outrage to force passage of an expanded Voting Rights Bill of 1965. Rather than leave town, SNCC workers focused their formidable skills on the organization's last major project in Lowndes County. Hasan Kwame Jeffries' forthcoming book on organizing in Alabama during 1965–66 provides a detailed picture of how SNCC, drawing on knowledge acquired from previous campaigns, worked with local leaders to create an entirely new political party, the Lowndes County Freedom Party, infamously symbolized by a Black Panther. SNCC entered Lowndes County, whose adult population was 82 percent African American, in February 1965. Stokely Carmichael led the effort that reshaped Alabama politics at the local and state levels; the third-party alternative made sense to many civil rights workers after the 1964 Democratic National Convention in Atlantic City, New Jersey. The quest to build the roots of an independent political party throughout the country would characterize the third and final era of SNCC projects.[3]

Bob Moses' path illustrates the perils of the single most difficult component of movement building in the aftermath of Waveland: sustaining energy. Perhaps more than anyone else in the organization, Moses recognized SNCC's need for an independent economic base both locally and, in the wake of the liberal Democrats' betrayal at Atlantic City, at the national level.[4]

"It was a weakness on our part, that we left the worries about fundraising to Jim [Forman,] so the whole weight of the fundraising fell on his shoulders,"

Moses stated in 1982. Although COFO staffers were capable of extraordinary ingenuity when motivated, most of them did not see SNCC's economic base as a pressing need. Consequently, as a group they "were not imaginative about fundraising" or about "how you put an economic base to an institution." Furthermore, there were no innovative models to work from: the other major civil rights groups all raised funds from Democratic Party members.[5] At Atlantic City, "we saw how those Democratic Party sources came down," asserted Moses. From that encounter, he made a simple — but culturally unsanctioned — discovery. "There's no sense in trying to launch a [alternative] political party in this country without an economic base, because you'd throw yourself back on the hands of whomever you're going out to for your funds." This was shown to be true: Betita Sutherland (Martinez) reported from New York that the SNCC office received $12,360 from direct mailings in 1965 but only $632 in 1966, after SNCC's articulation of "black power." Moses felt that the organization finally confronted the black-white issue during the summer of 1966. Yet "the question that we couldn't get out in the open and upon which we couldn't agree and on which I wouldn't continue to work with SNCC was this question of the economic base.... There was no chance, no sense of trying to embark on this radical program." By 1966, after waiting for nearly two years following Waveland, he could not justify expending his energy on SNCC work if the organization would not address this fundamental problem.[6] Indeed, most efforts remained in limbo, COFO worker Debbie Louis observed, as staff "faced increasing difficulty in continuing programs that might be suspended the next day, not knowing what to expect programmatically or financially in shaping future plans."[7] When the pressure and despair became too great, people left their projects. Some departed for only a few days; others never returned.

Charles McDew later explained that many SNCC staffers had always viewed the committee as a short-lived group of organizers who would eventually organize themselves out of a job. "We said if we go more than five years or if we go without an understanding or feeling that the organization would be disbanded, we will run the risk of becoming institutionalized and spending more time trying to perpetuate the institution than having the freedom to act and to do."[8]

Except in Lowndes County, Alabama, organizing among SNCC workers now took a back seat to the traditional idea of leadership. The energy of the people who remained came from the intellectual ferment within SNCC leadership to reinvent black culture, an effort so powerfully documented by historian Clayborne Carson. Over the next two years, SNCC became an organization of leaders telling people what to think, rather than developing individuals' capacities to think.[9]

Local Fallout

If staff members could not be candid with each other at Waveland, were they any better at discussing such matters back at their local base? Three weeks after the Waveland conference, at a Fifth Congressional District COFO meeting on 25 November 1964, staff confronted several issues that had stymied the Waveland summit.

The meeting began with eight people present. The topic was communication among staff members. Hattiesburg project director Doug Smith wanted the first order of business to be discussion of problems with his staff. Smith, a thoughtful and dedicated SNCC activist, had spent more time canvassing than almost anyone in the room. A Mississippi native, he was still a teenager, with an angular, skinny frame. "No one who's been down here for five months could know more about the district than Doug, but people are talking as if they had the right to give Doug his job or take it away," stated black staffer Charles Glenn, who worked in Moss Point and Pascagoula. Barbara Schwartzbaum, a summer holdover, noted the need for a training program so new volunteers "wouldn't be so quick to judge project directors and there might be a lot less policy friction in projects."[10]

Harry Bowie, a black Episcopal minister from New Jersey who had gone to McComb for the Summer Project under the auspices of the Delta Ministry and then stayed, raised the issue he felt underlay the entire discussion: race. "There really is a basic black-white problem here which you don't say but which is at the bottom of a lot of what you're saying." Doug Smith was black, whereas the holdover summer volunteers were white. Bowie advised his colleagues to be less concerned with their personal fear of saying something unsanctioned. Then he expressed a sentiment whose piercing echo reverberated through all the mass movements that had ever tried to change things and one repeated many times subsequently: "If as much bitterness could be directed at the white man out there as has been at each other and the Jackson office, things would really be moving here."[11]

In effect, Bowie was calling on people to examine their own social relations. The very size of the problem was intimidating. It would have been easy for everyone to draw back from the minister's suggestion, alarmed by the extent of the dilemma and its tendency to elicit volatile emotional responses, or to ask why honesty was, in fact, important. "Let's just get to work," someone might have said to dismiss Bowie's idea. Even though he had nailed the strategic importance of candor, in this particular staff meeting, the group's confusion was apparent. After Bowie spoke, Doug Smith said: "I strongly believe that this is the real problem, but what can you give us to go on?" Bowie suggested that the participants discard some of their bitterness, at least for the meeting. The two staffers having the most problems with each other could not remain on the same project, but Bowie did not want to say who should leave. Amid the personal tension, another participant scrambled back to firm ground: "I don't think the black-white issue can be solved, but the transportation, personnel, and finance problems can be solved. So we should deal with them."[12] Obviously, this intervention constituted a desperate effort to keep the project going. It proceeded from the assumption that people needed to avoid things they could not change and work on those things they could.

Doug Smith, though, did not respond to the call to "do the things we can do." He wanted to get to the heart of the problem. So he tried Bowie's suggestion to be candid. He blurted out: "We've got to stop being Muslims during the day and integrationists at night. One reason guys fight on projects is that some of the guys feel others are using the [white] girls they are bitching about during the day." The eight people sitting around the table in Mississippi's Fifth Congressional District now had race, gender, and interracial sex before them. Three of the most tangled, divisive, and opaque issues of the twentieth century now stood between the group members and their ability to work together. Everyone tried to balance the need for candor against the fear of pushing too hard.[13]

Charles Glenn tried to convey to the northern volunteers the difference in the stakes for native Mississippians: "No cat that comes here for three months is going to give me orders when he can go home next week or next month and I got to be here for the next 55,000 years if I live that long. No one like that is going to do me that way, and I don't care if he's white or black or polka-dotted with a green stripe up his back." Some people were "going to go home and have a family and [would forget] all about Charles Glenn." Known locally as the "come-here" and "been-here" people problem, "been-heres" had to stay and live; "come-heres" were just as likely to move on. The chuckles at his polka-dot comment made him angry. "Don't laugh, I mean this from the bottom of my heart." The differences in perspective were compounded by the divergent education and experience of the Mississippians and the northern volunteers. "A kid who's born and raised in Mississippi is working in the movement and he's never had a chance to get any kind of decent education and a kid from the North who's gotten a good education comes and works in the movement and then he uses that good education against the kid from Mississippi," continued Smith. "Then this guy is going to throw 55 curves in the way of experience, talking with education against the dude who really knows the score."[14]

Around the table, education, different grasps of "knowledge," and varying experiential understandings now joined race, gender, and interracial sex as issues to be worked through. How should the group decide which one to discuss first? Could these matters even be separated? The meeting broke up with a feeling that, finally, some real issues were being discussed. Yet this positive development was tainted by frustration at the inability to act on these concerns.

Everyone knew that when the group reached this level of internal conflict, it became almost impossible to decide what to do. It was understood that if SNCC stopped acting, its effort would collapse. Worse, other groups were quite willing to try to capitalize on the grassroots strength that the MFDP had so far been able to mobilize. As SNCC field secretary R. Hunter Morey reported in July 1965, the passage of the 1965 Voting Rights Bill unleashed "a large chunk of voting power which all types of people want to control." The Mississippi NAACP announced that it would run its own summer project, separate from COFO. It was "willing to be 'responsible' and happy to criticize the direct action/local people forces," Morey noted bitterly.[15]

Morey himself was involved in a struggle that—like the one confronting Doug Smith, Charles Glenn, and Reverend Bowie—illuminated larger patterns that SNCC organizers were observing in Mississippi after Waveland. A small-scale version of the conflict between the MFDP and regular Democrats at the Atlantic City convention played out before Morey's eyes. He worked with some young blacks, who called themselves the Whitefield group, who were attempting to gain recognition from the Young Democratic Clubs of America (YDCA). The YDCA president, J. Albert House of North Carolina, encouraged the Whitefield group to "voluntarily drop our application . . . and fall in under the direction of [President of the AFL-CIO of Mississippi Claude] Ramsey, and the Ol' Miss. group," as well as Charles Evers of the NAACP. "No one from FDP had been invited," nor from any other civil rights group. The skirmish ended when the YDCA refused the Whitefield group's offer to work together and Spencer Oliver, the "Hubert Humphrey" of the controversy, vowed to fight Whitefield's charter application to the end.[16]

The momentous debates that began within SNCC in the fall of 1964 now spread through the COFO staff and the MFDP. In the tense environment created by the conflicts between summer volunteers who remained in the state and native Mississippians, the effort to maintain the group's inner cohesion through face-to-face discussion encountered overwhelming hazards. Among them were differences in race, gender, experience, formal education, sexual expectations, and personal opinion. Few inside the movement knew how to control the emotional content these differences could provoke. It was hard to see the struggle for candor as the necessary prerequisite to solving SNCC's everyday issues. Still, if staffers could not reach a consensus on how to proceed, these more explosive issues would continue to surface in the seemingly unrelated business of "who will use the car" or "who will get paid this week." Moreover, such arguments over mundane day-to-day operations produced more frustration and alienation, which drove people out of the movement. All of this took place in the context of a vociferous, active, and unyielding attack by white Democrats on the rank-and-file power base that the MFDP had built up over the preceding two years. In the wake of the 1965 Voting Rights Act and Lyndon Johnson's War on Poverty, the federal government now began to funnel funds to such institutional sites as the Mississippi NAACP, the state AFL-CIO, and the state Democratic Party. All began to try to co-opt or otherwise outmaneuver the MFDP's grassroots organizations. Furthermore, money sources from the North were drying up.[17] The Mississippi movement was threatened both from within and from without.

Not Quite There
The Search for Enduring Ground

Julian Bond's caricature of the story told of the American civil rights movement, "Rosa sat down, Martin stood up, and the white kids came down and saved the day," contains a number of factual errors. It is a three-part fantasy Bond holds aloft for inspection. For starters, Rosa Parks was the third black woman in 1955 to refuse to move to the back of the bus. Dr. King did not "stand up" and start speaking. In a compromise gesture among themselves, a number of Montgomery's concerned black citizens asked him to speak. And as on-the-ground evidence starkly confirms, "white kids" did not come down and save Mississippi blacks. More white supremacy: conscious in some, unconscious in others, misleading in either instance.

The civil rights movement was built by and among the most marginalized citizens in the land and lasted only a decade, yet it succeeded in upending the legalized system of racial oppression and terror that replaced slavery one hundred years earlier. It was an extraordinary achievement, considering the slow, difficult sweep of American history, yet also saddening because the country was not transformed in the end, but instead settled into more comfortable terms of denial. How can we unravel such a massive cultural malfunction? Why did SNCC activists and their manifestly important democratic accomplishments not become part of the popular national legend? The reasons are many, but a central cause lies in the nature of SNCC's demise.

Those who had been "many minds but one heart" in SNCC, as Chuck McDew put it, splintered in the twenty months following the Waveland conference of November 1964. Quietly, with the departures and separations of old associates, SNCC simply faded away.

For a long time SNCC people had shared tumultuous experiences. At the height of the Greenwood movement in 1963, for instance, Charles McLaurin and James Forman served time in jail together. They sang old hymns and created new freedom songs, they argued over the day's schedule in the cell, they disagreed over when to turn off the light bulb, they debated the degree to which Henry David Thoreau's theories were applicable to their penal community. What kept them together was far stronger than what separated them. As one veteran put it, people with all kinds of skills entered SNCC, and "together we made a world."[1] These activists experienced joy and sorrow in one another's presence; they cooked meals and fixed hair and drank beer and made love and screamed at one another. They built lives together. Over many long staff meetings and the social activities that followed, they kept track of one another's trials and small triumphs. All of them believed that the movement was more important than the self and acted accordingly — as Debbie Louis put it, "facing cattle prods or simply running a mimeo machine until two A.M. because that's how long it took to get out a leaflet rather than stopping at six to eat dinner or at nine because that's when Mama said to be home." Through this shared experience, they created a language of words, gestures, jokes, and behavior so interior that it was only with other SNCC people that many felt truly comfortable.[2] From the Nashville sit-ins in 1959–60 to the Mississippi Summer Project in 1964, this was the movement of people who ended Jim Crow in America.

What happened between 1964 and 1967 overturned the premise on which these earlier undertakings were based. At Waveland, McLaurin and Forman's views of "where the revolution should go" pointed in fundamentally different directions. This, then, became the center of the trauma for many inside the movement. The people of SNCC who tore down old submissive habits and barriers to freedom no longer knew how to sustain their community. The more intense one's experiences in SNCC had been, the deeper the agony of the post-SNCC period. After working for several years in Albany, Georgia, Charles Jones was shot at as he returned to the city from Americus. "It got my attention," he said. "After that I made sure I was always in the presence of someone else, particularly the press, when we did things. Because people got lost. People got missing." Soon afterward, he moved to Mexico. "I was 145 pounds, I was taking Miltowns, ten milligrams, smoking a pack and a half of cigarettes a day, no appetite, emotionally shot." He had given the movement "everything I ever learned or felt." Now, he was "absolutely drained."[3]

Dave Dennis gradually disengaged from movement work in Mississippi and entered law school at the University of Michigan. He noticed something familiar about the woman who checked out his books at the law library. It turned out she had survived the abuse of Natchez police officers in 1964, who had played Russian roulette with a pistol to her head. Shortly thereafter she had entered a mental institution in Michigan, and eleven years later, when Dennis encountered her, she was still an outpatient at the institution. For others, the damage was physical, as in the case of Lawrence Guyot, who discovered on leaving an MFDP meeting that he was unable to move the left side of his body. The aftermath of living for too long under extreme tension took a variety of forms. Some used alcohol as a means of self-medication, some knocked down doors in a sudden burst of rage or frustration. In 1966, in Muir Woods north of San Francisco, after a group of former SNCC workers had used the drug LSD, one man began to run through the giant, rust-colored redwoods. Stopping every few minutes, he screamed epithets at the top of his lungs, then the name of a movement leader, followed by "Fuck him!" Amid the stares of tourists and nature lovers, the other SNCC veterans could only calm him down for short periods before he resumed his ranting. Things not said at Waveland now were screamed. Though a makeshift community of internists, psychiatrists, and psychoanalysts across the country was available to help the young people pull themselves together, some students drifted beyond reach. Alienated, they floated aimlessly from job to job. Some became mechanics or cab drivers or house cleaners — "anything which keeps you away from anything which deals with social commentary of any sort." The new society that SNCC activists thought they had been building had vanished.[4] It was a disturbing ending for the group that began with such promise.

Following Waveland, many SNCC people lived with a profound disappointment in white America — an emotion that could easily slide into cynicism, alienation, and a numbing anger that could find no coherent expression. Some former black staffers chose not to talk to whites, sometimes for as long as a decade. Others refused to converse with anyone outside the movement. Such disappointment produced a sense of profound isolation and haunted grief. A few young veterans, old at twenty-two or even nineteen, could find no sustained way to talk about the movement at all.

Former SNCC activists felt not only an all-encompassing loss, but also a sense of failure. What they had learned often could not be explained to others. In collapse, their original dreams were too heavy to share or even to examine privately. Too often, what outsiders had to say about the movement, about "civil rights" and "progress" or about the need for new strategies seemed so facile, so innocent as to render an engaged response impossible.[5]

Now, more than forty years later, we can ask how is it possible that this student movement crashed and burned before those inside could communicate its essential meaning to the rest of the country? James Lawson, Martin Luther King, Charles Sherrod, Prathia Hall, and numerous others in the black freedom church found a way in the late 1950s and early 1960s to mobilize certain aspects of the Judeo-Christian tradition for political ends. They introduced nonviolent direct action as a powerful concept and tool that animated the sit-ins and Freedom Rides. Secular civil rights workers like Ella Baker, Bob Moses, and Charles McLaurin joined them to organize a voting rights drive that broke apart the very foundation of segregation. These SNCC activities created schoolrooms — for the activists themselves, for the people they were talking to, and for visitors from other parts of the nation. A car carrying people to register to vote at a courthouse or the meeting in a church the night before symbolized a hidden American reality. People found out not just about Mississippi, or Georgia, but about America. Most of all they found ways they could perform significant political acts of their own.

In the months after Waveland, only people intimately invested in SNCC understood that the group's actual existence was threatened. Viewed from afar, the Voting Rights Act of 1965 could be seen as a sure sign of success. And it was. But it was not a culminating success for SNCC people. For them, it was merely a beginning. All the more agonizing, then, was the discovery that the movement could not fashion a coherent plan for what to do next.

How do people act when a movement is no longer moving? Not very well, it turns out.[6] Just to get through the day, coworkers and allies began to evade and lie to one another as if they had never experienced the candor that grew out of their common struggle. This was most visible in the withdrawal of black SNCC staff from interracial relationships, but it was also happening in intraracial relationships among all workers.[7] Understandably, SNCC had not developed ways to talk through different experiential realities. For some, a ritualized and empty rhetoric replaced politics. Others competed in what they hoped others would see as "militance." Though a common pattern in the late stages of social movements, it hardly softened the absurdities that soon began to surface in activists' conversations. One would hear, for example, that local leaders like Fannie Lou Hamer were "no longer relevant."[8]

In the endless postmortems, one could blame America, or white America, or the establishment, or some other abstraction, but this exercise did not provide a blueprint for daily life in the late 1960s. One could critique the movement, or certain individuals in it, but that, too, did not lead to a usable organizing plan. In sum, people who attempted to live by the lessons the movement had taught now lacked something concrete to do that would have a solid political impact.

Hanging over this entire situation was an immense sadness that was inseparable from the extraordinary experiences they had earlier shared.[9]

To communicate their knowledge to others, SNCC people needed poise, endurance, and a space for reflection — space that Bob Moses perceived was nonexistent in Mississippi. The only thing that came close, he said, was the work-study program at Tougaloo College. Here civil rights workers could attend school for a year and recuperate, but it "was not tailored to a person that had this intensive experience in the field. So you didn't take advantage of what they had learned. There was no program for tape recording or teaching them how to write, to term what they were doing." This was also true of the Fund for Educational and Legal Defense (FELD), created by Ella Baker, which provided college scholarships for some SNCC workers. While such options had given SNCC workers a temporary respite from the intensity of movement work, they did not teach people how to reflect on their movement experiences in ways that enabled organizers to return to the field rejuvenated and clear. Many SNCC people discovered that between the movement and the university, a chasm existed.[10]

In terms of political democracy, the long-term price of veteran activists' muteness has been that a wealth of practical information on grassroots democracy was not passed on to subsequent generations. This knowledge did not become a part of the history taught in the schools of America. Nor did most post-SNCC organizations manage to internalize the experience of the movement. Today, two generations of historians have struggled to understand and reconstruct this era. The introduction to this book described this challenge as the "sacred ground" problem. First, almost no historians have been able to clearly explain *how* civil rights or Black Power activists accomplished their feats, except through highly generalized abstractions about people transforming the social and political landscape of the nation.[11] The specifics have remained beyond reach. Second, activists are often regarded as superheroes. But our respect for SNCC people and their achievements should not prevent us from seeing where they made mistakes.

SNCC itself ceased to operate as a group of organizers after its last campaign in Lowndes County, Alabama. While they no longer organized together under the SNCC umbrella, most veterans of the movement entered occupations that demonstrated their determination to work with people at the bottom of the social hierarchy.[12] Outgrowths of the SNCC experience included participation in the Black Power, women's liberation, community organizing, draft-resistance, and labor movements.

Many initiatives resulting from SNCC activities can be loosely grouped under the rubric of Black Power — defined by Stokely Carmichael as a call for African Americans to unite and build their own political, economic, and social organizations. Fannie Lou Hamer started a multifaceted self-help program, Freedom Farm. Willie Peacock and Sam Block organized multiple folk festivals in Mississippi to develop "an appreciation of our rich heritage and cultural ties with Black Africa." As Block recalled, when he and Peacock worked as community organizers, "we discovered that the local adults knew many old songs that were part of our heritage and we wanted to present them to the people to show what a great story the songs tell." The Federation of Southern Cooperatives, another by-product of the freedom movement, marketed dashikis made from African-produced fabrics sewn by over thirty southern cooperatives. The Drum and Spear Bookstore in Washington, D.C., started by Charlie Cobb, Judy Richardson, Curtis Hayes (later Muhammad), and Courtland Cox, was by the early 1970s the largest black bookstore in the country. Tony Giddings, one of the leaders of the Howard University student movement in 1968, worked as the Drum and Spear's manager. Eventually, the Drum and Spear collective was instrumental in organizing Howard's historic 1969 conference, "Toward a Black University," which led to the formation of hundreds of Black Studies departments at universities and colleges nationwide.[13] Some SNCC people stayed in the rural South to organize such groups as the Mississippi Freedom Labor Union, adult literacy cooperatives, independent economic enterprises including the Madison County Sewing Firm, quilt cooperatives, woodworking cooperatives, and okra or bean cooperatives. Others tried to bring SNCC pilot programs to Harlem, Chicago, and other places in the urban North.[14]

At the same time, the 1964 – 68 experiences of SDS activists eerily reproduced the post-Waveland initiatives of SNCC veterans. Education and Research Action Projects (ERAPs) in the North generated "free spaces" from which other community-based institutions emerged. The most important of these were welfare rights organizations that sought to bring a democratic dimension to the national War on Poverty. ERAPs proved to be the training ground for organizers who later worked in the draft-resistance unions and women's liberation organizations that sprang up near the end of the sixties.

By 1965 ERAPers, similar to the SNCC field staff, had developed their own ways of speaking and dressing; to a large extent, they worked from assumptions (also similar to SNCC's) that separated them from their counterparts on college campuses. Their experientially based understanding of the way local people came to civic life conflicted with the intellectually based understanding of SDSers on campus and in the national office.[15] The closer ERAPers got to the grass roots, the less university-based conventional wisdom made sense: neither Marxist ideas about organizing workers nor liberal certitudes about government intervention appeared to improve the lives of the urban working poor. After SDS sponsored the first March on Washington against the Vietnam War in April 1965, campus activities and recruitment increased significantly. People struggled to connect welfare rights organizing to antiwar activities.[16] The juncture reached at Waveland — where activists in projects and those in the central office no longer communicated clearly enough to stay united on program — was repeated within the national SDS organization in 1965. It would recur over and over again throughout the decade in hundreds of local activist groups, as well as those at the regional and national levels.

SNCC work had other echoes. One of the first documents created by the "second-wave" of feminist movements that crested in the 1960s and 1970s was produced at the Waveland conference. SNCC staffers Casey Hayden, Mary King, and several others wrote what Hayden later called an "internal education" paper on women in the movement. "A novel idea at the time," it was an attempt to "bring forward the fact that sexism was comparable to racism."[17] The paper asked: Why were competent, qualified, and experienced SNCC women "automatically assigned to the 'female' kinds of jobs such as: typing, desk work, telephone work, filing, library work, cooking, and the 'assistant' kind of administrative work, but rarely the 'executive' kind"? Just as black labor underlay the entire cotton economy, "women are the crucial factor that keeps the movement running on a day to day basis." What could SNCC do to give women "equal say-so when it comes to day to day decision-making?"[18]

After Waveland, black women continued to fight sexism within SNCC in the context of the black struggle for equality. They did not publicly address the Hayden-King questions; for most, unity with their black brothers superseded a public break over the men's sexist behavior.[19] Those willing to openly break with their male allies at this point were SDS women, newly emboldened by their work in ERAPS. Thus it was white women, Hayden and King, while trying to make sense of the withdrawal of their black SNCC friends, who raised the first public call for women to be seen as equals within the student movement. The women who responded to this call were looking for a language to critique the intense intellectual jockeying that characterized SDS staff meetings. The conceptual language in the second memorandum Hayden and King wrote to movement women in 1965 gave SDS women a way to initiate the critical conversations that would lead to the emergence of a women's movement within the New Left. Still, the unexamined white supremacy of many early white feminists outside the civil rights movement made their debt to their feminist southern sisters — black and white — difficult to see.[20]

Nevertheless, the ideas expressed in these two memos by SNCC women both influenced and played out within the movement for women's liberation, bearing significant political fruit by the late 1960s. Applying the lessons of earlier movement experiences to their own lives, groups such as the Redstockings, the

Feminists, Sudsofloppen, Bread and Roses, Cell 16, the Chicago Women's Liberation Union, and the New York Radical Feminists focused action campaigns on challenging laws and cultural beliefs about abortion, marriage, the nature of sexual orientation and desire, work, medical practice, and religion.[21] Many of these groups possessed one or more members who had taken part in the southern freedom struggle. As women tried to talk to each other more openly as a way to identify and reevaluate the central issues of their own lives, they named these small gatherings "consciousness-raising" (CR) groups. CR groups mushroomed across the country.

In the growing opposition to the Vietnam War, SNCC men were the first to fly in the face of the John Wayne real-men-are-warriors mentality. In ways that many Americans gradually came to understand over the next two generations, SNCC field secretaries tested the exact intersection of U.S. foreign policy and the civil rights movement. When MacArthur Cotton tried to eat with white inductees in Jackson, Mississippi, the induction center was wholly segregated. Amazingly, Jim Crow was enforced even among those fighting to bring democracy to Vietnam.[22]

The ensuing draft resistance movement echoed the southern voter registration projects, sometimes in striking ways. Like their female counterparts, white men in SNCC were unsure how to find meaningful work after leaving the civil rights movement. They often landed in the North, joining peace movements largely centered on university campuses. SNCC veterans like Mendy Samstein, Staughton and Alice Lynd, John Wilhelm, and Jake Blum on the East Coast and David Harris and Dennis Sweeney on the West Coast formed "The Resistance," a draft resistance group they envisioned as a northern version of SNCC. ERAP staffers such as Carl Wittman, Vernon Grizzard, and Nick Egleson joined them. "Though the talk was politics," Harris recalled, "it was an intimate experience. We were carrying out big decisions in one another's company. Where our fathers had become men at war, charging a hill with a rifle in their hands, we were trying to do the same thing by dropping the rifle, stopping the war, and saving the hill. We had no models to go by, and it took courage to fly in the face of everything John Wayne stood for." Draft counselors tried to keep in daily contact with those who had pledged to resist the draft. Often resisters trained as counselors. Counseling, in this case, was a way to share life experiences. People in the draft resistance movement engaged in thousands of one-on-one conversations, building relationships in the same way SNCC organizers had built relationships with local people.[23]

Black men in SNCC had in fact been the first to lead in antiwar analysis and action. SNCC issued its first statement against the war on 6 January 1966 after Sammy Younge Jr., an early SNCC supporter from Mississippi just home from the navy, was shot to death in Tuskegee, Alabama, by a white filling station attendant for using a whites-only bathroom. SNCC launched the slogan "We Won't Go." David Gilbert of SDS later reflected that "SNCC was the one that said 'hell no, I won't go,' and raised draft resistance a lot earlier than we did. So they raised the stakes. They raised the clarity about identification with third world struggles."[24]

As in Mississippi, draft counselors placed a premium on each man making his own decision, rather than telling draftees what to do. In the course of counseling, the men would explore their deepest feelings about armed service and the nature of the conflict in Vietnam. Young men took the greatest risks: "If everybody refused to serve," one participant noted, "the war could not go on." Another man who had a secure deferment remarked: "I knew that meant someone was getting drafted in my place. I found that hard to live with, so I felt the only thing for me to do was to stand up and say 'no' publicly, and to join building a movement that is going to shut this Selective Service down permanently."[25]

As Bernice Reagon observed in the 1970s, SNCC gave birth to all of these movements — Black Power, ERAP, women's liberation, and the draft resistance movement.[26] Yet some veterans could not maintain their post-SNCC involvement. Elaine DeLott Baker was "asked by feminist historians why more of us who are considered to be 'early feminists' did not go on to leadership positions in the women's movement," she recalled in 2001. "My response is that despite the personal anger that I sometimes felt when confronted with sexist situations, and despite my yearning for equality between the sexes, it was always the freedom struggle that held me. To shift my identity, commitment and energy from the freedom struggle to the women's struggle was not something I could do, especially at a time when I was still grieving over my separation from the movement." Her response captures the sentiments of many SNCC workers who could not find a sustaining environment after their self-generated community in SNCC collapsed. As Baker concluded, "The freedom struggle was the flame; all else was shadow."[27]

Conclusion
Freedom as an Inside Job

For large numbers of Americans, the civil rights movement is a triumphant story. The movement stands tall as a significant landmark on the preordained American journey toward a more perfect union. Accordingly, we celebrate the movement through its most easily understood spokesman, Martin Luther King. We name bridges, highways, and public schools after him in communities across the land. And, in truth, we have reason to do so. The movement for which he became a symbol altered the racial landscape of the country. America did change, though in less profound ways than activists had envisioned. The task at hand, then, is to explore the gap between the two in order to come to grips with what SNCC people had internalized that the rest of the country, including participants in subsequent movements, found so difficult to emulate.

SNCC's vision of democratic relations warred with a deeply ingrained American understanding of how a true democracy functioned. Based on an unconsciously self-serving assumption, many white citizens believed that racial injustice lodged within uninformed and prejudiced sectors of the population and could therefore be fixed by U.S. experts and leaders; any remaining cultural gaps between whites and nonwhites persisted because of actions of the uneducated. A few barnacles from the past undoubtedly existed, but "we were working on them."

SNCC people learned firsthand that experts and leaders did not know how to break down Jim Crow. The great discovery of SNCC activists was that they themselves could dismantle the caste system — if they acted as if segregation did not exist when entering restaurants, movie theaters, roller rinks, hotels, churches, courtrooms, and voting booths. They found that they could create democratic interactions that had the potential (after a certain amount of cultural and judicial strain) to become habits absorbed into the American mainstream. Freedom was not a product of speeches or anthems proclaiming "the land of the free and the home of the brave." It was not a circumstance one experienced by writing the words "America is a free country." Freedom existed (or did not exist) in one's daily life. It was how one acted every day. It was an inside job.

SNCC people worked to share this way of being with black people in the South — some urban, but most rural — who subsequently began to regard themselves as leaders. Black southerners no longer looked to local whites. Nor to black ministers. Nor even to the movement veterans popularly known in the South as Freedom Riders. In 1963 a young Bob Dylan witnessed this work in Greenwood, Mississippi, as "the chimes of freedom flashing."[1]

Once at the heart of movement activity, individuals in SNCC were compelled to become what Antonio Gramsci termed "organic intellectuals," those whose experiences forced them to rethink everything they had previously understood about their own lives, their country, and indeed politics itself. As Bob Moses noted at Waveland in 1964, "There are people in this room who know more about the 1957 and 1960 Civil Rights Acts than anyone in Congress or the Justice Department — from being out in the field and trying to make use of [these acts]." "People . . . who know more about the . . . Civil Rights Acts" did not refer to those who were trained to understand legalese, but to SNCC workers who "know people for whom [the laws] were intended" and who were in a much better position than anyone else in the nation to assess the laws' effectiveness.[2]

People comfortable within the nation's intellectual-cultural elite often found such claims as those put forward by Moses to be naïve or even offensive.[3] They took offense that Moses could claim that a twenty-year-old black student from Mississippi like Curtis Hayes or an uneducated sharecropper like Fannie Lou Hamer knew more about civil rights politics than they did. Since very little if anything in the lives of politicians, intellectuals, and journalists had created room for such a possibility in the realm of comparative expertise, a controlling condescension came to mark their attitude. It could be seen garishly when Robert Kennedy ordered Charles Sherrod and Diane Nash to start a "cooling down period" during the Freedom Rides, but also when NAACP head Roy Wilkins told Mrs. Hamer to go on home from Atlantic City, he'd clean up the mess she had made at the Democratic National Convention. Journalists, politicians, and the academics who came along later all tended to quote the Kennedy/Wilkins version of events, one that consistently saw political elites as critical to any viable solution. The two versions of events, as well as the two separate understandings they generated, were directly at odds with each other. Movement activists like Bob Moses articulated the experientially tested view from within, whereas political elites expressed a view from afar, detached from the messy reality or the rich learning experiences on the ground. Unfortunate for both activists in the movement and subsequent generations of Americans, the elite view from afar also was, and continues to be, the culturally dominant view. As a consequence, central lessons of the movement have not been passed on. While the movement eventually failed to transform the political culture of the larger society, the larger society subsequently failed to see and understand the movement's accomplishments. Younger generations thus continue to hear the well-rehearsed and crippling sanitized version from afar.

Why the total misfire here, particularly when the civil rights era may well prove to be one of the most important moments of popular democratic striving in American history? What is so threatening about the civil rights movement? What qualities did it embody that render the answer to this question so uncomfortably awkward that, in the end, it becomes too much to swallow? Journalists, academics, and politicians recorded the civil rights movement for posterity. Repeatedly, almost all of them got it wrong. They got it wrong because they had not experienced a transforming moment when they discovered that their prior understanding of race in America had been fundamentally skewered by white supremacy. They also got it wrong because scholars and politicians belong to the very part of society the movement was trying to change, a society replete with hierarchy and unearned condescension.

Unlike natural scientists, social scientists and journalists can chronicle the happenings of the world on a day-to-day basis without having to test their assumptions against reality. Their findings cannot be verified or disproved by being experimentally "reproduced" by their peers, as natural science insights must be. Quite the contrary, because they live and work in a comfortable and hierarchical culture, intellectuals and political leaders far more often than not reproduce a vast accumulation of hierarchical assumptions. Hence, a prolific writer on the civil rights movement, Milton Viorst, can state that at Atlantic City, Bob Moses "chose not to take into account" the processes of democratic politics and assumed a position of "moral absolutism," which had a "place in abstract philosophy, but not in the political system." Moses was no "moral absolutist," but rather a battle-seasoned realist: he asked the Democratic Party to follow its own rules. Another widely respected scholar of the movement, Kirkpatrick Sale, can opine that the poor "want leaders, they do not want to lead; the poor are myth-ridden, enervated, cynical, and historically the least likely to rebel; the poor are powerless." Such descriptions, while carrying plenty of cultural authority, are not only ignorant, the historical evidence is impressive that they are plain wrong. Habits of condescension, once internalized, seem almost impossible to break.

Another difficulty for journalists, academics, or political commentators, especially when they write about political change generated by unexpected, nonelite actors, is that they operate in an environment in which certainty is expected and rewarded. Indeed, in academia as well as in the world of journalism and politics, the appearance of doubt or uncertainty is a great liability. Grimacing city editors admonish reporters to "get it right." The labor of academics is subjected to a similar form of peer review. And politicians have the most unassailable test of all: they either win the election or they exit the stage. But for the most compelling of reasons — survival itself — the entire history of SNCC was one of doubt. Movement activists constantly questioned, and then tested, their assumptions. If things did not work, one had to go back to the drawing board and refine or change one's idea in consultation with others. Not to remain flexible, open, and questioning could get one killed. Reminders of this truth were everywhere.

In American culture, journalists, academics, and politicians occupy leadership positions — they belong to a privileged group. From right to left, this group routinely condescends to ordinary people. Thus more often than not, in 1964, 1982, and today, those who have attained the "credentials" to tell the story of the movement have had trouble fathoming that Curtis Muhammad or Fannie Lou Hamer would have more sophisticated insights than they themselves about what is possible and what is not, and how American culture operates on multiracial terrain.

The difference is and was one of implementation: Movement intellectuals asked, over and over, "What can I do to get rid of the caste system?" It was a question not posed by other intellectuals. Reality forced movement people to reevaluate their ideas. Intellectuals based at newspapers, universities, or in political positions did not have to do this, and routinely did not.

Ella Baker, perhaps the movement's most outstanding organic individual, addressed this problem in a profound yet simple way: she encouraged others to listen. In so doing, however, she intended much more than what is ordinarily meant by "listening." For her, it included opening herself up to the views of others as a means to develop her ability to look at things from other perspectives. In short, she grew in herself a willingness to doubt and question her own thinking. She also believed that listening was an inherently communal act, one that capitalized on the fact that everybody contributed something to the civic conversation, and that everyone therefore is important. Historian Barbara Ransby summarized Baker's legacy in SNCC: "Baker spent many hours sitting silently through long and cumbersome SNCC discussions, making her interventions often at the very end of the meeting. She interrupted only to make sure that others were allowed to speak and that the more confident speakers were made to listen."[4] Quite simply, then, Ella Baker knew that one cannot hear, much less learn from, someone to whom one condescends. As she put it in 1980, "if there is any philosophy, it's that those who have walked a certain path should know some things, should remember some things that they can pass on, that others can use to walk the path a little better."[5] Lastly, years of organizing had taught Baker that small groups of people could not make a movement alone. Just "being" right is a losing proposition if you cannot make movement goals seem right, and *feel* right, to the people you are trying to reach. For Baker, the point was to encourage people to articulate and fight for their ideas, to create leadership in each community so that formal leaders would no longer be necessary. If your ideas and actions were no longer informed by the struggles in the community, you lost the people who make up a movement. Things no longer "move." You go nowhere.

If they had internalized the lessons of organic intellectuals like Ella Baker, journalists, academics, and politicians did not have to be in the movement to see and hear Bob Moses and know what he was talking about when he said SNCC workers knew more in 1964 about how effective the 1957 Civil Rights legislation had been than most everyone in Congress. Without such insights, or the personal experiences that come from participating in inclusive politics, however, Moses' conclusions were almost certainly missed. The evidence is overwhelming that the political lessons he learned in his years of struggle have ever since proved incomprehensible to the cultural gatekeepers of American society. Therefore, simply enough, these ideas have not been passed down. Every newspaper article, history textbook, or documentary that fails to grasp and therefore passes over SNCC's democratic insights continues to produce two results. First, it maintains the notion that American political culture, however hierarchical and flawed, is the best Americans can hope to achieve. Second, it robs all those who were not in the movement of a key model upon which future generations could build.

Even though their political achievements were largely invisible to the broader society, SNCC veterans' prior experiences in the freedom struggle were the formative building blocks of who they had now become — the essential memories that gave their lives meaning. This was true even though their work was largely invisible to subsequent generations. Collectively, for them, these images *were* the movement: students who calmly ignored whites when they spattered ketchup on their faces or poured salt in their hair during sit-ins; the Afro-Mississippians who never made a speech but who housed and fed young activists for weeks at a time and who kept guns in their closets for self-defense; those who drove people and fed people because, like Bernice Johnson walking around City Hall in Albany, Georgia, they could sing "Over My Head I See Freedom." There were the compelling images of Diane Nash and John Lewis insisting on returning to Birmingham, Alabama, to reignite the Freedom Rides, and of the Reverend Fred Shuttlesworth of the Sixteenth Street Baptist Church, alone of the entire black establishment, resolutely waiting in Birmingham to meet them; of Charles Sherrod in Mount Olive Church of Terrell County, Georgia, preaching "If God be for us, who can be against us?" as Sheriff Z. T. Matthews burst through the structure's wooden frame door; of Annell Ponder refusing to hate the Winona, Mississippi, policeman who brutally beat her for refusing to say "sir"; of Bob Moses and his band of black youths in Mississippi and their ingenious and perilous attempts to force the rest of the country to see the state through the Freedom Vote; of Roy Wilkins lecturing Fannie Lou Hamer at the 1964 Democratic National Convention in Atlantic City, New Jersey, that she was ignorant and should go home so he could take care of things; of the muddled, damaged insides of the movement spilling out in Doug Smith's anguished statement that "we can't be Muslims in the day and integrationists at night!"; and, perhaps most encouraging for the movement as a whole, of the remarkable self-activity in southwest Georgia and Mississippi then regenerating itself in places like Lowndes County, Alabama; Berkeley, California; and Newark, New Jersey.

These sustained experiences provided SNCC veterans with a new yardstick to measure political vitality. The majority of them who had participated in the freedom struggle before 1966 had too many vibrant memories of grassroots empowerment to participate with gusto in what many saw as the politics of rage, the politics of respectability, or the "personal-is-political" liberation movements that surfaced between 1966 and 1973.

For those who had been involved in the process of trial and error within SNCC, it was exasperating to realize that others — media, family members, college friends — considered SNCC's loss of faith in government institutions to be a product of what the popular press labeled "burnout." Such reasoning was exactly wrong: the federal government's inaction in the face of local abuses between 1960 and 1965 dramatized its deep complicity in Jim Crow. It was as true in Selma, Alabama, in 1965 as it had been in McComb, Mississippi, in 1961: a movement physician in Selma reported treating an average of twenty civil rights women a day whose vaginas had been burned by cattle prod – wielding police. The doctor sent affidavit after affidavit to Washington, but the papers "found their permanent resting places in Justice Department files."[6] The professed impotence of Justice Department liberals such as John Doar, Burke Marshall, and Robert Kennedy when COFO workers phoned in pleas for government protection reinforced the activists' sense of betrayal: Kennedy, for example, had promised protection for voter registration activities and then refused (or could not find a way) to deliver.

Subsequently, Kennedy Justice Department officials learned what movement workers already had suspected: that FBI agents often worked closely with local law enforcement and even the Ku Klux Klan. As long as extralegal violence could be hidden from national and international media outlets, those in positions of power ignored the contradiction between the U.S. Constitution and the existence of segregation.[7]

Lyndon Johnson's abuse of FBI technology at the Atlantic City convention took FBI collusion to a new level of corruption. The Bureau's surveillance of SNCC and the MFDP allowed Johnson unparalleled access to movement thinking. He capitalized on what can only be described as an illegal, unethical expansion of the wiretap's scope to prevent the MFDP challenge from reaching the convention floor. Loss of faith, in short, did not come from burnout. It was a result of government actions that betrayed government promises.[8]

Taken together, such interactions with appointed and elected officials between 1960 and 1965 fostered among movement workers a sobering awareness of the gap between themselves and the federal government. A sophisticated knowledge, which developed well before the release of the Pentagon Papers in 1971 and the Watergate hearings in 1973, prompted a response from the wider public that was similar though markedly less intense than the one that suffused the civil rights movement.

SNCC activities within the broader movement reshaped the republican tradition as it was widely understood in American life. From the colonial period forward, this tradition had depended on the vision of independent yeomen — each with a stake in society — gathering to stand together against distant, impersonal, and overbearing institutions. SNCC behavior revised this republican idea of standing up to demand one's natural rights to life, liberty, and property. The struggle to realize democratic social relations was an avenue of public work that was possible only in the company of others. SNCC workers demonstrated the simple proposition that one cannot live a democratic life alone. People like Bob Moses, Charles Sherrod, and Prathia Hall — along with early models of "womanist" practice such as Fannie Lou Hamer, Ella Baker, and Carolyn Daniels — offered concrete examples of how to act in public while pursuing broad popular goals. It was "womanist" because the skills required of these community organizers often overlapped with the previously sanctioned social training of females: warmth, empathy, compassion, and an ability to listen. Yet certainly men like Moses, Sherrod, Charles McLaurin, and Curtis Hayes were also among the more talented creators of such new social spaces for Americans.

SNCC's impact on wider American politics was initially minimal and not especially effective when national Democrats proceeded on conventional political assumptions. But the group did teach something belatedly useful to the Robert Kennedys and Burke Marshalls of the Democratic Party. From SNCC, they learned how America's massive burden of racial oppression undermined the democratic tradition. Kennedy, for one, moved to confront some of this burden once he transcended his traditional assumptions in the months before his assassination in 1968. The Democratic Party as a whole was receptive enough to become associated in the minds of many whites, North and South, with the civil rights movement itself. Indeed, this responsiveness ended the solid Democratic South and ushered in a racially conservative Republican Party augmented by millions of white southerners. Many of the inherited presumptions that had long guided the Jim Crow South found a convivial home in the numerically broadened southern Republican Party.

For better or worse, as Moses later pointed out, SNCC work raised the level of black Mississippians' civil rights to that of African Americans in the rest of the country. The Magnolia State was "no longer this defiant voice," both the symbolic and organized opposition "saying no to basic human rights [for] black people." And yet in their pursuit of raising Mississippi to a par with California, Ohio, or New Jersey, SNCC workers had glimpsed the possibility of a far more democratic politics for people in every part of the nation.

Moses' assessment of SNCC as the dominant creative force for the movements of the 1960s was both experientially informed and historically accurate. Careful analysis highlights SNCC's causative role in setting in motion the dynamics that led to multiple student movements in the North and on the West Coast, and to the women's movement nationally. It is also necessary to note the impact of SNCC on other civil rights groups such as SCLC. At key junctures — including the sit-ins, Freedom Rides, and early voter registration drives in Mississippi and Georgia — it became clear that SNCC internalized the organizing techniques of nonviolent direct action to a degree that SCLC could later approach only with great difficulty. Conversely, it is also true that SNCC staffers were routinely reluctant to give SCLC credit where, in fact, it was due — namely, SCLC's major role in Birmingham and, sequentially, Birmingham's role in helping create the preconditions for congressional passage of the 1964 Civil Rights Act.[9] The "Letter from the Birmingham Jail" represented Martin Luther King at his best; nevertheless, public and confrontational (nonviolent) direct action actually came to Birmingham through the work of Jim Bevel, a veteran of the Nashville workshops. Similarly, SNCC veterans Diane Nash and John Lewis played a key role in maintaining the momentum of the crucial Freedom Rides of 1961. Their effect on the consciousness of southern blacks was so galvanizing that thereafter the popular term for all young movement activists, regardless of their organizational affiliation, was "Freedom Rider." CORE deserves recognition for its contribution to the Freedom Rides, as does Bayard Rustin and the older generation of nonviolent direct action advocates. CORE additionally set up voter registration projects in Mississippi and even more in Louisiana. The magnificent role of Fred Shuttlesworth in Birmingham demands more than a mention:

he lived the statement he made in 1961 — "We mean to kill segregation or be killed by it!"[10]

It seems only fair to also credit SCLC's activities in Selma, along with everything that SNCC did there between 1963 and 1965, with creating a positive climate for the 1965 Voting Rights Act. Though federal pressure after the passage of these acts was directly responsible for many changes that took place, it was the civil rights movement that forced Washington to take such action. Beyond this impact on the civil rights struggle as a whole, SNCC was central in generating the political climate that produced SDS's historic conference in Port Huron, Michigan, in 1962 (see Chapter 4). SNCC also served as the channel through which movement tactics could be exported from the Deep South to the rest of the nation (see Chapters 5, 6, and 12; Appendix H).

P eople's hopes and visions about the future of race relations in America — as well as about the future of democracy — were informed by varied life experiences. Diane Nash and Ruby Doris Smith Robinson shared time in the Rock Hill, South Carolina, jail, as well as a fierce commitment to total noncooperation with segregation, but by 1966 they emerged with dramatically different ideas about how to proceed. Nonetheless, these and other activists formed an increasingly sophisticated understanding of how to organize local blacks in a hostile environment and how to relate to one another without giving in to constant threats of violence, exhaustion, and limited resources. As chronicled in this book, SNCC people had numerous disagreements, setbacks, and failures. SNCC workers in the Delta or southwest Georgia had no benefit of hindsight to indicate whether their efforts would eventually pay off, or even whether they would live to see another day.

The immediate, tangible goals of the movement had the power to recruit large numbers of people — if often only temporarily — to integrate buses, lunch counters, theaters; to employ more black drivers, waiters, teachers; to desegregate schools; to register blacks to vote. And it is precisely in this sense that observers, with some justification, have proclaimed the era of 1964 – 65 a triumph for civil rights. On paper, the combined thrust of the Civil Rights Act of 1964 and the Voting Rights Act of 1965 effectively broke apart America's legal caste system.

To the mounting alarm of movement activists, however, this success had distressingly little impact on the daily lives of many African Americans. At the very moment of presumed "triumph," most blacks still attended substandard schools, lived in segregated neighborhoods with far fewer resources than their white counterparts, endured racism practically wherever they came in contact with white America, were relegated to a second-class job market, and had no statistically significant new access to capital. At the same time, whites asked: "Didn't the civil rights era fix everything?"[11] This situation created a new set of circumstances for movement veterans and a new set of problems. It was one thing to address a visible obstacle like Jim Crow, but quite another to overcome the intangible manifestations of white privilege.

After the Civil Rights Act of 1964 and the Voting Rights Act of 1965, the wider movement's clarity about its tactical goal to end Jim Crow essentially vanished. The challenge of what to do next proved too much for activists to surmount together. Meanwhile, outside the movement, most observers who were pleased with the new civil rights laws of the 1964–65 era could not grasp why, at the height of its power, SNCC appeared to implode.

Yet, while both irony and tragedy may have been part of the unfolding events, the reasons for SNCC's rather sudden demobilization were multifaceted and both external and internal to the wider movement. The experiences of sit-ins, Freedom Rides, and voter registration drives did not routinely or automatically equip anyone to figure out what to do about poverty in the African American community. This remained true despite the fact that it was relatively easy to demonstrate that black poverty was a direct legacy of America's racist heritage.

Transparently, the question "now what should we do?" has not been answered to this very day. One can imagine that future historians will look back to our own era as a time when the country allowed a large proportion of a new generation of black people to suffer through substandard education, violent and drug-infested neighborhoods, a lack of real job opportunities, and mass incarceration as a uniquely American answer to social challenges. Despite this, as any survey of contemporary U.S. politics quickly reveals, there is no sustained public debate about this ongoing contemporary tragedy, much less any agreement on possible solutions.

The problems for SNCC members in 1965, however, were further compounded when they compared their own hard-earned experience in shared democratic decision-making with the dominant realities of politics in day-to-day America. SNCC experimented with the challenge of how to live democracy — and interracial democracy at that. Many activists entered the movement thinking that democracy consisted primarily of having a representative government. Yet after months or years of community organizing, they concluded that any substantive notion of democracy involved a lot more than structural reforms. It included changes in daily habits and ways of acting toward others at every level of public life. And while SNCC organizers became astute listeners to local people, they realized that the larger society was tone-deaf to the voices calling for such changes at the grass roots.

Band of Brothers, Circle of Trust

By 1965, when most observers saw SNCC at the peak of its success, its membership confronted mounting external obstacles in addition to internal problems. Many are issues that perennially haunt social movements; indeed, they routinely interrupt democratic attempts in our own time. Laws are easily passed, but cultures are hard to change.

The internal difficulties SNCC people faced, as described in this account, had to do with lack of patience with one another, lack of a format for self-evaluation, lack of a structure that made activists accountable, and lack of received traditions that enabled Americans to talk about race in a straightforward manner in "mixed" company.

Another problem was SNCC's movement-long tendency to occasionally let their eyes wander from people at the base, leading to the personal aggrandizement of field secretaries. This was evident early on in sometimes-loving, sometimes-derisive remarks about Martin Luther King as "De Lawd."[12] To SNCC's credit, this inclination was often domesticated; however, it is not mean-spirited but merely necessary to note that it was not always repressed. Some staffers used cars, funds, or fund-raising trips to increase their personal power at the expense of others. In contrast, King (if not all SCLC staffers) was always generous. One movement veteran once remarked: "That old man [King] knew a good number of democratic things — not as many as Bob Moses, certainly, but far more than most Americans of all races."[13]

Amid all these difficulties, activists had to learn to live with the discomfort of unpredictable lives and uncertain futures. Charles Sherrod, for example, made hundreds of drives between Albany and Atlanta and literally risked death on each one. Every movement woman who was arrested at night feared she would be sexually assaulted by prison guards. John Lewis did not know whether he would live to see the end of the Freedom Ride.

When the weight of unpredictability became too heavy, some turned to versions of communism or nationalism. It was a threatening and chaotic environment that raised more questions than answers. Antiwar and feminist activist Jane Alpert wrote, "I couldn't tolerate any form of ambivalence or the idea that there was no solution to the horrors I saw in the world." It was, perhaps, an understandable response, but one that warred fundamentally with the flexibility that was a central feature of SNCC's history.[14]

While communism did not find fertile soil in the southern movement, strains of separatism and nationalism did.[15] Whites had left an unpaid bill sitting on the table to gather dust. The bill's contents were summed up somberly by one woman who lived through Jim Crow: "White folks could do anything they wanted to in those days, and if one of our men said something, they'd just kill him." That was it. The way it had been. SNCC people had changed that — now it was different. But the bill was still there. And it had a human face when white guards at the Mississippi State Penitentiary at Parchman stripped seventeen-year-old Ruby Doris Smith naked, then scrubbed her with a wire brush; or when a Camilla, Georgia, police officer beat Marion King so badly she miscarried a seven-month fetus; when a group of whites in Selma, Alabama, pummeled Bernard Lafayette until pieces of his skull hung open; when white policemen in Rolling Forks, Mississippi, put a gun to Ivanhoe Donaldson's temple, raised the hammer and screamed, "Nigger, you ain't gonna get nothin' but a bullet in the head!"; when someone shot and killed Louis Allen on his front lawn in Amite County, Mississippi; when the whites who killed James Chaney left evidence for the forensics team at Old Miss that was so grotesque, so unprecedented, that it produced near incoherence in the doctor responsible for writing the autopsy report; or when a white officer murdered Jimmy Lee Jackson as he tried to protect his grandmother in Perry County, Alabama. Fay Bellamy, a black SNCC staff member, tried to convey the anguish of living through these events: "Can one write about pain? What I'm also attempting to ask is how does one get used to it? How many people will have to die before we can make it a two-way street?" She was afraid of war but "would much rather us die fighting to defend ourselves, since we die all of the time anyway." After James Forman's friend Sammy Younge, a Vietnam-era veteran, was gunned down at a gas station in Tuskegee, Alabama, for using a "whites-only" restroom, Forman wrote: "Crying will not help. If only we were in a shooting war with the crackers. If only we could kill some of *them*. Maybe then having a friend killed would not cause this kind of anguish. We would get some of them if they got some of us. The war ought to be open. But we weren't killing back. We were not in a shooting war."[16]

The constancy of white brutality — particularly police brutality — as the routine response to the civil rights movement across the Deep South led some blacks to see separatism as the only psychologically viable solution. For many, it was the cost they paid for their work during 1960–65, when they repeatedly demonstrated to other African Americans that no one had to remain compliant with segregation. Their endurance made segregation unfeasible; however, their very survival within this crucible of white hatred engendered for some SNCC people an enduring anger that left them nowhere to go. Movement veterans experienced conflicting loyalties: blacks had seen too many brothers and sisters killed by whites to believe in the simple idea of interracial democracy — thus the shift to black separatism. To other African Americans in the movement, whites like Bob Zellner and Bill Hansen who had been unswerving in their loyalty to the movement exposed black separatism as clumsy overkill. Yet some racially separate space had to be created. Fear and suspicion enveloped black and white alike: "The tradition developed between the two has dehumanized both," Sherrod had noted earlier. "On both sides, falsehoods have become the rule."[17]

Integration, moreover, was not the same as assimilation. African Americans wanted equal access to public and educational facilities, but they needed separate institutions as well "to protect and to make change in the black community." Martha Norman later explained that "certain things should be accessible to all. Once those rights are granted, a person should have the choice of whether to assimilate into white culture or to remain in their communities."[18]

Separatism made sense to many SNCC people, but the unalterable fact was that, by itself, it did not provide a long-term strategy. Even in 1965 and thereafter, when the majority of white workers had left the organization, SNCC activists still had to fashion an agenda of action and a structure to support it. As organizers, they struggled over how to empower local blacks. In the spring of 1965, Bob Moses laid out a vision of an organizer who created more links between people and no longer had to be the focal point of the grassroots effort, then asked: "How can we bring this about?" Few in SNCC had answers.

Stokely Carmichael's 1966 call for blacks to rally around "black power for black people" appealed to blacks as a means to "be in control of their own lives." The terms "black power" and "black people" were sweeping abstractions that urgently needed specific content. The words could excite, but they did not provide a concrete way to act. Moreover, as white journalists Pat Watters and Reese Cleghorn recalled, most people in the larger society saw Black Power as "a renunciation of integration and nonviolence." Further, they observed, it "touched the ultimate question of the voter effort: Could democracy and self-government as evolved in America be made to do the work in the South that had been shaped by the movement?"[19]

Once most whites and many blacks had left SNCC, the remaining organizers continued to debate fundamental questions of hierarchy versus decentralization. Was it better for people to be directed by an "all powerful leader who can reward or punish as he sees fit," asked William Porter, a black activist from Albany, Georgia, "or should the group determine its own goals and standards?" In May 1966 Porter dropped out

> because of the feeling of the Atlanta office director in that I must go to the field. . . . I think that SNCC is one of the best groups in the country and because of my love to the organization and the staff I feel as if there is no room for me. I am afraid to go into the field and to work on my own on the things that Forman wants me to work on. I think that in the last three or four years that I

1.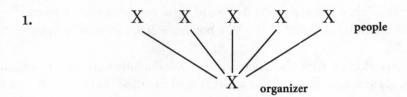

All people have talked to him and he is their reference point. Different groups will form like high school students, college, general etc. and you get something like this:

2.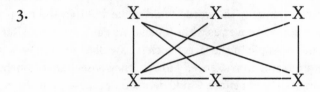

These different groups are not related. All look to organizer. If you want:

3.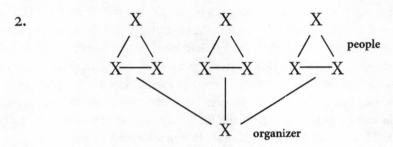

More hookup between people. The organizer needn't be the focal point of meetings. How can we bring this about?

Bob Moses' vision of an organizer. (Bob Parris Moses, 23 April 1965, Staff Meeting Minutes, Mary King Papers, State Historical Society of Wisconsin, Madison)

have tried to do the best that I can to help this organization toward progress. I am sick and need a rest and for the above reason I resign from this group.[20]

A stark reality becomes visible in hindsight. In voluntary social organizations committed to grassroots democracy, resorting to hierarchy was psychologically understandable and yet impractical — indeed, it was unfeasible. When ordered to do something they found untenable, members simply withdrew.

Finally, despite the fact that their efforts had transformed the social and political landscape of the South, SNCC workers never discovered an effective tactic
to dramatize the economic inequities of the region. (No one else has either.)
The best they were able to do was to raise a stunning series of questions on who
should make these economic decisions at the local, state, and national levels.
(Later, the global justice movement would address the issue of "who decides" at
the international level, involving the World Trade Organization, World Bank,
and International Monetary Fund). As one SNCC worker wrote from Natchez,
Mississippi, in July 1965: "I saw in the lighted eyes of an old lady, born and
raised to plantation farm work, the cruelty to the old of the Freedom Movement. 'I just hopes I live to see it,' she says, and sometimes I despair of the same
wish for myself, when we talk of the paradise of a free land."[21]

We Will Be Nonviolent with Those
Who Are Nonviolent with Us

Armed self-defense . . . nonviolent direct action — this story of the civil rights
movement necessarily is about both. Armed self-defense had a long tradition
in black southern politics.[22] After the Civil War, black farmers' first purchase
was often land and a rifle. When whites attacked blacks in the Atlanta race
riots of 1906, blacks were given sanctuary at Clark College. After a few days,
they pulled out guns and marched into the street, singing "Oh Freedom."[23] In
the 1960s some well-trained activists seized control of cultural mores and the
law from white supremacists through nonviolent direct action. Yet all was not
sweetness and sunlight. Many who showed up for nonviolent demonstrations
arrived with a switchblade or a pocketknife. The Klan threatened, the Klan
waved guns, the Klan killed. People in the movement carried guns, too. Others
stood on their porches, rifles pointed toward caravans of hollering Klansmen.
While none of these roads led by themselves to the promised land, all functioned as experiments in freedom.

Nonviolence was more than a "street theater morality play" that led to the
passage of the Civil Rights and Voting Rights Acts. As James Lawson originally
demonstrated, and as Martin Luther King later explained to Stokely Carmichael, "The beauty of nonviolence is that you never let any outside force, nothing outside of yourself, control what you do." The "morality play" description
treats nonviolent direct action as if it were only used to transform the law. Missing from that analysis is the way nonviolent direct action allowed its practitioners to act as *agents* rather than as victims. One had to accept accountability to
be nonviolent.[24]

Of course, nonviolence did not always work to change the law or transform those who enforced the law. One such witness surfaced in the person of Mississippi movement stalwart Hartman Turnbow. A farmer and fiery orator who spoke "with dancing fingers, hands, and phrases," Turnbow told King at Atlantic City that when night riders shot into his house, the only thing that saved his wife and fourteen-year-old daughter was a gun: "This nonviolent stuff ain't no good. It'll get ya killed." As SNCC member Julian Bond recalled, "Almost everybody we stayed with in Mississippi had guns, as a matter of course, hunting guns." It is clear that nonviolence helped people register to vote. It is unclear to what degree people who benefited from successful nonviolent techniques subsequently subscribed to nonviolence as a way of life. As several scholars have observed, many local blacks relied on armed self-defense in situations they felt required it. For them, this flexibility did not house a contradiction; it was simply a commonsense response to conditions. Thus it was never a question of either (self-defense) or (nonviolence), but a model of both-and: use nonviolence when it made sense and self-defense when it was necessary.[25]

This understanding put into perspective other inaccurate depictions by armed self-defense advocates of nonviolent protesters. Robert F. Williams, of Monroe, North Carolina, characterized nonviolent black men as "emasculated" for not protecting their wives and daughters from white mobs: "We most surely can be called the 'sissy race' of all mankind." Williams asserted that only elite African Americans practiced nonviolence. "Nor should we forget that [these] same deceiving pacifist-preaching well-to-do southern blacks profit from the struggle, living lives of luxury while most Afro-Americans continue to suffer." Yet in Mississippi, people at the grass roots practiced self-defense in the context of a nonviolent movement not only to acquire the vote but also to democratize the national party system. Williams also maintained that blacks' willingness to use armed self-defense protected nonviolent protesters: no one in Monroe's sit-ins was spat upon because everyone knew that the blacks in town had guns and would use them if required. Yet in 1961, after picketing a white swimming pool, Williams threatened to kill whites unless he was given protection. He barricaded himself in his home to defend himself, his family, and his neighborhood against night riders. The Klan did appear, but FBI reports indicated "scattered racial violence against isolated black citizens all over town." Despite Williams's intention to use armed self-defense, white racial brutality continued for weeks; beatings, stonings, and gun shots into black homes were reported "almost daily."[26] Importantly, this kind of self-defense differed dramatically from the use of armed struggle as a strategy for change in itself.[27]

In many situations, self-defense allowed voter registration work to continue. But it could also backfire, serving as justification for repression. Similarly, whereas in some situations nonviolent direct action protected people, in others it provoked attack. Given the overwhelming reach of cultural white supremacy, there was not and could never be a single approach that guaranteed defeat of Jim Crow.

Both nonviolent direct action and armed self-defense can be characterized as "militant."[28] Throughout the period 1960 – 65, these strategies, as well as boycotts, legal challenges, and protest marches, coexisted within the freedom struggle. The complexity of these interactions was apparent in Greenwood in the summer of 1964. Idell Graft, a young woman who had just been released from Parchman, shouted at a meeting that young people were fed up with the neatly businesslike discussion, that the boycotts should be an adult responsibility, too. People had been sitting around long enough. "This can be our Mississippi! If we stick together we can do it! And if it mean violent, we go violent!" Anna Mae added that block captains ought to stop blacks from breaking the boycotts: "If you see people goin' in those stores, you beat those jokers up! You smash the food on the ground, and they not goin' back there again." Such behavior was violent. Yet did this count as armed self-defense?[29] It was hard to tell. In any case, the best armed self-defense could do was maintain the status quo. It could not lead to a new day.

In the second half of the 1960s, the government's military response to uprisings in Harlem, Watts, Detroit, and other urban areas had an enormous impact on the ability and willingness of SNCC and ERAP workers to remain committed to their grassroots organizing projects. Newark's brutal police maneuvers seemed impervious to most nonviolent tactics, particularly when the same repression occurred almost simultaneously in Detroit, Chicago, and New York. In such cities, where African Americans were killed for walking in the street, how could blacks be trained to respond nonviolently within a few days? Increasing knowledge of U.S. military policy and its impact on Vietnamese civilians prompted some SNCC and SDS workers to focus greater attention on how they might — "by any means necessary" — prevent the federal government from pursuing the war in Southeast Asia.

Given the pace of these events, most SNCC and ERAP organizers now had only a one-to-three-year lifespan. When the grassroots' organizers drifted out of SNCC or SDS, the activists who took their place did not have the patience for community organizing. Rather, they were interested in a quick response. With the important exception of the comparatively few people who still participated in nonviolent direct action and draft resistance organizing, the antiwar movement did not foster the same kinds of significant social experiences as had the voter registration drives and ERAPs. Nonetheless, as President Johnson continued to escalate the U.S. commitment in Vietnam, many movement people felt compelled to turn their attention to the war. It "had to be fought with everything we could throw at it," recalled sDser Helen Garvy. "And as it became more horrible, that was even more true. And [the Vietnam War] totally distorted the movement, and made us drop a lot of other things that were important. But it had to be done."[30] The murder of Black Panthers in Chicago and Los Angeles prompted a similar response within several wings of the freedom struggle.

Even those transformed by their activities at the beginning of the decade began to doubt the efficacy of nonviolent resistance. Diane Nash remembered that in this period she decided that nonviolence was "probably an ineffective way to struggle for liberation." For a few years Nash — despite being perhaps the most creative nonviolent practitioner of the entire decade — could not imagine a way for the strategy to influence the politics of the later 1960s. sDs activist Dotson Rader attested to a sentiment that broadly emerged: "the meaning-lessness of nonviolent, 'democratic,' methods was becoming clear to us in the spring of 1967. The civil rights movement was dead. Pacifism was dead." It was only later that Nash "noticed that I hadn't killed anybody, I hadn't been to the rifle range, I hadn't blown up anything and truly, I had done very little during that period of time where I had decided that violence was the way to go." Decisively, she observed "that the movement had not attracted large numbers of people in the kind of meaningful social action that it had attracted while we were using the philosophy of nonviolence."[31]

Violence in the street — whether because of racial unrest or antiwar demonstrations — did however bring forth the government in battle dress. Washington paid its price, for it seemed that the country's system of government could no longer settle political disagreements within a civil forum. Yet as peace activist Barbara Deming noted in 1968, it was one thing "to be able to state the price the antagonist paid, another to be able to count your own real gains." It was an echo of the logic Jim Bevel had employed with the northern black leader who was stockpiling weapons. Will you use your resources to get better schools, housing, and health care, Bevel asked, or will you buy guns? At an early sNcc meeting Martin Luther King had warned that nonviolence was not a tactic, but a way of life. The movement's ultimate end had to be the beloved community, for "the tactic of nonviolence without the spirit of nonviolence may become a new kind of violence."[32] Early in the Nashville sit-ins, James Lawson had stressed that the greater the injustice, then the greater the force of the idea that opposed it. Action on behalf of one's conscience would recruit others. Without the essential component of nonviolence, this dynamic idea would morph in the late 1960s into movement outgrowths such as the Black Liberation Army and the Weather Underground — whose recruits were few indeed.[33]

The Loss of Democratic Patience

Even among its best practitioners, the complex and constantly changing problems created by life inside the movement made the continual development of democratic relations a tremendous challenge. For example, the external terror faced by SNCC led activists to experience their emotional lives at an intensified pitch. At times personal relations were too explosive to be handled with calm or grace. Few individuals and virtually no groups developed methods to place self-criticism — honest political assessment — in a context of goodwill and thoughtful caring. On this front, Ella Baker's reminders to ask questions and her observation that people needed time to develop and were at different places were extremely hard to replicate.[34] Further, the compelling nature of personal politics could sometimes work to exclude some activists from tight-knit circles. For many, it was difficult to see how to connect this mode of political activity with traditional strategic politics on a sustained basis.

As well, SNCC confronted the agonizing dilemma of what some veterans referred to as "movement quality control." Going to jail, organizing, surviving — all consumed significant amounts of time. Initially, anyone willing to share the terror of the work was welcomed, as ideological and racial differences paled in comparison to the external threat. Dona Richards noted that to prepare for the Mississippi Summer Project, SNCC had "the problem of hiring large numbers of people at one time." At an October 1964 staff meeting Richards recognized that SNCC had always been able to "absorb a few people at a time," but at Atlantic City she observed the consequences of working with those "who didn't have a SNCC orientation. There are people in the field who don't qualify. [We] must be particular as to people we attract." Quality control produced both a recruitment puzzle and a structural problem, as Bob Moses pointed out: "How does one determine who the good people are — who will decide who the good people are?" It was a stumper that closed the October 1964 staff meeting. A quarter of a century later — in 1988 — Diane Nash asserted that if SNCC had spent more of that time training new people to have a SNCC orientation, it might have remained "a band of brothers, a circle of trust."[35]

The combination of underdeveloped procedures for self-evaluation and the rapid growth of SNCC between 1964 and 1966 put a premium on verbal dexterity, not on grassroots recruiting skills. When SNCC people had problems after 1964, their posture of action and militancy often discouraged or even denied cultural approval of slow and patient work with people at the grass roots. This situation promoted movement workers' talents for rhetorical display rather than encouraging an ever-widening circle of ordinary people to become full participants in civic life.[36] The culture was proving agonizingly difficult to change. In fact, the received culture of hierarchical thinking, impatience with social experimentation, and false intellectual certitude had a tight grip even on activists who tried to change that very culture. As the SNCC experience brought into great relief, it was necessary for people to be persistent and patient with one another. Apparently, this was the single most important lesson that SNCC could not find a way to sustain.

Talking the Talk . . .

As a consequence of these internal and external pressures, SNCC people could not agree on how to proceed as a group. Speechifiers outshouted organizers. The result was that individuals continued to organize, but the group itself no longer focused on working with people at the base. In the end, the Charles McLaurins, Bob Moses, and Jean Wheelers of the movement by and large carried on their work, but did so in new contexts outside of SNCC. The rhetorical style loosened within SNCC got in the way of patiently and persistently growing leaders at the grass roots.

It follows that today it is hard for subsequent generations to see Dave Dennis working as an education organizer in Jackson, Mississippi, or John O'Neal organizing a theater-based community in New Orleans. SCLC's Reverend Jesse Jackson is much more visible. Naomi Wolf is the obvious spokesperson for the women's movement; the thousands of women who initiated and ran CR groups in the late 1960s have largely disappeared from the national civic stage. Public intellectuals like Toni Morrison, Cornel West, David Brooks, and Noam Chomsky enrich our collective civic discourse, but our culture has not yet figured out how to invite onto the stage organic intellectuals based in community movements such as Diane Nash, Hollis Watkins, and Casey Hayden. Today, orators like Wolf and West conduct our public dialogue on democracy and justice. Organizers and grassroots leaders who possess communitarian knowledge (gained through their work with people at the base) are largely, if not wholly, absent from the debate. People like Curtis (Hayes) Muhammad, Jean Wheeler, and Charles Sherrod are available to have the conversation. They just don't have many people inviting them to talk. Most people don't even know that these organizers are missing from the national conversation, much less how to support the work they do.

This is not to say that orators have no place in our public dialogue; certainly well-known SNCC veterans such as Bernice Johnson Reagon, Julian Bond, and John Lewis have shared what they learned in highly significant ways. More often, however, those who "speak" for socially disadvantaged groups are not organizers or leaders in relationship with local people. Most Americans therefore have not internalized what SNCC organizers had learned by 1965. The way to re-vitalize democracy at the base of society is not merely to give rousing speeches to the media or even preach in small churches and community centers. Instead, one might follow the example of the young Charles McLaurin, who found out what the elderly of Sunflower County, Mississippi, wanted — to vote. McLaurin then stood with them, encouraging them to take civic actions. He was "trans-formed" in the sense that this process — learning how to act — changed his life and his understanding of politics. He had long possessed ideas about a better way to live, but now, within SNCC, he learned how to act on them. When he proceeded, he experienced "freedom on the inside." It was freedom created by his own actions, freedom in that very moment. He no longer felt bound by any kind of subservience. It was freedom inside, freedom as an inside job.[37]

It is no striking observation that individuals and societies throughout the world await such a transformation.

Afterword
Beyond Sacred Ground

Why is there a gap between popular conceptions of the civil rights movement, the "sacred ground" versions, and the lessons the movement taught those who participated in it? Some would say it is enough merely to state the problem. If so, it is satisfactory to end on the down note that rhetoric bested grassroots organizing. Others might argue that the only alternative is to end in glory, by praising the changes wrought by the movement. One announces sacred ground and bows out.

Instead, let us return to Charles McLaurin for a brief moment. The descriptive word he used in 1962 was "transform." He was transformed by a new vision — *this is the way to live, this is the way I want to live. This feels like freedom.* What do we say to him now, and what is his response? Does he walk into the room and declare, "In order to give new birth to the democratic ideal like we did in the 1960s, you all need to be transformed"? Clearly he does not. How does he pass on what he learned to those who have *not* experienced the movement's discoveries of how to act politically? This is the biggest conceptual barrier faced by the citizens of this or any other country. McLaurin, Julian Bond, and their compatriots understood the dynamics of movement activity because they learned through experience how hard it is to act democratically.

It was McLaurin, along with hundreds of other black southern youths, who learned how to live by walking into "dusty towns visiting the preacher, and talked to the people about their flower patches and how it was on the plantation and sat in the cafes drinking bootleg liquor with the hustlers and tired farmers and finally got everyone to come to a meeting and talk about how the Lord might see you through by and by but ain't nobody gonna see your babies through today 'lessen it's you and if we *all* get together whitey just can't keep pickin us off one by one — we got to *help* each other, we got to get our rights."[1] Police beat them, shot them, put guns to their head and, in some cases, pulled the trigger. Yet far more stayed than died and became "prophets of a new religion, always, always walking the roads and listening." They built a movement.

Today, the black youths who created the movement are in their sixties and, when they look at America, often find themselves almost speechless with disappointment. The stark reality is that they cleared new spaces through their slow and patient work—the beginnings of new democratic terrain. They learned how to act as full citizens. They helped bring forth that same knowledge within others.[2] The irony is that we do not even have a name for this ground, this terrain, this space, this way of acting "as if" we are free to act.

It is still there.

Sobering though it is to end with the adversity of SNCC's disappointment, worse still would be if SNCC's hard-won knowledge died with them.

John Lewis called it democratic patience. It provides a glimpse of what democracy would mean, or could mean—the place not yet found.

To young people today, SNCC's legacy encourages: challenge any line that limits your full human capacities.

To people who have trouble imagining life beyond the narrow undemocratic boundaries of the present day, they offer a richer, more inclusive way to live.

To journalists, academics, and politicians, they propose the alternative stance of an organic intellectual.

To American politics, SNCC work provides a model to reverse professed ignorance or helplessness in the face of race-based violence, discrimination, and white privilege.

SNCC took on the colossal edifice of the American caste system, armed only with a dream for a new America. The democratic space it carved out is still there, open, waiting.

We'll Never Turn Back: Freedom Songs

Blacks in Albany, Georgia, discovered a way to publicly dramatize their total dissatisfaction with the custom of segregation and not be killed in the process. Bernice Johnson Reagon believed that once the community realized it could do this as a group, it "settled the issue of whether to go to jail."[1] Songs were pivotal in that process, "because in the songs you could just name the people" who were oppressive. Naming one's enemies in song was different from "every once in a while hav[ing] a crazy black person going up against some white person and they would hang him," Reagon explained. "Not only did you call their names and say what you wanted to say, but they could not stop your sound. They would have to kill me to stop me from singing." When the police pleaded with the protesters to stop singing in the paddy wagons or in jail, "you would just know that your word is being heard."[2]

Albany's thickly textured black community life gave birth to some songs that merit mention in any analysis of the dynamics of civic life in the United States. Given the wearisome hardships they faced with seven hundred people jailed, the solidarity that developed in this period is visible through the lyrics of Reagon's "Give Your Hands to Struggle":

If you see me stumble,
Don't stand back and look on
Reach out now, baby,
Give your hands to struggle
Give your hands to struggle
If you feel my heartbreak,
Don't just count the soundwaves
Hold me close now, baby,
Give your arms to struggle
If you see me crying,
Tears running down my face
Don't just pat my shoulder,
Help me go on right on
Give your strength to struggle
If you hear me singing this love song
Don't just stand back and listen
Help me sing it right now,
Give your voice to struggle

Then we'll be moving,
We'll be really moving
Building up our union
If you give your all to the Struggle.[3]

It was through the Albany struggle that church music became central to the civil rights movement as a whole. Freedom songs had always been vital to the struggle, "but the Albany songs carried greater emotional force and were more often rooted in the Afro-American cultural heritage than was earlier the case," Clayborne Carson found. The Albany movement was "basically an adult movement," and church-based songs helped older people make the transition to a position of insurgency. Frequently Charles Sherrod's first action on entering a new area was to teach freedom songs. Through song, civil rights workers were able to embody the idea that "everyone [was] pulling together with a spirit of love and togetherness," McCree Harris noted. As Reagon described it, "The singing was just an echo" of the new society SNCC was creating.[4]

Affidavits

The following grassroots affidavits illustrate more clearly than anything else the gap between American democratic rhetoric and daily reality in the early 1960s.

Affidavit of Mrs. Edith Simmons Peters

"On this 27th day of September, 1961, Mrs. Edith Simmons Peters, being first duly sworn, says as follows:"

"My name is Mrs. Edith Simmons Peters and I live at Box 106, Tylertown, Walthall County, Mississippi. I am a Negro. I am 63 years old, and have raised ten children. I was married in 1913 and divorced in 1943. All of my children now live in New Orleans, Louisiana. I have an eighth grade education from Mt. Moriah School, and have lived in the Mt. Moriah community all of my life.

"Since 1943, I have owned an eighty-acre farm and have run the farm since that time. I raise cotton, sugar, corn, sweet potatoes, sugar cane, and peas. I own ten head of cattle and sell butter and sour milk from them, and have five head of hogs. My property tax runs approximately six or seven dollars a year after my homestead exemption. I paid my poll tax from 1943 till I made sixty years in 1958.

"I have always wanted to register and vote, but never attempted because I was afraid to try.

"I heard in Tylertown that some boys were at Mt. Moriah teaching colored people how to qualify to register. Harrison Hall told me this about two weeks ago. I wanted to go and see and learn how to qualify myself to register that I may vote, so I got Lucius Wilson to carry me over to the school on Monday night, 4 September 1961. They had tables set up, but I sat in one of the pews and listened. They began with singing and praying. Then John Hardy[,] one of the boys who was teaching[,] gave us a talk on good citizens. He said to be a good citizen you had to be a good Christian because they went hand-in-hand and he was trying to encourage every colored person in that community to qualify himself and vote so that he may become a good citizen. . . . After these boys taught this school I made my mind up to go down and register. . . .

"Mr. Wood [registrar] was sitting at his desk typing. [Lucius] Wilson and I walked up to the desk and I said, 'Good morning, Mr. Wood.' He said, 'Good morning, how are you?' He kept typing and after about two minutes, he stopped typing and asked me, 'May I help you?' I told him, 'Yes, I came in to try to register this morning.' He said, 'I am not registering anyone now. You all have got me in court and I refuse to register anyone else until this court is cleared up.' I said, 'Thank you.' He said this loud enough for John Hardy, who was outside the door about five or six feet away, to hear.

"John Hardy then stepped in and said, 'I beg your pardon. My name is John Hardy.' He said this nice and politely. Before John could say anything else Mr. Wood said, 'I want to see you, John.' Mr. Wood got up from his desk and went past John who was in the door and moved aside while Mr. Wood came into the main room. All of us then went out behind Wood into the main room. Mr. Wood went behind a desk and pulled out what appeared to be the top left hand drawer and took a gun from the drawer. All of us were about three feet away from Mr. Wood at this time. Mr. Wood pointed to the door with his left hand and held the gun in his right hand down by his right side. He said to John with a rough voice, 'Do you see that door, John?' John said 'Yes.' Wood told him, 'You get out of it.' John said 'OK,' and turned and began walking out. He was about six feet away from the door leading to the hall. Mr. Wood followed him to the door and just as John got in the door Mr. Wood reached back with his right hand and struck John on the back of the head on the right hand side. Just as he hit him he said, 'Get out of here you damn son-of-a-bitch and don't come back in here.' . . .

"John told the sheriff what had happened. The sheriff told him he didn't have no business in that courthouse. [Lucius] Wilson walked up at this time. The sheriff then said to John, 'If that boy (pointing to Wilson) wants to register he know how to go down to that courthouse and he don't need you to escort him. You didn't have a bit of business in the world down there. You is from Tennessee, you was in Tennessee, and you ought to have stayed there.' The sheriff told him to 'Come on.' John asked him, 'Are you arresting me?' The sheriff said 'Yes.' John asked, 'On what charges?' and the sheriff said for disturbing the peace and bringing an uprising among the people. John said, 'Will you allow me to tell my side of the story[?]' The sheriff said, 'Don't give me none of your head boy, or I will beat you within an inch of your life.' After the sheriff took John, I went home."[1]

Affidavit of Mrs. Hazel T. Palmer

"On June 2 [1964] I was selected to be a poll watcher at Precinct 23 in Jackson [Mississippi] along with Mrs. Navry Taylor.

"I was elected to go to a 23rd precinct meeting held on June 16 for the purpose of electing delegates to the Hinds County Convention. At this meeting I was nominated as delegate but not elected.

"Today, June 23, at 10:00 A.M., I went to the Hinds County Convention at the Hinds County Courthouse, with the intention of being an observer. Mr. Welch, the chairman, came into the hall. He spoke politely but said that there wasn't any room for visitors and he turned us away (I was with Mrs. Nannie Benson). The door was guarded by about four persons — all white.

"I feel that Mrs. Benson and I were turned away because we are Negroes."[2]

Affidavit of Leonard Clay

"We arrived at the courthouse about 5 minutes to 10:00 A.M. We went up first to a room in the courthouse (Madison County), we weren't sure where the County Democratic

Convention was actually being held. So we took a seat [in] the rear with a large crowd outside and a small group inside of the court room. We then decided to split up. Rev. McCloud and I went outside to the Chancery Clerk's office. We were told there that the County Convention wasn't being held there. We had seen a large crowd of people go in, we therefore went to inquire about the Convention. Upon arrival we were told that it was not a meeting of the County Convention, but a meeting to bid on the hospital.

"Rev. McCloud and I left and went back to the court room, where we found that Mrs. [Annie] Devine had moved up to the front. There I took a seat right across from her. Then Rev. McCloud, Mrs. Kelly, and Mrs. Glover followed. This committee sitting around a table was talking and whispering and we couldn't find anything out. Later we found out that the chairman had appointed a credentials committee to go out, they went out. When they came back, they had made up a slate for the representatives to the District Democratic Convention. They asked that his slate be accepted unanimously. And it was accepted by the white committee. Then the chairman turned to us, and said that this is a meeting of the executive committee and not open to the public. When he asked us to leave Mrs. Devine asked to be recognized. And she was. She asked[,] Wasn't this a meeting of the County Convention[?] And he said there wouldn't be a County Convention. Only a meeting of the executive committee. Mrs. Devine said that we were delegates from the West Ward. And he said that he couldn't find our names on the credentials list. So we then left and went back to the COFO office and held our own County Convention. I was elected chairman of the Convention and Mrs. Devine the secretary. The following delegates were elected to go to the District Convention: Mrs. Devine, Rev. McCloud, and myself with Mrs. Kelly as alternate. Then the meeting was adjourned."[3]

Appendix C
The Other Sacred Ground

If the civil rights movement has often occupied a righteous plateau that seemed to soar beyond criticism, the same may be said of the New Left that emerged in the 1960s. This is especially true of its most energetic and influential organization, Students for a Democratic Society (SDS). On this terrain, too, calm reassessments appear to be in order.

It would be unfair to the historical reputation of SDS to suggest that its members were uniquely prone to error or confined by a special kind of narrowness, ideological or otherwise. It is the fate of each successive generation of "modern" people to be insensitive, or perhaps inappropriately indignant, or, even worse, to have one's enthusiasms subsequently seen as mere anachronisms. The militants of SDS cannot be faulted for attempting to tell the country that the emperor was appearing in far fewer clothes than advertised.

Despite their deeply felt call for a grassroots revival of democratic conduct across America, many SDS members possessed an Achilles heel in their very understanding of democracy. The early SDS produced the "Port Huron Statement," which offered a brilliant analysis of the democratic shortcomings of contemporary American society and called for the creation of a "participatory democracy" in which average citizens counted for something and had a right as Americans to be taken seriously. On college campuses, the "Port Huron Statement" was a much-admired document — and justly so.

But the subsequent history of SDS demonstrated conclusively that the ability to write well or to think grandly about democratic possibility did not in any causative way translate into personal democratic conduct or into a democratic conception of what political organizing necessarily entailed. The deepest irony of the history of SDS is that its members made speeches and wrote position papers, but the Jim Crow South could endure a thousand speeches and ten thousand position papers while holding the fort for segregation.

The process by which political ideas move to action is not something one learns from speeches, position papers, or sanctioned texts by Adam Smith, John Locke, Karl Marx, or anyone else. For example, a Michigan graduate student named Alan Haber paid close enough attention to the early sit-ins in February 1960 that he took it upon himself to attend the founding meeting of SNCC at Shaw University. It was an energizing experience, but whatever Haber learned about conferences of Afro-Americans, the debates that occurred at Shaw were organizational (or institutional, to be more precise) rather than operational. They thus did not succeed in bringing home to Haber finite instructions on how to act — at least not in language he could understand. Bluntly, Haber was quite "advanced," ideologically, but he did not know how to act. He subsequently played an essential role in the formation of SDS — but then SDS did not know how to act. Indeed, the well-known Haber-Hayden debates of 1963 juxtaposed different understandings of SDS's possible future actions.

Haber's antagonist in these debates, Tom Hayden, brought vigorous new ideas to the subject because he had been recruited by someone fresh from the Atlanta office of SNCC, Sandra Cason (later his wife, Casey Hayden). Hayden was then led by her to the movement action in Fayette, Tennessee, and in due course to the world that Bob Moses inhabited in Mississippi. Collectively, these experiences (including hiding in the back seat of Moses' car to avoid local police) brought home to Hayden the process through which ideas could move to action. This did not mean, however, that Hayden (or SDS) had acquired the wherewithal to teach recruits the possible new directions for participatory democracy. That is to say, had they decided to launch a Lawsonesque workshop in Michigan, they would not have known what to say or do in it. The libraries at Ann Arbor seemed of little help because neither Adam Smith nor Karl Marx had much to offer on the subject. There was a substantial difference between what could be learned about social life and politics in a college classroom and the teaching potential of an experientially grounded workshop. The necessary "classroom," it turned out, was in Cambridge, Maryland.

Just as it was crucial to trace the early education of James Lawson through the influence of his mother, his time with A. J. Muste at the Fellowship of Reconciliation, his decision to be a conscientious objector and go to prison rather than serve in the army, and his sojourn to India to learn about Gandhi, it is necessary to provide a link between Penny Patch, Mimi Feingold, Swarthmore College, SNCC's Albany project in southwest Georgia, and the style of Louisiana Jim Crow as practiced in Plaquemine Parish. Then one can connect them to Cambridge, Maryland, to nearby Chester, Pennsylvania, and in due course to SDS's most ambitious political undertaking, the Economic Research and Action Projects (ERAPS).

Patch and Feingold, the offspring of progressive white parents, met at Swarthmore College in 1961. Patch demonstrated her commitment to civil rights by joining legendary teacher-organizer Charles Sherrod's voter registration project in Albany, Georgia; Feingold showed her courage by participating in the Freedom Rides and later signing up for voter registration campaigns in Louisiana. Both women acquired extensive educations in the South; they learned how the movement recruited people from the rank and file of the population, how it sustained morale through songs, how people learned to speak for themselves and talk to each other at gatherings that in due course became mass meetings. Whereas Patch's early guide was Sherrod, Feingold's mentors were police officers led by one of the South's most notorious sheriffs, Leander Perez. Feingold wrote about life in Louisiana in letters to her classmates at Swarthmore and, when the movement desperately needed money, to her parents.

Sheriff Perez proved so repressive that the civil rights movement in Plaquemine organized a protest march to his house. The demonstrators were repelled by tear gas bombs and state troopers on horses with cattle prods. Feingold wrote home: "One girl, about 12 years old, was trampled by a horse" and died after a long delay in treatment because the hospital would not treat her without a $75 deposit. "HOW LONG MUST THIS GO ON???"[1]

A second march was organized against a local injunction to stop marching. Again, men on horseback with cattle prods dispersed the marchers and "white mobs" followed them back to the black church that was their base of operations. Feingold's chronicle read: "Tear gassed all around the church, rode the horses into the churchyard, and when the marchers packed into the church, they broke down the door and windows and threw tear gas inside." The leaders of the protest were unable to move the seriously injured to a waiting ambulance because of the tumult outside. Some escaped to a clergyman's home nearby, but "eventually the police and the mobs broke into the front of the house and tear gassed it." When the demonstrators, who had packed the clergyman's house "with a mass more solid than the NY City subway at rush hour," scattered across the row of backyards, the police gassed them, then turned high pressure hoses on them in front of the church. "White mobs then traveled throughout the neighborhood breaking into homes, overturning furniture and dragging out everyone with a black face. If they had prodders they used them. . . . They pulled down one girl's pants and prodded her between her legs; they prodded an 8 month pregnant lady until she dropped from pain." The mob found Feingold huddled in a shed behind the church with a fifteen-year-old "panic-stricken girl clinging to me . . . where we had listened for over an hour to the mobs." Feingold was arrested.[2]

Despite the terror, Feingold continued to work in rural Louisiana, moving north from Clinton to Iberville Parish, where she was put in charge of voter registration. "In a typical week, I contact 150 people, train 60 people, send 18 to the registrar's office, and have 9 people get registered." Even so, Leander Perez turned Plaquemine into "a police state." Two cars owned by CORE workers were impounded for having out-of-state plates. Feingold wrote that "it took a whole month to cut through the red tape necessary to get the cars out of hoc," cost two hundred dollars, and when the workers retrieved the cars, the police "had so tampered with them that they no longer run at all." The list of charges against one freedom worker was so extensive that Feingold included the litany in a letter home: "subversive activities, criminal anarchy, public intimidation, extortion, perjury, and having whites and Negroes in the same dwelling place."[3]

Cars were essential for canvassing rural Louisiana, where "rapid getaways" constituted an "imperative," and organizers sought the badly needed funds for operational expenses from outside sources. Feingold asked her parents to see if *their* friends and associates in New York would contribute to the car fund. "We cannot continue our work unless we have money and/or cars. We are ready to do anything to get the money, including selling our blood to a blood bank." As she engaged in this kind of fund-raising, Feingold replicated on a small scale the work people like Casey Hayden—and later, Mary King, Betty Garman, and Dinky Rommelly—had been doing on a national scale from Atlanta for SNCC.

If Feingold learned in Louisiana that agreements with police were meaningless unless they were in writing and held by movement lawyers for safekeeping, so Patch learned in Georgia that the movement had a chance to last only if people's trust in each other could be sustained by at least a bare minimum of day-to-day financial sustenance. As detailed in Chapter 6, this kind of experiential education led to extensive black-white cooperation in Cambridge, Maryland, and to the recruitment of students like Carl Whitman, who augmented the Cambridge movement by adding projects in nearby Chester. Whitman, duly instructed by what he had learned in both areas, convinced Tom Hayden that the undertakings in Cambridge-Chester provided at least the beginnings of a working model for SDS activity in northern cities. The influential Stokely Carmichael backed him up. Also a participant in the Cambridge effort, Carmichael lobbied Todd Gitlin and white activists to turn their attention to nearby cities. This was the genesis of SDS's ERAPS.

In the mid-1960s there was one constant in the northern ERAPS: the impact on workers of the harsh day-to-day realities encountered in the ghetto was strikingly similar to the effect of the voter registration drives in Dixie. Veterans of the ERAPS gained stunning insights into the ubiquitous reach of white nationalism in America. This other sacred ground is the unacknowledged debt of the New Left to the civil rights movement, which approaches something of a scandal in the scholarly literature.

Incidents of Violence against Voter Registration Activities in Mississippi, 1964

According to Aaron E. Henry, the white community responded to the 1964 voter registration campaign by taking the following actions.

Supplements to Testimony of Aaron E. Henry before the U.S. Commission on Civil Rights, Jackson, Mississippi, 16 – 20 February 1965[1]

16 January, McComb: "Armed nightriders shot into the homes of six Negro families, wounding a young Negro boy (*Atlanta Daily World*, Jan. 16, 1964)."

13 – 17 January, Clarksdale: "Negroes reported to courthouse daily. Total Negroes involved, 136. None permitted to take voter registration test. Reason given, court was in session and registrar was busy in courtroom. It is believed that white people were allowed to register during this period while Negroes were not permitted to take the test."

31 January: "Louis Allen of Amite County was killed with two shotgun blasts. Allen had been a witness to the 1961 slaying of Herbert Lee, active in voter registration, by E. H. Hurst, then a State legislator (ruled justifiable homicide)."

2 February, Vicksburg: "Seven crosses burned in various Vicksburg locations in what was termed 'evidence of the empire of the Ku Klux Klan in Mississippi.'"

15 February, Jackson: "Two voter registration workers, Arthur Harris and Will Galloway, were beaten by police."

7 April, Neshoba County: "12 crosses were burned throughout Neshoba County. One at the courthouse near the voter registration office. Three crosses were burned in the Negro section of Philadelphia, Miss."

26 April: "In 64 counties . . . crosses blazed across the State of Mississippi. Crosses were burned in most communities where voter-registration campaigns were being carried on."

22 May, Longdale community of Neshoba: "The Mount Zion Methodist Church was burned after a voter-registration clinic had been conducted in the church. Armed white men, some masked, some in law enforcement uniforms, had allegedly earlier surrounded the church and brutally beaten three Negroes who were attending a church meeting."

30 May, Natchez: "Clifford Walker, a Negro, was found dead with half of his face torn away by a shotgun blast."

30 May, Pike County: "The *New York Times* reported a cross had been burned in the yard of NAACP Pike County president, Curtis C. Bryant. He also received a note telling him to get out of town; a bomb was tossed through his barbershop window the next night."

31 May, Canton: "A Negro man was taken to the hospital after alleged beating by 8 policemen during arrest of 55 persons in voter rally outside a Negro church."

12 June, Canton: "Bombs shattered windows of a church used for civil rights meetings [at] voter-registration clinics.

22 June, Philadelphia: "James E. Chaney, Andrew Goodman, and Michael Schwerner were reported missing. The trio had driven from Meridian to investigate a church burning in Longdale community. Church had been used for voter-registration activity. The trio were [*sic*] never seen again, alive. Later found murdered."

24 June: "Voter-registration workers who are white are informed by public officials of Hollandale that they cannot stay in Negro section of town and work to register Negro voters. On same day in Drew, Miss., 30 voter-registration workers encountered open hostility from whites. Weapons exhibited by whites toward voter-registration workers."

25 June, Itta Bena: "Two voter-registration workers taken to a gas station by four white men and told, 'If you speak in town tonight, you'll never leave here.'"

26 June, Columbus: "Seven voter-registration workers arrested for distributing literature without a permit. Bond set at $400 each."

27 June, Ruleville: "Several whites attempted to fire-bomb a church. They drove through the Negro section of Ruleville throwing bottles. Some of the whites were armed. The same group are suspected of interfering with voter-registration activities in Drew, Miss., on the same day."

2 July: "Two voter-registration workers were followed and questioned by men describing themselves as state officials."

8 July, Ruleville: "Voter-registration worker ejected from county circuit clerk's office for accompanying local woman to attempt to register to vote."

8 July, Moss Point: "A shot from a passing car went through a church window and wounded in chest a 19-year-old Negro girl standing to sing at a rally of 300. Negroes pursued automobile suspected of firing the shot. Occupants of the car of Negroes were promptly arrested for reckless driving and possession of firearms."

13–17 July, Coahoma County: "Circuit clerk at . . . courthouse closed down and refused to permit Negroes to attempt to register. Reason given: court in session."

15 July, Drew: "25 arrested for willfully and unlawfully using sidewalks and the streets during voter-registration rally."

16 July, Greenwood: "111 arrested in front of courthouse . . . as they came to try to register to vote."

18 July, Lauderdale: "Two voter-registration workers arrested for willful trespassing while discussing voter registration on front porch of two Negro women; no complaint made by women."

19 July, Columbus: "Two voter-registration workers detained in jail in Aberdeen for 4 hours after being picked up as suspicious strangers and refusing to be driven out of town and left on highway by police."

19 July, Biloxi: "A voter-registration worker was chased and threatened by two white men in a pickup truck."

22 July, Greenville: "A local Negro was arrested while passing out voter-registration leaflets. He was questioned about his civil rights activity. He was subsequently charged with forgery. The forgery charge to this date has not been pushed."

23 July, Durant: "Voter-registration workers were assailed while canvassing for voter registration. Two white men approached them and asked what it would take to get them out of town. The voter-registration workers replied that they were not ready to leave town. They were struck several times by the men."

24 July, Holly Springs: "A voter-registration worker was arrested for disturbing the public peace. Held on $500 bond. Voter-registration worker was assisting in getting some 55 Negroes to the courthouse to try to register to vote. Police insisted that the 55 potential registrants walk to the courthouse to try to register. . . . Police insisted that the 55 potential registrants walk to the courthouse steps one by one, 8 feet apart, and have a police escort from steps to registrar's office. Approximately 60 helmeted highway patrolmen and 35 helmeted local police were stationed at the courthouse."

4 August, Moss Point: "Approximately 62 potential voters arrested during voter-registration rally held on a vacant lot. The orderly meeting had been in process for 15 min. when an assistant deputy sheriff gave the group 5 cars and 2 motorcycles, total of 40 officers accumulated. All at meeting were put in bus and taken to jail. They were held for breach of the peace on $300 cash or $600 property bond, each."

4 August, Cleveland: "13 persons arrested for handing out voter-registration literature."

7 August, Jackson: "Mary Zeno and Rommie Drain were chased by white men with pistol as they canvassed for voter registration."

8 August, Tallahatchie County: "Four members of a local family, the first Negro family to attempt to register to vote from the county in several decades, have been steadily harassed since they attempted to register. On the night of August 7, two truckloads of whites with guns drove by shouting obscenities and threats. They have been back several times and the family is now afraid to go to work in the fields."

11 August, Aberdeen: "Joel Bernard was attacked by a local white man while canvassing for voter registration."

11 August, Anguilla: "Louis Grant and Bob Wright were arrested by local officials for handing out voter-registration literature."

11 August: "24 Negro citizens in Charleston . . . attempted to register at Tallahatchie County courthouse. Approximately 100 armed whites gathered. Cars and trucks with guns prominently displayed were double and triple parked in front of the courthouse."

14 August, Columbus: "John Luther Bell was jailed in West Point . . . on charges of disturbing the peace. He was arrested while canvassing for potential Negro registrants."

15 August, Jackson: "Voter-registration worker beaten outside COFO office with baseball bat by carload of whites."

15 August, Meridian: "Voter-registration workers Sam Brown, David McClinton, and Preston Ponder fired upon while driving down Highway 11."

21 August, Belzoni: "Police cars followed voter-registration workers continuously, surrounding them at every house at which they stopped. Four to five carloads of white citizens also followed. Police chief ordered workers out of town."

23 August, Tupelo: "Voter-registration headquarters set afire. City investigators said there was evidence of arson."

24 August, Holly Springs: "Mr. J. T. Dean turned off his land in economic reprisal for trying to register to vote. He tried to vote on August 15, 1964. His credit was cut off and he was told by landowner he was no longer needed to work land. His water supply was also cut off. None of the 200 Negro citizens who took tests at Holly Springs on August 15 have been told whether or not they passed."

25 August, Amory: "Three young Negro voter-registration workers, Adair Howell, Andrew Moore, and Essie Carr, arrested as they canvassed for potential registrants. Police entered home and arrested workers, charging them with disturbing peace and forcing Negro woman to sign form. Local officials denied knowledge of whereabouts of workers after their arrest. Howell and Moore were located by the FBI in the Amory jail and Miss Carr was released to custody of her parents."

1 September, Belzoni: "Ellis Jackson, a voter-registration worker, was arrested by Chief of Police Nichols for lacking selective service identification and held for 5 hours, no bail set, turned over to FBI, who released him."

4 September: "Mrs. Mary Thomas of 279 Hayden Street was arrested on a charge of not having a beer license. This arrest came shortly after Mrs. Thomas went to the courthouse in Belzoni to try to register to vote. Bond set at $1000."

14 September, Philadelphia: "Voter-registration attempt met with violence and arrests. Cliff Vaughs was beaten over the head with a blackjack by a local white citizen when an auxiliary policeman demanded that Vaughs surrender his camera. Vaughs's camera was seized and smashed. Two civil rights voter-registration workers were arrested and released later that afternoon, Allan Schiffman and Tommie Collier. Four local Negroes were fired from their jobs for attempting to register to vote. They were employed by the Jack P. Eubanks firm."

21 October, Marks: "Dave Harris, a voter-registration worker, was told by the local police to leave town when he tried to help local Negro citizens to register to vote. Four white teenagers beat and urinated on Frank Morse after he was stopped by them and asked some questions about civil rights. The attack followed."

24 October, Jackson: "Four voter-registration workers arrested for passing out leaflets urging citizens to register and vote."

26 October, Indianola: "Bob Newell was beaten by whites as he tried to help Negro citizens to register to vote. A 6-footer, weighing at least 200 pounds, beat Newell directly in front of the Sunflower County courthouse."

27 October, McComb: "36 Negroes arrested upon entering courthouse to try to register to vote. They were met by the sheriff and highway patrolmen, several deputies, and a plainclothesman who read a court order ordering the registrar to close his office and appear in court in his capacity as county clerk. They were arrested for trespassing and held on $100 bond, each."

31 October, Sunflower County: "A cross was burned on the farm of Mr. R. Giles, early today. Mr. Giles, one of the few registered Negroes in Sunflower County is an active voter registration worker."

1 November, Ripley: "Voter registration clinic held in Antioch Baptist Church. . . . Church burned during the night. Voter-registration literature among the ruins of the building."

28 December [location not indicated]: "Three voter-registration workers arrested and charged with vagrancy while helping Negroes register to vote at the courthouse."

29 December, Clarksdale: "Five Negro citizens went to the courthouse to ask the circuit clerk if they had passed the test and could register. Without any reference to any notes or memorandum, the circuit clerk informed them that they had not passed. He told them simply, '"No you didn't pass.'"

"The month of December found many of the COFO voter-registration workers engaged in the election to county crop and acreage allotment committees. There were many instances of arrest and abuse including James Bates, Stan Boyd, and George Raymond. Many were ejected from polling places including Bill Forsyth, Bill Ware, Madeline McHugh, and Tom Ramsey in Canton. . . . Marvin Rich was approached by former Governor Ross Barnett at the polling place where he went to vote. He was verbally insulted by the former Governor. Rich was later beaten by two white men as he tried to observe the counting of the ballots. Others arrested included Elaine DeLott, Earistiss Crawford, Ann Darden, and Euvester Simpson."

James Forman's Speech at Waveland, November 1964

As indicated in Chapter 10, James Forman, executive secretary of SNCC, generated two historical versions of what he said at SNCC's pivotal 1964 staff conference. In his autobiographical account, *The Making of Black Revolutionaries*, published in 1985, he characterized the debate as one between "field staff" and a "freedom high" faction. The following is the text of the speech Forman delivered twenty years earlier at the SNCC staff retreat at Waveland, Mississippi, on 6 November 1964.[1]

There are many strong points about the Student Nonviolent Coordinating Committee. One of those strong points is our ability to look inwardly at ourselves, at our organization, and to criticize it honestly and openly without fear of anyone misconstruing, misunderstanding what we are doing. We have been relatively free, as someone has said, of power struggles within SNCC. Let us continue to be free of these struggles and of personality clashes. We have examined ourselves many, many times in the past. In 1961, when we decided to put on a staff of some 16 people[,] there was an intensive examination of our structure. It was found inadequate and a new structure emerged, where the Executive Committee was basically the staff. And it was in this new structure that I was granted the opportunity to serve as the Executive Secretary. On Easter weekend of 1962 we ended an extensive examination of that structure and we found it wanting in many respects. It was not workable because in fact, the Student Nonviolent Coordinating Committee still had a student base and there were students who had been intimately involved in the formation and early development of SNCC who felt that they had a right to be a part of SNCC. It was also felt by the small staff, not more than 20 at that moment, that it should be responsible to some other body than to itself. Consequently we all agreed as an operating procedure that the staff would have voice but no vote on any Executive Committee, on any Coordinating Committee. Time has changed this particular situation. We come to this meeting, November, 1964, 3 years since the staff was first formed, and find that, in effect, there is no student base to the Student Nonviolent Coordinating Committee, that the organization is composed primarily of a group of organizers, of people who operate within the Friends of SNCC, and of many other people associated indirectly with SNCC throughout the country. But that the nucleus, the people who do the most work, is the staff. And there has been within SNCC during the past 3 years a constant examination of the role of the staff in the overall decision-making. Now the word decision-making can confuse us. No one is questioning the fact that everybody within SNCC is a decision-maker, every project director makes decisions about his projects. There is no superstructure which sits in Atlanta or sits in Jackson and constantly says this project must do this and must do that. There have been suggestions and there have been rigorous attempts to make these suggestions the binding rule, the binding force, but no one has ever questioned the right of the staff to make decisions in the field, except for certain decisions dealing with fund-raising. In this respect we have been different from other organizations that have attempted to control decisions made by staff people in the field from a central point. On the other hand, that freedom to make decisions has created many problems and many strains within the organization.

In December of 1963 it became quite apparent at a staff meeting that the decision-making body of the organization had to be changed. A compromise was found in the amendment to the Constitution to allow the staff itself to elect 6 members to the Executive Committee. At the spring conference of 1964 this was done, but the student base was even weaker than it had been in 1963 and legitimate questions were raised later in a staff meeting in June of 1964 about that structure. At the staff meeting recently held, one month ago, there were attempts to deal with that problem. Many other problems came out and it was felt that another staff meeting, a staff retreat should be held to deal with the problems that were very basic to the organization. We are here today, we will be here this weekend, and we should remain here until this question is resolved. I call for internal cohesion. We can withstand the external pressures if we are together. I call for unity. I call for a consensus around the proposition that the staff and those here present consider themselves as the Coordinating Committee and elect at some point in this meeting an Executive Committee, the number to be determined. Also I suggest that the Coordinating Committee, we here assembled, elect a Call Committee to handle the arrangements for future meetings of the Coordinating Committee and to determine whom it wants to invite to sit in session with this body.

There may be some uncertainty about whether or not those people gathered in this room — the staff, the remnants of the Executive Committee, some Friends of SNCC — do have the right to change and alter the over-all decision-making body within the organization. We have the right and we must do that this weekend, for the organization for the past 3 to 4 weeks has been in limbo, because of the unresolved nature of this question. Someone has written that we are a boat which is afloat and that the boat has to be changed in order to stay afloat, and that it must stay afloat in order to be changed. There are some who say they don't understand that metaphor. Well, let me further confuse the picture by saying that we are on a river of no return. We do have an organization. We are committed to programs and to people in the bayous and in the Deltas, in the back woods, in the Black Belt, in Northern cities and Southern hamlets. And so, therefore, the longer we take to deal with this question, the longer we fail to give the kind of service to the people that we could. It becomes imperative that we solve this question. It also becomes imperative that we ask ourselves why do we exist? Spend some time on that, but not too much, because we only have 4 days, and then we must examine what is the structure that can help do whatever we exist for? Put another way, what are our goals? And what is the structure that we want to implement these goals? And what will be our program for the summer of 1965 and even up until 1968? Will we have a four-year plan? Will we have a summer project for the summer of 1965? And if we can accomplish these three things at the staff retreat, we will have done a momentous amount of work. We cannot answer all of the questions that were circulated on that staff memorandum. Some of the answers are in writing, and I sincerely urge every member to read the position papers that people have written, for they provide some answers to some of those questions.

Before I close, I should simply like to dovetail what I think are some other things that we have to deal with this weekend, or soon thereafter. We must rigorously examine the civil rights bill to determine what is there in that bill that we can use as tools and techniques to further the militant struggle we have started. We took the 1960 and 1957 civil rights acts with the provision basically of the federal government coming in and filing suit, and under the 1960 civil rights act supposedly providing protection for civil rights workers. We knew that the law was a sham in many respects, but we used the law in order to further the struggle and mobilize people. There is much within the civil rights bill that has just been passed that we can employ to further break down the barriers of segregation. We must examine the anti-poverty bill and find out if, in fact, there is anything in there which we can employ. We must begin to study more diligently the political and economic forces operating in this country, to continue to criticize those forces and to continue to construct new alternatives for the people and for ourselves. We must continue, not necessarily to work for the redemptive society, but to work toward a new spirit of brotherhood, a spirit that transcends both black and white, a spirit that supercedes, a spirit that goes above and a spirit that sees all of us simply as men and women, struggling for a sense of dignity. But above all, we must take the sense of injustice that burns deeply inside all of us, we must take the few tools and the few resources that we have and begin to organize that which we know is unorganized. And we must not be concerned too much with the theory of what we are doing, but rather begin to do some of the things we know that have to be done, a theory itself, for it is out of practice that a theory will evolve. We have enough practice for the past three years to develop a sort of theory about what we have been doing and it is our hope that in 3 years from now we can come back and further reexamine ourselves.

And now my brothers and sisters I should like to take this opportunity to say a few humble and honest words. I have tried to serve you in the capacity of Executive Secretary for the last 3 years. I have tried diligently and at all times to consider the best interests of SNCC, to do that which would make the organization alive and that which would make it survive, not for its organizational value itself, but rather for what it has done in the sphere of race relations, what it must do, what history demands of us. There have been mistakes made by all of us, we recognize that. Whether I continue to serve in the capacity of Executive Secretary is a decision which you should make, a decision that you must make, but it is with a profound regret that I must tell you, regardless of your decision, I absolutely, positively must take off at least 3 months for my state of health. I'm in bad shape. My dues are overpaid. In those three months I intend to be available for consultation, for various meetings, for occasional speaking engagements, but I must rigidly guard the use of my time. Also during those 3 or 4 months I will be working on a book, the title of which will be: A Band of Brothers; A Circle of Trust. I shall attempt to write a personal history of SNCC, because there are many things about this organization which only I can write, just as there are many things about the Indianola project which only Charles McLaurin can write, or just as there are many things about McComb which only Jesse Harris can write, or Bill Hansen about Arkansas or Cordell Reagon about Southwest Georgia. All of us have our little histories within us and I would wish that all of us could set them down on paper. But your deliberations this weekend should not take into account, necessarily what I will be doing months from now, or 1 year from now, or 2 years from now, nor should it take into account what anyone else in the organization will be doing. But rather you should take into account what it is that's best for all of us, for there are people who are waiting on us *right now* to return to our respective projects to begin work and to continue the work we started. People do see us as a band of brothers. We must decide if the circle will be unbroken. If we remain a band of brothers, a circle of trust, We Shall Overcome!

Suggested Structures for SNCC, November 1964

"Group 5 Francis Mitchell Chairman, Who Decides Program?" ("Proposal A" in the Minutes of the Waveland Conference)[1]

General Consensus: Coordinating Committee should make broad program decisions i.e., what organizations the organization should be committed to.

General Consensus: Coordinating Committee should invest in an Executive Committee the power to act for it between CC meetings.
   a. That committee should meet no less than once a month.

Majority: There should be an Executive Secretary.
   b. He would represent SNCC.
   c. He would make the day to day decisions that have to be made.
   d. He would be responsible both to the Ex. Co. and to the CC Comm.
   e. He would implement the decisions of both groups.

Minority View #1: There should be a three man Ex. Sec. who would have the function of the above one-man Ex. Sec.

Minority View #2: No need for an Ex. Sec. Day to day decisions should be made by people who are responsible for a particular program area.

General Consensus: There should be Program Coordinators, based in Atlanta, who are responsible for a particular program area. There should be a chairman of the organ. elected by CC who would chair all CC meetings and Ex. Co. meetings. He would be spokesman for the organization, an image public relations man.

Who decides how resources are shared?

General Consensus: CC should approve a general budget.

Ex. Co. should appoint a finance committee.

All program directors and state project directors submit a budget to Ex. Co.

Ex. Co. turns the budget over to the finance co. which investigates the budget, approves or rejects them and turns them over to the Ex. Co. which OK's them.

If the budget is rejected then program directors review and cut their budget and resubmit it to the finance co.

All decisions can be appealed to the CC.

Who will decide priorities?

General Consensus: The Executive Committee.

Casey Hayden, "Memorandum on Structure" ("Proposal B" in the Minutes of the Waveland Conference)[2]

Coordinating Committee: The Coordinating Committee would be the staff and these people [who] are invited by the staff to attend. It would be the basic decision-making body and would function pretty much as Jim [Forman] suggests.

Program Committees: At the Coordinating Committee meeting we would have committees meet. These committees would be the same as our workshops on program this time. The committees, in other words, would be composed largely of people working in a given program full time, with the addition of others who wanted to come. They would meet three times a year at the Coordinating Committee meeting.

The committees would be set up by each Coordinating Committee meeting. There would be a committee for each program we have or want to have. This time we had committees on Freedom Schools, Community Centers, Voter Registration, Unions, Political Organizing, Public Accommodations, Literacy. Before the meeting is over, we should have meetings of committees on our other program areas (most of which Jim [Forman] calls administration): Northern Support, Southern Campuses, Communications, Research, Education. We would be sure to set meetings of the committees so that people working in the field can go to meetings of committees that don't relate directly to field programs and vice versa. These committees will select someone to suggest to the body to coordinate the program they outline and help them carry it out. Sometimes this will mean they shift to Atlanta and travel from there; sometimes they can go on with work in their area, and still kind of see the program is carried out. So [Ralph] Featherstone and [Charlie] Cobb and Amanda will coordinate the Freedom School program and John Perdew, still in Southwest Georgia[,] will work on the union workshop.

This will provide for getting leadership for all our programs directly from the staff and will do away with the administration idea in Jim's paper, which makes many program areas responsible to one person rather than to all of us.

Executive Committee: Between the meeting of the Coordinating Committee there should be a group which can review the work of the people who are coordinating the work the committees have outlined. This group can be called an Executive Committee. It should be a workable size, maybe about fifteen people. It should call in anyone they need to have at the meeting part or all of the time to get information. But the people actually on the committee would not be there because they were the head of this or that. We would elect the Executive Committee from the staff at large and should elect people we trust to make sure what we wanted to happen at the last Coordinating Committee meeting is really happening. They might be people who were head of a program area (like Northern Coordinator) or a project director, but they would not be there because they were head of the area but because we might trust them to serve on the committee. People who were needed would be specifically invited, [cuts off for four or five words], that they are not there to act as the committee (which was elected by all of us at the Coordinating Committee). If there were decisions about crucial things that could not be made by the Exec. Comm., they would call a special staff meeting or would delay decision until the meeting of the Coordinating Committee.

Jim's proposal seems to try to give representation to program areas and project areas, but I think if the Coordinating Committee really functions (as it hasn't) then it will make basic decisions and the function of the Exec. Comm. will be to see they are carried out. If this is the case, we need good people we will trust to do that, rather than someone to go to and represent our views on crucial issues.

Maybe one of the reasons SNCC's functioning seems to [*sic*] confused is that the way we really work isn't reflected in our formal structure. I think the above plan doesn't impose any unnecessary structure on the way we really work and it allows for as much staff participation as possible.

There are some problems not included above because I don't understand them entirely:

1. The Executive Secretary and Chairman: I don't understand the difference. Maybe Chairman has been spokesman and Exec. Secretary responsible for the carving out of programs. If we have a lot of people responsible for carrying out programs and responsible to the staff as a whole[,] maybe we don't need such a strong exec.

2. Personnel: Personnel committees don't function because personnel decisions are day to day decisions. I suggest we outline at the Coordinating Committee personnel policies and have someone in Atlanta responsible for hiring, on an interim basis and with consultation with people working in the different program areas and projects. These hirings can be approved by the personnel committee.

3. Program Secretary: I do think we need someone, maybe the same person as the personnel person, to work directly with the field and kind of help the coordinators of program[s] that relate to the field with problems they might have. This would be the person you'd call if you needed a car and there was a hang-up with the transportation person or who would find out for you why you didn't get your check for a month and Chessie said it was sent. Maybe program secretary isn't the right word for this kind of person, but there really has to be someone to get people out of bureaucratic jams and help them with programs the program coordinators aren't already handling.

4. Who is on the Coordinating Committee: Jim suggests we solve this with a Call Committee. Again, I just don't think committees function well for us unless they are made up of people involved in the work. Maybe the Executive Committee should plan and call CC meetings by letting the staff know they are happening and by indicating they are only for staff, but if staff knows of anyone else who really should come, they can let X (the Exec. Secretary) know.

5. Finances: The Executive Committee should be responsible for outlining the budget and the financial report in such a way that everyone can understand it. Finances [are] probably the general responsibility of the Exec. Secretary, but the whole staff should be able to understand questions like how much are we spending on offices compared with the field? And what salaries are people getting and why?

"Memorandum on the Structure of the Student Nonviolent Coordinating Committee by James Forman" ("Proposal C" in the Minutes of the Waveland Conference)[3]

PURPOSE:

The purpose of this paper is to set forth some of my ideas on the question of structure. It will try to take into account many of the ideas raised by people from time to time. Some of these ideas are: How do you broaden the decision making process of the organization and what plans can be submitted for broadening the implementation of decisions made by the body? Some staff also say to us that we must try to educate ourselves and try to give those people who do not normally have administrative and committee responsibilities some function in the organization.

Before I do this, however, I would like to say that whatever structure is set up will have to be changed at some future time because the goals and programs of the organization will change and this will require some new structure for implementation. Also I think it is very important that we do not forget or that we remind ourselves that this is a long term struggle. We will always have some problems before us and that each time we engage in some new action that will create some new problem.

THE STRUCTURE:

I suggest the Coordinating Committee which will be the entire staff and those people [who] the Call Committee invite[s] should meet three times a year. At these meetings it should discuss problems and programs. The basic policy making body should be this body and it should vote upon programs that it wishes the organization to do in the periods of time when it is not meeting. For instance, the people here assembled or those present at this meeting should vote on whether or not [they wish] to extend the Freedom Schools into other projects. [They] should discuss the merits of the Federal Programs and the Freedom Democratic Party — to see if these should also be extended. Now if we do this, for instance, then it is necessary for the body to set up some structure for the implementation of this program across the south. The Coordinating Committee should elect an Executive Committee. The form of this election will vary from what is usually the form of elections. For instance I am proposing that elections take place within a circle of people who will work together on a series of programs in various areas. This will become more clear when the structure of the Executive Committee is presented. Also the Coordinating Committee should have certain Committees directly responsible to it. They are:

A. Personnel and Office Committee
B. Education Committee
C. Call Committee
D. Freedom School Committee
E. Community Centers Committee
F. Federal Programs Committee
G. Political Action Committee

STRUCTURE OF THE EXECUTIVE COMMITTEE:

A. All state project directors should be on the Executive Committee. The state project directors should be elected by an assembly of all the staff assigned to work in a particular state. If there is a state where there are not more than ten people working, then the Executive Committee should appoint that project director. (There is some concern on this proposal. I have shown a draft of this proposal to many people asking for ideas. Some say that if the project director was elected by the staff this might lead to a lot of politicking and that maybe better people may not get elected. There were other reasons. I am presenting the alternative proposal of having the state project directors appointed by the Executive Committee.)

B. Each state should have so many votes at large. These votes will be determined by the number of people who are working in Congressional districts. If in a state we are working in two Congressional districts with five or more staff people in each Congressional district, then those state field staff should elect two people at large to the Executive Committee. If we are working, as we are in Mississippi, in five Congressional districts, then there should be five votes at large from the state of Mississippi. In Arkansas there would be currently one vote at large and if that program expands into two Congressional districts with five or more staff in each district, then they would have two at large. In a state where there is not five people in a Congressional district, then there would only be the project director represented on the Executive Committee.

C. The Chairmen of all standing committees of the Coordinating Committee would be elected to the Executive Committee. The Chairman of these committees would be selected by the people working on these committees. Selection to these committees could be on the basis of those interested in working on the committees and suggestions from the floor.

D. Five delegates from the entire body should be selected. This election would come after all other elections have taken place.

The Executive Committee would have to elect or appoint a Planning Committee and a Finance Committee. Both of these committees would be responsible to report at a session of the Coordinating Committee, but the detail[ed] nature of their work sort of makes it imperative that they come from the smaller body. The Finance Committee should and must report broad categories of expected budget items, how this money will be raised. The Coordinating Committee itself should approve a yearly budget and must have reports on the state of the budget.

FUNCTIONS OF THE COMMITTEES OF THE COORDINATING COMMITTEE:

A. The Personnel and Office Committee will be responsible for the recommending of hiring people to the Executive Committee and the review of how the offices of the Student Nonviolent Coordinating Committee are functioning. The details of how this committee will work and where it will meet should be left out of this paper but could be discussed by those wanting to work on it and brought back to the body or to the Executive Committee.

B. The Education Committee: This needs working out in more details but I think we all know what we are talking about.

C. The Call Committee: This deals with who is invited to the meetings of the Coordinating Committee. Also the Call Committee is responsible for the preparation of an agenda. It does this in consultation with the Executive Committee. The Call Committee is responsible for the orderly working of all meetings of the Coordinating Committee. The Chairman of this committee is responsible to see that staff and other invitees of the Coordinating Committee get copies of the meetings of the Executive and Coordinating Committee[s].

D, E & F: These committees are self-explanatory. But the Political Action Committee deals with the various political programs that the sections of the organization will be working on.

The people here assembled should examine the role of the Chairman and the Executive Secretary, determine how they should be elected, and some general guidelines as to their roles.

Now I want to present a plan for the administration. The Executive Secretary should be asked by the body to be the overall administrative officer of the organization. He should have the right to select people who will assist in the administration subject to the approval of the Executive Committee. I suggest the following people be considered a part of the Administration: Executive Secretary, Administrative Assistant, Program Secretary whose role will be to travel in the field to examine how programs are carried out and to report to the Executive Secretary his findings and to the Executive Committee, the Administrator of the Jackson Office if this is a SNCC person, if not then SNCC must find a person who works in the Jackson office to serve as Administrative Assistant in Jackson; the Northern Coordinator, the Southern Campus Coordinator, the Director of Communications [cuts off].

Structure Debate at Waveland

When Casey Hayden's turn came to explain her group's ideas on structure (referred to as "Proposal B" in the Minutes of the Waveland Conference), she found it difficult to clarify an organizational form that was unfamiliar to people who were largely accustomed to hierarchies. She consequently drew a picture of seven or eight dots connected as a circle. Each dot represented a work group. Work groups consisted of people involved in the same programs: for example, a Freedom School work group, a community center work group, or a voter registration work group. Each work group would elect an administrator, who would communicate with other group administrators, exchanging ideas, coordinating plans, and distributing scarce resources. She then drew a triangle to represent the hierarchy of James Forman's structure. The executive secretary would be at the tip of the triangle, and he or she would direct subordinates how to proceed.[1]

When Hayden finished her talk, people laughed and booed. It was unclear why.[2] Although in this rancorous environment, it was impossible to resolve the issues concerning SNCC's identity and purpose. The three proposals by Mitchell, Varela-Hayden, and Forman all provided a strong framework for the organization; nevertheless, some regarded the decentralist models as having "no structure" or a "loose" structure compared to Forman's hierarchical prototype. "That is inaccurate," Hayden later wrote. "Both are tight." All three proposals, in other words, had the potential to hold people accountable and effectively distribute resources.[3]

Staff members at Waveland discussed the potential drawbacks in each of the proposed structures. Some believed that Forman's and Mitchell's plans ("Proposal C" and "Proposal A" respectively) would make SNCC an institution rather than serve the movement. Varela-Hayden's structure ("Proposal B") would serve the movement but would neither provide a formalized channel to interact with the outside world nor permit a check and balance on the Personnel/Finance Committee. Proposal B also assumed that people in the field had enough information to make day-to-day decisions, yet SNCC's communication channels were not efficient or dependable enough to furnish such information. Proposal A did not clarify responsibilities for personnel and budget decisions, and it required work specialization. Proposal C did not provide adequately for field needs.[4]

All three designs appeared to be sincere, legitimate structures and, in the tradition of SNCC, had been democratically developed by staff. Compared to traditional hierarchical models, the A and B plans offered a way for staff members to stay both "organized" and "accountable" to one another, without resorting to telling others what to do. B had flaws but amounted to a decentralized structure, not anarchy. All participants at Waveland noted the absence of a clear consensus. As one dismayed staffer put it, "What kind of a structure we are to have was left hanging."[5]

SNCC as the Borning Struggle

Key to understanding SNCC during the period 1964–67 was the worldwide intensification of decolonization movements and the dismantling of the British and French Empires. Beginning with the Vietnamese independence movement, African liberation struggles, and the Gandhian independence movement that drew James Lawson to India, previously colonized peoples began to experiment with nonviolent and armed methods of liberation. In the United States, Lawson tried to make "many Montgomerys," while Robert F. Williams and Gloria Richardson led local civil rights movements where armed self-defense played a central role. Yet regardless of tactical differences, black Americans had the same concern: as the mainstream National Council of Negro Churchmen asserted in 1966, "The issue is not one of racial balance but of honest interracial interaction." No longer did "integration" suffice as the solution. For integration to work, the middle-of-the-road ministers noted, "all people need power, whether black or white." Simply put, black nationalist perspectives, though as varied as the people who articulated them, were based on the idea that black people needed control over black lives. In some activist and institutional circles, black nationalism grew partly from suspicion of whites, but more generally as an impulse to maintain and extend African Americans' individual and collective integrity and self-determination. Movement activists had been pioneers in "integration" into white society, and their firsthand experiences often made them experts on the many flaws and contradictions of the dominant white society. Malcolm X captured this sentiment in his frequent refrain: "I don't want to integrate into a sinking ship."[1]

On 30 December 1965 John Lewis declared that SNCC people regarded the failure of the MFDP challenge as clear evidence of whites' disrespect for black people. After years of fund-raising on the liberal cocktail party circuit in the Northeast and Midwest and along the West Coast, he could no longer sustain this activity. "Too many of us are too busy telling white people that we are now ready to be integrated into their society," he had said in February 1965. "We must dig deep into the black centers of power throughout this nation not just for financial reasons but as a base of political support." Lewis wondered aloud: "Is it possible for Negroes and whites in this country to engage in a certain political experiment such as the world has never yet witnessed and in which the first condition would be that whites consented to let Negroes run their own revolution?"[2]

The experience of SNCC taught that U.S. society was merely protodemocratic due to its subconscious white supremacist assumptions. SNCC's early pursuit of a universal community striving to come together as "the moral responsibility of men and women with soul force, people of goodwill," now became submerged in the southern move-ment under the intense need black people felt "to get together by themselves."[3]

Racial separatism was only one strand of the larger Black Power movement, however. Some SNCC members, like Lewis and Fannie Lou Hamer, devoted themselves to "black nationalism and its various cultural, psychological and institutional manifestations" but refused to judge people based on race. As Hamer biographer Chana Kai Lee ex-plained, Hamer "subscribed wholeheartedly to the principle of black control over black lives" while maintaining her belief that white participation in the movement for racial equality was not at odds with black self-determination. She represented the strand of black nationalism that did not include separatism. The same conviction persisted among members of the Lowndes County [Alabama] Christian Movement for Human Rights, who held neighborhood elections for the majority-black county planning com-mittee but reserved a minority of the seats for whites. These movement activists "were willing to work with whites," historian Hasan Jeffries writes, "but [were] unwilling to surrender their right to make decisions."[4]

New cultural institutions such as the Free Southern Theater, Black Studies programs, and Black Arts and theater troupes emerged in succeeding years, creating space within hundreds of new institutions in which African Americans could question fundamental issues of identity, power, and history. The "black is beautiful" aesthetic, for example, shattered the societal norm of beauty as a blonde, blue-eyed European. Think tanks such as Atlanta's Institute of the Black World supported intellectuals who pushed to break through a body of scholarship created largely within majority-white institutions. Community-based organizations that formed around black nationalist ideas endeav-ored to support low-income black people's basic needs for education, housing, health care, and recreation.[5]

ERAP

In the urban North, where SDS tried to adapt SNCC's community organizing model, progress between 1964 and 1968 was agonizingly limited. Since community-based ERAPs coexisted with the government-sponsored poverty projects of the Johnson ad-ministration, tension quickly developed between the two. In Cleveland, in the mid-summer of 1965, a community leader associated with ERAP, Carole King, wrote an open letter to "CEO [Chief Executive Officer] People" asserting: "Seventeen subur-banites — Eight people from the city/This isn't representative of the poor." She asked: "What are you going through and experiencing to make you know what poverty is like? We are demonstrating to make you realize we are alive!" When city officials ignored the issue, King's group dropped rats, rubbish, and torn clothing on the poverty program director's desk.[6]

In Cleveland, Newark, and Chicago, ERAP people worked for the better part of three years to open city government to low-income community leaders like Carole King. In each place, the groups had similar results: while local officials had to include ERAPers in some way in order to qualify for federal monies, they proceeded to use manipulation of due process, ostracism, and delay tactics to prevent meaningful input from ERAP leaders. As one ERAP staffer said, "I sympathize with a guy here [in Cleveland] who said he has come to cease to believe in social change, and is only learning all the ways in which it is prevented."[7] Nonetheless, the process of becoming a part of city government served a purpose similar to that of the MFDP: local leaders began to act "as if" they had the right to self-government. The subsequent reactions of city officials then created a giant classroom where citizens could see firsthand that those officials typically did not respond to most of their constituents.

ERAP workers, like SNCC organizers before them, encountered such resistance from those in power that they literally did not know what to do next. They could not find people to recruit, and they did not know what to do with people who were interested in "doing something." Others were stopped in their tracks after organizing for several years, accumulating multiple victories but even more battle scars. In all cases, a wall had been created by the thinness of the democratic heritage. After enough workers were brought up short, they tended to leave the project.

Early Michigan activist Sharon Jeffrey, her classmate Carol McEldowney, and Kathy Boudin, a Bryn Mawr graduate who had been close to the Swarthmore activists, organized a formidable welfare union in the white neighborhoods of Cleveland's Near East Side. They worked in concert with a similar organization in a black area of the city, Hough, for over three years up to 1967.[8] For a time, the group flourished. Nevertheless, it was not universally welcomed within the wider ERAP experiment, as most SDS-ERAP people did not believe that welfare issues were capable of raising fundamental questions in society. In other words, welfare organizing did not appear — at least initially — to be sufficiently "radical" to those whose experience trying to change conditions remained limited to intellectual debate.[9] In the field, activists in the Cleveland welfare organizing project kept recruiting new people. They regarded training local people to help welfare clients as "our everyday job." Everyone worked to make the welfare system more democratic and responsive to citizen input.

By January 1966, Boudin and McEldowney noticed that local leaders showed signs of impatience. The welfare activist group had won two significant victories in the fall: it now held monthly negotiations with welfare department officials, and they sat on the department's new committee to evaluate difficult cases. In addition, the local people on the city's Welfare Committee had "gained a lot of recognition" in the city. However, the local leaders did not feel they were able to accomplish as much as Boudin and McEldowney. "We need more activities and aren't doing enough," some members emphasized. "We've been going to a lot of meetings, but not much else." Moreover, "we've been uncooperative with each other," suffered from poor communication, and "haven't coordinated enough of our activities." They felt "frozen," without new ideas or new people. "We still need more knowledge and education to be able to teach others about the welfare system, and so we can get others to feel as we do (to have dignity)."[10]

Boudin and McEldowney decided to hold a training program focusing on welfare department rules and regulations, budgets, grievance procedures, and office tasks like mimeographing in order to "level out the differences in knowledge and information between the welfare mothers and the two of us."[11] Originally scheduled for three or four days, it lasted four weeks. As the program began, Boudin and McEldowney "realized that it was taking on a new and unexpected character." They sat down together afterward and conducted a lengthy evaluation of the instruction. In many ways their program mirrored the Nashville workshops led by James Lawson seven years earlier. How, then, did they re-create this important innovation in the North?

Boudin and McEldowney's accumulated experience over four years pushed them on a new course in 1966. They "consciously decided *not* to recruit people to meetings, not to build a mass organization." They felt they needed local leaders and a program before they could recruit. Like Ella Baker, they felt more comfortable working in small groups. Some Welfare Committee members' bad experiences with large organizations "had a big influence on our decision to stay small for a while." They did not feel ready to confront the problem of membership turnover and did not know how to address leaders' lack of commitment to recruiting others. Instead, they decided to "work patiently in developing a small, strong, well-informed, competent leadership group" that could run its own client service organization.[12]

The Spring 1967 training program was a major success.[13] Like in the Lawson workshops, participants met regularly for an extended period. Morning and afternoon sessions lasted about two hours each; they usually started with an examination of written materials, followed by discussions led by Boudin and McEldowney as "question-askers." The two leaders "made a point of keeping the number of people per session small, and were not rigid about content." This flexibility not only allowed them to cover the scheduled material but also enabled participants to explore larger issues. "Talking about the legal structure of welfare led us into discussion of the American political party system; . . . talking about medical care led us to the topic of socialized medicine; talking about organizing tactics led us into broader discussion of the movement." In other words, people began to explore the possibilities of full citizenship. What did they want out of the organization? What did they want out of their lives? How could they get it through political participation?[14]

The regularity with which they met as well as the excitement of learning in meaningful ways made participants "feel a strong sense of responsibility to the program, and to demand of one another a commitment to it." This carried over to their feelings of obligation to recruit more people for the Welfare Committee. The most dramatic result was "the self-confidence [the training] inspired in people." As they became knowledgeable about welfare laws and policies, the women working with Boudin and McEldowney claimed the power to define or interpret the welfare law as they saw it, rather than retreating to caseworkers or even to Boudin and McEldowney for an interpretation. The process of leadership development that had occurred in Lawson's Nashville workshops and again in Mississippi had now taken real, if fragile, root in the burgeoning ghettos of the North.[15]

"Precisely because they were ADC mothers, they would be better than we at setting an example for other ADC mothers to stand up and fight for their rights," Boudin and McEldowney wrote. They also believed that "racial difference affected our effectiveness in organizing; that again, they could more effectively reach other welfare people — the majority of whom are black — and that there could be real problems for whites organizing in a Negro neighborhood, a problem we hadn't been very willing to confront head-on previously."[16]

The results were immediate. The Welfare Committee now created materials to help recruit other potential leaders. They wrote, reproduced, and distributed a booklet,

"How to Organize a Welfare Rights Local Group," to further energize the leadership; they identified new people with whom they wanted to start additional training; and they began a second round in June 1967. Welfare Committee members were now thinking, acting, reacting, and behaving as full citizens. The group eventually joined and assumed a leadership role in a statewide welfare rights organization. Boudin and McEldowney had accomplished every organizer's ultimate goal: they had worked themselves out of a job.

SDS

While ERAP attempts to work with local and federal officials in the "War on Poverty" did not succeed by traditional standards, they did afford leadership training for many local people. Angry reactions to exclusion then bolstered community efforts to organize local civic groups — paralleling the MFDP — leading to the creation of numerous such organizations in the black communities of the urban North. In the context of a post–World War II society, most urban areas were administered by a rising class of "expert" city managers. This trend, combined with the virulent anticommunism that tended to mute prewar civic groups geared to address urban problems, had the effect of excluding most nonexperts — citizens — from municipal government. In the long term, one Cleveland ERAPer recalled, ERAP organizations in Newark, Cleveland, and Chicago served as a major force in rejuvenating large-scale participation in city politics after World War II.[17] Yet the ERAP staffers who were able to build on these community successes did not find a way to teach what they had learned to others in SDS. McEldowney came close: she sustained ongoing dialogues with the men widely regarded as the "heavies" in the organization through 1966. But in the era preceding the women's movement, when there was no widespread understanding that the personal was political, successful ERAP organizers did not necessarily articulate the relational essence of community organizing.

Although some ERAPers like McEldowney and Boudin found modest success in welfare organizing and generated significant citizen participation in the federal War on Poverty programs, it became clear that the movement in the North would founder on the same shoals as its counterpart in the South: participants could not find ways to dramatize economic inequality. This reality prompted the development of a fateful dynamic spearheaded by Oberlin graduate and ERAP head Rennie Davis. In Chicago, as Davis tried to organize the young men of Uptown, he and those who worked with him were in danger of being beaten up by the very people they were trying to reach. Lacking criteria for political efficacy, the primary measure of valuable work became which activists were willing to risk the most. Thereafter, those like Davis — who risked bodily harm by working with the area's dangerous youth — dominated. Following this model, SDSers would explain the Days of Rage in 1969 as a way to "show people through struggle our commitment, our willingness to run risks, our willingness to die in the struggle to defeat US imperialism. We have to convey these things, and [rage] is a concrete way that we can do that." Again, the political models available to SDSers in the nation's living or written history had proved insufficient to sustain their activities.[18]

Though they failed to mobilize African Americans at the grass roots, they did manage to monopolize media attention later in the decade.

By no means did such activity constitute the whole of later activism. The most significant organizing efforts of the late 1960s and the 1970s were spearheaded by people who had taken part in, or whose political life had been largely shaped by, either SNCC or ERAP. Ivanhoe Donaldson, Stokely Carmichael, Bernice Johnson Reagon, and many other veterans of SNCC worked in organizations that were part of the larger Black Power movement. But lost in the powerful impetus to both black separatism and black nationalism after the 1964 Democratic National Convention in Atlantic City, the few whites who had broken through the caste system—people like Casey Hayden, Mary King, Bob and Dottie Zellner, Mendy Samstein, Penny Patch, and Bill Hansen—suddenly found that their "whiteness" now prevented them from living within the group that SNCC had become by the end of 1966.[19] In fact, the women's movement, grassroots labor organizing, counterculture institutions, and draft resistance movements trace their origins in part to the search for post-SNCC work. In these new organizations, people continued to honor the knowledge they had gained in SNCC.[20]

Women's Liberation

Casey Hayden did not consider the paper she wrote with Mary King for the November 1964 conference in Waveland, Mississippi, titled "The Position of Women in SNCC," an attack on her peers, but rather part of the "questioning and pushing back of limits in which we were engaged at all levels." It was an example of "the huge, anonymous, communal effort of which all of us in SNCC were so gladly a part [of] at all times. This is the true source of that paper about women in the movement, this process and energy of interaction, of giving of ourselves to each other and those we served in the freedom struggle."[21]

The paper's immediate impact was negligible; Hayden later described it as "action on the sidelines." The central issues at Waveland focused on program and structure. Yet as Hayden and King slowly withdrew from SNCC in the months following Waveland, they sought a place to work. Hayden temporarily moved to Chicago to organize women on welfare in an SDS-ERAP project. She did this partly to build a "white alliance" for the organizing she saw Stokely Carmichael, Ruth Howard, and Bob Mants doing in Alabama. Yet as she worked on the project, Hayden realized that such urban organizing would take years and required a feminist consciousness few of those she knew possessed. Moving from Chicago in the late fall of 1965, she reconnected with Mary King. Drawing on their Waveland paper, they wrote to forty black and white women organizers they knew in the movement. Hayden viewed this letter, titled "Sex and Caste: A Kind of Memo," as "an attempt to create conversations among us about what mattered to us. This strengthened the bonds between us which sustained us, and thus strengthened the movement from within by eliciting more openness and engagement by women toward their own issues, which were heretofore considered private and nonpolitical."[22]

In the letter, Hayden and King laid out ideas that would significantly influence the rise of "radical feminism" later in the decade. They wrote that "working in the movement often intensifies personal problems, especially if we start trying to apply things we're learning there to our personal lives." They suggested that if "we can start to talk with each other more openly," they might be able to "deal with ourselves and others with integrity and can therefore keep working." In the wake of the fragmentation of her marriage to Tom Hayden and of SNCC, as well as the bleak prospects for useful work in Chicago, Casey Hayden needed support to move on. The memo was an effort to foster this internal support *and* a self-conscious attempt to create a feminist consciousness within which new and meaningful work could take place.[23]

Interestingly, SNCC people had many conversations about gender and sex prior to the appearance of these memos. To mention only a few examples, Willie Peacock remembered that Helen O'Neal "beat the hell out of Dewey Green Jr." when he said something sexist to her around the Freedom House in Jackson, Mississippi; "she up and slapped the hell out of him — slapped him blind." Ruby Doris Smith Robinson called a meeting of women in the Atlanta SNCC office in the spring of 1964 and suggested a strike: "Women would do absolutely nothing until men recognized that first of all [they] couldn't grab your butts, couldn't grab your breasts. . . ." Bob Moses and Julian Bond, in charge of SNCC's press contacts from Atlanta, both read books given to them by SNCC women such as Doris Lessing's *The Golden Notebook* and Simone de Beauvoir's *The Second Sex* and passed them on to other men in the organization. They openly talked about gender in the course of daily work. Jane Stembridge noted that during the Work-Study Institute SNCC held in February – March 1965, "Vicki Levy and Phyllis Cunningham came and we all talked about sex. That was good because what we talked about was important and Vicki was free to talk about it freely, as was most of the class. No one seemed to assume that sex was anything but great!" Many SNCC people carried varying degrees of womanist and feminist thought into their work.[24]

Once SDS women built a movement in reaction to the ferment generated in part by the Hayden-King memo, women all over the country joined together in consciousness raising groups. To the outsider, CR groups appeared as "just talk" — ideas, not action. Yet action akin to the Lawson workshops was taking place within, as people redefined their relationships to one another, to their husbands, to their fathers, to their male friends, to the state. In many cases, it transformed their subsequent personal and public interactions.[25]

The politics feminist women engaged in — petitioning state and federal legislators, electing women to office, litigating civil rights cases for gender equity, fighting to open professions to women — reshaped the civic landscape and broadened the social relations possible inside the nation between genders in ways remarkably parallel to the freedom struggle's transformation of political and social relationships between people of color and whites.[26] For some men, "women's liberation came at one suddenly, like a Mack truck tearing into your land, totally unexpected, and quickly one discovered that in the most routing flirtations . . . danger lurked." Yet it provided many New Left women a safe harbor from the increasingly macho, apocalyptic rhetoric of the late sixties. Even at conventions, where factionalization and personal antagonisms raged, women of different political orientations often participated in women's caucuses in a respectful, even loving manner.[27]

Yet for all its transformative qualities, women's liberation did not come soon enough—nor was it broad enough—for Casey Hayden. "Looking for somebody who was still willing to see community as the big picture," she moved toward the counterculture, studying Hinduism and Buddhism. "Everybody splintered off into these various, narrow pictures of who they were—women or black people or gay people," she said later. Such activity seemed peripheral to who she had become. Thus, after writing "A Kind of Memo," Hayden dropped out of what she then knew as the movement and "went to the heart of the counterculture." Counterpolitical parties (MFDP), counterschools (Freedom Schools), counter–labor unions, and agricultural marketing services (co-ops) had sprung up throughout the South. The counterculture among youth nationwide followed that lead, and the direction Hayden took after 1965 seemed innately political to her, in harmony with the movement she had known in the South. Though "A Kind of Memo" had been an effort to make the movement stronger, she subsequently found the space within it lacking breadth. The women's movement served a critical purpose, but for her it fell short of the "beloved community."[28]

Flying in the Face of John Wayne

A veteran of the SNCC project in Cambridge, Maryland, and for several years an ERAP organizer, Vernon Grizzard worked in the Boston Draft Resistance Group by 1967. He accompanied young men he counseled to preinduction physicals and used this as a way to promote his mission. While they waited on the bus or in line, he would say: "We work against the draft, we use the law to keep guys out. I just wanted to explain to you what is happening today. We'd just like you to know that if any of you have a problem, you should come see us." He would hand out a card with a phone number of the Boston Draft Resistance and tell the men who had been called up: "I have friends over there, and I don't want them to be killed. The only way we'll be able to do anything about it is if we all stick together, and keep anyone else from having to go over." There were "a lot of guys" whom nobody reached, Grizzard later noted, "and their last stop is Vietnam."[29]

"The only comfort you can draw," reported one young man, "is that you are not alone." Members of the Draft Resistance Group met for dinner, held strategy sessions, and participated in many one-on-one conversations. "What we're trying to do is to take [to a meeting or a dinner] this turmoil of values" and help people learn "that a whole other sense of values, of community, is out there. If they're going into prison, it helps a whole lot to have a group of people supporting them." If they stayed together, another resistance organizer noted, "I may be going to prison, but I feel free, I feel great, this feeling of liberation is really what it's all about."[30]

Whereas most organizers of the draft resistance were white, black civil rights workers had been active in antiwar mobilizations from the onset of the movement. Bob Moses played an early, critical role in mobilizing civil rights activists to support the antiwar movement. As early as August 1964, he spoke against the war at a memorial service for James Chaney, Mickey Schwerner, and Andrew Goodman. Standing next to the ruins of the burned black church in Philadelphia that the three slain men had initially come to investigate, Moses compared the Tonkin Bay resolution—which had passed Congress on 10 August, six days after the bodies were found—to these killings in Mississippi. As someone remembered Moses saying: "If you don't understand that this country will allow black people to be killed without raising an eyebrow, then you won't understand that the country is planning to go to war with brown people in Vietnam fighting for their self-determination."[31]

This remarkable parallel between moments of day-to-day agony in the civil rights movement and the structural wretchedness of the Vietnam War provided one more example of the creative energy liberated among SNCC workers like Moses. Freedom School coordinator and Spelman professor Staughton Lynd was present at Moses' eulogy for Chaney, Schwerner, and Goodman. "When I think of Bob, and his people trying to get the right to vote, and three people killed, it just staggers me," Lynd said in 2001. He later remarked on Moses' determination to stand in solidarity with the Vietnamese people. According to Moses, the movement was surprisingly clear about its position on U.S. involvement in Vietnam — not because civil rights workers understood so much about foreign policy, but because "they understand so much about the United States. They understand just how much hypocrisy is wrapped up in our claim to stand for 'the free world.' They know how much they had to endure in beatings and bombings and murder before the American government acted to pass civil rights legislation."[32]

In the late spring of 1965, Bob Moses, his wife Dona Richards Moses, and other organizers, sent a memo to SNCC workers on "an idea for a project based in Washington D.C. this summer." After meeting with peace groups, civil rights group, community groups and churches, they felt the need to first, "muster mass support for the [MFDP's] congressional challenge," and second, "to address ourselves to the broader implications of our work in the South, such as its relation to foreign policy (South Africa, the Dominican Republic, South Vietnam.)" Because "a large amount of activity this summer will be concerned with protesting the war in Vietnam," they wanted to "tap that energy to support the [MFDP] challenge." Both peace and civil rights groups thought they might benefit from learning about each other's work. At its most basic, the connection could be seen by a mother in Mississippi who registered to vote on the very day her son was killed in Vietnam. Yet SNCC people still found "the idea very new and very difficult to get into working order." Nonetheless, over the summer an increasing number of SNCC and SCOPE workers refused to serve in the military. After John D. Shaw, a twenty-three-year old black man active in the movement in his hometown of McComb, Mississippi, was killed in Vietnam, the Mississippi Freedom Democratic Party circulated an antidraft petition. When critics questioned its patriotism, MFDP representatives responded "by pointing to the great sacrifices made by our members toward bringing true freedom and democracy to Mississippi." SNCC would go on to oppose the draft a full year before SDS did. And once again, one brutal result was that across the South, local draft boards called up almost all men associated with SNCC activities.[33]

The Counterculture

After returning to their college campuses between the fall of 1964 and 1966, Mississippi Summer Project volunteers created an array of "countercultural" institutions based on the experiences, knowledge, and skills they had acquired in the Deep South. For Mario

Savio, after spending two months in McComb, it was impossible to slip back into the life of an undergraduate math major at Berkeley. Instead, he set up a table on Sproul Plaza to raise money for SNCC. Administrative resistance to his efforts led to the Free Speech Movement: by December 1964, 30,000 people "sat in" at Sproul Plaza to protest the university's restrictions. Similarly, on arriving in Chicago and finding one of her friends suicidal over an unplanned pregnancy, Heather Tobias asked a doctor she knew through the civil rights movement to perform an abortion. Subsequently Tobias and a group of friends started JANE, an underground abortion service for women in the Midwest.[34]

Such counterculture projects often developed as reactions to emergencies: Savio wanting to aid SNCC's shoestring operation, Tobias responding to an unplanned pregnancy in the era before *Roe v. Wade*. Other projects sprang up to deal with the crisis of the Vietnam War and extreme poverty in rural and urban areas. Yet the wider thrust of the counterculture engaged what social commentator Theodore Roszak termed "'the technocracy.'" This was a rebellion against experts assuming authority over not just technical operations such as power plants and medical laboratories but "even the most seemingly personal aspects of life: sexual behavior, child-rearing, mental health, recreation." The onset of the age of technocracy prompted the average citizen, overwhelmed by "bewildering bigness and complexity," to defer to those who "knew better."[35]

It was this deference that outraged the children of the counterculture. An upswell of desire to find out for oneself, rather than be told by an expert, characterized all aspects of the movement, including spiritual searches, particularly of eastern religious traditions; alternative newspapers; movie collectives; art and theater troupes; and "free universities." It stretched to encompass sexual freedom leagues, communes, and groups coming together to explore alternative family structures. Marijuana and LSD were extolled as opening "the doors of perception" into other ways of thinking. Yoga classes, alternative healing therapies, organic food cooperatives, and "free medical clinics" questioned the assumptions on which most American medical care was based. Jimi Hendrix, Jefferson Airplane, the Grateful Dead, bell bottoms and dashikis, afros and men with long hair — these emerged as the sound, look, and feel of this revolt against deference to professional experts.[36]

Labor

Some former SNCC organizers joined the labor movement. After participating in a SNCC labor conference at Highlander, Casey Hayden and Mendy Samstein tried to work on a union campaign in North Carolina with Liz and Sam Shirah (both white SNCC workers) but found the hierarchical nature of the union too stifling. The Shirahs worked for the International Ladies' Garment Workers Union (ILG), but stopped organizing, as Liz put it, "because the sonovabitch-male supremacist state director of the ILG ordered me to." Their experience was typical when the union retained the organizational structure of the received culture. The state director told the Shirahs to hand out leaflet-surveys "bearing serial numbers" at different plants; he would determine interest in the union based on the number of people who bothered to mail the surveys back. "The organizer is not expected or permitted to take any initiative," Liz informed SDSer Paul Booth in

September 1965. "Decisions are made by people who have no knowledge of the real situation." The police used city ordinances that had been passed to prevent civil rights demonstrations — for example, antileafleting and antiassembly laws — against the organizers. Though "the unions know they must organize the South to survive," Shirah wrote, they refused to organize at the grass-roots" because they "cannot permit [grassroots] power to exist within their own framework."[37]

Some SNCC veterans — among them, Marshall Ganz, Dennis Sweeney, Mary King, and Elizabeth Hirshfeld — had better luck working with Cesar Chavez and Dorothy Huerta of the United Farm Workers (UFW). Indeed, Ganz and Hirshfeld spent a large part of their professional lives in the UFW. Others, like Curtis Muhammad, successfully worked for the AFL-CIO as grassroots organizers.

Notes

Abbreviations

CORE Papers
  Congress of Racial Equality Papers, microfilm
Ewen Papers
  Stewart Ewen Papers, State Historical Society of Wisconsin, Madison
Feingold Papers
  Miriam Feingold Papers, State Historical Society of Wisconsin, Madison
FOR Papers
  Fellowship of Reconciliation Papers, Swarthmore College Peace Collection,
  Swarthmore, Pa.
JFK Library
  John F. Kennedy Library, Boston
Kennedy Papers
  Robert F. Kennedy Papers, John F. Kennedy Library, Boston
KMS
  Kelly Miller Smith
KMS Papers
  Kelly Miller Smith Papers, Vanderbilt University Special Collections,
  Nashville, Tenn.
Mary King Papers
  Mary King Papers, State Historical Society of Wisconsin, Madison
Matthews Collection
  J. B. Matthews Collection, Special Collections Library, Duke University,
  Durham, N.C.
MFDP Papers
  Mississippi Freedom Democratic Party Papers, rolls 65 – 70, Student Nonviolent
  Coordinating Committee Papers, 1959 – 72 (Sanford, N.C.: Microfilming
  Corporation of America, 1982)
MFSR Papers
  "Mississippi's 'Freedom Summer' Reviewed: A Fifteen Year Perspective on
  Progress in Race Relations, 1964 – 1979" Papers, State Historical Society of
  Wisconsin, Madison
Project South Collection
  Project South Collection, Special Collections Library, Stanford University,
  Stanford, Calif.

Rauh Papers
  Joseph L. Rauh Papers, Manuscript Division, Library of Congress,
  Washington, D.C.
Romaine Papers
  Anne Romaine Papers, State Historical Society of Wisconsin, Madison
SB-SNCC Conference
  "'We Who Believe in Freedom Cannot Rest': Ella Baker and the Birth of SNCC"
  Conference, Shaw University, Raleigh, N.C., 15 Apr. 2000
SCLC Papers
  Southern Christian Leadership Conference Papers, microfilm
SDS Papers
  Students for a Democratic Society Papers, State Historical Society of Wisconsin,
  Madison
Sherrod Papers
  Charles Sherrod Papers, State Historical Society of Wisconsin, Madison
SHSW
  State Historical Society of Wisconsin, Madison
SNCC Papers
  Student Nonviolent Coordinating Committee Papers, 1959–72 (Sanford, N.C.:
  Microfilming Corporation of America, 1982)

Introduction

1. Charles McLaurin, "To Overcome Fear," frames 55–56, reel 40, SNCC Papers.
McLaurin and the twenty-odd other SNCC people named in this book are (for reasons
of space) "standing" for the over 400 SNCC (and some CORE) people whose experiences
I hope to represent. In no way does my selection of historical actors intend to slight the
contributions of those in SNCC who are not visible in the particular incidents that follow. Instead, this selection is based on available evidence and narrative flow. I hope this
work encourages others to tell the stories of those not present on these pages.

2. Charles McLaurin to Cleve Sellers, n.d. [August 1965], "Report on the Second
Congressional District," frames 165–66, reel 40, SNCC Papers.

3. In a field of literature already flowering with thousands of books, it is customary
to challenge traditional narratives, asserting the luminosity of the new work when
compared to the fading explanatory power of previous endeavors. I have no desire to
repeat this patricidal pattern. What follows is only one piece of the larger truth emerging from the activity known as the "civil rights movement": It is an attempt to uncover
the precise sequential dynamics of *how* individuals successfully insisted on the right
to their own lives. Barbara Deming's insightful approach in *We Are All Part of One
Another* has shaped my own. Deming's idea, that we all only have one piece of the truth,
does however open one to criticism — how does one's work interact with and reshape
the themes visible in previous work in the field? Rather than include this material in
the text, I have provided most of it in these endnotes. I ask the reader's patience with
this placement. Since such matters are of primary interest only to specialists, I have
tried to keep them in the notes, so as to direct the text toward the general reader. In

addition, some beautifully illustrative stories live in the notes rather than the text due to concerns of narrative pace and focus.

4. See also Reagon, "'Nobody Knows the Trouble I See.'"

5. Conley, *Being Black*, 25. On wealth, see also Darity and Myers, *Persistent Disparity*; Oliver and Shapiro, *Black Wealth/White Wealth*; and Massey and Denton, *American Apartheid*. On school segregation, see Orfield et al., *Dismantling Desegregation*, as well as the Harvard Civil Rights Project's online report on Metro Boston, ‹http://www.civilrightsproject.harvard.edu/research/metro/segregation_education.php›. For recent statistics on educational and residential segregation, see the PBS website, "Race: The Power of an Illusion," ‹http://www.pbs.org/race/001_WhatIsRace/001_00-home.htm›, and school statistics at ‹http://www.pbs.org/race/000_About/002_04-background-03-08.htm›.

6. See Charles W. Mills, *Racial Contract* and *Blackness Visible*.

7. Recent emphasis by historians on transnational scholarship illuminates the profound limitations of writing U.S. history in the post–World War II period. While the story that follows focuses on a movement within U.S. borders, many participants saw their activities in the context of global liberation efforts.

8. Bond has stated this at numerous public forums on the movement.

9. As one observer noted in 2004, "Perhaps this fact surprises me most: the civil rights movement required preparation, and could not merely rely on spontaneity and ideology to succeed." Participant in Larry Goodwyn's Duke University seminar, Spring 2004. On Buckley, see "Buckley Assailed on Selma Remarks," *New York Times*, 6 Apr. 1965, and his autobiography, *Miles Gone By* (2004), for his admission that conservatives might have been wrong about the movement.

10. Laue, *Direct Action*, 241 (King). Historian Chana Kai Lee (*For Freedom's Sake*, 44) later wrote: "Although it had a longtime interest in black suffrage, the NAACP conducted its main battles in the courtroom. This strategy had little mass appeal and was relatively slow and very time-consuming. However, when SNCC hit the scene, it came with a plan of action that produced consequences that were noticeable and appreciated without much delay." Charles Payne, Adam Fairclough, Emilye Crosby, Timothy Tyson, Stephen Tuck, and others have all demonstrated how local NAACP chapters often adopted programs and philosophies that included far more diversity than the national organization.

11. SCLC held numerous "institutes" on nonviolent practice. For brief documentation of "Institutes on Nonviolence" held in Petersburg, Va. (July 1960), Atlanta (August 1960), Birmingham (August 1960), and Lynchburg, Va. (March 1961), see Part II, reel 3, SCLC Papers. In 1955–56 Glenn Smiley trained Martin Luther King to run such workshops himself, so it is fair to say that King had experience with how difficult it was to move people to action. See Burns, *Daybreak of Freedom*, 292–95. In the upper echelons of SCLC, it was common knowledge that King's respect for Lawson was unmatched.

12. Charles M. Payne coined the term "organizing tradition" in his innovative study, *Light of Freedom*. This work would not have been possible without the careful scholarship that he and John Dittmer pioneered on the Mississippi movement in particular and on social movements more generally.

13. See Joyce Ladner to Julian Bond, "Zellner's Version – Black Panther Logo," posted

on SNCC – List Serve, 6 Mar. 2002. South African Z. K. Matthews wrote in the American pacifist journal *Liberation* of December 1956 that the Montgomery bus boycott was an "inspiration to others faced with similar problems in other parts of the world"; reprinted in Burns, *Daybreak of Freedom*, 317. On World War II veterans, see Charles Payne, *Light of Freedom*, chaps. 1–2. One such veteran was Mississippi activist Aaron Henry: "I soon found that there were NAACP chapters near every base where I was stationed. I always affiliated with these chapters, and many times it was helpful in working out racial disputes on the base. While individual Negro soldiers might be hesitant to speak up to a commanding officer about injustices, they were willing to allow an NAACP representative to speak for them. The NAACP officials were always available and made it their business to mediate. Negro soldiers who had never dreamed of joining the NAACP became enthusiastic members and started chapters when they returned home." Henry, *Fire Ever Burning*, 63.

Chapter One

1. Lawson interview, 14 Aug. 2001; Halberstam, *The Children*, 138, 413 (Lafayette). For a brief definition of nonviolent direct action and an overview of different ways to think about nonviolence, see Sharp, "Beyond Just War and Pacifism."

2. Kapur, *Raising Up a Prophet*, 155 (Lawson).

3. Lawson served as the FOR's southern field secretary from 1957 to 1960, then as national secretary in charge of Race and Nonviolence. He continued to participate in the FOR in a number of advisory capacities before being named executive secretary in 1995. Kapur, *Raising Up a Prophet*, 155; Smiley, "How Nonviolence Works." Following its establishment in 1915, the major focus of FOR's American branch was protecting the human rights of COs during World War I. Over the next four decades, FOR staff developed programs to counsel COs and their families. When Gandhi acolyte and Columbia University doctoral candidate Krishnalal Shridharani published *War Without Violence* in 1939 — introducing Gandhian nonviolence to a North American audience — longtime proponents of equality, including Muste, A. Philip Randolph of the Brotherhood of Sleeping Car Porters, and Dr. John Haynes Holmes of the Community Church of New York, saw its relevance to dismantling segregation in the United States. The FOR subsequently allowed three of its staff members — the irrepressible trio of Bayard Rustin, James Farmer, and George Houser — to begin experimenting with nonviolent techniques and conducting nonviolent workshops in the 1940s. Such workshops, combined with the group's publications, made the FOR a major channel for the transmission of Gandhian practices to U.S. activists, particularly those within the early civil rights movement. The early correspondence of Rustin, Houser, and Farmer can be found in the FOR Papers and CORE Papers. Rustin, as the FOR's college secretary in the early 1950s, lectured on "Non-Violence for America" during this period ("Gandhi Memorial Meeting," 30 Jan. 1952, box 9, FOR Papers); he had conducted "Interracial Workshops on Nonviolence" as early as 1943 ("Program of the New York Institute on Race Relations and Non-Violent Solutions," Grace Congressional Church, 2–4 Apr. 1943, clipping collection, Bayard Rustin Fund, New York). FOR's Glenn Smiley also conducted workshops and regularly visited colleges and divinity schools during

the 1950s (box 30, FOR Papers). On Rustin, see D'Emilio, *Lost Prophet*. On Rustin's workshops, see Daniel Levine, *Bayard Rustin*, 33–39, 79–80, 91; also Jervis Anderson, *Bayard Rustin*, 68, 81, 87–89, 112. See also Farmer, *Lay Bare the Heart*, and Houser, *No One Can Stop the Rain*.

4. Halberstam, *The Children*, 43–46.

5. Ibid., 46 (Lawson).

6. Lawson interview, 23 Mar. 2000; Kapur, *Raising Up a Prophet*, 155; Jack, *Gandhi Reader*, 316 (Gandhi).

7. Lawson interview, 14 Aug. 2001; KMS, "Pursuit of a Dream (The Nashville Story)," manuscript, n.p., folder 7, box 28, KMS Papers. See also Halberstam, *The Children*, 217, 16, and Garrow, *Bearing the Cross*, 89–90. On Montgomery, see Burns, *Daybreak of Freedom*; Robinson, *Montgomery Bus Boycott*; and Raines, *My Soul Is Rested*. On King's role in the boycott, see Garrow, *Bearing the Cross*, and Branch, *Parting the Waters*. In India, Sudarshan Kapur (*Raising Up a Prophet*, 155) notes, Lawson "met with such outstanding Gandhians as Vinoba Bhave, Gandhi's foremost disciple; JC Kumarappa, the leading Gandhian economist; and Asha Devi, a frontline Gandhian in the post-independence period."

8. See Lawson interview, 14 Aug. 2001; Student Workshop, Tennessee A&I State University, 11 Oct. 1960, folder 13, box 74, KMS Papers; and "Toward the Beloved Community: Story of the Nashville Christian Leadership Council" n.d., folder 13, box 75, KMS Papers. While still in India and months before meeting King, Lawson wrote FOR executive secretary John Swomley: "The hitch out here [in Nagpur] makes me want to return and dig in on the books. Yet FOR field work appeals to me. . . . There is a great deal on my heart and mind which will need expression in creative peace work." Lawson, Nagpur, India, to John M. Swomley Jr., New York, N.Y., 10 Apr. 1956, Lawson folder, temporary box 2, FOR Papers. Once he got into the field with Smiley, both men often held long discussions with students between workshop sessions. Frequently, they helped to sponsor North-South student exchanges. Smiley organized a conference in Atlanta in January 1957 to train southerners in nonviolence. See Glenn E. Smiley to "Friend," January 1957, reprinted in Burns, *Daybreak of Freedom*, 332–33. Smiley had been running workshops for many years. As part of the March on Washington movement in the early 1940s, his workshops had introduced thousands to the basic ideas of nonviolent direct action. Smiley and Lawson built on this experience, as well as techniques developed by Bayard Rustin and George Houser in the 1940s and 1950s. On Smiley's influence on Martin Luther King Jr. and the Montgomery bus boycott, see Burns, *Daybreak of Freedom*, 20, 22, 36. On the March on Washington movement, see Macdonald and Macdonald, *War's Greatest Scandal!*, and Herbert Garfinkle, *When Negroes March*. For CORE activities in the 1940s and 1950s, see reels 14, 16, CORE Papers. See also Laue, *Direct Action*, chap. 3; Kent Larrabee to Glenn Smiley, 21 Sept. 1955, box 30, FOR Papers; "August: Youth Conferences, camps, etc." and "Fellowship of Reconciliation Questionnaire," n.d., box 30, FOR Papers; Smiley [Montgomery] to [FOR] Staff, 7 Apr. 1956, reprinted in Burns, *Daybreak of Freedom*, 250–52; Charles Walker to "Smiley, Swomley, Larrabee and other staff," 5 Dec. 1955, and "North-South Student Exchange," n.d. [1957?], box 30, FOR Papers.

9. Lawson interview, 14 Aug. 2001; KMS, "Pursuit of a Dream." Smith also noted that

though the "courageous young college students sometimes speak as if there were no background to their thrust, old-timers in Nashville quickly remind them that, in their own way, oppressed Nashvillians have always struggled to erase the shame of their city," referencing J. C. Napier, one of two African American aldermen in the nineteenth century, and S. P. Harris, Sr., a black councilman from 1909 to 1911. See also Aldon Morris, *Origins*, 175–77, and Halberstam, *The Children*, 52, 56. For SCLC's working papers, dated 10–11 Jan. 1957, see SCLC Papers; for NCLC's statement of "Purposes and Principles," see folder 8, box 75, KMS Papers.

10. Lawson interview, 14 Aug. 2001. Glenn Smiley had worked extensively with the SCLC ministers in Montgomery during the bus boycott as well. Smiley, Rev. Ralph Abernathy, and Lawson subsequently traveled through the South, drawing together black leaders around the tactics and philosophy of nonviolence. KMS, Introduction to *Sit-In Nashville Tennessee*, Guy Carawan, Folkways Records, FH 5590, 1960, reprinted in folder 4, box 74, KMS Papers. Lawson's thinking during this time is visible in his late 1961 article, "Eve of Nonviolent Revolution."

11. Alfred Hassler to Walter Muelder, 2 Apr. 1958, box 20, FOR Papers; Lewis, *Walking with the Wind*, 83. The FOR pamphlet, published in 1957 as "Martin Luther King and the Montgomery Story," can be found in box 19, FOR Papers. See also Hassler to Edward Reed, 2 May 1956, box 17, FOR Papers, and Aldon Morris, *Origins*, 159–65, 176. "Dignity" and "justice," while universal concepts, are culturally specific in manifestation. For instance, a "dignified" or "just" way to treat a stranger in the U.S. South in 1957 might have differed from a "dignified" or "just" way to treat a stranger in the Republic of the Congo in 1993, or in Thailand in 2001. For further delineation of this important idea, see Scott, *Weapons of the Weak*.

12. Lewis, *Walking with the Wind*, 83.

13. Lawson interview, 14 Aug. 2001; KMS, "Pursuit of a Dream." Black police officers could arrest African Americans only.

14. Lawson interview, 14 Aug. 2001. Such a wide-ranging, calculated, and long-term plan as emerged from the Lawson workshops in 1959 disrupts the traditional understanding that the civil rights movement was relatively unconcerned with economic justice issues until after passage of the 1965 Voting Rights Act.

15. Lawson, Minutes, 17 Nov. 1959, folder 22, box 75, KMS Papers; Lewis, *Walking with the Wind*, 91.

16. Halberstam, *The Children*, 49–50 (Lewis), 147. Nash quoted in interview, "The Nashville Sit-In Story," *Sit-In Nashville Tennessee*, and Hampton and Fayer, *Voices of Freedom*, 55. Thanks to Hasan Jeffries for helping me to develop this portrait of Nash.

17. Hampton and Fayer, *Voices of Freedom*, 131–35 (description of Bevel); Carmichael, *Ready for Revolution*, 206–7; Halberstam, *The Children*, 49–59, 70, 96, 100.

18. Lawson interview, 14 Aug. 2001. See *The Journal of John Woolman* (London: Andrew Melrose, 1898) and William Penn, *A Letter from William Penn* (London, 1683).

19. A "Selected Bibliography" used by Lawson in Nashville at the time (in folder 14, box 75, KMS Papers) includes selections from Hinduism, Buddhism, Jainism, Henry David Thoreau, Leo Tolstoy, Richard Gregg, Joan Bondurant, R. R. Diwakar, T. K. N. Unnithan, and of course Gandhi. The rich and thought-provoking literature on the intellectual tradition and practice of nonviolence in the United States (and

elsewhere) includes Gregg, *Power of Nonviolence* and *Discipline for Non-Violence*; DeBenedetti, *Origins of the American Peace Movement* and *Peace Reform*; Chatfield, *For Peace and Justice* and *Americanization of Gandhi*; and Sharp, *Exploring Nonviolent Alternatives, Politics of Nonviolent Action*, and *Gandhi as a Political Strategist*. More recent work includes Epstein, *Political Protest*; Tracy, *Direct Action*; Smith, Chatfield, and Pagnucco, *Transnational Social Movements*; Zunes, Kurtz, and Asher, *Nonviolent Social Movements*; Steger and Lind, *Violence and Its Alternatives*; Banerjee, *The Pathan Unarmed*; Cavin, "Glenn Smiley Was a Fool"; and Peterson, *Linked Arms*.

20. Lawson interview, 14 Aug. 2001; Viorst, *Fire in the Streets*, 104 (Lewis). See also folders 3 – 4, 12 – 16, box 74, KMS Papers.

21. Lewis, *Walking with the Wind*, 87.

22. "Student Central Committee of the Nashville Nonviolent Movement," "Attention All Students: Why We Must Fight Segregation," 11 Oct. 1960, folder 12, box 74, KMS Papers; Halberstam, *The Children*, 75; Lewis, *Walking with the Wind*, 87. For an excellent primary source on the impact of segregation on individual lives and the way it fostered anger about Jim Crow, see Burns, *Daybreak of Freedom*, esp. 58 – 105.

23. Lewis, *Walking with the Wind*, 87.

24. In a modern context, Aung San Suu Kyi (*Freedom from Fear*, 180 – 85) has also articulated the political utility of concepts such as truth, justice, and compassion. She maintains that in an environment where fear is an integral part of everyday existence, "the burden of upholding the principles of justice and common decency falls on the ordinary people." Their cumulative efforts and endurance to live out a just and compassionate existence "are often the only bulwarks which stand against ruthless power." As such, "concepts such as truth, justice and compassion," she argues, "cannot be dismissed as trite."

25. Halberstam, *The Children*, 101 (Lawson). Lawson's understanding that it was personal insecurity that drove reactionaries to assault nonviolent protesters was an early and important articulation of an idea brought forward most forcefully later in the 1960s by the women's movement: the personal is political.

26. Bevel explains this dynamic at greater length in Hampton and Fayer, *Voices of Freedom*, 226. See also Halberstam, *The Children*, 77.

27. Lawson interview, 14 Aug. 2001; Halberstam, *The Children*, 78.

28. Lawson interview, 14 Aug. 2001; Lewis, *Walking with the Wind*, 87, Nash, "Inside the Sit-Ins," 45. Halberstam, *The Children*, 78.

29. We suffer no shortage of evidence on the sit-ins: one can find thousands of documents on these events in the papers of SNCC, SCLC, CORE, the Highlander Folk School, local NAACP youth groups, and various government agencies. These sources contain lists of workshop participants and materials sent to them, agendas for the workshops, and literature recommended to the participants. However, almost none of the crucial energizing dynamics — how topics were introduced and discussed, what parameters for discussion were established, and, above all, how participants were induced to move from idea to action inside these nonviolent workshops — is recoverable from the organizational papers of the major civil rights organizations that structurally attempted to employ nonviolent direct action — namely SCLC, FOR, CORE, and SNCC. The closest approximation are documents such as "Resolutions of July 22 – 24

Institute on Nonviolent Resistance to Segregation," and its subsequent "Manifesto," dated 11 Aug. 1959, in the SCLC Papers. These documents lay out the intellectual and philosophical underpinnings of nonviolent forms of social change, but reveal little else about how people came up with these ideas and how they planned to act on them. It follows, then, that such details are absent from the historical literature derived from these primary sources. Hundreds of oral histories exist as well, yet almost none explore the interior dynamics of the workshops.

30. Viorst, *Fire in the Streets*, 104 (Lewis). Challenges to Jim Crow indeed had existed since its onset. See Meier and Rudwick, "Boycott Movement"; J. Douglas Smith, *Managing White Supremacy*; Sullivan, *Days of Hope*; and Barnes, *Journey from Jim Crow*. Paul Ortiz's study of resistance to Jim Crow in Florida, *Emancipation Betrayed*, is particularly instructive.

31. Lawson, "Evaluation: Institute on Nonviolence, Spelman College," 22–24 July 1959, box 20, FOR Papers. The Nashville workshops drew on but also enriched the legacy of similar initiatives run by the Highlander Folk School and by local churches elsewhere in the South under the auspices of CORE and later by SCLC. Yet in 1958–60 the Nashville sessions constituted a genre of their own. In them, Lawson set out to prove that the Montgomery bus boycott had not been an accident, that it could be done at the grass roots "again and again." On the Highlander Folk School, see Myles Horton, *The Long Haul*, and Charles Payne, *Light of Freedom*, chap. 3. For other workshops in SCLC during this period, see Aldon Morris, *Origins*, chaps. 3–5, 8; Septima P. Clark, *Ready from Within*; Joanne Grant, *Ella Baker*, 102–21; and Powledge, *Free at Last?*, 201–24.

32. Lawson interviews, 27 Mar. 2000, 14 Aug. 2001; Lawson, "Evaluation: Institute on Nonviolence, Spelman College"; Lewis, *Walking with the Wind*, 85. See also Halberstam, *The Children*, 61–63.

33. Lawson interview, 14 Aug. 2001. Lawson stressed that some of his favorite examples to share were not only imaginative responses to violence by Gandhi and Martin Luther King, but also those of Bayard Rustin, A. J. Muste, Muriel Lester, and Magla and Andre Trocme. The Trocmes, who organized resistance to the Nazis in much of the Provence region in France, saved about 5,000 Jews from going to death camps. Lawson heard Magla Trocme speak in the late 1940s, when she toured the United States after World War II. She explained how she and her husband, a local pastor, had preached, taught, and lived. In their largely rural area, they and their associates openly resisted the Germans. Some of them did get thrown in jail, some of them got shot. But they resisted and survived the war intact. Lawson also frequently taught with Andre Trocme's book, *Jesus and the Nonviolent Revolution*.

34. Lawson interview, 14 Aug. 2001.

35. Ibid.; KMS, "Pursuit of a Dream."

36. Lawson, Projects Committee Report, NCLC Minutes, 3 Jan. 1960, folder 23, box 75, KMS Papers; Lawson interview, 14 Aug. 2001. After conducting a formal survey of black buying power in Nashville, NCLC estimated that if Harvey's annual sales volume in 1957 was $2 million, blacks contributed $300,000. "This is not to be sneezed at since such a dollar amount could be the difference between profit and loss or the difference between success and failure for many firms," NCLC determined. "Selected

Estimates on Negro Buying Power in Nashville as of January 1957," folder 7, box 28, KMS Papers.

37. Lawson interview, 14 Aug. 2001; Raines, *My Soul Is Rested*, 75 – 80 (McCain). The 1960 sit-ins were not the first such demonstrations in the United States; the tactic had in fact become a "time-honored" one by 1960. Bayard Rustin, George Houser, James Farmer, and other members of the FOR and CORE had pioneered the use of the sit-in throughout the North and West in the 1940s and 1950s. And according to sociologist Aldon Morris (*Origins*, 189, 202 – 5), between 1957 and 1960 civil rights activists had held sit-ins in at least sixteen southern cities. But it was not until the sit-ins of 1960 that students in large numbers challenged segregated public facilities throughout the region. For a detailed community study of the Greensboro sit-ins, see Chafe, *Civilities*. After Greensboro, veteran nonviolent teachers Gordon Carey and Jim McCain of CORE also began traveling from one southern community to another, running nonviolent workshops. On Carey and McCain, see Debbie Louis's extraordinary breakthrough movement account, *We Are Not Saved*, 99. For a list of cities that experienced sit-ins during February – May 1960, see Laue, *Direct Action*, app. F.

At the start of the sit-ins, students maximized the communications network developed among southern black church communities during SCLC's previous three years of organizing. Through these "movement centers," students gathered information on the sit-ins and spread the word in their communities. In places where the movement had not yet arrived, national publicity through the *New York Times* and other newspapers helped the sit-ins to increase. Longtime black activist Ella J. Baker, the "mother of SNCC," observed the Atlanta sit-ins from her post as executive secretary of SCLC. She felt that word of mouth was an even stronger impetus. "A sister to a brother, members of the same fraternity, girlfriend to boyfriend, or simply calling up contacts, friends asking, 'what is happening on your campus?'" impelled the protests to proliferate. Within a week of the Greensboro sit-in, students conducted sit-ins across North Carolina; within two months, the sit-ins had spread to sixty-nine cities. Two thousand students experienced arrest, fingerprinting, and jail. This, in turn, launched a national boycott of chain stores like Woolworth's and Kress. Places where James Lawson and Glenn Smiley had already presented "freedom workshops" proved particularly responsive. (Aldon Morris noted that SCLC movement centers were created with the assistance of CORE and NAACP Youth Councils.) Joanne Grant, *Ella Baker*, 131 (Baker). See Aldon Morris, *Origins*, 190, 200 – 201, 203, and Chafe, *Civilities*, 85.

38. Lewis interview ("ready response"); Raines, *My Soul Is Rested*, 98 (Lewis). The next morning Lawson reported to the NCLC: "Although we had been making preparations for this a long time, our timing was suggested by the action in North Carolina" (quoted in KMS, "Pursuit of a Dream"). Lawson and Moore were both active in SCLC. See also Paul LaPrad, "Nashville: A Community Struggle," in Jim Peck, ed., *The Sit-Ins* (pamphlet), frames 371 – 73, reel 49, CORE Papers, and Garrow, *Bearing the Cross*, 127.

39. Quotations by Diane Nash in "Ain't Scared of Your Jails" (video); by Lawson, from Lawson interview online; and by Lewis, in Raines, *My Soul is Rested*, 99. See also KMS, "Pursuit of a Dream." For Original "Rules of Action Proposed by Sit-In Participants," n.d., see folder 14, box 75, KMS Papers. Just how hard it was to adhere to such rules could be seen in the sit-in campaign in Portsmouth, Va., where whites

taunted those who were sitting-in by pulling out car chains and claw hammers and swinging them in the face of a black male activist. "The boy kept walking. Then, in utter frustration, the white boy picked up a street sign and threw it at a Negro girl. It hit her and the fight began. The white boys, armed with chains, pipes, and hammers, cut off an escape through the street. Negro boys grabbed the chains and beat the white boys, who went running back to their hot rods." Edward Rodman, "Portsmouth: A Lesson in Nonviolence," Jim Peck, ed., *The Sit-Ins*, frame 370, reel 49, CORE Papers.

40. KMS, "Pursuit of a Dream"; LaPrad, "Nashville," folder 4, box 75, KMS Papers. Access to Ben Houston's forthcoming local study on the movement in Nashville has enriched this account. I am grateful for his feedback and input on this chapter.

41. Peggi Alexander, "Report I," *Sit-In Nashville Tennessee*, Folkways Records, FH 5590, 1960; KMS, "Pursuit of a Dream."

42. KMS, "Pursuit of a Dream." See also "Ain't Scared of Your Jails." The capacity for living with the uncertainty of the immediate future would grow increasingly valuable and rare as the decade wore on. The failure of more movement people to develop this facility would in fact significantly contribute to the confusion of the student movement by the end of the 1960s.

43. Lawson interview, 14 Aug. 2001; "Ain't Scared of Your Jails"; Halberstam, *The Children*, 141, 9. The central committee consisted of Lawson, the core group of people who participated in the Fall 1959 workshops (among them Lewis, Nash, and Bevel), one or two representatives from each campus, and NCLC members like Andrew White, Delores Wilkerson, and C. T. Vivian. The committee's nonhierarchical ideas of leadership also emerged in the course of the Montgomery bus boycott, although they were never broadly visible. See Burns, *Daybreak of Freedom*, 72, 77.

44. Nash interview; Nash, "The Nashville Sit-In Story."

45. Halberstam, *The Children*, 10 (Nash); Powledge, *Free at Last?*, 208 (Nash); Lawson interview online; Louis, *We Are Not Saved*, 117 (southern student); Lewis, "The Student Speaks: Democracy as a Reality," paper presented in a panel discussion, 13 May 1960, folder 4, box 75, KMS Papers.

46. Shakur, *Assata*, 139 ("appealing to the conscience of whites"). See also Carmichael and Hamilton, *Black Power*, 51–53, 82. For an extended discussion of the concept of human nature among nonviolent practitioners, see Chappell, *Stone of Hope*, chaps. 3–4. As Chappell quotes Rustin and King: "Gradually the Negro masses in the South began to reevaluate themselves. . . . We discovered that we had never really smothered our self-respect and that we could not be at one with ourselves without asserting it" (p. 59).

47. "Ain't Scared of Your Jails" (Lewis) and Halberstam, *The Children*, 120 (Lewis). See also Lewis, "The Nashville Sit-In Story," Folkways Records, FH 5590, 1960, and Lewis, "The Student Speaks: Democracy as a Reality," speech at the United Student Protest Movement against Discrimination," 13 May 1960, Clark Memorial Church, Nashville, Tenn., folder 1, box 74, KMS Papers. On 9 Apr. 1960 CORE traveler Len Holt observed: "In this atmosphere of great unity there was one fly in the marmalade; to stay or not to stay in jail? On one side was the general fear of jail and dislike of jail so much a part of an American community. The feeling on this side was crystallized recently in a speech before 4000 by Thurgood Marshall in the gymnasium of Fisk U. . . . On

the other side was the youthful, indigenous leadership of the sit-ins, 'the new Negro.'" L. E. Holt, frames 1397–98, reel 42, CORE Papers.

48. Laue, *Direct Action*, 91 (Anne Braden); "Ain't Scared of Your Jails" (Vivian); Hampton and Fayer, *Voices of Freedom*, 66–67 (Diane Nash); Viorst, *Fire in the Streets*, 106 (John Lewis). See also KMS, "Pursuit of a Dream." Angeline Butler, "There We Were All Locked in Jail . . ." n.d., folder 7, box 28, KMS Papers.

49. Halberstam, *The Children*, 4, 284 (Nash).

50. "Ain't Scared of Your Jails" (West and Nash); Laue, *Direct Action*, 205 (Nash). Ben West had already been exposed to nonviolent direct action. As a young assistant district attorney in Nashville in 1942, he encountered African American pacifist Bayard Rustin in police custody after Rustin was arrested for sitting at the front of a bus. According to one of Rustin's biographers, the two men "discussed pacifism, FOR, and the *Christian Century* for a good half hour" before Rustin was released on West's initiative. Daniel Levine, *Bayard Rustin*, 33 (quotation); Carmichael, *Ready for Revolution*, 170–71. Nash later referred to her bravado as a result of "the feeling of right, the moral rejuvenation is the only thing that carries you over. . . . With the mayor in 1960 I had a moment of divine inspiration" (quoted in Laue, *Direct Action*, 205).

The victory fallout stunned those immediately affected. As a result of the sit-in campaign, Vanderbilt's chancellor Harvie Branscomb expelled Lawson from the Divinity School. Branscomb immediately fell under heavy fire, receiving letters condemning his action from religious, university, and cultural leaders nationwide. Branscomb stood his ground, maintaining that the university could not provide "a base of operation for an avowedly illegal and organized campaign," given Vanderbilt's "80 percent to 90 percent [white] southern alumni and its southern Board of Trustees and a city administration to which we must turn for protection." Branscomb to John M. Swomley Jr., 7 Apr. 1960, box 17, FOR Papers. On 9 Mar. 1960, 126 members of the Vanderbilt faculty, including 12 department heads, signed an open statement criticizing Branscomb and indicating that the university ought to reverse itself. In the weeks that followed, demonstrations were held and petitions circulated at Vanderbilt, Fisk, Tennessee State, Yale, Harvard, the University of Wisconsin, Rutgers, the University of Colorado, Shaw University, Alabama State, Hampton, the University of California, Williams College, Lehigh, Kansas State, and Florida A&M. Student Christian Federation, Kansas State University, "To the Kansas State University Students, Staff, and Faculty," folder 12, box 74, KMS Papers. Lawson briefly relocated to Boston to finish his degree before returning to the South.

51. Ransby, *Ella Baker*, 186, 237, 239.

52. Halberstam, *The Children*, 215–16 (Bond); "Youth Leadership Meeting: Shaw University," folder 23, box 75, KMS Papers. See also Shaw University agenda, Spring 1960, frame 987, reel 26, CORE Papers. According to her biographer, "Baker met with and consulted King, but she sent out the actual correspondence and made most of the final decisions. . . . The details in shaping the Raleigh meeting were important and ultimately politically significant" (Ransby, *Ella Baker*, 408). The NCLC also paid for the students to participate in SNCC conferences. See folders 3–4, box 74, KMS Papers.

53. Lewis interview; Nash interview. This, of course, is not to say that the entire thrust of the Judeo-Christian tradition has been one of love and nonviolence. Certainly

as it has been practiced in the United States, as my colleague Tim Tyson clarified, "Most Judeo-Christians through the ages have showed up for the wars, blessed the troops as they left, prayed for victory, praised the Lord and passed the ammunition." Thus, it is important to point out that Lewis's interpretation of nonviolence as a way of living a political life in harmony with his deep Christian beliefs was not shared by all of the original members of SNCC.

54. Greenberg, *Circle of Trust*, 34–35 (McDew); Ransby, *Ella Baker*, 193–94; Carmichael, *Ready for Revolution*, 172. Nash, Lewis, Lawson, and Bevel would go on to run workshops and create similar relationships within both SNCC and SCLC. Nash and Lawson in particular wielded this powerful tool early on to great effect. At a pivotal SNCC conference in October 1960, Nash led a workshop that covered a major issue inside the movement the following year: jail versus bail. Here, SNCC invited "resource people"—such as Ella Baker and Ralph Abernathy of SCLC, Tom Gaither of CORE, and David McReynolds of the War Resisters League—to participate in discussions alongside students unfamiliar with the nonviolent tradition. It was a workshop that would reverberate through the Freedom Rides in 1961, as students for the first time went beyond their own communities to challenge segregation en masse. SNCC held similar workshops through 1964. After the civil rights movement, Lawson continued to participate in nonviolent workshops through the 1990s. Bernard Lafayette, who had worked in Selma, Ala., and on other SNCC and SCLC projects in the 1960s, also offered workshops on nonviolence in South Africa in the 1990s. Lawson interview online; "Workshop G, Jail v. Bail, Diane Nash," frame 133, reel 1, SNCC Papers.

55. Greenberg, *Circle of Trust*, 34 (McDew); Lawson tried to insert Nashville workshop–type programming into SNCC conferences. In Fall 1960, he wrote Jane Stembridge to offer "one major suggestion" in response to Marion Barry's request that he comment on the draft agenda for the October meeting. There were too many topics on the agenda. Why not replace the new topics proposed for Saturday evening sessions with extended sessions of the morning workshops? People could read about a lot of the material in college libraries, "but continuing analysis of these matters from the perspective of an emerging non-violent movement is only available through what we are able to achieve in these workshops of the morning. I urge that we make it possible for thorough discussion from the point of our non-violent approach." Lawson, in other words, tried to give SNCC members the opportunity to discuss their own feelings in depth about the major issues facing the movement. Stembridge took him up on the suggestion. Lawson to Jane [Stembridge], 7 Sept. 1960 (frame 472), and Stembridge to Lawson, 9 Sept. 1960 (frame 471), reel 11, SNCC Papers.

56. Nash interview; Wells, "Southern Horrors"; Raines, *My Soul Is Rested*, 239 (Guyot). Even those Mississippi activists who were heavily armed largely agreed with Bob Moses, Ella Baker, and Amzie Moore in their respect for nonviolent practitioners such as Lawson, Bevel, and Nash.

57. Carmichael, *Ready for Revolution*, 165, 111; "Students Explore the Movement," 14 Apr. 1961, *Voice of the [Nashville Nonviolent] Movement*, vol. 1, no. 3, folder 3, box 74, KMS Papers; Robert F. Williams, *Negroes with Guns*, 40, 63, 68; Shakur, *Assata*, 138. As Alice Walker's fictional character Tommy Odds put it after being shot by a white terrorist as he came out of a church meeting: "Don't nobody offer me marching and preach-

ing as a substitute for going after these jokers *balls*." Walker, *Meridian*, 133. Robert Williams, biographer Timothy Tyson (*"Radio Free Dixie,"* 141) tells us, "denounced the 'emasculated men' who preached nonviolence while white mobs beat their wives and daughters." The historical literature has often further obscured our understanding of the roles of nonviolence and self-defense in the civil rights–black power movement, contrasting the "good" early 1960s, when activists were nonviolent, with the "bad" late 1960s, when black power and armed self-defense came to the fore. Such a narrative simply does not work, as Todd Moye (*Let the People Decide*) and Emilye Crosby (*A Little Taste of Freedom*) point out, when trying to make sense of local civil rights struggles. In fact, not only have practitioners of self-defense been inaccurately portrayed as the "bad boys" of the movement, but also nonviolent practitioners emerge in these histories as "morally superior," gentle, and weak. Both the bad boy and the gentle saint stereotypes distort the history. Neither helps people today figure out how to be fully actualized citizens.

58. Burns, *Daybreak of Freedom*, 195–96.

59. "Statement of Purpose," frame 648, reel 11, SNCC Papers. The Nashville sit-ins "launched what was a long-range process," said Lawson. Lawson interview, 14 Aug. 2001. Lewis personally stayed involved in the Nashville movement through 1964; see "Nashville Erupts as Protests Begin" (p. 1) and "Nashville Group Sustains Protests" (p. 1), both in SNCC's newspaper, *Student Voice*. For ten years SNCC continued pushing the circle of desegregated institutions ever wider into the surrounding areas. This was similar to the blueprint laid in the aftermath of the Montgomery bus boycott. See "Long Range Plan," in Burns, *Daybreak of Freedom*, 322. See also Bevel, quoted in Halberstam, *The Children*, 102, and Edward King to Diane Nash, 27 Dec. 1960 (frame 424, reel 4), Edward King to Sandra Cason, 27 Dec. 1960 (frame 419, reel 4), and Dottie Miller to Jim [Forman], 12 Dec. 1961 (frame 332, reel 8) — all in SNCC Papers.

60. Lawson interview, 14 Aug. 2001; Glenn Smiley to Marion Barry, 14 Sept. 1960, frame 184, reel 1, SNCC Papers; Powledge, *Free at Last?*, 88, 90, 247 (Jones).

61. Sherrod interview; Casey Hayden, "Fields of Blue," 347 ("dramatic, devout, daring"). "My grandmother used to tell me stories when I was a little boy," Sherrod related. "Stories about white people, and what they'd do. She told me about how my grandfather had to flee from Waverly [in Surrey County, Va.] for verbally protesting the killing of a black man, who was burned, hanging from a tree, while his genitals were burning in another tree. Stories like that were part of my consciousness. That's what was passed down."

62. Moses interview by Carson; Moses, *Radical Equations*, 3, 28. Moses also quoted in "Ain't Scared of Your Jails" and Ransby, *Ella Baker*, 251.

63. Greenberg, *Circle of Trust*, 115 (Bernice Johnson Reagon). On Albany's Freedom Songs, see Appendix A.

64. "Freedom Faith" (video) (Simmons). Martha Prescod Norman, a young black woman from Michigan, went further: "The first time I heard somebody line hymns, I said to myself, 'Oh. This is what this means.' All those years I knew the words, I didn't know what it meant. And I understood at that moment how music sustained us through slavery and through segregation and through everything. Just in those first few minutes" (quoted in "Freedom Faith"). See also Reagon, "The Lined Hymn."

65. Blacks living in the segregated South had to fight for institutions to call their own, and the only terrain they could consistently secure in the century following the Civil War was the church. Betty Fikes, one of the most extraordinary singers of the civil rights movement, has said that "the church was the center of the black community for the simple reason that we had no other place to go" (quoted in "Freedom Faith"). Lawrence Guyot agreed: "There couldn't have been a civil rights movement without the black church." The church "was the only institution controlled, run, financed, and dictated by black folks. The only question [for a movement worker] was getting in on them, getting into the church and moving it" (quoted in Powledge, *Free at Last?*, 44). Notwithstanding all the other institutions that African Americans did not control — governments, groceries, banks, insurance companies, medical centers — the black church served as the central touchstone for the majority of black people in each southern parish or town. In this atmosphere, southern blacks participated in nonviolent workshops to prepare for sit-ins and Freedom Rides. As eighth-grader Barbara Howard recalled, here "they would teach us how to act. What to say. How to protect ourselves." For her, "Song was the key, that was the spirit lifter. 'Ain't Gonna Let Nobody Turn Me 'Round,' 'We Shall Overcome,' of course, and 'O Freedom'" (quoted in Ellen Levine, *Freedom's Children*, 66). David Chappell's chapter, "The Civil Rights Movement as a Religious Revival," in *Stone of Hope*, 87–104, argues that religious ritual and particularly the conversion experience should be at the center of our understanding of how people found the determination and grit to continue in the movement. I would agree in part, but add that this is not to say that we can simultaneously ignore the practical, nuts-and-bolts ways they organized change: it will not help us to understand the movement if we say that it "swept over the land" or "moved through the minds of the masses" as if it were a force of nature or spirit beyond explanation.

The Black Freedom Church — a sustaining wellspring of the civil rights struggle — represented a strong current within African American religious institutions from the colonial period forward. It nurtured the spirit of resistance, providing through the examples of people in the Old and New Testament an inspiration, hope, and sustenance for a full humanity — despite the outward hold of slavery and segregation. The Freedom Church also fostered what Lawson called the "forces of spiritual and moral revolution," where, despite the indignities and inhumanities suffered at the hands of whites, African Americans could gather to pursue "relationships of rightness, of compassion, of care." At base, the Black Freedom Church was both a spirit and an institution, promoting and transmitting to future generations, as philosopher Cornel West defined it, "a sense of respect for others, a sense of solidarity, [and] a sense of meaning and value which would usher in the strength to battle against evil." Lawson, address to Annual Public Gathering of the American Friends Service Committee, 7 Nov. 1998, Philadelphia, ‹http://www.afsc.org/lawson.htm›, 21 Mar. 2000; West, Interview by bell hooks, reprinted in hooks and West, *Breaking Bread*, 51. There has been a great deal written about the Black Freedom Church; for an overview, see, e.g., Thurman, *Deep River*; Lincoln, *Race, Religion*; Lincoln and Mamiya, *The Black Church*; Cone, *A Black Theology of Liberation*; Jacquelyn Grant, *Perspectives on Womanist Theology*; Cannon, *Womanism*; Delores S. Williams, *Sisters in the Wilderness*; Collier-Thomas,

Black Women Preachers; Hopkins, *Up, Down and Over*, esp. introduction, chaps. 1–3; West, *Prophecy Deliverance!*; and Harding, *There Is a River*.

66. Sellers, *River of No Return*, 23.

67. The difficulties in the fall are discussed by SNCC people in staff meetings and correspondence. See esp. reels 1 and 3, SNCC Papers. In Nashville, C. T. Vivian noted that by August 1960 the Nashville workshops were sparsely attended as well. Vivian, NCLC Minutes, 6 Aug. 1960, folder 12, box 74, KMS Papers.

68. Countryman, "The Student Nonviolent Coordinating Committee," frames 204–5; Joanne Grant, *Ella Baker*, 136; Carmichael, *Ready for Revolution*, 304; Ransby, *Ella Baker*, 4; Nash remarks at SB-SNCC Conference (transcript).

69. Joanne Grant, *Ella Baker*, 137 (McDew); Carmichael, *Ready for Revolution*, 304–6. See also Ransby, *Ella Baker*, 44.

70. Joanne Grant, *Ella Baker*, 129. See also Ransby, *Ella Baker*, 242–43. James Lawson, interviewed separately by both Aldon Morris and David Garrow, gently but firmly disputed Baker's belief that King tried to take over the student group. Lawson felt that King could have taken over had he wanted to. But King, Walker, and Lawson "made an explicit decision that the students—the Conference would proceed as they wanted to proceed, and that we would encourage them in . . . the democratic process and in an open process. That we would not try to impose upon them our own analysis or our own determination of how they should go" (quoted in Aldon Morris, *Origins*, 217, and Garrow, *Bearing the Cross*, 132–33).

71. Moses interview by Carson. On the fact that no one wanted to travel in the Deep South, see Julian Bond interview. Baker, though on the SCLC payroll until she took the YWCA job, actually worked for SNCC during this period, typing minutes, drafting internal documents, maintaining a mailing list, and recruiting new students (Ransby, *Ella Baker*, 247). Baker included people on Moses' contact list who were "a world apart" from the SCLC leaders, including Amzie and Ruth Moore in rural Mississippi. "She wanted to put the students in touch as quickly as possible with a set of elders who represented a different class background and political orientation than the ministerial clique heading SCLC," Ransby found (pp. 176, 261). This work draws on the definition of "grass roots" or "local people" in Jeanne Theoharis and Komozi Woodard's important book, *Groundwork*: "By local people, we mean a political orientation, a sense of accountability and an ethical commitment to the community. As such, local people were those who struggled with, came out of, and were connected to the grassroots" (p. 3).

72. Bernice Johnson Reagon, " 'Let Your Light Shine'-Historical Notes," in Reagon and Sweet Honey in the Rock, *We Who Believe in Freedom*, 20. Barbara Ransby explores this aspect of Baker's practical philosophy with great insight in her biography, *Ella Baker*, 13–14, 284, 293.

73. Moses, *Radical Equations*, 32–37; Casey Hayden, "Fields of Blue," 345 (quotations); Carmichael, *Ready for Revolution*, 304–7. See also Moses interview by Carson and Ransby, *Ella Baker*, 113–14.

74. Baker, Ransby reveals, utilized this approach to leadership development at least as early as the 1940s. Anthropologist Karen Brodkin Sacks (*Caring by the Hour*), sociologist Belinda Robnett (*How Long?*), historian Chana Kai Lee (*For Freedom's Sake*), and

Ransby herself (*Ella Baker*, 364–70, 422), and) have all developed similar theories of African American women's leadership. On Baker's influence on Moses and the early SNCC, see Ransby, pp. 244–53.

75. Powledge, *Free at Last?*, 205 (Lewis).

76. Lawson interview, 14 Aug. 2001; Viorst, *Fire in the Streets*, 104 (John Lewis, 2d quotation). See also Aldon Morris, *Origins*, 190, and Halberstam, *The Children*, 35, 138.

77. Halberstam, *The Children*, 71 (Lafayette); Viorst, *Fire in the Streets*, 104 (Lewis). Lewis, Lafayette, and James Bevel were all divinity students. Nash was a devout Catholic.

78. Lawson interview online; Garry Fullerton, "King Delayed by Bomb Scare," *The Tennessean*, 21 Apr. 1960, A1 (King). See also Branch, *Parting the Waters*, 297.

Chapter Two

1. Moses, Foreword to *Delta Time*, xiv.

2. "Appeal for Freedom Riders," 30 June 1961, *Voice of the [Nashville Nonviolent] Movement*, vol. 1, no. 9, folder 2, box 74, KMS Papers (Lewis and Lafayette).

3. *Boynton v. Virginia*, 364 U.S. 454 (1960); Laue, *Direct Action*, 98–100; "Ain't Scared of Your Jails" (video) (Farmer); Carmichael, *Ready for Revolution*, 163–64; Peter B. Levy, *Civil War*, 36–38. CORE was an interracial group long committed to nonviolent direct action. After Adam Malik Sow, the ambassador from the Republic of Chad, informed Attorney General Robert Kennedy that he had been evicted from a Maryland restaurant while traveling between his Washington, D.C., embassy and United Nations headquarters in New York, Robert Kennedy declared that nothing less than the international credibility of the United States and the fate of the free world was at stake if Asian and African diplomatic personnel continued to be denied access to public accommodations in Maryland. In response, CORE and the Civic Interest Group of Baltimore (CIG) called for sit-ins along Maryland's Route 40. The Kennedys greeted the Route 40 sit-ins with a vague statement of support and quiet, cynical calls to restaurant owners encouraging them to learn to distinguish between Africans from the continent and those born in America. See Wofford, *Of Kennedys and Kings*, 127. For background on CORE's Freedom Rides, see Meier and Rudwick, *CORE*, 135–58. For more on the numerous Route 40 incidents, see Kennedy Papers. Robert F. Williams, an advocate of armed self-defense, also manipulated these Cold War tensions brilliantly. See Tyson, *"Radio Free Dixie"*, chap. 8. See also Borstelmann, *Cold War*, and Dudziak, *Cold War Civil Rights*.

4. Lewis, *Walking with the Wind*, 133, 137; Meier and Rudwick, *CORE*, 136. James Farmer assessed the courage it took to step forward: "I was frankly terrified with the knowledge that the trip to Jackson might be the last trip any of us would ever take. I was not ready for that." Before leaving Washington, Farmer had decided not to go. "It was only the pleading eyes and words of the teenage Doris Castle that persuaded me to get on that bus at the last minute." For Lewis, the departure was so daunting that their last meal in D.C. felt "like the Last Supper. You didn't know what to expect going on the Freedom Ride." Person, at age eighteen, was the youngest in the first group of CORE

volunteers. Farmer, *Lay Bare the Heart*, 197; Hampton and Fayer, *Voices of Freedom*, 76 (Lewis). For more on the Freedom Rides, see Arsenault, *Freedom Riders*.

5. Robert Kennedy forced FBI director J. Edgar Hoover to investigate events in Anniston. Five of the six men arrested served no time in jail. O'Reilly, *"Racial Matters"*, 85–86; Meier and Rudwick, *CORE*, 138; Lewis, *Walking with the Wind*, 132; Manis, *Fire You Can't Put Out*, 264; Eskew, *But for Birmingham*, 153–58. SCLC provided financial backing and logistical support for the Freedom Rides, since at this point CORE was based in the North and had few southern outposts (see Manis, pp. 262–77). As they went in to rescue the Freedom Riders, Shuttlesworth told his men: "Gentlemen, this is dangerous, but I know you mustn't carry any weapons. You must trust God and have faith." But the men disobeyed. Hank Thomas remembered that each car had a shotgun in the floorboard in case of trouble. They got out of Anniston and back to Bethel Baptist Church without incident (Manis, p. 264).

6. "Ain't Scared of Your Jails" (Nash); Lewis, *Walking with the Wind*, 147. The SNCC members who took over the Freedom Rides did not recognize at the time how momentous their actions would be. Examining in hindsight how these creative organizers were able to lever so much power on behalf of their cause, it is critical to remember the artificiality by which historians may impose on the chaos of the past a certain kind of order. In a significant number of instances the only order that is discernible is unpredictability. No one knows what to do next. Activists accept this. In fact, even when they have carefully planned an action, people never know where it will take them. Some of this process is visible in the story of the Freedom Rides.

7. On Hoover's antagonism toward the civil rights movement, see O'Reilly, *"Racial Matters"*. For an extensive examination of the Kennedys' response to the Freedom Rides and the dynamics between Robert Kennedy and the FBI during the Rides, see Niven, *Politics of Injustice*, chap. 2. Niven, a political scientist, convincingly argues that in terms of securing a victory in the 1964 elections, the Kennedys should not have equivocated in their support for the 1961 Freedom Rides — the white South was already "gone" by 1960, and the black vote strategically proved much more important to them (Niven, chap. 6). But the Kennedys also had to contend with the congressional seniority system, which granted chairmanships to those representatives and senators who had served the longest. White southern Democrats chaired committees the White House viewed as critical to moving their legislation through Congress before the 1964 elections. On the complex series of relationships between CORE and SNCC in this period, see Farmer, *Lay Bare the Heart*, and Louis, *We Are Not Saved*. While important and instructive, this issue remains unexplored in most of the literature on the movement.

8. Manis, *Fire You Can't Put Out*, 271 (Shuttlesworth); Lewis, *Walking with the Wind*, 149 (Nash); Farmer, *Lay Bare the Heart*, 207; Halberstam, *The Children*, 271, 322. Jim Bevel, chairman of the Nashville central committee, made the ultimate judgment as to who from Nashville would go, but the entire committee talked it through. During the complex chain of events between Nashville and Alabama, at least one parent went to Alabama to take his child home. See Arsenault, *Freedom Riders*. School administrators told Rodney Powell, a Meharry Medical College student, that if he participated in the action, he would not graduate. People had to make life-altering decisions in a very short period that not only defined their level of commitment to one another, but also

determined the direction of the rest of their lives. NCLC ultimately paid over $10,000 for transportation to Alabama and the resulting expenses. "When Carl Bush's clothing and luggage were burned in a Freedom Ride bus in Alabama, it was the NCLC that paid $197 to replace them. When William Barbee was so beaten by an Alabama mob that he had to be hospitalized, it was NCLC that picked up the tab." "Without Your Help Our Hands Are Chained." n.d, folder 10, box 75, KMS Papers. See also "Call Meeting" Minutes, NCLC Executive Board, 18 May 1961 (folder 12, box 74) and all check receipts (folder 5, box 74), KMS Papers. Farmer showed another important kind of courage in his autobiography, violating the "show no fear" code of American masculinity to explain candidly how much fear factored into his decision-making process during the Freedom Rides.

9. "Flash Flash Flash Birmingham, Alabama," *Voice of the [Nashville Nonviolent] Movement*, 20 May 1961, vol. 1, no. 7, folder 3, box 74, KMS Papers. As T. Eugene "Bull" Connor, Birmingham's commissioner of public safety, personally drove the Nashville students to the state line, those who believed in nonviolence as a way of life tried to converse and communicate with him, as they did other whites as volatile and brutal as Connor. " According to Barbara Ransby (*Ella Baker*, 266), Ella Baker was "in daily contact" with Diane Nash during these rushed and heated days between the first and second Freedom Rides, providing reassurance and a seasoned political analysis of publicity and negotiation strategy. See also Eskew, *But for Birmingham*, 161–65.

10. James Farmer, quoted in "Ain't Scared of Your Jails." See also Seigenthaler interview in Halberstam, *The Children*, 288, and Fred Shuttlesworth, quoted in Powledge, *Free at Last?*, 280–81.

11. See Niven, *Politics of Injustice*, 60, 74, 81–91. The primary evidence for both Kennedys' *realpolitik* response can be found in Oral History Interviews with Robert F. Kennedy, John Seigenthaler, Burke Marshall, John Patterson, Louis Oberdorfer, and Nicholas Katzenbach, as well as in the Kennedy Papers.

12. Halberstam, *The Children*, 307. See also King, *Freedom Song*, chap. 6.

13. "Ain't Scared of Your Jails" (Lewis and Leonard). Zwerg, an active participant in the Lawson workshops, wrote his parents a letter to warn them that he would probably be dead by the time they received it. Yet there was never a question in his mind of whether or not to go on the Freedom Ride. "My faith was never so strong as during that time," he declared. "I knew I was doing what I should be doing." After the beating, Zwerg remained unconscious in the hospital for three days. Only later did doctors diagnose that his injuries included a broken back. "There was nothing particularly heroic in what I did," Zwerg concluded in 1989. "If you want to talk about heroism, consider the black man who probably saved my life. This man in coveralls, just off of work, happened to walk by as my beating was going on and he said, 'Stop beating that kid. If you want to beat someone, beat me.' And they did. He was still unconscious when I left the hospital. I don't know if he lived or died" (Bausum, "Zwerg Recalls"). Zwerg went on to become a minister for many years, then a manager with IBM.

14. Branch, *Parting the Waters*, 451; "Ain't Scared of Your Jails." Seigenthaler was hit with a pipe as he tried to protect two female Riders who were being beaten. He lost consciousness. See Seigenthaler, Oral History Interview. The attack on Robert Kennedy's aide "was to effect profoundly the way the government of the US behaved

from then on," argued David Halberstam (*The Children*, 316, 321). The right-hand man of the president's right-hand man had been assaulted.

15. King, in a moment of great personal bravery, turned to the people in the church and, despite the enormous anxiety, spoke with absolute composure: "Fear not. We've gone too far to turn back. Let us be calm. We are together, we are not afraid. And we shall overcome." "Ain't Scared of Your Jails." King's fear on the telephone to Kennedy reported in Marshall, Oral History Interview. Kennedy's toleration of repeated violations of federal law is clearly laid out in Niven, *Politics of Injustice*, 88–91. See also Manis, *Fire You Can't Put Out*, 275–78.

16. Robert Kennedy and John Patterson, Oral History Interviews.

17. Kennedy brokered the deal with Sen. James Eastland of Mississippi. The attorney general's sense of prerogative and lack of concern over the fate of the Freedom Riders, once they were in police custody and thus out of the headlines, can be seen in his Oral History Interview. See also Niven, *Politics of Injustice*, 105–13. Dave Dennis, a CORE member, recalled that everyone on the first bus "was prepared to die." It was very strange when "we were just arrested and put in jail. One girl in particular just started pulling hands full of hair out. She just started screaming. Nothing happened, and there was the cold shock. One guy was beating his head up against the wall. *We didn't die....* It was just that right then and there everybody wanted to die. They had been willing to give up their lives" (quoted in Raines, *My Soul Is Rested*, 277).

18. Sherrod interview; Hirshfeld interview; "Freedom Ride Questionnaires," n.d. [Spring 1961] folder 11, box 75, KMS Papers (White and Herrick). See also Arsenault, *Freedom Riders*. The coordinating committee consisted of James Farmer, Wyatt T. Walker, Diane Nash, Gordon Cary, and Ed King Jr. ("Freedom Ride Coordinating Committee," folder 10, box 75, KMS Papers).

19. Meier and Rudwick, *CORE*, 143; Branch, *Parting the Waters*, 480 (Sherrod); Nash, "Inside the Sit-Ins," 44, 53, 57. Nash continued: "Montgomery has shown how far it has advanced on its own; we've seen this from the mob to the governor" (p. 57). For Sherrod, see also Carmichael, *Ready for Revolution*, 178–215. Sherrod may well have taken his lead from Ella Baker; see Ransby, *Ella Baker*, 266–67. For Burke Marshall, see Lewis, *Walking with the Wind*, 148. On the ICC regulations, see Barnes, *Journey from Jim Crow*, 169–71.

20. Moses, Interview comments, *Freedom Song*; Light, *Delta Time*, xiv (Moses). Diane Nash noted: "We created a climate in Mississippi where it's at least possible to keep an office open" (quoted in Laue, *Direct Action*, 109). Many authors have hailed the Freedom Rides as a turning point in the civil rights movement. See Rothschild, *Black and White*, 6; Chafe, *Civilities*, 71; Sitkoff, *Struggle for Black Equality*, 72; and Charles Payne, *Light of Freedom*, 77. As Timothy Tyson ("*Radio Free Dixie*," 104) insightfully observed, it was World War II and the Cold War "that shattered the Compromise of 1877, in which Northern Republicans and Southern Democrats had agreed to let the white South have its way on questions of race."

21. "Ain't Scared of Your Jails" (Leonard); Hampton and Fayer, *Voices of Freedom*, 94 (Farmer); Carmichael, *Ready for Revolution*, 205–6. Bevel and Lafayette were only two of the many talents in the movement who reworked songs from black sacred and secular worlds, transforming them into freedom anthems. When these two "freedom

people got [hold of] the song" by Little Willie John, "You'd Better Leave My Kitten Alone," they turned it into "You'd better leave segregation alone / Because they love segregation / Like a hound dog loves a bone." The men were addressing the black community, recalled movement historian and participant Bernice Johnson Reagon. While in the original song, the singer had warned away other men from his woman, Bevel and Lafayette were trying to get other blacks to join them. Leave segregation alone, it is poison to you, they sang. "You can't have segregation unless *we* participate," Reagon explained. The duo also reworked old spirituals. "I know we'll meet again," they sang to one another. "And then you and I / Will never say goodbye / When we meet again." This kind of love song, coming as it did out of the collective exhilaration of challenging segregation on the Freedom Rides and the shared hardships endured in Parchman, "makes you understand something about love songs," Reagon recalled years later. "Makes the little love songs you hear on the radio sort of light" (quoted in Greenberg, *Circle of Trust*, 121). For more on Freedom Songs, see Appendix A. For more on Parchman, see Oshinsky, *Worse Than Slavery*.

22. The sit-in movement waned over the winter of 1960–61. Despite the hundreds of sit-in victories, thousands of southern eateries in less-populated areas continued the humiliations of segregation, uninterrupted by the new rhythms of SNCC activities. To survive, the movement needed to keep evolving innovative ways to challenge the caste system. The jail–no-bail strategy used in Rock Hill was taken from the Pan Africanist Congress of Azania (South Africa). During the previous sit-ins, the students had challenged segregation in their own cities or towns. Now they traveled beyond their own communities, determined to challenge segregation en masse. In Rock Hill, they intended to "demonstrate that racial discrimination is no longer a local issue, that when segregation affects one of us, it affects all." Furthermore, they wanted to "fill the jails" to make it impossible for authorities to enforce the local segregation laws (quoted in "Attention!," *Student Voice*, 2).

23. Fleming, *Soon We Will Not Cry*, 13, 56, 73.

24. Powledge, *Free at Last?*, 248–49 (Jones); Sherrod, "Nonviolence," n.d., frames 1234–39, reel 7, SNCC Papers. See also Jean Wheeler Smith, in Greenberg, *Circle of Trust*, 136–39, and Casey Hayden, "Radical Roots of SNCC."

25. Sherrod interview.

26. Halberstam, *The Children*, 267–68 (Nash). Ruby Doris Smith also spent much of her time reading, including *The Ugly American*, *The Life of Mahatma Gandhi*, *Exodus*, *The Wall Between*, and *Elmer Gantry*. Fleming, *Soon We Will Not Cry*, 75–77. See also Peter Countryman, "The Student Nonviolent Coordinating Committee," 10 Nov. 1961, frame 205, reel 1, Feingold Papers.

27. Nash interview; Halberstam, *The Children*, 49–59, 70, 147. Nash continued the jail–no-bail policy even when her peers in Nashville did not. See "Sunday, Aug. 6, 1961," in *Voice of the Movement*, 11 Aug. 1961, vol. 1, no. 15, folder 2, box 74, KMS Papers. The Nashville movement continued through 1965.

28. African Americans raised in the white supremacist culture had experienced the equality of all people in the sit-ins. Possession of such rare experiences in a segregated world allowed activists to begin shedding their subservient acculturation and their subservient identity. As they created a new community space together, their sense of

what was possible inevitably expanded. Women in SNCC, likewise, were able to experience a release from subservient identity constructions and acculturation as women. Similarly, the few whites who joined early SNCC staff shed their white supremacist habits. These individual transformations experienced in the context of movement activity were then reinforced by their collective ethic — the way they treated one another. Each interaction within the group thus held in itself the small seed of a possibly different, and better, future. Bell hooks has written that people who have actually experienced such relationships not only need to give testimony, but also need to share "the conditions of change that make such an experience possible." One of those conditions is that "each individual . . . has made his or her own commitment to living an anti-racist life." A second condition is that "we do not surrender ties to precious origins," including class background, skin color, and cultural heritage. Since the idea that "we should all forsake attachment to race and/or cultural identity and be 'just humans'" has taken place within the framework of white supremacy, subordinate groups have felt that participation in beloved community means giving up their "identities, beliefs, values, and assimilate," creating an understandably "fierce cultural protectionism." Instead, hooks argues, beloved community can *only* take place when people maintain their deep rootedness in their communities of origin. hooks, "Beloved Community," 271–72. See also Lewis, *Walking With the Wind*, 87; Jean Wheeler Smith, in Greenberg, *Circle of Trust*, 136–39; and Ransby, *Ella Baker* 309, 368–69, 421, n. 51.

29. See esp. Carmichael, *Ready for Revolution*, 181.

30. Zinn, *SNCC*, 96 (Rogers and Glover), 98. The Mississippi jailers also engaged in other less dramatic but humiliating practices, such as forcing activists to drink huge quantities of laxatives, then denying them access to adequate toilet facilities, or bringing them rotted food full of insects. The blankets smelled of urine, sheets were soiled, and the mattresses were dirty. "Natchez Crisis," [Fall 1965], frame 14–15, reel 40, SNCC Papers; Meier and Rudwick, *CORE*, 140–41. Mississippi's Governor Ross was not known for his moderation on racial issues. An aide of his once told Winson Hudson, a black activist from Harmony, Miss., that "your children's blood would be spilled in the streets like water before integration came." See Hudson, "Bring Some Clean Drawers," in Henry, *Fire Ever Burning*, 235.

31. Carmichael, *Ready for Revolution*, 194; Meier and Rudwick, *CORE*, 141–42.

32. Hirshfeld interview. Like other northern Riders, Hirshfeld had been looking for some way to connect to the freedom struggle for a considerable time. A personal quest for meaning also compelled her. "Everybody I knew who was my age, women anyway, was married. I was single, my life had no meaning to me, for what I was doing, and I just was bound and determined my life was going to have some meaning." She "had this feeling like it's now or never. I got to do it now, or my life is useless." Ibid.

33. Ibid.

34. Ibid. Wrist-breaker cuffs and cattle prods were used on the men who refused to cooperate, and Farmer reported that they were "dragged across the floor in great pain." Meier and Rudwick, *CORE*, 141.

35. Seeger and Reiser, *Everybody Say Freedom*, 62; Fleming, *Soon We Will Not Cry*, 87.

36. Hirshfeld interview.

37. Ibid.; Louis, *We Are Not Saved*, 110. The Detroit contacts, called "Friends of the South," consisted of "old left people both black and white, including red diaper babies." Hirshfeld interview. The SNCC Papers are replete with examples of people like Hirshfeld who returned from the South to create new political forms in the North. See James Forman's correspondence with northern students, or the many hundreds of letters between Sandra "Casey" Hayden, Dinky Rommilly, or Betty Garman and such students, in the SNCC Papers. For a post–Freedom Ride experience of a group determined to test nonviolence against strategies of armed self-defense, see Tyson, *"Radio Free Dixie,"* chap. 10.

38. Braden, "Southern Freedom Movement," 99. August Meier and Elliott Rudwick (*CORE*, 135) found that the Rides "revived older [CORE] chapters and generated many new ones."

39. Laue, *Direct Action*, 108 (Dunbar). See also Laue, *Direct Action*, 113: "The most important message of the [Freedom] Rides came as a feedback to the civil rights leaders and organizations themselves. It was the realization that *without a carefully planned, concentrated, sustained attack, the movement would not come in force to the rural Deep South for many years"* (italics mine). In Sherrod's words, "The idea that would disrupt the system of segregation could not have been delivered to the rural Deep South without this realization." Ibid., 113.

Chapter Three

1. Sherrod interview; O'Neal interview.

2. Moses wrote in February 1963: "We know this plateau by now; we have had to crawl over it in McComb City, Amite and Walthall Counties, Hattiesburg, Greenwood, and Ruleville; you dig into yourself and the community and prepare to wage psychological warfare; you combat your own fears about beatings, shootings and possible mob violence; you stymie by your own physical presence the anxious fear of the Negro community seeded across town from paneled pine and white sunked sink [of the white community] to windy kitchen floors and rusty old stoves [of the Negro community], that maybe you *did* come only to boil and bubble and then burst, out of sight and sound; you organize, pound by pound, small bands of people who gradually focus in the eyes of Negroes and whites as people tied up in that mess; you create a small striking force capable of moving out when the time comes, which it must, whether we help it or not" (quoted in a VEP report reprinted in Watters and Cleghorn, *Climbing Jacob's Ladder*, 159).

Mississippi was divided into five congressional districts; SNCC eventually organized within the First, Second, Third, and Fifth, while CORE organized in the Fourth. The two groups worked together under COFO, an umbrella organization discussed later in this chapter. SNCC later developed significant voter registration projects in Arkansas (Little Rock, Pine Bluff, Helena, and Star City), central Alabama, and Cambridge, Md., as well as in Virginia, North Carolina, and South Carolina.

3. Sherrod interview by James Laue, 22 Mar. 1962, in Laue, *Direct Action*, 113, 127.

4. Dittmer, *Local People*, 58–60; Mrs. G. C. Trout (white resident), quoted in Slocum, "Ballots and Jobs," 10; Peter Countryman, "The Student Nonviolent Coordinating

Committee," 10 Nov. 1961, frame 207, reel 1, Feingold Papers. Like the sit-ins and the Freedom Rides, the story of what happened in southwest Mississippi in Summer and Fall 1961 is widely known among civil rights scholars thanks to the pioneering scholarship of John Dittmer, *Local People*, and Charles Payne, *Light of Freedom*; the 2000 release of TNT's *Freedom Song* made these events passably familiar to a wider audience. This chapter's focus is not, then, on what happened, but rather, on how SNCC recruited people into the organization. On early voter registration efforts in the 1950s, and on C. C. Bryant, a key figure, see Dittmer, *Local People*, chaps. 2–4, and Henry, *Fire Ever Burning*, 81–103. Dittmer and Payne have inspired an entire generation of younger historians with their work. See Theoharis and Woodard, *Groundwork*.

5. Moses, in Transcript of tape recording made in Fall 1962, reprinted in Moses, "Mississippi, 1961–1962," 12; Long, Preface to *We'll Never Turn Back*, 7; Zinn, *SNCC*, 72; Countryman, "The Student Nonviolent Coordinating Committee," frame 209.

6. Powledge, *Free at Last?*, 318–19 (Guyot); Forman, *Black Revolutionaries*, 222; Moses, *Radical Equations*, 44. Diane Nash said in 1988 that voter registration "really did amount to direct action" in Mississippi (quoted in Powledge, 308). See also Rothschild, *Black and White*, 14. For an overview of the initial disagreement among early SNCC activists over direct action vs. voter registration, see Clayborne Carson, *In Struggle*, 26, 31, 39–42.

7. Moses interview by Carson; Moses, *Radical Equations*, 45; Samstein interview; Dittmer, *Local People*, 103 ("Super Cool Daddy").

8. Dittmer, *Local People*, 104 (Moses); Moses interview by Carson.

9. Rogers, *Cold Anger*, 17 (Cortes).

10. Ibid.; McLaurin, "Notes on Organizing," frame 53, reel 40, SNCC Papers. Moses (*Radical Equations*, 32–33) emphasized Baker's commitment to making personal connections as the center of her organizing method. On Baker's prowess over a lifetime of testing out ways to bring people to civic life, see Ransby, *Ella Baker*, 250–51 and chaps. 8–10, 12. Prathia Hall (Wynn) reinforces McLaurin's approach with her own experience in Ransby, *Ella Baker*, 362. See also Lawrence Guyot in Raines, *My Soul Is Rested*, 239–40.

11. Moses, Foreword to *Delta Time*, xiii (Moore).

12. Ibid. For in-depth descriptions of how SNCC people built on these older networks in Mississippi, see Charles Payne, *Light of Freedom*, and Dittmer, *Local People*. SNCC would later duplicate this mode of operation in Albany, Ga.; Cambridge, Md.; and Lowndes County, Ala. On Cambridge, see Peter B. Levy, *Civil War*; on Lowndes County, see Jeffries, "Organizing for More Than the Vote."

13. Robert P. Moses, "Affidavit," frame 185, reel 40, SNCC Papers; Travis Britt, "Affidavit," frame 191, ibid.; Countryman, "The Student Nonviolent Coordinating Committee," frame 208; Moses, *Radical Equations*, 48.

14. Raines, *My Soul Is Rested*, 108 (quotations); Powledge, *Free at Last?*, 325; Dittmer, *Local People*, 106; Charles Payne, *Light of Freedom*, 117; Countryman, "The Student Nonviolent Coordinating Committee," frame 208; Moses, in Transcript of tape recording made in Fall 1962, reprinted in Moses, "Mississippi, 1961–1962," 8, 11. In early 1965 Moses asked people to call him Robert Parris. It was a change from "Moses the Myth to Robert Parris the Man," Courtland Cox observed. Cox, transcription of staff meeting by Mary King, February 1965, p. 7, Mary King Papers.

15. Zinn, *SNCC*, 170; Hampton and Fayer, *Voices of Freedom*, 143 (Zellner). Travis spent four months in reform school for her civil rights activities.

16. Thrasher interview. When Zellner joined SNCC, Charles McDew would quip, it ended three generations of family Klan membership (McDew quoted in Carmichael, *Ready for Revolution*, 307).

17. Viorst, *Fire in the Streets*, 246 (Zellner); Zinn, *SNCC*, 170–71.

18. McDew interview; Greenberg, *Circle of Trust*, 70 (McDew); Moses, in Transcript of tape recording made in Fall 1962, reprinted in Moses, "Mississippi, 1961–1962," 12, 14–15, and *Freedom on My Mind* (video); Dittmer, *Local People*, 109, 115. Despite the fact that "Lee's killing paralyzed the voter registration movement, stopped it cold, with no Black person in all of rural southwest Mississippi willing to make an attempt at registering," Herbert Lee's death was an event that "signed over in blood" the commitment of this small band of SNCC workers to keep chipping away at the edifice of state-sanctioned terror in Mississippi (Moses, *Radical Equations*, 50).

19. Casey Hayden interview, 7 Dec. 1996 (Zellner); Zinn, *SNCC*, 171.

20. Countryman, "The Student Nonviolent Coordinating Committee," frame 210; Moses, in Transcript of tape recording made in Fall 1962, reprinted in Moses, "Mississippi, 1961–1962," 14. See also Hollis Watkins, in Greenberg, *Circle of Trust*, 63. On the Freedom School, see Charlie Cobb to COFO Summer Program Committee, January 1964, frame 60, reel 40, SNCC Papers.

21. Jenkins, quoted in Laue, *Direct Action*, 114, 352, and Raines, *My Soul Is Rested*, 227. Thirty SNCC members participated in the three-week seminar. During the sessions, they identified four major problems in SNCC: (1) a "constant breakdown in communication and thus coordination" among one another, (2) a diminishment of actions in local protest centers as students did not feel they were part of anything larger, (3) the need to present a unified front to the South in demanding equal access, not just to lunch counters, but to broader social institutions such as education, employment, and the vote, and (4) the need for staff to administer projects like the voter registration program in Mississippi (Bob Moses had explored its possibilities and received encouragement and promises of assistance from Robert Kennedy, but how could he run such a program without staff?). Countryman, "The Student Nonviolent Coordinating Committee," frame 206; Carmichael, *Ready for Revolution*, 217–19. On Forman's recruitment, see Nash and Forman remarks, "Organizing in the Spirit of Miss Baker," 15 Apr. 2000, SNCC Conference, Raleigh, N.C., notes in the author's possession.

22. The role of whites in the field would soon become a pivotal issue. Critically, even at this early date, the Atlanta office viewed the situation differently from the workers in Mississippi. For example, well before Moses' first attempt to register black voters in McComb, the April–May 1961 *Student Voice* called for "Northern and Southern students to join hands and work for rehabilitation in our own country, in the state of Mississippi." In Fall 1961, after SNCC had left McComb but before those on staff had gathered to reach a consensus on what to do next, Oberlin student Dave Campbell wrote James Forman to ask how he could help SNCC. Forman replied: "The preliminary thinking regarding white Northern students participating in the movement in Mississippi is that all students throughout the nation could possibly be involved in some form. Students from the North will perhaps be asked to come in on the second

'tidal wave.'" In another letter, Forman mentioned that SNCC was considering the formation of a "Southern Peace Corps" to bring northern students to voter registration projects during Summer 1962. Yet several field workers in Mississippi were wary at best of such ideas. This difference in approach prefigured significant tensions that would emerge within SNCC by 1963. "Attention!," *Student Voice*, 2; Forman to Campbell, 7 Dec. 1961 (frame 762, reel 5), and Forman to Holland McSwain, 7 Dec. 1961 (frame 589, reel 7), SNCC Papers.

SNCC created an "inter-staff newsletter" to facilitate the exchange of information beginning in December 1962 (reel 15, SNCC Papers). There was indeed a great deal of movement. Individuals secured for the advisory board included Ella Baker; SNCC adviser Connie Curry, who was also southern project director of NSA; and entertainer Harry Belafonte, a personal friend of the Kennedys who set up the talks between SNCC and the Justice Department on the voter registration projects. Clayborne Carson, *In Struggle*, 43, 39; Powledge, *Free at Last?*, 305–7. On Forman's recruitment into SNCC, see Forman, *Black Revolutionaries*, 221–23, and Diane Nash remarks at SB-SNCC Conference (transcript).

23. Raines, *My Soul Is Rested*, 228–31 (Jenkins); Powledge, *Free at Last?*, 299–300 (Jones); Henry, *Fire Ever Burning*, chap. 8. Both Jenkins and Charles Jones recalled that Marshall assured SNCC that the federal government would protect people involved in voter registration. For a time, the Justice Department did in fact take the calls from SNCC workers, to the great surprise and consternation of local law enforcement officers. But when Mississippi senators complained, Justice backed off.

24. Dittmer, *Local People*, 114.

25. See Moses, in Transcript of tape recording made in Fall 1962, reprinted in Moses, "Mississippi, 1961–1962," 14–15; Dittmer, *Local People*, 115; Charles McDew, in Greenberg, *Circle of Trust*, 70; and Moses, in *Freedom on My Mind* (video) and in Watters and Cleghorn, *Climbing Jacob's Ladder*, 155.

26. Forman, *Black Revolutionaries*, 223; Casey Hayden, "Fields of Blue," 346.

27. Carmichael, *Ready for Revolution*, 224. See also Moses interview by Carson; Forman, *Black Revolutionaries*, 221–23; and Forman remarks at SB-SNCC Conference (transcript). Though Nash's later work is in great need of scholarly attention, I know of no treatment except that of David Halberstam's in *The Children*. For a brief account of her actions in the Jackson nonviolent movement, see "Judge Halts Diane Nash Bevel's Jail Try," *Student Voice*, June 1962; Zinn, *SNCC*; and boxes 74–75, KMS Papers.

28. Tillinghast interview.

29. Sherrod interview. See also Henry, *Fire Ever Burning*, which describes a similar environment for African American men in rural Mississippi.

30. Laue, *Direct Action*, 120; Zinn, *SNCC*, 125.

31. Laue, *Direct Action*, 121 (Sherrod); Sherrod interview; Hampton and Fayer, *Voices of Freedom*, 99 (Bernice Johnson Reagon). See also Hampton and Fayer, pp. 100–101, and Sherrod, in Forman, *Black Revolutionaries*, 250. Sherrod's advice to stay in jail was something he had learned during the earlier sit-ins, he explained. "Plus it costs so much to get people out. You've got to organize that whole thing. That's a lot of trouble and time" (Sherrod interview). For an example of the letter sent home informing the Albany State students of their expulsion, see Forman, *Black Revolutionaries*, 252.

32. Hampton and Fayer, *Voices of Freedom*, 100 (Anderson); Powledge, *Free at Last?*, 346 (Jones). Jones stated that, in addition to fear of their congregations being harmed, the ministers had a philosophical difference with the SNCC workers. The ministers believed that "God had chosen them and put them between Him and the masses for the purpose of providing the divine leadership and that any action of any significance had to be led by the ministers. And our position was that *everybody* made decisions. The ministers certainly should be a part of, individually, the leadership structure, but the decisions were made by a broad group of leadership, or a group of leaders."

33. Hampton and Fayer, *Voices of Freedom*, 104 (Sherrod).

34. Sherrod interview; Hampton and Fayer, *Voices of Freedom*, 104 (Sherrod). See also Casey Hayden, "Fields of Blue," 18 – 19.

35. Hampton and Fayer, *Voices of Freedom*, 104 (Sherrod). See also Sherrod, "Non-violence," n.d. [1962?], frames 1234 – 39, reel 7, SNCC Papers. As Juliette Morgan, editor of the *Montgomery Advertiser*, noted in 1955, white supremacists were "willing to fight all right, say cruel things, and to make others suffer, but the case is such that it calls for no suffering or sacrifice on their parts. That weakens their case" (quoted in Burns, *Daybreak of Freedom*, 102). King preached that "suffering teaches sympathy" and that while sacrifices might force some whites to concede, "unearned suffering is redemptive." For more on this topic, see Chappell, *Stone of Hope*, 50 – 52.

36. "Keep Your Eyes on the Prize," in *Sing for Freedom* (Sherrod and Culbreath). See also McCree Harris, in Ronald Fraser et. al., *1968*, 37. Nashville and Rock Hill, S.C., were two of the locales where large parts of the black community supported the struggle. See Clayborne Carson, *In Struggle*, 21 – 25, 31 – 35.

37. Hampton and Fayer, *Voices of Freedom*, 103 (Anderson); "No Easy Walk," *Eyes on the Prize* (Sherrod). For a comparative examination of how tensions among local leaders and between local and national organizations played out in another southern locale, see the important work of Glenn Eskew, *But for Birmingham*.

38. Hampton and Fayer, *Voices of Freedom*, 105. The FBI's alert is revealing. Pritchett confirmed that he was working closely with federal law enforcement at a time when the only federal law enforcement agency with contacts at the local level across the South was the FBI. Pritchett received detailed information on King's plans from the FBI in November 1961, one month after Robert Kennedy authorized a wiretap on King. See Branch, *Pillar of Fire*, 154. This is only one of the many startling and deeply disrupting effects such intervention had on the civil rights movement.

39. Hampton and Fayer, *Voices of Freedom*, 106 (Pritchett).

40. Ibid., 111 (Coretta Scott King).

41. In both cases, Sherrod sent a report to the Justice Department — and in both cases, heard nothing. "Albany July 1962," Sherrod Papers.

42. Hampton (111 – 12), Andrew Young (113), and Wyatt Tee Walker (105), in Hampton and Fayer, *Voices of Freedom*. See also Vickers, *Formation of the New Left*, 24.

43. Hampton and Fayer, *Voices of Freedom*, 110 (Marshall). Though in the 1980s Marshall blamed FBI director Hoover for the federal government's failure to vigorously prosecute civil rights violations, at the time he toed the same line. The Justice Department did not supply federal protection to civil rights workers, he wrote to the ACLU early in 1963, because "the protection of citizens against unlawful conduct on

the part of others is the responsibility of local authorities." Zinn, *SNCC*, 197. As Zinn noted in 1964 and scholars have subsequently reaffirmed, that meant Justice abdicated its responsibility to enforce its own laws.

44. Hampton and Fayer, *Voices of Freedom*, 110 (Marshall).

45. Local and state officials were bound by the Fourteenth Amendment not to deny individuals these rights.

46. Zinn, *SNCC*, 192–94. Zinn cataloged the series of specific federal laws violated (pp. 192–211). He suggested that the president establish a special force of federal agents to protect and defend the constitutional rights of any person against private or official action. The force would be present at all demonstrations and available for emergency calls for help.

47. Hampton and Fayer, *Voices of Freedom*, 112; Laue, *Direct Action*, 126.

48. Braden, "Images Are Broken," 1 (Sherrod).

49. Braden, "Images Are Broken," 1; Hall, quoted in Greenberg, *Circle of Trust*, 60, and "Freedom Faith" (video).

50. "Freedom Faith" (Hall). In his position paper in preparation for the SNCC conference at Waveland, Miss., in late 1964, Sherrod declared: "We must demand that the new society of Democracy for which we strive be based on the wisdom of the pinched toe and empty belly." He suggested that local people's experiential wisdom be at the center of SNCC's work. Charles Sherrod, untitled position paper, November 1964, Ewen Papers. For an in-depth examination of the role of local women in the civil rights movement, see Olson, "A Woman's War," *Freedom's Daughters*, 248–63.

51. Samuel Wells's ledger, quoted in Watters and Cleghorn, *Climbing Jacob's Ladder*, 121; Sherrod interview; O'Neal interview; "Freedom Faith" (Sherrod); Braden, "Images Are Broken," 3 ("strict personal discipline," etc.). For an important examination of how to overcome fear, see Charles McLaurin, "Notes on Organizing" and "To Overcome Fear," frames 52–55, reel 40, SNCC Papers.

52. Greenberg, *Circle of Trust*, 58 (Allen); Watters and Cleghorn, *Climbing Jacob's Ladder*, 164–67; "Freedom Faith" (Sherrod).

53. Greenberg, *Circle of Trust*, 58 (Allen); Zinn, *SNCC*, 139. Matthews later told Jack Chatfield: "When those newspapers got a hold of me they made me sound like Uncle Remus" (quoted in Watters and Cleghorn, *Climbing Jacob's Ladder*, 169).

54. Forman, *Black Revolutionaries*, 258; Watters and Cleghorn, *Climbing Jacob's Ladder*, 168.

55. Braden, "Images Are Broken," 3. See also Zinn, *SNCC*, 139.

56. Chatfield interview; Zinn, *SNCC*, 143–44, 141. See also Watters and Cleghorn, *Climbing Jacob's Ladder*, 178–79.

57. Zinn, *SNCC*, 227 (Sherrod). Kwame Ture sounded a similar note, recalling that when people brought up the communist affiliations of certain unions, lawyers, or activists, SNCC people decided "we can't afford to be hostage to any such sectarian history. . . . SNCC will work with anybody who supports our programs, shares our goals, honors our principles, and earns our trust. . . . Whenever reporters would raise [communist infiltrators] to me, I'd tell them, 'Hey, you don't worry about the Communists, worry about SNCC. We way more dangerous, Jack.'" Carmichael [Ture], *Ready for Revolution*, 304.

58. Sherrod interview. White activists brought resources that the Albany movement could use. The project acquired blankets because a white volunteer had a cousin who directed a factory; it received money because "this guy here is in jail, and his daddy is a corporation executive. And in order to get his son out," the father had to bail out all of the SNCC workers "because his son isn't going to want to get out unless he can help get the rest of them out" (ibid.).

59. Reagon interview, 23; Hampton and Fayer, *Voices of Freedom*, 113 (Anderson). Reagon went on to become Distinguished Professor of History at American University, curator of the Smithsonian National Museum of American History, and artistic director of Sweet Honey in the Rock, the renowned African American women's a cappella ensemble she founded in 1973. The creativity unleashed by the Albany movement can be observed in the Freedom Songs produced by the movement (see Appendix A).

60. Moses interview by Romaine. Smith's campaign allowed SNCC to make contacts in Hinds, Adams, Jefferson, Claiborne, Copiah, and Lincoln Counties. COFO was created by Aaron Henry of the state's NAACP and by Dennis and Tom Gaither of CORE. Henry served as COFO's president (Henry, *Fire Ever Burning*, 107–9, 115). COFO, Moses stated in June 1964, subsequently evolved in three stages: first, in Summer 1962, VEP asked Mississippi civil rights groups "to combine into an umbrella organization so that it would not have to exclude any of these groups when granting funds for voter education work. During this time COFO was just an expedient umbrella organization for the purposes of accepting VEP funds." The second stage, in Summer 1963, saw COFO become the vehicle to bring "various adult groups throughout Mississippi . . . into contact and communication with each other." This lasted until November 1963, when they entered the third stage for the "Freedom Vote." COFO set up district heads in each of the state's five congressional districts, and "COFO has become more political in outlook and has begun to take on its own image." SCLC participated through its citizenship teachers, but "the same relationship does not exist between SCLC workers [and COFO] and the SNCC and CORE staff." Moses to SNCC Executive Committee, Re: SNCC Mississippi Project, n.d. [Fall 1963], and Moses, Staff Meeting Minutes, June 9–11, 1964, pp. 15–16, frames 983–84, reel 3, SNCC Papers; Moses, in Transcript of tape recording made in Fall 1962, reprinted in Moses, "Mississippi, 1961–1962," 15; Zinn, *SNCC*, 79; Charles Payne, *Light of Freedom*, 62. SCLC was also a technical member of the group but did not play a significant role either in terms of staff or money until Summer 1965. Rothschild, *Black and White*, 15.

61. Dunbar, Interview by Stanford Students, box 7, Project South Collection; Sitkoff, *Struggle for Black Equality*, 116; Countryman, "The Student Nonviolent Coordinating Committee," frame 207. See also Watters and Cleghorn, *Climbing Jacob's Ladder*, 46–47. Aaron Henry (*Fire Ever Burning*, 115) also remembered that SNCC workers played the largest role in COFO operations.

62. Moses interview by Romaine.

63. McKinnie, 24 Mar. 1964, quoted in Laue, *Direct Action*, 204; Moses interview by Carson; Moses, in Transcript of tape recording made in Fall 1962, reprinted in Moses, "Mississippi, 1961–1962," 15; Moses, Foreword to *Delta Time*, xiii, xv. For more on Moore, see Charles Payne, *Light of Freedom*, and Dittmer, *Local People*. On the Highlander workshops, see Payne, *Light of Freedom*, 142–44.

64. Zinn, *SNCC*, 81 (Smith); Charles Payne, *Light of Freedom*, 236–64.

65. Chana Kai Lee, *For Freedom's Sake*, 24–25; Mills, *Light of Mine*, 24; Hampton and Fayer, *Voices of Freedom*, 178 (Guyot).

66. Hamer, transcript of speech at Cleveland Community Conference, 20 Feb. 1965, box 24, SDS Papers.

67. Chana Kai Lee, *For Freedom's Sake*, 25; Mills, *Light of Mine*, 24; Halberstam, *The Children*, 478. According to Lee's and Halberstam's accounts, Bevel quoted Luke 12:54, whereas Mills states that he quoted Matthew 16:3.

68. Reagon, "Women as Culture Carriers," 208, 204 (Hamer). Not insignificantly, Hamer noted that it was her mother who insisted that "we should be proud to be Black, telling us, 'nobody will respect you unless you stand up for yourself'" (p. 208).

69. Chana Kai Lee, *For Freedom's Sake*, 11.

70. The variety and depth of nonviolent thinking sparked in this period not only inspired the members of SNCC, but also brought together a large group of ministers under the SCLC umbrella, some of whom, like Martin Luther King, had studied Paul Tillich; others of whom, like Hosea Williams, had seen the transformative power of nonviolence in action and moved from there. Through their experiences — in Montgomery, Birmingham, and Selma, Ala.; Albany, Ga.; Danville, Va.; St. Augustine, Fla. — these clerics generated a wealth of practical wisdom on how to get people to act as if they were free.

71. Transcript of SCOPE Orientation, 15 June 1965, box 9, Project South Collection (this and next paragraph).

72. Ibid.

73. Transcript of SCOPE Orientation, 15 June 1965. (this and next paragraph). For more on Winona, see Watters and Cleghorn, *Climbing Jacob's Ladder*, 363–75, and Chana Kai Lee's important analysis of Hamer's multiple versions of the story in *For Freedom's Sake*, 59–60. For more on the theological basis of these ideas, see Chappell, *Stone of Hope*, chaps. 3, 5. Chappell notes that these "lamb" stereotypes "may have been less damaging, but they were not much less insulting, than antiblack stereotypes, to which they were historically related" (p. 103). For another perspective on the morality play, see Hale, *Making Whiteness*.

74. Charles Payne, *Light of Freedom*, 309 (Ponder); Raines, *My Soul Is Rested*, 253 (Hamer).

75. Transcript of SCOPE Orientation, 15 June 1965. In late 1963 the U.S. Department of Justice charged five law enforcement officers with violating the civil rights of Ponder and the other activists jailed in Winona: state highway patrolman John Basinger, Montgomery County sheriff Earle Wayne Patridge, Winona police chief Thomas Herod Jr., former state highway patrolman Charles Perkins, and Winona police officer William Surrell. Justice Department lawyers called six witnesses, including four demonstrators who had been beaten and two FBI officers. In addition to Ponder, Hamer, and fifteen-year-old June Johnson, Lawrence Guyot testified that when he went to post bond for the civil rights workers in Winona the next day, he was kicked, punched, and beaten because he refused to say "sir." The jury found the law officers innocent, despite the FBI agents' introduction of photographs and Johnson's bloody shirt as evidence. "Jury Frees Officers," *Student Voice*, 9 Dec. 1963.

76. Transcript of SCOPE Orientation, 15 June 1965.

77. Ibid.

78. Charles Payne, *Light of Freedom*, 373 (Baker), 366, 372 ("moral anchors"). This is not to say that Baker herself viewed nonviolence as a way of life. Indeed, while she supported nonviolence as a tactic and recognized its value in enhancing internal movement dynamics, she would not let anyone "step on my neck" (Ransby, *Ella Baker*, 193, 211–12, 323). Bob Moses had a similar approach.

79. Greenberg, *Circle of Trust*, 21 (Nash).

80. For examples of scholarship that focuses on the ways armed self-defense allowed people to come into their own and maintain their dignity, see Umoja, "Ballots and Bullets" and "1964"; Tyson, *"Radio Free Dixie"*; Strain, *Pure Fire*; Crosby, *Taste of Freedom*; and the account of the Cambridge, Md., movement in Chapter 5 of this book as well as in Peter B. Levy, *Civil War*.

81. Hamer interview.

82. Dittmer, *Local People*, 135, 129.

83. On White Citizens Councils, see Samuel DuBois Cook, "Political Movements." For another important and creative examination of the internal diversity of attempts to maintain white supremacy, see Chappell, *Stone of Hope*, chaps. 6–7.

84. Zinn, *SNCC*, 84.

85. Ibid. (Moses).

86. Moses, in Transcript of tape recording made in Fall 1962, reprinted in Moses, "Mississippi, 1961–1962," 15.

87. Transcript of SCOPE Orientation, 15 June 1965. Another person who used this tactic with great success was SCLC minister Fred Shuttlesworth, based in Birmingham. Stokely Carmichael explained that among movement veterans, Shuttlesworth "commanded a respect bordering on awe." He remembered that "it was Reverend Shuttlesworth who walked into the station [during the Freedom Rides] and carried the unconscious James Peck to the hospital. It was Reverend Shuttlesworth who would spend the night with the besieged students at the bus station that Friday night. In Montgomery, two days later, it was Reverend Shuttlesworth who met James Farmer and conducted him through the hundreds of angry whites surrounding the Reverend Mr. Abernathy's church. . . . We figured that sooner or later the racists would murder him," and there were countless attempts. But Shuttlesworth survived and today lives in Cincinnati. Carmichael, *Ready for Revolution*, 190.

88. Dittmer, *Local People*, 131; Moses interview by Romaine.

89. Moses interview by Romaine.

90. Guyot interview; Rothschild, *Black and White*, 16; Charles Payne, *Light of Freedom*, 158.

91. Despite the scale of the effort, it was "never enough": though hundreds of food boxes were handed out, "each time hundreds were standing in line when the food ran out." Rothschild, *Black and White*, 16.

92. Charles Payne, *Light of Freedom*, 164; Ellen Levine, *Freedom's Children*, 109 (Simpson). Wiley Branton, director of the VEP in Atlanta, was a native Mississippian and a descendant of Greenwood Leflore, the French-Indian slave trader for whom the

county and town were named. Branton's heritage included African, Native American, and French ancestors. The day after the Travis shooting, he called on voter registration workers throughout the state to converge on Greenwood: "Leflore County, Mississippi, has selected itself as the testing ground for democracy, and we shall meet the challenge there" (quoted in Henry, *Fire Ever Burning*, 139).

93. For a list of references on Montgomery, see Chapter 1, n. 7.

94. Raines, *My Soul Is Rested*, 61 (elderly woman).

95. McWhorter, *Carry Me Home*, 326 – 61; Eskew, *But for Birmingham*, 259 – 98.

96. Hampton and Fayer, *Voices of Freedom*, 141 (Moore).

97. McLaurin, Minutes, 8 Nov. 1964, p. 7, frame 939, reel 11, SNCC Papers; "Freedom in the Rain," *Ruleville Freedom Fighter*, July 1964, frame 36, reel 40, SNCC Papers (Johnson). Moore best summed up SNCC's great achievement between 1961 and 1963 in working on rural voter registration in the Deep South. Before SNCC, when he had served as vice president of the state conference of the NAACP, Moore had been required to do everything "according to law. Unless we were advised to do certain things, we didn't do it. But when SNCC came, it didn't seem to matter what these white people thought. When SNCC moved, SNCC moved in SNCC's way" (quoted in Hampton and Fayer, *Voices of Freedom*, 141). McLaurin said that simply watching three elderly women walk up the courthouse steps "did something to me. It told me something. It was like a voice speaking to me . . . although these old ladies knew the risk involved in their being there they were still willing to try." McLaurin, "To Overcome Fear," n.d. (frames 54 – 55, reel 40), McLaurin, Minutes, 8 Nov. 1964, p. 7 (frame 939, reel 11), and "Freedom in the Rain," *Ruleville Freedom Fighter*, July 1964 (frame 36, reel 40), SNCC Papers. Similar to the infantry soldiers who were later dropped into Vietnam with minimal training and inconsistent support, that unrelenting tension "stretched like a tight steel wire between the pit of the stomach and the center of the brain." Blurry vision, ulcers, asthma, migraine headaches, constipation, nervous twitches — "all these maladies plagued them," SNCC worker Cleveland Sellers (*River of No Return*, 51) recalled. Some went to Atlanta and other places outside the battleground to rest; others called friends to talk through the surreal world they had entered. Moses interview by Romaine.

Chapter Four

1. Magidoff interview, 17 Nov. 1999. This kind of influence is also visible throughout the SNCC Papers. For example, from Vassar, Adelaide Matteson and Susan Kent wrote Charles McDew and Charles Jones: "We have been interested in the Freedom Rides since they began, but were not aware of their full value or nature until Tom Hayden spoke at Vassar on Wednesday, December 13 . . . we would like to participate in this movement or help in anyway possible. We plan to arrive in Atlanta on January 18 with two or three other friends." Matteson and Kent to McDew and Jones, 15 Dec. 1961, frame 747, reel 7, SNCC Papers.

2. Magidoff interview, 17 Nov. 1999. Given the assumptions of conventional political culture, it may have been inconceivable to Magidoff at that time that the reverse could be true: that he, not Zellner, was being "absolutist" in labeling Zellner's behavior as pas-

sive. In fact, there was nothing passive about Zellner, a veteran of the front-line struggle against the southern caste system. On the issue of nonviolence as active, not passive, see Carmichael, *Ready for Revolution*, 165–66, and Nash, "Inside the Sit-Ins," 60.

3. Wayne Proudfoot [Harvard divinity student and president of the national Methodist Student Movement in the early 1960s] to James Forman, 10 Dec. 1961, frame 912, reel 7, SNCC Papers.

4. Casey Hayden interview; Casey Hayden, "Fields of Blue," 359. For a fully drawn portrait of the Christian Faith and Life Community, see Rossinow, "'Break-through to New Life'" and *Politics of Authenticity*. In Matthews's seminars, Casey also read "a wide range of writers: the gospels; the church fathers . . . the existentialism of contemporary Europeans, especially Camus, Sartre, contemporary drama and poetry and short stories, like *Waiting for Godot*, *Death of a Salesman*, and the work of e. e. cummings."

5. Casey Hayden interview (this and next paragraph). It was the beginning of a worldview that led Cason toward a lifelong study of eastern religions and philosophy. Individualism, she had concluded by the mid-1990s, was not only a lie but "the great western lie, the great Cartesian lie."

6. Ibid.

7. Casey Hayden: Speech for panel on "Feminists and Women," Interview by the author, "A Nurturing Movement," 5, and Remarks, panel on "How Do We Get to a Just Society?," SB-SNCC Conference (transcript). In 1965 Cason said: "Society thinks we're crazy because we present a reality the country thinks is crazy. I think we're sane because I have a group that thinks like I do." Casey Hayden, Staff Meeting Minutes, February 1965, 8, Mary King Papers.

8. Casey Hayden, "Fields of Blue," 340; Cason, e-mail to the author, 10 Apr. 2001. Though McDew, Bob Moses, Ruby Doris Smith Robinson, and others in SNCC contributed greatly to her thinking, Cason's mentors were Rosalie Oakes, a white woman who ran the Austin YWCA, and Ella Baker, under whom Cason also worked through the auspices of the YWCA, this time in Atlanta.

9. Casey Hayden, "Fields of Blue," 342.

10. Ibid., 346; Casey Hayden, e-mail to the author, 21 Nov. 1999. On the changes in commonly held understandings of leadership, see esp. Mansbridge, "Democracy, Deliberation"; Johnson, "Theoretical Foundations"; and Sirianni, "Learning Pluralism." Baker's model had an enormous influence on Hayden and numerous other SNCC workers. See Barbara Ransby's nuanced portrait of Baker's "horizontal" leadership in her *Ella Baker*, chap. 12 and p. 421.

11. Laue, *Direct Action*, 216 (Forman). Although there is a certain artificiality in listing some people while neglecting others, other key bridge builders with extensive contacts in both North and South over a long period included Bob Moses, Julian Bond, Stokely Carmichael, Ruby Doris Smith Robinson, Mendy Samstein, Dorothy Dawson Burlage, Martha Prescod, Mike Miller, Julia Prettyman, James Forman, and Jim Monsonis. Adults also linked students together through their national networks, in particular Ella Baker, James Lawson, Connie Curry, Vincent and Rosemarie Harding, Anne Braden, Staughton Lynd, and Howard Zinn.

12. Garvy interview, 14 June 1998. "All of a sudden, it wasn't this intellectual conference," Garvy said. Michigan freshman Sharon Jeffrey described the Greensboro men's

appearance: "A lot of people came, and there was a lot of excitement. It was the beginning of students coming together to discuss social [and] political issues" (Jeffrey interview). See also Haber to Charles Van Tassel, 31 Jul. 1958, in James Miller, "Democracy Is in the Streets," 30. For more on Haber-SNCC correspondence, see Haber to Charles Jones, Charles McDew, Diane Nash, Charles Sherrod, et al., 14 Oct. 1961 (frame 1150), and James Forman to Haber, 17 Oct. 1961 (frame 1149), reel 4, SNCC Papers; Haber to Supporters of the SNCC Fund-raising Program, 26 Oct. 1961, frame 1007, reel 27, CORE Papers. James Laue (Direct Action, 92–95) reported that hundreds, if not thousands, of local student groups formed in the North from the impetus of the sit-ins.

13. James Miller, "Democracy Is in the Streets," 34–36 (Ross, 36); Haber remarks, "Remembering SNCC and SDS," Organization of American Historians, 4 Apr. 2003, Memphis, Tenn., notes in the author's possession; Garvy interview, 14 June 1998. Haber continued to organize "conferences and gatherings where people from different colleges would get together with each other, [establishing] a network and foundation for a national student organization," noted Jeffrey. Though students initially organized around the civil rights movement, Haber continued to bring them together across different campuses *and* encourage them to see the connections between other issues like civil liberties, peace, and campus issues. Jeffrey interview.

14. Magidoff interview; Jeffrey interview; Ross interview. On the New Left in Ann Arbor during this period, see Eynon, "Community, Democracy."

15. James Miller, "Democracy Is in the Streets," 33 (Jeffrey); Magidoff interview. The CORE workshop was led by Gordon Carey, a longtime CORE trainer in nonviolent direct action. The group in Miami included Bernard Lafayette from Nashville's core group and Dorothy Miller, a later SNCC staff member (Powledge, Free at Last?, 220–21).

16. Magidoff interview; Jeffrey interview; Marti Smolin, "The North: We Walk So They May Sit," frame 375, reel 49, CORE Papers.

17. Roberts, "Will Tom Hayden Overcome?"; Tom Hayden, Reunion, 35 (quotation); James Miller, "Democracy Is in the Streets," 45.

18. Casey Hayden, speech at NSA conference, August 1960, quoted in Tom Hayden, Reunion, 41.

19. Tom Hayden interview.

20. Roberts, "Will Tom Hayden Overcome?" In Fayette County, near Memphis, blacks outnumbered whites three to one; in Haywood County, Tenn., three to two. When blacks registered to vote in increasing numbers in Fall 1960 and Spring 1961, sharecroppers were evicted from their homes. They relocated to tents in "Freedom City." See Cason and Hayden, "Keep Freedom City Alive," 2.

21. Tom Hayden interview; James Miller, "Democracy Is in the Streets," 38, 54–55, 185–86.

22. Tom Hayden interview; Casey Hayden, "Fields of Blue," 341.

23. Today Casey is known as both Sandra Cason and Casey Hayden. Casey Hayden, e-mail to the author, 29 Jan. 2000.

24. Casey Hayden, "Fields of Blue," 343–44; Casey Hayden to Joanne Meyerowitz, 31 Aug. 2001, e-mail, copy in the author's possession ("Great soul"). For Baker's impact on SNCC's gendered conceptions of political leadership, see Ransby, Ella Baker, 256–59.

25. Casey Hayden, "Fields of Blue," 345.

26. Casey Hayden interview.

27. Ibid.; Joanne Grant, *Ella Baker*, 137 (McDew); Greenberg, *Circle of Trust*, 139 (Ladner); Casey Hayden, "Fields of Blue," 346.

28. Bond interview; Sherrod interview.

29. Sellers, *River of No Return*, 53–54; Carmichael, *Ready for Revolution*, 145; Casey Hayden interview; Casey Hayden, Remarks, panel on "How Do We Get to a Just Society?." See also Louis, "The Freedom Community," *We Are Not Saved*, 62–75.

30. Greenberg, *Circle of Trust*, 71 (Tom Hayden); James Miller, *"Democracy Is in the Streets,"* 59.

31. James Miller, *"Democracy Is in the Streets,"* 59–60; Tom Hayden, "Revolution in Mississippi" [pamphlet first printed by SDS in January 1962], 5, SDS Papers, quoted in ibid., 60; Sale, *SDS*, 36.

32. Roberts, "Will Tom Hayden Overcome?" (Tom Hayden); James Miller, *"Democracy Is in the Streets,"* 60; Greenberg, *Circle of Trust*, 60 (Hall).

33. Magidoff interview.

34. Pardun interview.

35. James Miller, *"Democracy Is in the Streets,"* 76. Trying to reach new recruits, SDS leaders called people to their June convention to reform SDS's structure and programs. They wanted to build a movement that was "passionate and reflective," one that honored "the full movement of the human imagination," rather than encouraging "sectarian rigidity" or "stereotyped rhetoric." Membership included those "students and faculty" who were committed to democratic values "and to the ideas of cooperation and planning as crucial" to participation in the Left, as well as to "full responsibility of membership in a university community, both of serious scholarship and of democratic participation in the decision making and direction of the institution." They passionately wanted to avoid what they understood to be the divisive factions of the "Old Left." Anyone could be a member, if they were willing "to apply the same criteria of criticism and affirmation to nation-states, be they of the Sino-Soviet bloc or of the West, and to social movements, be they revolutionary movements of the left, liberal movements of reform, or reactionary developments on the right." "What Is the SDS?," n.d. [Spring 1962], box 515, Matthews Collection.

36. "What Is the SDS?" n.d. [Spring 1962], box 515, Matthews Collection. Alan Haber ("Remembering SNCC and SDS") recalled in 2003 that "our capacity is somehow to form the counter vision: not America ruling the world on our behalf, but somehow empowering the world, sharing the resources, share the wealth, heal the planet. More or less, that was what SDS's vision was way back. . . . We were people trying to come to an understanding of how to act as citizens in the world." For background on SDS, see Sale, *SDS*, and James Miller, *"Democracy Is in the Streets."*

37. The "Port Huron Statement" is reprinted in James Miller, *"Democracy Is in the Streets,"* 329. For an interesting reflection on the document forty years after the fact, see Hayden and Flacks, "Port Huron Statement," 18–20.

38. Casey Hayden interview. It was Maria Varela, Tom Hayden and Dick Flacks recalled, who came up with a compromise of "unfulfilled" rather than "unlimited" capacities for good. Hayden and Flacks, "Port Huron Statement at 40," 19. Casey said that repeated use of the pronoun "men" in the statement was a generic usage, not one reflecting

a particularly sexist perspective. Nonetheless, it is remarkable to note this usage in the context of the document's call for individual independence. Casey Hayden interview. Forty years later, Tom Hayden did not appear to understand Casey's Sisyphus analogy: "On the one hand, there were followers of the theologian Reinhold Niebuhr, influenced by the atrocities of the Holocaust and Stalinism, who had asserted that 'the children of darkness,' the political realists, were in their generation wiser than 'the foolish children of light,' the pacifists and idealists. On the other side were the Enlightenment humanists who believed in infinite perfectibility through education and nonviolence as adopted by Gandhi and Martin Luther King Jr. The dominant view was that we were children of light. We chose utopia and rejected cynicism." Casey Hayden interview.

39. Casey Hayden interview; Casey Hayden, e-mail to the author, 12 Apr. 2001; "Port Huron Statement," reprinted in James Miller, *"Democracy Is in the Streets,"* 332.

40. Flacks interview; Roberts, "Will Tom Hayden Overcome?" (Ross); Casey Hayden, "Fields of Blue," 348. Space limitations prohibit inclusion of more biographical material on some of these northerners. However, it must be noted at least in passing that the late Paul Potter was among the most extraordinary individuals of this northern SDS group. Potter's book, *A Name for Ourselves* (1971), is surely one of the most interesting reflections on the internal dynamics of SDS, its later ERAPs, and the contours of the New Left.

41. Norman interview. After participating in the food and clothing drive for Greenwood, Mississippi, in Winter 1962–63, Prescod determined to go South herself and that summer worked on the Greenwood voter registration project. The following year she did community work in Selma. While she did not see herself as part of the SDS group in Ann Arbor, she and Casey Hayden remained close and she attended some of the meetings in the Haydens' house in 1962. "A lot of ideas and feelings . . . were very similar at that point between SDS and SNCC people," she recalled. "Not the level but the kind of commitment" was different. SNCC people asked: " 'Where is your body?' and 'How much are you willing to risk?' " At this point, Prescod found SDS intellectually committed to change, but "as yet unsure of how to act." Political parents did not guarantee supportive parents. When Prescod announced later that she was going to Mississippi, her parents "really honest to God, believed that I had to be out of my mind to think that made sense" (quoted in Fleming, *Soon We Will Not Cry*, 61). The Greater Boston and Michigan FOS groups sent over twenty tons of food and clothing to Greenwood in Winter and Spring 1963 and Winter 1964. See *Student Voice*: "Friends Send Food, Clothes," 11 Feb. 1964, 2; "Food, Clothes Sent to Mississippi," 18 Feb. 1964, 2; "Registration Up since Food, Clothes Arrive," 25 Feb. 1964; and "News Roundup," 2 June 1964, 4. The other students in Ann Arbor's FOS group were Helen Jacobson of NSM and Sue Wender of SNCC.

42. "Civil Rights in the North; An Intercollegiate Conference," [Spring 1962], frames 560–62, reel 7, SNCC Papers; Casey Hayden, "Fields of Blue," 348.

43. Mickey Flacks, e-mail to author, 15 May 2001; Flacks interview.

44. Flacks interview. See also Norman interview.

45. Flacks interview. Martha Prescod Norman remembered that at the meetings the men would discuss politically relevant books "as if there were no women in the room. If the women said something, it would be overlooked or else some man would say it two minutes later. After awhile, most of the women just gave up, and we sat upstairs

and had coffee while the discussion went on." Norman interview. Sara Evans's *Personal Politics*, a classic book on the origins of second-wave feminism, remains very useful in laying out the conflicting social relations between men and women in SDS. On the ways gendered acculturation allows women to develop their social knowledge into political capital, see Bucholtz, Liang, and Sutton, *Reinventing Identities*; Luke, *Feminisms and Pedagogies*; Meyers, *Being Yourself*; Carol Lakey Hess, *Caretakers of Our Common House*; and Rinehart, *Gender Consciousness*. Although it does not direct all of its attention to this issue, *Women: A Feminist Perspective*, edited by Jo Freeman, contains a great deal of information useful to understanding the politics of gender socialization in the twentieth-century United States.

46. Casey Hayden, "Fields of Blue," 348.

47. Ibid., 347, 349; Tom Hayden, *Reunion*, 107 – 8. David Gilbert, though a full college cohort younger than the Haydens, fleshed out this "chauvinist's paradise" further: "The way it got played out until there was a stronger women's movement that challenged us was using the rhetoric of sexual liberation to really play out a more traditional male thing about scoring and sex as ego. In other words, how many women have you made it with or did you conquer this woman or not, rather than what are the terms of your relationship and what are you getting from each other, including close relationships with women that aren't necessarily sexual." Gilbert interview, 18 June 1985.

48. The Hayden's divorce was final in 1965. Casey Hayden, e-mail to the author, 29 Jan. 2000. At the time of their separation, however, none of these personal/political dynamics was articulated — and perhaps could not be articulated, since "the personal" was not widely understood to be a political issue before the women's liberation movement.

49. Tom Hayden, *Reunion*, 110 (Ross); Jeffrey interview.

50. In 1961 the Stern Family Fund and Taconic and Field Foundations gave $870,000 to the Southern Regional Council in Atlanta to disburse to NAACP, SCLC, the Urban League, CORE, and SNCC through the Voter Education Project. See "News Release: The Voter Education Project," 29 Mar. 1962, frame 934, reel 27, CORE Papers. Clayborne Carson, *In Struggle*, 70; Moses interview by Carson.

51. Casey Hayden, "Fields of Blue," 349.

52. Casey Hayden: Speech for panel on "Feminists and Women," "Fields of Blue," 350, Interview by the author, and E-mail to the author, 12 Apr. 2001. On the clothing and food drives, see Sandra Hayden to Sharon Jeffrey, to Richard Lorr, and to Ellen Macken, 15 Mar. 1963, frames 656 – 57, reel 8, SNCC Papers; and Casey [Hayden] to Peter Countryman, 27 Mar. 1963, and Casey Hayden to Countryman and Jeffrey, 4 Apr. 1963, frame 660, reel 8, SNCC Papers. The Mississippi Summer Project of 1964 resulted in the formation of hundreds of FOS groups. Prior to this period, FOS groups existed in the following locales: San Francisco Bay Area (1960), Los Angeles (September 1962), Denver (November 1963), Connecticut (August 1963), Chicago (July 1961), Africa (December 1963), England (October 1963), France (November 1963), Boston (April 1963), Michigan (December 1962), St. Louis (May 1963), New Jersey (September 1963), Ohio (November 1963), Portland, Ore. (August 1963), and Seattle (July 1963). Correspondence with these groups appears on reels 28 – 34, SNCC Papers. Much of the 1961 – 62 correspondence with northern groups can be found in Forman's executive secretary files, reels 5 – 10, SNCC Papers. Strangely enough, many of the meticulous records Casey kept during

her time as northern coordinator have disappeared from the SNCC Papers, though some carbons of her letters are in Forman's executive secretary files (reels 5–10).

53. Hewitt interview, 6 Apr. 1984; Casey Hayden, "Fields of Blue," 343, and Speech for panel on "Feminists and Women." Hewitt, also known as Masai, later went on to play a central role in the Black Panther Party.

54. Garvy interview, 22 June 1998.

55. Casey Hayden, e-mail to the author, 21 Nov. 1999. Ella Baker's' modus operandi since the 1940s modeled this kind of leadership, explicitly or implicitly, for Casey as well as for SNCC workers such as Bob Moses, Bernice Reagon, and Joyce Ladner. See Ransby, *Ella Baker*, 271. For examples, see Julian Bond's correspondence with Ron Dorfman, frames 45–49, reel 7, SNCC Papers. On the ways the draft resistance and women's liberation movements reconfigured these networks, see Chapter 11 and Appendix H.

56. For example, in April 1963 Casey wrote to Sharon Jeffrey and Peter Countryman that they could do SNCC fund-raising as an entrée into northern community organizing. "If you are trying to reach second level leadership, which I assume is your best bet (as it has been ours) increasing a constituency for yourselves, you will probably be working through civic clubs, churches, etc. That will probably mean you'll need lots of hand outs, pictures, etc." Casey Hayden to Countryman and Jeffrey, 16 Apr. 1963, frame 661, reel 8, SNCC Papers.

Chapter Five

1. Richardson interview; Patch interview. See also CNAC Summer Staff, "The Negro Ward of Cambridge, Maryland: A Study in Social Change," September 1963, Phillips and Fein Papers. SNCC field secretaries Reggie Robinson and Bill Hansen arrived in Cambridge in December 1961 and worked with the Civic Interest Group of Baltimore to investigate conditions on the Eastern Shore. Together they organized demonstrations beginning in January 1962, climaxing with violence against demonstrators at the Choptank Inn. After this, a local civil rights group, the Cambridge Nonviolent Action Committee (CNAC), formed around the St. Clair family, which opened its home to the SNCC secretaries as living and working space.

2. Prior accounts, particularly those by Clayborne Carson (*In Struggle*) and James Miller (*"Democracy Is in the Streets"*), provide invaluable intellectual histories of SNCC and SDS, respectively. Kirkpatrick Sale (*SDS*), who has written the most comprehensive account of SDS to date, argued that SNCC influenced SDS a great deal (though Miller vehemently disagreed). Despite their differences, these interpretations remain credible and authentic explanations. Yet these important studies leave unexplored the crucial question of precisely how democratic forms can develop in one region and spread to others. Both Miller and Sale treat SDS primarily as the creation of a group of young intellectuals influenced by scholars such as Albert Camus, C. Wright Mills, and Paul Goodman. The role of the civil rights movement in generating SDS's move toward activism has been aggressively challenged by Miller.

3. Cambridge erupted in the summer of 1963, when Governor J. Millard Tawes called in the national guard after crowds of whites and blacks threatened one another. For more on Cambridge, see Harley, "'Chronicle of a Death Foretold,'" and Peter B. Levy,

Civil War, chaps. 2–3. What follows is not a comprehensive history of the Cambridge movement; rather, my purpose is to trace the experiences of Swarthmore students who participated in that movement. SNCC people and those from the NSM "played a big role in the beginning of the Cambridge movement," Annette Brock ("Gloria Richardson," 123–27) found. Students came from nearby Morgan State, Howard, Maryland State, and Swarthmore, as well as Skidmore, Brown, and Harvard.

4. Patch interview; Richardson interview; Fein interview. On the NAACP lawsuit, see Legal Department Case Files, NAACP Papers.

5. The Eastern Shore sit-ins were organized by CIG. In the winter of 1961, SNCC workers Reggie Robinson and Bill Hansen were arrested on Christmas Day for trespassing on behalf of a sit-in. Frederick St. Clair had suggested that they investigate the situation in Cambridge. Peter B. Levy, *Civil War*, 37–44.

6. Patch interview; Brock, "Gloria Richardson," 123. See also correspondence between James Forman, executive secretary of SNCC, and Peter Countryman, head of NSM, frames 570–75, reel 8, SNCC Papers. At the time, SNCC both enabled cooperation among local direct action movements and ran its own voter registration projects. While not all of the Swarthmore activists were red-diaper babies, Carl Wittman, Jerry Gelles, and Michael Manove were (Fein interview). Cambridge's location—75 miles from Baltimore, 75 miles from Washington, D.C., 125 miles from Philadelphia, and 200 miles from New York—"gave the movement in Cambridge access to resources and publicity way beyond most of the rest of the South." CNAC Summer Staff, "Negro Ward of Cambridge, Maryland," 4.

7. CNAC Summer Staff, "Negro Ward of Cambridge, Maryland," 4; Brock, "Gloria Richardson," 125 (Richardson). See also Peter B. Levy, *Civil War*, 31. CNAC asked the Cambridge Board of Education to include commercial courses at the black high school to prepare more students for good jobs and demanded that the city institute fair-housing practices and pave the streets in black neighborhoods. The Swarthmore students reported that one reason for the Eastern Shore's resemblance to the Deep South was its isolation: until the 1950s, there was no road or rail transportation to the area except at the northern neck of the peninsula. After the Supreme Court's *Brown v. Board of Education of Topeka, Kansas* decision in 1954, Cambridge set up an advisory committee on desegregating the public schools. The authorities agreed on a plan for desegregation, beginning with the twelfth grade, but it was not attempted until 1962. That year two black juniors entered North Dorchester High School and stayed, while blacks at Cambridge High withdrew. During the spring of 1963, CNAC negotiated with the Board of Education, but these talks broke off in June when the board refused to speed up the pace of integration. Gloria Richardson remarks at SB-SNCC Conference (transcript); "OCAC Summary of the Conditions in Cambridge, Maryland," [1963], frame 375, reel 1, Feingold Papers; "Baltimore Civic Interest Group/Northern Student Movement Prospectus: Eastern Shore Project," frame 718, reel 8, SNCC Papers; CNAC Summer Staff, "Negro Ward of Cambridge, Maryland," 23. For more on Richardson and her influence on the emerging black movement after 1963, see Harley, "'Chronicle of a Death Foretold.'"

8. CORE Host Maryland Confab," *Student Voice*, June 1962, 2 (Lewis); Bob Moses, *Radical Equations*, 77 (NAG); Stokely Carmichael, *Ready for Revolution*, 112, 137–77.

See also Peter B. Levy, *Civil War*, 40–44, 51. NAG started nonviolent direct action against Jim Crow establishments along Route 40 in Maryland in 1960; CIG-CORE organized a larger campaign in 1961. In early 1962 Cambridge's first civil rights demonstrations began. In May 1962 a conference sponsored by the Baltimore Civic Interest Group brought together NAG, CORE, and several national civil rights leaders to plan "wade-ins," sit-ins, and Freedom Rides for Ocean City, Md., that June.

9. In 1961 Al Haber tried to persuade SPAC to become an SDS affiliate through Swarthmore contact Becky Adams. SPAC president Oliver Fein remembered that SDS, at first, seemed a little too focused on intellectual debate and not enough on political action. It was not until 1962–63 that SPAC became an SDS affiliate. Fein interview; Lewis, *Walking with the Wind*, 85, 212; Clayborne Carson, *In Struggle*, 90, 252.

10. CIG was a civil rights group with a large percentage of members from historically black Morgan State.

11. Richardson interview. As has been pointed out, this anecdote provides a vivid snapshot of racism in the North. In 1962 Swarthmore, which considered itself progressive on race issues, admitted only eight black students to the freshman class.

12. Richardson interview; Ron Dorfman to Julian Bond, 25 July 1963, frame 40, reel 7, SNCC Papers (one supporter).

13. Countryman worked with SNCC field staffers Reggie Robinson and Bill Hansen and with Clarence Logan of CIG. See Peter [Countryman] to Gentlemen, 10 Feb. 1962 (frame 571, reel 8), "Agenda for Executive Committee Meeting," NSM, 15 Feb. 1962 (frame 573, reel 8), Countryman to [Jim] Forman and [Jim] Monsonis, 28 Feb. 1962 (frame 573, reel 8), and [Peter Countryman] to Forman, McDew, Monsonis, 13 Mar. 1962 (frame 575, reel 8), SNCC Papers.

14. On Swarthmore's unique history, see Burton R. Clark, *Distinctive College*, 171–230.

15. Peter [Countryman] to "Gentlemen," 10 Feb. 1962, frame 571, reel 8, SNCC Papers; "Sit-in Report," [1962], frame 194, reel 1, Feingold Papers. This is not to say that such civil rights work was unique to Swarthmore, as significant FOS groups formed in Los Angeles, the San Francisco Bay area, Detroit, Chicago, Boston, and New York. However, because of their physical proximity to southern activism and Swarthmore's activist tradition, Swarthmore students could most immediately translate what they were learning from SNCC into their own community organizing project based at a northern college. Unlike SNCC workers in Nashville, those at Swarthmore had no institutional base such as James Lawson's nonviolent workshops in which issues could be hashed out. They also lacked a mentor to provide guidance and support. It is crucial to note that this chapter is not a historical endorsement of the Swarthmore students' view of the Cambridge project. Rather, it is an analysis of how the Swarthmore group reacted to the Cambridge movement and what the group did in the wake of these experiences.

16. [Carl Wittman], "Suggestions for Organization of Freedom Rides," [1962–63], frame 195, reel 1, Feingold Papers. Project Eastern Shore, run by GIC and CNAC, functioned between Summer 1962 and Spring 1963. Peter B. Levy, *Civil War*, 57–59.

17. Mimi Feingold, Journal in Cambridge, Md., jail, 30 Mar.–2 Apr. 1963, written on return to Swarthmore, Feingold Papers (contains Wittman's letter); CNAC Summer Staff, "Negro Ward of Cambridge, Maryland." The Dorset Theater, Cambridge's only

movie theater, had recently confined blacks to the back half of the balcony, whereas previously African Americans had been allowed to sit anywhere in the balcony. Gloria Richardson and Enez Grub of CNAC subsequently met with CIG, a representative from Fellowship House in Philadelphia, and students from Swarthmore, Beaver College, and the University of Maryland in March 1963, when "all committed themselves to assist CNAC in direct action, voter registration, and possibly a tutorial, if requested" (CNAC Summer Staff, "Negro Ward of Cambridge, Maryland"). Wittman and the other students were then jailed for sitting-in, some at the Dorset Theater and some at the Rescue Fire Company's Arena (skating rink).

18. "Freedom Singers Debut, to Appear at Feb. 1 Fete," *Student Voice*, 19 Dec. 1962, 2; Clayborne Carson, *In Struggle*, 63 – 64. The first group of Freedom Singers included SNCC field secretaries Bernice Johnson Reagon, Rutha Harris, Bertha Gober, Dorothy Vails, Chico Neblett, and Cordell Reagon. Their songs helped people connect to the broader currents of the Black Freedom Church (see Chapter 1, n. 65).

19. Charlotte Phillips to Mimi Feingold, 2 Apr. 1963, frame 227, reel 1, Feingold Papers. Phillips, Oliver Fein, Ann McCaghey, and Blake Smith — all Swarthmore students — had attended SNCC's October 1960 conference as observers. See frame 560, reel 11, SNCC Papers, and Peter B. Levy, *Civil War*, 42.

20. See, e.g., the civil rights activities listed by Grizzard and Levin in their applications to SNCC's leadership training institute in Nashville, Fall 1962, frames 731 – 32, reel 11, SNCC Papers.

21. Two other members key to the development of SDS — Kathy Boudin from Bryn Mawr and Cathy Wilkerson from Swarthmore — also worked with the Swarthmore group. Boudin likely knew a great deal about SNCC activities through the daughter of her father's law partner, Joni Rabinowitz, who worked in Albany, Ga., in 1963. Boudin and Wilkerson later became members of the Weather Underground. Preliminary research indicates that their journey to the politics of the Weather Underground was much more a product of their work in SDS-Chicago (1966 – 68) for Wilkerson and ERAP-Cleveland (1964 – 68) for Boudin than their experience in SPAC's Chester project, though that pushed them to greater involvement in SDS. Richardson interview; Feingold, Journal in Cambridge, Md., jail; Grizzard to Phillips and Fein, 30 July 1963, box 24, SDS Papers; Wittman, Broadmeadows Prison [Pennsylvania], to Mimi Feingold, 2 Apr. 1964, Feingold Papers; Fein interview. On Rabinowitz in Albany, see "Federal Jury Indicts Nine," *Student Voice*, October 1963, 3.

22. Feingold, Journal in Cambridge, Md., jail.

23. The fears of family members worried about their safety impeded or complicated students' involvement in the demonstration. As during the earlier sit-ins and Freedom Rides, some parents actively opposed or physically prevented their children's participation. Sophomore Vernon Grizzard fielded a phone call from his mother after he joined actions in Cambridge. From their home in Florida, she told him to leave Cambridge "with all this violence." "After long consideration," his friend Rachel Folsom reported to Feingold, "he told [his mother] he wouldn't [go home] and he didn't think she could make him." At that point his mother threatened to either send the Florida police to get him, force Swarthmore to cancel his scholarship, or get her psychiatrist to commit him to an institution. "So he went home. It really killed him." "I still want like hell to

depart for places of conflict," Grizzard wrote Feingold. Two weeks after his return to Jacksonville, he informed her of recent developments in the black community of St. Augustine, forty miles to the south. "Negro leaders there are saying that they will carry guns on their picket lines in case whites start any violence." It seemed no place in the South lacked conflict. After many long discussions, Grizzard persuaded his mother to allow him to work in SNCC's Albany or Atlanta offices. Grizzard's mother's reasons for asking him to return home were quite interesting. She felt that blacks deserved equal rights, but whites who participated with them in this quest were meddling and inciting passions that then resulted in violence, and this was against her belief that everyone has a duty in life "to do no harm." Somehow obscured from her view, it seems, was the harm done to African Americans by participating in the system of segregation. Grizzard to Feingold, 4 Apr. 1963, Folsom to Feingold, 16 June 1963, and Mark Suckle to Feingold, "Dear M. The situation is extremely tense," n.d. [Summer 1963], frame 265, reel 1, Feingold Papers; Grizzard to Charlotte Phillips and Oliver Fein, 30 July 1963, box 24, SDS Papers. For more on parents' response to the sit-ins and Freedom Rides, see Fleming, *Soon We Will Cry*, 60–61.

24. Suckle to Feingold, "Dear M. The situation is extremely tense"; CNAC Summer Staff, "Negro Ward of Cambridge, Maryland,' 49; "Desegregation Pact Signed after 18-Month CNAC Protest," *Student Voice*, August 1963, 1. The National Guard occupied Cambridge, enforcing militia law for twenty-five days in June and July 1963, and for another three weeks in August; martial law did not end until the following summer.

25. Grizzard to Feingold, 22 June 1963, frame 250, reel 1, Feingold Papers; CNAC Summer Staff, "Negro Ward of Cambridge, Maryland," 55. The Cambridge movement adopted nonviolence, the Swarthmore students believed, "not primarily because of philosophical conviction, but because non-violence is practicable," but a split occurred in April 1963, when members of Philadelphia's Fellowship House "objected to the lack of 'loving' and good will in the other demonstrators. They cited the defiant singing (with such verses as 'Ain't gonna let no dumb-cop turn me 'round') and undignified behavior in jails as evidence of this. When CNAC leaders did nothing to change the situation," the Swarthmore students observed, "the Fellowship House group discontinued its assistance." Carl Wittman to Mimi Feingold, 13 July 1963, and Mark Suckle to Feingold, "Dear M. I'm sure you've seen about the situation in Cambridge," n.d. [Summer 1963], frame 250, reel 1, Feingold Papers; CNAC Summer Staff, "Negro Ward of Cambridge, Maryland," 55.

26. Brock, "Gloria Richardson," 130–36; Carmichael, *Ready for Revolution*, 339; Vernon Grizzard to Mimi Feingold, 22 June 1963, frame 250, reel 1, Feingold Papers. The negotiations were extremely tense, reflecting the situation in Cambridge itself. The sessions, which were held in Washington under the aegis of the U.S. attorney general, included Robert Kennedy, Gloria Richardson, Diane Nash, SNCC chairman John Lewis, Reggie Robinson, local NAACP leader Stanley Branche, Kennedy's assistant for civil rights Burke Marshall, Maryland attorney general Thomas B. Finon and his deputy Robert C. Murphy, Brigadier General George M. Gelston, Governor Tawes's top aide Edmund C. Mester, and Robert Weaver, head of the federal Housing and Home Finance Agency. Marshall declined to invite city officials in order to prevent a collapse of the talks, which lasted from 3:00 P.M. to midnight on 22 July 1963.

27. Richardson claimed that she had agreed to the Cambridge Accord because she "wanted to prove that the moral suasion of the federal government would not make local [white] leaders keep the promises they made" (Brock, "Gloria Richardson"). The National Guard enforced more than twelve months of martial law, withdrawing on 7 July 1964. Almost a year later, presidential candidate and outspoken segregationist George Wallace came to Cambridge, sparking a series of protests from Cambridge blacks against Wallace's brand of Democratic politics. See "Wallace Sparks Cambridge Protests," *Student Voice*, 19 May 1964, 2. On the way the Cambridge race situation intersected with national politics, propelling Wallace's presidential candidacy, see Lesher, *George Wallace*, 298–301, and Carter, *Politics of Rage*. At a SNCC reunion in 2000, Gloria Richardson noted that Diane Nash had been instrumental in the meeting with Robert Kennedy. After he had given his final negotiated offer, Nash rose to pronounce the deal inadequate. "'I remember you,'" Richardson recalled Kennedy saying. "'You're the lady who ripped me up one side and down the other'" on the Freedom Ride. Richardson remarks at SB-SNCC Conference (transcript).

28. CNAC Summer Staff, "Negro Ward of Cambridge, Maryland" (Wittman and Grizzard); Grizzard to Charlotte Phillips and Oliver Fein, 30 July 1963, box 24, SDS Papers; Grizzard to Mimi Feingold, 4 Apr. 1963, frame 265, reel 1, Feingold Papers. Kirkpatrick Sale (*SDS*, 104) wrote that the Cambridge SNCC had a considerable impact on SPAC students. He also pointed out that events in Cambridge and Chester generated much of the evidence that was fundamental to the production of "An Interracial Movement of the Poor?" by Wittman and Tom Hayden (June 1964; found in frames 638–43, reel 2, Feingold Papers). However, it was not just Wittman's life trajectory that they crucially altered. It was the *network* of activists that emerged from this set of similar experiences that proved so influential on the directions subsequently taken by ERAP, and, as a result, SDS as a whole.

29. Richardson and CNAC indeed went on to address economic issues over the following year in ways that prefigured ERAP's emphasis on economic equity and civic reforms around housing, jobs, and education. See the *Student Voice*: "Cambridge Negroes Resume Protests," 3 Mar. 1964, 2; "Wallace Sparks Cambridge Protests," 19 May 1964, 2; and "Employment Programs Begin in Cambridge," 9 June 1964, 4.

30. A particularly useful component of the summer staff's report, "Negro Ward of Cambridge, Maryland," is the way the group compared the Cambridge Accord's provisions to the results visible two months later, just before an October referendum on a bill to desegregate public accommodations. It is possible to ascertain from this document why the Swarthmore group remained skeptical that the Cambridge Accord was a victory.

31. Feingold to "Family," 31 July 1863 [*sic*], Feingold Papers.

32. Fein interview; Larry Gordon and Vernon Grizzard, "Notes on Developing Organization in the Ghetto: Chester, Pennsylvania," [Summer 1964], box 44, SDS Papers; Danny Pope, Alain Jehlen, and Evan Metcalf, with Cathy Wilkerson, "Chester, Pennsylvania: A Case Study in Community Organization," n.d., box 1, SDS Papers (unprocessed, collection M96–081); Wittman to Mimi Feingold, 31 Oct. 1963, frame 335, reel 1, Feingold Papers. Paul Lauter later commented: "One of the lessons, I think, for people

who were involved in that group was the possibility of taking that individual action that really moved people and that gave people the freedom and the sense of possibility to break out of what people call apathy" (quoted in Greenberg, *Circle of Trust*, 30).

33. Pope et al., "Chester, Pennsylvania."

34. Mimi Feingold to Parents, 15 Oct. 1963, Feingold Papers.

35. The students who worked on the Cambridge project during the summer of 1963 reported that "with the increase of tensions," Reggie Robinson, Stanley Branche, and Phil Savage "became increasingly prominent" in CNAC's decision-making, "to some extent pushing out the executive committee and the student staff." CNAC Summer Staff, "Negro Ward of Cambridge, Maryland," 55–56.

36. Mimi Feingold to Parents, 15 Oct. 1963; Wittman to Feingold, 31 Oct. 1963, frame 365, reel 1, Feingold Papers.

37. In the 1980s and 1990s a new group of studies on community organizing helped to expand our collective vocabulary for civic participation movements. See, e.g., Benello, *From the Ground Up*; Boyte, Booth, and Max, *Citizen Action*; Boyte, *Commonwealth*; Rogers, *Cold Anger*; Delgado, *Beyond the Politics of Place*; and Gittell and Vidal, *Community Organizing*. See also Civic Practices Network, ‹http://www.cpn.org›, and COMM-ORG, ‹http://comm-org.utoledo.edu›.

38. Pope et al., "Chester, Pennsylvania."

39. On Baker and Moore, see Charles Payne, *Light of Freedom*, chaps. 3–4. Still, the students' focus on geographic area did take advantage of residents' neighborhood ties. They debated whether to organize "ten square blocks" or do "intensive" organizing in a smaller area, allowing organizers to "spend more time with each family" and foster "a sense of being a unit" that might then expand to include others. Swarthmore students led early meetings until there had been "a chance for leadership to emerge" from the group. They found that this might "not be the most efficient short-term structure," but they initially tried to stay true to the SNCC understanding of building organizations by supporting the leadership of people indigenous to the community. They hoped that block leaders would bring the issues that people wanted to act on to the executive committee of CFFN, in an effort to create a larger structure of block organizations that could mobilize the entire community. Pope et al., "Chester, Pennsylvania."

40. Pope et al., "Chester, Pennsylvania."

41. Gordon and Grizzard, "Notes on Developing Organization"; Pope et al., "Chester, Pennsylvania."

42. Pope et al., "Chester, Pennsylvania."

43. Sale, *SDS*, 102, 98 (Gitlin); Roberts, "Roberts, "Will Tom Hayden Overcome?" (Hayden). See also Haber to Mike Miller, n.d. [September 1963], box 16, SDS Papers; Richard Rothstein to Dorothy Burlage, 22 Mar. 1965, box 19, SDS Papers; Tom Hayden, *SDS Bulletin*, March–April 1963, quoted in Sale, *SDS*, 96–97; Hayden, *Reunion*, 126; Carl Wittman, *SDS Bulletin* (March 1964), quoted in Sale, *SDS*, 104. Those in graduate school were Gitlin, Hayden, Robb Burlage, Rennie Davis, Richard Flacks, Al Haber, Ken McEldowney, Paul Potter, Bob Ross, and Richard Rothstein.

Chapter Six

1. Roberts, "Will Tom Hayden Overcome?"
2. Gitlin interview. Gitlin had attended the prestigious Bronx Science High School with Carmichael in the late 1950s. At their Fall 1963 national council meeting, SDS used the $5,000 donated by the UAW to fund the work of their first organizer, Joe Chabot, a University of Michigan dropout. He asked how he would find people to recruit in Chicago. No one in the national SDS leadership had community organizing experience — except for Sharon Jeffrey, who was now working with NSM in Philadelphia. The grant also paid Al Haber to support Chabot from a central office in Ann Arbor. Haber would turn Chabot's reports into a newsletter and circulate these to a "small group of people for comment and advice." Haber, in other words, would provide some intellectual scaffolding and entice liberal allies to the project. The Economic Research and Action Project (ERAP) officially began that September, but Chabot had little success and soon disappeared. Sale, *SDS*, 97 – 98 (quotation above), 102. Ironically, Carmichael also met fellow Bronx resident Theresa del Pozzo in the Atlanta SNCC office that summer of 1963. "Racial fighting broke out in the fringe area separating our two neighborhoods" in Atlanta, del Pozzo ("The Feel of a Blue Note," 184) remembered. "We had a good laugh when he suggested, tongue in cheek, that since it was 'my people' rioting and attacking blacks, I should go there and try to 'organize' them. The mutually understood clear absurdity of such a suggestion made it funny."
3. Sale, *SDS*, 105; Gitlin interview.
4. Haber to Robb Burlage, 6 Dec. 1963, box 16, SDS Papers.
5. Sale, *SDS*, 107 (Booth, 106); Magidoff interview, 17 Nov. 1999; Haber, *SDS Bulletin* (March – April 1964), quoted in Sale, 110. At least one thoughtful ERAPer, Helen Garvy, felt that the anti-intellectualist label did not describe the ERAP staff (Garvy interview, 14 June 1998). Also present at the meeting were Harlem organizer Jesse Gray and Stanley Aronowitz from the newly formed National Committee for Full Employment, both of whom later served ERAP in an advisory capacity. The SDS national council "met in New York with a sense that big things were going to happen," sympathetic New York-based journalist Kirkpatrick Sale reported. The leaders felt, in SDSer Paul Booth's words, that they "were *it*. We were the wave of the future." Webb had staged the gathering, bringing in many people from Swarthmore whom he had met that fall. The Swarthmore students' commitment to organizing in Chester while still attending classes amazed and impressed many of the participants. "We had been involved in a little bit of community [organizing] in Ann Arbor," said Michigan student Dickie Magidoff, "but they were really immersed in it. Really energetic." Among the issues discussed was the extent to which SDS should organize the poor versus other students, a deliberation others remembered as the "Hayden-Haber Debate." Sale, *SDS*, 107 (Booth, 106); Magidoff interview, 17 Nov. 1999.
6. Countryman, remarks at SDS meeting, 1 – 2 Dec. 1962, tape 8, side 1, SDS Tapes, SHSW; Countryman to Jim Forman, 22 Jan. 1962 (frame 570), Countryman to Forman, 6 Feb. 1962 (frame 568), Countryman to Gentlemen, 10 Feb. 1962 (frames 571 – 72), Countryman to Forman and [James] Monsonis, 28 Feb. 1962 (frame 573), and Countryman to Forman, McDew, Monsonis, 13 Mar. 1962 (frame 575), all in reel 8,

SNCC Papers; "Foundation Grants Sought for Expansion of Tutorial Projects," *NSM News*, 14 Dec. 1962, frame 706, reel 27, CORE Papers.

NSM was founded after a June 1961 conference of the Student Christian Movement of New England. Inspired by the stories of Dr. John Maguire of Wesleyan University, a Freedom Rider, and Marian Wright (later Edelman) of Yale Law School, both of whom had spoken to conferees "on the dynamics of racial discrimination," the delegates appointed a committee to investigate how New England students might support civil rights activism. In October 1961 this committee held a seminar for twenty college representatives and established a basic structure for what became known as NSM. Through personal letters, publications, and campus visits, the organization expanded to new campuses, tapping into "groups already active on the local level" and developing new leadership. NSM, whose initial goal was "to provide an immediate opportunity for support — moral, physical and financial — of the Southern Student movement," concentrated on raising money for SNCC's voter registration program. Since its members "had been shown by Southern students in the past eighteen months that this is a struggle in which students can actively participate," they would no longer be "frustrated by striving to develop ideals which have no concrete application in the world." After "the tedious picket lines, and the shanty Citizenship schools and the wet, cold Mississippi jails," They were "witness to the reality of individual responsibility and the possibility of personal involvement." Students wanted "an education that has meaning because it lies within the context of a very real struggle for human fulfillment." Soon they would try to create a foundation for an ongoing student movement in the North, emphasizing "the entirety and urgency of the racial problem in the United States, with special focus on the dilemma of the Northern urban areas." Most often this meant setting up tutorial projects in northern ghettos. "The NSMCC: History, Structure, and Program," 5 Jan. 1962 (frame 202), and Countryman, "The Student Nonviolent Coordinating Committee," 10 Nov. 1961 (frame 204), both in reel 1, Feingold Papers.

7. Countryman, "Student Nonviolent Coordinating Committee," 10 Nov. 1961. See also Countryman-Forman correspondence, reel 8, SNCC Papers. Countryman prefigured ideas that would emerge in both the "Port Huron Statement" of SDS and the Free Speech Movement: practical application of democratic ideals, individual responsibility, and personal commitment.

8. Countryman, "Student Nonviolent Coordinating Committee," 10 Nov. 1961. This was the story of a revolution, Countryman wrote. Prefiguring the "Port Huron Statement," he said that this was a revolution that sought "to destroy the dominant institutions of dehumanization, [and] centers primarily around a re-creation of humanitarian institutions."

9. The North Carolina project was led by Casey Hayden's roommate at the Christian Faith and Life Community, Dorothy Dawson (later Burlage), another major bridge builder between South and North.

10. James Miller, *"Democracy Is in the Streets,"* 187 (Jeffrey). Even though SDS needed to be cautious about political action because of its continuing dependence for financial support on its parent organization, the tax-exempt League for Industrial Democracy, both Jeffrey and Tom Hayden believed that SDS needed to get involved in direct action, rather than remain focused on "just talk." Given SDS's funding limitations, then, NSM

provided a financial and organizational umbrella for sit-ins, boycotts, and sympathy pickets initiated by people returning home to the North after their involvement in southern civil rights actions.

11. Countryman, remarks at SDS meeting, 1–2 Dec. 1962. NSM had in fact sent two students, Bill Henry and Tom Kennedy, to the Eastern Shore of Maryland over the summer of 1962 to work on voter registration, recreation, and uniting labor and the civil rights movement. CNAC Summer Staff, "The Negro Ward of Cambridge, Maryland: A Study in Social Change," September 1963, Phillips and Fein Papers. An unidentified southern male participant at the December 1962 SDS meeting agreed but argued that SDSers lacked a concrete issue on which to proceed. Should they challenge bad housing? employment discrimination? inferior schools? "How do we get theory without some sense of context" and some experience on which to base that theory? "It's only through *being* with people who are experiencing conflict that we *can* develop theory," he added. Students were irrelevant "until we *are* the movement, not just supporting the southern movement." Unknown male voice, perhaps Robb Burlage, in the "Questions" section to Countryman's remarks at SDS meeting, 1–2 Dec. 1962.

12. Gitlin interview; "Over 300 Attend SNCC Conference," *Student Voice*, 9 Dec. 1963, 4 (Lewis). Tom Hayden articulated this emergent vision in his debate with Haber in December 1963. Since Hayden understood his own political identity to have developed from seeing SNCC activists at work in Mississippi and Georgia, he insisted that SDS people must live through organizing in order to write about it; this could make SDS relevant to the struggle for social justice in a way that the university model of education had not. After the debate, the national council voted 20–6 that henceforth the young organization invest its principal energies in ERAP. Haber resigned and Oberlin graduate Rennie Davis took over as director of ERAP. Sale, *SDS*, 107; Tom Hayden interview; Hayden, Ann Arbor, to Steve Johnson, Cambridge, [Mass.], 10 May 1963, box 6, SDS Papers. Todd Gitlin gave five reasons for the tilt toward ERAP: first, Carmichael had suggested that SDS organize whites as the natural allies of the civil rights movement. Second, by organizing the poor, SDS might rejuvenate a coalition of church, labor, and liberal forces. Third, students had to connect with others beside themselves, and poor people were the most angry and deprived constituency. Fourth, nobody else would do it and thus it was SDS's duty. Fifth, there "was a very strong feeling within SDS, and, on the part of black organizers, in both SNCC and NSM, that SDS was this bullshit talk organization that put out a lot of smart working papers and talked a lot, but didn't do anything. SDS had to do something. . . . And this was something to do: send people out. Send them out there, a hundred people, get them in community projects, and that will constitute action. We'd be taken seriously." Gitlin interview.

13. Garvy interview, 14 June 1998. A CORE staffer noticed the same thing the following year. In leaving Louisiana voter registration projects for CORE chapters in the North, "people just weren't attacking problems that were meaningful to people in the community and they didn't really know how to go about it — they were in a different place than we were. We were talking about community organization then, because that had come through from Mississippi. We were talking about organization as *a goal*, organization as an attempt to get people some power in order for them to be able

to decide what kinds of goals they had, rather than getting registered as voters as an avenue of power." "ML" quoted in Louis, *We Are Not Saved*, 263.

14. Casey Hayden, "Fields of Blue," 342; Danny Pope, Alain Jehlen, and Evan Metcalf, with Cathy Wilkerson, "Chester, Pennsylvania: A Case Study in Community Organization," n.d., box 1, SDS Papers (unprocessed, collection M96–081); Wittman to Mimi Feingold, 30 Jan. 1964, Feingold Papers.

15. Wittman to Feingold, 30 Jan. 1964, Feingold Papers. In Ann Arbor that January, Hayden and Wittman's conversations provoked energy and movement: Rennie Davis, Dickie Magidoff, and seniors Carol and Ken McEldowney, among others, began to dig into the planning of prospective ERAPs. Working from her NSM project in Philadelphia, Sharon Jeffrey agreed to take part.

16. Wittman to Mimi Feingold, 30 Jan. 1964, Feingold Papers; Hayden, *Reunion*, 126.

17. Wittman and Hayden, "An Interracial Movement of the Poor?," June 1964, frames 638–43, reel 2, Feingold Papers. The influence of the Cambridge experience on the ERAP paper is clear in the report Wittman coauthored in September 1963 on Cambridge: "Better housing, full employment, better working conditions, and better education are the demands of the residents of the Negro community, not public accommodations. It is this change which is going on at the present time (September 1963) and which foreshadows events to come elsewhere. It is our feeling that the particular factors which go into the Cambridge movement are not particular to Cambridge, and because of that, the directions of the movement are similarly not particular to Cambridge. This last contention, if true, makes a study of the details of the Cambridge situation most valuable; it is with this in mind that we present the material of this report." CNAC Summer Staff, "Negro Ward of Cambridge, Maryland," 3.

The working notes represented by "An Interracial Movement" oscillated between experimental open-ended questions and authoritative pronouncements, embodying the tensions the authors experienced between notions of participatory democracy and a more authoritarian leadership style. Hayden and Wittman took for granted that the South would soon desegregate. Next they wanted to enlist low-income whites as the allies of low-income blacks, rather than as agents of a white backlash. Their document shows the degree to which the black freedom struggle's tactics fundamentally shaped both men's approach to democratic practice; a single-spaced, eight-page analysis of the civil rights struggle provided the basis for the rest of their strategy. "Any discussion of the prospects for an interracial class movement should begin with an assessment of what people in the Negro movement are doing and care to do," they stated. First, the black freedom struggle "provides impetus for Negroes elsewhere, and precipitates action" in other parts of the country. Second, it "awakens conscientious individuals to the possibility of doing something right and effective . . . providing a model of commitment and action which challenges those who are taking it easy." Third, "the movement dramatically raises political and economic issues of a fundamental importance for the whole society . . . forcing Americans to return to an examination of their way of life after many Cold War years of foreign pre-occupations." Finally, as "organizations like SNCC are already talking and programming on economic issues which are of deep concern to poor white as well as most Southern Negroes . . . it is certainly possible to begin experiments in organizing whites into political alliance with the Negro community today."

Whites, they argued, had to be organized around class and economic hardships rather than racial injustice. Wittman and Hayden viewed industrial automation as the key, because it displaced hundreds of thousands of workers who could form the nucleus of a movement for fundamental social change. At the same time they recognized that not all blacks would support an interracial populist movement, which could be perceived as "a direct threat to the Negro organization to the extent that the organization is a means of finding and expressing a Negro identity." Yet they proceeded apace, warning only of the "immense difficulties" such a movement might encounter. Wittman and Hayden, "Interracial Movement of the Poor?"

After finishing the working notes, Wittman returned to Swarthmore. Throughout the spring of 1964, he developed close personal ties with Tom Hayden and Rennie Davis, the new national director of ERAP, while they prepared for the summer projects. They conferred on potential cities, organizations, and staffers. The events of the spring in Chester appeared to confirm the analysis in "An Interracial Movement of the Poor." As SDSers interested in ERAP visited the Chester-Swarthmore operation, it became the dominant model for people planning similar projects. Wittman to Davis, [February 1964], box 24, SDS Papers; Johnny Bancroft to Rennie [Davis], Paul [Potter], Clark [?], and Roxane Neal, 4 Aug. 1964, box 15, SDS Papers.

18. Pope et al., "Chester, Pennsylvania"; Wittman to Davis, [February 1964]; Wittman, Broadmeadows Prison [Pa.], to Mimi Feingold, 2 Apr. 1964, Feingold Papers. The city created a barrier to making bail by refusing to accept property equity after 3:00 P.M. on Fridays.

19. Vernon Grizzard, Swarthmore, Pa., to "Everybody" [SDS National Office], 2 May 1964, box 25, SDS Papers. Grizzard explained that after a "marathon meeting" a few nights earlier, the Swarthmore group decided to go ahead with the Chester summer project. They debated four issues: (1) Would they have enough time in the fall to continue to participate in organizing a rent strike? (2) Could they overcome their vulnerability as white students who lacked a power base in the community, without seeming to "cause trouble"? (3) Where would they find the money to support themselves? And (4) would they be able to have a full-time person to continue organizing in the fall? After lengthy debate, the SPAC group decided it could work on getting a full-time person and more money. The students would accept the time commitment. They knew of no way to address the race issue. As white organizers in a predominantly black neighborhood, they would simply be "praying about the vulnerability." The last would prove to be an unpromising strategy.

20. The ERAP efforts that began in the summer of 1964 eventually included thirteen locales, including Cleveland, Newark, Chicago, and Chester. Jennifer Frost (*Interracial Movement of the Poor*) has written an important account of the four-year experiment in community organizing.

21. "Wallace Sparks Cambridge Protests," *Student Voice*, 19 May 1964 (italics mine). In 1963–64 SNCC work on economic issues included not only Cambridge but also the Washington, D.C., SNCC office's organization of a local rent strike and Tuskegee student protests over unpaved streets, the absence of garbage collection, and inadequate

street lighting in their city. Potter, *A Name for Ourselves*, 150; Wildflower interview, 7 June 1988. Another interesting difference between North and South emerges from Grace Hale's (*Making Whiteness*, 292–96) compelling examination of the public and performative nature of southern segregated culture. In the civil rights movement, southern blacks "rewrote the drama of racial meaning," refusing "to play their parts as scripted in the play of segregation." African Americans had "finally found a way to counter the black mammy and the black whore, the Uncle Remus and the rapist, with more modern and more persuasive images: white customers pouring ketchup and abuse on black college students at lunch counters, police dogs biting black children in public parks, and firehose torrents rolling black bodies down city sidewalks." Yet in the North, "the movement's performative tactics found no clear drama to subvert, no transparently white spaces to seize, and no embodiments of evil like Bull Connor to attack." Instead, whites used terms like "inner city" and "the City" to dehumanize and demonize blacks.

22. Casey Hayden, "Raising the Question of Who Decides," 10; Richard Rothstein to Robb Burlage, 16 Mar. 1965, box 19, SDS Papers.

23. Brightman interview, 79; Potter, *A Name for Ourselves*, 152–53; Frost, *Interracial Movement of the Poor*, chap. 7.

24. Sale, *SDS*, 143–44.

25. Ibid. James Miller (*"Democracy Is in the Streets,"* 212–13), echoing Sale, regarded the projects as inconsistent, fluctuating "between alliances with liberal institutions such as the Office of Economic Opportunity and hostile attacks on them." While their most tangible victories involved winning concrete concessions from these institutions, they also tried "to build 'counter-societies' and 'counter institutions.'" There is always a danger of distortion when viewing these movements from afar. Sale and Miller, among other commentators, set up a false dichotomy between strategic and prefigurative politics. In fact, ERAP tried to live both in the world as it should be and in the world as it was. Wini Breines first made this point in her path-breaking study, *Community and Organization in the New Left*.

26. Breines, *Community and Organization*, 62.

27. Miller, *"Democracy Is in the Streets,"* 214; Mansbridge, *Beyond Adversary Democracy*; Sirianni, "Democracy and Diversity."

28. Many learned how to listen to each other, learn from each other, before attempting to act collectively. Originating with SNCC, both an understanding and a set of actions — what we might call a democratic understanding of how to be a citizen — had traveled North. The story of the Swarthmore student activists makes it possible to specify precisely when and how SDSers adapted innovative democratic practices developed within the SNCC affiliate in Cambridge, Maryland — first through the Eastern Shore sit-ins, then through the Cambridge project, and finally in Chester. Moreover, Swarthmore's tight-knit activist network attracted the attention of national SDS leaders. Carl Wittman's work in Cambridge and subsequently in Chester gave him the experiential authority to draw up a blueprint for northern urban organizing, which he then laid out with Tom Hayden, whose political vision had been fundamentally refocused as a result of his experiences with SNCC in Georgia and Mississippi. Swarthmore students such as Nick Egleson and Connie Brown, who had been involved intensely in

Chester in 1963 and 1964, had a full year of experience as community organizers prior to the launching of ERAP. They formed the backbone of several ERAP staffs — and then draft resistance and women's liberation groups — in the years to come. Though not always successful, a very different understanding of collective human striving, fashioned after the blueprints provided by SNCC, had opened spaces for more democratic social relations in American society.

Chapter Seven

1. Zinn, *SNCC*, 99–100 (Donaldson). On Muddy Waters, see the unsurpassed Albert Murray's *Blue Devils of Nada*, *Stomping the Blues*, and *Conjugations*; see also Welding and Byron, *Bluesland*. On increasing violence, see Henry, *Fire Ever Burning*, 141–42. In response to the increased police brutality in 1963, black physicians in Mississippi created the southern Medical Committee for Human Rights (MCHR) to investigate, document, and treat civil rights workers who were beaten, as most local physicians — black and white — were afraid to care for these workers. The doctors who did treat them had loans recalled or lost hospital privileges; many black doctors left the state. The MCHR also arranged for physicians from outside the state to "serve the SNCC and CORE kids and NAACP people." The Medical Committee thus became a critical movement institution. See Robert Smith, "Staying the Course," 213–17.

2. Moses to SNCC Executive Committee, Re: SNCC Mississippi Project, n.d. [Fall 1963], frame 7, reel 40, SNCC Papers.

3. Ibid.

4. Martha Prescod Norman interview. Prescod noted that by Summer 1963, no one in Greenwood still talked about "knocking it out" and going back to school. "SNCC people talked about going to communities and living there for ten or fifteen years. There was a sense of protracted struggle." By 1963 at Yale Law School, Tim Jenkins had been involved in the original push for voter registration projects within SNCC. See Peter Countryman, "Northern Student Movement Coordinating Committee," 10 Nov. 1961, 2, Feingold Papers. On the Freedom Ballot, see "Mississippi Freedom Vote Henry: Planning Details for Freedom Vote for Governor," frames 510–13, reel 27, CORE Papers. See also Watters and Cleghorn, *Climbing Jacob's Ladder*, 66. One mainstay of the Greenwood office was even called "Freedom Smith." He explained to a summer volunteer how he got his name: "Well, I used to be Henry. But I said Freedom so much that my friends jus' said it back to me. Don't matter what people call you, nohow. In my life, I been called everythin' but human" (quoted in Belfrage, *Freedom Summer*, 203).

5. The board of the U.S. Department of Agriculture's Agricultural Stabilization and Conservation Service (ASCS) now determined cotton allotments in the South, a decision traditionally made by local white farmers. "The result of this," explained a SNCC worker, "is that most of the extra acres allotted to each county goes to the big farms and plantations. The small farmers, especially the black small farmers, can hardly get more than a half to two acres over his allotted acres to plant cotton. Cotton money multiplies for those who already have it." The first blacks ran for the ACSC in Mississippi in 1964, and others followed in Alabama and Georgia. Maria Varela, "Report to Mrs. Deborah

Cole . . .," 20 Feb. 1965, p. 5, Varela Papers. For more on the ASCS board elections, see "Negroes Win ACSC Post, but Irregularities Charged," *Student Voice*, 20 Dec. 1965, 1.

6. Moses, *Radical Equations*, 81, 87; Belfrage, *Freedom Summer*, 233; Stokely Carmichael, Staff Meeting Minutes, 23 Apr. 1965, Mary King Papers. Ubiquitous written evidence of this self-activity can be found in reels 36 – 42 of the SNCC Papers, where local people created their own newspapers and newsletters, leaflets, coops, etc.

7. Greenberg, *Circle of Trust*, 63 (Hollis Watkins). The NAACP, CORE, SCLC, and SNCC all needed money to continue their efforts, and COFO provided an umbrella under which all of them could work together rather than compete for scarce resources.

8. Moses interview by Romaine.

9. Moses adopted this device in part from his experiences working on the R. L. T. Smith campaign in Jackson in 1962. Aaron Henry served as COFO's gubernatorial candidate, and Ed King, a white Methodist minister working at Tougaloo, ran as his lieutenant governor. See Henry, *Fire Ever Burning*, chap. 12.

10. As a brief reminder, SNCC took primary responsibility for the First, Second, Third, and Fifth Congressional Districts. CORE workers, led by David Dennis, had the Fourth District. The groups worked as one under the COFO umbrella.

11. Chafe, *Never Stop Running*, 180 – 82; Moses interview by Romaine; Moses, *Radical Equations*, 72. As early as April 1962, Moses noted that "you can't realistically expect action from folks down there [in the rural Deep South] without outside help" (quoted in Laue, *Direct Action*, 219).

12. Moses interview by Carson; Henry, *Fire Ever Burning*, 161; Moses, comments on National Public Radio's "Talk of the Nation," 21 June 2005. See also Moses to "Friend," 2 Aug. 1963, frame 6, reel 40, SNCC Papers.

13. Moses interview by Carson. The clash between Lowenstein and Baker foreshadowed the central political debate of the decade: what were the limits of liberalism? This issue would emerge most visibly in the Democratic National Convention at Atlantic City in 1964 and then again in the presidential election of 1968. During that period, historian William Chafe (*Never Stop Running*, 253) explained, people accused Lowenstein of being "indistinguishable 'from the Hubert Humphreys of the world, working for the LBJs of the world, [who] were manipulating the Aaron Henrys of the world — [all as part of] a massive conspiracy to destroy, or at least subvert, the revolution.'" Lowenstein, on the other hand, saw those who would "hate America rather than [work to] save it" as the ultimate threat. In his view, the Democratic Party was, and should be, "'an instrument of salvation rather than of oppression'; if only people would enter the political process and work to turn things around, the system would respond and peace would come." See Chapter 9 for an examination of what happened when black Mississippians did try to enter the political process. Lowenstein's habit of calling "big name people" did get him out of trouble at least once in Mississippi. Curtis Wilkie, a journalist with the *Clarksdale Press Register* in 1963, was told by a Clarksdale police officer in early 1964 that Lowenstein had been arrested at Aaron Henry's house, but "do you know who that son of a bitch Lowenstein called? He calls Franklin Delano Roosevelt Jr. So we said, 'Holy God! We have to let these guys go.'" Wilkie, "Chicago Insurgents," in Henry, *Fire Ever Burning*, 223.

14. Baker, transcript, "Implications of the Mississippi Civil Rights Movement for America and the World," 1 Nov. 1979, in Mississippi Revisited Papers.

15. Moses interview by Romaine; Dittmer, Introduction to Henry, *Fire Ever Burning*, x. Henry, who worked tirelessly as an advocate for human dignity and progress in Mississippi from his return as a World War II veteran until his death in 1997, hung a sign over the door to his pharmacy: "Through this portal pass the best of the persons on the cutting edge of changing for the better life's opportunities for all citizens." McClinton, "The Legacy," 249.

16. Louis, *We Are Not Saved*, 155; Middlebrook to Miller, 27 Oct. 1963, frame 514, reel 27, CORE Papers.

17. "Notes on Mississippi," n.d. [November 1963], Samstein Papers.

18. Ibid. Highlander served as an important movement house. For background on its role, see Myles Horton, *The Long Haul*; Charles Payne, *Light of Freedom*, chap. 3; Glen, *Highlander*; and Aimee Isgrig Horton, *Highlander Folk School*.

19. Sherrod, Transcript, 30 Oct. – 2 Nov. 1979, MFSR.

20. Moses interview by Romaine; Sherrod, Transcript, 30 Oct. – 2 Nov. 1979, MFSR; Moses in Hampton and Fayer, *Voices of Freedom*, 181; Rothschild, *Black and White*, 21; "Notes on Mississippi," Samstein Papers; Greenberg, *Circle of Trust*, 80 – 81 (Guyot). At the Greenville staff meeting in November 1963, attended by thirty-five blacks and seven whites, Guyot, David Dennis, Fannie Lou Hamer, and Dorie Ladner were among those who argued in favor of the Summer Project. Guyot had an incredibly strong sense of self and was not likely to be cowed by anyone from the North. As SNCC coworker Theresa del Pozzo ("The Feel of a Blue Note," 202 – 3) wrote: "Guyot was able to listen to and work with anyone. He treated a Delta sharecropper, a New York lawyer, a minister, a barber, a high school activist, or a white volunteer with equal respect — or disdain, depending on their actions." Though evidence does not indicate that the following incident was widespread, Jesse Harris reported the opposite: he observed that civil rights workers were arrested "right away" in Yazoo City during the Freedom Vote, despite the presence of whites. Harris, Staff Meeting Minutes, 9 – 11 June 1964, frame 991, reel 3, SNCC Papers.

21. Moses interview by Romaine. See also Moses to SNCC Executive Committee, n.d. [Summer 1963], frames 6 – 8, reel 40, SNCC Papers. Moses argued that even SNCC was unprepared to relocate its headquarters from Atlanta to Mississippi.

22. Hampton and Fayer, *Voices of Freedom*, 183 (Watkins). Ella Baker reported that others in Mississippi felt the same way. See Hattiesburg Meeting Minutes, 24 Jan. 1964, reel 11, SNCC Papers.

23. Hampton and Fayer, *Voices of Freedom* (Watkins, 183; Blackwell, 180).

24. Jane Stembridge to Mary King, 5 – 6 Apr. 1964, Mary King Papers; Holt, *Summer That Didn't End*, 80; Hampton and Fayer, *Voices of Freedom*, 183 (Watkins); *Freedom on My Mind* (video) (Hayes). These sentiments were highly visible in the minutes of the SNCC Hattiesburg meeting at the end of January 1964 to consider the Summer Project. See frames 829 – 30, reel 3, SNCC Papers. I am grateful to Tim Tyson for helping me develop this point.

25. Branch, *Pillar of Fire*, 157.

26. Moses interview by Carson; Moses, in Hampton and Fayer, *Voices of Freedom*,

181; Moses, *Radical Equations*, 73. Jean Wheeler Smith later explained that she and Prescod moved from Albany to Greenwood also in part because Sherrod "wanted to keep and protect us," while the women wanted to be in Greenwood, which they perceived as more "exciting and dramatic and powerful" (quoted in Greenberg, *Circle of Trust*, 138).

27. Peacock described how he was poised to go to Meharry Medical School in Nashville. He had been home "about a week, when Bob Moses and Amzie Moore said to me, 'We need you, man.' So I said, 'OK.' I went and talked to my mother. She was scared. She was definitely disappointed. My father was pretty happy about it because his old partner, his old buddy Amzie Moore was there. They were Master Masons and they were giving signs, and they were like just having a good time about it, you know. But my mother was really upset." Eventually Mrs. Peacock gave her blessing, and Peacock began registering people to vote. Peacock, ‹http://www.crmvet.org/nars/waziri.htm›.

28. Peacock, Transcript of remarks on "Genesis of the Mississippi Summer Project," 30 Oct. 1979, MFSR; Fraser, *1968*, 42 (Sherrod). See also Peacock, ‹http://www.crmvet .org/nars/waziri.htm›. For further background on Peacock, see Charles Payne, *Light of Freedom*, 152.

29. Fraser, *1968*, 42 (Sherrod); Peacock remarks, "Genesis of the Mississippi Summer Project"; "Notes on Mississippi," Samstein Papers. Peacock's reasons for advocating a majority-black or all-black SNCC staff were not "nationalist" so much as practical. This complicates the already-complex project to understand the historical development of black nationalism in the 1960s that Komozi Woodard carefully laid out in *Nation within a Nation*, 5–7. Woodard notes that nationalism emerged in the 1960s as a combination of factors at the urban grass roots, where black community leaders criticized the federally led urban renewal that threatened their neighborhoods' integrity, and African American students, artists, and intellectuals rebelled against bureaucracies that "demanded that African Americans replace their black identities with white ones in order to find a slot in the land of opportunity" (p. 7).

30. Peacock, Personnel Committee Meeting, 10 May 1964, frame 476, reel 12, SNCC Papers. For more historical background, see Giddings, *When and Where I Enter*, 33–37, 43–46, 87, 321–22; Lee, *For Freedom's Sake*, 9–10; Hudson and Curry, *Mississippi Harmony*, 20–23; Olson, *Freedom's Daughters*, 35, 273–76; White, *Ar'n't I a Woman?*, 27–46, 78–81, 165–67; Wells-Barnett, *Selected Works*; Kunzel, "White Neurosis, Black Pathology"; D'Emilio and Freedman, *Intimate Matters*, 35–36, 86, 93, 107; and Henry, *Fire Ever Burning*, 29–31, 70–73.

31. "Notes on Mississippi," Samstein Papers.

32. Greenberg, *Circle of Trust*, 81 (Samstein); "Notes on Mississippi," Samstein Papers. Samstein noted that "there was a lot of back and forth discussion," and he felt that the approval of the Summer Project could have gone either way (quoted in Greenberg, p. 82).

33. Warren, *Who Speaks for the Negro?*, 96 (Moses). As movement historian and adviser Vincent Harding put it, How could blacks be "freed even from the need to hate"? (quoted in Belfrage, *Freedom Summer*, 78). See also Belfrage, 183.

34. Moses interview by Romaine. Another reason why Moses might have used this organizational form was because it was more compatible with patterns of action and

visions of change common among working-class black women — as well as his own background, and that of one of his most important mentors, Ella Baker. Most of the people Moses worked with in Mississippi, whether organizers or community leaders, were people of limited means, and many of the leaders were women. A similar pattern emerges in Nancy A. Hewitt's work on the differences between working-class and middle-class activist styles. See Hewitt, *Women's Activism*, esp. chaps. 4 – 5 and p. 256, and "In Pursuit of Power," 199 – 217. Middle-class reform groups' hierarchical structures did not always resonate for these women, but that did not make working-class protests "spontaneous," as they are often referred to in survey literature.

35. Moses interview by Carson. Moses said the exceptions were Lawrence Guyot and Dorie Ladner.

36. Moses interview by Carson. Comparatively, Moses observed at the time, "the full resources of the state will continue to be at the disposal of local authorities to fight civil rights gains." Moses, Memo to SNCC Executive Committee, n.d. [Summer 1963], frame 7, reel 40, SNCC Papers. The only thing they had that was close, he said, was the work-study program at Tougaloo, Miss. He noted a desperate need for internal education programs in the 27 – 31 Dec. SNCC Executive Committee Meeting Minutes, reel 3, SNCC Papers.

37. Victoria Gray Adams, quoted in *Freedom on My Mind* (video).

38. Moses comments on National Public Radio's "Talk of the Nation," 21 June 2005. Allen's brother, who lived in Milwaukee, reported that Louis Allen planned to move the next day. *Student Voice*, 3 Feb. 1964, 1.

39. Moses interview by Carson. Moses' decision was, in fact, causal: people in the state had begun to mobilize for the Summer Project. He turned to the Atlanta office to try to "sell SNCC" on the endeavor. Ruby Doris Smith Robinson, now working with James Forman, "had a lot of questions about it," Moses recalled (quoted in Hampton and Fayer, *Voices of Freedom*, 184). Forman, however, soon began to lend support, as he realized its potential to draw northern funds into the organization. Lawrence Guyot stated at a conference in 1988 that the first Greenville meeting, chaired by David Dennis, decided against a Summer Project, and that Moses "came in on the second day and threw his mantle in support of the Summer Project and reversed the staff's position — there are tapes of both of these meetings" (quoted in Greenberg, *Circle of Trust*, 80). The *Student Voice* reported that Moses did say, at a conference in Washington, D.C., in late November 1963, that "the experience of SNCC workers in the hard core areas of the South showed that the only hope for Negroes lay in creating a situation which would force a confrontation of federal and state authorities." "Over 300 Attend SNCC Conference," *Student Voice*, 9 Dec. 1963. Moses said that he "favored the Summer Project but held back after the Greenville meeting as the Mississippi staff continued to wrestle with the question." After Allen's death, "there had to be a response, a larger response than we had been able to provide two years before. . . . I spoke up for the summer project, threw all my weight behind it." Moses, *Radical Equations*, 75 – 76.

40. See Michael Thelwell, Transcript of a panel on "Implications of the Mississippi Civil Rights Movement for America and the World," 1 Nov. 1979, MFSR; Moses, quoted in Hampton and Fayer, *Voices of Freedom*, 183; and Henry, *Fire Ever Burning*, 162 – 63. These same questions — whether to focus on local empowerment or bring visibility to

the South — animated other civil rights organizations at the time as well, especially CORE, the only other organization putting significant numbers of people in the field to register rural southern blacks.

Chapter Eight

1. *Freedom on My Mind* (video) (White Citizens Council member).

2. Ibid. (Johnson). See the *Student Voice*: "Police Enlarged; Whites Organize," 26 May 1964, 1, and "Legal Barriers to Greet Workers," 9 June 1964, 2; Rothschild, *Black and White*, 60; and Lee, *For Freedom's Sake*, 77. The state also passed six new laws to frustrate civil rights activity, including a curfew, riot control acts, a ban on the distribution of boycott literature, antipicketing measures, and increased fines for traffic violations.

3. Greenberg, *Circle of Trust*, 64 (Watkins). See also "SNCC Calls on Government to Probe 5 Mississippi Murders," *Militant*, 25 May 1964, Schomburg Center Clipping File, SNCC, fiche 004, 762–1.

4. Committee members sent out promotional materials to northern colleges, set guidelines for volunteer recruitment, arranged a training institute for the volunteers in Oxford, Ohio, in June, and began to prepare Mississippi communities for the volunteers' arrival.

5. Written evidence of Moses' thinking about the necessity of this strategy can be traced to the summer of 1963, though he says that the strategy came out of his work in the winter of 1961–62 on the R. L. T. Smith campaign in Jackson. See Moses to SNCC Executive Committee, Re: SNCC Mississippi Project, n.d. [Summer 1963], frame 6–8, reel 40, SNCC Papers. For an example of the enormous amount of work the MFDP summer challenge entailed, see Moses and FDP Coordinators to All Field Staff, "Emergency Memorandum," 19 July 1964, frames 62–68, reel 40, SNCC Papers.

6. Dittmer, *Local People*, 223 (Cox).

7. Cobb, McLaurin, Guyot, Peacock, Robinson, Watkins, and Harris, Staff Meeting Minutes, 10 June 1964, pp. 12–13, frames 981–82, reel 3, SNCC Papers. See also Tyson, *"Radio Free Dixie,"* 290, 297. Stanford, a part of the Revolutionary Action Movement (RAM), later changed his name to Akbar Muhammed Ahmed. On RAM, see Revolutionary Action Movement Papers, and Sales, *From Civil Rights to Black Liberation*, 100, 130.

8. Block, Cox, Cobb, and Sayer, Staff Meeting Minutes, 10 June 1964, pp. 14–15, frames 982–83, reel 3, SNCC Papers; Belfrage, *Freedom Summer*, 176 (Lynd). See also Ransby, *Ella Baker*, 322–24.

9. At the end of June, Sally Belfrage reported that Moses told the summer volunteers: "No COFO workers, staff or volunteers, would be permitted to carry guns. The police could murder those armed and then claim self-defense. 'We don't preach that others carry guns or refrain from carrying them. You may find some difficult, limiting situations. If you were in a house which was under attack, and the owner was shot, and there were kids there, and you could take his gun to protect them — should you? I can't answer that. I don't think anyone can answer that.'" Belfrage, *Freedom Summer* (Moses, 10).

10. McLaurin and Samstein, Staff Meeting Minutes, 9–11 June 1964, pp. 14–15, frames 982–83, reel 3, SNCC Papers; Belfrage, *Freedom Summer*, 56 (Gregory).

11. Ella Baker, Staff Meeting Minutes, 9–11 June 1964, p. 27, frame 989, reel 3, SNCC Papers. White people's projects in the South failed for the same reason that ERAP projects failed in the North: despite repeated attempts, no one came up with a tactic that dramatized the economic or personal damage that segregation inflicted on the white community. White volunteers in Mississippi tried to work with human relations groups, women's groups involved in public education, and poor whites. In southwest Georgia during 1964, two white women worked full time on "community interpretation" of the civil rights struggle, focusing on white ministers and white women's church groups. They could not find a way to cut through white fear. Mendy Samstein worked on preparations for white people's projects in Mississippi and found what others like Sue Thrasher, Bob Pardun, Katherine Havice, and Edith Snyder would find in both states: liberal whites "were in such despair over the situation that they were unable to function. These groups of whites are generally shocked when we say that we're interested in the problems of poor whites." It was not until the 1970s and 1980s that white communities were organizable, Bob Moses reflected, but by that time they were "out of phase" with the civil rights movement. Samstein, Staff Meeting Minutes, 9–11 June 1964, p. 28, frame 990, reel 3, SNCC Papers; Moses interview by Carson. See also Bruce Maxwell, "COFO's Experimental White Community Project in Biloxi," frames 451–53, reel 40, SNCC Papers; H. Katherine Havice, "Review and Prospectus of Albany Project," 1 Nov. 1964, Sherrod Papers; Pardun interview; and Thrasher, "Circle of Trust," 233–36.

12. Lynd, e-mail to the author, 19 May 2001. "'We Shall Overcome' and 'Kumbaya' are the songs that more than any others were later viewed as corny, both by hardliners in the movement and by smartass folks in the larger culture. Yet this is what SNCC people in extremis elected to sing."

13. Jane Stembridge to Mary King, 5–6 Apr. 1964, Mary King Papers; Holt, *Summer That Didn't End*, 80.

14. Moses interview by Romaine.

15. Sellers, *River of No Return*, 56 (field secretary); Harris, *Dreams Die Hard*, 51.

16. Moses, Staff Meeting Minutes, 9–11 June 1964, p. 10, frame 980, reel 3, SNCC Papers. Moses said that in Mississippi all staff had a general idea of the planned programs. "The tougher problems are the internal ones: is the whole program worthwhile? What are the goals? What is the black-white relationship? Is there a fear by blacks that the movement will be taken over by whites?"

17. King, *Freedom Song*, 327; Rothschild, *Black and White*, 96; Watkins, Staff Meeting Minutes, 9–11 June 1964, frame 991, reel 3, SNCC Papers; Silver, *Mississippi*, 341–42 (Hamer). The orientation sessions were organized by Moses, James Forman, and Mendy Samstein.

18. Rothschild, *Black and White*, 57. Carmichael's disagreements with Lawson grew out of a history of intramovement contention. See Carmichael, *Ready for Revolution*, 306. In Ruleville, Miss., Fannie Lou Hamer's hometown church, Williams Chapel, the site of many movement meetings, was bombed at the end of June 1964, and whites rode

around the black community throwing bottles at homes and cars. The local police never responded to calls for assistance (Lee, *For Freedom's Sake*, 74).

19. Ward Churchill's *Pacifism as Pathology* illustrates in vivid detail the ongoing miscommunication between those who took an unbending view of either armed struggle or nonviolent direct action. A more fruitful way forward would be to go back and debate the advantages and disadvantages of a proposal made by Diane Nash in 1963 that SNCC create a nonviolent army, 25,000 strong, "uniformed and militant, that would undertake such campaigns as surrounding and paralyzing southern state capitals where governors set their faces utterly against integration, stopping transportation by blocking airports, highways, and railroads with their bodies" (quoted in Waskow, *From Race Riot to Sit-In*, 244).

20. "You have to tell people to be very careful," Casey Hayden told Moses. Even as the words left her mouth, she thought: "This is so silly, it doesn't matter how careful they are. There was just nothing to do" (quoted in Hampton and Fayer, *Voices of Freedom*, 189). Chaney and Schwerner worked for CORE and were based in Meridian. They had traveled to Philadelphia, Miss., thirty-five miles away, to investigate a church burning. For more on the Chaney, Schwerner, and Goodman murder, see Huie, *Three Lives*; "Mississippi: Is This America? 1962–1964," *Eyes on the Prize*; and Cagin and Dray, *We Are Not Afraid*.

21. *Freedom on My Mind* (Moses, Parker, and Ganz). The Tolkien reference is from Staughton Lynd, personal interview, 14 July 2001, and Belfrage, *Freedom Summer*, 26–27. The burden of this leadership has been explored in fiction and nonfiction; see, e.g., Burner, *Gently He Shall Lead Them*, and Heath, *The Children Bob Moses Led*. Moses himself consistently pursued a vision of group-centered leadership. See Moses et al., "Algebra Project."

22. Belfrage, *Freedom Summer*, 27; Coles, *Farewell to the South*, 248; *Freedom on My Mind* (Ganz, Wheeler's song). Staughton Lynd recalled that earlier in the day, there was a smaller gathering of SNCC staff. All assumed that the three men were dead. "The meeting began with verse after verse after verse of 'Kumbaya.' 'People are missing Lord, kumbaya.' 'We all need you Lord, kumbaya.'" Lynd, e-mail to the author, 19 May 2001.

23. Holt, *Summer That Didn't End*, 22, 25, 50; Jeannette Parker, unsent letter to the mother of Andrew Goodman, n.d., [ca. 1964–65], Allen Papers (unprocessed). "Unaware of the voter registration workers' efforts in Mississippi—of Herbert Lee, of Louis Allen—and thus inactive during the previous two and a half years, now these parents could not seem to do enough to petition the government for assistance to those in the state." News Roundup," *Student Voice*, 30 June 1964, 4.

24. Stembridge, "Open Letter to America . . . our country," 31 June 1964, King Papers, SHSW; Evans, *Personal Politics*, 73. Four girls, aged eleven to fourteen, were killed in September 1963 when whites bombed Birmingham's Sixteenth Street Baptist Church. The crime was publicized nationwide. See Eskew, *But for Birmingham*, 319–20, and McWhorter, *Carry Me Home*, 518–30. The WATS line digest in the SNCC Papers kept a running summary of incidents. See reel 40, SNCC Papers. According to Watters and Cleghorn (*Climbing Jacob's Ladder*, 139), during the summer there were "35 shooting

incidents with 3 injured; 30 homes and other buildings bombed; 35 churches burned; 80 persons beaten; 3 other murders [in addition to Goodman, Chaney, and Schwerner]." Now, after more than forty years have passed, it might seem reasonable to establish an even more accurate account of attacks on civil rights workers and church burnings in Mississippi during the summer of 1964. However, local law enforcement officers rarely reported such incidents (having committed a good many of these crimes themselves); state agencies did not record whether or not assaults, arson, or murder cases were connected to civil rights work; and the FBI's records are notoriously erroneous in matters of fact on the civil rights movement in general and SNCC in particular. Though the SNCC Papers contain numerous police reports from local law enforcement agencies as well as affidavits petitioning the Justice Department to intervene, there is no way to know if this is "all there was." What seems more pertinent to the story than the exact number of violent attacks on civil rights workers is, How did movement workers respond tactically and strategically to the many incidents of violence that *did* occur?

25. Sellers, *River of No Return*, 102 (sheriff); "Freedom Faith" (video) (Simmons); Testimony of Wiley A. Branton, 16–20 Feb. 1965, *Hearings before the United States Commission on Civil Rights*, vol. 1, Jackson, Miss., 184; "Sabotage in Hattiesburg," *Student Voice*, 18 Feb. 1964, 3 (syrup incident). See also McAdam, *Freedom Summer*, 90, and Belfrage, *Freedom Summer*, chaps. 7–8. For a rundown of incidents, see internal "Staff Newsletter," July–August 1964, frames 12–24, reel 15, SNCC Papers, as well as the 1964 summer issues of the *Student Voice*.

26. Belfrage, *Freedom Summer*, 135; Raines, *My Soul Is Rested*, 283 (Bowie).

27. Staff and volunteers did not always adhere to these guidelines. See Belfrage, *Freedom Summer*, 40–42, 216; Rothschild, *Black and White*, 61–63; Sellers, *River of No Return*, 95; McAdam, *Freedom Summer*, 90; and Evans, *Personal Politics*, 72.

28. Adams interview in Chepesiuk, *Sixties Radicals*, 62.

29. Moses, Staff Meeting Minutes, 9–11 June 1964, p. 10, frame 980, reel 3, SNCC Papers; "SNCC Calls on Government to Probe 5 Mississippi Murders," *Militant*, 25 May 1964, Schomburg Center Clipping File, SNCC, fiche 004, 762–1; Belfrage, *Freedom Summer*, 9; Branch, *Pillar of Fire*, 393 (Moses).

30. Harris, *Dreams Die Hard*, 62, 84; Dittmer, *Local People*, 306–10 (Watkins); Branch, *Pillar of Fire*, 504–5 (Hoover). See also Davies, "J. Oliver Emmerich," 130–31. Interestingly, by November 1964, 650 McComb residents—many of them white—signed a "statement of principles" renouncing violence and supporting "equal treatment under the law for all" (Davies, 131).

31. Sellers, *River of No Return*, 106.

32. Coles, *Farewell to the South*, 211.

33. Sellers, *River of No Return*, 106.

34. "Progress Report I," *Student Voice*, 15 July 1964, 3. Over 2,000 students attended Freedom Schools in the summer of 1964. The saga of the Mississippi Freedom Schools is important in itself. See Taylor Branch's remarkable chapter, "Crime, War and Freedom School," in his *Pillar of Fire*, 427–42; Rothschild, "Volunteers and the Freedom Schools"; Belfrage, *Freedom Summer*, 89–97; and Barbara Ransby, *Ella Baker*, 326–29. Perhaps most important is SNCC's own material on the Freedom Schools. See Charlie Cobb, "Some Notes on Education," n.d., Mary King Papers; Cobb to SNCC Executive

Committee, COFO Summer Program Committee, Re: Summer Freedom Schools, 14 Jan. 1965, frames 60–61, reel 40, SNCC Papers; "The Poor in America: Questions for Discussion in Freedom Schools," n.d. [1964], Mary King Papers; and Freedom Schools, subgroup E, reel 13, CORE Papers.

35. Greenberg, *Circle of Trust*, 83. Examples of how work in the movement's Freedom Schools fundamentally reshaped the educational philosophies of northern volunteers can be found in the Allen Papers; Robinson Papers; and Feingold Papers.

36. The ASCS committee elections were the only ones in the state that had registration, literacy test, or poll tax requirements. The major function of committee members was to tell each farmer how much acreage she or he could allot to cotton. When it became obvious that serious irregularities had taken place during the elections, COFO members reported them to the U.S. Department of Agriculture. In some cases, the federal department ruled that new elections could take place, but it did not change the composition of any ASCS committee. McAdam, *Freedom Summer*, 77; Dittmer, *Local People*, 333–34. SNCC workers imported the information and organizing skills they had acquired in Mississippi in 1963–64 to Lowndes County, Ala., in 1965. See Jeffries, "Organizing for More Than the Vote," 149–50.

37. The MFDP got off the ground on 26 Apr. 1964. For more on the party, see Dittmer, *Local People*; Henry, *Fire Ever Burning*; and Crawford, "African American Women."

38. These black institutions prefigured those formed over the next ten years in the Black Power, counterculture, Chicano, and women's liberation movements, among many others. For example, in January 1964 John Lewis announced that SNCC would support a multicity boycott of public schools in Chester, Pa., Cambridge, Md., Boston, Chicago, New York, Cleveland, Gary and Indianapolis, Ind., Philadelphia, and St. Louis. The boycott, he stated, "should serve to remind the nation as well as local school boards across the country that conditions in Negro schools, North and South, are still separate and unequal." At a November 1964 Freedom School conference, the idea and statewide endorsement of public school boycotts were widely recognized as a legacy from the summer's Freedom School experiments. Rothschild, *Black and White*, 114–15. These anticipated the 3 March 1968 boycott of Los Angeles public high schools by over 10,000 Latino teenagers protesting racist teachers and school policies, lack of freedom of speech, lack of Mexican American teachers, and the absence of classes on Mexican and Mexican American culture and history. According to scholar Carlos Muños (*Youth, Identity, Power*, 64), this was the first major mass protest explicitly against racism undertaken by Mexican Americans in the history of the United States. See *Student Voice*: "SNCC Backs Boycott," 20 Jan. 1964, n.p., and "Boycott Succeeds in Moultrie," 5 Mar. 1965, 1; Dittmer, *Local People*, 336; and Hudson and Curry, *Mississippi Harmony*, 88–131.

39. Hamer, Interview by Stanford students, n.d. [Summer 1965], box 7, Project South Collection. The transcriber could not get Bill's last name. Len, spelled "Lynn" by the transcriber, was Len Edwards, the son of Congressman Don Edwards of California. For more on the reaction of local people to summer volunteers, see Charles Payne, *Light of Freedom*, 306–8; Belfrage, *Freedom Summer*; and Mills, *Light of Mine*, 98–104.

40. *Freedom on My Mind* (Dorsey); King, Transcript of a panel, 1 Nov. 1979, MFSR; Aaron Henry, *Fire Ever Burning*, 170–71. See also Belfrage, *Freedom Summer*, 235–36.

41. Forman quoting Flowers in Greenberg, *Circle of Trust*, 79. The tension between COFO staffers and northern volunteers was visible in bold relief when veteran southern journalists Pat Watters and Reese Cleghorn (*Climbing Jacob's Ladder*, 169) noticed the significant change in McLaurin's staff reports between 1962 and 1964. In 1962–63 they were bowled over by "Mr. McLaurin's reports of obviously deep-felt belief in his work and enthusiasm." But during the 1964 Summer Project, volunteers described him as "withdrawn and hard to get along with." With the benefit of hindsight, the reporters felt they understood the cause of McLaurin's frustration: "The contrast, observed in 1964 by one of the authors, between Mr. McLaurin's handling of a voter registration meeting and the same task undertaken by the white volunteers was the difference between a virtuoso and earnest beginning students." Curtis Hayes noted this as well in *Freedom on My Mind*. See also Joyce Ladner, who reported that Ivanhoe Donaldson, Stokely Carmichael, and Courtland Cox — all northern college-educated blacks — were dubbed the "Howard University crew" because "they studied with Bayard Rustin in New York and they were much more ideological than we locals" (quoted in Greenberg, *Circle of Trust*, 139).

42. "The killing of white mothers' sons" was a phrase used by Ella Baker in August 1964. Angered by the rapid response of the federal government to the killing of Goodman and Schwerner compared to its indifference to the killing of black men, she said: "We who believe in Freedom cannot rest until the killing of black men, black mothers' sons, is as important as the killing of white men, white mothers' sons" (quoted in Reagon and Sweet Honey in the Rock, *We Who Believe in Freedom*, 21).

43. Penny Patch to Mimi Feingold, 7 July 1962, Feingold Papers.

44. Evans, *Personal Politics*, 77–78; *Circle of Trust*, 145–46 (Ladner and Hall). For other SNCC opinions on this issue, see Fleming, *We Will Not Cry*, 154–57, and Olson, *Freedom's Daughters*, 271–74. Bob Moses laid out a decision-making structure for the Summer Project at the 9 June 1964 staff meeting in Atlanta: "In each project area there will be a five man administrative council with the Freedom School Director, the head of voter registration, director of the community center, the lawyer and the minister in the area. In Jackson there will be a group who would have the final review. If SNCC moves to Greenwood, that office would have the review in the Northeast area. CORE would be the group in the 4th district, Hattiesburg for the 5th, and Jackson for the southwest." Moses, Staff Meeting Minutes, p. 11, frame 980, reel 3, SNCC Papers.

45. Rothschild, *Black and White*, 132, 136. The work of Freedom Schools was critical by any measure. They taught children how to act "as if" they were full citizens. Years later, for example, Tougaloo professor and pathbreaking movement historian John Dittmer remembered that he could always tell which of his students had been in Freedom Schools: they did not hesitate to ask questions and challenge the professor, they were comfortable in discussions, and they were not intimated by white professors. Nevertheless, at the time, "the field" was regarded by many in SNCC as the most crucial activity. Remarks from presentations by Dittmer, Charles Payne, and Judy Richardson, "Conversation in the Discipline," 24–26 March 2006, State University of New York–Geneseo, N.Y., notes in the author's possession.

46. Brecht, ["To Posterity"], 74.

47. Feingold, [Summer 1962], Feingold Papers; Sweeney remarks at Stanford, 2 Oct.

1963, Stanford University Archive of Recorded Sound, quoted in Branch, *Pillar of Fire*, 156.

48. See Peter Countryman, "The SNCC," 10 Nov. 1961, frame 205, reel 1, Feingold Papers; Payne, *Light of Freedom*, chap. 6 (quotation, 206); McAdam, *Freedom Summer*, 102, 104; and Belfrage, *Freedom Summer*, 79–80. In fact, the tension between SNCC's southern student core and northern students extended all the way back to its inception, when the students elected Marion Barry as SNCC chairman, in part, as a reaction against "bossy" whites who had been delegates from northern colleges. The missionary attitude of some whites did not bypass northern blacks, Barry believed. Following the Freedom Ride experience, the original SNCC members, nearly all of whom were southern, grew wary of northern blacks as well as whites. "Most of us who were Southerners had become suspicious of a lot of the Northern blacks who were coming down. There was a barely concealed contempt and condescension on their part in the way they treated the local people, as if they saw themselves as liberators," he said. "They thought they were there to teach us everything and they had little sense of how we lived and the danger of our lives in those small towns" (quoted in Halberstam, *The Children*, 306).

49. Casey Hayden interview; Hayden, Speech for panel on "Feminists and Women." The reality led to serious political repercussions in subsequent decades: Why were so few whites able to sustain long-term political relationships across racial lines? How did these few get to be that way? Some communities had to ask volunteers to leave "after incidents such as the white male volunteer in Clarksdale who stayed with a family and insisted on stripping and sprawling over the bed without closing the door in a house full of daughters, or the girl who moved in uninvited with another family and refused to clean up after herself, let alone help with the household chores." When a white volunteer criticized the daughter of a long-term community activist "for not having group spirit when the volunteers had come down to free her, she replied, 'I'm already free — worry about people who aren't!'" (Mrs. Vera Pigee of Clarksdale, NAACP youth adviser, quoted in Louis, *We Are Not Saved*, 193). In the summer of 1964, Hayden, Patch, and Samstein were working out of the Jackson, Miss., office. Hansen, after a stint in Cambridge, Md., and for a time in southwest Georgia, started a project in Arkansas that he directed in the summer of 1964. Bob Zellner was in graduate school in Boston.

50. Here it is important to distinguish the way the veteran SNCC staff felt about the volunteers from the way the local people did. Whereas many staffers grew frustrated by the volunteers, many local people found the volunteers' contributions to be overwhelmingly beneficial. Historians who have previously examined SNCC's work in the state, namely Clayborne Carson (*In Struggle*, 1981), John Dittmer (*Local People*, 1994), and Charles Payne (*I've Got the Light of Freedom*, 1995), have not portrayed the white volunteers in such blunt terms. This seems to me a result of the fact that Payne and Dittmer focused on the interaction between local people and SNCC workers and not as much on the impact that white volunteers had on the internal dynamics of SNCC. Carson, on the other hand, simply had to cover too many other topics in this first, pathbreaking book on SNCC to address the issue at length. Yet the evidence in the SNCC and MFDP Papers is overwhelming, and it comes from both black and white staffers. Furthermore, a clear understanding of this reality is essential to recovering the dynam-

ics leading to SNCC's internal difficulties after 1964, as covered in Chapters 10 and 11.

51. McAdam, *Freedom Summer*, 88 (unidentified Summer Project volunteer); *Freedom On My Mind* (Booth and Gray Adams).

52. *Freedom On My Mind* (Ganz).

53. Fraser, *1968*, 42 (O'Neal).

54. McAdam, *Freedom Summer*, 93.

55. Fraser, *1968*, 42 (O'Neal); Sherrod interview. Sherrod did not separate the men and women to maintain the reputation of the project with either the black or white local people. "What about this community of thirty or forty young people? What about us?" One could not "just allow things to go any way they went, because one little spark, one of us getting mad because one of them was taking another one's girlfriend or boyfriend, and you got an explosion out of proportion to the problem."

56. Sherrod interview. Chana Kai Lee's insightful article ("Anger, Memory," 157–60) on Fannie Lou Hamer considers the tangled issues of sexuality during the Summer Project and the way Hamer's knowledge of her family's own history shaped her anger about some young white women's behaviors. See also Lee, *For Freedom's Sake*, 74–76. Cynthia Griggs Fleming has written an interesting chapter on the complexities of race, gender, and sexual activity during the summer of 1964 for one African American woman, Ruby Doris Smith Robinson. See "Freedom Summer and Sexual Politics," *We Will Not Cry*, 101–41. Lynne Olson has considered these issues in *Freedom's Daughters*, 308–12. On the history of the lack of choice for African American women, see, e.g., Harriet Jacobs, *Incidents*; White, *Ar'n't I a Woman?*; Clinton, *Half Sisters of History*; Clinton and Gillespie, *Devil's Lane*; and Demaratus, *Force of a Feather*. For a particularly useful example of the way sex between white women and black men served as the lynchpin of Jim Crow in this period, see Tyson, *"Radio Free Dixie,"* chap. 4.

57. Fleming, *We Will Not Cry*, 102, 134; Walker, *Meridian*, 106, 220; Peacock, in "Women & Men in the Freedom Movement, A Discussion" (transcript); Rothschild, *Black and White*, 137, 149, 152; Belfrage, *Freedom Summer*, 13 (Harding). Walker's fictional account of Meridian Hill's life between 1963 and 1973 is an important exploration of one woman's attempt to live through the interior disputes that emerged in the movement, "bearing the conflict in her own soul." For a full picture of SNCC to appear, a good deal more work needs to be done to persuade activists, especially African American women, to tell their own stories. One particularly valuable effort, spearheaded by Judy Richardson, Martha Norman, Betty Garman Robinson, and Dottie Zellner, is a collection called "Hands on the Freedom Plow: The Untold Story of Women in SNCC" (manuscript). Until these stories surface, our collective understanding will necessarily be incomplete.

58. Snitow, Stansell, and Thompson, *Powers of Desire*, 25.

59. McAdam, *Freedom Summer*, 106. If a black female activist accused a white or black man of rape, she was unlikely to be "believed" by white authorities. If a white female activist accused a black man of rape, however, there was no way for her to avoid playing into the lethal stereotypes such an accusation by a white woman against a black man always caused. For an overview of these historical burdens, see Giddings, *When and Where I Enter*, and Hall, *Revolt against Chivalry*. Movement veterans learned early that talking about negative interpersonal interactions among themselves was sometimes useful. Talking about these interactions to people outside the movement often

boomeranged against the movement itself. Thus while some women reported when they were sexually assaulted by movement men, the overwhelming number of such assaults went unreported. Yet such stories circulated then and continue to circulate today. Similar issues still rip through the global justice movement. Few women are willing to go on record with details about these incidents. Yet enough women talked about them "off the record" to make them noteworthy.

60. Hall, Cox, Harris, Cobb, and Moses, Staff Meeting Minutes, 9–11 June 1964, pp. 6–8, frames 978–79, reel 3, SNCC Papers.

61. Evans, *Personal Politics*, 72 (Rogoff); Belfrage, *Freedom Summer*, 135 (Carmichael); Watters and Cleghorn, *Climbing Jacob's Ladder*, 53–54 (worker). See also Rothschild, *Black and White*, 61–63, and Sellers, *River of No Return*, 95. Many volunteers tried to vary the tasks they performed each day so as to not be "stale" when they talked to new people. After finding citizens who wanted to register, the volunteers organized classes covering "everything from the particulars of how to fill out the form, to an analysis of the Mississippi Constitution." In some locales, these classes became the basis of adult literacy programs. Since the people most likely to cooperate with the civil rights workers were older women and teenagers, on nearly every project the voter registration classes became a vital connection between COFO voter registration and Freedom School programs.

62. The congressional caucuses also nominated delegates to the Democratic National Convention in Atlantic City—though these delegates were subject to approval by the state convention. Brief Submitted by MFDP for Consideration of Credentials Subcommittee of the DNC, DNC Committee, Credentials Committee of the DNC, prepared by Joseph L. Rauh, Eleanor K. Homes, and H. Miles Jaffe, [August 1964], box 86, Rauh Papers; Holt, *Summer That Didn't End*, 162.

63. "The Democratic Party in Mississippi," n.d. [Spring 1964], frame 553, reel 27, CORE Papers; Brief Submitted by MFDP for Consideration of . . ., [August 1964]; "Over 800 Meet at MFDP Convention," *Student Voice*, 12 Aug. 1964, 4; Mills, *Light of Mine*, 107; Henry, *Fire Ever Burning*, 171–72; Holt, *Summer That Didn't End*, 162. See also Charles Sherrod, "Mississippi at Atlantic City," 12 Oct. 1964, in "The Grain of Salt" (Union Theological Seminary student paper), Sherrod Papers. At its 1960 convention, the regular Mississippi Democratic Party had voted to support both the Constitution and the Bill of Rights but stated: "We believe in the segregation of the races, and are unalterably opposed to the repeal or modification of the segregation laws of this State, and we condemn integration and the practice of non-segregation. We unalterably oppose any and all efforts to repeal the miscegenation laws" (quoted in Joanne Grant, *Ella Baker*, 169).

64. Greenberg, *Circle of Trust*, 77–78 (Hayden). For the WATS line reports, see reels 40–41, SNCC Papers. See also Casey Hayden, "Fields of Blue," 357–58.

65. Aaron Henry to John M. Bailey, Chairman, DNC, 17 July 1964, Rauh Papers; Brief Submitted by MFDP for Consideration of . . ., [August 1964].

66. Belfrage, *Freedom Summer*, 202 (Greene); Watters and Cleghorn, *Climbing Jacob's Ladder*, 16; *Freedom on My Mind* (Dorsey).

67. *Freedom on My Mind* (Gray Adams and Holland); Henry, *Fire Ever Burning*, 175.

68. *Freedom on My Mind* (Gray Adams). At the MFDP convention, five at-large delegates were selected: Lawrence Guyot from Hattiesburg, Fannie Lou Hamer from Ruleville, Dr. Aaron Henry from Clarksdale, Yvonne McGowan from Summit, and a Dr. Miles from Panola County. These at-large delegates accompanied the sixty-eight regular delegates to Atlantic City. "Over 800 Meet at MFDP Convention," *Student Voice*, 12 Aug. 1964, 1.

69. See "Biographical Sketches of Delegates to the National Convention of the Democratic Party," MFDP files, reel 41, SNCC Papers; Claude Sitton, "Mississippi Freedom Party Bids for Democratic Convention Role," *New York Times*, 21 July 1964; Mills, *Light of Mine*, 108–11; and McAdam, *Freedom Summer*, 81. Aaron Henry noted that the MFDP did not have the funds to open a Washington, D.C., office, even after "it became clear that we needed to open an office" there. Ella Baker, he recalled, volunteered to do the job. Henry, *Fire Ever Burning*, 166.

Chapter Nine

1. Dennis, quoted in Hampton and Fayer, *Voices of Freedom*, 195, and in Dittmer, *Local People*, 280 (this and next paragraph). A week before Dennis's speech, SNCC chairman John Lewis and SNCC program director Courtland Cox had met with long-time nonviolent activist Bayard Rustin based in New York, Martin Luther King Jr. of SCLC, Jack Greenberg of the NAACP Legal Defense Fund, Whitney Young of the Urban League, James Farmer of CORE, A. Philip Randolph of the Negro American Labor Council, and Roy Wilkins of the NAACP. Wilkins had called the meeting after the eruption of unrest in Harlem following the police shooting of a thirteen-year-old black boy. The discussion provided a good measure of just how wide and deep yawned the experiential gap between SNCC and CORE on the one hand and other civil rights organizations on the other. Wilkins got everyone in the group except SNCC to agree to a moratorium on nonviolent direct action until after the November 1964 election. Lewis and Cox were stunned: Chaney, Schwerner, and Goodman had been killed, as well as thousands beaten and harassed, in Mississippi over the last three months. Lewis stated: "Negroes must be allowed to protest, for they are very frustrated, desperate and restless. There is a need for some sort of creative expression." "SNCC, CORE Refuse Action Moratorium," *Student Voice*, 5 Aug. 1964, 1.

2. Raines, *My Soul Is Rested*, 276–78 (Dennis).

3. David M. Spain, M.D,, "Post Mortem Examination Report of the Body of James Chaney," Mary King Papers; Branch, *Pillar of Fire*, 509 (statements of James Jordan, 5 Nov. 1964, and Horace Doyle Barnette, 20 Nov. 1964, in a prosecutive summary of 19 Dec. 1964, found in FBI file no. 44-25706-1613). In 2005 *Jackson Clarion-Ledger* reporter Jerry Mitchell wrote that all three had been shot. It is unclear why Chaney's postmortem injuries were so severe. Nevertheless, the fact remains that in August 1964 the movement participants who heard about Dr. Spain's report felt that egregious torture had been inflicted on Chaney *before* he died. See Mitchell's stories on 1 May, 12, 26 June, 17 July 2005, *Jackson Clarion-Ledger*, ‹http:www.clarionledger.com›.

4. Belfrage, *Freedom Summer*, 180.

5. At the Democratic National Convention in 1948, Humphrey confronted the Dixiecrats in a rousing address that excoriated states' rights: "To those who say, my friends, that we are rushing this issue of civil rights, I say to them we are 172 years late! To those who say, to those who say this civil-rights program is an infringement on states' rights, I say this: the time has arrived in America for the Democratic party to get out of the shadow of states' rights and walk forthrightly into the bright sunshine of human rights!" Humphrey, "1948 DNC Address," 14 July 1948, ‹http://www.americanrhetoric.com/speeches/huberthumphey.html› (30 May 2004). In 1964, as Waskow (*From Race Riot to Sit-In*, 268) wrote, "Precisely because Humphrey's greatest strength was among the most vigorous racial equalitarians in the convention, he was expected [by Johnson] to prevent the equalitarians from disturbing the equilibrium of the convention and the party by voting to seat the Freedom delegation." Humphrey reversed his 1948 position in 1964 in order to secure his post as Johnson's running mate.

6. Casey Hayden interview; Rothschild, *Black and White*, 58; *Freedom on My Mind* (video) (Moses). Chana Kai Lee (*For Freedom's Sake*, 79) later wrote: "For local activists, capturing national attention seemed to be based on a rather simple, self-evident premise: Influential outsiders needed only to hear about the political atrocities endured by honest, freedom-loving citizens, and instantly they would move to help by deploying resources and soliciting federal pressure."

7. The Two-Seat Compromise is capitalized to distinguish it from the Green Compromise addressed later in this chapter. It had five components: (1) The regular Mississippi delegation would be fully seated and recognized, (2) The MFDP would get two at-large seats, (3) the MFDP seats had to be filled by Aaron Henry and Ed King, (4) the DNC would form a committee to review each delegation to the 1968 DNC convention to determine whether a state had prevented black participation, and (5) the DNC would challenge delegations to the 1968 convention that prevented black participation. Privately, some members of the Credentials Committee told the MFDP that "it would not guarantee a single registered voter added to the lists in the next four years." Since the Two-Seat Compromise only addressed "voters," it did not guarantee that blacks would be allowed to vote before 1968. MFDP to "All Friends of the MFDP," n.d. [Fall 1964], Rauh Papers.

8. Waskow (*From Race Riot to Sit-In*, 273) reported that to some MFDP delegates, "the Administration offer seemed reminiscent of the old southern etiquette of race relations, in which it was whites who decided whom to recognize as Negro leaders. To some, the offer of two seats rather than a full complement seemed reminiscent of token desegregation, in which a few 'well-scrubbed' Negroes were allowed into southern schools and conferences so long as the much larger number of poor, awkward, and unsophisticated Negroes stayed out."

9. For the formal refusal, see Aaron Henry, Chairman [MFDP], and Edwin King, Committeeman, to John McCormack, Chairman, Democratic National Convention, 26 Aug. 1964, Rauh Papers. For other accounts of Atlantic City, see *Freedom on My Mind*; Branch, *Pillar of Fire*, 465–72; Dittmer, *Local People*, 268–306; and Gitlin, *The Sixties*, 152–62.

10. Waskow (*From Race Riot to Sit-In*, 272) explained further: "To many of the na-

tional [Democratic Party] leaders, ... when 'protest' movements entered party politics they must and should give up their 'protest' style and their purity of conviction, and must be prepared to compromise."

11. Moses interview by Carson; "Bridge to Freedom, 1965" (video) (Forman).

12. Moses, *Radical Equations*, 81.

13. Moses interview by Carson.

14. Hundreds of these affidavits can be found in MFDP reels 40–42 and 63–70 of the SNCC Papers. Excerpts from the affidavits appear in Appendix B; incidents of violence against people attempted to register are cited in Appendix D.

15. A transcript of their testimony, as well as that of others who appeared before the Credentials Committee, can be found in the Rauh Papers.

16. Sherrod, "Mississippi at Atlantic City," 12 Oct. 1964, in "'The Grain of Salt" (Union Theological Seminary student paper), Sherrod Papers. Heightening their sense of a double cross, Humphrey offered the MFDP the Two-Seat Compromise in a suite at the Pageant Motel. Hamer, Aaron Henry, King, and Moses, representing the Mississippi party, "rejected it right there in front of Humphrey and Reuther," Moses recalled, when "suddenly someone knocked on the door, leaned in, and shouted, 'It's over!' and when we looked at the television, there was Walter Mondale announcing that the MFDP had accepted the 'compromise.'" Moses, *Radical Equations*, 81–82; Henry, *Fire Ever Burning*, 186–91.

17. Rauh, quoted in Mills, *Light of Mine*, 112, 114, and in Henry, *Fire Ever Burning*, 177; Jenkins interview by Theodore White, 1 Dec. 1975, quoted in Congress, Senate, *Final Report of the Select Committee to Study Governmental Operations*, book II, 10, 117–18. Johnson's preoccupation with the MFDP seems more a result of pride than political calculation. While there is plenty of evidence that many southern white Democrats would flee the party if it seated the MFDP, Johnson's earlier signing on 2 July 1964 of the Civil Rights Bill left little doubt in the minds of white southern politicians as to where the Democratic Party was headed on race issues. Furthermore, David Niven (*Politics of Injustice*) has argued persuasively that the Democrats had "lost" the white southern vote as early as 1960. More likely, Johnson was concerned that he would lose his native Texas in the November election. That would be a personal embarrassment, but it would not prevent his election in November. See Waskow, *From Race Riot to Sit-In*, 249–56. John Dittmer (*Local People*, 292) found that FBI agents posing as NBC correspondents were able to obtain "off the record information" from MFDP delegates by pretending to interview them. According to Dittmer, correspondence in the president's papers "reveals a constant stream of memoranda to the president's desk during convention week" in which FBI assistant director Deke DeLoach "passed on the FBI reports to Johnson's operatives on the floor, Walter Jenkins and Bill Moyers."

18. Jenkins interview by Theodore White, 1 Dec. 1975. See also Dallek, *Flawed Giant*, 162–64.

19. Jenkins interview by Theodore White, 1 Dec. 1975. See also Dittmer, *Local People*, 292, and Mills, *Light of Mine*, 113. For a vivid portrait of President Johnson's attitudes on race relations, see Moyers, *Moyers on America*, 159–80.

20. *Freedom on My Mind* (Rauh and Sellers); Henry, *Fire Ever Burning*, 177; Rebuttal

of Joseph L. Rauh Jr., counsel, MFDP, before Credentials Committee, DNC, 22 Aug. 1964, box 86, Rauh Papers.

21. Ransby, *Ella Baker*, 332, 340–42; Henry, *Fire Ever Burning*, 198; Sherrod, "Mississippi at Atlantic City," 12 Oct. 1964.

22. Sherrod, "Mississippi at Atlantic City," 12 Oct. 1964. See also Henry, *Fire Ever Burning*, 194.

23. Sherrod, "Mississippi at Atlantic City," 12 Oct. 1964.

24. Ibid. (quotation). Ten delegations supported seating the MFDP prior to the national convention: California, Colorado, Massachusetts, Michigan, Minnesota, New York, Oregon, Washington, Wisconsin, and the District of Columbia. See "Demo Convention Faces Showdown," *Student Voice*, 19 Aug. 1964, 1, 4; "Mississippi: Is This America? 1962–1964" (video); Henry, *Fire Ever Burning*, 193–96; Ransby, *Ella Baker*, 332.

25. Mary King notes on staff meeting in Atlanta, February 1965, Mary King Papers (Hamer).

26. *Freedom on My Mind* (Ganz); Hampton and Fayer, *Voices of Freedom*, 199 (Cox); Belfrage, *Freedom Summer*, 238 (Henry). See also Henry, *Fire Ever Burning*, 183, 191–92, and Lee, *For Freedom's Sake*, 96. Only 17 of the 110 Democrats on the Credentials Committee supported the MFDP after President Johnson offered the Two-Seat Compromise and the MFDP rejected it. See Aaron Henry, Position Paper, 29 Aug. 1964, Rauh Papers. The Rauh Papers also contain a list of the members of the Credentials Committee.

27. Sherrod, "Internal Memorandum," n.d., [Fall 1964], frame 350, reel 41, SNCC Papers. Immediately following the convention, Aaron Henry wrote that of 1,067 telegrams sent to the MFDP about the compromise, 1,011 supported the MFDP's rejection of the Two-Seat Compromise. Nevertheless, after the convention the MFDP sent a letter to "All Friends of the MFDP" giving specific reasons why the compromise was unacceptable. See Henry, Position Paper, Atlantic City, N.J., 29 Aug. 1964, and MFDP to "To All Friends of the MFDP," n.d., Rauh Papers. Sherrod presciently warned: "The real question is whether America is willing to pay its dues. We are not only demanding meat and bread and a job but we are also demanding power, a share in power! Will we share power in this country together in reconciliation or, out of frustration, take a share of power and show it, or the need for it, in rioting and blood?"

28. The MFDP had to fight hard to make this part of the Two-Seat Compromise a reality by 1968. See box 86, Rauh Papers, for the voluminous correspondence, briefings, and back-door politicking it took to make the change. The 1968 Mississippi delegation was half black, half white, and half male and half female. Aaron Henry and Hodding Carter cochaired the delegation; Fannie Lou Hamer was there, and Charles Evers and Patricia Derian were national committee members. The old, all-white Mississippi Democrats sued in federal court and lost. Still, Humphrey asked the integrated delegation to give up some of their seats to the all-white regulars in 1968, with no luck. See Derian, "Moment of Grace," 219–21, and Lee, *For Freedom's Sake*, 162–63.

29. Ellen Levine, *Freedom's Children*, 114 (DeBerry); Fannie Lou Hamer interview.

30. Hamer had been raising this question since at least 1963, effectively organizing others to register by explaining what had happened to her and moving from personal testimony to "sharply focused analysis," as Bernice Johnson Reagon described. In a

Hattiesburg mass meeting in 1963, Hamer said much the same thing she said to the Democratic National Convention: "Now the question I raise, is this America? The land of the free and the home of the brave? Where people are being murdered, lynched, and killed because we want to register to vote!" (quoted in Reagon, "Women as Culture Carriers," 209). A transcript of her testimony in Atlantic City is available in the Rauh Papers.

31. Aaron Henry (*Fire Ever Burning*, 197) reported that 70 percent of the MFDP delegates — 48 people — refused the Two-Seat Compromise.

32. Moses interview by Carson; Viorst, *Fire in the Streets*, 268. Green's proposal had a precedent in 1944, when Texas sent two rival delegations to the Democratic National Convention. President Franklin D. Roosevelt seated both, giving each half of the seats. Lyndon Johnson was in the delegation challenging the regulars. Mills, *Light of Mine*, 117. See also Lee, *For Freedom's Sake* (90–95), whose information on the Green Compromise quotes Arthur Waskow, "Notes on the Democratic National Convention, Atlantic City, August 1964," Romaine Papers, Atlanta. Waskow, at the time a resident fellow of the left-of-center Institute for Policy Studies (IPS) in Washington, D.C., had a doctorate in history and worked on Capitol Hill before moving to IPS. He was present for many of the FDP/Democratic negotiations at Atlantic City. According to Waskow's (*From Race Riot to Sit-In*, 269) account in 1966, the *original* Green Compromise was even more significant: "An oath of loyalty to the Democratic nominees and platform [should] be administered publicly to each delegate from the regular and from the Freedom Party delegation; that each delegate who assented to the oath be seated and all others sent home; and that all the acceptable delegates share the total vote to which Mississippi was entitled." Green had supported the civil rights movement in ways large and small over the previous three years. When SNCC's Cambridge, Md., affiliate, CNAC, brought a group of Cambridge schoolchildren to Washington in Summer 1963, it was Green who spoke with them, as well as arranged a tour of the capitol and a meeting with other sympathetic members of Congress. CNAC Summer Staff, "The Negro Ward of Cambridge, Maryland: A Study in Social Change," September 1963, 19, Phillips and Fein Papers.

33. Henry, *Fire Ever Burning*, 192–95. In December 1964 Rauh wrote to Congresswoman Green: "At a meeting of the Leadership conference on civil rights this past Tuesday evening, William Higgs quoted you as having said, 'Joe Rauh double dealed the MFDP at the convention.' You of course have the right to say that if you believe it. I am wondering if you really said it." Rauh to Green, 18 Dec. 1964, Rauh Papers.

34. Hamer interview (recollection of conversation with Wilkins), Romaine Papers; *Freedom on My Mind* (Moses). Unita Blackwell supported Hamer's contention that Wilkins had called the MFDP delegates "ignorant" (see Hampton and Fayer, *Voices of Freedom*, 203). Moses (*Radical Equations*, 83) noted in 2001 that "to this day I don't think the Democratic Party, which has primarily organized around the middle class, has confronted the issue of bringing poor people actively into its ranks." See also Moses interview by Carson; Sherrod, "Mississippi at Atlantic City," 12 Oct. 1964. For a tirade against SNCC, the MFDP, and Moses in particular by the NAACP's Gloster Current, see Dittmer, *Local People*, 317. And see Ransby, *Ella Baker*, 339–41. In multiple essays, Rustin attempted to convey why he thought the MFDP refusal was a strategic

error. See Rustin, *Strategies for Freedom*, 50–54, and "From Protest to Politics: The Future of the Civil Rights Movement," *Commentary*, February 1965, 25–31, reprinted in Rustin, *Down the Line*. See also Rauh interview by Romaine. Aaron Henry's view of the Wednesday afternoon meeting between the MFDP and the regular Democrats and of SNCC during this period can be found in his *Fire Ever Burning*, 196–98 and 199–203, respectively.

35. Worth Long, *We'll Never Turn Back*, 17 (Varela). Despite these sobering realities, the Voting Rights Act passed in 1965 would increase the percentage of black registrants to 59 percent by 1968. Sitkoff, *Struggle for Black Equality*, 197; Belfrage, *Freedom Summer*, 245.

36. In a 1964 study of 29 of the 82 counties in Mississippi, the U.S. government found that the percentage of white persons registered to vote varied from a low of 52 percent in Lowndes County to 100 percent in Holmes, Issequena, Madison, Marion, and Walthall Counties. The percentage of blacks registered to vote varied from a low of 0 percent in Lamar, Humphreys, Walthall, and Chickasaw Counties, to a high of 26 percent in Tallahatchie County (app. 1–2, *Hearings before the United States Commission on Civil Rights, Hearings Held in Jackson, Mississippi* 1:263–64).

Chapter Ten

1. The staffer was Judy Richardson, reading from her unpublished memoir, 25 March 2006, "Local Studies: A National Movement," State University of New York–Geneseo, notes in the author's possession.

2. Meanwhile, some rank-and-file staffers tried to regroup from the grueling pace of the summer by returning to school. Others continued to work with local leaders, encouraging the fledgling agricultural co-ops, Freedom Schools, and local campaigns for sheriff and school boards. Those who went with Belafonte to Guinea included Moses, Forman, Lewis, Hamer, Dona and Julian Bond, Ruby Doris Smith Robinson, Donald Harris, William Hansen, Prathia Hall, and Matthew Jones. See Forman, *Black Revolutionaries*, 408; Lewis, *Walking with the Wind*, 284; Carmichael, *Ready for Revolution*, 317–18; and Lee, *For Freedom's Sake*, 104. For a detailed interview with Belafonte about his civil rights activities, see *Democracy Now* (radio program), 20 Mar. 2006, ‹http:www.democracynow.org›.

3. Theresa del Pozzo [writing] for Guyot, 19 Sept. 1964, frame 626, reel 1, SNCC Papers.

4. McLaurin, Staff Meeting Minutes, 9–11 June 1964, frame 991, reel 3, SNCC Papers. See also "Report on Selma Workshop: December 13–16, 1963," prepared by Phil Davis, frame 112, reel 6, SNCC Papers. The FCC obligated national TV stations that aired political commentaries to allot equal time to opposing views. Consensus on the objectives of SNCC was problematic for all involved. Two of SNCC's slightly older advisers, Howard Zinn and Staughton Lynd, also found themselves arguing the merits of either federal intervention (Zinn) or building people at the grass roots (Lynd). See Polsgrove, *Divided Minds*, 226–27. McLaurin's objective, building on SNCC's prior experience, was to act in ways that revealed to the nation the repressive imperatives built into the system of segregation.

5. Jeffries, "Organizing for More Than the Vote," 142.

6. Zellner to SNCC-List-serv, 6 Jan. 2005, ‹https://list.mail.virginia.edu/mailman/listinfo/sncc-list›.

7. See Appendix E, "Forman's Speech at Waveland." SNCC's earlier formal layout of structure and the de facto structure that evolved between 1961 and 1964 never totally coincided. In May 1961 the Nashville students described SNCC's structure as follows: "The Coordinating Committee is composed of representatives from the sixteen southern states and the district of Columbia. The making of policy is the responsibility of the general conference, and the execution of fundamental policy is the responsibility of the coordination committee. The twenty-six committee members are elected by the conference and additions or replacements are made by the coordination committee. The annual conference is held in the early fall and the committee meets bimonthly. Policy decisions are handled by an advisory committee between meetings of the conference and of SNCC" ("SNCC," *Voice of the [Nashville Nonviolent] Movement*, vol. 1, no. 3, folder 3, box 74, KMS Papers). This fairly consistently reflected the idea put forward between May and December 1961 in the SNCC papers. After 1961, SNCC office workers often bypassed this structure out of a loyalty to address the urgent needs of field workers in local communities. There is some evidence that Forman developed these ideas very early in his tenure as SNCC executive secretary. In an interview with James Laue on 31 Mar. 1962, Forman said: "There are certain periods in all revolutions when functions have to be taken over. . . . There comes a time when certain transitory powers have to be exercised to carry a movement over." In 1962 Laue interviewed Forman's friend Paul Brooks, who put it more plainly: "SNCC needs a dictator to organize and pull strings and tell us what to do — and I've been trying to get Forman to do this." Laue, *Direct Action*, 217.

8. Martha Norman summarized these traditions: "Everybody ran their own project. Bob Moses used to say, 'When people are volunteering to do things, you can't tell them what to do.' And they were risking their lives. The combination meant that the people doing it made the decisions about what they were going to do." Norman interview. In his autobiography, *The Making of Black Revolutionaries* (p. 430), James Forman noted that it was not until this period that he realized "the gap between my ideas of what SNCC should be and the ideas of most SNCC workers." Stokely Carmichael (*Ready for Revolution*, 429) "agreed with Forman in principle, but the devil was in the details. Besides I couldn't really think of anyone in SNCC with either the desire or the personality to impose that kind of bureaucratic control."

9. Sherrod, "From Sherrod," [November 1964], Ewen Papers (this and next paragraph). This document is one of the few records of the retreat available to the public. All of these records are incomplete, highly abbreviated, and were never voted on by the staff as official minutes of the meeting; they were simply one person's best shot at capturing events during the week-long retreat. Furthermore, no known public archive contains the entire body of position papers from Waveland, but most of them can be found in the Stewart Ewen and Mary King Papers at the SHSW and the SNCC Papers at the King Center in Atlanta.

10. [Moses], "We are on a boat in the middle of the ocean . . .," n.d. [Fall 1964], Mary King Papers.

11. One SNCC staffer wrote: "The confusion that surrounds the working and talking of the committee which met following the [October 1964] staff meeting is very unfortunate. It threatens to tear us apart — to harm the people we are working with — and to waste our time, in that, we *will* be talking about people's personalities and personal relationships rather than the crucial issues that we all agreed were so important." "There was (general agreement) on the question of whether or not, . . ." frames 958 – 59, reel 11, SNCC Papers.

12. Moses interview by Carson. From working alongside other civil rights groups, some SNCC people had been aware of these dynamics for some time. James Farmer worried that SNCC's "projection" after the Freedom Rides would take away money from CORE. His worries reemerged in the spring of 1964 as planning for the Summer Project proceeded. As Dona Richards (Moses) recognized in June 1964, "We should consider the wisdom of SNCC concentrating all its resources in Miss. when it receives comparatively little in return as an organization." The recognition, instead, was going to COFO. "Realize SNCC doesn't want to project itself" the way the other organizations did, she noted, "but we need funds." Dona [Richards Moses], Staff Meeting Minutes, 9 – 11 June 1964, p. 16, frame 984, reel 3, SNCC Papers. Forman's perspective can be found in *Black Revolutionaries*, 429. As early as 1962, he had noted that "this lack of money and lack of organization is responsible for the decline of the so-called spontaneity. . . . There is no social revolution in this country or in the world which can survive without organization. It may *arise* spontaneously, but it cannot survive unless it is encouraged" (interview by James H. Laue, 31 Mar. 1962, quoted in Laue, *Direct Action*, 220).

13. Estimates of SNCC's budget are from the incomplete budget information on reels 11 – 12 and estimates of staff are from reels 3 – 4 and 11, SNCC Papers. As Betty Garman, a former Berkeley student who had worked in Atlanta as northern coordinator during 1964 – 65, had noted earlier in the summer, the "problem with funds is that no system of priority has ever been set up." According to the "Summary of Cash Transactions" for 1 Jan. – 31 Oct. 1964, SNCC had a balance of $86,359.66 on 30 Sept. 1964 and $77, 304.45 on 31 Oct. 1964, but as Forman stated in November, it spent $30,000 each month on salaries (frames 22, 120 – 22, reel 12, SNCC Papers). In June 1964 Don Harris reported that this money crunch did not extend to Mississippi alone; in fact, at the beginning of the summer, the pinch could be felt more acutely in SNCC's other project areas such as southwest Georgia, Arkansas, and Alabama. The executive committee had directed the southwest Georgia project to expand, Harris noted, but did not give it any money. "Have no indication of how many people will be coming to S.W. Ga. nor how they will be supported. Reason our staff took vacations in May was that we couldn't afford to support them. Five of our four cars are broken down and there are no phones. [Willie] Ricks spent 30 days in jail; wouldn't have if [he] had important post in SNCC — some excuse would have been found to get him out fast and money would have been found from somewhere. If you're not going to support us then tell us." Arkansas project director Bill Hansen then said, "Put ditto marks on everything Don said." Staff Meeting Minutes, 9 – 11 June 1964, pp. 22 – 23, frame 987, reel 3, SNCC Papers (Harris and Hansen). For more detail, see Louis, *We Are Not Saved*, 190 – 91. Charles Payne's interviews reveal that the tension over funds in the Mississippi project

actually reached back to 1963. In *Light of Freedom* (p. 366), Payne wrote: "We are still far from fully understanding the causes" of the changes in the organization in 1964 – 65. See also "WATS line report, 4 May 1964, frame 299, reel 15, SNCC Papers. The debate over the purchase of the Atlanta building is in the Executive Committee Minutes, 4 – 6 Sept. 1964, reel 3, and in a Waveland position paper ("The New Building," Mary King Papers), which revealed that SNCC paid $125,000 for the Bethany Methodist Church at the corner of Elizabeth Place and Bankhead Highway in Atlanta, planning to use it for SNCC's administrative offices, printing and publication operations, and an education institute.

14. Forman, interview by Laue, 31 Mar. 1962, quoted in Laue, *Direct Action*, 222.

15. Betty Garman to Ruby Doris Robinson, Chessie Johnson, LaVern Lilly, et al., "Please consider this my resignation from the SNCC Finance Committee," "Summary of Staff Retreat Minutes," [November 1964], frame 716, reel 12, SNCC Papers; Forman to All Staff Members, n.d. [late November – early December 1964], "This is a short memorandum concerning the financial situation . . .," frames 120 – 22, reel 12, SNCC Papers.

16. Dittmer, *Local People*, 329 – 30; [Elaine DeLott Baker], "Name Withheld by Request: Introduction: Semi-Introspective," n.d. [Fall 1964], Sherrod Papers (Baker later claimed authorship of this paper in "They Sent Us This White Girl," 271). In November 1964 the executive committee consisted of 6 staff members, 10 coordinating committee members, 2 advisers, and 3 at-large members (Bernard Lafayette, Marion Wright, and Courtland Cox). Ivanhoe Donaldson had been working for some time as Forman's administrative assistant out of Atlanta. Since the early summer, he noted, the executive committee "doesn't take decisions seriously" and did not follow through on decisions made by the larger group. "Information from one project should be disseminated throughout the others. We only talk about structural weaknesses," he noted. "We never do anything about them." The Jackson office had a similar problem. It had served as the nerve center of the Summer Project, allocating funds from Atlanta, alerting the FBI and press to the ongoing terror faced by local people and staff in the state, and coordinating all COFO programs. Now it too was in disarray. Donaldson, Staff Meeting Minutes, 9 – 11 June 1964, frame 987, reel 3, SNCC Papers.

17. Sherrod, untitled position paper prepared for Waveland staff meeting, November 1964, Ewen Papers.

18. Peacock, remarks, "Genesis of the Mississippi Summer Project," 30 Oct. 1979, MFSR; Norman interview. See also Moses interview by Robert Penn Warren, quoted in Warren, *Who Speaks for the Negro?*, 95 – 97.

19. Dittmer, *Local People*, 330. The CORE troubleshooter was Matt(eo) Suarez, who worked in New Orleans and Canton, Miss. Thirty-five years later, white Jackson staffer Theresa del Pozzo would note that the scholarly literature has highlighted racial strains above the other divisions and tensions within SNCC at this time, "because it's the 'juiciest' subject and feeds America's prurient racial obsession. Therefore, it has been blown out of proportion" (Del Pozzo, "The Feel of a Blue Note," 196 – 97). Del Pozzo's point is an important one, and I hope to do it justice by fleshing out the ways race functioned as only one of a number of stumbling blocks for SNCC in this period. It should be noted that CORE staffers found themselves confronting a similar problem when their own philosophy of nondiscrimination sat uncomfortably against voting majorities of

inexperienced volunteers who had precipitated "scores of incidents in which programs and projects had been severely jeopardized or destroyed by their presence" (Louis, *We Are Not Saved*, 202).

20. Braden, "Images Are Broken,"3; Zinn, *New Abolitionists*, 139 (quotations); Sherrod, untitled position paper prepared for Waveland staff meeting, November 1964, Ewen Papers. At Waveland, Sherrod added still another nuance to his evolving and alarming analysis of the movement: that "our commitment to change in this society has got to be stronger than our feeling for self." As with most of the views offered by Sherrod — and by Nashville veterans like John Lewis and Diane Nash — such philosophical understandings owed at least part of their power to the depth to which the ideology of nonviolence had been internalized in workshops, staff meetings, and nonviolent direct actions in the early 1960s. The only way Waveland participants could stay afloat on Moses' "ocean," observed Sherrod, was "to be honest during this conference." Furthermore, "there is a great need to curse and swear and fight and tear away at the masks which each of us wears." If they were unable to reestablish the strong interior lines of communication, he warned, how could they remain strong enough to fight their opponent outside of the movement? Without internal honesty, they would be crushed like "grasshoppers fighting the sleeping giant. When the giant awakens and puts on a unified armor, we're going to have hell to pay." (It is important to distinguish Forman's call for *unity* from Sherrod's call for *honesty*. Sherrod had earlier asserted: "Nonviolence as a way of life is a long way off for most of us. The best that can be said is that our great advantage is the work of the church in the South, or lack of the same. . . . The point where the church stops must be *our* point of entry." Sherrod, "Non-Violence," n.d. [1962?], frame 1235, reel 7, SNCC Papers). See also Lynd, Introduction to Moses, transcript of a tape recording made in Fall 1962, reprinted in "Mississippi, 1961–1962," 7; Moses interview by Carson; Moses, "We are on a boat in the middle of the ocean . . .," n.d. [Fall 1964], Mary King Papers, SHSW. Sherrod's commitment to interracial organization has been explored at length in Chapter 3.

21. Sherrod, Minutes, "Report on Selma Workshop: December 13–16, 1963," prepared by Phil Davis, frame 110, reel 6, SNCC Papers; Sherrod, Transcript, 30 Oct. 1979, folder 2, MFSR.

22. [Elaine DeLott Baker], "Name Withheld by Request: Introduction: Semi-Introspective," n.d. [Fall 1964], Sherrod Papers.

23. Norman, "What Is the Importance of Racial Considerations among the Staff?," Ewen Papers.

24. This need intensified after SNCC staff witnessed the nation's genuine concern for movement workers, as John Lewis stated, "only after two white boys are missing." He echoed Schwerner's wife Rita, who said "if Chaney had been alone when the disappearance occurred no one would ever have noticed" (quoted in "Chairman Requests Federal Marshals," *Student Voice*, 30 June 1964). This search for space to talk out of the earshot of whites was a dynamic repeated later in the decade when the women's and gay liberation movements split from other New Left organizations. As Andrea Eagan reported of her time in the film collective, Newsreel, "It was in Newsreel that I achieved the revelation that it was a no-win situation for women. If you didn't say anything, you were accused of not saying anything; if you said anything you were accused of talking

too much and thinking incomprehensible goop. That's when I went into the women's movement for ten years. Didn't work in a mixed group until the writer's union" (Eagan interview).

25. Moses interview by Carson.

26. Dona [Richards Moses], Staff Meeting Minutes, 9–11 June 1964, p. 16, frame 984, reel 3, SNCC Papers. "Can you make integration a goal and not live it? Could SNCC integrate itself and live as kind of an island of integration in society's sea of separation? Of course, it's a still unresolved problem of this country and in the end SNCC foundered on the question," Moses (*Radical Equations*, 73) wrote in 2001. Others had also tried to get the issue of race out and talk about it. Stokely Carmichael noted in the October 1964 staff meeting that the group "must consider the color question" when hiring summer volunteers who had expressed the desire to stay on. The next five speakers at the staff meeting ignored Stokely's point until, again, Moses spoke to it: "Motion doesn't speak to problem. Are mechanisms set up for absorption of additional staff to be based solely upon one year's commitment and work in the field? We must consider color question, the sophistication of the volunteer, the possible fall out." Carmichael, Moses, Staff Meeting Minutes, 11 Oct. [1964], pp. 10–11, frames 1020–21, reel 3, SNCC Papers. Moses later insisted that this separatist impulse was most fruitfully viewed in the context of events across the globe in this period—including anticolonial freedom movements in Africa, Asia, and Latin America, and in particular the emergence of independent African nations. Clayborne Carson, *In Struggle*, 37; Moses interview by Carson.

27. Ella Baker, Staff Meeting Minutes, 9–11 June 1964, p. 31 [mistakenly labeled pp. 30–32], frames 991–92, reel 3, SNCC Papers.

28. Atlanta Office to Friends of SNCC, Re: McComb, Miss., 24 Sept. 1964, frames 200–202, reel 14, SNCC Papers.

29. Forman to "All Staff, Friends of SNCC, and Potential Members of the Freedom Corps," n.d. [early Fall 1964], frame 679, reel 12, SNCC Papers. Forman had mentioned the Black Belt Project in a June 1964 staff meeting: "We should begin to view MSP [Mississippi Summer Project] as pilot project and after summer begin a black belt project." In a memo to all SNCC staff before he left for Guinea, he listed six positions that would be opening on the Black Belt Project. Despite the fact that the full staff had not yet agreed to it, Forman's memo indicated that the project had been approved by the executive committee in September 1964. Forman, Staff Meeting Minutes, 9–11 June 1964, pp. 24–25, frame 988, reel 3, SNCC Papers; Forman, *Black Revolutionaries*, 414, 416, 426, 429. Forman writes that "Moses and I were [the Black Belt Project's] chief proponents"; however, in his interview with Clayborne Carson in 1982, Moses specifically stated that he did not support the project. And at the time Ella Baker advised: "We should accept the concept that our first consideration is to solidify the programs we have; and the second step is to establish a nucleus in one or two areas in which we can develop programs via workshops and exploratory meetings. Do not commit selves to summer [Black Belt] project." Baker, Staff Meeting Minutes, 11 Oct. [1964], p. 6, frame 1018, reel 3, SNCC Papers. The October 1964 debate on the Black Belt Project can be found on frames 1016–21, reel 3, SNCC Papers. From the minutes, it appears that among those who supported it in the fall of 1964, in addition to Forman, were

Courtland Cox, Mendy Samstein, and Ivanhoe Donaldson; those cautious, hesitant, or skeptical included Baker, Ed Brown, Charles McLaurin, Tom Brown, Lawrence Guyot, Ruby Doris Smith Robinson, and Marion Barry.

30. Forman suffered from bleeding ulcers. See "SNCC [Interstaff] Newsletter," 21 Jan. 1963, frame 4, reel 15, SNCC Papers. On Forman's confrontations with southern sheriffs and other authorities, see *Student Voice*, October 1962, 20 Jan. 1964, and 20 Dec. 1965, as well as Forman, *Black Revolutionaries*, 197, 257, 303, 329.

31. See Appendix E, "Forman's Speech at Waveland."

32. Though many academic attempts have been made to explain this relationship between self-activity and changes in individual consciousness, I know of none better than the description given by Debbie Louis (*We Are Not Saved*, 114), herself a COFO worker: "But the *words* we use — 'intensity,' 'determination,' 'commitment' — are simply not enough to communicate what they meant to southern movement workers. It was *a change in oneself*, perhaps also impossible to describe, that essentially resulted from this experience. . . . It is essential also to define that 'something,' for it is *the* key to understanding the nature of those we are concerned with here. It has been called a 'quality of suffering' a 'loss of fear,' and I have often seen the transition likened to a deep religious experience.

"Perhaps it can be viewed as the sudden discovery of one's own individual power, perhaps of one's own individuality itself, or perhaps more simply one's ability to determine his own existence. For the experience itself came from one's *own* decision to act in a particular way upon one's *own* conception of truth, and accept the consequences of that act. The ensuing discovery, once that decision had been made and irrevocably acted upon, was *that those consequences could be survived. What this leads to is the recognition of the act, and not the consequence, as the important thing in relation to oneself. It is, in other words, learning that one can do what one wants* to do; if the reason for an act justifies it to oneself, if the ultimate purpose in which one is convinced (even if only at the time of decision, and later regarded as an objective mistake) is served by that act, its consequences to one's person are in fact irrelevant. It is, less philosophically, discovering that one *can* act contrary to 'reason,' to social sanctions, to overwhelming physical power, and still function in their midst, not be destroyed by them."

But this understanding was not then, nor is it now, widely shared in U.S. political culture. David Chappell (*Stone of Hope*, 2), for instance, has separated organizing/action from culture and consciousness. He writes that the "civil rights struggle did not consist entirely of politics and grassroots organizing, as books and documentaries on the subject have so far implied. It also involved a change in American culture, a change in what Americans thought and felt when they talked about things like freedom, equality, and race."

33. For this incident, see Introduction.

34. Sherrod pressed the activists to examine SNCC after five years in the field. Who were they as organizers, and who did they want to organize next? to what end? These questions "flowed out" of what was for them "the central issue": What was SNCC? "Who we are and who we will be should determine what we want, what direction we go in." Sherrod, "From Sherrod," n.d. [November 1964], Ewen Papers.

35. Smith, Staff Meeting Minutes, 11 Oct. [1964], p. 4, frame 1017, reel 3, SNCC Papers.

36. Moses, Staff Meeting Minutes, 9–11 June 1964, p. 11, frame 980, reel 3, SNCC Papers. See also Moses interview by Carson.

37. Forman, *Black Revolutionaries*, 416–17; Moses, Staff Meeting Minutes, 9–11 June 1964, p. 11, frame 980, reel 3, SNCC Papers (quotation); Moses interview by Carson. Moses supported the concept of group leadership, rather than leadership by individuals. A telling example was his decision to reject CBS Television's proposal to interview Governor Paul Johnson, then Moses. Moses declined "because I didn't want myself projected as [a] leader as [I] would be if [I sat] next to Johnson. Concept of group leadership more important to get across. Decided we'd focus on a group which was representative not necessarily of the decision-making group in COFO but of COFO itself." Moses, Staff Meeting Minutes, 9–11 June 1964, p. 21, frame 986, reel 3, SNCC Papers. These ideas of nondirective leadership are also clearly articulated in the position paper Maria Varela wrote for Waveland, "Training SNCC Staff to Be Organizers," in Sherrod Papers. Ivanhoe Donaldson ("A True Believer," 218) reiterated this years later: "SNCC often pooh-poohed existing leaders no matter how we loved them, even our own. I remember us thinking that to be chairman of SNCC was the worst thing and that the chairman's only purpose was so the outside world would have someone to talk to. Within SNCC, the chairman was just a co-equal; people didn't have to pay any attention to the chair." For an example of how Forman's view of leadership did not just dominate but wholly colored the historiography of the movement in the eyes of some historians, see Chappell, *Stone of Hope*, 78–80, who writes that Moses had a "nearly pathological aversion" to the use of power. That is incorrect—Forman's and Moses' definitions of power and beliefs in how to wield it simply diverged.

38. Forman, *Black Revolutionaries*, 422. "Freedom High" surfaces in the SNCC Papers for the first time, to my knowledge, in May 1965, in Mary King's minutes of the staff meeting at Gammon Theological Seminary, SNCC Papers. Forman uses the term in *Black Revolutionaries*, 422.

39. Forman, *Black Revolutionaries*, 413, 416–19, 425, 436–37, 552. Prior to the staff meeting in October 1964, Forman himself provided evidence that he had been making many administrative, financial, and program decisions unilaterally rather than by consensus, though he often called particular field staffers first for consultation (ibid., 429, 431, 438). Forman also laid much of the problem for the dissolution of trust at this point to a "vote" to add eighty-five volunteers to the staff (ibid., 420–21). It remains unclear from the SNCC Papers and from oral histories as to whether such a vote ever took place at the October 1964 staff meeting. Instead, some staff members said that they simply received a memo at the end of the summer that mentioned the volunteers who were "staying in the state," a change not discussed with the staff as a whole. On the issue of "middle-class impact," Forman claimed that it particularly influenced Moses (ibid., 416–19). Given Moses' insistence on working with local leaders in the MFDP, this charge seems impossible to sustain.

40. The number of references to "middle-class" SNCC workers as part of the problem in this crucial section of Forman's history of SNCC is staggering. See Forman, *Black Revolutionaries*, 413–14, 416–19, 425, 431, 434–35, 437, 440, 444. The weight that Forman gives to class as an explanation for people's actions indicates that we as a culture need more precise terms of description to explain why people do the things they do

in addition to whatever class they come from or reside within. Certainly more precise descriptors would illuminate in finer detail the complex reasons why the staff began to fracture at this point. Class orientation simply cannot account for the entirety of the reasons why they began to split. For instance, Moses, Sherrod, and Casey Hayden were all from families without great means. Furthermore, they did not adhere to middle-class lifestyles or values.

41. Ibid., 412.

42. Ibid. Lawrence Guyot later voiced the impact this divide had on staff in February 1965, as the group still struggled over the structure question. Guyot asserted: "I'll work with anyone willing to work" rather than "polarize about structure. . . . We were told what we needed was a structure to operate. That's intimidation, only we didn't know it" (quoted in Staff Meeting Minutes, February 1965, 9, Mary King Papers).

43. For the complete text of Forman's proposal, see Appendix E.

44. Clayborne Carson, Charles Payne, Barbara Ransby, Cleve Sellers, David Chappell, and Stokely Carmichael all use either these terms or the similar "hard-liners and float-ers" formulation.

45. Forman, *Black Revolutionaries*, 436. It was following the October 1964 staff meeting, Forman recalled in his memoirs, that he felt for the first time that "careful planning and control of SNCC meetings" was an "absolute necessity." There is some contradiction in Forman's account about when he began to perceive a faction working against him. On p. 419, he puts it following the Gammon conference in October 1964. On p. 433, it is between his return from Atlanta and the Waveland conference. On p. 436, he says it is immediately after Waveland. The matter is relevant because at whatever point he began to feel a faction was being organized against him, he responded in a way that fundamentally changed the organization. His opening speech at Waveland represented a departure from usual SNCC practice, a departure that became more common in subsequent years.

46. Smith, "Position Paper #1," Ewen Papers.

47. "Report on Selma Workshop: December 13–16, 1963," prepared by Phil Davis, frame 110, reel 6, SNCC Papers.

48. Individuals who had been a part of SNCC continued to pioneer new democratic forms, but the organization had reached its limit.

49. Carmichael presents one of the most efficient and clear portraits of this breakdown of SNCC culture in *Ready for Revolution*, 429–33. No individual can be saddled with sole blame for the predicament that engulfed SNCC. Every voluntary organization must struggle with these issues.

50. Charles Payne, *Light of Freedom*, 367 (Baker); Forman, *Black Revolutionaries*, 412–14, 418–19, 425, 431, 434–35, 437, 440, 444. See also Sellers, *River of No Return*, 133.

51. Greenberg, *Circle of Trust*, 139 (Wheeler Smith).

52. Group interview [Muriel Tillinghast, Kathy Archibald, Bill Hansen] by Carson, 6 Nov. 1976, Atlanta. The second unidentified woman continued: "And if you look at it that way, then the hierarchical stuff just doesn't matter that much, and I don't think it mattered at least until 1965."

53. Greenberg, *Circle of Trust*, 22 (Nash); Nash interview. According to Doug McAdam (*Freedom Summer*, 112), 80 volunteers stayed on in Mississippi at the end of the Summer

Project. The question of how summer volunteers joined the SNCC staff has never been fully resolved. In May 1964 there were 136 staff members ("Support SNCC Now," *Student Voice*, 5 May 1964, 3); by September that number had grown to over 200. Forman later claimed that he and Ruby Doris Smith Robinson led the group opposing the retention of summer holdovers for fear they were FBI informants. As he remembered, a vote was taken and the summer people were put on the staff. See Forman, *Black Revolutionaries*, 421. Some SNCC people did not recall such a vote. All other sources cite Forman. See Dittmer, *Local People*, 318, and Chappell, *Stone of Hope*, 236. At the 11 Oct. 1964 staff meeting, in which a good deal of time was spent talking about this issue, Betty Garman noted that "there are 61 people who are now in need of support. 30 of these people have been put on staff by Jesse Morris as of Sept. 28. There has been fund raising by support groups that are not FOS groups. These support groups are demanding letters from volunteers whom they support — letters are not forthcoming. This is not a reliable way of soliciting funds." Staff Meeting Minutes, 11 Oct. [1964], p. 9, frame 1020, reel 3, SNCC Papers.

54. Powledge, *Free at Last?*, 205 (Lewis).

55. Forman, Minutes, 27–28, frames 951–52, reel 11, SNCC Papers.

56. Jemott, Minutes, 10 Nov. 1964 (p. 29, frame 953, reel 11), and "Summary of Staff Retreat Minutes," [November 1964] (p. 4, frame 718, reel 12), SNCC Papers.

57. Forman, "Memorandum on the Structure of the Student Nonviolent Coordinating Committee," submitted to staff at Waveland [November 1964], Mary King Papers; Forman, *Black Revolutionaries*, 435–37. See also Appendix E, "Forman's Speech at Waveland," and Forman, "What Is the Student Nonviolent Coordinating Committee: A Band of Brothers, A Circle of Trust," prepared for the SNCC staff retreat of Nov. 1964 ...," in Mary King Papers. This had been Forman's job during the previous four years. Forman suggested that the executive secretary appoint at least seven administrative people who would report to him: an administrative assistant, a program secretary, someone to run the Jackson office, a northern coordinator, a southern campus coordinator, a director of communications, and a research director.

58. "Group 5, Francis Mitchell Chairman," n.d. [November 1964], Mary King Papers, and; Mitchell, Minutes, 10 Nov. 1964, pp. 32–35, frames 954–55, reel 11, SNCC Papers; Appendix F, "Suggested Structures for SNCC." The latter two groups differed in their decentralized structure. A decentralized structure would later be suggested by Greg Calvert within SDS. Indeed, Charles Payne (*Light of Freedom*, 369) argues that such a structure was endorsed by Ella Baker: "She envisioned small groups of people working together, but also retaining contact in some form with other such groups, so that coordinated action would be possible whenever large numbers were really necessary. I know of no place where she fully explains her thinking, but, given her values, it is almost certain that she would have been put off by the undemocratic tendencies of larger organizations as well as by their usual failure to provide the kind of environment that encouraged individual growth. I suspect that she also favored smaller organizations precisely because they were less likely to factionalize or develop climates of distrust." Baker's position on structure, however, is made a bit more obscure by her remarks at a Personnel Committee Meeting in May 1964, where SNCC people discussed a wide range of structural problems within the organization. Baker noted: "Some jobs are

more specific, i.e., well run offices, fund raising, bookkeeping, etc. [SNCC people] have been running away from structure, established procedure" (Baker, frame 480, reel 12, SNCC Papers).

59. Moses, "We are on a boat in the middle of the ocean," n.d. [Fall 1964], Mary King Papers. The decentralized model mirrored several of the position papers prepared for Waveland. "All persons and officers involved in SNCC programs should be nominated and elected by the staff," wrote Frank Smith, for "the only way for the staff to make its own program and to make sure that the programs get run the way it wants them run is to make sure that it puts people into positions that it trusts and has confidence in" (Smith, "Position Paper #1," Ewen Papers). Prathia Hall asserted the same idea at the last staff meeting before the Summer Project in June 1964. SNCC could hold staff accountable for implementing decisions only "if people feel a part of the decision making process." Decisions must "come from the project up" (Hall, Staff Meeting Minutes, 9 June 1964, reel 3, frame 976, SNCC Papers). See also Casey Hayden, "Fields of Blue," 363–64, and James Pittman, untitled paper, n.d. [November 1964], Mary King Papers.

60. For this discussion, see Appendix G, "Structure Debate at Waveland." And see Minutes, 12 Nov. 1964, 39, frame 957, reel 11, SNCC Papers. At the subsequent Planning Committee Meeting, held in Pine Bluff, Ark., staff disagreed about what had actually been decided or not decided at Waveland. See, e.g., John Lewis's memo to staff over "alleged coup" in SNCC and "red-baiting of SNCC" and Mary King's response in Lewis to All SNCC Staff, n.d. [Winter 1964–65] (frame 23, reel 2), and King to Lewis, 10 Jan. 1965 (frame 650, reel 1), SNCC Papers.

The discussion of structure continued at the next full staff meeting, held in Atlanta in February 1965 (for partial minutes, see Mary King Papers). It is unclear if or when a structure was actually decided upon, or if the alternatives presented at Waveland ever received a vote. "Summary of Staff Retreat Minutes," [1964], frame 716, reel 12, SNCC Papers; Clayborne Carson, *In Struggle*, 149. Though in hindsight Waveland can be seen as a pivotal moment for the grassroots southern movement, no one has ever noted that Forman's plan was actually a "minority position." In the minutes of the retreat, a majority of those voicing their opinion were highly skeptical of centralization; indeed, two of the three proposals for a new SNCC structure rejected hierarchy, and Forman himself admitted that his ideas were out of sync with those of most SNCC people. Most accounts merely say that over the course of 1965, a hierarchical structure was implemented. South Carolinian and summer recruit Cleve Sellers (*River of No Return*, 131) wrote that during this period SNCC workers lost the "zip and enthusiasm that had kept us going in previous times."

Chapter Eleven

1. For chronicles of other groups that experienced the same tensions between hierarchical and decentralized forms within the all-black Detroit Revolutionary Union Movement and the women's group JANE, see Georgakas and Surkin, *Detroit, I Do Mind Dying*, and Kaplan, *Story of JANE*. Within SDS, these debates over structure took on labyrinthian proportions. Ominously, debates often ended with the slogan to "Let the People Decide," which did not provide specific democratic processes through which

people could hold others accountable. See Sale, *SDS*, and James Miller, *"Democracy Is in the Streets."* Within CORE, the same tension between project people and structure people occurred at its national convention in Durham in the summer of 1965. See Louis, *We Are Not Saved*, 266–67, and Meier and Rudwick, *CORE*, 379–408.

2. Emmie Schrader Adams ("From Africa to Mississippi," 322) points out that "this was a period of prolonged lull," but what struck her about the histories of the movement "are the lulls. The focus shifts from place to place. . . . No one writes much about what was happening in the lulls when the focus moved elsewhere." The attempts to increase Atlanta/field contacts can be found in the papers of SNCC's Communications Department, reel 14, SNCC Papers.

3. Marion Barry, Minutes, 9 Nov. 1964, p. 26, frame 951, reel 11, SNCC Papers. On Lowndes County, see Jeffries, "Standing Up for Freedom" and "Organizing for More Than the Vote"; Hullet and Carmichael, *Black Panther Party*; Minnis, *Lowndes County Freedom Organization*; and *Lowndes County Freedom Movement* and "The Time Has Come, 1964–1966" (videos). The MFDP also spun off organizations to work on issues including welfare distribution, low-income housing, and education. Evidence of their activities can be found in MFDP Papers and WATS Line Reports (frame 520 passim, reel 14), Marion Barry, Minutes, 9 Nov. 1964 (frame 951, reel 11), and Minutes, 12 Nov. 1964 (frame 955, reel 11), SNCC Papers, as well as in Charles Sherrod, "From Sherrod," [November 1964], Ewen Papers. The issue of different values and priorities between SNCC staff and MFDP organizations emerges throughout the SNCC minutes. See, e.g., Ed [Brown], "Transcription of MEK Notes, Feb '65 Atlanta SNCC Meeting [historic]," Mary King Papers.

4. See "Rough Minutes of a Meeting Called by the National Council of Churches to Discuss the Mississippi Project," 18 Sept. 1964, Mary King Papers. Moses said that these minutes, which showed the clear danger of SNCC's lack of an independent economic base, were distributed within SNCC but no one responded to the warning (interview by Carson). Paralleling this thinking, Sherrod noted in November that "the dollar will increasingly become hard to get." The problem was that one could not simultaneously fight state policies and ask the state for economic support. "That's the mistake we made in SNCC and CORE and SCLC," he stated years later. "An organization could not bite the hand that fed it." Sherrod, Untitled Position Paper Prepared for Waveland Staff Meeting, November 1964, Ewen Papers; Sherrod interview. "They're still making the same mistake," Sherrod said of the major civil rights organizations in the 1980s.

5. Moses interview by Carson; Forman, *Black Revolutionaries*, 430. It is interesting that most social insurgent groups that have been able to carry on over the long haul have developed their own economic base; prominent among these are religious institutions, labor unions, and, most recently, gay and lesbian advocacy organizations.

6. Moses interview by Carson. Moses said that Forman was unwilling to get the question of the problematic financial base out into the open and discuss it. Following Atlantic City, Moses saw no point in organizing with SNCC if it did not have an economic base of its own. "It wasn't possible to get people to see" how important this question was until SNCC issued its first self-consciously "radical" statement. At this point, he recalled, their funds were "completely swept out from under them with no prepara-

tion, no anticipation of an alternative source of support." He had waited nearly two years for these "basic problems" to surface, but when they had not been addressed by 1966, Moses chose to stop working with SNCC. For evidence that Moses saw SNCC as the energy source at the time as well as in hindsight, see his comments in Staff Meeting Minutes, 9–11 June 1964, p. 12, frame 981, reel 3, SNCC Papers: "COFO isn't a source of energy for change. . . . SNCC is committed to develop groups like COFO, which is similar to the Albany and Cambridge movements." For corroboration of how quickly liberal funding dried up, see Elizabeth Sutherland [Martinez], "Desperation Memorandum" to Stokely Carmichael and Ruby Doris Robinson, 23 May 1965 [*sic*: should be 1966], frame 76, reel 12, SNCC Papers. Moses moved to Canada, then taught math in Tanzania for a decade. At this writing he served as the director of the Algebra Project (started with a grant from the MacArthur Foundation), spending half of his time in Cambridge, Mass., and half in Mississippi. For more on his post-SNCC trajectory, as well as his views on the movement, see Moses, *Radical Equations*, and Moses interview by Carson, 48. In November 1964 Moses had been more specific: "When labor is organized, it can only discuss a narrow aspect of the problem: wages. [Founding director of the United Auto Workers, Walter] Reuther sat in the meeting with [Martin Luther] King, [Hubert] Humphrey, and others to urge the [M]FDP to accept the compromise, talking anti-Goldwater, keep morality out of politics, etc. Two weeks later the union struck in the middle of the campaign on the issue of 'human dignity.'" Moses, Minutes, 9 Nov. 1964, frame 948, reel 11, SNCC Papers. SNCC's executive committee minutes of 4–6 Sept. 1964 show how hard it was to generate an independent economic base. "There is a need for people to engage in Fund Raising only," the group decided. "This type of creativity has to be continued." Moses suggested meetings and workshops on how to best manage funds, but it is unclear if such events ever took place. SNCC people also agreed that they needed a structure but were wary of the building Forman had in mind. Several people — Marion Barry, Frank Smith, Jack Minnis, Prathia Hall — opted for a committee to investigate alternatives. SNCC Executive Committee Meeting Minutes (incomplete], 4–6 Sept. 1964, pp. 4–6, Casey Hayden Papers. In the wake of the Waveland meeting, Forman put together a finance committee in the Atlanta office that consisted of Prathia Hall (chair), Betty Garman, Ruby Doris Robinson, and Chessie Johnson. The group was set up to work with people traveling in the field — Courtland Cox, Ivanhoe Donaldson, and John Lewis — to assess needs and disburse funds. James Forman to All Staff Members, n.d. [Late November – Early December 1964], "This is a short memorandum concerning the financial situation . . .," frames 120–22, reel 12, SNCC Papers. See also Joann Gavin, "Position Paper: Funds-Sources and Staff Salaries," n.d. [November 1964], frame 787, reel 12, SNCC Papers.

7. Louis, *We Are Not Saved*, 232.

8. Greenberg, *Circle of Trust*, 36 (McDew). See also Sherrod interview. This understanding was indeed shared by others. As Charles Jones asserted at a staff meeting in 1962: "Our unique emphasis is that we establish clear identity with the local community by living in it to the point where we are no longer outsiders. It is only this way that we will be able to crack the *deep* South. In order to build up the confidence of the local community we must really identify." Julian Bond added: "And when we leave, we leave

behind a community movement with local leadership, not a new branch of SNCC." Jones and Bond, Minutes of SNCC Regional Meeting, Atlanta, 24 Mar. 1962, p. 3, frame 802, reel 3, SNCC Papers. During a 9 June 1964 staff meeting in Atlanta, Frank Smith said: "SNCC originally formed to give impetus to the organization of indigenous local groups in the South. We were actually trying to work ourselves out of a job." Smith, Staff Meeting Minutes, 9 – 11 June 1964, p. 16, frame 984, reel 3, SNCC Papers. See also Jane Stembridge, quoted in Ransby, *Ella Baker*, 280.

9. On SNCC's intellectual contributions to the black cultural movement, see Clayborne Carson, *In Struggle*, chaps. 11, 13 – 14. For a brilliant account of the loss of the organizing tradition, see Charles Payne, *Light of Freedom*, chap. 13.

10. "Minutes of Meeting of Fifth District, 25 Nov. 1964," presented as a working paper for the COFO Mississippi Staff Conference, Mary King Papers. On other COFO projects at the time, see Dittmer, *Local People*, 317.

11. "Minutes of Meeting of Fifth District, 25 Nov. 1964."

12. Ibid.

13. Ibid.

14. Ibid. "Come-here" and "been-here" appear in Watters and Cleghorn, *Climbing Jacob's Ladder*, 115.

15. "Young Democratic Clubs of Mississippi," *ERAP Newsletter*, 23 July 1965, box 6, Lynd Papers (Morey). For how this struggle unfolded in Sunflower County, see Lee, *For Freedom's Sake*, 144 – 45, and Moye, *Let the People Decide*. In Alabama, as the research of Hasan Jeffries ("Organizing for More Than the Vote," 147 – 48) shows, the process of white co-optation was less subtle.

16. "Young Democratic Clubs of Mississippi," *ERAP Newsletter*, 23 July 1965. Similar dynamics — where traditional organizations moved in to take over organizations generated from within the movement — could be seen throughout areas where SNCC and CORE had been active in voter registration projects. See, e.g., letters of 1965 – 66 to Mimi Feingold from local blacks she had worked with in West Feliciana Parish, La., in reel 1, Feingold Papers.

17. See, e.g., Charles McLaurin to Cleve Sellers, n.d. [Summer 1965], "Report" (frames 165 – 67, reel 40), Sanford R. Leigh to Executive Committee, 18 Mar. 1965 (frames 995 – 97, reel 7), and Herman Kitchens to Atlanta SNCC, 19 Jan. 1965 (frame 968, reel 7), SNCC Papers. A chronicle of the increasingly tense exchanges between projects and the Atlanta office over money, staff, and resource distribution can be found in reels 36 – 42, SNCC Papers.

Chapter Twelve

1. Forman, *Black Revolutionaries*, 301 – 2; Tillinghast interview (quotation). I would like to thank Bill Greider for his invaluable help on this chapter.

2. Louis, *We Are Not Saved*, 119. Interestingly, Joseph Ellis (*Founding Brothers*, 7) has argued that such daily shared experiences were a major factor holding the generation of "founding brothers" together through the war of independence and the creation of permanent federal institutions. See also Carmichael, *Ready for Revolution*, 428 – 29.

3. Powledge, *Free at Last?*, 419 (Jones).

4. Raines, *My Soul Is Rested*, 273, 290 (Dennis and Guyot), 259 (Ivanhoe Donaldson). From 1964 through the 1970s, those who drifted out of their core relationships as the movement they knew collapsed found that the more one's identity was interwoven in the movement community, the greater the loss and the more exposed one felt. Many never found their way back to a sense of wholeness. "You just hop and go off out there and next thing you know you're on the edge of the world," Casey Hayden recalled. "Wouldn't have missed it for the world, but it was an expensive ride." Hayden interview by the author. Activists who returned to the university were struck by how deeply unaware most academics seemed of the knowledge movement workers had internalized. Charles Jones eventually went to Howard Law School. See also Powledge, *Free at Last?*, 419 (Jones), and Patch interview.

5. David Chappell (*Stone of Hope*, 86) notes: "The movement's hope was something very different from the liberals' optimism. Liberals' bright future was automatic. The moral improvement of their world would come as a function of increased economic growth, scientific discovery, and educational dissemination of new ideas. The movement's hope, by contrast, was forged by years of disappointment. . . . Activists in the movement believed, or came to believe, that they had to act. They believed that they had to set themselves off from the general drift of social development."

6. In her 1970 memoir of the movement, *We Are Not Saved* (p. 70), Debbie Louis encouraged readers to view the withdrawal of movement veterans with due consideration: "Far from being rigid dogmatists, their attitude simply reflects their past experience, which has been that the reasons for their decisions can neither be understood nor accepted by the non-[movement] audience." Louis believed it necessary to explain why SNCC veterans "feel no need to justify themselves and no interest in embarking upon an argument or indictment they know must follow and which they also know would hardly be constructive. If we understand this, we might then understand, and with compassion, a major reason why those who left the movement have isolated themselves: such lessons (to them, the most fundamental in life) are simply not generally learned outside of the kind of experience they have had, which makes communication with those outside of the struggle impossible, even on the most trivial level."

7. Ibid., 80. The most sustained exploration that I have found of this most difficult terrain is Louis's. The emotional price is suggested by her title, *And We Are Not Saved*. A similar situation from a different racial perspective is explored in Theresa del Pozzo ("The Feel of a Blue Note," 197–98). Del Pozzo writes that the process was uneven but visible at staff meetings that, as whites suddenly discovered, were black-only or at gatherings where a black woman stood stock-still, looking through her white woman confidante as the latter, unsuspecting, went up to greet her. Whites often honored the new wishes of their old friends by leaving, usually in silence. Blacks and whites "all were caught at a cultural crossroads." The best effort white movement workers could make "was [to] try to understand this new form of racial separation in its historical context and deal with its painful exclusion with the same dignity that African Americans had done for so long."

8. Charles Payne's unrivaled chapter, "Mrs. Hamer Is No Longer Relevant: The Loss of the Organizing Tradition," in his *Light of Freedom*, touches on this development.

9. Louis, *We Are Not Saved*; Del Pozzo, "The Feel of a Blue Note," 178–79.

10. Moses interview by Carson; Joanne Grant, *Ella Baker*, 157.

11. There are notable exceptions: Chafe, *Civilities and Civil Rights*, Dittmer, *Local People*, and Charles Payne, *I've Got the Light of Freedom* are among the pioneers in this effort to understand *how* movements succeed and fail. As more local studies appeared in the last decade, more historians began to ask "How did these movements succeed?" as opposed to chronicling what happened.

12. SNCC activists went on to a variety of endeavors but often kept the same values and experientially tested beliefs. It is essential, as Judy Richardson later commented, to "combat the idea that once SNCC fell apart, nothing else happened." Richardson interview.

13. Sam Block, "Folk Festival in Mississippi," n.d. [1965], frame 51, reel 40, SNCC Papers. See also Carmichael and Hamilton, *Black Power*, 44. The bulk orders for books from these Black Studies departments were then purchased largely at Drum and Spear. These efforts led to the formation of the Drum and Spear Press, which published children's literature including a coloring book called *Children of Africa*. The press also printed the first book of the prominent black author of children's literature, Eloise Greenfield.

14. For more on post-SNCC activities, see Appendix G, Structure Debate at Waveland. Also working on the folk music festivals were Julius Lester, Worth Long, and Jimmy Travis. See Long, *We'll Never Turn Back*, 36; Peacock, "Folk Song Festivals," n.d. [Spring 1965] (frames 50 – 52, reel 40), and Block, "Folk Festival in Mississippi," n.d. [1965] (frame 51, reel 40), SNCC Papers. See also Judy Richardson to SNCC Executive Committee, "RE: Residential Freedom School," n.d. [1965?], frame 696, reel 12, SNCC Papers. For early ideas, see Jim Monsonis, "Report to SNCC Executive Committee, RE: New York Office," n.d. [end of 1963] (frames 289 – 91, reel 3), and Monroe Sharp, Minutes, 9 Nov. 1964, p. 14 (frame 944, reel 11), SNCC Papers; and "Minutes of the First Membership Meeting of the Poor People's Corp.," 21 Sept. 1965, frames 544 – 47, reel 27, CORE Papers. On the Mississippi Freedom Labor Union, see Donald Janson, "Striking Negroes Are Evicted from Plantation in Mississippi," 4 June 1965, *New York Times*; Janson, "Negro Walkouts in Delta Spurred," 6 June 1965, *New York Times*; and *Student Voice*, 6 June 1965, 20 Dec. 1965. Chana Kai Lee (*For Freedom's Sake*, chap. 8) explores Fannie Lou Hamer's continuing involvement in this post – 1964 work on Freedom Farm. Komozi Woodard's book on Amiri Baraka's role in developing similar local institutions as well as national ones like the Modern Black Convention Movement is a revealing study of how these institutions were created in the North.

15. Fruchter and Kramer, "Approach to Community Organizing Projects."

16. Carol McEldowney, "I will try in this letter to set down some general ideas," 19 May 1965, Webb Papers; Johnny Bancroft to "Cleveland People" (16 May 1965, box 15) and Dickie Magidoff to CCPnicks (29 Nov. 1964, box 24), SDS Papers. Magidoff, homesick for ERAP, read all of the ERAP correspondence "rather assiduously" and found that the projects all lacked significant growth during the fall except for those in Chicago and Philadelphia, "[which] started at a pretty low point." No one quite knows what to do now, he wrote to colleagues in Cleveland, "with the possible exception of Newark." ERAP's major accomplishment, he stated, was that the organization had proven a few of its original hypotheses: poor whites could be brought into organiza-

tions and would work with blacks given the right conditions, as the Cleveland welfare organizers had found.

17. Casey Hayden, "Fields of Blue," 365; Emmie Schrader Adams, "From Africa to Mississippi," 327. The women's paper was entitled "The Position of Women in the Movement" (frame 785, reel 12, SNCC Papers). According to Hayden, Maria Varela helped draft it, though Varela does not recall this, whereas Elaine DeLott Baker and Emmie Schrader Adams remember being in the group. While the paper may have been one of the first documents produced by second-wave feminism, this was not the first time women's issues emerged within SNCC or the New Left. Hayden and Mickey Flacks had discussed these issues with SDS women as early as January–February 1962, and, as Adams points out, early in July 1964. Women's concerns were regularly discussed by women and men in SNCC. Most persuasive on this issue, however, is the fact that at Waveland, Ruby Doris Smith Robinson was widely believed to have been the primary writer of the position paper on women. She never denied it, and no one challenged her on it. This was testament to the strength of Robinson's position in the organization. In terms of long-term historical impact, the paper did draw an enormous amount of scholarly attention as well as responses to that attention from activists. Cynthia Griggs Fleming (*We Will Not Cry*, 152) maintains there is evidence both that Robinson did not support the paper and that she may have supported it. See also Evans, *Personal Politics*, and Cynthia Washington's letter to *Southern Exposure* in 1977, "We Started from Different Ends of the Spectrum," in Evans, 238–40. The comparison between racial oppression and gender oppression often took disfigured forms as adapted in the later New Left and women's movement. For one interpretation, see bell hooks, *Ain't I a Woman*, 143.

18. [Name withheld by request], "SNCC Position Paper," n.d. [Fall 1964], Sherrod Papers.

19. Giddings, *When and Where I Enter*, 302–3; Casey Hayden, "Fields of Blue," 371; Washington, "We Started from Different Ends of the Spectrum." Barbara Omolade ("Ella's Daughters," *Rising Song*, 170) noted that by the end of the 1970s, "virtually every Black organization or initiative seemed to break down over the appropriate place of Black women in its leadership. Some organizations, such as the National Black Independent Political Party, tried to create a formal approach by requiring that Black women co-lead with Black men in each of its chapters." The essay chronicles her struggle to place the quest for gender equity within a nationalist framework. For evidence of gender emerging earlier among nationalist organizations, see Fleming, "Black Women and Black Power," and Matthews, "'No One Ever Asks What a Man's Role in the Revolution Is,'" 230–56. On Ericka Huggins's and Elaine Brown's pivotal roles in the Black Panther Party, see Elaine Brown, *Taste of Power*, 137, 191. Robyn Spencer's new work, *Mothers of the Revolution* (forthcoming), provides one of the most promising approaches to uncovering these gendered dynamics.

20. Evans, *Personal Politics*, 161–69. These women forced a dialogue on the memo at the SDS National Council meeting in December 1965; *Liberation* subsequently published the "Kind of Memo" in April 1966. One of the more egregious examples of this unconscious white supremacy can be seen in Brownmiller, *In Our Time*.

21. Reproductive control, interestingly enough, had already emerged as an issue in the freedom struggle, but in ways that would cripple black-white coalition on the topic in the future. In the spring of 1964, as SNCC prepared for the Mississippi Summer Project, the all-white Mississippi legislature considered (but ultimately scrapped) measures that would have enforced sterilization or jail terms on the parents of two or more illegitimate children. John Lewis argued that the "bill was aimed at eliminating the state's Negroes." State representative Stone Barfield of Forrest County, the site of a concerted SNCC voter registration drive, told the Mississippi house: "When they start cutting [reproductive organs], they'll head for Chicago." "Pamphlet Weakens Genocide Measure," *Student Voice*, 26 May 1964.

22. Gregory Calvert, an SDS leader opposing the draft, said that during the summer of 1966, he believed Mendy Samstein "was very convinced that draft resistance was the issue which would convince SNCC organizers that white students in the North were willing to take the same kinds of risks they were. I thought I should say that that was a very bad basis for making one's decisions about draft resistance strategy, to prove to SNCC that we were as tough as they were." Calvert interview. Though it is unclear whether or not this was Samstein's intention — and it is unlikely that it was — it is relevant to note Calvert's interpretation, for this dynamic shaped a good deal of activity in the late 1960s within the movement. See Moses, quoted in Howard Zinn, "Should Civil Rights Workers Take a Stand on Vietnam?" *Student Voice*, 30 Aug. 1965, and "SNCC Raps Service Bias," *Student Voice*, 30 Dec. 1963. See also John Ross's statement before refusing induction in San Francisco in December 1964: "I am not alone in this contention. All over America, young men of draft age are refusing to divorce the issue of war and peace from that of human dignity, Vietnam from Mississippi." Ross to Sir, 8 Dec. 1964, frame 72, reel 40, SNCC Papers.

23. Harris, *Dreams Die Hard*, 145–46 (quotation, "SNCC North"). On draft resistance generally, see Ferber and Lynd, *The Resistance*; Calvert, *Democracy from the Heart*; Foley, *Confronting the War Machine*; Unseem, *Conscription, Protest*; Thorne, "Resisting the Draft"; and Franklin Stevens, *If This Be Treason*.

24. Gilbert interview, 17 Jan. 1985. See Clayborne Carson, *In Struggle*, 183–86, and Ferber and Lynd, *The Resistance*, 127. See also Stokely Carmichael to Lorna D. Smith, 14 Mar. 1967, Carmichael–Smith Papers, and Sellers, *River of No Return*, 190.

25. Harris, *Dreams Die Hard*, 251. Other quotations are from John Douglas, Norman Fruchter, Allen Graubard, Mickey Morgan, Mike Robinson, Allan Siegel, Rhodie Streeter, and Shawn Walker, who appeared in a fifteen-minute movie, "RESIST/Resistance," for Newsreel; a copy of the film is listed as VBB 020 at the Film and Video Archives, SHSW. At a Resistance gathering in March 1969, Michael Ferber (Introduction to Lynd, "The Movement," 6) wrote, "long sessions in workshops or plenaries led to long personal raps with each other, or to singing movement songs, or to games outdoors. When they left for home, they hugged one another. I was amazed: at this late date, with the movement factionalized and uptight, the open and experimental groups uncertain and the disciplined cadres more arrogant than ever, national SDS meetings reduced to empty ideological debates, and even some Resistance groups split over tactics and hassled over personalities, 150 movement people actually managed to hold a healthy conference."

26. See Appendix H for a more complete description of the movements directly born from SNCC activity.

27. Baker, "They Sent Us This White Girl," 279 – 80.

Conclusion

1. Dylan, "Chimes of Freedom." SNCC staff lived with local people, working to register voters for subsistence wages. Other groups like CORE, NSM, SCLC, and SDS subsequently adopted this approach. By Summer 1965, even the previously critical NAACP had set up voter registration projects where students lived with local people. Though the dangers of the work had by no means disappeared by mid-decade, in 1961 – 62 it had been SNCC activists and no one else who had been willing to begin the work where the terror was greatest and allies most scarce. Their efforts inspired Dylan; in turn, his music "operated as a sort of grapevine, spreading ideas around about political and social values." Mick Gold, quoted in Fraser et al., *1968*, 65.

2. Bob Moses, Minutes, 9 Nov. 1964, 17 – 18, SNCC Papers. On "organic intellectuals," see Gramsci, *Letters from Prison*, and Lipsitz, *A Life in the Struggle*. Lipsitz makes extended and creative use of Gramsci's work. The 1957 Civil Rights Act for the first time gave the Department of Justice authority to issue injunctions against people who intimidated others who were trying to vote in federal elections. It created a division within the Justice Department to monitor civil rights abuses and called for a joint report on race relations from representatives of the two major political parties. However, the department's burden of proof was "very difficult to sustain," Burke Marshall testified in *Hearings before the United States Commission on Civil Rights*, Jackson, Miss., 16 – 20 Feb. 1965, vol. 1, 258 – 62. The 1960 Civil Rights Act provided that penalties be levied against any one who obstructed attempts to register or to actually vote, and created a Civil Rights Commission.

3. On how narrowly the term "intellectual" has been defined in movement histories, see Chappell, *Stone of Hope*, 229, 313 – 14.

4. Ransby, *Ella Baker*, 362.

5. Ibid., 357 (Baker).

6. Louis, *We Are Not Saved*, 222.

7. Charles Payne, "The View from the Trenches," in Lawson and Payne, *Debating the Civil Rights Movement*, 116. Much research remains to be done on the interactions between local, state, and federal law enforcement agencies and movement organizations. For more on the FBI's role, see Blackstock, *COINTELPRO*; Churchill, *Agents of Repression*; Donner, *Age of Surveillance*; Swearingen, *FBI Secrets*; and O'Reilly, *"Racial Matters."*

8. As the MFDP launched its congressional challenge the year after Atlantic City, movement workers traveled to Washington to lobby their representatives to support the effort. Those activists originally from the North realized that many members of Congress either did not know or did not care about the betrayal of democracy in the South. One northern white congressman came off the floor with Prentiss Walker, a

Republican member from Mississippi, to meet with SNCC lobbyists. Both congressmen proceeded to tell the SNCC workers that their support for black people's human rights could be seen in their devotion to their "Negro maids." Another midwestern congressman informed his SNCC constituent that "I would never vote against such a fine legislator as [Mississippi representative] Jamie Whitten, especially when my state's agricultural appropriations must come from his committee." Thelwell, "MFDP Congressional Challenge," 3.

9. Arthur I. Waskow's front-row seat in Washington and his close connections to Democratic Party leaders allowed him an unparalleled vantage point during the period between 1962 and 1965 to assess which movement activities placed the most pressure on top Democrats. On the role of Birmingham in the federal legislative process, see Waskow, *From Race Riot to Sit-In*, 231, 235. For the impact of SNCC and MFDP, see ibid., 251.

10. Manis, *A Fire You Can't Put Out*, 255 (Shuttlesworth).

11. Conley interview on *RACE* (newsreel).

12. Belfrage, *Freedom Summer*, 166.

13. Quotation not for attribution. As Taylor Branch wrote in *Parting the Waters* (p. 185), King's "air of humility" contrasted sharply with the "circus of adulation surrounding him."

14. Alpert, *Growing Up Underground*, 346.

15. Separatism as distinct from black nationalism. I have used Komozi Woodard's (*A Nation within a Nation*, 9) definition of nationalism: "an ideological movement for the attainment and maintenance of autonomy and individuality for a social group, some of whose members conceive it to constitute an actual or potential nation." Woodard further notes that "although many intellectuals yearn for a pure nationalist ideology, they are probably longing for the impossible, because nationalism is heterogeneous." People who wanted to be separate from whites did not necessarily see themselves as black nationalists.

16. Sellers, *River of No Return*, 205 (Bellamy); Forman, *Sammy Younge*, 66. On Jimmy Lee Jackson, see Carmichael, *Ready for Revolution*, 446–48. Others had a strong distaste for retaliatory violence. Aaron Henry (*Fire Ever Burning*, 151) reported on his friend Medgar Evers's funeral, where the procession ran into highway patrolmen blocking the street in Jackson, Miss., in 1963. Henry recalled an incident Evers had earlier related: "He once told me about an experience when he was only fourteen years old at his home in Decatur, Miss. A close friend of his father had been lynched for allegedly insulting a white woman, and young Medgar and his brother, Charles, had seen them bring in the body. He had heard his father say that his friend had done nothing—not even spoken to the woman. Yet he was dead and nothing could be done. Medgar told me that for him it was the turning point—from then on he felt a deep bitterness toward a system that allowed this. During his ten years in the civil rights movement he saw case after case of raw brutality against Negroes, and he abhorred the violence. His funeral should not have been an occasion for further violence."

17. Sherrod, "Nonviolence," n.d., frame 1235, reel 7, SNCC Papers.

18. Norman interview.

19. Watters and Cleghorn, *Climbing Jacob's Ladder*, 69. See also Carmichael and Hamilton, *Black Power*.

20. Porter to SNCC Staff, "Group Relationships," n.d. (frames 1065–66, reel 14), and Porter, "To Members of the Central Committee of the SNCC," [May 1966] (frame 506, reel 12), SNCC Papers. For another portrait of the splits among black SNCC workers and the personal trauma involved, see Sellers, *River of No Return*.

21. Jim Kares to People, 7 July 1965, frame 10, reel 40, SNCC Papers.

22. Malcolm X, "The Bullet or the Ballot.

23. Bernice Johnson Reagon, with Bill Moyers, "The Songs Are Free" (Princeton, N.J.: Films for the Humanities and Sciences, 1997) (videorecording).

24. Tyson, *"Radio Free Dixie,"* 191; Carmichael, *Ready for Revolution*, 166.

25. Sue Sojourner (Lorenzi), "Some People of That Place: 1960s Holmes County, Mississippi," ‹http://www.crmvet.org/images/imgms.htm›, 19 Feb. 2005 ("dancing fingers"); Raines, *My Soul Is Rested*, 266–67 (Turnbow and Bond); Charles Payne, *Light of Freedom*, 402; Tyson, *"Radio Free Dixie,"* 291.

26. Tyson, *"Radio Free Dixie,"* 256; Robert F. Williams, *Negroes with Guns*, 114.

27. See Crosby, *Taste of Freedom*, for more on this point.

28. This becomes clearer when one considers Diane Nash's 1963 proposal, disregarded both by her peers in the movement and by the mainstream *Washington Post*. Following the murder of four African American girls in Birmingham, she proposed that SNCC create a nonviolent army, 25,000 strong, "uniformed and militant, that would undertake such campaigns as surrounding and paralyzing southern state capitals where governors set their faces utterly against integration, stopping transportation by blocking airports, highways, and railroads with their bodies" (quoted in Waskow, *From Race Riot to Sit-In*, 244). Nevertheless, nonspecific terms like "radical" and "militant" often obscure more than they clarify how to proceed in concrete political activity. For examples of such obfuscations, see the way Lance Hill juxtaposes nonviolence and self-defense in *Deacons for Defense*, 2–9, 258–73.

29. Tyson, *"Radio Free Dixie,"* 191–96. A summer volunteer related a conversation between herself and her host, Cora Lou Amos: Mrs. Amos went to bed after lining up the buckshot capsules in a row on the table by her husband's bed. "They been shootin' into the windows on Broad," Amos said (Belfrage, *Freedom Summer*, 200, 233).

30. Garvy interview, 22 June 1998. See also Sale, *SDS*.

31. Greenberg, *Circle of Trust*, 19 (Nash); Sale, *SDS*, 335 (Rader).

32. Deming, "On Revolution and Equilibrium"; Sellers, *River of No Return*, 35 (King). On Jim Bevel, see Chapter 3.

33. Deming, "On Revolution and Equilibrium."

34. Carmichael, *Ready for Revolution*, 304–6; Ransby, *Ella Baker*, 44; Joanne Grant, *Ella Baker*, 137. I am grateful to Emilye Crosby for these examples and for developing this point further.

35. Dona Richards Moses and Bob Moses, 11 Oct. 1964, frames 1020–22, reel 3, SNCC Papers; Nash, comments at SNCC's 1988 reunion, Trinity College, Hartford, Conn., quoted from Greenberg, *Circle of Trust*, 22. Stevie Schwenn, who worked at SDS's central office in Chicago during the winter of 1965, noted the same problem as it developed

a little later in that organization: "We want the whole world, but if we go too fast, people will join when they don't really understand and we will be unable to work as well and we will destroy our lovely society." Schwenn, "Criteria and Procedures for Staff Selection," n.d., [early 1965], box 19, SDS Papers.

36. See, e.g., Ransby (*Ella Baker*, 351) on Baker's "concern about the excesses and reckless use of black power rhetoric" when employed as an "empty slogan" rather than a settled reflection emerging from life-altering experiences such as those Stokely Carmichael and other SNCC field secretaries had lived through. See also Woodard, *A Nation within a Nation*, 264, and Tyson, "*Radio Free Dixie*," 304.

37. McLaurin, "To Overcome Fear," frames 55 – 56, reel 140, SNCC Papers.

Afterword

1. Louis, *We Are Not Saved*, 197.

2. If the rest of the country thought that segregation had been destroyed because "Rosa sat down, Martin stood up, and the white kids came down and saved the day," only a few stray voices in the wilderness were heard in opposition. Then SNCC people, sometimes in groups, sometimes alone, went to see the 1988 Hollywood adaptation of the Mississippi Summer Project, *Mississippi Burning* (video). Imagine you are Bob Moses or Dave Dennis, the former director and codirector of the Mississippi COFO project. You go and sit in a darkened theater and watch your story told through Hollywood's eyes. First you see that every central character — hero and villain alike — is white. There is no Herbert Lee, no Fannie Lou Hamer, no Annell Ponder, no Ivanhoe Donaldson, no you. Black people provide only a backdrop to the story. The sole place they dominate is the gospel music score. It appears that what America has internalized about the civil rights movement twenty-five years after the fact is that the Ku Klux Klan was bad, blacks were too scared to move, and two hardscrabble white FBI agents arrived on the scene to restore justice. The world turned upside down. Worse, in one scene a young black boy convinces a peer that "it's alright Willie, tell the FBI agents what you saw." The boy does, and it breaks the case wide open — that is, in the film. But in reality, Moses and Dennis had lived through it. They knew that Louis Allen told the FBI what he knew, and that got him killed for his trouble. Moses and Dennis watched the white FBI agents on screen slog through the swamps for an hour and a half, determined as ever to nail the bad guys. At the end of the movie, when several Klansmen are convicted on federal civil rights violations, one of the heroes who won the convictions, an FBI agent played by Willem Dafoe, ponderously announces that "maybe we are all guilty." Moses and Dennis jumped up from their seats determined to convey what they had not been able to communicate in the late 1960s: namely, their understanding of the meaning of the civil rights struggle. Moses brought his current initiative, the Algebra Project, to Mississippi; Dennis left his law practice to spearhead a new "Southern Initiative" of the Algebra Project based in Jackson. Today, the Algebra Project develops new curricula for math literacy — a necessity for entry into the information economy — directed at underserved youth throughout the South. It directly combats what Moses has called the legacy of segregation — the "sharecropper education" reserved for children on track to become minimum-wage workers. Other

SNCC veterans' revulsion at *Mississippi Burning* prompted attempts to get a different history before the public. In 1988 Jack Chatfield and other SNCC workers organized a conference and reunion at Trinity College, in Hartford, Conn., where they insisted that movement veterans get their version of events on the record. SNCC scholar and activist Martha Norman and historian Charles Payne followed with a second major conference at Shaw University in Raleigh, N.C., in 2000. Moses, Chuck McDew, Bob Zellner, and others brought *their* story to the big screen with the feature film *Freedom Song* (Turner Network Television) in 2000.

Appendix A

1. Hampton and Fayer, *Voices of Freedom*, 108 (Reagon).
2. Ibid.
3. Reagon, "Give Your Hands to Struggle," [1970], Sweet Honey in the Rock, CD 942522-2.
4. Carson, *In Struggle*, 63–64; Ronald Fraser et al., *1968*, 37 (Harris); Hampton and Fayer, *Voices of Freedom*, 98 (Reagon). Clayborne Carson notes that Reagon and others went on to form the Freedom Singers, who brought the songs of the Albany movement to the rest of the nation through their fund-raising tours for SNCC. Sherrod did indeed advocate for workers to "teach the songs of freedom" as the number one activity when moving into a community. See Sherrod, "Non-violence," n.d. [1962?], frames 1234–39, reel 7, SNCC Papers.

Music renewed the courage of SNCC workers in times of great stress throughout the early 1960s. As plans for the Mississippi Summer Project of 1964 proceeded frantically from Jackson, students on white campuses in the city ran a few small, sporadic, uncoordinated actions to support the movement. Because few white southerners were willing to risk a break with home and family, only a tiny number of white students went so far as to work with SNCC. Yet attending folk concerts enabled some students to show their identification with and support of the movement. When Pete Seeger, Joan Baez, or the Freedom Singers sang in town, white students attended. These integrated havens in small churches and auditoriums proved quite powerful. Jane Stembridge attended a Baez concert in a Jackson church in April 1964. Six hundred people witnessed "the beauty and the courage of Joan making protest and affirmation." Baez "never let up," singing Bob Dylan's "Birmingham Sunday," and "Blowin in the Wind," and then the "very hard Dylan," "With God on Our Side." "I figured if people can take Baez singing Dylan so clear, they can begin to take freedom," Stembridge observed. When Baez finished, "the people stood. Mendy [Samstein] was first over in the choir loft which Ivanhoe [Donaldson] and Bob [Moses] and Dona [Moses] and the rest of us occupied. I saw Mendy stand up and I didn't know what would happen at all." But then everyone else in the room stood as well and "gave a very long ovation. If people stood for "With God on Our Side," and "the way Baez did this song with no let-up," then maybe, Stembridge thought, there was reason to hope. "Freedom Singers," *Southern Patriot*, December 1962, 4; Stembridge to Mary King, 5–6 Apr. 1964, Mary King Papers.

At the intermission, Baez announced to the integrated audience that a photographer was present. During the second set, he would take pictures which might include people in the first two rows. "If anybody sitting there figured to be kicked out of school as a result, they should move and it'd be okay," wrote Stembridge. No one moved at all. "I heard a lot of people laugh the way you laugh at such absurd real awful possibilities. Nobody from [predominantly white] Old Miss moved and nobody from [predominantly white] Millsaps [College] and we didn't move of course," said Stembridge. "You could feel inside those people making a big decision at that moment and it was a decision about being and nonbeing about tomorrow and Mississippi. It was new people saying we shall not be moved." Stembridge to Mary King, 5–6 Apr. 1964, Mary King Papers.

Appendix B

1. Affidavit of Mrs. Edith Simmons Peters, frames 188–89, reel 40, SNCC Papers.
2. Affidavit of Mrs. Hazel T. Palmer, frame 440, reel 41, ibid.
3. Affidavit of Leonard Clay, frame 444, reel 41, ibid.

Appendix C

1. Feingold to Danny, Port Allen [La.] Jail, 5 Sept. 1963, Feingold Papers.
2. Ibid.
3. Feingold to Parents, 16 Nov. 1963, frame 343, reel 1, ibid.

Appendix D

1. Supplements to Testimony of Aaron E. Henry, 16–20 Feb. 1965, *Hearings before the United States Commission on Civil Rights*, vol. 1, Jackson, Miss., 264–66. This list covers only violence specifically aimed at voter registration activities. None of the hundreds of examples of violence against sit-ins or other direct actions are included.

Appendix E

1. Forman's speech is available in the Ewen Papers.

Appendix F

1. "Proposal A" is available in the Mary King Papers.
2. "Proposal B" is available in the Casey Hayden Papers.
3. "Proposal C" is available in the Casey Hayden Papers.

Appendix G

1. Casey Hayden, "Memorandum on Structure," n.d. [November 1964], Casey Hayden Papers; Casey Hayden, "Fields of Blue," 361–64; Casey Hayden interview. Hayden's plan is reprinted as "Proposal B" in Appendix F of this text.
2. For years after Waveland, Hayden felt that the people who had booed wanted a

strong leader and reacted to her as a white woman, rather than to her idea. By 2000, she felt the explanation was more complex than race and gender. This is one moment where it would be important to determine exactly at what point Forman began to organize against what he perceived to be a faction organizing against him within SNCC. If it was prior to the Waveland meeting, then this might have been part of the reason Hayden's ideas were dismissed. But certainly at Waveland, when Forman stated, "I want to deal with the idea in Casey's mind of where power in the organization resides" (Minutes, 12 Nov. 1964, p. 36, frames 955–56, reel 11, SNCC Papers), he had recognized the differences between his own and Hayden's approach.

3. Casey Hayden, "Fields of Blue," 363. It was not until a staff meeting three months later that the decentralized structure was recognized as "not being 'no structure' but [a] different structure," Mary King's notes indicate. But it was clear that many of those present felt that hierarchical structure was a "hard line" position, "with all its phallic appeal and connotations," recalled Emmie Schrader Adams ("From Africa to Mississippi," 327). Atlanta SNCC Meeting, February 1965, transcription of Mary King's notes, Mary King Papers. Forman referred to weak versus strong structures in *Black Revolutionaries*, 424. One of the more interesting examples today of this structure of a horizontal network of projects with a coordinating center is the Frente Autentico del Trabajo union in Mexico. See Hathaway, *Allies across the Border*.

4. Minutes, 12 Nov. 1964, pp. 35–39 (frames 956–57, reel 11), and "Summary of Staff Retreat Minutes," [November 1964], p. 4 (frame 718, reel 12), SNCC Papers. The Mitchell and Forman plans are reprinted as "Proposal A" and "Proposal C," respectively, in Appendix F of this text.

5. Minutes, 12 Nov. 1964, p. 39 (frame 957, reel 11), SNCC Papers. The Planning Committee Meeting for the next staff meeting (February 1965) was held in Pine Bluff, Ark., where participants disagreed about what had actually been decided at Waveland. See, e.g., Mary King's response to John Lewis's memo to staff over "alleged coup" and "red-baiting of SNCC": Lewis to All SNCC Staff, n.d. [Winter 1964–65] (frame 23, reel 2), and King to Lewis, 10 Jan. 1965 (frame 650, reel 1), SNCC Papers.

Appendix H

1. The title of this appendix is drawn from "The Borning Struggle: An Interview with Bernice Johnson Reagon," in Cluster, *They Should Have Served That Cup of Coffee*. The National Council of Negro Churchmen and Malcolm X are quoted in Carmichael and Hamilton, *Black Power*, 34–35. A later definition of black nationalism comes from Cornel West, Interview by bell hooks, reprinted in hooks and West, *Breaking Bread*, 47. In 1991 West felt that preservation of black cultural integrity and acknowledgment of black cultural distinctiveness were "indispensable for a progressive Black politics. Yet a progressive Black politics must go beyond them for purposes of principled coalition and alliance." He criticized the dominant forms of black nationalism of the period for being "too narrow and sometimes even xenophobic," though he maintained that these attitudes were often reinforced by whites' racist attitudes.

Early SNCC members viewed their support of international solidarity with oppressed peoples as part of—not opposed to—their commitment to interracial solidarity. For example, in early 1961, when twelve new African and Asian nations were admitted to the United Nations in one day, the SNCC newspaper *Student Voice* noted that not only were two-thirds of the citizens of the planet nonwhite, but also admission of these countries to the world body "literally shifted the weight of international authority from white to nonwhite hands." Charles McDew asserted in 1962 that "the morally underdeveloped people are not necessarily across the sea. What is the difference between restricted travel in Berlin and Jackson, or between free speech in Poland and Talladega, or between the atrocities in Hungary and the murder of Mack Parker and Herbert Lee?" (quoted in "SNCC Conference Report," *NSM News*, 14 Dec. 1962, frame 707, reel 27, CORE Papers). "It matters not whether it is in Angola, Mozambique, Southwest Africa, or Mississippi, Alabama, Georgia and Harlem USA," John Lewis told the SNCC staff in 1965. "The struggle is . . . the same. . . . It is a struggle against a vicious and evil system that is controlled and kept in order for and by a few white men throughout the world" (quoted in Clayborne Carson, *In Struggle*, 37). Moses insisted on putting this separatist impulse in the context of international events across the globe. See Moses interview by Carson.

2. "Statement on 1966 by John Lewis, Chairman, SNCC, Dec. 30, 1965" (frame 163, reel 1), and "Statement by John Lewis, Chairman," February 1965 (frames 1065–66, reel 1), SNCC Papers.

3. Moses interview by Carson.

4. Lee, *For Freedom's Sake*, 139; Jeffries, "Organizing for More Than the Vote," 147.

5. On the first articulation of "Black Power," see Carmichael and Hamilton, *Black Power*, 44; Allen, *Black Awakening*; and Cone, *Black Theology*. Though we are still far from understanding the full scope and impact of the Black Power era, relevant studies include Myrick-Harris, "Behind the Scenes"; Craig, *Ain't I a Beauty Queen*; Collier-Thomas and Franklin, *Sisters in the Struggle*; Tyson, *"Radio Free Dixie"*; Woodard, *A Nation within a Nation*; Charles E. Jones, *Black Panther Party (Reconsidered)*; and Walters, *Pan-Africanism*. For community studies of the impact of the Black Power movement in Atlanta, see Grady-Willis, "A Changing Tide." In Chicago, see Fish, *Black Power/White Control*. Black Studies programs have also received scholarly attention. For the effect of such a program on a large, midwestern land grant, see Williamson, "'We Demand Everything.'" See also McEvoy and Miller, *Black Power and Student Rebellion*. Many more community studies need to be done before we have a clear picture of the impact of black nationalist community-based organizations in the 1960s and 1970s. Examples of this nascent body of literature are Woodard, *A Nation within a Nation*; Van DeBurg, *New Day in Babylon*; Yohuru R. Williams, "No Haven"; Cynthia Ann Young, "Soul Power"; Countryman, "Civil Rights and Black Power in Philadelphia"; Scot D. Brown, *Fighting for US*; Rice, "Black Radicalism on Chicago's West Side; and Bowen, "Who Said It Was Easy?"

6. Phyllis Jackson, "CUFAW Speaks for Itself," Cleveland Community People's Conference, 19–21 Feb. 1965, McEldowney Papers; Carole King, *ERAP Newsletter*, 21 Aug. 1965, box 6, Lynd Papers.

7. Evan Metcalf to Larry Gordon and Nick Egleson, *ERAP Newsletter*, 23 Jul. 1965, box 6, Lynd Papers.

8. The first summer in Cleveland in 1964, Jeffrey found that the one thing that seemed

to draw people into the ERAP organization was helping them negotiate the dangerous shoals of the welfare bureaucracy. She had stumbled onto welfare as a recruiting device when she noticed that every Tuesday, there was a long line of people at the welfare office. "As an organizer, I knew immediately that this was an ideal place," she recalled. "We had a captive audience; they were standing in line, having to wait for their welfare check, being humiliated—they *loved* having somebody to talk to" (quoted in James Miller, *"Democracy Is in the Streets,"* 203).

9. Over the summer of 1964, the Cleveland group had two drawn-out meetings to discuss whether or not welfare organizing should continue. They agreed to keep working on the project but also determined to devote internal educational sessions to exploring alternative visions of future economies. It turned out that this involved reading works of Karl Marx, Gunnar Myrdal, Robert Theobald, and other theorists.

10. McEldowney to Greg Calvert, 5 Dec. 1966, box 34A, SDS Papers; Welfare Grievance Committee Minutes, 18 Jan. 1967, 4, 12 Jan. 1967, and Boudin and McEldowney, "Welfare Grievance Committee Training Program: An Evaluation," [April 1967], all in McEldowney Papers.

11. Boudin and McEldowney, "Welfare Grievance Committee Training Program: An Evaluation."

12. Ibid.

13. First, Boudin and McEldowney had wished to develop a welfare manual for clients for some time. As they pulled together materials for the training, they realized "that we were in fact developing precisely the material we wanted for a Manual," so production of the manual itself became a goal of the program. Second, ERAP staff initially handled grievances because it was a needed service and a way of training people to respect themselves and others—to learn and to teach; in essence, to be organizers. Now they needed to put grievances "in perspective by showing people how many grievances resulted from bad laws or policies" that needed to be changed. Third, by training leaders, they hoped to strengthen the group so it could grow. Ibid.

14. Ibid.

15. Ibid.

16. Ibid.

17. Magidoff interview, 19 Nov. 1999.

18. Bill Ayers, speech at SDS conference in Cleveland, August 1969, reprinted in *New Left Notes*, 12 Sept. 1969, box 515, Matthews Collection.

19. Bill Hansen resigned as Arkansas project director in September 1964 in favor of James Jones, a longtime black staffer on the project. He continued to work in the state but felt that the movement had to have black leadership. "Arkansas," *Student Voice*, 23 Sept. 1964, p. 4.

20. Since these pioneering white organic intellectuals are essential to building democratic practice, some elaboration of their thinking process might be useful. Connie Curry ("Wild Geese to the Past," *Deep in Our Hearts*, 31) "understood the new emphasis on Black Power within some ranks of the movement; dashed dreams, broken heads, and loss of faith can demand a new strategy." She was "neither frightened nor threatened." For Joan Browning ("Shiloh Witness," 79–80), the Black Power movement added richness to her world and expanded her understanding. Mary King wrote

that "the demonic-Stokely-of-the-news-media has been one of the most ardent people in trying to keep the last whites from being driven out of SNCC"; she urged those who did not appreciate Black Power "to understand how deeply hurt and alienated is Black America. We have got to try to understand the feelings *behind* Black rejection of white help" (quoted in M. King to Poppa, 21 June 1967, and to Bishop Lloyd C. Wicke, 1 Aug. 1967, Mary King Papers). See also Lorna Smith's correspondence with Stokely Carmichael throughout the 1965–77 period in Carmichael-Smith Papers. Smith, a San Jose resident in her mid-sixties, had been active in Greenwood, Miss., during the summer project of 1964.

21. Casey Hayden, Speech for panel on "Feminists and Women."

22. "The point was to keep creating work, profession, self, and family. This was not a rebellion. It was an attempt to sustain. Thus was the seed of feminism rooted in the nonviolent movement." Casey Hayden: "Nurturing Movement," 53; "Fields of Blue," 367, 370; and e-mail to the author, 6 Aug. 2002. Hayden's work in the SDS-ERAP project provided an important woman-centered counterbalance to Carl Wittman and Tom Hayden's formulations about ERAP.

23. Hayden and King, "Sex and Caste: A Kind of Memo," reprinted in Evans, *Personal Politics*, 237; Casey Hayden, e-mail to the author, 12 Apr. 2001. On radical feminism, see Echols, *Daring to Be Bad*; Casey Hayden, Speech for panel on "Feminists and Women"; Mary King, *Freedom Song*, 460; and Casey Hayden, "Fields of Blue," 370. See also Nina S. Adams, "The Women Who Left Them Behind," 185–86.

24. Peacock, in "Women & Men in the Freedom Movement (transcript); Fleming, *We Will Not Cry*, 151 (Stanley Wise, on Ruby Doris Smith Robinson); Stembridge, "Waveland: Work-Study Institute," February–March 1965, p. 3, frame 695, reel 12, SNCC Papers. "Womanist," a term coined by Alice Walker (*In Search of Our Mother's Gardens*), reformulated "feminist" to take into account African American women's concerns and historical experiences.

25. One "recipe" for CR groups was an accurate, if tongue-in-cheek, representation of how these groups worked: "Recipe: Ingredients: sharing, analysis, action. Take experience from your private life (family) and share with other women. Let rise. Extract common elements. Knead political analysis in oiled free space. Add action relevant to first two processes. Mix well. Let political organization emerge. Let grow and develop." Peggy Quinn to Pam Allen, 1 Sept. 1969, and "Recipe," n.d., box 1, Allen Papers. Pam Allen had been a Mississippi Summer Project volunteer, and Sudsofloppen emerged directly out of her quest to apply movement lessons learned in Mississippi to her life in the San Francisco Bay area. See also Nina S. Adams, "The Women Who Left Them Behind," 191–94.

26. Alice Echols's useful study, *Daring to Be Bad*, makes clear that by no means should these different radical women's groups be considered synonymous. Instead, it was their variety that sparked so much intellectual energy and evoked such a positive a response. This said, radical feminists differed, sometimes a great deal, over the importance of CR, "personal solutionism," and the degree to which "the personal is political" should be interpreted prescriptively. Some wanted more collective action and less talk. It was a debate over means and ends that echoed in important ways the discussions centered at Waveland in 1964. See ibid., 142–43, 156, 170, 185. For other relevant work on

the women's liberation movement, see DuPlessis and Snitow, *Feminist Memoir Project*; Kaplan, *Story of Jane*; Berkeley, *Women's Liberation Movement*; Cohen, *The Sisterhood*; Farrell, *Yours in Sisterhood*; Gerhard, *Desiring Revolution*; Rosen, *The World Split Open*; and Ryan, *Feminism and the Women's Movement*.

27. Rader, *Blood Dues*, 11 (quotation). See also Whalen and Flacks, *Beyond the Barricades*, 139; Sale, *SDS*, 526; and Jane Adams (p. 71) and Bernardine Dohrn (p. 234) interviews in Chepesiuk, *Sixties Radicals*. A few males found that the youth and women's liberation movements allowed them to move away from the "brittle, rigid, defensive competitiveness they normally experience whenever they are together" (Potter, *A Name for Ourselves*, 156–57).

28. Evans, *Personal Politics*, 101, 155, 164–65; Casey Hayden interview; Hayden, e-mail to the author, 11 Apr. 2001.

29. "Boston Draft Resistance Group," n.d. [1967?], Newsreel Productions, 20 min., Film and Video Archives, SHSW (Grizzard).The draft resistance movement was certainly not a homogeneous entity. In fact, much like the women's movement, while it may have taken initial impetus from SNCC and ERAP people, it soon mushroomed into thousands of different organizations. At the 10 Mar. 1968 meeting of the SDS Southwest Regional Conference, the group advocated "going into the army" over jail, underground, or Canada: "The army is the only logical choice for the serious radical who is forced into this situation. The advantages are obvious: (a) familiarization with weapons and military technique, (b) contact with working-class youth, (c) the breakdown of barriers between middle-class radicals and workers, and (d) the possibility of creating a degree of radical political sentiment amongst GI's." "Draft Resistance Resolution," box 36, SDS Papers. The repeated use of the word "radical" as a substitute for a more precise description of the "sentiment" they wished to "create" within the population highlights the conceptual limitations of the movement's development as of 1969.

30. "RESIST/Resistance," 15 min. film., VBB 020, Film and Video Archives, SHSW. Of the estimated 26,800,000 young men subject to the draft throughout the U.S. involvement in Vietnam, 8,720,000 chose to enlist and 2,215,000 were drafted. Of these, 1,600,000 served as combatants and 550,000 as noncombatants. Of the 15,980,000 who registered with the Selective Service and saw no military service, 15,410,000 were deferred, exempted, or disqualified. Of the 570,000 young men who violated the Selective Service Act, 209,517 were prosecuted, 8,750 were convicted, about 3,000 became fugitives, and 197,750 had their cases dropped. Of those convicted, 3,250 were imprisoned and 5,500 were given probation or suspended sentences. Of those in prison, 1,500 served less than 6 months, 1,500 served between 7 and 24 months, and 250 served 25 months or more. Harris, *Dreams Die Hard*, 286. The Pentagon admitted to at least 500,000 incidents of desertion between 1963 and 1973. H. Bruce Franklin, *Back Where You Came From*, 212.

31. Moses' quotation recalled by Staughton Lynd, who was present — Lynd interview. Moses made this statement on the same day that Dave Dennis eulogized Chaney at his memorial service in Meridian, quoted at some length at the beginning of Chapter 9. It is interesting, Lynd pointed out, that Dennis foretold a direction toward despair and violence, whereas Moses was imagining a new way to move forward. Lynd, e-mail to

the author, 9 June 2001. Sally Belfrage also reported Moses comparing Mississippi to Vietnam at the beginning of the summer of 1964. She recalled that he said: "'When you come South, you bring with you the concern of the country—because the people of the country don't identify with Negroes. The guerrilla war in Mississippi is not much different from that in Vietnam. But when we tried to see President Johnson, his secretary said that Vietnam was popping up all over his calendar and he hadn't time to talk to us.' Now, because of the Summer Project, because whites were involved, a crack team of FBI men was going down to Mississippi to investigate. 'We have been asking for them for three years. Now the federal government is concerned; there will be more protection for us, and hopefully for the Negroes who live there'" (quoted in Belfrage, *Freedom Summer*, 10).

32. Lynd interview; Moses, quoted in Lynd's introduction to Moses, "Mississippi, 1961–1962," *Liberation* 14 (January 1970), 7.

33. Memo from Walter Tillow, Bob Parris, Francis Mitchell, Courtland Cox, Dona Richards, and others, Re: An Idea for a Project Based in Wash., D.C., This Summer, "Staff Newsletter," 12 June 1965, frame 29, reel 15, SNCC Papers. See also Sale, *SDS*, 220. The project would "provide a forum for discussion between different 'interest groups' by setting up workshops in the D.C. area that would run continuously all summer." The goal was "that out of such discussion and exchange of opinions we could begin to see our way to developing common programs as part of a new and broad social movement." See also Ronald J. Young to Rev. J. M. Lawson, 11 Aug. 1965, box 66, FOR Papers; Norman interview; and "The MFDP and Vietnam," 31 July 1965, frame 529, reel 27, CORE Papers. At Tom Hayden's request, Moses spoke at an antiwar rally in 1965. When Moses was drafted after that speech, he recalled, "on the one hand, I really didn't want to go back to jail, and on the other hand, I really didn't want to get any more involved in the fight against the war than I had been, so I left the country. I went to Montreal, and I stayed there for almost two years, dropped my identity, got a new identity, figured out a way to get a passport, under that identity, and left with the person who is my wife now, Janet, and we went to Tanzania, and we taught over there." Moses remarks at panel, "How Do We Get to a Just Society?," SB-SNCC Conference (transcript). For more on SNCC and the draft, see Clayborne Carson, *In Struggle*, 184–85, and Dittmer, *Local People*, 349.

34. On Savio and the Free Speech Movement, see Brett Eynon's insightful article, "Community in Motion"; on JANE, see Kaplan, *The Story of Jane*. Hundreds of similar stories abound. At the very least, volunteers organized supply drives: COFO handed out a "Materials Needed by COFO" sheet to departing volunteers that contained a long list of sports equipment, books, films, community center supplies, clothing, trucks, sound equipment, etc. The flier advised workers: "You are in the unique position of having been in Mississippi, and of returning to 'normal civilian life,' and the spectrum of contacts, friends, and relatives you undoubtedly know. You can function as a bridge between the Mississippi project and its needs and the people you know who can help fill these needs. . . . Be ingenious—we need practically everything!" "Materials Needed by COFO," September 1964, frame 980, reel 11, SNCC Papers.

35. Roszak, *The Making of a Counterculture*, 5–7.

36. Hundreds of books and thousands of pamphlets on the counterculture testify to

the many breathtaking challenges it made to all facets of modern society. For a more extensive bibliography, see Roszak's Bibliographic Notes, ibid., and Bloom and Breines, *Takin' It to the Streets*. They include Romm, *Open Conspiracy*; Rossman, *Wedding within the War*; Weissman, *Big Brother and the Holding Company*; Obst, *The Sixties*; Albert and Albert, *The Sixties Papers*; Sculatti and Seay, *San Francisco Nights*; Jay Stevens, *Storming Heaven*; Adler, *Heretic's Heart*; Ellwood, *Sixties Spiritual Awakening*; Unger and Unger, *The Times Were a Changin'*; Whitmer, *Aquarius Revisited*; Richard Goldstein, *Reporting the Counterculture*; and Law, *Flashing on the Sixties*.

37. Liz Shirah to "Paul [Booth] and Everybody," 20 Sept. 1965, box 34, SDS Papers. On the SNCC Labor Conference, see "To Walt from Judy," n.d. [1965], frames 977–78, reel 7, SNCC Papers.

Bibliography

Manuscript and Archival Sources

Pamela Parker Allen Papers. State Historical Society of Wisconsin, Madison.

Emile de Antonio Papers. State Historical Society of Wisconsin, Madison.

Karin Ashley, Bill Ayers, Phoebe Hirsh, Johnny Lerner, Terry Robbins, Mark Rudd, Mike Spiegel, and Bill Willet. "Foggy Bottom Breakdown: Nixon's Inauguration or the Pigs' Parade." J. B. Matthews Collection. box 518, Special Collections Library, Duke University, Durham, N.C.

Stokely Carmichael – Lorna D. Smith Papers. Department of Special Collections, Stanford University, Stanford, Calif.

Congress of Racial Equality Papers. Microfilm.

Stewart Ewen Papers. State Historical Society of Wisconsin, Madison.

FBI File of the Student Nonviolent Coordinating Committee. Wilmington, Del.: Scholarly Resources, 1990 – 91.

Miriam (Mimi) Feingold Papers. State Historical Society of Wisconsin, Madison. Microfilm.

Fellowship of Reconciliation Papers. Swarthmore College Peace Collection, Swarthmore, Pa.

Casey Hayden (née Sandra Cason) Papers. Private Collection of Casey Hayden.

Legal Department Case Files, 1960 – 72. Supplement to Part 23, series B.1, National Association for the Advancement of Colored People Papers. Microfilm.

Robert F. Kennedy Papers. Attorney General Files, John F. Kennedy Library, Boston.

Mary King Papers. State Historical Society of Wisconsin, Madison.

Staughton Lynd Papers. State Historical Society of Wisconsin, Madison.

J. B. Matthews Collection. Special Collections Library, Duke University, Durham, N.C.

Carol McEldowney Papers. State Historical Society of Wisconsin, Madison.

Mississippi Freedom Democratic Party Papers. Reels 63 – 70, SNCC Papers. Microfilm.

"Mississippi's 'Freedom Summer' Reviewed: A Fifteen Year Perspective on Progress in Race Relations, 1964 – 1979," sponsored by Tougaloo and Millsaps Colleges, Jackson, Miss. State Historical Society of Wisconsin, Madison.

A. J. Muste Papers. Swarthmore College Peace Collection, Swarthmore, Pa.

New Left Collection. Hoover Institution on War, Revolution, and Peace, Stanford, Calif.

Pacifica Collection. Freedom Archives, San Francisco.

Charlotte Phillips and Oliver Fein Papers. Courtesy of Phillips and Fein, in their personal collection.

Project South Collection. Special Collections Library, Stanford University, Stanford, Calif.

Joseph L. Rauh Papers. Manuscript Division, Library of Congress, Washington, D.C.

Revolutionary Action Movement Papers, 1963–96. Microfilm.

Jo Ann Ooiman Robinson Papers. State Historical Society of Wisconsin, Madison.

Anne Romaine Papers. Archives Department, Martin Luther King Jr. Center for Nonviolent Social Change, Atlanta, and State Historical Society of Wisconsin, Madison.

Mendy Samstein Papers. State Historical Society of Wisconsin, Madison.

John Nevin Sayre Papers. Swarthmore College Peace Collection. Swarthmore, Pa.

Charles Sherrod Papers. State Historical Society of Wisconsin, Madison.

Sixties Collection. Columbia Oral History Project, Butler Library, Columbia University, New York.

Kelly Miller Smith Papers. Vanderbilt University Special Collections, Nashville, Tenn.

Southern Christian Leadership Conference Papers. Microfilm.

Robert Starobin Papers. State Historical Society of Wisconsin, Madison.

Student Nonviolent Coordinating Committee Papers, 1959–72. Sanford, N.C.: Microfilming Corporation of America, 1982.

Students for a Democratic Society Papers. State Historical Society of Wisconsin, Madison.

Walter Tillow Papers. State Historical Society of Wisconsin, Madison.

Maria Varela Papers. State Historical Society of Wisconsin, Madison.

Lee Webb Papers. State Historical Society of Wisconsin, Madison.

Interviews

Adams, Jane. Interview by Ron Chepesiuk. In *Sixties Radicals, Then and Now: Candid Conversations with Those Who Shaped the Era*. Jefferson, N.C.: McFarland and Co., 1995.

Archibald, Kathy. Interview by Dr. Clayborne Carson, Atlanta, 6 Nov. 1976. Courtesy of Carson, Martin Luther King Jr. Papers Project, Stanford University, Stanford, Calif.

Ayers, Bill. Interview by Ron Chepesiuk. In *Sixties Radicals, Then and Now: Candid Conversations with Those Who Shaped the Era*. Jefferson, N.C.: McFarland and Co., 1995.

Bond, Julian. Interview by Gwen Gillan, 6 July 1967, tape 487, Civil Rights Collection. State Historical Society of Wisconsin, Madison.

Bowen, Robert. Interview by Ronald Grele, Los Angeles, 23 June 1984. Columbia Oral History Project, Butler Library, Columbia University, New York.

Brecher, Jeremy. Interview by Bret Eynon, New York, N.Y., 20 Sept. 1983. Columbia Oral History Project, Butler Library, Columbia University, New York.

Brightman, Carol. Interview by Ronald Grele, New York, N.Y., 12 Dec. 1984. Columbia Oral History Project, Butler Library, Columbia University, New York.

Calvert, Greg. Interview by Ronald Grele, Eugene, Ore., 1–3 July 1987. Columbia Oral History Project, Butler Library, Columbia University, New York.

Chatfield, Jack. Interview by the author, telephone, 6 Jan. 2001.

Eagan, Richard, and Andrea Eagan. Interview by Ronald Grele, Brooklyn, N.Y., 18 Feb. 1985. Columbia Oral History Project, Butler Library, Columbia University, New York.

Fein, Oliver. Interview by the author, 19 May 2002.

Flacks, Mickey. Interview by Bret Eynon, Santa Barbara, Calif., 25 Sept. 1978. Bentley Historical Library, University of Michigan, Ann Arbor.

Friedman, Paula. Interview by the author, Berkeley, Calif., 28 June 1998; telephone, 4 Oct. 1998.

Garvy, Helen. Interview by the author, Los Gatos, Calif., 14, 22 June 1998.

Gilbert, David. Interview by Ronald Grele, Auburn Correctional Facility, Auburn, N.Y., 16–17 Jan., 18 June 1985. Also present: Lieutenant Riley. Columbia Oral History Project, Butler Library, Columbia University, New York.

Gitlin, Todd. Interview by Bret Eynon, Berkeley, Calif., 16 Sept. 1978. Bentley Historical Library, University of Michigan, Ann Arbor.

Gonzales, Juan. Interview by Ronald Grele and Bret Eynon, Philadelphia, 6 Aug. 1984. Columbia Oral History Project, Butler Library, Columbia University, New York.

Guyot, Lawrence. Interview by Anne and Howard Romaine, 1966. Anne Romaine Papers, State Historical Society of Wisconsin, Madison.

Haber, Barbara. Interview by Bret Eynon, n.d., n.p., Contemporary History Project (The New Left in Ann Arbor, Mich.), Bentley Historical Library, Ann Arbor.

Hamer, Mrs. Fannie Lou. Interview by Anne and Howard Romaine, 1966 (transcript). Anne Romaine Papers, State Historical Society of Wisconsin, Madison.

Hamilton, Steve. Interview by Ronald Grele and Bret Eynon, Oakland, Calif., 9 Apr. 1984. Columbia Oral History Project, Butler Library, Columbia University, New York.

Hansen, Bill. Interview by Dr. Clayborne Carson, Atlanta, 6 Nov. 1976. Courtesy of Carson, Martin Luther King Jr. Papers Project, Stanford University, Stanford, Calif.

Hayden, Casey (née Sandra Cason). Interview by the author, Tucson, Ariz., 7 Dec. 1996.

Hayden, Tom. Interview by Bret Eynon, Los Angeles, 29 Sept. 1978. Bentley Historical Library, University of Michigan, Ann Arbor.

Hewitt, Ray. Interview by Ronald Grele and Bret Eynon, Los Angeles, 6–7 Apr. 1984. Columbia Oral History Project, Butler Library, Columbia University, New York.

Hirshfeld, Elizabeth. Interview by the author, Oakland, Calif., 27 June 1998.

Huggins, Ericka. Interview by Ron Chepesiuk. In *Sixties Radicals, Then and Now: Candid Conversations with Those Who Shaped the Era.* Jefferson, N.C.: McFarland and Co., 1995.

Jeffrey, Sharon. Interview by Bret Eynon, San Rafael, Calif., October 1978. Bentley Historical Library, University of Michigan, Ann Arbor.

Jones, Jeff. Interview by Ronald Grele, New York, N.Y., 24 Oct. 1984. Columbia Oral History Project, Butler Library, Columbia University, New York.

———. Interview by the author, telephone, 21 June 1999.

Katzenbach, Nicholas. Oral History Interview. John F. Kennedy Library, Boston.

Kennedy, Robert F. Oral History Interview, John F. Kennedy Library, Boston.

Lawson, James. Interview by the author, telephone, 23, 27 Mar. 2000; 14 Aug. 2001.

———. Interview online. ‹http://www.pbs.org/weta/foremorepowerful/nashville/interview.html›, 18 July 2001.

Lewis, John. Interview by Dr. Clayborne Carson, Atlanta, 17 Apr. 1972. Courtesy of Carson, Martin Luther King Jr. Papers Project, Stanford University, Stanford, Calif.

Lynd, Staughton. Interview by the author, Niles, Ohio, 14 July 2001.

Magidoff, Dickie. Interview by the author, Oakland, Calif., 26 June 1998; telephone, 17, 19 Nov. 1999.

Marshall, Burke. Oral History Interview. John F. Kennedy Library, Boston.

McDew, Charles. Interview by Katherine M. Shannon, Washington, D.C., 24 Aug. 1967. Transcript in the author's possession.

Metcalf, Evan. Interview by James O'Brien, n.d., tape 573A, reel 44. James O'Brien Papers, State Historical Society of Wisconsin, Madison.

Morales, Iris. Interview by Ronald Grele, New York, N.Y., 19 Nov. 1984. Columbia Oral History Project, Butler Library, Columbia University, New York.

Moses, Robert P. Interview by Dr. Clayborne Carson, 29–30 Mar. 1982. Courtesy of Carson, Martin Luther King Jr. Papers Project, Stanford University, Stanford, Calif.

———. Interview by Anne Romaine, Highlander Center, New Market, Tenn., 5 Sept. [1965?]. Anne Romaine Papers, State Historical Society of Wisconsin, Madison.

Nash, Diane. Interview by the author, telephone, 31 Aug. 2001.

Norman, Martha Prescod. Interview by Bret Eynon and Eileen Fishman, Ann Arbor, April 1979. Bentley Historical Library, University of Michigan, Ann Arbor.

Oberdorfer, Louis. Oral History Interview. John F. Kennedy Library, Boston.

Oglesby, Carl. Interview by Bret Eynon, Boston, July 1978; Cambridge, Mass., 12 Dec. 1984. Columbia Oral History Project, Butler Library, Columbia University, New York.

O'Neal, John. Interview by Dr. Clayborne Carson and Jean Wiley, New Orleans, 20 Sept. 1978. Courtesy of Carson, Martin Luther King Jr. Papers Project, Stanford University, Stanford, Calif.

Pardun, Robert. Interview by the author, Los Gatos, Calif., 22 June 1998.

Patch, Penny. Interview by the author, telephone, 19 Nov. 1999.

Patterson, John. Oral History Interview. John F. Kennedy Library, Boston.

Rabinowitz, Victor. Interview by Lenore Bredeson Hogan, New York, N.Y., 10, 17, 25 Oct., 8, 14, 21 Nov., 6 Dec. 1978; 2, 7, Mar., 7 Nov., 5, 11 Dec. 1979. Columbia Oral History Project, Butler Library, Columbia University, New York.

———. Interview by Norman I. Silber, New York, N.Y., 13, 20, 28 June, 2 Nov. 1989; 27 Apr. 1990. Columbia Oral History Project, Butler Library, Columbia University, New York.

Rauh, Joseph L. Interview by Anne Romaine, n.d. Rauh Papers, Library of Congress.

Reagon, Bernice Johnson. Interview by Dick Cluster. In *They Should Have Served That Cup of Coffee*. Boston: South End, 1979.

Richardson, Judy. Interview by the author, telephone, 20 Aug. 2000.

Ricks, Willie. Interview by Dr. Clayborne Carson, Stanford, Calif., 10 May 1976. Courtesy of Carson, Martin Luther King Jr. Papers Project, Stanford University, Stanford, Calif.

Ross, Bob. Interview by Bret Eynon, Worcester, Mass., July 1978. Bentley Historical Library, University of Michigan, Ann Arbor.

Rudd, Mark. Interview by Ronald Grele, New York, N.Y., 30 Mar. 1987. Columbia Oral History Project, Butler Library, Columbia University, New York.

Samstein, Mendy. Interview by Anne Romaine, n.d. [1966?]. Anne Romaine Papers, State Historical Society of Wisconsin, Madison.

Seigenthaler, John. Oral History Interview. John F. Kennedy Library, Boston.

Shapiro, Peter. Interview by Ronald Grele, Oakland, Calif., 21 June 1984. Columbia Oral History Project, Butler Library, Columbia University, New York.

Sherrod, Charles. Interview by Bret Eynon, Albany, Ga., 12 May 1985. Courtesy of Eynon, Columbia Oral History Project, Butler Library, Columbia University, New York.

Thrasher, Sue. Interview by Ronald Grele, Tennessee, 1986. Columbia Oral History Project, Butler Library, Columbia University, New York.

Tillinghast, Muriel. Interview by Dr. Clayborne Carson, 6 Nov. 1976. Courtesy of Carson, Martin Luther King Jr. Papers Project, Stanford University, Stanford, Calif.

Wildflower, Leni. Interview by Ronald Grele, Santa Monica, Calif., 7, 13 June 1988. Columbia Oral History Project, Butler Library, Columbia University, New York.

Winslow, Barbara. Interview by the author, Brooklyn, N.Y., 16 Aug. 1998.

Government Publications

Commission on CIA Activities within the United States. *Report to the President*. Washington, D.C.: Government Printing Office, 1975.

Extent of Subversion in Campus Disorders, Testimony of Ernesto E. Blanco, Hearings before the Subcommittee to Investigate the Administration of the Internal Security Act and Other Internal Security Laws of the Committee on the Judiciary, Senate. 91st Cong., 1st sess., pt. 1, 19 June 1969.

Extent of Subversion in Campus Disorders, Testimony of John F. McCormick and William E. Grogan, Hearings before the Subcommittee to Investigate the Administration of the Internal Security Act and Other Internal Security Laws of the Committee on the Judiciary, Senate. 91st Cong., 1st sess., pt. 3, 26 June 1969.

Extent of Subversion in Campus Disorders, Testimony of Max Phillip Friedman, Hearings before the Subcommittee to Investigate the Administration of the Internal Security Act and Other Internal Security Laws of the Committee on the Judiciary, Senate. 91st Cong., 1st sess., pt. 2, 12 Aug. 1969.

Extent of Subversion in the "New Left," Testimony of Robert J. Thoms, Hearings before the Subcommittee to Investigate the Administration of the Internal Security Act and Other Internal Security Laws of the Committee on the Judiciary, Senate. 91st Cong., 2d sess., pt. 1, Jan. 20, 1970.

Extent of Subversion in the "New Left," Testimony of Inspector Cecil M. Pharris, SFPD, Hearings before the Subcommittee to Investigate the Administration of the Internal Security Act and Other Internal Security Laws of the Committee on the Judiciary, Senate. 91st Cong., 2d sess., pt. 2, 21 Jan. 1970.

Extent of Subversion in the "New Left," Testimony of Marjorie King and Mike Soto, Hearings before the Subcommittee to Investigate the Administration of the Internal Security Act and Other Internal Security Laws of the Committee on the Judiciary, Senate. 91st Cong., 2d sess., pt. 3, 31 Mar. 1970.

Extent of Subversion in the "New Left," Testimony of Charles Siragusa and Ronald L. Brooks, Hearings before the Subcommittee to Investigate the Administration of the Internal Security Act and Other Internal Security Laws of the Committee on the Judiciary, Senate. 91st Cong., 2d sess., pt. 4, 10 June 1970.

Extent of Subversion in the "New Left" (Fall River, Mass.), Hearings before the Subcommittee to Investigate the Administration of the Internal Security Act and Other Internal Security Laws of the Committee on the Judiciary, Senate. 91st Cong., 2d sess., pt. 5, 11 June, 9 July 1970.

Extent of Subversion in the "New Left," Testimony of James W. Rutherford, Louis Szabo, and Charles H. Gilmore, Hearings before the Subcommittee to Investigate the Administration of the Internal Security Act and Other Internal Security Laws of the Committee on the Judiciary, Senate. 91st Cong., 2d sess., pt. 6, 1 July 1970.

Extent of Subversion in the "New Left," Testimony of Hugh Patrick Feely and Harry F. Port Jr., Hearings before the Subcommittee to Investigate the Administration of the Internal Security Act and Other Internal Security Laws of the Committee on the Judiciary, Senate. 91st Cong., 2d sess., pt. 8, 3 Aug. 1970.

Extent of Subversion in the "New Left," Testimony of Allen Crouter and Paul Chambers, Hearings before the Subcommittee to Investigate the Administration of the Internal Security Act and Other Internal Security Laws of the Committee on the Judiciary, Senate. 91st Cong., 2d sess., pt. 9, 6 Aug. 1970.

Extent of Subversion in the "New Left," Testimony of Clifford A. Murray and Richard M. Schave, Hearings before the Subcommittee to Investigate the Administration of the Internal Security Act and Other Internal Security Laws of the Committee on the Judiciary, Senate. 91st Cong., 2d sess., pt. 8, 25 Sept. 1970.

FBI Counterintelligence Programs, Hearing before the Civil Rights and Constitutional Rights Subcommittee of the Committee on the Judiciary, House of Representatives. 93d Cong., 2d sess., 20 Nov. 1974. Serial no. 55.

Final Report of the Select Committee to Study Governmental Operations with Respect to Intelligence Activities. 94th Cong., 2d sess., 26 Apr. 1976. Report no. 94-755.

Hearings before the United States Commission on Civil Rights, Hearings Held in Jackson, Miss., 16 – 20 Feb. 1965. Vols. 1 and 2. Washington, D.C.: Government Printing Office, 1965.

Hearings relating to HR 959, Amending the Internal Security Act of 1950 (Obstruction of Armed Forces), Hearings before the Committee on Internal Security, House of Representatives. 91st Cong., 1st sess., 15–16 Sept. 1969.

Hearings regarding the Administration of the Subversive Activities Control Act of 1950 and the Federal Civilian Employee Loyalty-Security Program, Hearings before the Committee on Internal Security, House of Representatives. 91st Cong., 2d sess., pt. 1, 23, 30 Sept. 1970.

Hearings regarding the Administration of the Subversive Activities Control Act of 1950 and the Federal Civilian Employee Loyalty-Security Program, Hearings before the Committee on Internal Security, House of Representatives. 92d Cong., 1st sess., pt. 2, 21–22, 27–29 Apr. 1971.

Hearings regarding the Administration of the Subversive Activities Control Act of 1950 and the Federal Civilian Employee Loyalty-Security Program, Hearings before the Committee on Internal Security, House of Representatives. 92d Cong., 1st sess., pt. 3, 2–3, 8–10 June, 27–29 July, 3 Aug. 1971.

Hearings regarding the Administration of the Subversive Activities Control Act of 1950 and the Federal Civilian Employee Loyalty-Security Program, Hearings before the Committee on Internal Security, House of Representatives. 93d Cong., 1st sess., pt. 4, 25, 27 Jan., 23, 29 Feb., 16 Mar. 1972.

Illinois Crime Investigating Commission. *Report on the SDS Riots* (April 1970). Reprinted in *Extent of Subversion in the "New Left," Testimony of Robert J. Thoms, Hearings before the Subcommittee to Investigate the Administration of the Internal Security Act and Other Internal Security Laws,* Committee on the Judiciary, U.S. Senate. 91st Cong., 2d sess., pt. 1, 20 Jan. 1970.

Intelligence Activities, Senate Resolution 21, Hearings before the Select Committee to Study Governmental Operations with Respect to Intelligence Activities of the U.S. Senate. 94th Cong., 1st sess., vol. 2, Huston Plan, 23–25 Sept. 1975.

Intelligence Activities, Senate Resolution 21, Hearings before the Select Committee to Study Governmental Operations with Respect to Intelligence Activities of the U.S. Senate. 94th Cong., 1st sess., vol. 3, Internal Revenue Service, 2 Oct. 1975.

Intelligence Activities, Senate Resolution 21, Hearings before the Select Committee to Study Governmental Operations with Respect to Intelligence Activities of the U.S. Senate. 94th Cong., 1st sess., vol. 4, Mail Opening, 21–22, 24 Oct. 1975.

Intelligence Activities, Senate Resolution 21, Hearings before the Select Committee to Study Governmental Operations with Respect to Intelligence Activities of the U.S. Senate. 94th Cong., 1st sess., vol. 5, The National Security Agency and Fourth Amendment Rights, 29 Oct., 6 Nov. 1975.

Intelligence Activities, Senate Resolution 21, Hearings before the Select Committee to Study Governmental Operations with Respect to Intelligence Activities of the U.S. Senate. 94th Cong., 1st sess., vol. 6, Federal Bureau of Investigation, 18–19 Nov., 2–3, 9–11 Dec. 1975.

Investigation of Students for a Democratic Society, Part 1-A (Georgetown University), Hearings before the Committee on Internal Security, House of Representatives. 91st Cong., 1st sess., 3–4 June 1969.

Investigation of Students for a Democratic Society, Part 1-B (Georgetown University),

Hearings before the Committee on Internal Security, House of Representatives. 91st Cong., 1st sess., 5, 17 June 1969.

Investigation of Students for a Democratic Society, Part 2 (Kent State University), Hearings before the Committee on Internal Security, House of Representatives. 91st Cong., 1st sess., 24–25 June 1969.

Investigation of Students for a Democratic Society, Part 3-A (George Washington University), Hearings before the Committee on Internal Security, House of Representatives. 91st Cong., 1st sess., 22 July 1969.

Investigation of Students for a Democratic Society, Part 3-B (George Washington University), Hearings before the Committee on Internal Security, House of Representatives. 91st Cong., 1st sess., 23–24 July 1969.

Investigation of Students for a Democratic Society, Part 4 (American University), Hearings before the Committee on Internal Security, House of Representatives. 91st Cong., 1st sess., 24 July 1969.

Investigation of Students for a Democratic Society, Part 5 (University of Chicago; Communist Party Efforts with Regard to SDS), Hearings before the Committee on Internal Security, House of Representatives. 91st Cong., 1st sess., 6–7 Aug. 1969.

Investigation of Students for a Democratic Society, Part 6-A (Columbus, Ohio, High Schools), Hearings before the Committee on Internal Security, House of Representatives. 91st Cong., 1st sess., 20–22 Oct. 1969.

Investigation of Students for a Democratic Society, Part 6-B (Akron, Ohio; Detroit, Mich.; and Pittsburgh, Pa.), Hearings before the Committee on Internal Security, House of Representatives. 91st Cong., 1st sess., 28–30 Oct. 1969.

Investigation of Students for a Democratic Society, Part 7-A (Return of Prisoners of War, and Data concerning Camera News, Inc., "Newsreel"), Hearings before the Committee on Internal Security, House of Representatives. 91st Cong., 1st sess., 9 Dec. 1969.

Investigation of Students for a Democratic Society, Part 7-B (SDS Activities at Fort Dix, N.J.; Washington, D.C.: and Chicago, Ill.), Hearings before the Committee on Internal Security, House of Representatives. 91st Cong., 1st sess., 17–18 Dec. 1969.

The New Left: Memorandum Prepared for the Subcommittee to Investigate the Administration of the Internal Security Act and Other Internal Security Laws of the Committee on the Judiciary, Senate. 90 Cong., 2d sess., 9 Oct. 1968.

Notification to Victims of Improper Intelligence Agency Activities, Hearings before a Subcommittee of the Committee on Government Operations, House of Representatives. 94th Cong., 2d sess. on HR 12039, HR 13192, and HR 169 to Amend the Privacy Act of 1974, 28 Apr., 11 May 1976.

Riots, Civil and Criminal Disorders, Hearings before the Permanent Subcommittee on Investigations of the Committee on Government Operations, Senate. 91st Cong., 1st sess., pt. 18, 16–17 June 1969.

Riots, Civil and Criminal Disorders, Hearings before the Permanent Subcommittee on Investigations of the Committee on Government Operations, Senate. 91st Cong., 1st sess., pt. 20, 26, 30 June 1969.

Riots, Civil and Criminal Disorders, Hearings before the Permanent Subcommittee on

Investigations of the Committee on Government Operations, Senate. 91st Cong., 1st sess., pt. 21, 1–2, 8 July 1969.

Riots, Civil and Criminal Disorders, Hearings before the Permanent Subcommittee on Investigations of the Committee on Government Operations, Senate. 91st Cong., 1st sess., pt. 22, 9–10, 15–16 July 1969.

Riots, Civil and Criminal Disorders, Hearings before the Permanent Subcommittee on Investigations of the Committee on Government Operations, Senate. 91st Cong., 1st sess., pt. 23, 22 July, 4–5 Aug. 1969.

SDS Plans for America's High Schools, Report by the Committee on Internal Security, House of Representatives. 91st Cong., 1st sess., 1969.

Subversive Influences in Riots, Looting, and Burning, Part I, Hearings before the Committee on Un-American Activities, House of Representatives. 90th Cong., 1st sess., 25–26, 31 Oct., 28 Nov. 1967.

Subversive Influences in Riots, Looting, and Burning, Part II, Hearings before the Committee on Un-American Activities, House of Representatives. 90th Cong., 1st sess., 31 Oct., 1 Nov. 1967.

Subversive Influences in Riots, Looting, and Burning, Part III (Los Angeles – Watts), Hearings before the Committee on Un-American Activities, House of Representatives. 90th Cong., 1st sess., 28–30 Nov. 1967.

Subversive Influences in Riots, Looting, and Burning, Part IV (Newark, N.J.), Hearings before the Committee on Un-American Activities, House of Representatives. 90th Cong., 2d sess., 23–24 Apr. 1968.

Subversive Influences in Riots, Looting, and Burning, Part V (Buffalo, N.Y.), Hearings before the Committee on Un-American Activities, House of Representatives. 90th Cong., 2d sess., 20 June 1968.

Subversive Influences in Riots, Looting, and Burning, Part VI (San Francisco – Berkeley), Hearings before the Committee on Un-American Activities, House of Representatives. 90th Cong., 2d sess., 27–28 June 1968.

Subversive Involvement in Disruption of 1968, Democratic Party National Convention, Pt. 1, Hearings before the Committee on Un-American Activities, House of Representatives. 90th Cong., 2d sess., 1, 3–4 Oct. 1968.

Subversive Involvement in Disruption of 1968, Democratic Party National Convention, Pt. 2, Hearings before the Committee on Un-American Activities, House of Representatives. 90th Cong., 2d sess., 2–3 Dec. 1968.

Subversive Involvement in Disruption of 1968, Democratic Party National Convention, Pt. 3, Hearings before the Committee on Un-American Activities, House of Representatives. 90th Cong., 2d sess., 4–5 Dec. 1968.

Subversive Involvement in the Origin, Leadership, and Activities of the New Mobilization Committee to End the War in Vietnam and Its Predecessor Organizations. Staff Study by the Committee on Internal Security, House of Representatives. 91st Cong., 2d sess., 1970.

U.S. Congress. House. Committee on Internal Security. *Investigation of Students for a Democratic Society, Part 6-A (Columbus, Ohio, High Schools).* 99th Cong., 1st. sess., 20–22 Oct. 1969.

U.S. Congress. House. Select Committee on Intelligence. *CIA: The Pike Report.* Spokesman Books for the Bertrand Russell Peace Foundation, 1977.

U.S. Congress. Senate. Committee on the Judiciary. Subcommittee on Administrative Practice and Procedure. *Hearings on Oversight of the Freedom of Information Act.* 95th Cong., 1st sess., 15 – 16 Sept., 6 Oct., 10 Nov. 1977.

U.S. Congress. Senate. Committee on the Judiciary. Subcommittee to Investigate the Administration of the Internal Security Act. *Report of the Subcommittee to Investigate the Administration of the Internal Security Act and Other Internal Security Laws.* 94th Cong., 2d sess., January 1975.

U.S. Congress. Senate. Select Committee to Study Governmental Operations with Respect to Intelligence Activities. *Final Report of the Select Committee to Study Governmental Operations with Respect to Intelligence Activities.* 94th Cong., 2d sess., 1976.

Books, Articles, and Dissertations/Theses

Abbott, Sidney, and Barbara Love. *Sappho Was a Right-On Woman.* New York: Stein and Day, 1973.

Acuna, Rodolfo. *Occupied America: A History of Chicanos.* New York: Harper and Row, 1981.

Adams, Emmie Schrader. "From Africa to Mississippi." In Constance Curry et al., eds. *Deep in Our Hearts: Nine White Women in the Freedom Movement,* 289 – 332. Athens: University of Georgia Press, 2000.

Adams, Nina S. "The Women Who Left Them Behind." In Melvin Small and William D. Hoover, eds., *Give Peace A Chance: Exploring the Vietnam Antiwar Movement,* 182 – 95. Syracuse, N.Y.: Syracuse University Press, 1992.

Adelson, Alan M. *SDS.* New York: Scribner, 1972.

Adler, Margot. *Heretic's Heart: A Journey through Spirit & Revolution.* Boston: Beacon Press, 1997.

Ahmann, Matthew H., ed. *The New Negro.* Notre Dame, Ind.: Fides, 1961.

Albert, Judith Clavir, and Stewart Edward Albert, eds. *The Sixties Papers: Documents of a Rebellious Decade.* New York: Praeger, 1984.

Alinksy, Saul D. *Reveille for Radicals.* Chicago: University of Chicago Press, 1946.

——. *Rules for Radicals.* New York: Random House, 1971; New York: Vintage Books, 1989.

Allen, Robert L. *Black Awakening in Capitalist America: An Analytic History.* Garden City, N.Y.: Doubleday, 1969.

Alpert, Jane. *Growing Up Underground.* New York: Morrow, 1981.

Anderson, Jervis. *Bayard Rustin: Troubles I've Seen: A Biography.* New York: HarperCollins, 1997.

Anderson, Reynaldo. "Practical Internationalists: The Story of the Des Moines, Iowa, Black Panther Party." In Jeanne Theoharis and Komozi Woodard, eds., *Groundwork: Local Black Freedom Movements in America,* 282 – 99. New York: New York University Press, 2005.

Anthony, Earl. *Picking Up the Gun: A Report on the Black Panthers*. New York: Dial Press, 1970.

Aptheker, Bettina. *The Academic Rebellion in the United States*. Charleston, S.C.: Citadel Press, 1972.

———. *Higher Education and the Student Rebellion in the United States, 1960–1969: A Bibliography*. New York: American Institute for Marxist Studies, 1969.

Aronowitz, Stanley. "Toward Radicalism: The Death and Rebirth of the American Left." In David Trend, ed., *Radical Democracy: Identity, Citizenship, and the State*, 81–101. New York: Routledge, 1996.

Arsenault, Raymond. *Freedom Riders*. New York: Oxford University Press, 2005.

"Attention! Join Our Own Peace Corps of the South." *Student Voice*, April–May 1961.

Avorn, Jerry L., with Andrew Crane, Mark Jaffe, Oren Root Jr., Paul Starr, Michael Stern, and Robert Stemberg. *Up Against the Ivy Wall: A History of the Columbia Crisis*. New York: Atheneum, 1969.

Ayers, William. *The Good Preschool Teachers: Six Teachers Reflect on Their Lives*. New York: Teachers College Press, 1989.

Baker, Elaine DeLott. "They Sent Us This White Girl." In Constance Curry et al., eds. *Deep in Our Hearts: Nine White Women in the Freedom Movement*, 253–88. Athens: University of Georgia Press, 2000.

Banerjee, Mukulika. *The Pathan Unarmed: Opposition and Memory in the Northwest Frontier*. Sante Fe, N.Mex.: School of American Research Press, 2000.

Barber, Benjamin. *Strong Democracy: Participatory Politics for a New Age*. Berkeley: University of California Press, 1984.

Barbour, Floyd B., ed. *The Black Power Revolt: A Collection of Essays*. Boston: Extending Horizons Books, 1968.

Barnes, Catherine A. *Journey from Jim Crow: The Desegregation of Southern Transit*. New York: Columbia University Press, 1983.

Baruch, Ruth-Marion, and Pirkle Jones. *The Vanguard: A Photographic Essay of the Black Panthers*. Boston: Beacon Press, 1970.

Bates, Tom. *RADS: The 1970 Bombing of the Army Math Research Center at the University of Wisconsin and Its Aftermath*. New York: HarperCollins, 1992.

Bausum, Ann. "James Zwerg Recalls His Freedom Ride." *Beloit College Magazine* (Winter–Spring 1989), ‹http://www.beloit.edu/~belmag/fall02/features/02fa_zwerg.htm›. 28 May 2004.

Belfrage, Sally. *Freedom Summer*. New York: Viking Press, 1965.

Benello, George. *From the Ground Up: Essays on Grassroots and Workplace Democracy*. Boston: South End Press, 1992.

Bennett, Lerone, Jr. *Before the Mayflower: A History of Black America*. New York: Penguin, 1984.

Bennett, Scott H. "'Pacifism Not Passivism': The War Resisters' League and Radical Pacifism, Nonviolent Direct Action, and the Americanization of Gandhi, 1915–1963." Ph.D. diss., Rutgers University, 1998.

Berkeley, Kathleen C. *Women's Liberation Movement in America*. Westport, Conn.: Greenwood Press, 1999.

Blackstock, Nelson. *COINTELPRO: The FBI's Secret War on Political Freedom*. New York: Pathfinder, 1975.

Bloom, Alexander, and Wini Breines, eds. *Takin' It to the Streets: A Sixties Reader*. New York: Oxford University Press, 1995.

Bookchin, Murray. "Between the '30s and the '60s." In Sohnya Sayres et al., eds., *The 60s without Apology*, 247–51. Minneapolis: University of Minnesota Press, 1984.

Borstelmann, Thomas. *Cold War and the Color Line: American Race Relations in the Global Arena*. Cambridge: Harvard University Press, 2001.

Boudin, Jean. "Jean Boudin Talks about Her Fugitive Daughter." *Ms.*, August 1976.

Boudin, Kathy. "Participatory Literacy Education behind Bars: AIDS Opens the Door." *Harvard Educational Review* 63, no. 2 (Summer 1993): 207–32.

Boudin, Kathy, Bernardine Dohrn, and Terry Robbins. "Bringing the War Home: Less Talk, More National Action." *New Left Notes*, 28 Aug. 1969.

Bowen, Angela. "Who Said It Was Easy? Audre Lorde's Complex Connections to Three United States' Liberation Movements, 1952–1992." Ph.D. diss., Clark University, 1997.

Boyd, Herb, ed. *Autobiography of a People: Three Centuries of African American History Told by Those Who Lived It*. New York: Doubleday, 2000.

Boyd, Malcolm, ed. *The Underground Church*. New York: Penguin, 1969.

Boyte, Harry. *Commonwealth: A Return to Citizen Politics*. New York: Free Press, 1989.

Boyte, Harry C., Heather Booth, and Steve Max. *Citizen Action and the New American Populism*. Philadelphia: Temple University Press, 1986.

Braden, Anne. "The Images Are Broken: Students Challenge Rural Georgia." *Southern Patriot* 20 (December 1962): 1.

———. "The Southern Freedom Movement: The Student Revolt 1960–61." *Monthly Review* (July–August 1965). Reprinted in Massimo Teodori, ed., *The New Left: A Documentary History*. Indianapolis: Bobbs-Merrill, 1969.

Branch, Taylor. *Parting the Waters: America in the King Years, 1954–1963*. New York: Simon and Schuster, 1988.

———. *Pillar of Fire: America in the King Years, 1963–1965*. New York: Simon and Schuster, 1998.

Brecht, Bertolt. "An Dei Nachgebornen" ["To Posterity"], trans. H. R. Hays. Quoted in Howard L. Parson, *The Critique of War: Contemporary Philosophical Explorations*, ed. Robert Ginsberg. Chicago: Henry Regnery Co., 1969.

Breines, Wini. *Community and Organization in the New Left, 1962–1968: The Great Refusal*. New York: Praeger, 1982.

———. Review of *Personal Politics*, by Sara Evans. In *Feminist Studies* 5, no. 3 (Fall 1979): 495–506.

———. "Whose New Left?" *Journal of American History* 752 (September 1988): 528–45.

Brock, Annette K. "Gloria Richardson and the Cambridge Movement." In Vicki L. Crawford, Jacqueline Anne Rouse, and Barbara Woods, eds., *Women in the Civil Rights Movement: Trailblazers and Torchbearers, 1941–1965*, 121–44. Bloomington: Indiana University Press, 1993.

Broderick, Francis L., and August Meier, eds., *Negro Protest Thought in the Twentieth Century.* Indianapolis: Bobbs-Merrill, 1965.

Brown, Elaine. *A Taste of Power: A Black Woman's Story.* New York: Pantheon, 1992.

Brown, Richard. *Strain of Violence: Historical Studies of American Violence and Vigilantism.* New York: Oxford University Press, 1975.

Brown, Scot D. *Fighting for US: Maulana Karenga, the US Organization, and Black Cultural Nationalism.* New York: New York University Press, 2003.

———. "The US Organization: African American Cultural Nationalism in the Era of Black Power, 1965 to the 1970s." Ph.D. diss., Cornell University, 1999.

Browning, Joan C. "Shiloh Witness." In Constance Curry et al., eds. *Deep in Our Hearts: Nine White Women in the Freedom Movement,* 37–84. Athens: University of Georgia Press, 2000.

Brownmiller, Susan. *In Our Time: Memoir of a Revolution.* New York: Dial Press, 1999.

Bucholtz, Mary, A. C. Liang, and Laurel A. Sutton, eds. *Reinventing Identities: The Gendered Self in Discourse.* New York: Oxford University Press, 1999.

Buckley, William F., Jr. *Miles Gone By: A Literary Biography.* Washington, D.C.: Regnery Publishers, 2004.

Bunzel, John H., ed. *Political Passages: Journeys through Two Decades of Change.* New York: Free Press, 1988.

Burner, Eric. *And Gently He Shall Lead Them: Robert Paris Moses and Civil Rights in Mississippi.* New York: New York University Press, 1994.

Burns, Stewart, ed. *Daybreak of Freedom: The Montgomery Bus Boycott.* Chapel Hill: University of North Carolina Press, 1997.

———. *Social Movements of the 1960s: Searching for Democracy.* Boston: Twayne Publishers, 1990.

Bush, Rod. *We Are Not What We Seem: Black Nationalism and Class Struggle in the American Century.* New York: New York University Press, 1999.

Cagin, Seth, and Philip Dray. *We Are Not Afraid: The Story of Goodman, Schwerner, and Chaney and the Civil Rights Campaign for Mississippi.* New York: Bantam Books, 1991.

Calvert, Greg. *Democracy from the Heart: Spiritual Values, Decentralism, and Democratic Idealism in the Movements of the 1960s.* Eugene, Ore.: Communitas Press, 1991.

———. "Democratic Decentralism." *New Left Notes,* 20 Feb. 1967.

———. "From Protest to Resistance." *New Left Notes,* 13 Jan. 1967.

———. "In White America: Radical Consciousness and Social Change." In Massimo Teodori, ed., *The New Left: A Documentary History,* 412–18. Indianapolis: Bobbs-Merrill, 1969.

———. "Participatory Democracy, Collective Leadership, and Political Responsibility." *New Left Notes,* 18 Dec. 1967.

———. Review of *The Great Refusal: Community and Organization in the New Left,* by Wini Breines. In *Telos* (Winter 1982–83): 194–98.

Calvert, Greg, and Carol Neiman. *A Disrupted History.* New York: Random House, 1971.

Cannon, Katie G. *Womanism and the Soul of the Black Community.* New York: Continuum, 1995.

Carmichael, Stokely (Kwame Ture), with Ekwueme Michael Thelwell. *Ready for Revolution: The Life and Struggles of Stokely Carmichael (Kwame Ture).* New York: Scribner, 2003.

Carmichael, Stokely, and Charles Hamilton. *Black Power: The Politics of Liberation in America.* New York: Vintage Books, 1967.

Carson, Clayborne. *In Struggle: SNCC and the Black Awakening of the 1960s.* Cambridge: Harvard University Press, 1981.

Carson, Josephine. *Silent Voices: The Southern Negro Woman Today.* New York: Delacorte Press, 1969.

Carter, Dan T. *The Politics of Rage: George Wallace, the Origins of the New Conservatism, and the Transformation of American Politics.* New York: Simon and Schuster, 1995.

Cason, Sandra, and Thomas Hayden. "Keep Freedom City Alive." *Student Voice,* January 1961.

Castellucci, John. *The Big Dance: The Untold Story of Kathy Boudin and the Terrorist Family That Committed the Brink's Robbery Murders.* New York: Dodd, Mead, 1986.

Cavin, Margaret. "Glenn Smiley Was a Fool: The Use of the Comic as a Strategy of Nonviolence." *Peace and Change* 26 (April 2001): 223–42.

Chafe, William H. *Civilities and Civil Rights: Greensboro, North Carolina, and the Black Struggle for Freedom.* Oxford: Oxford University Press, 1980.

———. "The End of One Struggle, the Beginning of Another." In Charles Eagles, ed., *The Civil Rights Movement in America: Essays.* Jackson: University Press of Mississippi, 1986.

———. *Never Stop Running: Allard Lowenstein and the Struggle of Save American Liberalism.* New York: Basic Books, 1993.

Chapman, Mark L. *Christianity on Trial: African American Religious Thought before and after Black Power.* Maryknoll, N.Y.: Orbis Books, 1996.

Chappell, David L. *A Stone of Hope: Prophetic Religion and the Death of Jim Crow.* Chapel Hill: University of North Carolina Press, 2004.

Chatfield, Charles. *For Peace and Justice: Pacifism in America, 1914–1941.* Knoxville: University of Tennessee Press, 1971.

———, ed. *The Americanization of Gandhi: Images of the Mahatma.* New York: Garland Publishing, 1976.

Chepesiuk, Ron. *Sixties Radicals, Then and Now: Candid Conversations with Those Who Shaped the Era.* Jefferson, N.C.: McFarland and Co., 1995.

Churchill, Ward. *Agents of Repression: The FBI's Secret War against the Black Panther Party and the American Indian Movement.* Boston: South End Press, 1988.

———. *Pacifism as Pathology: Reflections on the Role of Armed Struggle in North America.* Winnipeg, Canada: Arbeiter Ring, 1998.

Clark, Burton R. *The Distinctive College: Antioch, Reed, and Swarthmore.* Chicago: Aldeen Publishing, 1970.

Clark, Septima P. *Ready from Within: Septima Clark and the Civil Rights Movement.* Trenton, N.J.: Africa World Press, 1990.

Clecak, Peter. *Radical Paradoxes: Dilemmas of the American Left, 1945–1970.* New York: Harper and Row, 1973.

Clinton, Catherine, ed. *Half Sisters of History: Southern Women and the American Past.* Durham, N.C.: Duke University Press, 1994.

Clinton, Catherine, and Michele Gillespie, eds. *The Devil's Lane: Sex and Race in the Early South.* New York: Oxford University Press, 1997.

Cluster, Dick. *They Should Have Served That Cup of Coffee.* Boston: South End Press, 1979.

Cohen, Joshua, and Joel Rogers. *On Democracy: Toward a Transformation of American Society.* New York: Penguin, 1986.

Cohen, Marcia. *The Sisterhood: The True Story of the Women Who Changed the World.* New York: Simon and Schuster, 1988.

Coles, Robert. *Farewell to the South.* Boston: Little, Brown, 1972.

Collier-Thomas, Bettye. *Black Women Preachers and Their Sermons, 1850–1979.* San Francisco: Jossey-Bass, 1998.

Collier-Thomas, Bettye, and V. P. Franklin, eds. *Sisters in the Struggle: African American Women in the Civil Rights–Black Power Movement.* New York: New York University Press, 2001.

Commission of Inquiry into the Black Panthers and the Police. *Search and Destroy: A Report.* New York: Metropolitan Applied Research Center, 1973.

Cone, James H. *Black Theology and Black Power.* New York: Seabury Press, 1969. Reprint, Maryknoll, N.Y.: Orbis Books, 1997.

———. *A Black Theology of Liberation.* Maryknoll, N.Y.: Orbis Books, 1986.

———. *Risks of Faith: The Emergence of a Black Theology of Liberation, 1968–1998.* Boston: Beacon Press, 1999.

———. *Speaking the Truth: Ecumenism, Liberation, and Black Theology.* Grand Rapids, Mich.: William B. Eerdmans, 1986.

Conley, Dalton. *Being Black, Living in the Red: Race, Wealth and Social Policy in America.* Berkeley: University of California Press, 1999.

Cook, Blanche Wiesen, and Gerald Markowitz, "History in Shreds: The Fate of the Freedom on Information Act." *Radical History Review* 26 (1982): 173–78.

Cook, Samuel DuBois. "Political Movements and Organizations." *Journal of Politics* (February 1964).

Cooney, Robert, and Helen Michaelowsi, eds. *The Power of the People: Active Nonviolence in the United States.* Philadelphia: New Society Publishers, 1987.

Countryman, Matthew J. "Civil Rights and Black Power in Philadelphia, 1940–1971." Ph.D. diss., Duke University, 1999.

Craig, Maxine B. *Ain't I a Beauty Queen: Black Women, Beauty, and the Politics of Culture.* New York: Oxford University Press, 2002.

———. "Black Is Beautiful: Personal Transformation and Political Change." Ph.D. diss., University of California at Berkeley, 1995.

Crawford, Vicki. "African American Women in the Mississippi Freedom Democratic

Party." In Vicki L. Crawford, Jacqueline Anne Rouse, and Barbara Woods, eds., *Women in the Civil Rights Movement: Trailblazers and Torchbearers, 1941–1965*, 121–38. Bloomington: Indiana University Press, 1993.

Crawford, Vicki L., Jacqueline Anne Rouse, and Barbara Woods, eds. *Women in the Civil Rights Movement: Trailblazers and Torchbearers, 1941–1965*. Bloomington: Indiana University Press, 1993.

Crosby, Emilye. "'God's Appointed Savoir': Charles Evers's Use of Local Movements for National Stature." In Jeanne Theoharis and Komozi Woodard, eds., *Groundwork: Local Black Freedom Movements in America*, 165–92. New York: New York University Press, 2005.

———. *A Little Taste of Freedom: The African American Freedom Struggle in Claiborne County, Mississippi*. Chapel Hill: University of North Carolina Press, 2005.

Crowley, Walt. *Rites of Passage: A Memoir of the Sixties in Seattle*. Seattle: University of Washington Press, 1995.

Curry, Constance. *Silver Rights*. Chapel Hill, N.C.: Algonquin Books, 1995.

Curry, Constance, et al., eds. *Deep in Our Hearts: Nine White Women in the Freedom Movement*. Athens: University of Georgia Press, 2000.

Dallek, Robert. *Flawed Giant: Lyndon Johnson and His Times, 1961–1973*. New York: Oxford University Press, 1998.

Darity, William A., and Samuel L. Myers. *Persistent Disparity — Race and Economic Inequality in the United States since 1945*. Northhampton, Mass.: Edward Elgar, 1998.

Darnovsky, Marcy, Barbara Epstein, and Richard Flacks, eds. *Cultural Politics and Social Movements*. Philadelphia: Temple University Press, 1995.

Davidson, Carl. "Toward a Student Syndicalist Movement, or University Reform Revisited." *New Left Notes*, 9 Sept. 1966.

Davies, David R. "J. Oliver Emmerich and the McComb *Enterprise-Journal*." In Davies, ed., *The Press and Race: Mississippi Journalists Confront the Movement*, 111–36. Jackson: University Press of Mississippi, 2001.

Davies, David R., and Judy Smith. "Jimmy Ward and the Jackson *Daily News*." In Davies, ed., *The Press and Race: Mississippi Journalists Confront the Movement*, 85–110. Jackson: University Press of Mississippi, 2001.

Davis, David Brion, ed. *The Fear of Conspiracy*. Ithaca, N.Y.: Cornell University Press, 1971.

DeBenedetti, Charles. *Origins of the American Peace Movement, 1915–1929*. New York: KTO Press, 1978.

———. *The Peace Reform in American History*. Bloomington: University of Indiana Press, 1980.

DeBenedetti, Charles, with Charles Chatfield. *An American Ordeal: The Antiwar Movement of the Vietnam Era*. Syracuse, N.Y.: Syracuse University Press, 1990.

Defiance #2. Paperback Library, March 1971.

Delgado, Gary. *Beyond the Politics of Place: New Directions in Community Organizing*. Berkeley: University of California Press, 1997.

del Pozzo, Theresa. "The Feel of a Blue Note." In Constance Curry et al., eds., *Deep in*

Our Hearts: Nine White Women in the Freedom Movement, 171–206. Athens: University of Georgia Press, 2000.

Demaratus, DeEtta. *The Force of a Feather: The Search for a Lost Story of Slavery and Freedom*. Salt Lake City: University of Utah Press, 2002.

D'Emilio, John. *Lost Prophet: The Life and Times of Bayard Rustin*. New York: Free Press, 2003.

———. *Making Trouble: Essays on Gay History, Politics, and the University*. New York: Routledge, 1992.

———. *Sexual Politics, Sexual Communities: The Making of a Homosexual Minority in the United States, 1940–1970*. Chicago: University of Chicago Press, 1983.

D'Emilio, John, and Estelle Freedman. *Intimate Matters: A History of Sexuality in America*. New York: Harper and Row, 1988.

Deming, Barbara. "On Revolution and Equilibrium." *Liberation* (February 1968): 10–21.

———. *We Are All Part of One Another: A Barbara Deming Reader*. Philadelphia: New Society Publishers, 1984.

Derian, Patricia. "A Moment of Grace." In Aaron Henry, with Constance Curry. *The Fire Ever Burning*, 219–22. Jackson: University Press of Mississippi, 2000.

Dhaliwal, Amarpal K. "Can the Subaltern Vote? Radical Democracy, Discourses of Representation and Rights, and Questions of Race." In David Trend, ed., *Radical Democracy: Identity, Citizenship, and the State*, 42–61. New York: Routledge, 1996.

Dickstein, Morris. *Gates of Eden: American Culture in the Sixties*. New York: Basic Books, 1977.

Dittmer, John. Introduction to Aaron Henry, with Constance Curry, *The Fire Ever Burning*, ix–xviv. Jackson: University Press of Mississippi, 2000.

———. *Local People: The Struggle for Civil Rights in Mississippi*. Urbana: University of Illinois Press, 1994.

Dohrn, Bernardine. "International Woman's Day." *New Left Notes*, 7 Mar. 1969.

Dohrn, Bernardine, Jeff Jones, Billy Ayers, and Celia Sojourn for the Weather Underground. *Prairie Fire: The Politics of Revolutionary Anti-Imperialism: The Statement of the Weather Underground*. Brooklyn, N.Y.: Communications, Co., 1974.

Donaldson, Ivanhoe. "A True Believer." In Aaron Henry, with Constance Curry, *The Fire Ever Burning*, 217–19. Jackson: University Press of Mississippi, 2000.

Donner, Frank. *The Age of Surveillance: The Aims and Methods of America's Political Intelligence System*. New York: Knopf, 1980.

———. *Protectors of Privilege: Red Squads and Police Repression in Urban America*. Berkeley: University of California Press, 1990.

Douglas M. Davis. "Tom Hayden — The White Stokely." *New York World Journal Tribune*, 1 Jan. 1967.

Duberman, Martin. *Midlife Queer: Autobiography of a Decade, 1971–1981*. New York: Scribner, 1996.

———. *Stonewall*. New York: Plume, 1994.

Dudziak, Mary. *Cold War Civil Rights: Race and the Image of American Democracy*. Princeton, N.J.: Princeton University Press, 2000.

DuPlessis, Rachel Blau, and Ann Snitow, eds. *The Feminist Memoir Project: Voices from Women's Liberation*. New York: Three Rivers Press, 1998.

Echols, Alice. *Daring to Be Bad: Radical Feminism in America, 1967–1975*. Minneapolis: University of Minnesota Press, 1989.

———. "'Women Power' and Women's Liberation: Exploring the Relationship between the Antiwar Movement and the Women's Liberation Movement." In Melvin Small and William D. Hoover, eds., *Give Peace A Chance: Exploring the Vietnam Antiwar Movement*, 171–81. Syracuse, N.Y.: Syracuse University Press, 1992.

Eichel, Lawrence E., et al. *The Harvard Strike*. New York: Houghton Mifflin, 1970.

Ellis, Joseph J. *Founding Brothers: The Revolutionary Generation*. New York: Knopf, 2000.

Ellwood, Robert S. *The Sixties Spiritual Awakening: American Religion Moving from Modern to Postmodern*. New Brunswick, N.J.: Rutgers University Press, 1994.

Epstein, Barbara. *Political Protest and Cultural Revolution: Nonviolent Direct Action in the 1970s and 1980s*. Berkeley: University of California Press, 1991.

Epstein, Barbara, and Richard Flacks, eds. *Social Movements and Cultural Politics*. New York: Oxford University Press, 1994.

Eskew, Glenn T. *But for Birmingham: The Local and National Movements in the Civil Rights Struggle*. Chapel Hill: University of North Carolina Press, 1997.

Euben, J. Peter. "Taking It to the Streets: Radical Democracy and Radicalizing Theory." In David Trend, ed., *Radical Democracy: Identity, Citizenship, and the State*, 62–80. New York: Routledge, 1996.

Evans, Sara. *Personal Politics: The Roots of Women's Liberation in the Civil Rights Movement and the New Left*. New York: Vintage Books, 1980.

Eynon, Bret N. "Community, Democracy, and the Reconstruction of Political Life: The Civil Rights Influence on New Left Political Culture in Ann Arbor, Michigan, 1958–1966." Ph.D. diss., New York University, 1993.

———. "Community in Motion: The Free Speech Movement, Civil Rights, and the Roots of the New Left." *Oral History Review* (Spring 1989): 39–69.

Fairclough, Adam. *Race and Democracy: The Civil Rights Struggle in Louisiana, 1915–1972*. Athens: University of Georgia Press, 1995.

———. *To Redeem the Soul of America: The Southern Christian Leadership Conference and Martin Luther King Jr*. Athens: University of Georgia Press, 1987.

Farber, Jerry. *The Student as Nigger*. New York: Pocket, 1970.

Farmer, James. *Lay Bare the Heart: An Autobiography of the Civil Rights Movement*. New York: Arbor House, 1985.

Farrell, Amy Erdman. *Yours in Sisterhood: Ms. Magazine and the Promise of Popular Feminism*. Chapel Hill: University of North Carolina Press, 1998.

Feldman, Paul. "New Wind on the Campus: A Report on the SDS National Conference." *Dissent* (March–April 1966): 183–89.

Ferber, Michael, and Staughton Lynd. *The Resistance*. Boston: Beacon Press, 1971.

Findley, Tim. "Tom Hayden: The Rolling Stone Interview." *Rolling Stone*, 26 Oct., 9 Nov. 1972.

Fish, John Hall. *Black Power/White Control: The Struggle of the Woodlawn Organization in Chicago*. Princeton, N.J.: Princeton University Press, 1973.

Flacks, Richard. *Making History: The Radical Tradition in American Life*. New York: Columbia University Press, 1988.

———. "Making History vs. Making Life: Dilemmas of an American Left." *Working Papers for a New Society* 2 (Summer 1974): 56–73.

———. "Reviving Democratic Activism: Thoughts about Strategy in a Dark Time." In David Trend, ed., *Radical Democracy: Identity, Citizenship, and the State*, 102–16. New York: Routledge, 1996.

———. "What Happened to the New Left?" *Socialist Review* 19 (January–March 1989).

———, ed. *Conformity, Resistance, and Self-Determination: The Individual and Authority*. Boston: Little, Brown, 1973.

Fleming, Cynthia Griggs. "Black Women and Black Power: The Case of Ruby Doris Smith Robinson and the Student Nonviolent Coordinating Committee, in Bettye Collier-Thomas and V. P. Franklin, eds., *Sisters in the Struggle: African American Women in the Civil Rights–Black Power Movement*, 197–213. New York: New York University Press, 2001.

———. *Soon We Will Not Cry: The Liberation of Ruby Doris Smith Robinson*. Lanham, Md.: Rowman and Littlefield, 1998.

Foley, Michael S. *Confronting the War Machine: Draft Resistance during the Vietnam War*. Chapel Hill: University of North Carolina Press, 2003.

Foner, Philip, ed. *The Black Panthers Speak*. Philadelphia: Lippincott, 1970.

Forman, James. *The Making of Black Revolutionaries*. Seattle: Open Hand Publishing, 1985.

———. *Sammy Younge Jr.: The First Black College Student to Die in the Black Liberation Movement*. New York: Grove Press, 1968.

Foster, Julian, and Durward Long, eds. *Protest! Student Activism in America*. New York: Morrow, 1970.

Franklin, H. Bruce. *Back Where You Came From: A Life in the Death of the Empire*. New York: Harper's Magazine Press, 1975.

Franklin, John Hope. *From Slavery to Freedom: A History of African Americans*. 7th ed. New York: McGraw-Hill, 1994.

Fraser, Nancy. "From Redistribution to Recognition? Dilemmas of Justice in a 'Post-Socialist' Age." *New Left Review* 212 (July–August 1995): 68–93.

Fraser, Ronald, et al., eds. *1968: A Student Generation in Revolt*. London: Chatto and Windus, 1988.

Freeman, Jo. "On the Origins of Social Movements." In Freeman, ed. *Social Movements of the Sixties and Seventies*. New York: Longman, 1983.

———, ed. *Women: A Feminist Perspective*. Mountain View, Calif.: Mayfield, 1995.

Frost, Jennifer. *An Interracial Movement of the Poor: Community Organizing and the New Left in the 1960s*. New York: New York University Press, 2001.

Fruchter, Norm, "Mississippi: Notes on SNCC." *Studies on the Left* 5 (Winter 1965): 77.

———. "SDS: In and Out of Context." *Liberation* 16 (February 1972): 19–32.

Fruchter, Norm, and Robert Kramer. "An Approach to Community Organizing Projects." *Studies on the Left* 5, no. 5 (Winter 1965).

Gans, Herbert J. "The New Radicalism: Sect or Action Movement?" *Studies on the Left* 5, no. 3 (September 1965): 126–31.

Garfinkle, Adam. *Telltale Hearts: The Origins and Impact of the Vietnam Antiwar Movement.* New York: St. Martin's Press, 1995.

Garfinkle, Herbert. *When Negroes March: The March on Washington Movement in the Organizational Politics for FEPC.* New York: Atheneum, 1969.

Garrow, David J. *Bearing the Cross: Martin Luther King Jr. and the Southern Christian Leadership Conference.* New York: Morrow, 1986.

Georgakas, Dan, and Marvin Surkin. *Detroit, I Do Mind Dying.* Cambridge, Mass.: South End Press, 1998.

Gerhard, Jane. *Desiring Revolution: Second-Wave Feminism and the Rewriting of American Sexual Thought, 1920–1982.* New York: Columbia University Press, 2001.

Gerson, Deborah Ann. "Practice from Pain: Building a Women's Movement through Consciousness Raising." Ph.D. diss., University of California at Berkeley, 1996.

Giddings, Paula. *When and Where I Enter: The Impact of Black Women on Race and Sex in America.* New York: Morrow, 1984.

Gitlin, Todd. "The Achievement of the Anti-War Movement." In R. David Myers, ed., *Toward a History of the New Left: Essays from within the Movement,* 183–94. Brooklyn. N.Y.: Carlson Publishing, 1989.

———. "The Dynamics of the New Left." *Motive* 31, no. 2 (November 1970): 43–67.

———. "On Organizing the Poor in America." *New Left Notes,* 23 Dec. 1966.

———. *The Sixties: Years of Hope, Days of Rage.* New York: Bantam, 1987.

———. *The Whole World Is Watching: Mass Media in the Making and Unmaking of the New Left.* Berkeley: University of California Press, 1980.

Gitlin, Todd, and Nanci Hollander. *Uptown: Poor Whites in Chicago.* Harper and Row, 1970.

Gittell, J. Ross, and Avis Vidal. *Community Organizing: Building Social Capital as a Development Strategy.* Thousand Oaks, Calif.: Sage Publications, 1998).

Glassman, Carol. "Women and the Welfare System." in Robin Morgan, ed., *Sisterhood Is Powerful: An Anthology of Writings from the Women's Liberation Movement,* 112–27. New York: Vintage Books, 1970.

Glen, John M. *Highlander: No Ordinary School.* Knoxville: University of Tennessee Press, 1996.

Glick, Brian. *War at Home: Covert Action against U.S. Activists and What We Can Do about It.* Boston: South End Press, 1989.

Goldman, Peter, with Gerald C. Lubenow. "The Underground Nation." *Newsweek,* 31 Mar. 1975.

Goldstein, Richard. *Reporting the Counterculture.* Boston: Unwin Hyman, 1989.

Goldstein, Robert. *Political Repression in Modern America, 1870 to the Present.* Cambridge, Mass.: Schenkman Publishing, 1978.

Goodman, Mitchell, ed. *The Movement toward a New America: The Beginnings of a Long Revolution.* Philadelphia: Pilgrim Press, 1970.

Goodwyn, Lawrence. *Breaking the Barrier: The Rise of Solidarity in Poland.* New York: Oxford University Press, 1991.

———. *The Populist Moment: A Short History of the Agrarian Revolt in America.* New York: Oxford University Press, 1978.

Gosse, Van. *Where the Boys Are: Cuba, Cold War America and the Making of a New Left*. London: Verso, 1993.

Grady-Willis, Winston A. "A Changing Tide: Black Politics and Activism in Atlanta, Georgia, 1960–1977." Ph.D. diss., Emory University, 1998.

Gramsci, Antonio. *Letters from Prison*. Trans. Lynne Lawner. New York: Harper and Row, 1973.

Grant, Jacquelyn. *Perspectives on Womanist Theology*. Atlanta: ITC Press, 1995.

———. *White Women's Christ and Black Women's Jesus: Feminist Christology and Womanist Response*. Atlanta: Scholars Press, 1989.

Grant, Joanne. *Ella Baker: Freedom Bound*. New York: Wiley, 1998.

Grathwohl, Lawrence. *Bringing Down America: An FBI Informer with the Weathermen*. New Rochelle, N.Y.: Arlington House Publishers, 1976.

Greenberg, Cheryl Lynn, ed. *A Circle of Trust: Remembering SNCC*. New Brunswick, N.J.: Rutgers University Press, 1998.

Gregg, Richard. *A Discipline for Non-Violence*. Wallingford, Pa.: Pendle Hill, 1941.

———. *The Power of Nonviolence*. Philadelphia: J. B. Lippincott, 1934.

Grele, Ronald. *Envelopes of Sound: The Art of Oral History*. Rev. ed. New York: Praeger, 1991.

Grier, Peter. "Federal Use of Wiretaps Continues Rapid Rise: Drug Figures Are Major Targets." *Christian Science Monitor*, 10 May 1984.

Halberstam, David. *The Children*. New York: Random House, 1998.

Hale, Grace Elizabeth. *Making Whiteness: The Culture of Segregation in the South, 1890–1940*. New York: Pantheon, 1998.

Hall, Jacqueline Dowd. *Revolt against Chivalry: Jesse Daniel Ames and the Women's Campaign against Lynching*. New York: Columbia University Press, 1979.

Hamer, Fannie Lou, et al. *To Praise Our Bridges: An Autobiography*. Jackson, Miss.: KIPCO, 1967.

Hampton, Henry, and Steve Fayer, with Sarah Flynn. *Voices of Freedom: An Oral History of the Civil Rights Movement from the 1950s through the 1980s*. New York: Bantam, 1990.

Harding, Vincent. "Healing at the Razor's Edge: Reflections on a History of Multicultural America." *Journal of American History* (September 1994): 571–84.

———. *Hope and History: Why We Must Share the Story of the Movement*. Maryknoll, N.Y.: Orbis Books, 1990.

———. *There Is a River: The Black Struggle for Freedom in America*. New York: Harcourt Brace Jovanovich, 1981.

Harding, Vincent, and Staughton Lynd. "Albany, Georgia." *Crisis* 70 (February 1963).

Harley, Sharon. "'Chronicle of a Death Foretold': Gloria Richardson, the Cambridge Movement, and the Radical Black Activist Tradition." In Bettye Collier-Thomas and V. P. Franklin, eds. *Sisters in the Struggle: African American Women in the Civil Rights–Black Power Movement*, 174–96. New York: New York University Press, 2001.

Harris, David. *Dreams Die Hard*. New York: St. Martin's Press, 1982.

Hathaway, Dale. *Allies across the Border: Mexico's "Authentic Labor Front" and Global Solidarity*. Boston: South End Press, 2000.

Hayden, Casey. "Fields of Blue." In Constance Curry et al., eds., *Deep in Our Hearts: Nine White Women in the Freedom Movement*, 333–76. Athens: University of Georgia Press, 2000.

———.Memorandum to ERAP newsletter, n.d. [ca. Summer 1965]. In the author's possession.

———."Notes on Organizing Poor Southern Whites in Chicago," August 1965. Paper in the author's possession.

———."A Nurturing Movement: Nonviolence, SNCC, and Feminism." *Southern Exposure* (Summer 1988): 48–53.

———."The Radical Roots of SNCC: Non-violence and Existentialism." Paper in the author's possession.

———."Raising the Question of Who Decides." *New Republic* 154 (22 Jan. 1966): 9–10.

———.Speech for panel on "Feminists and Women: Their Roles, Rights and Opportunities during the Movement." 12th Annual Fannie Lou Hamer Memorial Symposium Lecture Series, Jackson State College, Jackson, Miss., 4 Oct. 1995. Transcript in the author's possession, courtesy of Sandra Cason.

Hayden, Casey, and Mary King. "Sex and Caste: A Kind of Memo." *Liberation* 10 (April 1966): 35–36. Reprinted in Sara Evans, *Personal Politics: The Roots of Women's Liberation in the Civil Rights Movement and the New Left*, 235–38. New York: Vintage Books, 1980.

Hayden, Casey, and Mary King, with Maria Varela. "SNCC Position Paper: Women in the Movement." In Sara Evans, *Personal Politics: The Roots of Women's Liberation in the Civil Rights Movement and the New Left*, 233–35. New York: Vintage Books, 1980.

Hayden, Casey, Richie Rothstein, Judy Bernstein, Rennie Davis, and David Palmer. "Chicago: JOIN Project." Interview by Stanley Aronowitz and Norman Fruchter. *Studies on the Left* 5, no. 3 (September 1965): 107–25.

Hayden, Tom. *Rebellion in Newark*. New York: Random House, 1967.

———."Report." *SDS Bulletin*, March–April 1963.

———.*Reunion: A Memoir*. New York: Random House, 1988.

———.*Trial*. New York: 1970.

Hayden, Tom, and Dick Flacks. "The Port Huron Statement at 40." *Nation*, 5 Aug. 2002.

Hayden, Tom, and Staughton Lynd. "Reply to Herbert J. Gans." *Studies on the Left* 5, no. 3 (September 1965): 132–36.

Heath, William. *The Children Bob Moses Led*. Minneapolis: Milkweek Editions, 1995.

Heineman, Kenneth J. "'Look Out Kid, You're Gonna Get Hit!': Kent State and the Vietnam Antiwar Movement." In Melvin Small and William D. Hoover, eds., *Give Peace a Chance: Exploring the Vietnam Antiwar Movement*, 201–22. Syracuse, N.Y.: Syracuse University Press, 1992.

Henig, Peter, with Cathy Wilkerson. "Manpower Channeling." *New Left Notes*, 20 Jan. 1967.

Henry, Aaron, with Constance Curry. *The Fire Ever Burning*. Jackson: University Press of Mississippi, 2000.

Hersh, Seymour M. *My Lai 4: A Report on the Massacre and Its Aftermath*. New York: Random House, 1970.

Hess, Carol Lakey. *Caretakers of Our Common House: Women's Development in Communities of Faith*. Nashville, Tenn.: Abingdon Press, 1997.

Hess, Gary R. "The Unending Debate: Historians and the Vietnam War." *Diplomatic History* 18 (Spring 1994): 239–64.

Hewitt, Nancy A. "In Pursuit of Power: The Political Economy of Women's Activism in Twentieth-Century Tampa." In Hewitt and Suzanne Lebsock, eds., *Visible Women: New Essays on American Activism*, 199–222. Urbana: University of Illinois Press, 1993.

———. "Multiple Truths: The Political, the Personal, and the Postmodernist in Contemporary Feminist Scholarship." Center for Research on Women, Memphis State University, Memphis, Tenn., January 1992.

———. *Women's Activism and Social Change: Rochester, New York, 1822–1872*. Ithaca, N.Y.: Cornell University Press, 1984.

Hill, Lance. *The Deacons for Defense: Armed Resistance and the Civil Rights Movement*. Chapel Hill: University of North Carolina Press, 2004.

Hilliard, David, and Lewis Cole. *This Side of Glory: The Autobiography of David Hilliard and the Story of the Black Panther Party*. Boston: Little, Brown, 1993.

Hinks, Peter. *To Awaken My Afflicted Brother: David Walker and the Problem of Antebellum Slave Resistance*. University Park: Pennsylvania State University Press, 1997.

Holt, Len. *The Summer That Didn't End*. New York: Morrow, 1965.

hooks, bell. *Ain't I a Woman: Black Women and Feminism*. Boston: South End Press, 1981.

———. "Beloved Community." In *Killing Rage: Ending Racism*, 263–72. New York: Holt, 1995.

———. *Yearning: Race, Class, Gender, and Cultural Politics*. Boston: South End Press, 1990.

hooks, bell, and Cornel West. *Breaking Bread: Insurgent Black Intellectual Life*. Boston: South End Press, 1991.

Hopkins, Dwight. *Up, Down and Over: Slave Religion and Black Theology*. Minneapolis: Fortress Press, 2000.

Horne, Gerald. *Fire This Time: The Watts Uprising and the 1960s*. Charlottesville: University Press of Virginia, 1995.

Horton, Aimee Isgrig. *The Highlander Folk School: A History of Its Major Programs, 1932–1961*. Brooklyn, N.Y.: Carlson Press, 1989.

Horton, Myles, with Judith Kohl and Herbert Kohl. *The Long Haul: An Autobiography*. New York: Doubleday, 1990.

Houser, George. *No One Can Stop the Rain*. New York: Pilgrim Press, 1989.

Hudson, Winson, and Constance Curry. *Mississippi Harmony: Memoirs of a Freedom Fighter*. New York: Palgrave, 2002.

Huie, William Bradford. *Three Lives for Mississippi*. New York: WCC Books, 1965.

Hullet, John, and Stokely Carmichael. *The Black Panther Party: Speech by John Hullet, Interview with Stokely Carmichael, Report from Lowndes County*. New York: Merit Publishers, 1966.

Hunter, Allen. "Rethinking Revolution in Light of the New Social Movements." In Marcy Darnovsky, Barbara Epstein, and Richard Flacks, eds., *Cultural Politics and Social Movements*, 320–43. Philadelphia: Temple University Press, 1995.

"Interview with John Lewis." *Militant*, 5 Apr. 1965.

Isserman, Maurice. *If I Had a Hammer . . . The Death of the Old Left and the Birth of the New Left*. New York: Basic Books, 1987.

———. "1968 and the American New Left." *Socialist Review* 18 (October–December 1989): 94–104.

———. "You Don't Need a Weatherman but a Postman Can Be Helpful." In Melvin Small and William D. Hoover, eds., *Give Peace a Chance: Exploring the Vietnam Antiwar Movement*, 22–34. Syracuse, N.Y.: Syracuse University Press, 1992.

Jack, Homer A. Jack, ed., *The Gandhi Reader: A Source Book of His Life and Writings*. New York: Grove Press, 1994.

Jacobs, Harold S. *The Personal and the Political: A Study of the Decline of the New Left*. Ph.D. diss., University of California at Berkeley, 1978.

———, ed. *Weatherman*. Berkeley, Calif.: Ramparts Press, 1970.

Jacobs, Harriet. *Incidents in the Life of a Slave Girl*. New York: Oxford University Press, 1988.

Jeffries, Hasan Kwame. "Freedom Politics: The Civil Rights Movement in Lowndes County, Alabama, and the Making of Black Power." Manuscript.

———. "Organizing for More Than the Vote: The Political Radicalization of Local People in Lowndes County, Alabama, 1965–1966." In Jeanne Theoharis and Komozi Woodard, eds., *Groundwork: Local Black Freedom Movements in America*, 140–65. New York: New York University Press, 2005.

———. "Standing Up for Freedom: The Civil Rights Movement in Lowndes County, Alabama." Ph.D. diss., Duke University, 2002.

Jetter, Alexis. "Mississippi Learning." *New York Times Magazine*, 21 Feb. 1993.

Johnson, Julia Hitchcock Barrett. "Theoretical Foundations for a Study of Women's Leadership in Higher Education." M.A. thesis, University of Arizona, 1996.

Jones, Charles E., ed. *The Black Panther Party (Reconsidered)*. Baltimore: Black Classic Press, 1998.

Jones, Jeff, ed. *Brigadista: Harvest and War in Nicaragua*. New York: Praeger, 1986.

Jones, Patrick. "'Not a Color, but an Attitude': Father James Groppi and Black Power Politics in Milwaukee." In Jeanne Theoharis and Komozi Woodard, eds., *Groundwork: Local Black Freedom Movements in America*, 259–81. New York: New York University Press, 2005.

Kahn, Roger. *The Battle for Morningside Heights*. New York: Morrow, 1970.

Kaiser, Charles. *1968 in America: Music, Politics, Chaos, Counterculture and the Shaping of a Generation*. New York: Weidenfeld and Nicolson, 1988.

Kaplan, Laura. *The Story of Jane: The Legendary Underground Feminist Abortion Service*. New York: Pantheon, 1995.

Kapur, Sudarshan. *Raising Up a Prophet: The African American Encounter with Gandhi*. Boston: Beacon Press, 1992.

Katsiaficas, George. *The Imagination of the New Left: A Global Analysis of 1968*. Boston: South End Press, 1987.

Kelman, Steven. *Push Comes to Shove*. New York: Houghton Mifflin, 1970.

Kempton, Murray. *The Briar Patch: The People of the State of New York v. Lumumba Shakur et al.* New York: E. P. Dutton, 1973.

Keniston, Kenneth. *Young Radicals: Notes on Committed Youth.* New York: Harcourt, Brace, 1968.

King, Mary. *Freedom Song: A Personal Story of the 1960s Civil Rights Movement.* New York: Morrow, 1987.

Kirk, John A. *Redefining the Color Line: Black Activism in Little Rock, Arkansas, 1940–1970.* Gainesville: University Press of Florida, 2002.

Kissack, Terence. "Freaking Fag Revolutionaries: New York's Gay Liberation Front, 1969–1971." *Radical History Review* 62 (Spring 1995): 104–35.

Knight, Michael. [Untitled]. *New York Times*, 4 Mar. 1975.

Kunzel, Regina G. "White Neurosis, Black Pathology, and the Ironies of Professionalization: The 1940s." In *Fallen Women, Problem Girls: Unmarried Mothers and the Professionalization of Social Work, 1890–1945*, 144–70. New Haven, Conn.: Yale University Press, 1993.

Kwitny, Jonathan. *The Crimes of Patriots: A True Tale of Dope, Dirty Money, and the CIA.* New York: Norton, 1987.

Kyi, Aung San Suu. *Freedom from Fear and Other Writings.* Rev. ed., trans. Michael Aris. London: Penguin, 1991.

Ladner, Joyce. "Return to the Source." *Essence* (June 1977).

Langer, Elinor. "Notes for the Next Time: A Memoir of the 1960s." *Working Papers for a New Society* 1 (Fall 1973): 48–81.

Laue, James H. *Direct Action and Desegregation, 1960–1962: Toward a Theory of the Rationalization of Protest.* Brooklyn, N.Y.: Carlson Publishing, 1989.

Lauter, Paul, and Florence Howe. *The Conspiracy of the Young.* World Pub. Co., 1970.

Law, Lisa. *Flashing on the Sixties: Photographs.* San Francisco: Chronicle Books, 1987.

Lawson, James. Address to the Annual Public Gathering of the American Friends Service Committee, Philadelphia, 7 Nov. 1998, ‹http://www.afsc.org/lawson.htm›. 21 Mar. 2000.

———. "Eve of a Nonviolent Revolution." *Southern Patriot*, November 1961.

———. "From a Lunch Counter Stool." In Francis L. Broderick and August Meier, eds., *Negro Protest Thought in the Twentieth Century*, 274–81. Indianapolis: Bobbs-Merrill, 1965.

Lawson, Steven F. *Black Ballots: Voting Rights in the South, 1944–1969.* New York: Columbia University Press, 1976.

———. *Running for Freedom: Civil Rights and Black Politics in America since 1941.* New York: McGraw-Hill, 1997.

Lawson, Steven F., and Charles Payne. *Debating the Civil Rights Movement, 1945–1968.* Lanham, Md.: Rowman and Littlefield, 1998.

Layton, Azza Salama. *International Politics and Civil Rights Policies in the United States, 1941–1960.* Cambridge, England: Cambridge University Press, 2000.

Lazarre, Jane. "Conversations with Kathy Boudin." *Village Voice*, 14 Feb. 1984.

Lee, Chana Kai. "Anger, Memory, and Personal Power: Fannie Lou Hamer and Civil Rights Leadership." In Bettye Collier-Thomas and V. P. Franklin, eds., *Sisters in* the Struggle: African American Women in the Civil Rights – Black Power Movement, 139 – 70. New York: New York University Press, 2001.

———. For Freedom's Sake: The Life of Fannie Lou Hamer. Urbana: University of Illinois Press, 1999.

Lee, Martin A., and Bruce Shlain. Acid Dreams: The CIA, LSD, and the Sixties Rebellion. New York: Grove Weidenfeld, 1985.

Lesher, Stephan. George Wallace: American Populist. Reading, Mass.: William Patrick, 1994.

Lester, Julius. All Is Well. New York: Morrow, 1976.

———. Revolutionary Notes. New York: Grove Press, 1969.

Levine, Daniel. Bayard Rustin and the Civil Rights Movement. New Brunswick, N.J.: Rutgers University Press, 2000.

Levine, Ellen. Freedom's Children: Young Civil Rights Activists Tell Their Own Stories. New York: Putnam, 1993.

Levy, David W. The Debate over Vietnam. Baltimore: Johns Hopkins University Press, 1991.

Levy, Peter B. Civil War on Race Street: The Civil Rights Movement in Cambridge, Maryland. Gainesville: University Press of Florida, 2003.

———. The New Left and Labor in the 1960s. Urbana: University of Illinois Press, 1994.

Lewis, John, with Michael D'Orso. Walking with the Wind: A Memoir of the Movement. New York: Simon and Schuster, 1998.

Light, Ken. Delta Time: Mississippi Photographs by Ken Light. Washington, D.C.: Smithsonian Institution Press, 1995.

Lincoln, C. Eric. The Negro Pilgrimage in America: The Coming of Age of Black Americans. New York: Praeger, 1969.

———. Race, Religion and the Continuing American Dilemma. New York: Hill and Wang, 1984.

Lincoln, C. Eric, and Lawrence H. Mamiya. The Black Church in the African American Experience. Durham, N.C.: Duke University Press, 1990.

Lipsitz, George. A Life in the Struggle: Ivory Perry and the Culture of Opposition. Philadelphia: Temple University Press, 1988.

Long, Worth L. We'll Never Turn Back: A Photographic Exhibit Created by Worth L. Long. Washington, D.C.: Smithsonian Performing Arts, 1980.

Louis, Debbie. And We Are Not Saved: A History of the Movement as People. Garden City, N.Y.: Doubleday, 1970.

Luke, Carmen, ed. Feminisms and Pedagogies of Everyday Life. Albany: State University of New York Press, 1996.

Lynd, Staughton. Introduction to Robert P. Moses, "Mississippi, 1961 – 1962." Liberation 14 (January 1970): 7 – 17.

———. "The Movement: A New Beginning." Liberation (May 1969).

———. "The New Radicals and Participatory Democracy." Dissent (Summer 1965).

———. "A Radical Speaks in Defense of S.N.C.C." New York Times Magazine, 10 Sept. 1967.

———. "Towards a History of the New Left." In Priscilla Long, ed., The New Left: A Collection of Essays. Boston: Extending Horizons Books, 1969.

Lynn, Susan. *Progressive Women in Conservative Times: Racial Justice, Peace, and Feminism, 1945 to the 1960s.* New Brunswick, N.J.: Rutgers University Press, 1992.

Lyon, Danny. *Memories of the Southern Civil Rights Movement.* Chapel Hill: University of North Carolina Press, 1992.

Macdonald, Nancy, and Dwight Macdonald. *The War's Greatest Scandal! The Story of Jim Crow in Uniform.* New York: March on Washington Movement, 1943.

MacPherson, Myra. *Long Time Passing: Vietnam and the Haunted Generation.* Garden City, N.Y.: Doubleday, 1984.

Malcolm X, "The Bullet or the Ballot." Speech, 3 Apr. 1964. Reprinted in George Breitman, ed., *Malcolm X Speaks: Selected Speeches and Statements.* New York: Grove Press, 1965.

Manis, Andrew. *A Fire You Can't Put Out: The Civil Rights Life of Birmingham's Reverend Fred Shuttlesworth.* Tuscaloosa: University of Alabama Press, 1999.

Mansbridge, Jane J. *Beyond Adversary Democracy.* New York: Basic Books, 1980.

———. "Democracy, Deliberation, and the Experience of Women." In Bernard Murchland, ed., *Higher Education and the Practice of Democratic Politics.* Dayton, Ohio: Kettering Foundation, 1991.

Marable, Manning, and Leith Mullings, eds. *Let Nobody Turn Us Around: Voices of Resistance, Reform and Renewal.* Lanham, Md.: Rowman and Littlefield, 2000.

Marcus, Eric. *Making History: The Struggle for Gay and Lesbian Equal Rights, 1945–1990: An Oral History.* New York: HarperCollins, 1992.

Marine, Gene. *The Black Panthers.* New York: Signet, 1969.

Massey, Douglas S., and Nancy A. Denton. *American Apartheid: Segregation and the Making of the Underclass.* Cambridge: Harvard University Press, 1993.

Matthews, Traceye A. "No One Ever Asks What a Man's Role in the Revolution Is: Gender Politics and Leadership in the Black Panther Party, 1966–1971." In Bettye Collier-Thomas and V. P. Franklin, eds., *Sisters in the Struggle: African American Women in the Civil Rights–Black Power Movement,* 230–56. New York: New York University Press, 2001.

McAdam, Doug. *Freedom Summer.* New York: Oxford University Press, 1988.

McClinton, Aaron. "The Legacy." In Aaron Henry, with Constance Curry, *The Fire Ever Burning,* 247–49. Jackson: University Press of Mississippi, 2000.

McDew, Charles. "'What's the Problem, Sport?'" *Southern Exposure* (Summer 1988): 50.

McEvoy, James, and Abraham Miller, eds. *Black Power and Student Rebellion.* Belmont, Calif.: Wadsworth Publishing, 1969.

McLoughlin, William G. *Revivals, Awakenings, and Reform: An Essay on Religion and Social Change in America, 1607–1977.* Chicago: University of Chicago Press, 1978.

McPherson, Harry. *A Political Education.* Boston: Little, Brown, 1975.

McWhorter, Diane. *Carry Me Home: Birmingham, Alabama: The Climactic Battle of the Civil Rights Revolution.* New York: Simon and Schuster, 2001.

Meier, August, and Elliott Rudwick. "The Boycott Movement against Jim Crow Streetcars in the South, 1900–1906." In James C. Curtis and Lewis L. Gould, eds., *The Black Experience in America,* 87–115. Austin: University of Texas Press, 1970.

Meier, August, and Elliott Rudwick. *CORE: A Study in the Civil Rights Movement, 1942–1968*. New York: Oxford University Press, 1973.

Melville, Samuel. *Letters from Attica*. New York: Morrow, 1972.

Mendel-Reyes, Meta. *Reclaiming Democracy: The Sixties in Politics and Memory*. New York: Routledge, 1995.

Meyers, Diana Tietjens. *Being Yourself: Essays on Identity, Action, and Social Life*. Lanham, Md.: Rowman and Littlefield, 2004.

Miller, C. Wright. "Letter to the New Left." In Irving Louis Horowitz, ed., *Power, Politics and People: The Collected Essays*, 247–59. New York: Ballantine, 1963.

Miller, Frederick D. "The End of SDS and the Emergence of the Weathermen." In Jo Freeman, ed., *Social Movements of the Sixties and Seventies*. New York: Longman, 1983.

Miller, James. *"Democracy Is in the Streets" from Port Huron to the Siege of Chicago*. New York: Touchstone, 1987.

Mills, Charles W. *Blackness Visible: Essays on Philosophy and Race*. Ithaca, N.Y.: Cornell University Press, 1998.

———. *The Racial Contract*. Ithaca, N.Y.: Cornell University Press, 1997.

Mills, Kay. *This Little Light of Mine: The Life of Fannie Lou Hamer*. New York: Dutton Books, 1993.

Minnis, Jack. *Lowndes County Freedom Organization: The Story of the Development of an Independent Political Movement on the County Level*. Louisville, Ky.: Southern Conference Educational Fund, 1967.

Miyazaki, Hirokazu. "Sansei Radicals: Identity and Strategy of Japanese American Student Activists in Hawaii." In Franklin Ng, Judy Yung, Stephen S. Fugita, and Elaine H. Kim, eds., *New Visions in Asian American Studies: Diversity, Community, Power*, 173–87. Pullman: Washington State University, 1994.

Moore, Barrington, Jr. *Authority and Inequality under Capitalism and Socialism*. New York: Oxford University Press, 1987.

Moore, Gilbert. *A Special Rage*. New York: Harper and Row, 1971.

Morgan, Edward P. *The 60s Experience: Hard Lessons about Modern America*. Philadelphia: Temple University Press, 1991.

Morris, Aldon. *The Origins of the Civil Rights Movement: Black Communities Organizing for Change*. New York: Free Press, 1984.

Morris, Tiyi. "Local Women and the Civil Rights Movement in Mississippi: Re-visioning Womanpower Unlimited." In Jeanne Theoharis and Komozi Woodard, eds., *Groundwork: Local Black Freedom Movements in America*, 193–214. New York: New York University Press, 2005.

Morrison, Joan, and Robert K. Morrison. *From Camelot to Kent State: The Sixties Experience in the Words of Those Who Lived It*. New York: Times Books, 1989.

Moses, Robert P. Foreword to *Delta Time: Mississippi Photographs*, by Ken Light. Washington, D.C.: Smithsonian Institution Press, 1995.

———. "Mississippi, 1961–1962." With an introduction by Staughton Lynd. *Liberation* 14 (January 1970): 7–17.

———. "Questions Raised by Moses." *The Movement* 1 (April 1965): 1.

————, with Charles E. Cobb Jr. *Radical Equations: Math Literacy and Civil Rights*. Boston: Beacon Press, 2001.

Moses, R., M. Kamii, S. Swap, and J. Howard. "The Algebra Project: Organizing in the Spirit of Ella." *Harvard Educational Review* 59 (November 1989): 423–43.

Moye, J. Todd. *Let the People Decide: Black Freedom and White Resistance Movements in Sunflower County, Mississippi, 1945–1986*. Chapel Hill: University of North Carolina Press, 2004.

Moyers, Bill. *Moyers on America*. New York: New Press, 2004.

Mueller, Carol. "Ella Baker and the Origins of 'Participatory Democracy.'" In Vicki L. Crawford, Jacqueline Anne Rouse, and Barbara Woods, eds., *Women in the Civil Rights Movement: Trailblazers and Torchbearers, 1941–1965*, 51–70. Bloomington: Indiana University Press, 1993.

Mungo, Raymond. *Famous Long Ago*. Boston: Beacon Press, 1970.

Muños, Carlos, Jr. *Youth, Identity, Power: The Chicano Movement*. London: Verso, 1989.

Murray, Albert. *The Blue Devils of Nada: A Contemporary American Approach to Aesthetic Statement*. New York: Penguin, 1996.

————. *Conjugations and Reiterations*. New York: Pantheon, 2001.

————. *Stomping the Blues*. New York: McGraw-Hill, 1976.

Myers, R. David, ed. *Toward a History of the New Left: Essays from Within the Movement*. Brooklyn, N.Y.: Carlson Publishing, 1989.

Myrick-Harris, Clarissa. "Behind the Scenes: Doris Derby, Denise Nicholas and the Free Southern Theater." In Vicki L. Crawford, Jacqueline Anne Rouse, and Barbara Woods, eds., *Women in the Civil Rights Movement: Trailblazers and Torchbearers, 1941–1965*, 219–32. Bloomington: Indiana University Press, 1993.

Nash, Diane. "Inside the Sit-Ins and Freedom Rides: Testimony of a Southern Student." In Mathew Ahmann, ed., *The New Negro*. Notre Dame, Ind.: Fides Publishers, 1961.

"Nashville Erupts as Protests Begin." *Student Voice*, 5 May 1964.

"Nashville Group Sustains Protests." *Student Voice*, 19 May 1964.

Neruda, Pablo. "Ode to a Guitar." *Ode to Common Things*. 3d ed. Boston: Bullfinch Press, 1994.

Neumann, Osha. "Motherfuckers Then and Now: My Sixties Problem." In Marcy Darnovsky, Barbara Epstein, and Richard Flacks, eds., *Cultural Politics and Social Movements*, 55–73. Philadelphia: Temple University Press, 1995.

Newfield, Jack. *The Education of Jack Newfield*. New York: St. Martin's Press, 1984. (Interview with Bob Moses.)

————. *A Prophetic Minority*. New York: New American Library, 1966.

Newton, Huey P., with J. Herman Blake. *Revolutionary Suicide*. New York: Harcourt Brace Jovanovich, 1974.

Niezing, Johan, ed. *Urban Guerrilla: Studies on the Theory, Strategy and Practice of Political Violence in Modern Societies*. Rotterdam: Rotterdam University Press, 1974.

Niven, David. *The Politics of Injustice: The Kennedys, the Freedom Rides, and the*

Electoral Consequences of a Moral Compromise. Knoxville: University of Tennessee Press, 2003.

Obst, Lynda R., ed. *The Sixties: The Decade Remembered Now, by the People Who Lived It Then*. San Francisco: Rolling Stone Press, 1977.

Off the Pigs!: The History and Literature of the Black Panther Party. Metuchen, N.J.: Scarecrow Press, 1976.

Oglesby, Carl. "Notes on a Decade Ready for the Dustbin." *Liberation* 14 (August – September 1969): 5 – 19.

———. "Will Success Spoil SDS?" *Motive* (November 1968): 12 – 20.

Oliver, Melvin L., and Thomas M. Shapiro. *Black Wealth/White Wealth — A New Perspective on Racial Inequality*. New York: Routledge, 1997.

Olson, Lynne. *Freedom's Daughters: The Unsung Heroines of the Civil Rights Movement from 1830 to 1970*. New York: Scribner, 2001.

Omolade, Barbara. *The Rising Song of African American Women*. New York: Routledge, 1994.

O'Reilly, Kenneth. *"Racial Matters": The FBI's Secret File on Black America, 1960 – 1972*. New York: Free Press, 1989.

Orfield, Gary, Susan E. Eaton, and the Harvard Project on School Desegregation. *Dismantling Desegregation: The Quiet Reversal of Brown v. Board of Education*. New York: New Press, 1996.

Ortiz, Paul. *Emancipation Betrayed: The Hidden History of Black Organizing and White Violence in Florida from Reconstruction to the Bloody Election of 1920*. Berkeley: University of California Press, 2005.

Oshinsky, David M. *Worse Than Slavery: Parchman Farm and the Ordeal of Jim Crow Justice*. New York: Free Press, 1996.

Paret, Peter, and John W. Shy. *Guerrillas in the 1960s*. New York: Center of International Studies, Praeger, 1966.

Pascual, Diosdado Leon. "The Struggles for Gay Rights in the United States since 1945: Toward Rethinking the State and the Politics of Social Movements through the Discourse of Rights." Ph.D. diss., University of Hawaii, 1996.

Payne, Bruce. "SNCC: An Overview Two Years Later." In Mitchell Cohen and Dennis Hale, eds., *The New Student Left*. Rev. ed. Boston: Beacon Press, 1967.

Payne, Charles. Foreword to *Groundwork: Local Black Freedom Movements in America*, edited by Jeanne Theoharis and Komozi Woodard, ix – xv. New York: New York University Press, 2005.

———. *I've Got the Light of Freedom: The Organizing Tradition and the Mississippi Freedom Struggle*. Berkeley: University of California Press, 1995.

Peake, Thomas. *To Keep the Dream Alive: A History of the Southern Christian Leadership Conference from King to the 1980s*. New York: P. Lang, 1987.

Pearson, Hugh. *The Shadow of the Panther: Huey Newton and the Price of Black Power in America*. New York: Addison-Wesley, 1994.

Pepper, William F. *Orders to Kill: The Truth Behind the Murder of Martin Luther King*. New York: Carroll and Graf Publishers, 1995.

Peterson, Thomas. *Linked Arms: A Rural Community Resists Nuclear Waste*. Albany: State University of New York Press, 2002.

Piercy, Marge. "The Grand Coolie Damn." In Robin Morgan, ed., *Sisterhood Is Power-ful: An Anthology of Writings from the Women's Liberation Movement*, 473–92. New York: Vintage Books, 1970.

Polsgrove, Carol. *Divided Minds: Intellectuals and the Civil Rights Movement*. New York: Norton, 2001.

Potter, Paul. *A Name for Ourselves: Feelings about Authentic Identity, Love, Intuitive Politics, Us*. Boston: Little, Brown, 1971.

Powers, Thomas. *Diana: The Making of a Terrorist*. New York: Houghton Mifflin, 1971.

Powledge, Fred. *Free at Last? The Civil Rights Movement and the People Who Made It*. Boston: Little, Brown, 1991.

Rader, Dotson. *Blood Dues*. New York: Knopf, 1973.

———. *I Ain't Marchin' Anymore*. D. McKay Co., 1969.

Raines, Howell. *My Soul Is Rested: The Story of the Civil Rights Movement in the Deep South*. New York: Penguin, 1977.

Ransby, Barbara. "A Behind-the-Scenes View of a Behind-the-Scenes Organizer: The Roots of Ella Baker's Political Passions." In Bettye Collier-Thomas and V. P. Frank-lin, eds., *Sisters in the Struggle: African American Women in the Civil Rights – Black Power Movement*, 42–58. New York: New York University Press, 2001.

———. *Ella Baker and the Black Freedom Movement: A Radical Democratic Vision*. Chapel Hill: University of North Carolina Press, 2003.

Raskin, Jonah. *Out of the Whale: Growing Up Left in America*. New York: Link Books, 1974.

Reagon, Bernice Johnson. "The Lined Hymn as a Song of Freedom." *Black Music Re-search Bulletin* 12, no. 1 (Spring 1990): 4–7.

———. "'Nobody Knows the Trouble I See,' or 'By and By I'm Gonna Lay Down My Heavy Load.'" *Journal of American History* (June 1991): 111–19.

———. "Women as Culture Carriers in the Civil Rights Movement: Fannie Lou Hamer." In Vicki L. Crawford, Jacqueline Anne Rouse, and Barbara Woods, eds., *Women in the Civil Rights Movement: Trailblazers and Torchbearers, 1941–1965*, 203–18. Bloomington: Indiana University Press, 1993.

Reagon, Bernice Johnson, and Sweet Honey in the Rock. *We Who Believe in Freedom: Sweet Honey in the Rock . . . Still on the Journey*. New York: Anchor, 1993.

Rice, Jon Frank. "Black Radicalism on Chicago's West Side: A History of the Illinois Black Panther Party." Ph.D. diss., Northern Illinois University, 1998.

Richardson, Judy, Martha Norman, Betty Garman Robinson, and Dottie Zellner. "Hands on the Freedom Plow: The Untold Story of Women in SNCC." Manuscript.

Rinehart, Sue Tolleson. *Gender Consciousness and Politics*. New York: Routledge, 1992.

Roberts, Steven V. "Will Tom Hayden Overcome?" *Esquire*, December 1968.

Robinson, Armstead L., and Patricia Sullivan, eds. *New Directions in Civil Rights Studies*. Charlottesville: University of Virginia Press, 1991.

Robinson, Jo Ann. *The Montgomery Bus Boycott and the Women Who Started It: The Memoir of Jo Ann Robinson*. Edited, with a foreword, by David J. Garrow. Knox-ville: University of Tennessee Press, 1987.

Robnett, Belinda. *How Long? African-American Women in the Struggle for Civil Rights*. New York: Oxford University Press, 1997.

Rogers, Mary Beth. *Cold Anger: A Story of Faith and Power Politics*. Denton: University North Texas Press, 1990.

Romm, Ethel Grodzins. *The Open Conspiracy: What America's Angry Generation Is Saying*. Harrisburg, Pa.: Stackpole Books, 1970.

Rosen, Ruth. *The World Split Open: How the Modern Women's Movement Changed America*. New York: Viking Press, 2000.

Ross, Robert. "Lions and Lambs." *In These Times*, 14 Sept. 1977.

———. "Primary Groups in Social Movements: A Memoir and Interpretation." *Journal of Voluntary Action Research* 6 (July 1977): 139–51.

Rossinow, Doug. "'The Break-through to New Life': Christianity and the Emergence of the New Left in Austin, Texas, 1956–1964." *American Quarterly* 46, no. 3 (September 1994): 309–40.

———. *The Politics of Authenticity: Liberalism, Christianity and the New Left in America*. New York: Columbia University Press, 1998.

Rossman, Michael. *The Wedding within the War*. New York: Doubleday, 1971.

Roszak, Theodore. *The Making of a Counterculture: Reflections on the Technocratic Society and Its Youthful Opposition*. Berkeley: University of California Press, 1995.

Roth, Benita. "On Their Own and For Their Own: African American, Chicana and White Feminist Movements in the 1960s and 1970s." Ph.D. diss., University of California at Los Angeles, 1998.

Rothman, Stanley. *Roots of Radicalism: Jews, Christians, and the New Left*. New York: Oxford University Press, 1982.

Rothschild, Mary Aickin. *A Case of Black and White: Northern Volunteers and the Southern 'Freedom Summers,' 1964–1965*. Westport, Conn.: Greenwood Press, 1982.

———. "The Volunteers and the Freedom Schools: Education for Social Change in Mississippi." *History of Education Quarterly* 22, no. 4 (Winter 1982): 401–20.

Rothstein, Richard. *Representative Democracy in SDS*. Chicago, 1971.

———. [Untitled]. *Liberation* 16 (February 1972): 10–18.

Rudd, Mark. "Sixties' Lesson: Guilt-Motivated Militancy Can Be Dangerous." *The Guardian* (New York), 18 Jan. 1989, 19.

Rustin, Bayard. *Down the Line: The Collected Writings of Bayard Rustin*. Chicago: Quadrangle Books, 1971.

———. *Strategies for Freedom: The Changing Patterns of Black Protest*. New York: Columbia University Press, 1976.

Ryan, Barbara. *Feminism and the Women's Movement: Dynamics of Change in Social Movement Ideology and Activism*. New York: Routledge, 1992.

Sacks, Karen Brodkin. *Caring by the Hour: Women, Work, and Organizing at Duke Medical Center*. Urbana: University of Illinois Press, 1988.

Sale, Kirkpatrick. *SDS*. New York: Random House, 1973.

Sales, William, Jr. *From Civil Rights to Black Liberation: Malcolm X and the Organization of Afro-American Unity*. Boston: South End Press, 1994.

Scarry, Elaine. *The Body in Pain: The Making and Unmaking of the World*. New York: Oxford University Press, 1985.

Schaar, John. *Legitimacy and the Modern State*. New Brunswick, N.J.: Rutgers University Press, 1981.

Scott, James. *Domination and the Arts of Resistance: Hidden Transcripts*. New Haven, Conn.: Yale University Press, 1990.

———. *The Weapons of the Weak: Everyday Forms of Peasant Resistance*. New Haven, Conn.: Yale University Press, 1985.

Sculatti, Gene, and Davin Seay. *San Francisco Nights: The Psychedelic Music Trip, 1965–1968*. New York: St. Martin's Press, 1985.

Seeger, Pete, and Bob Reiser. *Everybody Say Freedom: A History of the Civil Rights Movement in Songs and Pictures*. New York: Norton, 1989.

Segrest, Mab. *My Mama's Dead Squirrel: Lesbian Essays on Southern Culture*. Ithaca, N.Y.: Firebrand Press, 1985.

Sellers, Cleveland, with Robert Terrell. *The River of No Return: The Autobiography of a Black Militant and the Life and Death of SNCC*. 1973. Reprint, Jackson: University Press of Mississippi, 1990.

Shakur, Assata. *Assata: An Autobiography*. Westport, Conn.: Lawrence Hill and Co., 1987.

Sharp, Gene. "Beyond Just War and Pacifism: Nonviolent Struggle towards Justice, Freedom, and Peace." In Manfred B. Steger and Nancy S. Lind, eds., *Violence and Its Alternatives: An Interdisciplinary Reader*, 317–24. New York: St. Martin's Press, 1999.

———. *Exploring Nonviolent Alternatives*. Boston: Porter Sargent, 1970.

———. *Gandhi as a Political Strategist, with Essays on Ethics and Politics*. Boston: Porter Sargent, 1979.

———. *The Politics of Nonviolent Action*. Boston: Porter Sargent, 1973.

Shugar, Dana R. *Separatism and the Women's Community*. Lincoln: University of Nebraska Press, 1995.

Silver, James. *Mississippi: The Closed Society*. New York: Harcourt, Brace, 1966.

Singh, Nikhil. "Rethinking Politics and Culture: Social Movements and Liberation Politics in the U.S., 1960–1976." *Radical History Review* 57 (Fall 1993): 197–201.

Sirianni, Carmen. "Democracy and Diversity in Feminist Organizations: Learning from Three Decades of Practice," 1995, ‹http://www.cpn.org/sections/topics/family-intergen/index.html›. 21 Mar. 2000.

———. "Learning Pluralism: Democracy and Diversity in Feminist Organizations." In Ian Shapiro and John Chapman, eds., *Democratic Community: NOMOS XXXV*. New York: New York University Press, 1993.

Sitkoff, Harvard. *The Struggle for Black Equality, 1945–1980*. New York: Hill and Wang, 1981.

Slate, William. *Power to the People: New Left Writings*. New York: Tower Publications, 1970.

Slocum, Kenneth G. "Ballots and Jobs." *Wall Street Journal*, 7 May 1965.

Small, Melvin. *Johnson, Nixon and the Doves*. New Brunswick, N.J.: Rutgers University Press, 1988.

Small, Melvin, and William D. Hoover, eds. *Give Peace a Chance: Exploring the Vietnam Antiwar Movement*. Syracuse, N.Y.: Syracuse University Press, 1992.

Smiley, Glenn. "How Nonviolence Works." *Fellowship* 56 (October – November 1990): 18.

———.*Nonviolence: The Gentle Persuader*. Nyack, N.Y.: Fellowship Publications, 1991.

Smist, Frank J. *Congress Oversees the United States Intelligence Community, 1947–1994*. 2d ed. Knoxville: University of Tennessee Press, 1994.

Smith, J. Douglas. *Managing White Supremacy: Race, Politics, and Citizenship in Jim Crow Virginia*. Chapel Hill: University of North Carolina Press, 2002.

Smith, Jackie, Charles Chatfield, and Ron Pagnucco. *Transnational Social Movements and Global Politics: Solidarity beyond the State*. Syracuse, N.Y.: Syracuse University Press, 1997.

Smith, Robert. "Staying the Course." In Aaron Henry, with Constance Curry, *The Fire Ever Burning*, 213–17. Jackson: University Press of Mississippi, 2000.

Snitow, Ann, Christine Stansell, and Sharon Thompson, eds. *Powers of Desire: The Politics of Sexuality*. New York: Monthly Review Press, 1983.

Spencer, Robyn Ceanne. "Inside the Panther Revolution: The Black Freedom Movement and the Black Panther Party in Oakland, California." In Jeanne Theoharis and Komozi Woodard, eds., *Groundwork: Local Black Freedom Movements in America*, 300–317. New York: New York University Press, 2005.

———.*Mothers of the Revolution: Women in the Black Panther Party, 1966–1982*. Forthcoming.

Spender, Stephen. *The Year of the Young Rebels*. New York: Random House, 1969.

Spiegel, Mike, and Jeff Jones. "Don't Take Your Guns to Town." *New Left Notes*, 4 Mar. 1968.

Steger, Manfred B., and Nancy S. Lind, eds. *Violence and Its Alternatives: An Interdisciplinary Reader*. New York: St. Martin's Press, 1999.

Stein, Marc. "The City of Sisterly and Brotherly Loves: The Making of Lesbian and Gay Movements in Greater Philadelphia, 1948–1972." Ph.D. diss., University of Pennsylvania, 1994.

Stern, Susan. *With the Weathermen*. Garden City, N.Y.: Doubleday, 1975.

Stevens, Franklin. *If This Be Treason: Your Sons Tell Their Own Stories of Why They Won't Fight for Their Country*. New York: Wyden, 1970.

Stevens, Jay. *Storming Heaven: LSD and the American Dream*. New York: Atlantic Monthly Press, 1998.

Stoper, Emily. *The Student Nonviolent Coordinating Committee: The Growth of Radicalism in a Civil Rights Organization*. New York: Carlson Publishing, 1989.

Strain, Christopher B. *Pure Fire: Self-Defense as Activism in the Civil Rights Era*. Athens: University of Georgia Press, 2005.

Sullivan, Patricia. *Days of Hope: Race and Democracy in the New Deal Era*. Chapel Hill: University of North Carolina Press, 1996.

Sutherland, Elizabeth, ed. *Letters From Mississippi*. New York: McGraw-Hill, 1965.

Swearingen, M. Wesley. *FBI Secrets: An Agent's Exposé*. Boston: South End Press, 1994.

Swift, Jeannine, ed. *Dream and Reality: The Modern Black Struggle for Freedom and Equality*. Westport, Conn.: Greenwood Press, 1991.

Teodori, Massimo, ed. *Duties, Pleasures, and Conflicts: Essays in Struggle.* Amherst: University of Massachusetts Press, 1987.

———. *The New Left: A Documentary History.* Indianapolis: Bobbs-Merrill, 1969.

Tepperman, Jean. "Two Jobs: Women Who Work in Factories." In Robin Morgan, ed., *Sisterhood Is Powerful: An Anthology of Writings from the Women's Liberation Movement,* 127–36. New York: Vintage Books, 1970.

Thelwell, Michael. "MFDP Congressional Challenge." *Student Voice,* July 1965.

———. "The Organizer." In *Duties, Pleasures, and Conflicts: Essays in Struggle.* Amherst: University of Massachusetts Press, 1987.

Theoharis, Athan. *Spying on Americans: Political Surveillance from Hoover to the Huston Plan.* Philadelphia: Temple University Press, 1978.

Theoharis, Jeanne, and Komozi Woodard, eds. *Groundwork: Local Black Freedom Movements in America.* New York: New York University Press, 2005.

Thompson, E. P. *The Making of the English Working Class.* New York: Vintage Books, 1963.

Thorne, Barrie. "Resisting the Draft: An Ethnography of the Draft Resistance Movement." Ph.D. diss., Brandeis University, 1991.

Thrasher, Sue. "Circle of Trust." In Connie Curry et al., eds., *Deep in Our Hearts: Nine White Women in the Freedom Movement,* 207–52. Athens: University of Georgia Press, 2000.

Thurman, Howard. *The Creative Encounter: An Interpretation of Religion and the Social Witness.* 1954. Richmond, Ind.: United Friends Press, 1997.

———. *Deep River: Reflections on the Religious Insight of Certain of the Negro's Spirituals.* New York: Harper, 1955.

———. *Jesus and the Disinherited.* Richmond, Ind.: United Friends Press, 1981.

Tracy, James. *Direct Action: Radical Pacifism from the Union Eight to the Chicago Seven.* Chicago: University of Chicago Press, 1996.

Tuck, Stephen G. N. *Beyond Atlanta: The Struggle for Racial Equality in Georgia, 1940–1980.* Athens: University of Georgia Press, 2001.

Turner, Wallace. "Tip Leads to Arrest of Radical Sought in 1970 Case." *New York Times,* 22 Jan. 1987.

Tyson, Timothy B. *"Radio Free Dixie": Robert F. Williams and the Roots of Black Power.* Chapel Hill: University of North Carolina Press, 1999.

Umoja, Akinyele. "Ballots and Bullets: A Comparative Analysis of Armed Resistance in the Civil Rights Movement." *Journal of Black Studies* 29, no. 4 (March 1999): 558–78.

———. "1964: The Beginning of the End of Nonviolence in the Mississippi Freedom Movement." *Radical History Review* (January 2003): 201–26.

Unger, Irwin, and Debi Unger, eds. *The Times Were a Changin': The Sixties Reader.* New York: Three Rivers Press, 1998.

Unseem, Michael. *Conscription, Protest and Social Conflict: The Life and Death of a Draft Resistance Movement.* New York: Wiley, 1973.

Valk, Anne M. "Separatism and Sisterhood: Race, Sex and Women's Activism in Washington, D.C., 1963–1980." Ph.D. diss., Duke University, 1996.

Van DeBurg, William L. *New Day in Babylon: The Black Power Movement and American Culture, 1965–1975*. Chicago: University of Chicago Press, 1992.

Venceremos Brigade, edited by Sandra Levinson and Carol Brightman. New York: Simon and Schuster, 1971.

Vickers, George. *The Formation of the New Left: The Early Years*. Lexington, Mass.: Lexington Books, 1975.

Viorst, Milton. *Fire in the Streets: America in the 1960s*. New York: Simon and Schuster, 1979.

Walker, Alice. *In Search of Our Mother's Gardens: Womanist Prose*. San Diego: Harcourt Brace Jovanovich, 1983.

———. *Meridian*. New York: Pocket Books, 1976.

Wallace, Michael, and Richard Hofstader, eds. *American Violence: A Documentary History*. New York: Knopf, 1970.

Walters, Ronald W. *Pan-Africanism in the African Diaspora: An Analysis of Modern Afrocentric Political Movements*. Detroit: Wayne State University Press, 1993.

Warren, Robert Penn. *Who Speaks for the Negro?* New York: Random House, 1965.

Washington, Cynthia. "We Started from Different Ends of the Spectrum." *Southern Exposure* 4, no. 4 (Winter 1977): 14–15. Reprinted in Sara Evans, *Personal Politics: The Roots of Women's Liberation in the Civil Rights Movement and the New Left*, 238–40. New York: Vintage Books, 1980.

Waskow, Arthur I. *From Race Riot to Sit-In: 1919 and the 1960s*. Garden City, N.Y.: Anchor Books, 1966.

Watters, Pat. *Down to Now: Reflections on the Southern Civil Rights Movement*. New York: Random House, 1971.

Watters, Pat, and Reese Cleghorn. *Climbing Jacob's Ladder: The Arrival of Negroes in Southern Politics*. New York: Harcourt, Brace, 1967.

Weather Underground Organization. *Osawatomie*, no. 1 (Spring 1975), no. 4 (Winter 1974–76), vol. 2, no. 1 (April–May 1976), vol. 2, no. 2 (June–July 1976). Historical Society Library Pamphlet Collection. Madison: Historical Society of Wisconsin.

Weigand, Kathleen Anne. "Vanguard of Women's Liberation: The Old Left and the Continuity of the Women's Movement in the United States, 1945–1970s." Ph.D. diss., Ohio State University, 1995.

Weissman, Steve, ed. *Big Brother and the Holding Company: The World behind Watergate*. Palo Alto, Calif.: Ramparts Press, 1974.

Welding, Pete, and Toby Byron, eds. *Bluesland*. New York: Dutton, 1991.

Wells, Ida B. "Southern Horrors." In Jacqueline Jones Royster, ed., *Southern Horrors and Other Writings: The Anti-Lynching Campaign of Ida B. Wells, 1892–1900*, 49–72. Boston: Bedford Books, 1997.

Wells-Barnett, Ida B. *Selected Works of Ida B. Wells-Barnett*. Ed. Trudier Harris. New York: Oxford University Press, 1991.

West, Cornel. *Keeping Faith: Philosophy and Race in America*. New York: Routledge, 1993.

———. *Prophecy Deliverance! An Afro-American Revolutionary Christianity*. Philadelphia: Westminster Press, 1982.

———. *Prophetic Fragments*. Trenton, N.J.: Africa World Press, 1988.

Whalen, Jack, and Richard Flacks. *Beyond the Barricades: The 60s Generation Grows Up*. Philadelphia: Temple University Press, 1989.

White, Deborah Gray. *Ar'n't I a Woman? Female Slaves in the Plantation South*. New York: Norton, 1985.

Whitmer, Peter O. *Aquarius Revisited: Seven Who Created the Sixties Counterculture That Changed America*. New York: Macmillan, 1987.

Wigginton, Eliot, ed. *Refuse to Stand Silently By: An Oral History of Grass Roots Social Activism in America, 1921–1964*. New York: Doubleday, 1991.

Wilkie, Curtis. "Chicago Insurgents." In Aaron Henry, with Constance Curry, *The Fire Ever Burning*, 222–28. Jackson: University Press of Mississippi, 2000.

Williams, Delores S. *Sisters in the Wilderness: The Challenge of Womanist God-talk*. Maryknoll, N.Y.: Orbis Books, 1993.

Williams, Patricia J. *The Rooster's Egg: Imagining How It Might Be Different in the Time of Democracy's Doldrums*. Cambridge: Harvard University Press, 1996.

Williams, Robert F. *Negroes with Guns*. New York: Marzani and Munsell, 1962.

Williams, Yohuru R. "No Haven: Civil Rights, Black Power, and Black Panthers in New Haven, Connecticut, 1956–1971." Ph.D. diss., Howard University, 1998.

Williamson, Joy Ann. "'We Demand Everything; We Hope for Nothing': Black Students at the University of Illinois at Urbana-Champaign." Ph.D. diss., University of Illinois at Urbana-Champaign, 1998.

Wittman, Carl. "A Gay Manifesto." *Liberation* (February 1970): 18–24.

———. "Waves of the Resistance." *Liberation* (November 1968): 29–33.

Wittner, Lawrence. *Rebels against War: The American Peace Movement, 1933–1983*. Philadelphia: Temple University Press, 1984.

Wofford, Harris. *Of Kennedys and Kings*. New York: Farrar, Straus, Giroux, 1980.

Wolin, Sheldon. "Editorial." *democracy. Journal of Political Renewal and Radical Change* (January 1981): 3–5.

———. "Norm and Form and the Constitutionalizing of Democracy." In Peter Euben, John R. Wallach, and Josiah Boer, eds., *Athenian Political Thought and the Reconstitution of American Democracy*. Ithaca, N.Y.: Cornell University Press, 1994.

———. *Politics and Vision*. Boston: Little, Brown, 1960.

———. "What Revolutionary Action Means Today." In Chantal Mouffe, ed., *Dimensions of Radical Democracy*, 240–53. London: Verso, 1992.

Woodard, Komozi. *A Nation within a Nation: Amiri Baraka and Black Power Politics*. Chapel Hill: University of North Carolina Press, 1999.

Young, Andrew. *An Easy Burden: The Civil Rights Movement and the Transformation of America*. New York: HarperCollins, 1996.

Young, Cynthia Ann. "Soul Power: Cultural Radicalism and the Formation of a United States Third World Left." Ph.D. diss., Yale University, 1999.

Young, Henry J. *Major Black Religious Leaders, 1755–1940*. Nashville, Tenn.: Abingdon, 1977.

Zaroulis, Nancy, and Gerald Sullivan. *Who Spoke Up? American Protest against the War in Vietnam, 1963–1975*. Garden City, N.Y.: Doubleday, 1975.

Zinn, Howard. *SNCC: The New Abolitionists*. Boston: Beacon Press, 1964.

Zunes, Stephen, Lester R. Kurtz, and Sarah Beth Asher, eds. *Nonviolent Social Movements: A Geographical Perspective*. Oxford, England: Blackwell Publishers, 1999.

Other Sources

"Ain't Scared of Your Jails, 1960–1961." *Eyes on the Prize: America's Civil Rights Years, 1954–1965*. Produced and directed by Orlando Bagwell. 60 min. Pacific Arts, 1992. Videocassette.

Berkeley in the Sixties. Produced by P.O.V. Theatrical Films. Directed by Mark Kitchell. 117 min. First Run Films, 1990. Videocassette.

"Bridge to Freedom, 1965." *Eyes on the Prize: America's Civil Rights Years, 1954–1965*. Produced, directed, and written by Callie Crossley and James DeVinney. 60 min. Blackside, Inc., 1987. Videocassette.

Chomsky, Noam. "Prospects for Democracy." Excerpts of a speech given at Massachusetts Institute of Technology. Compact disc AK002CD. AK Press, 1994.

Conley, Dalton. Interview. *RACE: The Power of an Illusion*. California Newsreel, 2003. ‹http://www.pbs.org/race/000_About/002_04-background-03-03.htm›. 29 Nov. 2005.

Deacons for Defense. Produced by Nick Grillo. Directed by Bill Duke. Written by Michael D'Antonio. 95 min. Showtime Entertainment, 2003. Videocassette.

Dylan, Bob. "Chimes of Freedom." *Another Side of Bob Dylan*. LP, Columbia, C-2193, 1964.

"Freedom Faith." *This Far by Faith*. Produced and directed by Alice Markowitz. 60 min. Blackside Productions, 2003. Videocassette.

Freedom on My Mind. Produced and directed by Connie Field and Marilyn Mulford. 110 min. California Newsreel, 1994. Videocassette.

Freedom Song. Produced, directed, and written by Phil Alden Robinson. 118 min. Turner Network Television, 2000. ‹http://tnt.turner.com/movies/tntoriginals/freedomsong/ypp/history.html›.

Fundi: The Story of Ella Baker. Written and directed by Joanne Grant. 45 min. First Run Films, 1981. Videocassette.

Grathwohl, Lawrence. Testimony at W. Mark Felt–Edward S. Miller Trial, Washington, D.C., 14 Oct. 1980. Videocassette.

Lowndes County Freedom Movement: The Rise of the Black Panthers. 25 min. Films for the Humanities and Sciences, Princeton, N.J., 1995. Videocassette.

Mississippi Burning. Directed by Alan Parker. Written by Chris Gerolmo. 127 min. Orion Films, 1988. Videocassette.

"Mississippi: Is This America? 1962–1964." *Eyes on the Prize: America's Civil Rights Years, 1954–1965*. Produced, directed, and written by Orlando Bagwell. 60 min. 1987. Videocassette.

"A Nation of Law?" *Eyes on the Prize: America's Civil Rights Years, 1954–1965*. Produced and directed by Terry Kay Rockefeller, Thomas Ott, and Louis Massiah. 60 min. Pacific Arts, 1992. Videocassette.

"No Easy Walk, 1961–1963." *Eyes on the Prize: America's Civil Rights Years, 1954–1965.* Produced and directed by Judith Vecchione. 60 min. Pacific Arts, 1992. Videocassette.

"The Promised Land, 1967–1968." *Eyes on the Prize: America's Civil Rights Years, 1954–1965.* Produced and directed by Paul Stekler and Jacqueline Shearer. 60 min. Pacific Arts, 1992. Videocassette.

"Putting the Movement Back into Civil Rights Teaching." ‹http://www .civilrightsteaching.org›.

Reagon, Bernice Johnson. "Give Your Hands to Struggle," [1970]. Sweet Honey in the Rock, *In This Land.* Compact disc CD 942522-2. Earth Beat, 1992.

Rebels with a Cause. Produced, directed, and edited by Helen Garvy. Shire Films, 1999. Videocassette.

Sing for Freedom: The Story of the Civil Rights Movement through Its Songs. Compact disc CD SF40032. Smithsonian/Folkways, 1990.

Sweeney, Dennis Remarks at Stanford University, 2 Oct. 1963, tape 631002-S1-2, Stanford University Archive of Recorded Sound, Stanford, Calif.

Sweet Honey in the Rock. "Ella's Song." *Breaths.* Compact disc CD FF70105. Flying Fish Records, 1990.

"The Time Has Come, 1964–1966." *Eyes on the Prize: America's Civil Rights Years, 1954–1965.* Produced and directed by James DeVinney and Madison Davis Lacy Jr. 60 min. Pacific Arts, 1992. Videocassette.

Underground. Produced and directed by Emile de Antonio, Mary Lampson, and Haskell Wexler. 1975. Videocassette.

The Weather Underground. Directed by Sam Green and Bill Siegel. 92 min. Creative Capital/Independent Television Service, 2003. DVD.

"'We Who Believe in Freedom Cannot Rest': Ella Baker and the Birth of SNCC" Conference. Shaw University, Raleigh, N.C., 15 Apr. 2000. Transcript in the author's possession.

Will the Circle Be Unbroken? An Audio History of the Civil Rights Movement in Five Southern Communities and the Music of Those Times. ‹http://unbrokencircle.org›.

"Women & Men in the Freedom Movement, A Discussion." June, August, September 2004. Transcript, ‹http://www.crmvet.org/disc/women1.htm›.

Acknowledgments

Nothing worthwhile on the preceding pages could have appeared without interviews — those done by others and those I conducted. Interviews can drain people, eat up time, and sometimes revisit the most difficult territory of a person's life. As one movement veteran recalled:

> The problem is that we've told all the stories so many times and under so many conditions that telling them is pain. I'm not even sure what *happened* any more. When I hit Louisiana from Arizona, I was nineteen years old and brought with me books by Ayn Rand and Robert Heinlein — that was my bag — and I was looking forward to six weeks of paying my dues and hastily returning to my career as a television announcer. And it just didn't come down that way. I ended up there better than a year and it changed my whole life. So it's a very hard year for me to talk about.

Moreover, movement people have watched their stories turn up misunderstood, mistakenly framed, or just plain abused for many years, so the payoff can seem limited even under the best circumstances. To this end, my first and most significant intellectual debt is to the civil rights activists who agreed to be interviewed, and to Clay Carson, Bret Eynon, and Ron Grele for sharing their invaluable interviews with me. Dr. Carson also kindly allowed me to use photos from the *Student Voice*. I regret that photographs of Robert Moses, James Forman, Prathia Hall, Charles Sherrod, and other key people could not be included. Of those I interviewed, Jim Lawson, Diane Nash, Casey Hayden, Judy Richardson, Staughton Lynd, and Dickie Magidoff deserve particular thanks.

Larry Goodwyn, Bill Chafe, Nancy Hewitt, Sucheta Mazumdar, and Tami Biddle served as a scholarly powerhouse early in the project. I wish to thank them for years of wise counsel, patient rereading, and their generosity of spirit and time; each provided intellectual wellsprings that sustained me — as well as encouragement, contacts, and compelling models of collegiality. I first met Mike Zuckerman in 1990, when we undergraduates nicknamed him "Zeus" as a token of our respect for his unmatched knowledge base and flair with the written word. Over the last decade, he has always appeared at the right time with a lightning bolt of encouragement and radiant enthusiasm. Eric O'Neil read the manuscript and passed it on to Staughton and Alice Lynd. All three rejuvenated the effort with their careful readings, making both detailed and general comments that allowed me to cut through huge swaths of the original draft. Eric, Staughton, and Alice all provide a working model for activism from which I benefit greatly.

Thank God for the Memphis trolley and Emilye Crosby. By her absence this project would have suffered in aspects too numerous to mention, but especially her model of scholarship and teaching, her keen eye for detail, and her gentle reminders to "show" not "tell." Tim Tyson's thorough, direct, and beautifully phrased comments enabled me to produce a richer and more textured work. Hasan Jeffries's encyclopedic knowledge of the SNCC papers, SNCC work in Alabama, and the civil rights – Black Power literature have made his reading of this material particularly sharp-eyed. His collegiality and suggestions have improved the book conceptually and factually. Ray Arsenault caught errors of fact and provided new avenues of vision. John Dittmer kindly pointed me in numerous fruitful directions that improved both the specific content and the broader conclusions of the later manuscript. I benefited enormously from working with Ben Houston and Peter Kuryla on a panel on the Nashville movement. Noah Buhayar read the manuscript for clarity over the course of 2002 and provided innumerable connections, suggestions, and well-timed humor. I am honored that Bill Greider took time to make many substantial and thoughtful contributions to this work. Finally, Dirk Philipsen did a fabulous edit (twice) in the final stages. His analytical talent and thoughtfulness made the homestretch one of creative joy rather than strain.

For making the publication process possible, my sincerest gratitude to David Perry, editor-in-chief of the University of North Carolina (UNC) Press. I believe he possesses a patience for the creative process that even the Dalai Lama might admire. His wry humor and deft observations clarified and strengthened both the work and my thinking. Paula Wald, Stevie Champion, and David Hines at the UNC Press polished and made the book presentable when it seemed jumbled and tattered at the edges.

For pointing out ways to improve parts of the text, I thank Candice Jimerson-Johnson, Nelson Johnson, Curtis Muhammad, Mike Miller, Tiyi Morris, Jeff Spain, Robyn Spencer, Ian Lekus, Rhonda Mawhood Lee, Shan Holt, Jeanne Theoharis, Peter Linebaugh, Benj DeMott, Lorry Swain, Jesse Lemish, Fred Carey, Betsy Stephens Ellsworth, Sara Amma-Leland, Scott Ellsworth, Liz Kieff, Jerry Thornberry, Kelly Hammond, Katie Heins, David Hines of the UNC Press, Paul Ortiz, Candace McClelland, Elizabeth Warshawsky-Ricanati, Tiana Brown, Kish Beckford, Chris Haskins, Kenya Ramey, Ben Moynihan, the students in Emilye Crosby's 2003 – 04 civil rights seminars at SUNY-Geneseo, Lawrence Goodwyn's 2004 FOCUS seminar at Duke University (particularly Jenn Tanaka), and anonymous readers at the *Pennsylvania Magazine of History and Biography*, the *Journal of Southern History*, the *Journal of American History*, and the UNC Press. My debt to Shanita Payne, Jeremy Guttman, Emily Geier, and Annie L. Barrett remains vast for pulling the title of this work out of the morass and making it accessible to a wider audience. The wonderful brainiacs listed above made many suggestions for which I was always grateful but did not always follow; I assume responsibility for all errors of judgment and fact.

My colleagues at Virginia State welcomed me in January 2003 and kept me in good cheer despite my rants down the hallway throughout the long publication process; for their advice and humor, I extend my gratitude to Renée Afanana Hill, Shelia Lassiter, Joe Goldenberg, Majid Amini, Olwyn Blouet, Arthur Abraham, Steven Ramold, Christina Proenza-Coles, Richard Chew, Jo Kukendall, Cheri Tucker, Cheryl Adeyemi, and my incomparable office mate, Paul Alkebulan.

Thanks to those who made the research task easier: the Lefferts family for countless nights spent in their guest room, Tim Tyson and Perri Morgan, Mike Miller, Staughton Lynd, Oli Fein, Wendy Chemielski at the Swarthmore College Peace Collection, the entire staff of the Stanford University Special Collections Library, Elaine Ignatius at the University of Cincinnati, Richard Johnson of the University of Washington who extended library privileges in the long winter of 1996, Kathy Bennett and Beth Odle at the Nashville Public Library, and T. J. Hogan who took several afternoons away from the lure of Wall Street to photocopy nearly all of the Fellowship of Reconciliation records pertaining to James Lawson in the basement of the Swarthmore Library. John Wagner brought his magic to the restoration of several key photographs.

In 2001, I saw a Toshi Reagon – Bernice Reagon concert benefiting Cincinnati's non-profit workers. The experience taught me that perhaps I lacked the experience to understand music's pivotal role in nourishing any long-term engagement, be it a relationship, a creative project, or even a movement. They may achieve fame and fortune, but musicians rarely get thanked for helping to sustain belief in the world as it could be. To this end, I could not have maintained this decade-long endeavor without the sounds of Toshi Reagon and Sweet Honey in the Rock, or without the music of Ben Harper, Nina Simone, Ani DiFranco, Ed Vedder, Parliament, All Natural, Spearhead, Marvin Gaye, and Greg Brown coursing through my daily routine.

Those who provided housing, child care, and travel money made the project possible on the most practical level. In this respect my debt is unpayable to Lola Rosensteel, Bill Rosensteel, and Merritt Hogan. I could not have written the book without traversing the country — from the Delta to Wisconsin, Seattle to Georgia, New York, and San Francisco. No way to do that with two young children without your help. You three made pursuing this project feasible countless times when I thought it would otherwise derail, and you did so with a constant stream of support, warmth, and kindness. I love you. I also extend open appreciation and gratitude on this score to the late John W. McWilliams Jr., Tom Main, Charlie Clark, T. J. and Karen Hogan, and Stevie and Marshall Wishnack.

Loving, sane people continued to remind me superwoman was only a fairytale so stop trying to keep her pace and come live. On this front, thanks go to Samantha and Josh Wishnack, Melissa Beitz Waters, Lillie Haffey, Gracie Haffey, Briana Boyer, Claire and Larry Pinnow, Hilary Mosher, Libby Benton, Elizabeth Warshawsky-Ricanati, Betsy Stephens Ellsworth, Elizabeth Kieff Levinson, Julia and Andrea Rogers, Paula Butler, Nell Goodwyn, Theresa Hirschauer, Eileen Barrett, Melonee Ridgeway, Leff and Jenny Lefferts, Sarah Nicole Johnson, Kim Burden, Hillery Shay, Shanita Payne, Emily Geier, Jeremy Guttman, Annie Barrett, Heidi and Scott Sullivan, Jarrod and Kelly Becker, Candice Jimerson-Johnson, Jeff Spain, Kelly Hammond, Karen Lee Hogan, Peter Andruss, Betsy Bullitt, Charlotte Wishnack, Renée and Oliver Hill, Niloufar Jafari, Susan Scovil and John Wagner, Majel Stein and Barry Friend, Sara Amma-Leland, Nik Philipsen, Sven Philipsen, John, Añe, and Bohdan Esteban Hundman, and particularly Lola Rosensteel and Merritt Hogan. Paula Friedman patiently gave me the most amazing interview I have recorded. Unfortunately its content was outside the scope of this book, yet Paula remained encouraging. Paula, I am so grateful.

With Bohdan I shared the steepest price, the tears of going dutch on the price of the ticket. Above all, Shamus and Chloë Hogan kept me rooted in practicing respect and kindness — not chronicling them. Finally, the energy spilling out of my conversations with Corbett fueled my little engine over the steepest inclines — without him I would have sputtered and stalled. I could not have asked for a finer intellectual compañero.

Index

for MFDP, 193; as mentor to SNCC, 35, 40–42, 68, 104, 238, 309 (n. 71), 326 (nn. 8, 10), 348 (n. 34); as Mississippi Summer Project Committee member, 155; on nonviolence and self-defense, 36, 85; on nurturing leadership in communities, 59, 239; on rhetoric, 384 (n. 36); on Shaw University conference, 34–35, 101, 305 (n. 52); and SNCC's gendered conceptions of political leadership, 327 (n. 24); on SNCC's internal culture of nonviolence, 84, 213, 324 (n. 78); speech to MFDP, 192

Baldwin, James, 91

Banking institutions: role in movement, 79, 85

Barbee, William, 48

Barnett, Ross, 272, 315 (n. 30)

Barry, Marion (chair of SNCC, 1960–61), 61, 64, 355 (n. 48), 375 (n. 6)

Bates, James, 272

Bay of Pigs incident, 46

Beauvoir, Simone de, 290

Belafonte, Harry, 197, 319 (n. 22)

Belfrage, Sally, 187

Bell, Emma, 79, 149, 169

Bellamy, Fay, 246

"Beloved community," 22–23, 25; confused with assimilation, 314–15 (n. 28); and women's liberation, 291

Benson, Nannie, 262

Bergman, Walter, 46

Bevel, Diane Nash. *See* Nash, Diane

Bevel, James (Jim), 19, 22, 30, 47, 51, 65, 66, 80–82, 252; brings nonviolent direct action to Birmingham campaign, 53, 90–91, 242; chairs Nashville central committee during Freedom Rides, 47–48; on freedom songs, 313 (n. 21)

Birmingham, Alabama, 7, 136, 239; Freedom Rides in, 46–48; murder of four girls in 16th St. Baptist Church bombing in, 164, 351 (n. 19); role in generating 1964 Civil Rights Act, 90, 242

Black Arts movement, 285, 376 (n. 9)

Black Freedom Church, 14, 73, 74, 307 (n. 64), 320 (n. 32); as force for spiritual and moral revolution, 44, 308 (n. 65); mobilized for political ends, 80, 229,

261; as institution controlled by blacks, 168

"Black is beautiful" aesthetic, 285

Black Liberation Army, 252

Black nationalism, 37, 126, 245–46, 284, 289; defined, 382 (n. 15); defined by West, 387 (n. 1); as distinct from black separatism, 285; all-black staff as practical, not nationalist, 347 (n. 29)

Black Panthers: killed by law enforcement, 252; as symbol of Lowndes County Freedom Party, 220

Black Power movement, 10, 221, 230–31, 234, 247, 284–85, 289, 353 (n. 38), 376 (n. 9), 378 (n. 14), 379 (n. 19), 388 (n. 5); antiracist white response to, 389 (n. 20); white misinterpretation of, 247

Black separatism, 150–53, 203–7, 285, 289, 377 (n. 7); as alternative to assimilation, 247; coexists with integration of public facilities, 247; in context of anticolonial freedom movements worldwide, 387 (n. 1); contributions evaluated, 247; as distinct from black nationalism, 382 (n. 15); dynamic repeated in women's and gay liberation movements, 367 (n. 24); as overkill, 246; and politics of anger, 207; as solution to racial terror, 245–46; and withdrawal from interracial relationships, 228

Black Studies programs, 231, 285, 378 (n. 13), 388 (n. 5)

Blackwell, Randolph, 88

Blackwell, Unita, 150

Blair, Ezell, Jr., 27, 100

Block, Sam, 79, 85–88, 91, 149, 157, 204; and folk festivals, 231

Bombings. *See* Racial terror

Bond, Julian, 35, 104, 254, 256; as bridge-builder, 326 (n. 11); on building local leadership, 375 (n. 8); on gender equality in SNCC, 290; satire of popular understandings of movement, 7, 226; on self-defense, 250

Booth, Heather. *See* Tobias, Heather

Booth, Paul, 293

Boston Draft Resistance Group, 291

Boudin, Kathy: "How to Organize a Welfare Rights Local Group," 287–88; runs

which ordinary people acquire, 75,
209–10; reproducible nature of, 209;
and SCLC ministers on acting free, 323
(n. 70); and shedding subservient acculturation, 314–15 (n. 28). *See also* Experiential education of civil rights workers;
Public life; Self-activity; Slave mentality
Consciousness-raising groups, 233, 254,
390 (n. 25); early versions of, 112; simi-
larities to Lawson workshops, 290
Consensus, 26, 42, 104, 158, 160, 168, 189–
90, 211, 213, 224, 274, 283
Constitution. *See* United States
Constitution
CORE. *See* Congress of Racial Equality
Cornell University, 54
Cortes, Ernesto, 59, 60
Cost of movement work, 61, 62, 91, 206,
246, 286; during Freedom Rides, 313
(n. 17); and identity in movement com-
munity, 227–29, 377 (nn. 4, 6, 7); during
Mississippi Summer Project, 167; ten-
sion causes physical and mental prob-
lems, 227–30. *See also* Burnout; Racial
terror
Cotton, Dorothy, 82
Cotton, MacArthur, 53; integrates Jackson
induction center, 233
Council of Federated Organizations
(COFO), 77, 87, 144, 145, 166, 169, 208,
221, 263, 322 (n. 60), 345 (n. 7); Fifth
Congressional District meeting (November 1964), 222–24; and groundwork
for MFDP, 156, 160; statewide meetings
(December 1963–June 1964), 147
Counterculture, 3, 139, 353 (n. 38); and
institutions created by Mississippi Summer Project volunteers, 292–93; institutions of, 284–85, 291; misrepresentation
of, 116; origins of, 116, 168, 289; as rebellion against experts, 293
Countryman, Peter, 111, 122, 123, 134–36;
links northern students to movement,
100, 116, 333 (n. 13); prefigures ideas
in "Port Huron Statement" and Free
Speech Movement, 135, 339 (n. 7)
Courage: as misunderstood ingredient of
political activism, 210. *See also* Fear
Cox, Courtland, 158, 366 (n. 16), 375 (n. 6);

on Credentials Committee, 193; as
Drum and Spear Bookstore founder,
231; meets with Big Six, 358 (n. 1); on
working in Democratic Party, 177
Cox, Harold, 156
Crawford, Earistiss, 272
Crawford, James, 76
Credentials Committee. *See* Democratic
National Convention of 1964
Culbreath, Janie, 69
Cunningham, Phyllis, 290
Curry, Constance (Connie), 61, 172, 205;
as bridge-builder, 98–99

Daniels, Carolyn, 72–73, 241
Darden, Ann, 272
Davis, Phil, 213
Davis, Rennie, 110; as organizer in Chi-
cago, 288
Dawson, Charles, 192
Dawson, Dorothy. *See* Burlage, Dorothy
Dawson
Days of Rage (1969), 288
Deauville Hotel, 192. *See also* Mississippi
Freedom Democratic Party
DeBerry, Roy, 194
Decentralist structure of institutions, 387
(n. 3)
Decolonization movements, 284
Deference, 1, 293. *See also* Slave mentality
DeLott, Elaine. *See* Baker, Elaine DeLott
Delta Ministry, 167, 168, 222
Deming, Barbara, 252, 296 (n. 3)
Democratic culture, 189, 241; cohesion in
face of disagreement, 197, 217; role of
candor in, 213, 229, 255, 290. *See also*
Freedom songs; Movement culture;
Student Nonviolent Coordinating
Committee: culture
Democratic experiment, 116, 182, 212,
213, 219, 237. *See also* Freedom Bal-
lot; Student Nonviolent Coordinating
Committee
Democratic heritage, 9, 140, 237; absence
as price of burnout, 240; gap between
reality and rhetoric of, 261–63; SNCC's
democratic accomplishments absent
from national legend, 239; thinness of,
286, 288; white supremacy undermines,

Federal Communications Commission
(FCC), 199, 363 (n. 4)
Federation of Southern Cooperatives, 231
Fein, Oliver (Oli), 118, 125, 126, 129
Feingold, Miriam (Mimi), 118–25 passim,
130; description of northern whites, 171;
and Plaquemine Parish, 265–67
Fellowship of Reconciliation (FOR), 14,
15, 38, 265; as channel for transmission
of Gandhian practices to United States,
14; pamphlet on nonviolence in Montgomery, 17, 300 (n. 11); pioneers sit-ins
in North and West in 1940s, 298 (n. 3),
303 (n. 37)
Feminism: development of feminist perspective in SDS, 109–14; development of
feminist perspective in SNCC, 232–33;
difficulty of seeing debt to civil rights
movement, 232; and immobilization of
women by U.S. culture, 109–10; origins
of second wave of feminism in SNCC,
232–33, 289–90, 390 (n. 22); radical
feminism, 289–90, 390 (nn. 23, 26); and
SNCC "internal education" paper, 232,
289; unexamined white supremacy of,
232, 379 (n. 20)
The Feminists, 233
Field Foundation, 78
Fifteenth Amendment, 156
Fisk University, 8, 19
Flacks, Mickey, 110, 111–14
Flacks, Richard (Dick), 110
Fleming, Cynthia Griggs, 54, 174
Flowers, Dickie, 169
FOR. See Fellowship of Reconciliation
Forman, James, 80, 100, 169, 227, 278; on
alternatives when people are not allowed to share power, 189; background,
64; bravery of, 208; as bridge-builder,
209; calls for unity in SNCC, 275, 367
(n. 20); concept of revolution, 208–12,
227; controls funds in SNCC, 202–3;
on death of Younge, 246; describes
SNCC as on "river of no return," 274;
fall 1964 trip to Africa, 197; on forming
centralized executive structure, 200,
202, 217, 373 (n. 60); health problems,
209, 275; *Making of Black Revolutionar-*

ies, 211, 273; as mentor to SNCC people,
199; on Moses' "refusal to lead," 211;
recruitment of, 64; sets up fund-raising
network, 66, 114, 220; as SNCC administrator, 64–65; suggestion for SNCC
direction at Waveland, 199, 273–76,
280–82; on Two-Seat Compromise, 194;
work ethic, 203, 208
Forsyth, Bill, 272
Freedom: defined as daily acts, 2, 235–36,
255
Freedom Ballot, 144; provides opportunity
to act in politically meaningful ways,
145–47; as public context to dramatize
disfranchisement, 145. *See also* Council
of Federated Organizations; Freedom
Vote; Mississippi Freedom Democratic
Party; Student Nonviolent Coordinating Committee
Freedom Democratic Party. *See* Mississippi Freedom Democratic Party
Freedom Farm, 378 (n. 14). *See* Hamer,
Fannie Lou
"Freedom High," 211–12, 273
Freedom Riders, 7, 45–55, 236, 242; as tag
for civil rights workers, 50–51
Freedom Rides, 3, 9, 14, 20, 45–55, 57, 58,
61, 66, 229, 236, 242, 245, 265, 311 (n. 5),
313 (n. 17); in Anniston, 45; central message of, 50–51, 316 (n. 39); Nashville
students' role in, 7, 148, 159; workshops'
role in sustaining, 47–48
Freedom Schools, 157, 168, 291; origins
of, 63; pedagogy of, 167; impact of, 167;
teach children to act free, 352 (n. 34), 354
(n. 45)
Freedom Singers, 124, 334 (n. 18); provide
opportunity for whites to break with
racist culture, 385 (n. 4)
Freedom Song (TNT, 2000), 317 (n. 4), 384
(n. 2)
Freedom songs, 39, 45, 51, 54, 86, 197, 231,
239, 249; help older Americans join
movement, 308 (n. 65); role in combating fear, 40; role in movement, 91, 204,
259–60, 313 (n. 21); role in sustaining
people through slavery, 307 (n. 64);
sung *in extremis*, 159, 163, 350 (n. 12), 351

(n. 22). *See also* Freedom Singers; Lining songs; Movement culture

Freedom Summer. *See* Mississippi Summer Project

Freedom Vote (November 1963), 3, 145–50, 203, 240; primary goal of, 146

Free Southern Theater, 285

Free Speech Movement, 293

Frente Autentico del Trabajo, 387 (n. 3)

Friends of SNCC (FOS) groups, 111, 114, 115, 273, 333 (n. 15); demand federal protection, 164; and Greenwood food and clothing drive, 87, 329 (n. 41); Mississippi Summer Project results, 293, 330 (n. 52), 392 (n. 34)

Fund for Educational and Legal Defense (FELD), 230

Gandhi, Mohandas, 8, 15, 20, 53, 69, 201, 265, 284, 329 (n. 38); Lawson's use of as example, 20–21, 33

Ganz, Marshall, 163; appeal to rule of reason or law in Mississippi, 173; and Credentials Committee, 193; and UFW, 294

Garman, Betty, 266; on fund-distribution system in SNCC, 365 (n. 13); as member of SNCC finance committee, 375 (n. 6); on summer volunteers joining staff, 372 (n. 53)

Garvy, Helen, 100, 137; view that ERAP staff was mislabeled as "anti-intellectual," 338 (n. 5); view that Vietnam caused distortion of New Left, 252

Gelles, Jerry, 118, 121, 126

Gendered acculturation, 112, 233, 250, 330 (n. 45)

Gendered division of labor. *See* Mississippi Summer Project; Student Nonviolent Coordinating Committee; White antiracism

Giddings, Tony, 231

Gilbert, David, 234

Gitlin, Todd, 136; background, 338 (n. 2); on university as cage, 132; on why SDS moved toward ERAP, 266, 340 (n. 12)

Glenn, Charles, 222–23

Global justice movement, 249

Glover, Jesse James, 53

Goldwater, Barry, 196

Goodman, Andrew, 162–64, 165, 185, 191, 196, 207, 269, 291

Goodman, Paul, 109

Gordon, Larry, 126

Graft, Idell, 251

Gramsci, Antonio, 236

Grant, Joanne, 41

Grass roots, 150, 196, 230, 231, 240, 289; defined, 209, 309 (n. 71); difficulty of identifying and training leaders, 253, 264; grassroots organizations, 167, 225, 248, 302 (n. 31); grassroots strategy, 212, 219, 244, 250, 251, 254, 293–94

Gray, Victoria. *See* Adams, Victoria Gray

Green, Edith, 194

Green Compromise, 195; 1944 precedent with two rival Texas delegations, 362 (n. 32); original Green Compromise, 362 (n. 32). *See also* Democratic National Convention of 1964

Greene, Dewey, Jr., 179, 290

Greene, Dewey, Sr., 179

Greene, George, 148

Greensboro sit-in (February 1960), 26–27, 101, 303 (n. 37)

Greenwood, Miss., movement, 3, 85–87, 136, 146, 157–59, 227, 236; Block arrives in, 85; and discontinuation of federal food program, 87; and police threat to SNCC office, 86; SNCC food program in, 88

Gregory, Dick, 158

Greyhound Bus Lines, 47–49, 61

Grizzard, Vernon, 125, 127, 128; in Boston Draft Resistance Group, 291; joins The Resistance, 233; parent resistance after Cambridge sit-ins, 334 (n. 23)

Groundwork, 60, 91, 172. *See also* Baker, Ella; Bryant, Curtis C.; Horton, Myles; Jordan, Cleveland; Moore, Amzie; Napier, J. C.; Owens, Webb; Smith, Kelly Miller; Steptoe, E. W.; Wells, Samuel

Group-centered leadership. *See* Leadership

Guinea, 197

Guyot, Lawrence, 37, 58, 79, 80, 149, 358 (n. 68); cost of movement work on, 325 (n. 97); on 1964 Democratic National Convention, 198; supports Mississippi Summer Project, 346 (n. 20)

Haber, Alan, 100–101, 108, 110, 111, 134–35, 264
Halberstam, David, 48
Hale, Grace, 343 (n. 21)
Hall, Prathia, 72, 107, 126, 229, 241; background, 73; on decision-making process in SNCC, 373 (n. 59); on Democratic Party, 177; on gendered division of labor in SNCC, 171; investigates alternatives to SNCC's buying building, 375 (n. 6); power of sermons of, 73
Hamer, Fannie Lou, 85, 156, 177, 194, 229, 236, 240, 241, 285, 356 (n. 56), 384 (n. 2); analysis of white supremacy, 161; Atlantic City testimony, 190, 195; fall 1964 trip to Africa, 195; and Freedom Farm, 231; mother's insistence on black pride, 323 (n. 68); on Rauh's betrayal at Atlantic City, 193; recruitment of, 80; supports Mississippi Summer Project, 346 (n. 20); and Winona jail incident, 83
Hamilton College, 39
Hamlett, Ed, 158
Hampton Institute, 39
Hansen, Bill, 172, 246, 276; difficulties of getting funds from Atlanta, 365 (n. 13); as organizer in Cambridge, 331 (n. 1); as project director in Arkansas, 355 (n. 49); resigns as Arkansas project director, 389 (n. 19)
Harding, Rosemarie: as bridge-builder, 326 (n. 11)
Harding, Vincent: as bridge-builder, 326 (n. 11); on freedom from hate, 347 (n. 33); on interracial sex, 175
Hardy, John, 61; beaten by registrar, 262; and Nashville workshop, 61; teaches voter registration classes, 261
Harris, David, 166, 271; joins The Resistance, 233
Harris, Don, 157; and money crunch in Albany, 365 (n. 13)
Harris, Doug, 177

Harris, Fred, 54
Harris, Jesse, 209, 276
Harris, McCree, 91; on freedom songs, 260
Harris, Rutha, 91
Harvard University, 39, 96, 115
Havice, Katherine, 350 (n. 11)
Hayden, Casey (Sandra Cason), 96–100, 102, 108–16, 162, 172, 190, 215, 254, 265, 266, 289; on developing new models of leadership, 137; divorce of, 114; enters counterculture, 291; and International Ladies' Garment Workers Union campaign, 293; as Mississippi Summer Project Committee member, 155–60, 178; "Position of Women in SNCC," 232, 289; role in "Port Huron Statement," 109; "Sex and Caste: A Kind of Memo," 232, 289; as SNCC's Northern Coordinator, 96, 114–15; structure proposal at Waveland, 216, 278–80, 283, 387 (n. 3); as welfare rights organizer, 289; and woman-centered leadership, 111–12
Hayden, Tom, 102–3, 111, 133, 265, 267; as author of "Port Huron Statement," 110; and basement discussions, 111–12; and Chester as model for ERAP, 134; divorce of, 114, 290; formation of political identity, 103–4; "An Interracial Movement of the Poor," 137, 341 (n. 17); as president of SDS, 132; visit to McComb, 105–6, 108, 158
Hayes, Curtis. See Muhammad, Curtis
Health care, 285
Henry, Aaron, 143, 156, 169, 191, 192, 196, 268, 382 (n. 16); background, 147; MFDP gubernatorial candidate, 189, 190; and NAACP chapters during World War II, 298 (n. 13); on Two-Seat Compromise, 194
Herrick, Jeanne, 50
Hewitt, Raymond, 115
Highlander Folk School, 9, 68; hosts SNCC workshops, 57, 79, 148, 293
High school student activism, 58, 60–63, 88, 90, 130, 136
Hill, Lance, 383 (n. 28)
Hirshfeld, Elizabeth, 54–55; personal quest for meaning, 54; and UFW, 294
Holland, Endesha Ida Mae, 181

with local people, 375 (n. 8); post-SNCC career, 377 (n. 4)

Jones, James, 79, 389 (n. 19)

Jones, Matthew, 204

Jordan, Cleveland, 85

Journal and Guide, 38

Justice, 38, 43, 46, 69, 86, 254, 300 (n. 11), 301 (n. 24)

Justice Department. *See* United States Justice Department

Katzenbach, Nicholas, 199

Kennedy, John F., 46, 47

Kennedy, Robert, 48–49, 241; betrays voter registration workers, 65, 240; and Cambridge Accords, 335 (n. 26); and elite attitude toward grassroots movement, 236; forces FBI to investigate Anniston attack on Freedom Ride, 311 (n. 5); on Jim Crow between United Nations in New York and Washington, D.C., 310 (n. 3); promises to protect voter registration, 58, 65; requests cooling-off period in Freedom Rides, 49, 50; secret deal with Mississippi officials, 49

Kerouac, Jack, 102

Khrushchev, Nikita, 46

King, Carole, 285

King, Coretta Scott, 70

King, Ed, 189, 196

King, Jeannette, 169

King, Marion, 71, 246

King, Martin Luther, Jr., 7, 16, 35, 36–37, 69–71, 89, 101, 102, 202, 226, 229, 250, 297 (n. 11), 358 (n. 1); advice to MFDP on Two-Seat Compromise, 194, 195; bravery during Freedom Rides, 49, 313 (n. 15); illegal wiretapping of, 191; "Letter from a Birmingham Jail," 90, 108, 242; as movement symbol, 235; on Nashville, 44; on nonviolence as way of life, 249, 252; relationship to Lawson, 9, 15; relationship to SNCC workers, 78, 88, 245; role in SNCC formation, 34, 41, 118, 309 (n. 70); on SNCC as storm troopers, 8

King, Mary, 266, 289; "Position of Women in SNCC," 232, 289; "Sex and Caste: A Kind of Memo," 232, 289; and UFW, 294

King, Slater, 71

Kress stores, 101

Ku Klux Klan (KKK). *See* Racial terror

Kunstler, Kathy, 164

Labor movement, 289, 375 (n. 6)

Ladner, Dorie, 79, 174; on Mississippi Summer Project, 346 (n. 20)

Ladner, Joyce, 104; on gendered division of labor in SNCC, 171

Lafayette, Bernard, 44, 45, 246, 366 (n. 16); background, 13; as Freedom Rider, 47, 48; on freedom songs, 313 (n. 21); and Nashville workshops, 20; runs workshops in South Africa in 1990s, 306 (n. 54)

Lafayette, Colia, 79

"Last shall be first," 181–82

Lauter, Paul, 336 (n. 32)

Law enforcement collusion in white supremacy, 60, 68–71, 82, 86, 90, 246, 252, 261, 265–66; in North, 251; and Pritchett innovation in Albany, 69–71, 320 (n. 38). *See also* Racial terror

Lawrence, David, 193

Lawson, James M., 9, 13–31, 39, 42–44, 53, 57, 81, 86, 127, 131, 215, 229, 265, 287; ability to listen, 24; background, 13–16; as bridge-builder, 326 (n. 11); defines revolutionary nonviolence, 36, 84, 99, 249; expelled from Vanderbilt Divinity School, 305 (n. 50); and idea that greater injustice calls for greater force opposing it, 43, 252; introduces workshops to SNCC, 306 (n. 55); on making "vital human connection," 83–85, 187; meets with Gandhians on India trip, 15, 284, 299 (n. 7); and Nashville Laboratory, 17, 31, 215, 302 (n. 31); sanctification experience, 14; on significance of Montgomery, 17; trains SNCC volunteers for Mississippi Summer Project, 162; and workshops with Smiley, 15, 299 (n. 8)

Leadership, 43, 123; Baker's model in SNCC, 41–42, 150, 195; group-centered in SNCC, 73, 146, 211, 213, 351 (n. 21), 370 (n. 37); and innovations in movement, 24; as organizing people to be their own

McCarthyism, 33, 288

McComb, Miss., 56–58, 240; center of statewide rollback action, 207–8; weekly firebombing in, 166; residents renounce violence, 352 (n. 30)

McComb, Miss., movement, 56–66, 292; and Greyhound sit-in, 61; and high school walkout, 62

McComb Enterprise Journal, 58

McDew, Charles (Chuck) (chair of SNCC, 1961–63), 35, 41, 61, 62, 64, 96, 102, 104, 135, 136, 200, 215; background, 36; compares U.S. morality to international standards, 387 (n. 1); description of SNCC as "many minds, one heart," 99, 227; sees SNCC as short-lived, 221

McEldowney, Carol, 286; and booklet on welfare rights, 287; and workshop in Cleveland, 286–88

McGhee, Laura, 157

McGowan, Yvonne, 358 (n. 68)

McHugh, Madeline, 272

McKinnie, Lester, 79; as Nashville workshop participant, 78

McLaurin, Charles, 1–4, 79, 143, 149, 169, 200, 209, 210, 227, 229, 241, 255, 256, 276; on nonviolence in Mississippi movement, 157–58; on purpose of Mississippi Summer Project, 199; on revolutionary nature of voter registration, 91, 227; as virtuoso organizer, 60, 353 (n. 38)

McNamara, Robert, 50

McNeil, Joseph, 27, 101

Media coverage of movement, 115, 116, 162, 289; contacts with SNCC, 74–75, 77; failure to understand central issues of 1964 Democratic National Convention, 195–96; ignores voter registration, 143, 146, 148–49, 156, 241

Media misinterpretation of movement, 7, 42, 88, 139, 195, 226, 367 (n. 20), 384 (n. 2); and Black Power, 389 (n. 20); and burnout, 240; caused by viewing movement from afar, 236; consequences for movement legacy, 236–37; misrepresentation of leadership, 370 (n. 37); in *Mississippi Burning*, 384 (n. 2); as naïve in rejecting Two-Seat Compromise, 195, 196; on political elites as critical to

viable solutions to racism, 235–36; and reporting of missing white civil rights workers but not black, 187; SDS monopolizes attention at end of 1960s, 252; as spontaneous, 348 (n. 34); on white volunteers, 172, 366 (n. 19)

Medical Committee for Human Rights (MCHR), 344 (n. 1)

Medical supplies and treatment: for SNCC workers, 61

Meharry Medical College, 8, 19

Meredith, James, 144

Meridian, Miss., 185

MFDP. *See* Mississippi Freedom Democratic Party

Michigan Daily, 102, 103

Michigan State University, 110

Middlebrook, Jonathan, 148

Militancy, 162, 209, 264; empty rhetoric posing as, 229, 253, 383 (n. 28); nonviolence and armed self-defense as, 251; rejection of slow work with grass roots, 251–53

Miller, James, 106, 140, 343 (n. 25)

Miller, L. K., 148

Miller, Mike: as bridge-builder, 326 (n. 11)

Mills, C. Wright, 108

Ministers: participation in movement, 67, 68, 89, 284; and SNCC, 320 (n. 32). *See also* African American Freedom Church; King, Martin Luther, Jr.; Lawson, James M.; Leadership

Minnis, Jack, 375 (n. 6)

Mississippi Burning, 384 (n. 2)

Mississippi Child Development Group, 168

Mississippi Freedom Democratic Party (MFDP), 1, 10, 139, 176, 177, 178, 180, 191, 198, 225, 241, 286, 288, 292; antidraft petition of, 292; at Atlantic City, 190, 192; blueprint for, 87; building of, 156, 189; county conventions, 181; daily life in, 166–69; gendered leadership in, 189; as largest twentieth-century civic experiment, 167, 179, 181, 345 (n. 6); lessons of 1964 Democratic National Convention, 284; long-term results for Democratic Party, 196; precinct meetings as political education, 179, 262; rejection of

Two-Seat Compromise, 194–96; sacrifices of participants in, 178, 188; second congressional challenge, 220, 381 (n. 8); as source of new political culture in Mississippi, 194; state convention, 181, 185; theoretical achievements of, 196. *See also* Council of Federated Organizations; Student Nonviolent Coordinating Committee

Mississippi Freedom Labor Union, 231, 291

Mississippi Free Press, 168

Mississippi movement, 56, 57–92, 143–82, 219–25; first SNCC workers in, 57–58

Mississippi State Sovereignty Commission, 57

Mississippi Student Union, 219

Mississippi Summer Project (1964), 63, 76, 173, 214, 227; conflict in, 169; contributions to counterculture in North and West, 292–93; decision-making structure of, 354 (n. 44); debate over, 150–54; debate over nonviolence and self-defense in, 349 (n. 9); gendered division of labor in, 170–71; involvement of whites as threatening, 171–73, 203–7, 372 (n. 53); Mississippi Summer Project Committee, 155; origins of, 148–51; planning for, 155–60; reaction of local people to, 160, 168–96; role of volunteers' parents in, 163–64, 351 (n. 23); training for, 155, 160–63; white response to, 269–71, 349 (n. 2). *See also* Council of Federated Organizations; Freedom Schools; Mississippi Freedom Democratic Party; Parker, Pam; Racial terror; Savio, Mario; Student Nonviolent Coordinating Committee; Tobias, Heather

Mitchell, Francis: structure proposal at Waveland, 217, 277–78, 283

Monsonis, Jim, 326 (n. 11)

Montgomery, Ala., 48–49

Montgomery bus boycott, 7, 15, 53, 71, 89, 226, 302 (n. 31); as inspiration worldwide, 284, 298 (n. 13)

Moore, Amzie, 37, 60, 84, 131, 133, 152, 156; assesses SNCC's achievements, 91, 325 (n. 97); background, 60; house as center, 78–79; Moses' "movement father," 60

Moore, Andrew, 271

Moore, Douglas, 27

Morehouse College, 46, 79, 169, 210

Morey, R. Hunter, 224

Morgan State University, 119

Morrison, Toni, 254

Morse, Frank, 271

Morse, Wayne, 194

Moses, Robert (Bob) Parris, 45, 57–66 passim, 77–91, 96, 106, 122, 131, 144–54, 155–78, 200, 201, 206, 214, 229, 240, 241, 242, 265, 384 (n. 2); background, 39, 41, 51; Baker as mentor, 41–42; as bridge-builder, 326 (n. 11); as chief negotiator for MFDP at Atlantic City, 189, 193; on collective black identity, 207, 368 (n. 26); on combating fear, 316 (n. 2); compares Tonkin Bay resolution to murders of activists, 291, 391–92 (n. 31); cost of movement work on, 61; on democratic process in Democratic Party, 196; describes SNCC's lifeblood as "slow and patient work" with local people, 209; on experientially tested view from within movement versus view from afar, 236, 239; fall 1964 trip to Africa, 197; leadership ideas misconstrued by historians, 370 (n. 37); leadership style, 61, 163, 370 (n. 37); leaves SNCC, 221, 374–75 (n. 6); and math literacy project against "sharecropper education," 375 (n. 6), 384 (n. 2); on media misrepresentation of MFDP rejection, 196; memo at Waveland, 201, 217, 274; on movement quality control, 253; on name change, 317 (n. 14); post-SNCC career, 375 (n. 6); on priorities of movement, 188; reads feminist literature, 290; reasons for opposing Black Belt Project, 211, 368 (n. 29); rejection of role of "front man," 202; role in decision for Mississippi Summer Project, 148–54; and SNCC's weakness in creating independent economic base, 220–21; strategy in Mississippi, 144, 345 (n. 9); in Tanzania, 375 (n. 6) on Two-Seat Compromise, 194, 237; understanding of MFDP challenge, 177; uses Tolkien's Ring of Power analogy, 163; vision of organizer, 248; and Washington, D.C., summer project on peace, 292

Mount Olive Church, 74

Movement building, 72, 117–18; church-based music helps older Americans join movement, 260; reactions when movement stops, 229; recruitment as essential component of, 238–39, 243. *See also* Sustaining energy

Movement culture, 21, 41–42, 118–19, 124, 169, 171; cultural resistance to, 176; deteriorating morale in, 365 (n. 11); flexibility as central to, 41–42, 245; and "movement quality control," 253; role of freedom songs in, 259–60; role of nonviolence in, 21, 22, 24, 80–85, 213, 324 (n. 78); role of patience in, 41–42, 253–54; role of reflection in, 20, 215, 230, 245; shortcomings of, 113. *See also* Democratic culture; Local leadership; Student Nonviolent Coordinating Committee

Moving people to act, 9, 20, 23, 43, 64, 91, 129, 181, 209–10, 229, 255, 297 (n. 11), 336 (n. 32); difficulty of in SDS, 133, 139, 244, 264–65; recovering in movement documents, 301 (n. 29)

Muhammad, Curtis (Curtis Hayes), 61, 62, 79, 91, 149, 161, 165, 210, 236, 241, 254; and AFL-CIO, 294; as Drum and Spear Bookstore founder, 231; Moses as mentor, 170; recruited to SNCC staff, 66; recruits northern students, 95, 111, 150

Music. *See* Fear; Freedom Singers; Freedom songs; Lining songs; Mass meetings

Muste, A. J., 14–15, 265

NAACP. *See* National Association for the Advancement of Colored People

Napier, J. C., 300 (n. 9)

Nash, Diane, 7–8, 35, 44, 50, 52–53, 84, 126, 148, 236, 239, 242, 243, 253, 254; analysis of loss of SNCC's internal culture, 215; background, 19; Baker as mentor, 40; and Cambridge Accords, 335 (n. 26), 336 (n. 27); confronts West, 33–34, 305 (n. 50); continues jail-no-bail strategy, 52–53; gives up on nonviolence, 252; leadership skills, 31; as Nashville workshop participant, 19–33; nonviolent leadership in Jackson, 66; proposal to

create nonviolent army after Birmingham church bombing, 351 (n. 19); reignites Freedom Rides, 7, 47–48; returns to nonviolence, 252

Nashville Christian Leadership Conference (NCLC), 16, 311 (n. 8)

Nashville era of SNCC (1960–62), 35

Nashville movement, 7–9, 18, 25–33, 49, 159; black boycott in, 26–34 passim, 302 (n. 36)

Nashville workshops, 8, 18–31, 35, 42, 47–49, 53, 68, 97, 158, 176, 207, 215, 216, 227, 242

National Association for the Advancement of Colored People (NAACP), 8, 15, 40, 138; branches established near World War II bases, 298 (n. 13); in Mississippi, 59, 60, 77, 84, 146, 147, 225; and youth councils, 8, 67, 118

National Council of Negro Churchmen, 284

National Student Association (NSA), 64, 102, 114, 134–37; Southern Student Leadership Seminar, 98

Neshoba County, Miss., 185

Newark, N.J.: brutal police maneuvers in, 251; ERAP project in, 9, 285

Newell, Bob, 271

New Left, 100; debt to movement, 264–67; sacred ground of, 264; women's movement emerges in, 232, 290

New Orleans, La., 46

New World Foundation, 64

New York Radical Feminists, 233

New York Times, 74

Nixon, E. D., 89

Nonviolence, 8, 13–55 passim, 67–68, 157–59, 284, 306 (n. 57); counterintuitive nature of, 14, 24; cultural intimidation of, 204, 251; difficulty of conveying concepts of, 37, 95–96, 162; discredited after 1960s, 81; examples of failure of, 71, 127; impact on SNCC culture, 21, 22, 24, 80–85, 213, 324 (n. 78); as major component of democratic practice, 17, 21–24, 31, 80–85, 104, 127, 204, 213, 324 (n. 78); misunderstood, 36; and National Guard, 127; need for consensus in, 104; nonviolent direct action, 27, 46–50, 56,

63, 90, 118, 229, 242, 351 (n. 19); nonviolent method, 17, 47, 83; protection by, 22, 84, 86; retaliation undermines, 186, 246, 306 (n. 57); revolutionary nonviolence, 52; role in strengthening voter registration projects, 80–85; role of communication in, 187; role of suffering in, 69, 83, 186; rules of, 27–28, 303 (n. 39); self-defense objections to, 186; and shift from victim to actor, 32, 84, 325 (n. 2); as way of life versus tactic, 28, 32, 164. *See also* Self-defense

Nonviolent Action Group (NAG), 61; and Cambridge project, 121; role of nonviolence in, 121

Nonviolent ethos, 31, 127, 204

"Nonviolent High School," 63

Nonviolent *realpolitik*, 47, 70

Nonviolent workshops, 16–31, 57, 67–68, 127, 233, 251, 265, 298 (n. 3), 306 (n. 54), 367 (n. 20); difficulty of recovering dynamics of, 301 (n. 29); difficulty of sustaining, 215; importance of small groups to, 287; joint ownership of, 23–24, 99; as laboratory for nonviolence, 215, 302 (n. 33); role-playing in, 25; and sociodrama, 20, 25; and welfare training program, 286–88

Norman, Martha Prescod, 91; background, 111; as bridge-builder, 326 (n. 11); and conference on SNCC in 2000, 384 (n. 2); on gender in SDS, 329 (n. 45); in Greenwood, 144; moves from Albany to Mississippi Project, 151; on SDS activities in Ann Arbor, 329 (n. 41); in Selma, 329 (n. 41); on structure of SNCC, 364 (n. 8); at University of Michigan, 110; on volunteers, 203

Norman, Silas, 205

North: community organizing in, 285–88; potential of, 378 (n. 14)

North Carolina A&T State University, 27, 101

Northern Student Movement (NSM), 100, 114–16, 339 (n. 6)

Northern students, 114–16, 146; alienation of, 170; conflicts with, 355 (n. 48); experiential lessons of, 117–40; limitations of exporting movement's lessons to public,

96, 169–70; recruited by southern black movement, 9, 102, 130, 136, 264–67; resources of, 87, 96, 115, 266, 392 (n. 34). *See also* Northern Student Movement; Students for a Democratic Society

NSM. *See* Northern Student Movement

Oberlin College, 9, 288

Old Left, 95, 124; role in Friends of SNCC groups, 316 (n. 37)

Oliver, Spencer, 224

Omolade, Barbara, 379 (n. 19)

O'Neal, Helen, 290

O'Neal, John, 56, 173–74; in theater, 254

Organic intellectual, 236, 238. *See also* Baker, Ella; Consciousness; Experiential education of civil rights workers

Organizers, 126; importance of listening among, 238–39, 257; limited lifespan in context of rapid pace in 1960s, 251; models of, 112, 288–89, 390 (n. 22). *See also* Community organizing; Trial-and-error democratic approach

Organizing tradition, 9

Overcoming fear. *See* Fear

Owens, Webb, 59, 60

Palmer, Hazel T., 262

Pan-Africanism, 314 (n. 22), 388 (n. 5)

Parchman Penitentiary, 45, 49, 51–55, 136, 246

Pardun, Robert, 350 (n. 11)

Parker, Pam, 163, 164, 390 (n. 25)

Parks, Rosa, 7, 226

Participatory democracy: accountability in, 140; and "Port Huron Statement," 110–12; problems with, 140

Patch, Penny, 117, 118, 121, 129, 172, 204, 265, 289; background, 120

Patterson, John, 48, 49

Payne, Bruce, 147

Payne, Charles, 84, 87, 172; and conference on SNCC in 2000, 384 (n. 2)

Peace movement, 233–34, 291–92, 380 (n. 22). *See also* Antiwar movement; Draft-resistance movement

Peacock, Willie (Wazir), 79, 149, 150, 157, 161, 204; analysis of slave mentality, 152; background, 151–52; father's friendship with Moore, 347 (n. 27); and folk festivals, 231; on gender relations in SNCC, 174–75, 290; and practicality of advocating majority-black staff, 347 (n. 29); on volunteers, 203

Peck, James (Jim), 46

Penn, William, 8, 20

Pentagon Papers release, 241

Perez, Leander, 265–66

Person, Charles, 46

"Personal is political," 109–14, 253–54, 288, 289–91, 301 (n. 25). See also Feminism

Peters, Edith Simmons, 261–62

Petersburg, Va., 67, 76

Philadelphia, Miss., 164, 185, 191, 291

Phillips, Charlotte, 118, 119, 124, 129

Pike County, Miss., 57

Pittsburgh Courier, 38

Plaquemine Parish, La., 265–66

Political consciousness. See Consciousness

Political culture. See Movement culture; Received culture

Poll tax, 261

Ponder, Annell, 82–83, 240, 384 (n. 2)

Popular politics. See Public life

Porter, William, 247–48

"Port Huron Statement." See Students for a Democratic Society

Potter, Paul, 110, 111, 391 (n. 27); movement memoir, 329 (n. 40)

Poverty, 5, 143, 243–44, 249, 293

Prescod, Martha. See Norman, Martha Prescod

Press coverage. See Media coverage of movement

Prettyman, Julia, 326 (n. 11)

Pritchett, Laurie, 68, 69–71, 88; collusion with federal law enforcement, 70, 320 (n. 38)

Public life, 23, 254–55; Baker's role in bringing people to, 317 (n. 10); community organizing expands, 73, 129–32, 147, 337 (n. 37); creation of egalitarian relationships in, 24, 99, 181, 196, 210, 215; developing democratic understanding of citizenship in, 87, 145, 169–70, 194, 254–55, 343 (n. 28); MFDP as largest twentieth-century civic experiment in, 179, 181; and mobilization of civic actors, 116, 117, 253; Nashville workshops as building blocks of, 31–33, 216; and precinct meetings in Mississippi, 179, 190; realities of, 254–55; relationships in, 190, 210; role of organizers in, 254–55; role of workshops in, 99; transformative possibilities of, 181, 209–10. See also Civil rights movement: causal dynamics of; Consciousness; Experiential education of civil rights workers; Local leadership; Movement culture

Public relations: role of spokesmen in movement, 202

Public school democratization, 116

Public services. See Racial terror; Voter registration

Questions. See Baker, Ella; Moses, Robert Parris

Quilt cooperatives, 231

Rabinowitz, Joni, 334 (n. 21)

Rabinowitz, Marcia, 163

Racial terror, 21, 28, 46–49, 61, 62, 71, 74–76, 90, 103, 128, 143, 146–48, 205, 207–9, 226, 228, 240, 249, 256, 265–66; and civil rights workers, 72, 261–62; difficulty of gathering accurate statistics on, 352 (n. 24); impact on democratic social relations in movement, 253–54; lacks appeal to rule of reason or law in Mississippi, 59; parents' stories of, 25–26, 67, 307 (n. 61), 382 (n. 16); in response to MFDP, 181; in response to Mississippi Summer Project, 155–79, 269–71; role in bringing Mississippi Summer Project, 150, 154; role in immobilizing citizens, 57, 58; role in producing black anger and separatism, 164, 186, 203–7; as unpaid bill, 245. See also Burnout; Clark, Jim; Connor, Eugene; Fear; Humor; Perez, Leander; Pritchett, Laurie; White Citizens Councils; White supremacy

Racism. See Economic intimidation; Racial terror; White supremacy

Radcliff College, 137

Rader, Dotson, 252

"Radical": as substitute for more precise description, 383 (n. 28), 391 (n. 29)

Sacred ground, 4–6, 10, 230, 256, 264, 267

St. Augustine, Fla., 90

Sale, Kirkpatrick, 343 (n. 25); on poor as "myth-ridden, enervated, cynical," 139, 237

Samstein, Mendy, 153, 172, 190, 289; as bridge-builder, 326 (n. 11); and International Ladies' Garment Workers Union campaign, 293; joins The Resistance, 233, 380 (n. 22); as Mississippi Summer Project Committee member, 155, 178

Sarah Lawrence College, 111

Savage, Philip, 138

Savio, Mario, 166, 293

Sayer, Mike, 158

Schwartzbaum, Barbara, 222

Schwerner, Mickey, 162–64, 165, 185, 191, 196, 207, 269, 291; final words of, 187

SCLC. *See* Southern Christian Leadership Conference

SDS. *See* Students for a Democratic Society

Seeger, Pete, 385 (n. 4)

Segregation, 2, 5, 15, 43, 45, 72, 196, 207, 264; African American response to, 20–21, 75, 89, 216, 229, 243; customs of, 25–26, 146, 241; and legacy of "share-cropper education," 384 (n. 2); as limit on whites, 50, 98, 172; modern-day, 5, 297 (n. 5); in North, 118. *See also* Racial terror; Voter registration

Seigenthaler, John, 49, 312 (n. 14)

Selective Service System, 234

Self-activity, 10, 24, 27, 32–33, 77, 89, 181, 209–10, 235, 284, 345 (n. 6); relationship to consciousness, 209–10, 255, 314–15 (n. 28), 369 (n. 32), 389 (n. 13); SNCC activities as public classrooms that teach, 68, 75, 91, 98, 103, 229, 265; and welfare rights, 286–88. *See also* Consciousness; Public life

Self-criticism, 253–54. *See also* Reflection; Trial-and-error democratic approach

Self-defense, 22, 38, 85, 127, 239, 246, 306 (n. 57); allows voter registration work to continue, 165; contributions evaluated, 249–52; in debates over nonviolence, 36–37, 162; differs from use of armed struggle as strategy, 250; limited impact

on daily lives of many African Americans, 22, 81–82; nonviolent objections to, 81–84; practical need for, 157–59, 166; psychological need for, 82; and respect for nonviolent practitioners, 306 (n. 56); and rural southern black tradition, 36, 81; used by police to justify abuse, 251–52

Sellers, Cleveland, 40, 105; on Atlantic City, 192; on toll of violence against movement, 166–67

Selma, Ala., movement, 220; and Pettis Bridge, 220; sexual assault by police, 240

"Serious politics": conflict over definitions of, 108–14. *See also* Consciousness

Sexism: in movement, 175, 232, 234; in U.S. society, 293

Sexual assault and rape, 160, 164, 245; black women's historical burden of, 175, 356 (n. 59); in movement, 175; white women's historical burden of, 175, 356 (n. 59)

Sexuality inside movement, 173, 223, 224, 233, 290, 356 (n. 56); and birth control, 175; black women in leadership compelled to deny, 174; difficulty of for women, 175; and difficulty of keeping personal relationships private, 174; double standard concerning, 175; historical background, 347 (n. 30); interracial sex, 174; provides democratic vista, 176; sex test, 175; "talking black and sleeping white," 175

Shakur, Assata (Jo Anne Chesimard), 37

Sharecropper education, 244, 384 (n. 2). *See* Moses, Robert Parris

Shaw, John D., 292

Shaw University, 35, 101, 198, 264

Sherrod, Charles, 50, 52, 56, 57, 61, 66–77, 96, 126, 149, 151, 236, 240, 245, 254, 265, 385 (n. 4); addresses sexuality inside movement, 173; analysis of slave mentality, 52, 72; on Atlantic City, 190, 194; background, 38, 67, 76–77; demands share in power, 361 (n. 27); on independent economic base, 374 (n. 4); on keeping lines of communication open in SNCC, 367 (n. 20); on racial tension

169, 244; contributions evaluated, 78, 242; culture of, 38, 57, 63–64, 74, 84, 136, 144, 169, 197, 210, 213, 215, 227, 239–40, 245, 260, 265, 284–85, 289, 314–15 (n. 28); decision-making in, 104, 150–54, 160, 203, 211–18, 232, 244; dissolving of culture of, 197, 198, 202, 203, 205n, 213, 215, 218, 227–30, 234, 365 (n. 11), 371 (n. 49), 377 (nn. 4, 6); distance from peers in college, 126, 135, 169; and dream for new America, 31, 77, 107, 192, 203, 228, 260; and erroneous "Field Staff" versus "Freedom High" distinction, 211–12; formation of, 35; fund-raising, 54, 59, 66, 100, 116, 203, 220–21, 284; gendered division of labor in, 170–71, 289, 379 (n. 19); Greenville staff meeting (November 1963), 148–53, 206, 346 (n. 20); Greenwood model, 85–87; hierarchy as "hardline," 283; and hope that MFDP justifies costs of movement, 187–88, 203; impact on SDS, 102, 133–40, 283–88; inability to act on lessons learned, 229, 230, 244, 245, 254; independent political party era (1965–68), 220; internal education in, 36, 65, 151, 155–62, 214, 215, 222–24, 232, 253, 318 (n. 22), 348 (n. 36); and international solidarity, 234, 387 (n. 1); Jackson office, 153, 164, 203, 204, 222; lack of money, 114, 198, 202–3, 213, 365 (n. 13), 375 (n. 6); lessons learned in South, 57, 62–64, 68–69, 90–92, 160, 165, 212, 215; local people as focus of, 57, 68, 78, 80, 105, 189, 201, 213, 234, 244, 254, 321 (n. 50), 375 (n. 8); Mississippi era (1962–65), 56, 145; Mississippi staff, 63, 66, 78, 84, 149–54, 169–70, 240, 354 (n. 41); Mississippi Summer Project, 148–82; mistakes of, 215, 230, 245; monetary conflicts in, 202–4; moral anchors of, 84, 215, 370 (n. 40); Nashville era (1960–62), 31, 204; Nashville seminar (August 1961), 64–65, 318 (n. 21); nonviolence in, 35–37, 84–85, 157–59, 204, 208, 249–52, 305 (n. 53); northern projects, 119, 129–31, 137–38, 231; as open to all, 76, 253; permanent staff created, 64, 78; as pipeline for northern students, 9, 114–16, 117–40; post-SNCC work, 230,

289–94, 378 (n. 12); race relations in, 67–77, 150–53, 161, 173, 176, 198, 201, 203–7, 222–24, 245, 247; relations with MFDP, 220; role in movement, 8, 78, 90–92, 160; SNCC identity, 104–5, 160–61, 227, 234; Southwest Georgia project, 67–77; splits among black staff in, 229, 247–48, 383 (n. 20); staff meetings, 73, 197–218; statement of purpose, 35, 38; as "storm troopers" of movement, 8; strategy to develop local long-term leadership, 77, 112, 133, 139, 146, 172, 176–78, 181, 189, 194, 209–10, 215, 233, 254–55; structural debates of, 40, 64–65, 200, 210–18, 277–83, 373 (n. 60); structural weaknesses of, 198, 197–218, 253–54, 364 (n. 7); undemocratic procedures in, 66, 197–218, 247–48; urged to work in white communities, 205; and vision of democracy at war with traditional American assumptions, 107, 110, 235, 241, 256–57; volunteers in, 148–53, 169–70, 222–24, 253, 372 (n. 53); Waveland (November 1964), 145, 197–218, 227, 229, 273–77, 289; Waveland as crucial juncture, 219, 231–32, 236, 373 (n. 1); white participation in, 62–63, 114, 149–53, 160, 203–7, 318 (n. 22), 377 (n. 7); and women's liberation, 232, 289–91; workshop experience as central to, 23–24, 36, 104, 253; work style in, 137. *See also* Friends of SNCC groups

Student Peace Union, 108

Students for a Democratic Society (SDS), 9, 96, 98, 100–102, 108–14, 119, 133–40; Achilles heel of, 264, 380 (n. 25); Carmichael's challenge to, 133–34; cultural limitations of, 113, 135, 288; definition of democracy in, 111; dynamics visible at Waveland, 231–32; ERAPs, 118–40 passim, 231–32, 251, 285–88, 340 (n. 12); evaluation of, 264–67; and Hayden-Haber debate, 134–35, 265; imitates SNCC, 137; links northern students to SNCC, 105–6, 119; misrepresentation of as giving SNCC ideas about participatory democracy, 211; "Port Huron Statement," 100, 108, 112, 133, 242, 264; SNCC recruits members of, 106; staff quality control in, 253, 383 (n. 35); structure debates in, 288–89, 372 (n. 58), 373 (n. 1); Swarthmore as magnet in, 132; women's response to SNCC memo, 290

Suckle, Mark, 127, 129

Sudsofloppen, 233, 390 (n. 25)

Summer Project. *See* Mississippi Summer Project

Sunflower County, Miss., 80, 255

Sustaining energy, 43, 101, 144, 148, 221, 222

Sutherland (Martinez), Elizabeth, 221

Suu Kyi, Aung San, 300 (n. 11)

Swarthmore College, 9, 117, 122, 123, 265

Swarthmore Political Action Club (SPAC), 118–32, 336 (n. 28); absence of Lawson workshops in, 132, 333 (n. 15); lack of mentors in, 131; role in bringing SNCC to North, 119, 121

Sweeney, Dennis: joins The Resistance, 233; lacks experiential knowledge, 171–72; in McComb, 166; and UFW, 294

Taconic Foundation, 78

Taylor, Navry, 262

Temple University, 119

Tennessee State College, 19, 48

Terrell County, Ga., 69, 74

Terror. *See* Racial terror

Thomas, Hank, 46

Thomas, Mary, 271

Thoreau, Henry David, 227

Thrasher, Sue, 350 (n. 11)

Tillinghast, Muriel, 66, 120, 121

Tobias, Heather, 173, 293

Tocqueville, Alexis de, 116

Tougaloo College, 119, 189; work-study program at, 230

Touré, Sékou, 197

Transformation, 3, 10, 13, 32, 89, 168–69; individual transformations reinforced by collective ethic, 98, 167, 241, 314–15 (n. 28); voter registration efforts as, 52, 147, 210

Travis, Brenda, 61

Travis, Jimmy, 88; and folk festivals, 378 (n. 14)

Trial-and-error democratic approach, 9, 15, 20, 68, 90, 105, 132, 140, 219, 240, 249;

necessary for survival, 238; at war with intellectual-cultural elite, 237–38

Trinity College, 76

Trocme, Andre, 302 (n. 33)

Trocme, Magla, 302 (n. 33)

Tucker, Mary, 80

Ture, Kwame. *See* Carmichael, Stokely

Turnbow, Hartman, 250

Tutorial projects, 116, 135

Two-Seat Compromise. *See* Democratic National Convention of 1964

UFW. *See* United Farm Workers

United Automobile Workers, 134, 191

United Farm Workers (UFW), 294

United States Constitution: Jim Crow laws as violation of, 72, 241; role of MFDP in upholding, 195

United States Department of Agriculture's Agricultural Stabilization and Conservation Service, 79, 145, 167, 344 (n. 5); and elections in Mississippi, 168, 272, 353 (n. 36)

United States foreign policy in Southeast Asia, 391 (n. 30); prompts "by any means necessary," 251; relation to civil rights work in South, 233, 251–52, 291–92

United States Justice Department, 48, 50, 58, 146, 149, 156, 187, 198, 199, 236, 323 (n. 75); affidavits sent by SNCC to, 72, 86, 320 (n. 41); betrayal of SNCC workers, 65, 208, 240; divergence with FBI over civil rights, 71; ignores Constitution, 49; inaction during Mississippi Summer Project, 207; professed impotence of, 65; takes SNCC calls until Mississippi senators complain, 319 (n. 23)

United States Supreme Court, 46

University of California at Berkeley, 9, 95, 293

University of Illinois, 104

University of Michigan at Ann Arbor, 9, 95, 100, 228

University of Mississippi Medical School Hospital, 186

University of North Carolina–Greensboro, 27

University of Rhode Island, 122

University of Texas at Austin, 97

University of Wisconsin at Madison, 95, 205

Urban unrest, 251

Vanderbilt University, 8, 16, 19

Varela, Maria, 116, 205; background, 100; proposes compromise on "Port Huron Statement," 328 (n. 38); role in connecting SDS and SNCC, 100; and structure proposal at Waveland, 217, 278–80, 283; and Waveland position paper on training organizers, 370 (n. 37)

Vaughs, Clifford, 271

Vietnam independence movement, 284

Vietnam War, 3, 143, 233, 291–92, 293; draft numbers, 391 (n. 30); effect on civil rights movement, 251

Viorst, Milton, 195, 237

Virginia Human Relations Commission, 77

Vivian, C. T., 33, 54

Vorhees Junior College, 40

Voter Education Project (VEP), 78, 88, 114, 165

Voter registration, 56–92, 143–82 passim, 210, 229, 242, 250, 363 (n. 36); and disfranchisement, 57, 261–63, 268–72; failure to offer clear path after Atlantic City, 197; and nature of canvassing, 177; and Vietnam, 292. See also Lee, Herbert; Moore, Amzie; Voting Rights Act of 1965

Voting Rights Act of 1965, 198, 199, 220, 243, 244, 249; lack of enforcement of, 199; limited impact of, 229, 243; role of SCLC in generating, 242; unleashes voting power, 224, 225

Walker, Alice: creates term "womanism," 390 (n. 24); fictional account of Meridian Hill, 175, 356 (n. 57)

Walker, Wyatt T., 41

Walthall County, Miss., 57

Ware, Bill, 272

War on Poverty, 225, 285–88

Watergate hearings, 241

Waters, Muddy, 143

Watkins, Hollis, 61, 62, 79, 91, 144, 149, 157, 200, 254; and grassroots organizing,

150; on Mississippi Summer Project, 155, 161; recruited to SNCC staff, 66

Watkins, William, 166. See also Racial terror; White supremacy

Watters, Pat, 247

Waveland staff meeting (November 1964), 197–218, 219, 222, 227, 229, 231–32, 236, 273–77, 289

Wealth distribution, 5

Weather Underground, 252, 334 (n. 21)

Webb, Lee, 132, 134, 137

Welfare rights: and Cleveland ERAP, 285–88, 388 (n. 8); and democratization of War on Poverty, 285; welfare rights organizations, 116, 139, 232. See also Boudin, Kathy; McEldowney, Carol

Wells, Samuel, 73

"We Shall Overcome." See Freedom songs

West, Ben: encounter with Nash, 33–34, 44; encounter with Rustin, 305 (n. 50)

West, Cornel, 254

West Virginia State College, 137

Wheeler, Jean, 254; background, 163; describes work in Mississippi, 215; leads song after news of murders of activists, 163; moves from Albany Project to Mississippi, 151, 347 (n. 26)

White, Lula Mae, 50

White antiracism, 207, 289, 377 (n. 7); cost of, 206; difficulty of development of, 96, 172, 222–24, 287, 350 (n. 11); difficulty of sustaining, 203–7; as response to Black Power, 389 (n. 20); and risk of break with home and family, 62; self-interest of, 98, 172–73; successful development of, 172–73; variations of, 168–70, 355 (n. 49)

White Citizens Councils, 4, 57, 85, 155, 324 (n. 83). See also Economic intimidation; Racial terror; White supremacy

White Folks Project, 158; and difficulty of dramatizing economics, 350 (n. 11); out of phase with movement, 350 (n. 11)

White nationalism, 6, 267

White primary. See Democratic Party; United States Justice Department; Voter registration

White supremacy, 5, 23, 57, 58, 80, 96, 117, 143, 193, 203, 226, 244, 250; in Congress,

381 (n. 8); effect on black psyche, 205–7; around globe, 10; historical burden of, 72, 153, 284; impact on democratic tradition, 207, 237; and killing of white mothers' sons versus black mothers' sons, 146, 149, 170, 354 (n. 42); media coverage of, 187, 384 (n. 2); in movement, 169–70; as no longer an issue, 244; as problem that can be solved by experts, 235–37; repercussions in movement, 156–59, 170, 203–7, 237; unexamined by white feminists, 232, 379 (n. 20)

White volunteers, 148–53, 170, 203–7, 222–24; "perfect obnoxiousness" of, 152, 171, 355 (nn. 48, 49); portrayed as saving the day, 7, 172, 226. *See also* Civil rights movement; Student Nonviolent Coordinating Committee

Wilhelm, John, 233

Wilkerson, Cathy: in Chester ERAP, 334 (n. 21); in Weather Underground, 334 (n. 21)

Wilkins, Roy: calls for movement moratorium, 358 (n. 1); comment to Hamer, 196, 236, 240

Williams, Robert F., 64, 284; on nonviolence as "emasculating," 250; on self-defense as protection, 37, 250

Wilson, Lucius, 261

Winona, Miss., 82–83, 240

Wittman, Carl, 121, 126, 129, 137, 266; convinces Tom Hayden to follow Chester model, 134; impact of black freedom struggle on, 341 (n. 17); "An Interracial Movement of the Poor," 137; jail experience of, 124; joins The Resistance, 233

Wolf, Naomi, 254

Womanism, 232; Walker coins term, 390 (n. 24); womanist practice, 241, 290

Women's movement, 10, 140, 175, 230, 353

(n. 38), 367 (n. 24); debt to civil rights movement, 232; gains momentum "like a Mack truck," 290; reshapes civic landscape, 233; as safe harbor from macho rhetoric, 290; SDS as seedbed of, 112, 231, 232; SNCC as wellspring of, 234, 242, 289–91; and SNCC "internal education" paper, 232. *See also* Feminism

Woodard, Komozi, 347 (n. 29), 378 (n. 14)

Woodworking cooperatives, 231

Woolman, John, 20

Woolworth's, 55, 61, 101, 118

Workshops. *See* Freedom Schools; Leadership; Nonviolent workshops

World Bank, 249

World Trade Organization, 249

World War II, 120; black veterans of, 15, 85, 298 (n. 13); Christian existentialism and, 97, 105; and global uprising against white supremacy, 297 (n. 7); resistance to Nazis in, 8

Wright, Marian. *See* Edelman, Marian Wright

Yale University, 9, 100, 122, 148, 151, 161; Law School, 144, 146, 344 (n. 4)

Young, Andrew, 82–83

Young Democratic Clubs of America, 224

Younge, Sammy, 233, 246

Young Women's Christian Association (YWCA), 97, 114, 172

Zellner, Dottie, 172, 289

Zellner, Robert (Bob), 62–63, 64, 91, 95–96, 136, 158, 172, 246, 289; on Forman, 200

Zinn, Howard, 63, 76, 321 (nn. 43, 46), 363 (n. 4)

Zwerg, Jim, 48–49; letter to parents, 312 (n. 13); on real hero of Freedom Rides, 312 (n. 13)

CPSIA information can be obtained
at www.ICGtesting.com
Printed in the USA
LVHW111912280722
724616LV00004B/453

9 780807 859599